D1261032

MODERN PROSE | Form and Style

ALSO BY WILLIAM VAN O'CONNOR

SENSE AND SENSIBILITY IN MODERN POETRY, 1948

THE SHAPING SPIRIT: A STUDY OF WALLACE STEVENS, 1950

AN AGE OF CRITICISM, 1900–1950, 1952

THE TANGLED FIRE OF WILLIAM FAULKNER, 1954

MODERN PROSE
Form and Style

William Van O'Connor
UNIVERSITY OF MINNESOTA

THOMAS Y. CROWELL COMPANY
NEW YORK · ESTABLISHED 1834

First Printing, November, 1958
Second Printing, January, 1960

Manufactured in the United States of America
By the Vail-Ballou Press, Inc., Binghamton, N.Y.

The Library of Congress has catalogued this publication as follows:

O'Connor, William Van, 1915– *ed.* Modern prose, form and style. New York, Crowell [1959] 562 p. 24 cm. 1. English language—Rhetoric. 2. Authorship. 3. American literature (Selections: Extracts, etc.) 4. English literature (Selections: Extracts, etc.) I. Title.
PE1417.O25 808 59–5071 ‡ Library of Congress

ACKNOWLEDGMENTS

Acknowledgment is gratefully made to the following authors, agents, and publishers who have granted permission to use selections from copyrighted publications.

America (National Catholic Weekly Review) for "Sound and Sense of Words" (*America*, Vol. 96, February 9, 1957, pp. 530–31), by John P. Sisk.

American Association of University Professors for "Scholarly Style, or the Lack Thereof" (*AAUP Bulletin*, Autumn, 1956) by Sheridan Baker.

American Civil Liberties Union for "Censorship of Comic Books: A Statement in Opposition on Civil Liberties Grounds." Published as a pamphlet by the American Civil Liberties Union, 170 Fifth Avenue, New York 10, New York, in 1955.

American Library Association for the ALA Bill of Rights and the Labeling Resolution.

Mrs. Joseph Warren Beach for "The Dirty Street" from *The Meek Americans and Other European Trifles* (University of Chicago Press, 1925) by Joseph Warren Beach. Reprinted by permission.

Beacon Press, Inc., for "The Future of Censorship" from *The Right to Read* by Paul Blanshard. Copyright 1955 by the Beacon Press, Inc.

Confluence for " 'Bloody-Minded Professors': The Anti-Social Role of Some Intellectuals," (*Confluence,* Volume 1, No. 3) by Peter Viereck, and "Bloody-Minded Professors?" (*Confluence,* Volume 1, No. 4) by Richard H. Rovere.

Curtis Brown, Ltd., for "Story, Theme and Situation" from "The Novelist's Craft" (*The Listener,* October 25, November 1 and 8, 1956) by Elizabeth Bowen. Reprinted by permission of the author.

Doubleday & Company, Inc., for "Writing Prose" from *The Summing Up* by W. Somerset Maugham. Copyright 1938 by W. Somerset Maugham. Reprinted by permission of Doubleday & Company, Inc.

E. P. Dutton & Co., for selections from the book *Samuel Butler's Notebooks.* Published by E. P. Dutton & Co., Inc. Reprinted by permission of the publishers.

William Faulkner for "Impressions of Japan." Reprinted by permission of William Faulkner.

Harcourt, Brace and Company, Inc., for: "Politics and the English Language" from *Shooting an Elephant And Other Essays* by George Orwell, copyright, 1945, 1946, 1949, 1950, by Sonia Brownell Orwell; reprinted by permission of Harcourt, Brace and Company, Inc. "Sir John Harington" from *Portraits in Miniature,* copyright, 1931, by Lytton Strachey. Reprinted by permission of Harcourt, Brace and Company, Inc.; and excerpts from *A Writer's Diary* by Virginia Woolf, copyright, 1953, 1954, by Leonard Woolf. Reprinted by permission of Harcourt, Brace and Company, Inc.

Harper & Brothers for "Here Is New York" by E. B. White. Copyright 1949 by the Curtis Publishing Company.

Henry Holt and Company for "*An Outline of Biography: From Plutarch to Strachey,* by Wilbur L. Cross. Reprinted by permission of Henry Holt and Company, Inc. Copyright 1924.

Christopher Isherwood for his article "Virginia Woolf." This article originally appeared in *Decision* (Volume 1, No. 5, May 1941).

Alfred A. Knopf, Inc., for: "Autobiographical Sketch" reprinted from *Assorted Articles* by D. H. Lawrence, by permission of Alfred A. Knopf, Inc.; copyright 1930 by Alfred A. Knopf. "The Nature of Slang," from *The American Language* by H. L. Mencken, by permission of Alfred A. Knopf, Inc.; copyright 1919, 1921, 1923, 1936 by Alfred A. Knopf.

Life for "Wanted: An American Novel" (Life, September 12, 1955). An Editorial from *Life* Magazine. Reprinted by permission; copyright 1955, *Time* Inc.

Little, Brown & Co., for "The Cliche Expert Testifies on Baseball" from *The Night the Old Nostalgia Burned Down* by Frank Sullivan. Copyright 1949, by Frank Sullivan. This piece first appeared in *The New Yorker.*

Archibald MacLeish for his article "Why Do We Teach Poetry?" originally published in *The Atlantic Monthly.*

The Macmillan Company for "Recent Prose" from *The Reader Over Your*

Shoulder by Robert Graves and Alan Hodge; copyright, 1943 by Robert Graves and Alan Hodge and used with The Macmillan Company's permission.
Mrs. Lester Markel for four essays from *Under Whatever Sky* by Irwin Edman.
Mr. Fred B. Millett for "The Vigilantes" originally published in the *AAUP Bulletin.*
Geoffrey Moore for his article "American Prose Today" originally published in the *8th Mentor Selection, New World Writing.*
National Council of Teachers of English for "Notes on Reading American Literature Abroad" (*College English*, January, 1957) by Ruth Myers; and for "Poets of the English Language" (*College English*, February, 1951) by Robert A. Hume.
New Directions for: "Early Success" from *The Crack-Up* by F. Scott Fitzgerald. Copyright 1945 by New Directions, reprinted by permission of New Directions; and "Letters to His Daughter" from *The Crack-Up* by F. Scott Fitzgerald. Copyright 1945 by New Directions, reprinted by permission of New Directions.
The New Yorker Magazine for: "Hall Continued" (*The New Yorker*, September 28, 1957). Reprinted by permission, © 1957 The New Yorker Magazine, Inc.; "The Nightingale Song" (*The New Yorker*, March 16, 1957). Copyright © 1957 by The New Yorker Magazine, Inc. Reprinted by permission of the author; and "Three in One (*The New Yorker*, May 12, 1956). Reprinted by permission, © 1956 The New Yorker Magazine, Inc.
The New York Times for: the book reviews: "Capital" (The New York Times, May 1, 1887) and "Maggie, A Girl of the Streets" (The New York Times, May 31, 1896); the articles: "Close-up of Britain's Censor" (The New York Times, September 2 and 16, 1956) by George Steiner; "French Fiction and American Reality" by Raymond Leopold Bruckberger; "A Lesson Read in American Books," (The New York Times, December 11, 1955) by Robert Penn Warren; "Ugly Words" (The New York Times, September 30, 1956) by J. Donald Adams; and "More Ugly Words" by J. Donald Adams.
The New York Times Book Review and Aileen Pippett for "Eminent Post-Victorian" (New York Times Book Review, December 8, 1957) by Aileen Pippett.
Oxford University Press for selections from *The Notebooks of Henry James* edited by F. O. Matthiessen and Kenneth B. Murdock; copyright 1947 by Oxford University Press, New York, Inc. Reprinted by permission.
Partisan Review for "Miss Porter's New Stories" by Gertrude Buckman; copyright 1945 by *Partisan Review.*
The Public Trustee and The Society of Authors (London, England) for "My Mother and Her Relatives" from *Sixteen Self Sketches* by Bernard Shaw.
Random House, Inc., for "American Pronunciation" from *Words and Ways of American English* by Thomas Pyle. Copyright 1952 by Random House, Inc.
The Reporter for "Sociological Habit Patterns in Linguistic Transmogrification" (*The Reporter*, September 20, 1956) by Malcolm Cowley. Reprinted by permission of *The Reporter*.
Charles J. Rolo for "Readers Choice" from *The Atlantic Monthly*.
Russell & Volkening, Inc., for "The Reading and Writing of Short Stories" by Eudora Welty, copyright © 1949 by Eudora Welty. Reprinted by permission

of Russell and Volkening, Inc. This article first appeared in *The Atlantic Monthly.*

Charles Shain for his article "American and British English." Reprinted by permission of Charles Shain.

Simon and Schuster, Inc. for "Joseph Conrad" from *Portraits from Memory* by Bertrand Russell. Copyright © 1951, 1952, 1953, 1956 by Bertrand Russell. Reprinted by permission of Simon and Schuster.

Time Inc., for: "Bloomsday's Child" (*Time,* February 3, 1958). Reprinted by permission from *Time,* The Weekly Newsmagazine; copyright Time Inc. 1958. "The Legend of Dylan Thomas" (*Time,* May 30, 1955). Reprinted by permission from *Time,* The Weekly Newsmagazine; copyright Time Inc. 1955.

The Times Literary Supplement (London) for: the book reviews: *The Great Gatsby, An American Tragedy, Soldier's Pay, A Farewell to Arms, The Grapes of Wrath;* and the articles: "The Comic Strip in American Life; and The Art of the Short Story."

Lionel Trilling for " 'Inner-Directed' and 'Other-Directed' " from *A Gathering of Fugitives* (Beacon Press, Inc., 1956) by Lionel Trilling.

The Viking Press, Inc., for: excerpts from *The Journals of Arnold Bennett.* Copyright 1932, 1933 by The Viking Press, Inc., New York; "Former Students" from *Philosopher's Holiday* by Irwin Edman. Copyright 1938 by Irwin Edman. Reprinted by permission of The Viking Press, Inc., New York; and seven essays from *Under Whatever Sky* by Irwin Edman. Copyright 1945, 1947, 1948, 1951 by Irwin Edman. Originally published in The American Scholar. Reprinted by permission of The Viking Press, Inc., New York.

The World Publishing Company for: "Ernest Hemingway" from *The Writer Observed* by Harvey Breit. Copyright 1956 by Harvey Breit. Reprinted by permission of The World Publishing Company; and "English: His Sisters and His Cousins and His Aunts" from *Miracle of Language* by Charlton Laird. Copyright 1953 by Charlton Laird. Reprinted by permission of World Publishing Company.

In memory of

Jewett McKellar Allen

Preface

The freshman English course for which *Modern Prose: Form and Style* is designed sets for its students these goals: to learn to observe and to reflect upon what one sees, to read intelligently and critically, and to write with precision, force, and style.

The readings in this text, very few of which have appeared in other textbooks, are by eminent twentieth century writers. They should broaden the students' knowledge, sharpen their wits, and set them thinking about writing, about writers, about language, and about literature. The readings serve, too, as models of expository writing intended for both analysis and emulation. And finally, not only the introductions and questions but many of the selections themselves provide instruction in the techniques of writing.

As arranged in the ten sections of the book, the readings provide a sequence to pace the student's progress from his first freshman theme to his final term paper. The first four sections represent forms of prose which the student may appropriately attempt early in the course. The instructor may wish to have each student begin his own "writer's notebook" upon which he can draw for later themes. He may also assign biographical and autobiographical sketches, book reviews, and essays that establish or prove a thesis.

Section V emphasizes theme, and shows how the proper management of such elements as tone, coherence, and emphasis helps to create a unified impression. Section VI considers appropriateness as a criterion of style, and points out stylistic pitfalls to be avoided. Section VII provides a glimpse into the history of our changing language, contrasts American and British usage, and helps answer the question, "What determines correctness in English?" Section VIII is a miniature anthology of famous prose stylists illustrating the two major traditions of English and American prose, the simple and the ornate. Section IX, Analysis of Imaginative Literature, links the discussion in this book to the study of short stories, novels, and poetry.

The final section, X, is designed to guide the student in the preparation of a term paper. It provides basic information on how to conduct research and includes practical advice on writing and revising. The broad area selected for research is censorship, a problem of universal and constant concern to everyone interested in literature and in our inherited freedoms. There is a list of forty-five possible term paper subjects. The seven reading selections offer a general introduction to the problem of censorship. These may be used as a controlled-sources research project, in which each student bases his research on these selections only; or each student may be required to compile his own bibliography of sources for his topic. Should the instructor favor having the student write in an altogether different subject area, the general procedures for research and writing as outlined here will nevertheless provide practical help.

The general introductions preceding the sections provide background for the readings and also suggest to the student some of the tools for analysis. The headnotes contain information about the authors and the selections themselves. Exercises at the end of each selection test the student's understanding of content and style, and may be used as the basis both for discussion and for written assignments.

A number of persons have helped me with this text. My wife discussed many of its problems with me, and she typed many sections of it. Mrs. Rita Gregory and Miss Janet Roche also helped with the typing. Mr. John F. Gallagher, who invited me to edit the book, made many valuable suggestions. Frank Buckley, Leonard Unger, Theodore Hornberger, Franz Montgomery, and Martin Steinman, my colleagues, read and criticized a few of the introductions. Mrs. Shirley Kenny worked very hard and ably on parts of the Teacher's Manual. Philip Winsor caught a number of errors, of various kinds, in reading page proof. My chief debt is to Mrs. Fannia Weingartner. She has been a skillful, creative, and always considerate editor.

WILLIAM VAN O'CONNOR

University of Minnesota

Contents

I. Notebooks and Journals

II. Biographical and Autobiographical Sketches

III. Book Reviews

VI. Naturalness and Pretentiousness in Writing

VII. The English Language

VIII. Traditions of English and American Prose

IX. Analysis of Imaginative Literature

X. Writing and Revising the Term Paper

I | Notebooks and Journals

Writing well demands more than a facility with words. It also depends on having something to say. A writer must possess a storehouse of information and observations, and be aware of their quality and significance. A great many impressions flow through our minds in a single day, and sometimes it is difficult to know which will be meaningful later on. We may see or hear something that strikes us as significant—but within a day or two it has slipped from memory. Many writers keep notebooks as a way of storing up and giving significant order to their experiences and observations.

Henry James' advice to a young writer was: "Try to be one of those on whom nothing is ever lost." While James believed a writer should take a good many notes, he did not believe that mere accumulation of notes was enough. A writer, he said, "has to take a great many in order to select a few." In pondering a series of notes, the writer will often see a pattern of meaning that might otherwise escape him, and in keeping a notebook he will undoubtedly develop a sense for the curious, the singular, the evocative.

The notebook or journal consists of a series of entries. The length of the entries depends on the writer and the occasion. He records whatever seems to him of more than passing interest, in the degree of detail necessary to stimulate, to elicit old and new associations. He may record a word that interests him, an anecdote, or write a vignette. Writers sometimes use a notebook to reflect on an idea, to develop a theme, or to analyze their reaction to an experience. The entry may be a rough jotting or a well-turned epigram, a phrase, or a fully developed essay. There are no rules:

the writer's taste and needs dictate the form and the character of his notebook or journal.

In the following selections we will see how individual a thing the notebook or journal is, how its one function is to please or serve the author. Samuel Butler drew on his notebooks for his novel, *The Way of All Flesh*. Arnold Bennett used his journal as a storehouse of raw material—incidents and observations—for essays and stories. The story Henry James entered in his notebook about Mrs. Kemble's sister became the germ for his novel, *Washington Square*. Virginia Woolf's reflections on people and literature are similar to those found in her novels and essays.

None of these writers intended to publish his notebook or journal. Other writers, however, have exploited the possibilities of the form in writing for publication. In his little sketches, Irwin Edman has brought it close to the informal essay. The anonymous authors of the "My Man Stanley" and "My Man Hall" reports in *The New Yorker* use the personal, informal quality of the notebook entry as a means of writing humorously about public events.

The jottings to be found in notebooks might seem too casual and fragmentary ever to be thought of as literature. Yet we often read notebooks with a sense that we are getting at a vital part of a man's thought and are seeing his life or even his age from a perspective that more formal modes of writing fail to provide. A good example of this is Samuel Pepys' *Diary*, one of the most famous in our language. Pepys (1633–1703) kept his diary during the Restoration, a period which handbooks of literature tell us was marked by a love of wit and gaiety as well as an intense interest in science. These qualities become real for us through the pages of Pepys' diary. Here are a few entries:

October 11, 1660—. . . . To walk in St. James Park where we observed the several engines at work to draw up water, with which sight I was very much pleased. Above all the rest, I liked that which Mr. Greatoress brought, which do carry up the water with a great deal of ease. Here, in the Park, we met with Mr. Salisbury, who took Mr. Creed and me to the Cockpit to see *The Moore of Venice*, which was well done. Burt acted the Moore; by the same token, a very pretty lady that sat by me, called out, to see Desdemona smothered.

January 1, 1662—Waking this morning out of my sleep on a sudden I did with my elbow hit my wife a great blow over her face and neck which waked her with pain, at which I was sorry, and to sleep again. . . .

March 1, 1662—My wife and I by coach, first to see my little picture that is a-drawing, and thence to the Opera, and there saw *Romeo and Juliet*, the first time it was ever acted, but it is a play of itself the worst that ever I saw these people do, and I am resolved to go no more to see the first time of acting, for they were all of them out more or less. . . .

Pepys wrote informally and with relish. He kept his diary from January 1, 1660, to May 31, 1703, and through it posterity has a fuller understanding of its author than it does of any of his more highly placed contemporaries. Pepys kept his diary purely for his own edification: other writers, as we shall see, have kept notebooks and journals as storehouses of material for future use, or have used the notebook form when writing casual pieces for publication.

1 *from* THE NOTE BOOKS
by Samuel Butler

Samuel Butler (1835–1902) was known by his contemporaries as an eccentric controversialist and as the author of Erewhon, *a satiric fantasy on English customs. Ironically, it is his posthumously published works, the autobiographical novel* The Way of All Flesh, *and* The Notebooks of Samuel Butler, *which have been most widely read and most influential. Many of the finest twentieth-century writers, among them George Bernard Shaw, E. M. Forster, and Virginia Woolf have acknowledged their debt to Butler.*

Butler's revolt against the moral attitudes of Victorian England is implicit in many of the entries in his Notebooks; *we find, there, in embryo, themes developed in his major works. He attacks false modesty (Our Conceit); he rejects the notion that poverty makes for virtue and claims, indeed, that possession and not lack of money opens the way to personal and intellectual cultivation (Money and Culture). The impersonal form of his aphorisms is deceptive: a careful reading reveals an intense passion artfully veiled by polished phrases.*

Opening For My Biography

Jones laughingly talked of writing my life. I said I would give him an opening sentence, thus: "The subject of this memoir was born of wealthy but dishonest parents, Dec. 4th, 1835. He inherited the dishonesty, but not the wealth of his family."

Hogarth's "Idle and Virtuous Apprentice" [1] is an immoral work for it

[1] A comment on William Hogarth's moralistic series of engravings, "Industry and Idleness" (1747), in which the fates of two apprentices, the one industrious, the other lazy, are pictured. The former becomes Lord Mayor of London, the latter is executed as a thief.

represents virtue and its consequences in a light nearly as odious as vice. Those are best who are neither virtuous nor idle.

"God is Love"

I like "Love is God" better.

Our Conceit

He is a poor creature who does not believe himself to be better than the whole world else. No matter how ill we may be, nor how low we may have fallen, we would not change identity with any other person. Hence our self-conceit sustains and always must sustain us till death takes us and our conceit together so that we need no more sustaining.

Good Breeding the Summum Bonum

When people ask what faith we would substitute for that which we would destroy, we answer that we destroy no faith and need substitute none. We hold the glory of God to be the summum bonum and so do Christians generally. It is a question of what is the glory of God. It is here that we join issue. We say it varies with the varying phases of God as made manifest in his works, but that so far as we are ourselves concerned the glory of God is best advanced by advancing that of man. If asked what is the glory of man, we answer "Good breeding"—using the words in their double sense, and meaning both the continuance of the race and that grace of manner which the words are more commonly taken to signify.

The double sense of the words is all the more significant for the unconsciousness with which it is passed over.

Physical Excellence

The question whether such and such a course of conduct does or does not do physical harm is the safest test by which to try the question whether it is moral or no. If it does no harm to the body, we ought to be very chary of calling it immoral, while if it tends towards physical excellence, there should be no hesitation in calling it moral. Overwork is as immoral in the case of those who are not forced to overwork themselves (and there are many who work themselves to death for the mere inability to restrain the passion for work which masters them as the craving for drink masters a drunkard)—overwork in these cases is as immoral as overeating or drinking. This, so far as the individual is concerned; as regards the body politic as a whole it is no doubt well that there should be some men and women so built that they cannot be stopped from working themselves to death, just as it is unquestionably well that there should be some who cannot be stopped from drinking themselves to death, if only that they may keep the horror of the habit well in evidence.

Purse, Person and Reputation

A man will feel money losses more keenly than loss even of bodily health. Take his money away, and deprive him of the means of earning any more, and his health will soon break up, but leave him his money, and even though his health breaks up and he dies, he does not mind it so much as we think. Money losses are the worst, bodily pain is next worst, and loss of reputation comes in a bad third. All other things are amusements, provided money, health and good name are untouched.

Greatness

He is greatest who is most often in man's good thoughts.

Money and Culture

People oppose money to culture, and imply that if a man has spent his time in making money he will not be cultivated. Fallacy of fallacies! As though there could be a greater aid to culture than the having earned an honourable independence, and as though any amount of culture will do much for the man who is penniless, except make him feel his position more deeply. The young man who was told to sell all his goods and give to the poor, must have been an entirely exceptional person if the advice was given wisely, either for him or for the poor. How much more often does it happen that we perceive a man to have all sorts of good qualities except money, and feel that his real duty lies in getting every halfpenny that he can persuade others to pay him for his services, and becoming rich. It has been said that the love of money is the root of all evil. The want of money is so quite as truly.

EXERCISES

1. After studying these passages from Butler's *Notebooks,* select one that interests you (you don't have to agree with it) and write a short paper expressing your views on it.
2. Would Butler's views be considered controversial today?
3. Analyze the quality of Butler's irony. What part does it play in communicating his views?

2 *from* THE NOTEBOOKS

by Henry James

Henry James (1843–1916) was born in New York and educated there and abroad. Much of his life was spent in Europe, and in 1915, he became a British subject. James is most widely known for his novels, among them, Daisy Miller, The Portrait of a Lady, The Princess Casamassima, *and* The Ambassadors, *but he also wrote short stories, literary criticism, plays, travel books, and several autobiographical works.*

The Notebooks of Henry James, *as Joseph Warren Beach pointed out, enable us "to follow the stages of that mysterious process by which, out of the untidy, ambiguous stuff of life, is fashioned, by infinite patient strokes of art, the ordered cosmos, the brave new world of the imagination." Here is an unusual record of how a writer develops ideas for his stories. Sometimes there is just a phrase; sometimes, as in the entry dated February 21, 1881, a story with characters and plot almost fully realized. James' reflections on his return to America (November 25, 1881) are particularly revealing when we remember that the impact of European culture and traditions on Americans forms the central theme of many of his novels and short stories.*

February 21st, 1881. Mrs. Kemble[1] told me last evening the history of her brother H.'s engagement to Miss T. H. K. was a young ensign in a marching regiment, very handsome ('beautiful') said Mrs. K., but very luxurious and selfish, and without a penny to his name. Miss T. was a dull, plain, common-place girl, only daughter of the Master of King's Coll., Cambridge, who had a handsome private fortune (£4000 a year). She was very much in love with H. K., and was of that slow, sober, dutiful nature that an impression once made upon her, was made for ever. Her father disapproved strongly (and justly) of the engagement and informed her that if she married young K. he would not leave her a penny

[1] Frances Anne Kemble, the actress and writer, was 69 when James made this entry. He had written to his mother a month before: 'She is certainly one of the women I know whom I like best. . . . It is . . . a kind of rest and refreshment to see a women who (extremely annoying as she sometimes is) gives one a positive sense of having a deep, rich, human nature and having cast off all vulgarities.' In April 1893, shortly after her death, he published an essay on her in *Temple Bar*.

of his money. It was only in her money that H. was interested; he wanted a rich wife who would enable him to live at his ease and pursue his pleasures. Miss T. was in much tribulation and she asked Mrs. K. what she would advise her to do—Henry K. having taken the ground that if she would hold on and marry him the old Doctor would after a while relent and they should get the money. (It was in this belief that he was holding on to her.) Mrs. K. advised the young girl by *no means* to marry her brother. 'If your father does relent and you are well off, he will make you a kindly enough husband, so long as all goes well. But if he should not, and you were to be poor, your lot would be miserable. *Then* my brother would be a very uncomfortable companion—*then* he would visit upon you his disappointment and discontent.' Miss T. reflected a while; and then, as she was much in love with <him>, she determined to disobey her father and take the consequences. Meanwhile, H. K., however, had come to the conclusion that the father's forgiveness was not to be counted upon—that his attitude was very firm and that if they should marry, he would never see the money. *Then* all his effort was to disentangle himself. He went off, shook himself free of the engagement, let the girl go. She was deeply wounded—they separated. Some few years elapsed—her father died and she came into his fortune. She never received the addresses of another man—she always cared in secret for Henry K.—but she was determined to remain unmarried. K. lived about the world in different military stations, and at last, at the end of 10 years (or more), came back to England—still a handsome, selfish, impecunious soldier. One of his other sisters (Mrs. S.) then attempted to bring on the engagement again—knowing that Miss T. still cared for him. She tried to make Mrs. K. join her in this undertaking, but the latter refused, saying that it was an ignoble speculation and that her brother had forfeited every claim to being thought well of by Miss T. But K. again, on his own responsibility, paid his addresses to Miss T. She refused him—it was too late. And yet, said Mrs. K., she cared for him—and she would have married no other man. But H. K.'s selfishness had over-reached itself and this was the retribution of time.

* * *

In a story, some one says—'Oh yes, the United States—a country without a sovereign, without a court, without a nobility, without an army, without a church or a clergy, without a diplomatic service, without a picturesque peasantry, without palaces or castles, or country seats, or ruins, without a literature, without novels, without an Oxford or a Cambridge, without cathedrals or ivied churches, without latticed cottages or village ale-houses, without political society, without sport, without fox-hunting or country gentlemen, without an Epsom or an Ascot, an Eton or a Rugby . . . !'

Brunswick Hotel, Boston, November 25th, 1881

If I should write here all that I might write, I should speedily fill this as yet unspotted blank-book, bought in London six months ago, but hitherto unopened. It is so long since I have kept any notes, taken any memoranda, written down my current reflections, taken a sheet of paper, as it were, into my confidence. Meanwhile so much has come and gone, so much that it is now too late to catch, to reproduce, to preserve. I have lost too much by losing, or rather by not having acquired, the note-taking habit. It might be of great profit to me; and now that I am older, that I have more time, that the labour of writing is less onerous to me, and I can work more at my leisure, I ought to endeavour to keep, to a certain extent, a record of passing impressions, of all that comes, that goes, that I see, and feel, and observe. To catch and keep something of life—that's what I mean. Here I am back in America, for instance, after six years of absence, and likely while here to see and learn a great deal that ought not to become mere waste material. Here I am, *da vero*, and here I am likely to be for the next five months. I am glad I have come—it was a wise thing to do. I needed to see again *les miens*, to revive my relations with them, and my sense of the consequences that these relations entail. Such relations, such consequences, are a part of one's life, and the best life, the most complete, is the one that takes full account of such things. One can only do this by seeing one's people from time to time, by being with them, by entering into their lives. Apart from this I hold it was not necessary I should come to this country. I am 37 [2] years old, I have made my choice, and God knows that I have now no time to waste. My choice is the old world—my choice, my need, my life. There is no need for me today to argue about this; it is an inestimable blessing to me, and a rare good fortune, that the problem was settled long ago, and that I have now nothing to do but to act on the settlement.—My impressions here are exactly what I expected they would be, and I scarcely see the place, and feel the manners, the race, the tone of things, now that I am on the spot, more vividly than I did while I was still in Europe. My work lies there—and with this vast new world, *je n'ai que faire*. One can't do both —one must choose. No European writer is called upon to assume that terrible burden, and it seems hard that I should be. The burden is necessarily greater for an American—for he *must* deal, more or less, even if only by implication, with Europe; whereas no European is obliged to deal in the least with America. No one dreams of calling him less complete for not doing so. (I speak of course of people who do the sort of work that I do; not of economists, of social science people.) The painter of manners who neglects America is not thereby incomplete as yet; but a

[2] He was actually 38.

hundred years hence—fifty years hence perhaps—he will doubtless be accounted so. My impressions of America, however, I shall, after all, not write here. I don't need to write them (at least not *à propos* of Boston); I know too well what they are. In many ways they are extremely pleasant; but, Heaven forgive me! I feel as if my time were terribly wasted here! . . .

February 9th, 1882, 102 Mt. Vernon St., Boston

When I began to make these rather ineffectual records I had no idea that I should have in a few weeks to write such a tale of sadness as today. I came back from Washington on the 30th of last month (reached Cambridge the next day), to find that I should never again see my dear mother. On Sunday, Jan. 29th, as Aunt Kate sat with her in the closing dusk (she had been ill with an attack of bronchial asthma, but was apparently recovering happily), she passed away. It makes a great difference to me! I knew that I loved her—but I didn't know how tenderly till I saw her lying in her shroud in that cold North Room, with a dreary snow-storm outside, and looking as sweet and tranquil and noble as in life. These are hours of exquisite pain; thank Heaven this particular pang comes to us but once. On Sunday evening (at 10 o'clock in Washington) I was dressing to go to Mrs. Robinson's—who has written me a very kind letter—when a telegram came in from Alice (William's): 'Your mother exceedingly ill. Come at once.' It was a great alarm, but it didn't suggest the loss of all hope; and I made the journey to New York with whatever hope seemed to present itself. In New York at 5 o'clock I went to Cousin H. P.'s—and there the telegram was translated to me. Eliza Ripley was there—and Katie Rodgers—and as I went out I met Lily Walsh. The rest was dreary enough. I went back to the Hoffman House, where I had engaged a room on my way up town and remained there till 9:30, when I took the night-train to Boston. I shall never pass that place in future without thinking of the wretched hours I spent there. At home the worst was over; I found father and Alice and A. K.[3] extraordinarily calm—almost happy. Mother seemed still to be there—so beautiful, so full of all that we loved in her, she looked in death. We buried her on Wednesday, Feb. 1st; Wilkie arrived from Milwaukee a couple of hours before. Bob[4] had been there for a month—he was devoted to mother in her illness. It was a splendid winter's day—the snow lay deep and high. We placed her, for the present, in a temporary vault in the Cambridge cemetery—the part that lies near the river. When the spring comes on we shall go and choose a burial place. I have often walked there in the old years—in those long, lonely rambles that I used to take about Cambridge,

[3] 'A. K.' was 'Aunt Kate'—James' mother's sister, Katherine Walsh.
[4] Henry James' youngest brother, Robertson.

and I had, I suppose, a vague idea that some of us would some day lie there, but I didn't see just that scene. It is impossible for me to say—to begin to say—all that has gone down into the grave with her. She was our life, she was the house, she was the keystone of the arch. She held us all together, and without her we are scattered reeds. She was patience, she was wisdom, she was exquisite maternity. Her sweetness, her mildness, her great natural beneficence were unspeakable, and it is infinitely touching to me to write about her as one that *was*. When I think of all that she had been, for years—when I think of her hourly devotion to each and all of us—and that when I went to Washington the last of December I gave her my last kiss, I heard her voice for the last time—there seems not to be enough tenderness in my being to register the extinction of such a life. But I can reflect, with perfect gladness, that her work was done—her long patience had done its utmost. She had had heavy cares and sorrows, which she had borne without a murmur, and the weariness of age had come upon her. I would rather have lost her forever than see her begin to suffer as she would probably have been condemned to suffer, and I can think with a kind of holy joy of her being lifted now above all our pains and anxieties. Her death has given me a passionate belief in certain transcendent things—the immanence of being as nobly created as hers—the immortality of such a virtue as that—the reunion of spirits in better conditions than these. She is no more of an angel today than she had always been; but I can't believe that by the accident of her death all her unspeakable tenderness is lost to the beings she so dearly loved. She is with us, she is of us—the eternal stillness is but a form of her love. One can hear her voice in it—one can feel, forever, the inextinguishable vibration of her devotion. I can't help feeling that in those last weeks I was not tender enough with her—that I was blind to her sweetness and beneficence. One can't help wishing one had only known what was coming, so that one might have enveloped her with the softest affection. When I came back from Europe I was struck with her being worn and shrunken, and now I know that she was very weary. She went about her usual activities, but the burden of life had grown heavy for her, and she needed rest. There is something inexpressibly touching to me in the way in which, during these last years, she went on from year to year without it. If she could only have lived she should have had it, and it would have been a delight to see her have it. But she has it now, in the most complete perfection! Summer after summer she never left Cambridge—it was impossible that father should leave his own house. The country, the sea, the change of air and scene, were an exquisite enjoyment to her; but she bore with the deepest gentleness and patience the constant loss of such opportunities. She passed her nights and her days in that dry, flat, hot, stale and odious Cambridge, and had never a thought while she did so but for father and Alice. It was a perfect mother's life—the life of a perfect wife. To bring her children into the world—to expend herself, for years, for their happiness and welfare—then, when they had reached a full maturity and were absorbed in the world and in their own interests—to lay herself down in her ebbing strength and yield up her pure soul to the celestial power that had given her this divine commission. Thank God one knows this loss but once; and thank God that certain supreme impressions remain! . . .

EXERCISES

1. James used the story Mrs. Kemble told him in his novel *Washington Square*. Write about an incident you saw or heard of as if you were entering it into a notebook with the thought that you might use it as the basis for a long short story or novel.
2. James was proud of being an American, but he felt that as a novelist his work lay in Europe. Read his comment on this carefully and explain in your own words what his reasons for this were.
3. There is a controlled quality about James' account of his mother's life; does it follow that he did not feel strongly toward her? How much do we learn about James' mother? How much about James?

3 *from* THE JOURNALS
by Arnold Bennett

Arnold Bennett (1867–1931) is most famous for The Old Wives' Tale *and the "Clayhanger" series of novels about his birthplace, the "Potteries" region of Staffordshire. At twenty-one, Bennett moved to London and subsequently spent several years in Paris. After the success of his early works, particularly* The Grand Babylon Hotel, *Bennett devoted himself entirely to writing.*

Bennett began his journal as a young man and kept it faithfully, whether at home, abroad, or on the high seas. Matters both significant and trivial were recorded with care: his state of health, the amount of money he earned, reflections on what he heard or read, anecdotes, and personal impressions. Some of these entries were obviously made for his own pleasure, others as potential material for stories and articles. From his painstaking analysis of the progress of a headache to his amusing account of his visit to the mysterious Mrs. L., one senses Bennett's resolution to waste nothing of what he experienced.

1896: Friday, May 15th.—At noon precisely I finished my first novel, which was begun about the middle of April last year; but five-sixths of the work at least has been performed since the 1st October. Yesterday, I sat down at 3 p.m. to write, and, with slight interruptions for meals etc., kept at it till 1 a.m. this morning. The concluding chapter was written between 9 and 12 to-day.

My fears about *In the Shadow* [published as *A Man from the North*] are (1) that it is not well-knit, (2) that it is hysterical, or at any rate strained in tone. Still, I should not be surprised if it impressed many respectable people. The worst parts of it seem to me to be in front of my *Yellow Book* story ['A Letter Home'], which came in for a full share of laudation.

Thursday, October 15th.—Does there, I wonder, exist a being who has read all, or approximately all, that the person of average culture is supposed to have read, and that not to have read is a social sin? If such a being does exist, surely he is an old, a very old man, who has read steadily that which he ought to have read sixteen hours a day, from early infancy. I cannot recall a single author of whom I have read everything—even of Jane Austen. I have never seen *Susan* and *The Watsons*, one of which I have been told is superlatively good. Then there are large tracts of Shakespeare, Bacon, Spenser, nearly all Chaucer, Congreve, Dryden, Pope, Swift, Sterne, Johnson, Scott, Coleridge, Shelley, Byron, Edgeworth, Ferrier, Lamb, Leigh Hunt, Wordsworth (nearly all), Tennyson, Swinburne, the Brontës, George Eliot, W. Morris, George Meredith, Thomas Hardy, Savage Landor, Thackeray, Carlyle—in fact every classical author and most good modern authors, which I have never even overlooked. A list of the masterpieces I have *not* read would fill a volume. With only one author can I call myself familiar, Jane Austen. With Keats and Stevenson, I have an acquaintance. So far of English. Of foreign authors I am familiar with de Maupassant and the de Goncourts. I have yet to finish Don Quixote!

Nevertheless I cannot accuse myself of default. I have been extremely fond of reading since I was 20, and since I was 20 I have read practically nothing (save professionally, as a literary critic) but what was 'right'. My leisure has been moderate, my desire strong and steady, my taste in selection certainly above the average, and yet in ten years I seem scarcely to have made an impression upon the intolerable multitude of volumes which 'everyone is supposed to have read'.

Essential characteristic of the really great novelist: a Christ-like, all-embracing compassion.

Wednesday, December 9th.—I have just finished reading J. M. Barrie's account of his mother, *Margaret Ogilvy*. This book is a picture of a grave, mighty, passionate family of men and women. Instinctively, and all the time, I was comparing it with my own, and in particular comparing

Margaret Ogilvy and J. M. Barrie with my mother and myself. Again and again, I had to acknowledge inferiority—inferiority of essential 'character', apart from inessential talent—a lack of bigness, and a presence of certain littlenesses. Yet at the same time, I found us sturdy enough not to be ashamed of shortcomings. What we are, we are! 'I exist as I am, that is enough.' To hold such a creed religiously is in one way to be great.

A proud, self-unconscious self-esteem: that is what few people have. If at times it deserts me and mine, it always returns the stronger for having retreated. We are of the North, outwardly brusque, stoical, undemonstrative, scornful of the impulsive; inwardly all sentiment and crushed tenderness. We are of the North, incredibly, ruthlessly independent; and eager to say 'Damn you' to all the deities at the least hint of condescension.

1897: Tuesday, October 5th.—To wake up at midnight, after an hour's sleep, with a headache, slight but certainly indicative of the coming attack; to hear the clock strike, every note drilling a separate hole into your skull; to spend the rest of the night uneasily between sleeping and waking, always turning over the pillow, and tormented intermittently by idiotic nightmares, crowded with action, which fatigue the brain: this is a disturbed liver. Towards morning comes the hope, caused by the irregularity of the pain, that the headache will pass away on getting up. But it never does so. Then one comes downstairs, eyes as it were in red-hot sockets, and gulps some effervescing saline. One rises from breakfast with a mouth full of reminiscences—butter, cocoa, porridge, and the headache remains. One walks to the office in the fresh autumn air; the headache remains. Towards noon, one seeks the last remedy, a draught which weakens the action of the heart. It is effective, and after half an hour's somnolence in a chair, one recovers, half-dazed, but without the headache; weak, silly, nerveless, but without the headache. The impulse to work is alive again, and one accomplishes an hour. But after lunch and dinner one has a consciousness that a new headache is lying in wait, and, one's resolves worn away by the constant sense of fatigue in the eyes and of rapid pulsation round the back of the head, one weakly lapses into idleness, trusting that to-morrow will be different.

1898: Tuesday, January 11th.—It seems to me that only within the last few years have we absorbed from France that passion for the artistic shapely presentation of truth, and that feeling for words as words, which animated Flaubert, the de Goncourts, and de Maupassant, and which is so exactly described and defined in de Maupassant's introduction to the collected works of Flaubert. None of the (so-called) great masters of English nineteenth-century fiction had (if I am right) a deep artistic interest in form and treatment; they were absorbed in 'subject'—just as the 'anecdote'-painters of the Royal Academy are absorbed in subject, and in my view they are open to the same reproach as these. Certainly they had not the feeling for words to any large degree, though one sees traces of it sometimes in the Brontës,—never in George Eliot, or Jane Austen, or Dickens, or even Thackeray or Scott.

Yet that this feeling for words existed independently in England is proved by the prose of Charles Lamb and John Ruskin. The novelists cared little for form, the *science* of construction,—*Composition*. They had not artistic taste; they lacked this just as Millais lacked it. Millais may have been a great painter; these novelists may have been great writers, but neither (to use de Maupassant's distinction) were great artists in the sense in which I understand the word. An artist must be interested primarily in presentment, not in the thing presented.

Saturday, March 12th.—On my way to seeing Mrs L. [who had a 'cure' for stammering] I called at a bread-shop in Holborn. To judge from the exterior one could desire no place of refreshment more fastidiously neat and dainty. But when I was inside I found the shop and the room at the back occupied by women and girls in various conditions of *déshabillé*. The place was being cleaned, and the hour being only 11 a.m. customers were clearly not expected. The girls all looked up surprised, and with a show of indifference I picked my way amongst kneeling figures into the inner room. When I had sat down, I heard a rummaging noise under the table, and presently a fat young girl appeared therefrom. She hurried away laughing, but came back shortly and produced from under the table a tin bowl of dirty water which she carried away, with a giggle. I ordered a glass of milk and a sandwich, and then waited. A girl, tall, thin and vacuous, ran upstairs and came down soon afterwards pinning on an apron at the back. She brought me my food. I ate it, while looking at a dirty newspaper placed to protect the newly-washed floor, and at the crimson petticoat showing through the placket-hole of a girl who was washing the floor behind the counter. I could feel about me the atmosphere of femininity. The dirt and untidiness spoilt the taste of my food, and I thought: 'This is a bad omen for the result of my interview with Mrs L.'

The room into which I was shown in Gower Street was, I think, the ugliest, the most *banal* I have seen. From the twisted columns of the furniture to the green rep of the upholstering, everything expressed Bloomsbury in its highest power. This was a boarding-house. My hopes sank, and they were not raised by the appearance of Mrs L. who combines the profession of a landlady with that of a 'mental healer'. She looks the typical landlady, shabbily dressed, middle-aged, and with that hardened, permanently soured expression of eyes and lips which all landladies seem to acquire. She fitted with and completed the room.

She asked me about my stammering and my health generally, talking in a quiet, firm, authoritative voice. I noticed the fatigue of her drooping eyelids and the terrific firmness of her thin lips. She told me how she had been cured of nervousness by Dr Patterson of America, and gave a number of instances of his success and her own in 'mentally treating' nervous and physical disorders. Some of them were so incredible that I asked myself what I, notorious as a sane level-headed man, was doing in that galley. However, as Mrs L. talked I was rather impressed by her sincerity, her strong quietude, and her sagacity. I asked what the patient had to do. 'Nothing,' she said. I explained my attitude towards 'mental healing'—that I neither believed nor disbelieved in it, that certainly I could not promise her the assistance of my 'faith'.

'Can you cure me of my stammering?'

'I am quite sure I can,' she answered with quiet assurance, 'but it will take some time. This is a case of a lifelong habit, not of a passing ailment.'

'Shall you want to see me often?'

'I shall not want to see you at all; but if you feel that you want to see me, of course you can do so. I shall look after your general health too. If you have a bad headache, or a liver attack, send me a word and I will help you.'

I nodded acquiescence but I was nearly laughing aloud, and telling her that I preferred to dispense with these mysterious services. As I was arranging terms with her, I marvelled that I should be assisting at such an interview. And yet—supposing there were after all something in it! I was not without hope. She had distinctly impressed me, especially by odd phrases here and there which seemed to indicate a certain depth of character in her. I went away smiling—half believing that the whole business was a clever fraud, and half expecting some happy result.

To-night I sent her a cheque. I wondered, as I wrote it out, whether twelve months hence I should be wanting to burn these pages which recorded my credulity, or whether with all the enthusiasm of my nature I should be spreading abroad the report of Mrs L's powers.

1901: Sunday, May 26th.—Talking about the Potteries with me, Billy Bennett told me that his father had once pointed out to him, that no potting firm, except Wedgwoods, had survived to the third generation. The first generation was of the people, industrial, simple; the second, though raised in the social grade, was still plodding and energetic and kept the business together; the third was a generation of wastrels coming to grief. He said that the usual condemnatory phrase of potters for bad clay was 'Nowt but moss-muck'.

1907: Sunday, October 20th.—A curious instance of avarice from Calvocoressi. An old lady living in a 9,000 fr. apartment in the Avenue de la Grande Armée, who pays two servants 150 fr. per month each in order to induce them to stand her avaricious ways. There is a story in this. If a piece of mutton was bought that was too much for one day and not enough for two, she would say to the servant: 'Supposing I don't eat any to-day will there be enough for to-morrow?' 'Yes, madame!' And she would starve. If her son was reading the paper in the evening she would say: 'Anything interesting in the paper?' 'No, nothing special.' 'Then let us turn off the light, and sit in the dark and talk.' When alone in the evening, in order to save the electric light, she would spend her time in promenading on the staircase.

1912: Wednesday, November 6th.—Day before yesterday, after having written about 6,000 words of new novel, I decided to begin it again, in a somewhat different key, but with exactly the same construction. And I did begin it again, and at once felt easier in my mind. I also decided that I would not make a fine MS. of it. The regularity of the lines and handwriting does not seem to accord with style in which this novel is to be written. A freer style than before—a little more capricious and swinging.

Tuesday, November 19th.—

A Conductor's Phrases in taking a Rehearsal

Must be all dubious.
I want a savage staccato.
Nice and limpid.
Nice and stormy.
Nice and gusty.
Nice and manifold.
Weep, Mr Parker, weep. (Mr Parker weeps.) That's jolly.
Press that 'A' home.
Don't handicap the crescendo.
It's not a bee's wedding, it's something elemental.
Gentlemen of the first fiddles.
Try it slurred, a sort of dot and carry two.
Not a wind you can cut with a knife, you must come and die.
This echo is so teasing.
Sorry to tease you.
An intimate 'cello solo.
Sixth desk forward, please. (Somebody in the orchestra, 'Sign, please.')
Sigh and die.
Now, side-drum, assert yourself.
Everybody must be shadowy together.
I want it mostly music.
That regular rum-tum which you do so ideally.
Let the pizzicato act as a sort of springboard to the passage.
A freshness inside the piano.
A sudden exquisite hush.

1929: London, May 27th.—My birthday. I celebrated it by going to

Portland Place and undergoing what for some inexplicable reason is called a thorough 'overhaul'. I had been warned that every man over fifty ought to be 'overhauled' every few years, whether he thinks he needs it or not. Dire maladies may unobtrusively begin their awful work within you, and develop and develop quite unsuspected, and then suddenly declare open war on you, and you are dead before you are prepared for death. Moreover, had I not been suffering from chronic insomnia for many years, and must not insomnia have a cause? And so on. The advice seemed sensible. As regards insomnia, my overhauler suggested that I should take a drug, 'medinol', every night for three months or six months. Yes, such was the advice I paid for!

London, June 5th.—I received the detailed report of my overhauler, via my ordinary doctor, in accordance with medical etiquette. There was nothing the matter with me at all. Blood pressure right. Heart very fine. Lungs very fine. Arteries suitable to the age of 32 instead of 62. The liver somewhat less brilliant than the other parts of the body, but still an excellent specimen of this great organ. No light thrown on my chronic insomnia. As a fact, another doctor, not professionally consulted, had once uttered to me the final word about my insomnia: 'It's simply this,' he said. 'You happen to be a bad sleeper.' I have never got beyond that!

EXERCISES

1. Bennett once said of himself, "I don't care what anyone says, I am a nice man." On the basis of these notes, write a short paper characterizing Bennett. You might want to compare him with Butler and with James.
2. How is Bennett's interest in literature reflected in these entries? Is there a special quality about them which reveals that this was a Journal kept by a professional writer?
3. Which of these entries might have been used as the basis for a short story or article? Write a brief account of an anecdote or incident from your own experience that could be the germ of a story or article.

4 *from* A WRITER'S DIARY
by Virginia Woolf

Virginia Woolf *(1882–1941) was the daughter of biographer and literary critic Sir Leslie Stephen. With her husband, Leonard Woolf, she was part of the Bloomsbury Group of writers, artists, journalists, and critics (page 62). She committed suicide in 1941. Virginia Woolf is known both for her literary criticism, much of which appeared in* The Common Reader *and* The Second Common Reader, *and her novels, particularly* Mrs. Dalloway, To the Lighthouse, *and* Orlando.

A Writer's Diary, *edited by her huband, was published after her death. In it she discussed her interests, her friends, her reading, and the progress of her work. Virginia Woolf's sensitivity, her probing self-analysis, and her concern with artistic values, so much a feature of her fiction and criticism, are very clearly revealed in these diary excerpts. Whether she was reflecting on* Paradise Lost, *commenting on the personality of Arnold Bennett, or wondering about her own literary reputation, her writing is penetrating, intelligent, and always intensely personal.*

Tuesday, September 10, 1918

Though I am not the only person in Sussex who reads Milton, I mean to write down my impressions of *Paradise Lost* while I am about it. Impressions fairly well describes the sort of thing left in my mind. I have left many riddles unread. I have slipped on too easily to taste the full flavour. However, I see, and agree to some extent in believing, that this full flavour is the reward of highest scholarship. I am struck by the extreme difference between this poem and any other. It lies, I think, in the sublime aloofness and impersonality of the emotion. I have never read Cowper on the sofa, but I can imagine that the sofa is a degraded substitute for *Paradise Lost*. The substance of Milton is all made of wonderful, beautiful and masterly descriptions of angels' bodies, battles, flights, dwelling places. He deals in horror and immensity and squalor and sublimity but never in the passions of the human heart. Has any great poem ever let in so little light upon one's own joys and sorrows? I get no help in judging life; I scarcely feel that Milton lived or knew men and women;

except for the peevish personalities about marriage and the woman's duties. He was the first of the masculinists, but his disparagement rises from his own ill luck and seems even a spiteful last word in his domestic quarrels. But how smooth, strong and elaborate it all is! What poetry? I can conceive that even Shakespeare after this would seem a little troubled, personal, hot and imperfect. I can conceive that this is the essence, of which almost all other poetry is the dilution. The inexpressible fineness of the style, in which shade after shade is perceptible, would alone keep one gazing into it, long after the surface business in progress has been despatched. Deep down one catches still further combinations, rejections, felicities and masteries. Moreover, though there is nothing like Lady Macbeth's terror or Hamlet's cry, no pity or sympathy or intuition, the figures are majestic; in them is summed up much of what men thought of our place in the universe, of our duty to God, our religion.

Wednesday, March 19, 1919

Life piles up so fast that I have no time to write out the equally fast rising mound of reflections, which I always mark down as they rise to be inserted here. I meant to write about the Barnetts and the peculiar repulsiveness of those who dabble their fingers self-approvingly in the stuff of others' souls. The Barnetts were at any rate plunged to the elbow; red handed if ever philanthropists were, which makes them good examples; and then, unquestioning and unspeculative as they were, they give themselves away almost to the undoing of my critical faculty. Is it chiefly intellectual snobbery that makes me dislike them? Is it snobbery to feel outraged when she says "Then I came close to the Great Gates"—or reflects that God = good, devil = evil. Has this coarseness of grain any necessary connection with labour for one's kind? And then the smug vigour of their self-satisfaction! Never a question as to the right of what they do—always a kind of insensate forging ahead, until, naturally, their undertakings are all of colossal size and portentous prosperity. Moreover, could any woman of humour or insight quote such paeans to her own genius? Perhaps the root of it all lies in the adulation of the uneducated, and the easy mastery of the will over the poor. And more and more I come to loathe any dominion of one over another; any leadership, any imposition of the will. Finally, my literary taste is outraged by the smooth way in which the tale is made to unfold into fullblown success, like some profuse peony. But I only scratch the surface of what I feel about these two stout volumes.[1]

[1] *Rev. Canon S. A. Barnett; His Life, Work and Friends.* By his wife, Mrs. Barnett, C. B. E. (Murray).

Wednesday, August 16, 1922

I should be reading *Ulysses*, and fabricating my case for and against. I have read 200 pages so far—not a third; and have been amused, stimulated, charmed, interested, by the first 2 or 3 chapters—to the end of the cemetery scene; and then puzzled, bored, irritated and disillusioned by a queasy undergraduate scratching his pimples. And Tom, great Tom, thinks this on a par with *War and Peace!* An illiterate, underbred book it seems to me; the book of a self-taught working man, and we all know how distressing they are, how egotistic, insistent, raw, striking, and ultimately nauseating. When one can have the cooked flesh, why have the raw? But I think if you are anaemic, as Tom is, there is a glory in blood. Being fairly normal myself I am soon ready for the classics again. I may revise this later. I do not compromise my critical sagacity. I plant a stick in the ground to mark page 200.

For my own part I am laboriously dredging my mind for *Mrs. Dalloway* and bringing up light buckets. I don't like the feeling. I'm writing too quickly. I must press it together. I wrote 4 thousand words of *Reading* in record time, 10 days; but then it was merely a quick sketch of Pastons, supplied by books. Now I break off, according to my quick change theory, to write *Mrs. D.*[2] (who ushers in a host of others, I begin to perceive). Then I do Chaucer; and finish the first chapter early in September. By that time, I have my Greek beginning perhaps, in my head; and so the future is all pegged out; and when *Jacob*[3] is rejected in America and ignored in England, I shall be philosophically driving my plough fields away. They are cutting the corn all over the country, which supplies that metaphor, and perhaps excuses it. But I need no excuses, since I am not writing for the *Lit. Sup.* Shall I ever write for them again?

Saturday, March 28, 1931

Arnold Bennett died last night; which leaves me sadder than I should have supposed. A lovable genuine man; impeded, somehow a little awkward in life; well meaning; ponderous; kindly; coarse; knowing he was coarse; dimly floundering and feeling for something else; glutted with success; wounded in his feelings; avid; thicklipped; prosaic intolerably; rather dignified; set upon writing; yet always taken in; deluded by splendour and success; but naive; an old bore; an egotist; much at the mercy of life for all his competence; a shopkeeper's view of literature; yet with the rudiments, covered over with fat and prosperity and the desire for hideous Empire furniture; of sensibility. Some real understanding power, as well as a gigantic absorbing power. These are the sort of things that I think by fits and starts this morning, as I sit journalising; I remember his

[2] *Mrs. Dalloway*, one of Mrs. Woolf's best-known novels.
[3] *Jacob's Room*, a novel.

determination to write 1,000 words daily; and how he trotted off to do it that night, and feel some sorrow that now he will never sit down and begin methodically covering his regulation number of pages in his workmanlike beautiful but dull hand. Queer how one regrets the dispersal of anybody who seemed—as I say—genuine: who had direct contact with life—for he abused me; and I yet rather wished him to go on abusing me; and me abusing him. An element in life—even in mine that was so remote—taken away. This is what one minds.[4]

Thursday, October 11th, 1933

A brief note. In today's *Lit. Sup.*, they advertise *Men Without Art*, by Wyndham Lewis: chapters on Eliot, Faulkner, Hemingway, Virginia Woolf. . . . Now I know by reason and instinct that this is an attack; that I am publicly demolished; nothing is left of me in Oxford and Cambridge and places where the young read Wyndham Lewis. My instinct is not to read it. And for that reason: Well, I open Keats and find: "Praise or blame has but a momentary effect on the man whose love of beauty in the abstract makes him a severe critic on his own works. My own domestic criticism has given me pain beyond what Blackwood or Quarterly could possibly inflict. . . . This is a mere matter of the moment—I think I shall be among the English poets after my death. Even as a matter of present interest the attempt to crush me in the Quarterly has only brought me more into notice."

Well: do I think I shall be among the English novelists after my death? I hardly ever think about it. Why then do I shrink from reading W. L.? Why am I sensitive? I think vanity: I dislike the thought of being laughed at: of the glow of satisfaction that A., B. and C. will get from hearing V. W. demolished: also it will strengthen further attacks: perhaps I feel uncertain of my own gifts: but then, I know more about them than W. L.: and anyhow I intend to go on writing. What I shall do is craftily to gather the nature of the indictment from talk and reviews; and, in a year perhaps, when my book is out, I shall read it. Already I am feeling the calm that always comes to me with abuse: my back is against the wall: I am writing for the sake of writing, etc.; and then there is the queer disreputable pleasure in being abused—in being a figure, in being a martyr, and so on.

Wednesday, January 15, 1941

Parsimony may be the end of this book. Also shame at my own verbosity, which comes over me when I see the 20 it is—books shuffled to-

[4] There is an entry in Arnold Bennett's diary for 1930 in which he records that he went to a dinner party at which V. W. was another guest, and adds: "Virginia is all right; other guests held their breath to listen to us."

gether in my room. Who am I ashamed of? Myself reading them. Then Joyce is dead: Joyce about a fortnight younger than I am. I remember Miss Weaver, in wool gloves, bringing *Ulysses* in typescript to our tea-table at Hogarth House. Roger [5] I think sent her. Would we devote our lives to printing it? The indecent pages looked so incongruous: she was spinsterly, buttoned up. And the pages reeled with indecency. I put it in the drawer of the inlaid cabinet. One day Katherine Mansfield came, and I had it out. She began to read, ridiculing: then suddenly said, But there's something in this: a scene that should figure I suppose in the history of literature. He was about the place, but I never saw him. Then I remember Tom [6] in Ottoline's [7] room at Garsington saying—it was published then—how could anyone write again after achieving the immense prodigy of the last chapter? He was, for the first time in my knowledge, rapt, enthusiastic. I bought the blue paper book, and read it here one summer I think with spasms of wonder, of discovery, and then again with long lapses of intense boredom. This goes back to a pre-historic world. And now all the gents are furbishing up their opinions, and the books, I suppose, take their place in the long procession.

We were in London on Monday. I went to London Bridge. I looked at the river; very misty; some tufts of smoke, perhaps from burning houses. There was another fire on Saturday. Then I saw a cliff of wall, eaten out, at one corner; a great corner all smashed; a Bank; the Monument erect: tried to get a bus; but at such a block I dismounted; and the second bus advised me to walk. A complete jam of traffic; for streets were being blown up. So by Tube to the Temple; and there wandered in the desolate ruins of my old squares: gashed, dimantled; the old red bricks all white powder, something like a builder's yard. Grey dirt and broken windows. Sightseers; all that completeness ravished and demolished.

EXERCISES

1. After studying these notes, write two or three paragraphs in which you characterize Mrs. Woolf's personality and temperament. Quote passages in support of your view.
2. How does Isherwood's sketch of Mrs. Woolf (see pages 62–64) stand up against the impression you get of her from the *Diary*?
3. What is the over-all impression created by Mrs. Woolf's comments on Arnold Bennett?
4. Is it your impression that Mrs. Woolf is being honest with herself when she writes that she rarely thinks of what her reputation as a novelist will be?

[5] Roger Fry, an art critic and friend of Mrs. Woolf.
[6] T. S. Eliot.
[7] Lady Ottoline Morrell.

5 | *from* UNDER WHATEVER SKY

by Irwin Edman

Irwin Edman (1896–1954) was educated at Columbia University and spent most of his academic career there as a member of the philosophy department. In addition to his scholarly works, he wrote several books of general interest; his semi-autobiographical Philosopher's Holiday *is probably the best known. Many of his essays appeared in* The American Scholar, *and he frequently contributed light verse to* The New Yorker.

Edman exploited the informal notebook style for his short sketches on diverse topics from Commencement oratory to a visit to the doctor. Though these sketches were written for publication, their easy, reflective tone endows them with the casual and personal quality of the journal entry.

Quieter, Please

The other day I picked up an earnest non-commercial periodical which boasted an article whose title contained the phrase: "dynamic democracy." There are certain words that have come to be used in our time as terms of implied moral praise. "Dynamic" is one of these, "vitality" another, and "life" itself is intended to connote a value and a good. I confess these words always make me a little uneasy. They are practically accusations of lethargy and deliberate torpor. At the end of a long day or at the beginning of a rainy one, to pick up an essay that feverishly exhorts one to "dynamic democracy" or to "vital philosophy" or to "living thought" or to "creative individuality" is a shock and a kind of indictment. As this is written, it is a dark, dull, foggy morning without the slightest trace of anything "dynamically creative" or "vital" about it—or in my own psyche. I know if I were worth preserving in the world, I should snap into "creativeness" and burst with "dynamicness." I often envy the writers of such homilies, though I cannot help wishing some of the qualities they recommend would overflow into their own prose. The tones in which they counsel such exuberant virtues are like the tones in the sky this morning.

By the time these lines get into print, I hope everybody, including the reader, is feeling "dynamic"; that is the "vital" thought with which I should like to close these meditations for the quarter.

On Hearing a Pin Drop

Many of the readers of THE AMERICAN SCHOLAR must have had the experience, at once quiet and tense, of sitting before a microphone in a radio studio in the thirty seconds before a program is about to go on the air. It makes no difference whether one is participating in the program or not. There is an awed hush about the studio, as if it were the eve of a transcendental revelation, as if at the end of half a minute some final insight or ultimate judgment were to be delivered. There are other reasons for the tension, of course. Everyone present, including the hardboiled radio engineers and the casually calloused announcers have the terrible fear (immortalized in many a classic radio anecdote) that some untoward word, some *negligé* private observation, intended for the intimacy of the studio or the control room only, may be heard by thousands or millions over a national network.

It is bad enough if one is only a visitor, but it is worse by far, as I have found out, if one is actually participating on a broadcast. In some ways, speaking over the radio is the least taxing of forms of public address. It is hardly necessary to raise one's voice; the radio engineers take care of that. If there is no studio audience, it is as simple as soliloquizing in a study. But in the moment just before going on the air, there comes a terrible brief *crise de nerfs*. In a moment one is going to speak into the unknown, and perhaps split an infinitive in the ears of who knows how many, who knows where. If it is a program without a script, the thought comes: "Suppose, with all those listening ears, I shall have *nothing* at all to say." In the excitement, it hardly enters the mind that there may not *be* any listening ears.

The minute before going off the air is equally tense, too. There is a tradition in radio that one must hit it on the nose, and end promptly with the sharply defined half hour of the radio clock. And then the uneasy tiny interval. Is one off the air yet or not? Dare one speak in normal relaxed tones? Is it certain that there are but a handful of flesh and blood listeners, not the assumed ghostly millions? "You could hear a pin drop" used to be the last word about silence. A new metaphor is now in order: "It was silent in the room, as if everyone in it were about to go on the air." I presume you are not allowed to drop a pin in a radio studio. Probably it sounds like the clang of a prison gate.

Hardy Perennial

Many things are going to be normal again, including the academic calendar. Commencements will flourish again this year, and the Commencement orators will flourish, too. The tone, I suspect, will be more Cassandra than Pollyanna, or even Matthew Arnold, this year. Sweetness and light will yield place to warnings and alarums. I wonder if it will really make much difference to the young in any case. The Commencement address—dare I say it in these pages, even the Phi Betta Kappa oration—is part of the time-honored ritual (like the word "time-honored"). Eloquence on such occasions has a certain suasion, and wit—possibly because it is not anticipated—is doubly welcome. Once in a century an address may be a classic, like Emerson's "The American Scholar" or, to a lesser degree, Woodrow Wilson's neglected classic "The Spirit of Learning." But I cannot believe that the young generally are much affected by the substance of what is said on such occasions. The newest Phi Beta Kappa members are still too set up by their recent distinction, the current bachelors of arts by their immediate problems of love or their summer jobs. They are accustomed to the voice of Polonius among the older generation, whether it be disguised as Cassandra or Pollyanna.

In my own college generation, the tone of Commencement addresses was generally optimistic; today it is likely to be grim and foreboding. The young were not too much impressed then, nor will they be too much depressed now. But people miss a great many sermons in church these days. It is good to have a secular sermon now and then, particularly in the long slanting light of a late afternoon in June, outdoors on an ivy-clad campus, in the shadow of a chapel. It makes no difference what the tone of the address; the tones themselves, albeit of a trustee, at such a time, in such a place, in such a mood, are musical.

Spiritual Snobs

If one were doing a book of snobs, such as Thackeray once did, it would be necessary, I think (though difficult), to describe the Spiritual Snob, who is now beginning to be in vogue again. The snob of wealth, of position, of blood, is familiar. So is the spiritual snob, though he is sometimes so disguised that he seems really to be on the height on which he fancies himself to be. The transcendental Pharisee I think of, is masqueraded as a model of pure and disinterred detachment. He is above all the temptations of the world, beyond all the distractions of time. He is a pure spirit beholding pure essences, for their own sweet sake. From his proud eminence there is no such thing as good and evil in this world; everything is smoothed out in his perspective, which is that of eternity. He can survey even the tragedy of our time with quietude, for he holds that the form of tragedy is always the same; and in any case, in light of timelessness, there is really no such thing as tragedy at all. The Spiritual Snob of our day has quite a battery of great names to quote. They include, of course, Spinoza, though it is conveniently forgotten that Spinoza was passionately concerned with civil liberties. Those in the spiritual top drawer of our time quote the mystics, though they forget that some of them—like Saint Theresa—were very busy and socially active people. They quote Plato on contemplation of the One, forgetting that Plato insisted that the philosopher go into the cave and the market place to test and apply his wisdom.

Were I writing such a Book of Snobs as I have described, I should like to include the Political Snob, too, who will not brook less than perfection; who will not be spotted by pacts and charters and documents, or traffic with actual political institutions. At the extreme he is, of course, an anarchist, all for a society of free spirits, beyond the gross instrumentalities of government. Today he is a nationalist who will not soil his mind with any imperfect world organization, something for starry-eyed global visionaries.

Then there is, finally, the Snob who looks down on Snobs. That is, perhaps, as far as the theme can logically be explored.

Diagnosis

The doctor carefully took temperature, blood pressure, blood count, sounded the chest, scrupulously inquired concerning all possible symptoms, and with great precision explained the possible causes of the malaise. He exhibited perfectly all the requisites of the responsible, scientific medical man.

I heard him being described a few weeks later by a lady of my acquaintance. "He is an excellent doctor," she said. "He has such a lovely manner, and such nice enunciation."

Mélange of Culture

There is an attractive scheme afoot to exchange on a large scale of both students and professors among different nations of the world. It is a very happy idea, certainly, and Sudanese in Kansas and Californians in Norway studying each other's sciences and arts, and perhaps more particularly philosophies, would certainly contribute to international understanding. Perhaps part of the understanding would come from the discovery that the academic mind is, for better or worse—possibly for worse—the same all over the world. Professors cannot help getting passionately attached to their pet theories, acquired in their youth from their favorite professors. Students all over the world find the same difficulties, the same quick enthusiasms, and perhaps go through the same periods of disillusion. Probably one of the greatest values of cultural exchange would be the discovery that we are all in the same boat, and that the boat is leaking. That might be even more useful than the delightful exchange of picturesque variations in language and customs and choice of headdress or of colors.

Standards

A group of us were discussing the degeneration of the standards in the field of literature and the arts. Contemporary criticism, we said, for the most part had no sense of the past and therefore no proper perspective on the present. A shoddy sensation could pass for a work of at least talent, even among reputable readers and reviewers. It was particularly true, some of us added, of the theatre, where time and again our attention was called to some major work that turned out to be a most tenuous triviality. Both books and plays, somebody remarked, acquired celebrity for the most purely topical and contemporary of reasons. And in the midst of the conversation, it suddenly came to me that in the 1830's or the 1840's a group similar to our own must have been making the same complaints while a whole flock of masterpieces was appearing in literature, music and the arts. Who knows, perhaps we have been neglecting something.

On Watching the Self

A little while ago, during an attack of the grippe, I was given by my doctor a mild sleeping tablet which he had prescribed in answer to my complaint that a cough kept me restlessly awake. He was quite enthusiastic about the merits of the medicament; he said that its great virtue was that it acted within ten minutes, and that some of his patients had to be careful to be in bed before they took it, because otherwise they fell asleep before they got into bed. My excellent physician, I am afraid, defeated his own ends. His description of the prompt power of his soporific was a challenge to me. I kept myself awake watching very carefully whether this really would work in ten minutes or not, and I kept myself awake nearly an hour and a half. To the writer of little moral essays such as these, everything becomes a parable. I could not resist keeping myself awake longer by deciding that it was the role of self-awareness, this watching of the self and what happens to it, that is one of the great distractions, interruptions and, if the phrase be not too strong, curses of the modern world. Some people call it subjectivism, some Existentialism—but whatever it is, it is hard to get over it. One watches oneself go to sleep, and thus one does not go to sleep; one watches oneself fall in love, and thus one does not fall in love; one watches oneself writing a paragraph like this, and thus one comes to end it.

As We Were

One of my earliest memories is Theodore Roosevelt's campaign for simplified spelling, and only the other day George Bernard Shaw revived his propaganda for the same end. What interests me at the moment is not the virtue of the campaign, but its periodicity, and the cyclic character of other and larger ideas. There are many things to be said for a short life and a merry one, but there is this to be said for a reasonably long tenure upon earth: one lives long enough to observe ideas come full cycle. Thus, I notice in an intellectual London weekly that one of the best of critics has come out for Stevenson and pure narrative again. People are beginning to speak with respect of the John Stuart Mill kind of individualism once more. Good words are being found for the small town; Victorian furniture has become modish. Dieticians are mentioning food again as well as vitamins. It is once more being suggested that babies should be heeded when they cry. Orders are given and obeyed in progressive schools.

The moral to be drawn is not the obvious one that all ideas are simply passing fashions and none should be taken as ultimate. Recurrence does not mean futility. It is natural enough that ideas should recur at given times, and under given circumstances. Umbrellas naturally come oftener to mind in a rainy season, and we forget galoshes in July. What I am led to think of is that there are themes that never go out of fashion: death and disillusion and love and happiness. I have not noticed these come suddenly into vogue again. I seem to have heard just about the same amount about them during the boom and the depression, during the two wars and now during the anxious peace. There may be no "perennial philosophy," but there are perennial themes. And one or another of them seems to intrude itself into any climate of thought or feeling.

Variation from a Theme

The seventeen-year-old boy had come to me partly at his own instigation and partly on that of his father, a house painter. I had not looked forward too much to the interview for, as I understood it, it was something about entering college and something, also, about a poor high school record. I did not anticipate with pleasure the prospect of having to tell the young man it was hard enough to get into a good college—or any college—with a poor high school record at any time, but especially so these days.

The youth came in, looking shy and troubled and rather winning in a not too brilliant way.

"Ah, he knows," I said to myself, "that he is asking help in a rather difficult matter."

He was asking aid, but not about what I expected. "Could you help me," he said earnestly, soon after we began talking, "to persuade my parents that I *oughtn't* to go to college?"

The habits of a lifetime made me, almost automatically, start to remind him of the values of a liberal education, about how important the great books were, about what a resource it was in time of trouble and unhappiness to have the arts and science and philosophy as a refuge. I glanced at him and checked myself. It was a safe bet he had already had some experience in the great books, had already been bored to death by Hamlet and Macbeth and Homer, had had a chance over WQXR to feed his soul on Beethoven and Mozart—and had already rejected these golden opportunities. Who was I to urge him to have some more stuffed down his throat? It turned out in the course of further conversation that what the boy wanted desperately to be was a dental technician, and that the thought of college was nothing less than revolting to him. His parents, I gathered, felt very strongly that he should have the blessings of higher education, even though he found them a curse.

The situation put a college teacher in an embarrassing spot. "In the confidence of this room," I felt like saying, "don't go to college. Stick by your guns. Be a pure and unsullied dental technician. Don't let them force a higher life upon you. But don't tell anybody I said so." Instead, I was academically fair-minded. In the best tradition of the noncommittal, I pointed out the advantages of both sides, knowing the colleges' admission offices would probably settle the boy's problem for him.

One never knows what ripples one's falling pebble will cause. A few days later I met the boy's father. "My boy wants to come to see you again," he said. "He says you made college sound very nice."

Homesick for Heaven

The nostalgia industry is growing by leaps and bounds. In plays, in novels, in autobiographies and softly retrospective histories, our eyes are asked to wander back over fairer vistas only a generation old, but now psychologically a part of pre-history.

It is coming to appear now that just around the turn of the century the most comfortable forms of bliss were epidemic. Magic carpets in the form of bicycles enabled one to ride, with decent slowness, moderate distances through unspoilt countryside. There were huge dinners, punctuated halfway through by Roman punch, to give a cooling interval so that one could apply oneself freshly to the second part of the grandiose meal. Gentlemen —and little boys—wore proper stiff collars. Street cars clattered deliciously along cobblestoned streets. Life was uncorrupted by ice cubes, automobiles, subways. There were no income taxes (or social security); there were no noisy airplanes overhead—also, it must be admitted, no penicillin or sulfa drugs.

Obviously even the most nostalgic, when pressed, will make two admissions: if they are old enough actually to remember, they recall many of the discomforts and inconveniences of a now softly fabled past; they know also, as many a middle-class child knew when occasionally he passed through slums, that the notion of universal security and serenity was a myth for all but the comfortable classes—and a myth, too, for some members of those classes. Around 1900, even the small boy could detect the tensions and insecurities in a so-called "happy family." We did not have the language of Freud to help us understand in those days, but there were other languages of understanding simpler and not altogether simple minded.

There is more than one variety of historical homesickness—the heart, disenchanted with the present, has turned back to the Middle Ages, to Greece, to the Garden of Eden. But the current mode is a yearning for the immediate past. The last generation is gilded in the memories of those who spent their childhood in it. It is aureoled also for younger people, who trustingly believe the sentimental tales of their elders, and are quite ready to agree that fifty years ago must certainly have been better than the present, and at least could not be worse. It is perfectly clear that around 1900 nobody except eccentric fanatics thought the world might be coming to an end any minute. The insane dreams of a generation ago have become standard sanity now.

At all times of desperation and crisis, people have had to look to "a world elsewhere." It might as well be the world of yesterday. A dreamed-of heaven may be placed anywhere, any time. Yesterday is as good a spot for Heaven as tomorrow, and Utopia, perhaps to the surprise of those who remember Lot's wife, is sometimes most vividly seen by a backward glance.

EXERCISES

1. In "Quieter, Please," Edman explains why the phrase "dynamic democracy" makes him uneasy. List several words or phrases one sees in advertisements or in magazines that connote modernity. Describe your reactions to the use of these words.

2. In "Spiritual Snobs" Edman has made a list of snobs of various sorts. Make your own list, and characterize each.

3. Using these little essays as models, write a short paper on a topic that you think would have interested Edman.

6 | *from* "TALK OF THE TOWN"
The New Yorker

"Talk of the Town," a weekly section in The New Yorker, *is a collection of comments on matters of current interest, and ranges from observations on human quirks to political editorials. The style is knowledgeable, sophisticated, and often humorous. Frequently, the section includes a report of a visit to some special show, a stockholder's meeting of unusual interest, or a celebrity, by "My Man Stanley" or "My Man Hall." The style of these reports echoes that of the Pepys* Diary*—a breathless account consisting of seemingly rough jottings. But in fact, these reports are carefully organized, neatly turned pieces of exposition.*

In the excerpts reprinted here, we join "My Man Stanley" on a visit to the Motorshow and "My Man Hall," an Anglophile, on a visit to the London Zoo. There is a distinct difference in tone between the almost jazzy reportage of "Stanley" and the dignified, laconic tone of "Hall."

Three in One

Who but our indefatigable Stanley would have had the gumption to make a non-stop tour of all three of the giant exhibitions that opened the Coliseum last week—philatelic, automotive, and photographic, the first two being international shows and the last, though merely national, nonetheless occupying seventy-six thousand square feet of floor space? Here are Stanley's notes of his trek:

"John Landy, Australian miler, says trackwork just matter of training. Took his advice, went to bed early, slept late, had wholesome breakfast, then on to Coliseum. Largest indoor track in the world. Visited auto show first. Admission one-fifty. Up escalator to second floor. At Amoco gas pump, saw photographers surrounding Jaguar with six girls in bathing suits prone on hood. What a car! Girls' feet dirty. Eyecatching vehicles on display—Packard Predictor, Lincoln Futura, Cadillac Eldorado. Wonderful names of automobiles—Saab and Volvo, Borgward and Triumph, Sunbeam and Gaylord. Gaylord equipped with unborn-calf upholstery. Nice red Dual-Ghia, $7,646, F.O.B. Detroit. 'When you ask this kind of money, you got to give the best,' salesman told prospect. Agreed. High-school kids staggering under weight of free literature. 'I've been clocked at one three eight point nine two,' supercharger salesman saying as passed by. Congratulated him, moved on to tiny three-wheeled vehicle, saw name Messerschmitt on it, blinked, pushed ahead. Alongside Jaguar exhibit, two sculptured jaguars, with mouths open. Small boy stuffed paper in jaws. Retrieved it. Brochure for Astra-Gnome, car shaped like spaceship. Has 'integra-luggage system,' many other otherwordly features. Filled cigarette lighter with free Esso fluid. Passed up chance to win M.G. for a dollar. Couple of miles farther on, came to stage, being prepared for fashion show. Sign: 'Dancing Waters.' Name of couturière? Indian princess? Salesman telling woman Rolls-Royce and Bentley almost exactly alike, except Rolls costs five hundred dollars more. Worth it. Onstage, fountains began to splash. Of course—dancing waters. Fashion-show models same girls as on hood of Jaguar. Shoes on now; couldn't tell if feet clean. 'Note the 1912 look in the linen overblouse,' said announcer's voice. Couldn't see for tall girl in blouse—maybe overblouse—standing front of me, with 'Cure-Ride Shock Absorbers' label on her back. Member of company bowling team? 'The elegant black umbrella is from George,' announcer's voice droned on.

"Out to street, back in through different new entrance, bought ticket (fifty cents) to Fifth International Philatelic Exposition. 'Fipex' for short. On third and fourth floors. Separate escalators. Stamps to the right, stamps to the left, stamps down endless corridors crossing the horizon. One collector specializing in U.S. one-cents, 1857 only. Dealers everywhere specializing in Grace Kelly Monacos—a quarter a set. Suddenly found self in Hall of Color. 'By reading the cards along this wall, you will gain quick and helpful knowledge of the mysteries of color change,' sign said. Read cards. Learned most butterfly wings have no pigment; color comes from a grating structure on wing surface. Sign warning philatelists not to stare at stamps too long—colors seem to change. Stared at man carrying bright-blue ladder. Ladder turned green. Man turned green. Rushed hastily past him. Sure did love that red Dual-Ghia. Passed dealers from Basle, London, Turin. At Montreal booth, middle-aged lady shopping. For grandson? 'This is the King,' salesman told her. 'Edward?' she asked. Salesman winced. 'George Sixth,' he said. 'I'll take it anyway,' lady said. No specialization there. Into International Salon, full of diplomatic types with briefcases. 'If China's cheap, buy China,' man telling companion. 'Hungary's cheap, buy Hungary. I have wonderful connections in Bolivia.' United Stamp Company, in Tuckahoe, has connections, too—offering chance on hand-woven rug from King Farouk's collection to every buyer of five dollars' worth of merchandise. On pedestal, under glass, world's rarest stamp—British Guiana one-cent, 1856. Hovering guard, Burns detective, said worth a hundred grand. On to U.S. Post Office corner, bought six-cent stamped envelope, just out. Fipex airmail issue. Sent first-day cover to cousin's boy. Would give him big kick. Enclosed Astra-Gnome brochure. To fourth floor. On pedestal, under glass, stuffed dog—postal mascot. Walked mile and a furlong, found Francis Cardinal Spellman Collection. Guestbook. First signature F. Cardinal Spellman's. Signed it. U.S. Post Office exhibit in a tunnel. Placard said worth a million. Man told me entire Coliseum for sale, for thirty-five million. Worth it. Nearby, big Swiss exhibit, on table, under glass—moving belt with stamps. Chairs! Sat down. Watched flowing procession of 'Pro Juventute Charity Stamps—Illustrious Swiss Citizens.' Chair comfortable. God bless Helvetia and all her illustrious citizens! God bless Alexandre Vinet, philosopher; Stefano Franscini, federal councillor; Daniel Jeanrichard, watch-industry founder; Niklaus von der Flüe, peacemaker and hermit.

"No more time to tarry. Out to street, sun going down. Back in, by separate, photography-show entrance. One dollar. Main floor. Girl in gold bathing suit, guarded by Burns detective, perched on gunwale of Mercury-powered Trojan outboard. How much girl worth? A hundred grand, F.O.B. Detroit? Girl surrounded by photographers, bent over under weight of their equipment. Some had balloons attached to shoulder straps. Looked like parachutists. Guess number of flash bulbs in giant flash bulb, win prize. Forget what prize was. Rolls-Royce? Stuffed dog? Carnival mood prevailing here. Boys in Indian war paint, man dressed like pirate, Japanese lady in kimono and *obi;* Japanese salesman said didn't need frash to take her picture. Man snapped Indians, snapped pirate, snapped *obi,* snapped me. Visitor with long white beard, bright-red shirt, cowboy hat, picture of Santa Claus on lapel. Santa Claus? Vistascope breaks the vision barrier. Webcor thinks as it plays. *Popular Photography* offers me chance on free Austin-Healy. Who needs Austin-Healy when he already has Dual-Ghia? Marionette show at Sylvania display. Puppet saying, 'One flash bulb does all *that?* Im*poss*ible!' Big glass tank full of water. Girl in gold bathing suit putting on cap. Same girl! Girl climbed to top of tank, made pretty *moue,* donned Aqua-Lung, submerged. Feet nice and clean. Photographers shooting madly as girl smiled through mask, through glass. Wonder what her hours are. Pick her up in my Rolls, drive her around third floor, show her my stamps. Specialize in 1912 overblouses, imperforate. Worth thirty-five million, C.O.D., Eastman Kodak, Bolivia."

"When I received your cablegram yesterday morning," writes our old-timey and cranky operative Hall, who is managing to extend his vacation in London by doing, with reluctance, some work for us, "instructing me to visit the London Zoo, in what you described as a 'follow-up' to the visit I paid recently to Madame Tussaud's (also at your explicit direction), I must confess that I put the message aside with something close to exasperation and went on reading the *Times* of London, which, along with a wholesome English breakfast, represents one of my greatest pleasures of the forenoon in the service flat I have taken in Half Moon Street, with its view of Piccadilly and the Green Park, beyond. Thanks to the *Times*, however, I was enabled to visit the Zoo with a clear-cut purpose, instead of simply going there and being engulfed by crowds of excitable children, doting parents, and wild animals.

"Turning a page in the *Times*, I was astonished to find myself confronted with a photograph of a monkey—or, to be accurate, a chimpanzee—holding a framed abstract painting in one hand while dangling with the other from a perpendicular rope. In a most interesting and well-written article accompanying what at first glance had appeared to me to be an abominably repulsive photograph, the *Times* informed me that on the previous evening Dr. Julian Huxley had opened an exhibition of paintings by Congo, the chimpanzee in the photograph, and Betsy, a chimpanzee of the zoo in Baltimore, Maryland—a city with which I am unfamiliar. Congo (neither animal appears to have a last name) is a resident, or inmate, of the London Zoo. The *Times* said that a scientist named Dr. Desmond Morris, an Oxford man, had been 'closely associated with him [Congo] in this activity [and] sees the patterns [of the paintings] as an important new source of information in tracing the origins of human art.'

"With a lightened heart, I took up my bowler and umbrella, hailed a cab in Piccadilly, and directed the driver to take me to the Zoo, which appeared to delight the good fellow unconscionably, as well it might, for the Zoo, at the extreme end of Regent's Park, is far outside my accustomed neighborhood here, as you will see from the expense account attached hereto. After first making the mistake of attempting to enter the place by means of a gate that I later saw was plainly marked 'Pram Gate,' I paid the adult's rate of three shillings and, thinking to avoid as much of what was on display inside as possible, asked a uniformed guard to direct me to the office of Dr. Desmond Morris. 'You'll find him in the television unit,' the man said. 'You walk right along through the reptiles, past the pelicans, and on to the eagles, sir.' Not without some difficulty, I found the television unit, and there I was received by Dr. Morris, a conservatively dressed youngish gentleman, who placed a chair for me at the opposite side of the room from his desk. 'Had a bout of Asian flu,' he explained. 'It's past the infectious stage, but it's just as well to be prudent. Suspect I picked it up from a young gibbon from Malaya, and passed it on to Congo. He developed pneumonia. Gave us quite a scare. Still convalescent. Afraid the head of the Institute of Contemporary Arts caught it from him when we were preparing for the exhibition that opened this week. Well, now, the pioneer in this new field, of course, was Alpha, a female chimpanzee at the famous Yerkes Laboratory, in your country, who produced several hundred drawings. In 1951, when she was eighteen weeks old, an analytical study of her work was published in your *Journal of Comparative and Physiological Psychology*—Volume Forty-four, pages a hundred and one to a hundred and eleven, in case you wish to refer to it.'

"In response to a number of questions I put to him, Dr. Morris went on to say that he himself had been a painter in his youth but after the war had had to choose between living in a garret and becoming something else, so at Oxford he had specialized in zoology and psychology and had taken a Doctor of Philosophy degree in the former. About a year ago, he was asked by one of the independent television companies, in conjunction with the Zoological Society of London, to take charge of a weekly half-hour program to be called 'Zoo Time.' Congo, who was approximately two years old—the exact date of his birth is unknown, because he was born in the place that bears his name—became a major attraction of the program, and has thus far appeared on it forty-seven times, frequently painting pictures for the television audience. 'I knew about Betsy of Baltimore,' said Dr. Morris, 'and arranged with Mr. Arthur Watson, the director of the zoo there, to send a dozen of her pictures over, to be shown along with a selection of Congo's work. The exhibition will probably go around to some other cities here, and then Mr. Watson plans to put it on in your country. Betsy has also performed on television, as you know.'

"I was taken to Congo's private cage—he is not on public exhibition except by way of television—and he appeared to me to be much like any other chimpanzee, although, of course, I have observed few, if any, chimpanzees in my lifetime. Afterward, I put some key questions to Dr. Morris concerning the connection between abstract art and the work of Congo, Betsy, and Alpha, and gathered that the abstract-art world is in something of a ferment, because it would appear that the work of these and lesser-known chimpanzees is regarded by many as the only truly abstract art; i.e., as the *Times* phrased it, 'It is comforting to know for certain, as one gazes at a painting, that it contains no image.' Feeling that it was my professional duty to see the exhibition itself, in spite of my distaste for abstract art, I went by cab to Claridge's for a leisurely luncheon and a causerie, and then strolled down Piccadilly to Dover Street and into the Institute of Contemporary Arts Gallery. Betsy, as I have perhaps neglected to tell you, paints only with her fingers, whereas Congo uses a brush. The difference in technique could be readily seen, for, as the *Times* aptly put it, 'Betsy's paintings have a more linear effect; some of them could remind one of groves of trees or even a cathedral nave. Congo's paintings, on the other hand, are somewhat richer daubs of colour that turn the mind toward exotic cacti and succulents.'

"In conclusion, I might add that while my purely personal attitude toward zoos has been perceptibly softened by this assignment, my negative attitude toward abstract art remains—but I'm sure that is of no interest to you and your readers, and besides I must hasten to catch the post before teatime."

EXERCISES

1. Employing a tone similar to "Stanley's," write five or six paragraphs about some event you have witnessed recently.

2. Write a short paragraph explaining the sort of person you take "Hall" to be.

II | Biographical and Autobiographical Sketches

Readers have been attracted to biography from Plutarch's *Lives* (the end of the first century A.D.) to a profile in a recent *New Yorker*. We read biographies for several reasons: because we are interested in human conduct; or because of a desire to identify ourselves with another human being—particularly someone famous; or, as Wilbur Cross suggests, because "we want to learn how to do the very same things that someone else has done—how, say, to write a novel like Thackeray's or how to amass a fortune and die a philanthropist like Carnegie." For the same reasons, there has always been a widespread interest in autobiography. Carlyle said that if you want "to interest your readers—that is to say, idle neighbours and fellow creatures in need of gossip—there is nothing like unveiling yourself." Doubtless, we are particularly attracted by a man's account of his own drama. Naturally, not all biographies and autobiographies are equally engaging. As in all literature, much depends on the writer's art, the keenness of his perceptions, and the inherent interest of his subject.

Selection, interpretation, and evaluation are tasks the biographer and autobiographer face in common. Each must assess experiences and incidents. The autobiographer is likely to be the less objective of the two. Examining and evaluating one's own life poses great difficulty. Inevitably we are likely to see in a heightened and exaggerated way whatever has happened to *us*. For another matter, at different periods in one's life the same incident assumes different meanings. This is illustrated in F. Scott Fitzgerald's "Early Success," reprinted in this section. Yet the barriers to complete self-awareness and a disinterested perspective need not detract seriously from the interest autobiography has for us. The autobiographer's view of himself and his past is often perhaps more significant than are the objective facts.

Nor can the biographer be wholly objective. The fact that he must select from a mass of material—he would never finish otherwise—already rules out complete "objectivity." To achieve coherence requires a point of view. The most we can expect of the biographer and autobiographer is a sense of *responsibility* in selecting and evaluating their materials.

The autobiographer and biographer differ in the sources of their information. The autobiographer depends, to a large extent, upon his memory, although he may also have diaries and letters to aid him. If the biographer is writing about a contemporary he, too, can call on his memory, but he will also have to draw copiously on other sources. The biographer writing about someone from another period must depend entirely on documents, legal records, photographs, and portraiture. He will search particularly for letters and journals, not only of his subject but of the latter's friends and contemporaries. He must also inform himself about the political, social, and intellectual climate in which his subject lived. He must see his subject living in a particular society, a particular world.

Biography in various periods has followed different patterns. Modern biography, commonly called the "new biography," is greatly indebted to the work of Lytton Strachey. In his preface to *Eminent Victorians* (1918), Strachey stated his tenets. He rejected the staid, factual, sentimentalized, white-washing biographies typical of the Victorian era—"those two fat volumes with their ill-digested mass of material, their slipshod style . . . their lamentable lack of selection, of detachment, of design." He advocated, instead, "a becoming brevity—a brevity which excludes everything that is redundant and nothing that is significant." In his own work, he ignored unimportant facts, telescoped uneventful years, and strove to catch the controlling trait and unique quality of his subject. Strachey's techniques have been adapted—used and abused—by many modern biographers. The *Time* biography of Dylan Thomas is an example of one type of adaptation.

The writer of short biographical and autobiographical sketches has to be particularly selective. He may emphasize certain aspects of his subject's life: the subject's ideas, achievements, relation to his society, or personal problems—in fact, whatever seems most significant or interesting about that person. The selections reprinted below illustrate the wide range of emphases possible. D. H. Lawrence, in his autobiographical sketch, talks both of the events of his life and of his overriding personal problem in his relation to his fellow-men. Bertrand Russell writes of his impressions of Joseph Conrad and his ideas. Christopher Isherwood describes Virginia Woolf in what to him seemed a characteristic setting for her. In his candid account of his family, George Bernard Shaw incorporates his own views on education.

The large number of interests which compete for the time of modern readers has led to an increasing dependence on journalistic media for information, for the quick satisfaction of their curiosity about people and events. Responding to the popularity of biography and autobiography, many magazines and newspapers regularly feature short sketches of people in the news. Full-length biographies and autobiographies continue to be written and widely read, but in short form they are probably more prevalent today than ever before.

1 AN OUTLINE OF BIOGRAPHY FROM PLUTARCH TO STRACHEY

by Wilbur Cross

Wilbur Cross (1862–1948) had two careers, one as a professor of English literature, the other as a politician. He was a professor at Yale and a Governor of Connecticut. James Truslow Adams said of him: "He was a politician when a scholar and remained a scholar when a politician. In a word, he has always been in the best Platonic and Greek sense a 'whole man.'" Much of his scholarly effort was devoted to the criticism of the English novel, but he also wrote a pleasant and witty autobiography, Connecticut Yankee.

This survey of biography is characteristic of Cross' writing. It is learned, urbane, and sprightly. A great deal of information is presented, and the various types of biography are deftly sorted out and evaluated. First delivered as an address at Columbia University in 1921, this essay was later published in the Yale Review *and then in book form.*

Biography next to fiction is the kind of reading most people now like best. As I once wrote a book on the novel and have since written the lives of two humorists, I naturally go with the majority.

But this is not the main reason. When a man (or a woman) accomplishes something worth while in art, letters, science, statesmanship, or business, I try to find out what I can about his life and personality. Behind this desire which I have with the rest of the modern world is more than mere curiosity. Life for most people is a rather difficult piece of business. So we want to know not only how others have turned the trick against fortune; we want to know also all the details of the game as they have played it. Perhaps we want to learn how to do the very same thing that somebody else has done—how, say, to write a novel like one of Thackeray's or how to amass a fortune and die a philanthropist like Carnegie.

Surely, too, we all have the impulse to vary and lengthen our own lives by living several other lives vicariously at the same time. Biography is thus a sort of Life Extension Bureau. A man who has read many biographies should have acquired a fairly good working knowledge of human nature, though he may never have mastered the Freudian psychology or wandered very far from a small university town.

This modern love for biography, intense as it now is, is no new thing. Someone, perhaps, will some day write a little treatise and call it "The Development of Biography" after the name of similar books on the drama and the novel. That man (or woman), who perhaps is living somewhere even now, may try to show how biography like fiction disengaged itself from history of the kind we have in the Old Testament or such as Herodotus wrote; but if he is wise he will come quickly to those wonderful *Parallel Lives* by Plutarch, which one may read in the late Professor Perrin's exact and beautiful English. If he be a Dr. Dryasdust, he will dwell on the fact that the Greek biographer gives few dates for the events he describes, and that there are no footnotes telling how the anecdotes concerning Caesar or Alcibiades or the rest can be run down to their sources.

It must be a relief to Plutarch, wherever he may be, to know that, quite apart from hearsay and anecdote, many of the documents he used, have been lost beyond recovery, so that he can no longer be checked up at all points by the scientific historians of the present age. But Dr. Dryasdust even, though he may lament that he has no field here for the exercise of his gifts, will hardly fail to see how perfect are the art and workmanship within those limits that Plutarch set for himself.

Only the personalities of the men and women he wrote about concerned Plutarch. The lines which he drew may not always be correct, and others may seek to rectify them; but such as they are, the portraits have come down to us directly and through Shakespeare; and they can never fade.

The historian of biography will have to tell about the impetus that Plutarch gave to biographical writing throughout Western Europe during and after the Renaissance, showing by the way how Vasari and Walton, for example, varied the art they learned from their master. He will probably say that these writers fixed the form of a biography which, though it still survives, as in Mr. Strachey's portraits of eminent Victorians, is really but an enlarged character-sketch with a brief summary at the end. He may turn aside to tell how the biographical method was taken over into hundreds of novels through the seventeenth and eighteenth centuries. He will be tempted to write some interesting pages on death-bed scenes from Cleopatra to Colonel Newcome, closing with the remark that they are less frequent now, perhaps because death has been robbed of its romance by modern science—by our knowledge of the streptococcus and what it does.

After an aside like this, the historian of biography will pass on through memoirs and diaries and letters until he reaches Boswell, where he will stop for a very long chapter. Eventually, after traversing the careers of Gladstone and Disraeli, he will arrive at our own time, when any man who can pay the price may have his life written and published in two stout volumes including his correspondence—all illustrated with portraits of himself from youth to age and with pictures of the houses where he has lived and thrived. This degradation of biography the historian will note, observing at the same time also the immense amount of biographical material, formless, incoherent, often irrelevant, that now gets into print when a great man like Roosevelt goes down into the grave.

The scope of biography has ever expanded to meet the requirements of new civilizations. Plutarch's heroes were the conquerors and rulers of the ancient world—statesmen, politicians, orators, and demagogues, whose conduct the biographer subjected, without being too severe with them, to the test of Greek ethics and philosophies as embodied in the teachings of Socrates and Plato and Aristotle. For him the center of the world vibrated between Athens and Rome. When Vasari came upon the stage the old states and empires had long since gone; and for the Italian mind questions concerning art had become of supreme importance. Accordingly, he described the painters, sculptors, and architects of that great brotherhood to which he himself belonged. In turn Izaak Walton lived in an age when men were immensely anxious about the salvation of their souls. So his heroes were mainly churchmen distinguished for their piety. Charming is the word to characterize his portraits of Hooker and Herbert and Donne. The old angler, though honest enough to allude to the worldliness, follies, and vices of his churchmen in youth, passed them by lightly that he might have room enough to display all the Christian virtues they practiced in their prime. No one could ask for a more satisfactory biographer to describe the perfect circle of a well-spent life, from a genteel birth to a happy death.

Thus far, few English men of letters, so far as I recall, had been honored by a biography, unless we include those sketches by Bale in his Latin copendium of illustrious writers of a past age. Vagabonds, highwaymen, and sharpers of all kinds were often written up for the masses, who then loved, as much as they do now, a story ending on the gallows-tree. But among these gentlemen I find no secular poet, no dramatist except Robert Greene, if "A Groatsworth of Wit" may be regarded as autobiography. Shakespeare had no contemporary biography. Ben Jonson had none. Dryden had none. Milton's were partial and fragmentary. Pope's were poor things. Nor was there any life of Richardson or Sterne or Smollett until long after they were dead.

To the twentieth century this may seem amazing. But the fact is that men of letters had not yet established themselves as members of an honorable profession; nor were they quite low enough in the social scale to awaken the curiosity of people with delight in picturesque crime. Nevertheless interest was beginning to be shown in them by anecdotes and stories about them, half true, half false, which became the basis of future biographies. Historically at least, Dr. Johnson did a fine piece of work when he composed from such materials as were at hand the lives of the British poets of his own and the previous age. And then Boswell in his life of Dr. Johnson first depicted with fullness the career of a man of letters. His success showed that the life of an essayist and lexicographer may be of the highest interest. Since his time we have had biographies of all sorts of persons; but the man of letters is the most certain of the honor or dishonor of having his entire career laid open to the public gaze either before or after death. A century ago, a poet or novelist (Thackeray, for instance) stood in fear of the biographer, not knowing what he might uncover. This fear he should have no longer, for faults of character, in the present temper of the world, are mostly excused on the ground that they show the subject to have been human like the rest of us.

With a few capital exceptions, I prefer to read a man's life as written by himself. Dr. Johnson went so far as to declare such a biography the best to be had, since the writer knows all the particulars and no one else can know them. Autobiography, of course, has its limitations. The view a man takes of himself, though he has all the facts, must be partial and one-sided; he puts into the account and leaves out what he pleases with equal unconcern; usually he does not see his career in true perspective, and he often deceives himself on the why and wherefore of his conduct at the crucial points of his history. The incidents of his life as he gives them need to be supplemented, and the motives underlying his acts need to be canvassed by an outsider. Moreover, he can hardly hope to escape the charge of vanity, of merely appearing to be frank where no frankness really is, and of suppressing facts that would damage his case if he has one.

Still, these limitations do not always appear; and any man who writes his own life, however much he may try to conceal himself, gives himself away. Herbert Spencer's autobiography is hardly more than a restatement of his philosophy and as such it has little value; and yet it shows him to have been almost a purely intellectual being of colossal egotism in whom the human affections ran low. From Darwin's autobiography a reader might not infer that the man gave the world an hypothesis which has revolutionized natural science, but he would see at once that Darwin was the most modest of men, really underrating his great achievements, and that he possessed all those human characteristics which Spencer lacked. Rousseau in his "Confessions" did not really shrive himself, but his sophistry and emotional psychology betrayed him as a complete sentimentalist; whereas St. Augustine in his "Confessions" was over-emphatic on the dissoluteness of his youth in order to gain a dark background for the splendor of the virtues he developed later. Tolstoi, I think, did the same thing. If none of us may hope for the fame of Tolstoi or St. Augustine, we may, I trust, take some satisfaction in having begun life with a cleaner record.

The man who relates his own life, though he may go much as he pleases, must have some motive for what he does. He may write out a brief story merely for the information of his family or descendants, as did Darwin and Sterne and Scott. Huxley wrote his delightful autobiography in order to set readers right on the facts of his life which were in danger of being perverted by the maker of a biographical dictionary. John Stuart Mill had two reasons for his autobiography. His first reason was to expose "the wretched waste" of time in the English system of education. He showed how in his own case a great mind was built up, under the guidance of a stern father, by a thorough study of the ancient classics, philosophy, economics, and science; so that at the age of fourteen he had gone far beyond any graduate of Oxford or Cambridge. His second reason was to tell posterity how much he was indebted to a platonic affection for Mrs. Taylor. This is the hallucination that makes Mill mortal. All his thoughts when in the presence of this not very remarkable woman he attributed to her inspiration, unaware that they were the product of his own fertile brain. Like Mill's, Henry Adams's main motive, as he put it into his title, was to let the world know how he had been educated from youth to mature manhood—only by a humorous perversity, he sought to prove that his education was a complete failure. On the other hand, Franklin sought to show how a poor boy may rise by thrift and shrewdness to competency, and afterwards weed out faults and vices acquired on the way, ridding himself of them one at a time at sufficiently long intervals until he grows into a respectable and honorable gentleman, perhaps a diplomat or a statesman.

How difficult it is to write a good autobiography one may learn from Gibbon, who composed parts of his own six or seven times over, so determined was he to give an exact account of his "moral and literary character." "Many experiments," he says, "were made before I could hit the middle tone between a dull chronicle and a rhetorical declamation." Everybody should know how the magnificent theme of his history came to Gibbon on a visit to Rome, as he "sat musing amidst the ruins of the Capitol, while the bare-footed friars were singing vespers in the Temple of Jupiter." Almost equally eloquent is the passage in which he tells of the completion of his great work twenty-odd years later on a June evening in his garden at Lausanne: "After laying down my pen, I took several turns in a *berceau*, or covered walk of acacias, which commends a prospect of the country, the lake, and the mountains. The air was temperate, the sky was serene, the silver orb of the moon was reflected from the waters, and all nature was silent. I will not dissemble the first emotions of joy on the recovery of my freedom and perhaps the establishment of my fame." What memorable words! For words like these from Shakespeare on "Hamlet," or "Lear," or "the dark lady" of the Sonnets we would surrender without reluctance all that Sir Sidney Lee has written of him.

Now and then a man, like General Grant or Mr. Bok, has given almost perfect objectivity to an autobiography while keeping himself in the foreground. This is a rare combination. Goethe, for another instance, took a cool survey of his youth, as if he had but a scientific interest in what he then did or in what then happened to him. His mind was in the main intent upon discovering the influences of youth upon the mature man. There was, as I remember, no remorse for any phase of his conduct, not even for his treatment of Friederike. Much the same is true of Benvenuto Cellini, who, though himself the hero, wrote as if he were describing the adventures of another man, and drew a broad and living picture of Italy at the time of the Renaissance, when art and crime were equally glorious. Nor should we forget Trollope, who wrote for money, who laid his watch on the table before him and wrote down 250 words every fifteen minutes. One by one he passed in review his many novels composed in this way, pointing out the defects and excellences of each precisely as if he were writing of Dickens or Thackeray. Trollope's aloofness was so triumphant as to be amusing.

The most amusing biographies, however, are among intimate personal narratives pervaded with harmless vanity, and often with some scandal. When Colley Cibber's "Apology" appeared, Fielding remarked that the "great man" appeared to have lived the life therein recorded only in order to write an apology for it. Again, some time ago, Margot Asquith lost the place she had long held in the sun and at the same time saw her husband's reputation for statesmanship challenged. So "the Woman with the Serpent's Tongue" published an autobiography, and came back gloriously like Napoleon from Elba, bringing with her a vindication of Mr. Asquith's policies. The seventeenth century also had a Margot Asquith. She was the Margaret, Duchess of Newcastle, whom Charles Lamb called "a dear friend of mine, of the last century but one . . . the somewhat fantastical and original-brained, generous Margaret Newcastle." Lamb's sentence perhaps sufficiently characterizes the first Margot's vainglorious autobiography, written, she informed the public, so that "after ages" might know that she "was the second wife of the Lord Marquis of Newcastle; for my Lord having had two wives, I might easily have been mistaken, especially if I should die, and my Lord marry again." Her husband, tutor to the young Prince of Wales (afterwards Charles the Second), a brave general and competent statesman, she celebrated in "The Life of the Thrice Noble, High and Puissant Prince, William Cavendish . . . By the thrice Noble, Illustrious, and Excellent Princess, Margaret, Duchess of Newcastle." Not only was the Duke, as he appears in this biography, "a pattern for all gentlemen," but all his children (born of the first marriage) were "dutiful and obedient, free from vices, noble and generous, both in their natures and actions." On reading the book the year after its publication, Pepys wrote in his Diary: "Stayed at home reading the ridiculous History of my Lord Newcastle, wrote by his wife, which shows her to be a mad, conceited, ridiculous woman, and he an asse to suffer her to write what she writes to him and of him."

The relation between husband and wife is so intimate that it is hazardous for either to write the biography of the other. The most that either can do with decorum is to publish the general correspondence of the other, properly arranged with the necessary connecting links. Mrs. Kingsley tried to do this for her husband, Charles Kingsley, and she succeeded fairly well except in spots and near the end, where she described him as "a most true and perfect knight," whose love for her "never stooped from its own lofty level to a hasty word, an impatient gesture, or a selfish act, in sickness or in health, in sunshine or in storm, by day or by night." This sort of sentimental rhetoric John Walter Cross escaped in his life of George Eliot by merely publishing letters and journals with just enough comment to make them understandable, never with any personal reflections on his wife's career. Neither of these books, however, is biography; they are but books containing material for biographies to be written by somebody else.

Nowhere in English is there, I think, a first-rate biography of a man by his wife. On the whole, husbands have perhaps done rather better with their wives. At once comes to mind Carlyle on Jane Welsh; but even here attention finally rests not upon the wife but upon the husband in his gloom after her death. I remember quite well, too, the "impressionistic portrait" which Professor Palmer drew of his wife, Alice Freeman. He called it "a personal estimate, an evolutional study." But here again there was eventually too much of the husband and his sabbatical years when he and his wife traversed Europe. What Professor Palmer and others have attempted, cannot be done. Wives and husbands cannot be outspoken of one another in print.

Sometime, no doubt, the existing restraint will be removed from their pens, and then we shall have some entertaining biographies. In the meantime, anyone who desires may read in a privately published volume Lady Lytton's highly spiced comment on her husband, the novelist, or what Pepys put down in cipher after quarrels with his wife—whose nose he tweaked on two occasions and who in turn threatened to pinch his with red-hot tongs. This is what we shall get if the muffler is ever cut out.

Nor can a son or daughter write freely of a father or mother. Censure would be regarded as impiety; and praise, though perfectly just, would be viewed with suspicion. Aware of this attitude of the public, Hallam Tennyson in the memoir of his father rarely let his own hand become visible, and then mostly in anecdotes, and depended on reminiscences of Lord Tennyson's friends for an estimate of the man and his works. With rather better taste, Francis Darwin dealt in a similar manner with the life and letters of his father, the great naturalist; and his sister, Henrietta Litchfield, likewise with the correspondence of their mother, the charming Emma Darwin. Only in fiction can a son or daughter do more. Dickens transferred some of the humorous characteristics of his father and mother to Mr. and Mrs. Micawber; and Samuel Butler, who hated his father, put him into "The Way of All Flesh." Although it is but fiction in each case, Dickens, it has been felt, did not behave quite like a gentleman; and Butler's conduct has been denounced as "base and dishonorable." The conclusion is that children of great men may well collect the correspondence of their fathers as a debt they owe to posterity. If they have the literary ability they should also publish it with all other important memorials, remembering always the limitations under which they assume their task. What a loss to the world it is that a son of Henry Fielding did not gather in the letters of the novelist; or that Mrs. Ritchie did not tell the plain story of her father's life in her own delightful way, including the best among those countless letters which Thackeray sent to his friends and which we should like to read forever.

Inevitably psychological errors creep into the estimate that one member of a family forms of the others. The closer the relationship, the less trustworthy the judgement. But as one leaves wife or husband, son or daughter, for the more remote members of a family, errors in judgement tend to fade, sometimes leaving behind only that sympathy necessary to all good biography. The perfection of such sympathy pervades Trevelyan's "Life and Letters of Lord Macaulay," wherein it is a nephew who speaks. Naturally Trevelyan was rather shy of praise or blame, but the book is a wonderfully fine piece of work, with everything in the proper place, beginning with Macaulay's childhood and ending with the inscription on his tomb in Westminster Abbey. On a smaller scale there is also the very interesting life of Jane Austen by her nephew Austen-Leigh, which has been expanded into many dull books on "the divine Jane." Likewise two sons-in-law, uncontaminated by the blood of the family, have written biographies admired by all who know them. A whole row of books and monographs on Pasteur may be found in any scientific library, but the only one that a man would sit up at night to read is the volume on Pasteur's life and labors by his son-in-law, Rene Vallery Radot. This is a book wherein one gets at the very heart of the great scientist. M. Radot was charged by Professor Tyndall and others with showing a certain bias towards Pasteur when dealing with the scientists who paved the way for his discoveries. No similar charge could be sustained, I think, against Lockhart who, though he loved and honored the memory of Scott, was a trained critic accustomed to an independence of judgement which he could not lay aside in favor of his father-in-law, whose character he let develop through letters and diaries, with his own just comment.

It would be well for all cocksure biographers (such as Mr. Archibald Stalker, who published not long ago "The Intimate Life of Sir Walter Scott") to read Lockhart's final words, where he says that no man can "pronounce *ex cathedra* on the whole structure and complexion of a great mind" from any materials he may have at hand; that there always remain behind mysteries of personality which a man like Scott never discloses and which no outsider can ever penetrate. Likewise, when Mrs. Carlyle told her husband that Darwin had asked her who would write her husband's "Life," Carlyle began to reflect how impossible it would be for any creature ever to write that "Life"; for "the *chief* elements of my little destiny have all along lain deep below view or surmise, and never will or can be known to any son of Adam." Nevertheless Froude sought to sound the depths of Carlyle's nature with the aid of what would now be called a Freudian complex, and in the process floundered amid domestic infelicities and lost his man. Similar results within a year or two have attended the labors of those psychoanalysts who have sought to pluck out the hearts of three American writers. Margaret Fuller, we learn from one, loved her father, if not too well, at least too long; and Mark Twain, we learn from another, was "a victim of arrested development," who in accordance with well-known psychic processes eventually "withered into a cynic" and a sort of "spiritual valetudinarian." Poe, according to Dr. John W. Robertson, inherited "a dipsomaniac compulsion" from his father, who, while a student of the law, had developed "an alcoholic syndrome."

While waiting for the Freudians to produce something better, the world, I fear, will have to fall back on Boswell's "Life of Samuel

Johnson" as the most complete portrait of a man ever put into words. So great a book we owe to a happy conjunction of art and circumstance. No biographer ever had a finer subject for the display of his talents. As a mere narrative, any career like Johnson's passing through poverty on to eminence arrests the attention of all who read. And this particular man was, besides, peculiar in dress, manners, speech, way of walking even; he was a "humorist" in the old sense of the word. He had read in a multitude of books of all kinds, ancient and modern; he had reflected on what he read, and so was ever ready with an opinion on any subject that might be broached. His opinions were likely to be colored by prejudice; but prejudice gave piquancy to his words, and behind them was always a truth which the most judicious could not ignore. Out of an honest heart he spoke always, whether with friends or foes. Withal he was generous, kind-hearted, and sound in his affections. Nor was Boswell the fool that Macaulay describes. His perceptive powers were acute and accurate. His memory was exact. His intellectual processes were honest. If he was a hero-worshiper, he chose a man worthy of homage; nor did he hesitate to call the great man to account when he became wild in his talk. Boswell knew Dr. Johnson as well as any man may know another. He traveled with him and hung about him for years; he asked all sorts of questions about his early life and spurred him on to talk in endless streams; he listened to his conversations at the club and elsewhere, with Burke and Garrick and Goldsmith, and wrote down, immediately or soon after, the best parts of the conversations with a concise description of the scene. Boswell knew that if he could arrange as it should be all that he had seen and heard he would have Dr. Johnson's personality, so far as it was ever disclosed in his presence, clinched forever.

Boswell's art was akin to Sterne's in "Tristram Shandy," wherein the characters are portrayed by the opinions they express on a great variety of subjects, the theory being, I suppose, that if you know what a man really feels and thinks, you know him essentially as he is. Add as Sterne and Boswell did the clash of opinions with others, and the man, half dead before, becomes alive. Neither in fiction nor in biography have we anywhere a book more truly dramatic than Boswell's "Life of Samuel Johnson." Others have tried to do what Boswell did and they have failed utterly. Forster missed his chance with Dickens. Froude missed a rarer chance with Carlyle.

Numerous attempts have been made in these latter years to construct the biographies of great men whose lives for one reason or another were not written by their contemporaries. I myself have tried my hand at Sterne and Fielding, and have thereby learned the difficulties that confront the man who is sometimes facetiously called "a pseudo-biographer."

Between him and the true biographer there exists a difference similar to that between the novelist who would depict men and women of his own time and the novelist who aims to restore the life and manners of a past age. The one derives his knowledge directly and perhaps easily from what he sees and hears. The other must depend upon his reading; he thus works in the manner and spirit of an historian. He must know the period in which his man lived in all its aspects—social, religious, and political; and this knowledge, if it is to be intimate, must be gained at first hand from the general literature of the period—from letters, diaries, and newspapers as well as from books. He must know down to the veriest detail everything his author published and all the memorials of him that have survived. He must consider the traditions that have grown up about his personality, and the anecdotes related of him, how far they may be true and how far false. He must search for unpublished writings of his author, and for new documents concerning him, always weighing their importance. If he discovers letters, or a diary, or a piece of an autobiography never before published, he is happy.

He cannot quiz Sterne or Fielding as Boswell quizzed Dr. Johnson, but he can bring under survey everything that got into print about his man and thus learn what his contemporaries in various walks of life, friends and foes, thought of him and his books. The "pseudo-biographer" must thus substitute for his own perceptions the eyes and ears of others long since dead and not to be questioned further. His ultimate success will depend upon his ability to project himself into another age as completely as Thackeray did when he wrote "Henry Esmond." If his subject is Fielding he must in imagination grow up with him, go to Eton College with him, watch from the roadside as the young man attempts to abduct an heiress, sit with him in the greenroom drinking champagne when a play succeeds or is damned, ride with him on the Western Circuit, watch him as he presides over the Bow Street Court, be with him through all his literary labors, have words of comfort for him in his bereavements, and take the last voyage with him to Lisbon. Perhaps it is impossible to make a living being out of a man one has never seen. But it is only by an imaginative process such as I have described that anything resembling life can be breathed into his nostrils.

A biographer who has no personal acquaintance with the man he writes about may proceed in one of several ways. If he is a pioneer he will be tempted to put into his book everything discoverable. I have been thus tempted. I had to settle the question what I should do with Sterne's Journal to Eliza and many other manuscripts which had long lain in obscure places. Eventually I decided to make what appeared to be a proper use of them in the biography and to publish them as a whole separately.

With Fielding, of whose career so little had been known, I dealt more liberally, though I avoided, I hope, the fatal example set by the late Professor Masson. It is fifty-odd years since Masson startled the literary world with the first two of seven volumes on the life of Milton. After groaning through nearly fourteen hundred pages of this work, and discovering that Masson had brought Milton down to only his thirty-fifth year, Lowell called for "a phial of *elixir vitae*," and afterwards remarked: "We envy the secular leisures of Methuselah, and are thankful that *his* biography at least (if written in the same longeval proportion) is irrecoverably lost to us." What was the result of Masson's lifelong labors on Milton? He collected and published everything relating to Milton and may have rightly interpreted the documents. Thereby he did an immense service to English letters. But Milton himself he submerged in a mass of political and ecclesiastical history from which it is difficult to rescue him.

And even if one takes the *via media*, as I did with Sterne and Fielding, it is still difficult, because of the documents, to keep the man always in sight. A pioneer must, however, include in his book the main documents with exact references, else he will not be believed. He may later rewrite his biography in shorter form, merely referring to his sources, and thus concentrate his efforts as did Plutarch on the personality of his subject. He will fail if he tries to condense; he must write a new book, using the old one only for his facts. If he does not do this himself, it will in the course of time be done by another. The biography of Lincoln that people read is not the standard work by Nicolay and Hay in ten volumes supplemented by twelve volumes of writings; it is Lord Charnwood's which, though it contains few new facts, gives within reasonable compass the salient lines of Lincoln's career and character, with narrative and comment evenly balanced. The only man who ever wrote a long biography that cannot be done over is Boswell.

"A well-written life," Carlyle remarked humorously, "is almost as rare as a well-spent one." What makes Lord Charnwood's "Abraham Lincoln," aside from its style and technique, a first-rate biography, is the author's clear understanding. The biologists warn us that "no one can satisfactorily explain *function* in terms of *structure*"; that from the constitution of the brain, for example, no one can predict all the phenomena of consciousness, though we are certain that the two are intimately related. So a biographer who has never known the man he would write about, may have at hand, or may discover, every pertinent fact about him and every essential document relating to his physical and spiritual history, and yet even then fail to present the hero in the habit as he lived. Why? He has never heard his man speak or seen him in action; he must divine as well as he can all those lights and shades which play over personality giving a distinctive quality to an act or even a word. However "scientifically" facts and documents may be interpreted, the living man will elude the biographer unless he has extraordinary insight and a constructive imagination of the first order. In the most favorable circumstances he only partially succeeds. Lord Charnwood's Abraham Lincoln is a consistent whole; and yet the portrait cannot be altogether true.

And there is always the question of style; by which I mean, of course, not mere phrasing, for style includes innumerable things besides that. Style is hardly more analyzable than personality; in a well written book it is all-pervading like the air we breathe. Walton was equally happy in his phrasing and in creating an atmosphere of gentle piety. Boswell succeeded by sheer directness and honesty. Lockhart, the professional man of letters, sometimes strove for effects which now seem artificial; whereas Trevelyan, a less conscious artist, charms by his perfect naturalness and ease.

Mr. Strachey has been justly praised for the style of his "Queen Victoria." So, too, Mr. Guedalla for his brilliant portraits in "The Second Empire." Like Lord Charnwood, Mr. Strachey is one of those biographers who, making little or no claim to discover, rely upon what has already been printed, with some verification of statements where manuscripts are available. The aim is not new knowledge, but a new interpretation of facts already known. Mr. Strachey, who had at hand many books including the Queen's diary and a scandalous chronicle, had but to read, absorb, and then select and recombine what would contribute to the portrait of Victoria which he desired to present. His method is more that of a novelist than of a biographer. Indeed, his book is dedicated to a novelist. Nothing is admitted that might appear dull; nothing is excluded that can give piquancy to the narrative. In temper, Mr. Strachey's art is not so much English as French. It has none of the genial humor that Thackeray let play over the Queen's ancestors among the Georges. It has rather the wit and irony almost of Voltaire.

Victoria was a symbol. She did not impress her personality upon her age as did the cultivated Elizabeth upon the age of Shakespeare and Spenser and Bacon. Without her the Victorian era, except for minor details, would have been precisely as it was. She did not read much. The amazing discoveries in science which she heard about left her cold, for her intelligence could not rise to an understanding of them. Even a novel like George Eliot's "Middlemarch" was too difficult for her. She preferred Marie Corelli. Nor did she care for poetry, except the resonant verse of Tennyson celebrating the blameless life of the Prince Consort. She had little imagination, and her sense of humor was rudimentary. She enjoyed a farce, but there is no record here of her reading Dickens or

Thackeray. So far as she was concerned, the world might have stood still. Though a woman, she thought the suffragists of her day should be whipped. She persuaded the editor of the *Times* to write on *"the immense* danger and evil of the wretched frivolity and levity" among the higher classes of society. The warning, it would seem, did not have the salutary effect she expected. She likewise interfered in the policies of her ministers: and sometimes prevailed; and yet "at the end of her reign the Crown was weaker than at any other time in English history."

There is doubtless another Victoria. It yet remains for a finer if less brilliant mind to trace the Queen in all her subtle influences on her age. No one, however, can deny that the book has atmosphere as well as arresting phrases. So has Lord Charnwood's "Abraham Lincoln." But note the difference. Lord Charnwood idealizes Lincoln, nearly always giving him the benefit of the doubt in matters uncertain. Mr. Strachey throws the emphasis on Victoria's limitations. His biography belongs to the literature of disenchantment, which always leaves something out. When we read of Spoon River and Gopher Prairie, we are apt to forget that men like Grant and Lincoln grew up in places as drab and sordid as these really were minus the exaggeration. On the heels of the realistic poets and novelists now comes Einstein, who overthrows an infinite universe, by somehow proving that space rolls back on itself and that something, which I do not understand, has happened to time. So, six centuries after Dante, it has become impossible to follow the great Florentine as his mind is lifted from the earth and borne through the unending heavens, on from light to light, under the guidance of Beatrice. Did not Henry Adams seek all his life for those lights and did he not fail to see them?

In the literature of disenchantment there is no mysticism, and immortality goes by the board. Old Izaak Walton's churchmen had souls which were to find eternal rest in Paradise; and "the small quantity of Christian dust" they left behind them was sometime to be re-animated. Death-bed scenes, I have remarked, are not so common now as they were when Montaigne judged of a man by the manner of his dying. But Mr. Strachey has revived them. Victoria dies scientifically, recalling, as she lies "blind and silent," the outstanding events of her career back to girlhood. These shadows of the past hovering over the fading mind of the Queen, though they may appear as the fancies of a romancer, are supposed to be in full agreement with modern psychology. Albert and his friend Stockmar die in an agnostic phrase; they "explored the shadow and the dust"; while the Princess Charlotte, in the style of the realistic novel, "tossed herself from side to side; then suddenly drew up her legs, and it was over."

Victoria would be shocked beyond measure could she see the glamour that once surrounded her throne thus fade and disappear.

EXERCISES

1. Why does the author of this essay prefer autobiographies to biographies? What are some of the limitations he recognizes in a man's attempts to write about his own life?

2. What does the author mean by the term "pseudo-biographer"? In what ways does the pseudo-biographer differ from the biographer?

3. Would this essay help a prospective biographer or autobiographer learn how to go about his project? How? If not, why?

4. This essay covers a great deal of ground. Does the author's style help the reader to grasp the content of the essay? What are some of the distinctive qualities of his style?

2 SIR JOHN HARINGTON

by Lytton Strachey

Giles Lytton Strachey (1880–1932) was, like the Woolfs, a member of the Bloomsbury Group. His first literary ventures in poetry, fiction, and drama were unsuccessful and he then turned to biography. He studied the art of biography and worked out certain principles which he applied in a series of biographical sketches, Eminent Victorians, *published in 1918. Almost alone, Strachey turned biography away from cold, factual records to a presentation of integrated character.* Queen Victoria *is probably his best work.*

In his biographies, Strachey attempts not only to portray a specific character, but also to imbue his sketch with the flavor of the period in which his subject lived. In Eminent Victorians, *this leads to harshness because Strachey wanted to blast the stodginess of that era. In his sketch of Harington, however, he had no axe to grind; the Elizabethans lacked the religiosity and moral fervor of his eminent Victorians; the gaiety, frivolity, and fast pace of court life did not call for the satirical acidity with which he toppled Victorian idols. "Sir John Harington" exemplifies Strachey's art at its best: a skillful selection of significant details, lucid exposition, and pervasive irony.*

An old miniature shows a young man's face, whimsically Elizabethan, with tossed-back curly hair, a tip-tilted nose, a tiny point of a beard, and a long single earring, falling in sparkling drops over a ruff of magnificent proportions. Such was John Harington, as he appeared in the happy fifteen-eighties, at Greenwich, or at Nonesuch—a courtier, a wit, a scholar, a poet, and a great favourite with the ladies. Even Gloriana [1] herself usually unbent when he approached her. She liked the foolish fellow. She had known him since he was a child; he was her godson—almost, indeed, a family connection, for his father's first wife had been a natural daughter of her own indefatigable sire. Through this lady the young man had inherited his fine Italian house at Kelston, in Somersetshire, where one day Elizabeth, on her way to Bath, paid him the honour of an extremely expensive visit. He had felt himself obliged to rebuild half the house to lodge his great guest fittingly; but he cared little for that—he wrote a rhyming epigram about it all, which amused the ladies of the bedchamber. He wrote, he found, with extraordinary ease and pleasure; the words came positively running off the end of his pen; and so—to amuse the ladies again, or to tease them—he translated the twenty-eighth book of Ariosto's *Orlando Furioso,* in which the far from decorus history of the fair Fiametta is told. The Queen soon got wind of this. She read the manuscript and sent for the poet. She was shocked, she said, by this attempt to demoralize her household; and she banished the offender from Court until—could there be a more proper punishment?—he should have completed the translation of the whole poem. Harington hurried off to Kelston, worked away for a month or two, and returned with a fine folio containing the entire Orlando in English, together with notes, a life of Ariosto, "a general allegory of the whole," and "apologie of Poetrie," and "epistle dedicatorie to the Queenes Majestie," and an engraved title-page with the portrait of himself and his dog Bungay. The book was printed in 1591. The exquisite elegance and mature serenity of the original are nowhere to be found in it; but Harington himself, bringing with him the natural abundance, the charming ingenuousness, the early morning freshness of his wonderful generation, comes to us delightfully on every page.

The translation was well received, and the gay young man looked about for new worlds to conquer. Not to be talked of was his only fear. A curious notion struck him. His nose was sensitive as well as impudent, and he had been made to suffer agonies by the sanitary arrangements in the houses of the great. Suddenly inspired, he invented the watercloset. Then, seizing his pen, he concocted a pamphlet after the manner of Rabelais—or, as he preferred to call him, "the reverent Rabbles"—in which extravagant spirits, intolerable puns, improper stories, and sly satirical digs at eminent personages were blended together into a preposterous rhapsody, followed by an appendix—written, of course, by his servant—could a gentleman be expected to discuss such details?—con-

[1] Elizabeth.

taining a minute account, with measurements, diagrams and prices, of the new invention. *The Metamorphosis of Ajax*—for so the book, with a crowningly deplorable pun, was entitled—created some sensation. Queen Elizabeth was amused. But then some malicious courtier told her that one of the satirical digs was aimed at the memory of Leicester, whereupon her smiles changed to frowns, the Star Chamber was talked of, and Harington made a strategic retreat to Somersetshire. "The merry poet, my godson," the Queen declared, "must not come to Greenwich, till he hath grown sober and leaveth the ladies' sports and frolics." But before very long she relented. With her supreme sense of the practical, she saw that, as she put it, "the marrow of the book" was not entirely ludicrous; she sent down word to the poet that she approved of his invention; and eventually she set the fashion for the new contrivances by installing one of them in Richmond Palace, with a copy of the Ajax hanging from the wall.

Harington's next adventure was more serious. He was summoned by Essex to join his ill-fated expedition to Ireland, in command of a troop of horse. In Ireland, with a stretch of authority which was bitterly resented by the Queen, Harington was knighted by the rash Lord Deputy, and afterwards, when disaster came thick upon disaster, he followed his patron back to London. In fear and trembling, he presented himself before the enraged Elizabeth. "What!" she cried, "did the fool bring you too?" The terrified poet fell upon his knees, while the Queen, as he afterwards described it, "chafed much, walked fastly to and fro, and looked with discomposure in her visage." Then, suddenly rushing towards him, she caught hold of his girdle. "By God's Son," she shouted, "I am no Queen, and that man is above me!" His stammering excuses were cut short with a "Go back to your business!" uttered in such a tone that Sir John, not staying to be bidden twice, fled out of the room, and fled down to Kelston, "as if all the Irish rebels had been at his heels."

It is clear that poor Harington never quite recovered from the shock of that terrific scene. The remainder of his life passed in ineffectiveness and disillusionment. In the bosom of his family he did his best to forget the storms and shipwrecks of "the Essex coast"; he wrote incessantly; he cracked scandalous jokes with his mother-in-law, old Lady Rogers; he busied himself over the construction of a curious lantern for King James of Scotland. But his happy vein had deserted him. His Discourse shewing that Elyas must personally come before the Day of Judgment could never get finished, and he threw aside his Treatise on Playe as a failure. His epigrams, no doubt, were more successful; he scribbled them down on every possible occasion, and the most scurrilous he invariably dispatched to old Lady Rogers. She roared with laughter, but omitted to leave him a legacy. He dashed into her house as she was dying, broke open the chests, tried to get possession of everything, and was at last ignominiously ejected by his brother-in-law. King James was equally disappointing. Even the curious lantern, even a learned, elaborate, and fantastic dissertation On the Succession to the Crown, failed to win him. After he had been a year in London, the new King granted Sir John an interview, but, though his Majesty was polite, he was not impressed. "Sir John," he said, with much gravity, "do you truly understand why the Devil works more with ancient women than others?" And, unluckily, on that, Sir John "could not refrain from a scurvy jest." Nevertheless, though he felt that he had made no headway, he would not despair; a little later, the Lord Chancellorship of Ireland and the Archbishopric of Dublin fell vacant, and the author of Ajax bravely requested that he should be appointed to both offices. Oddly enough, his application received no answer. He solaced himself with an endeavour to win the good graces of the young Prince Henry, to whom he addressed a discourse, full of pleasant anecdotes, concerning all the bishops of his acquaintance, followed by a letter describing "the good deedes and straunge feats" of his "rare Dogge," Bungay—how he used to carry messages from London to Kelston and how, on one occasion, he took a pheasant from a dish at the Spanish Ambassador's table, and then returned it to the very same dish, at a secret sign from his master.

But in truth the days of Bungay were over, and the new times were uncomfortable and strange. "I ne'er did see such lack of good order, discretion, and sobriety." There had been jollities and junketings, no doubt, in his youth, but surely, they were different. He remembered the "heroicall dames," the "stately heroyns" whom he had celebrated aforetime—

These entertayn great Princes; these have learned
The tongues, toys, tricks of Rome, of Spayn, of Fraunce;
These can correntos and lavoltas daunce,
And though they foote it false 'tis ne'er discerned.

More and more his thoughts reverted to his old mistress. "When she smiled, it was a pure sunshine, that everyone did choose to bask in, if they could; but anon came a storm from a sudden gathering of clouds, and the thunder fell in wondrous manner on all alike." Yes! . . . he was "olde and infirme"; he was forty-five; he must seek a quiet harbour and lay up his barque. He lingered at Kelston, impoverished, racked by various diseases; he vainly took the Bath waters; he became "stricken of a dead palsy"; until, in 1612, at the age of fifty-one, he passed into oblivion. And in oblivion he has remained. Nobody reads his Orlando; his letters are known to none but a few learned historians; his little books of epigrams lie concealed in the grim recesses of vast libraries; and Englishmen to-day, reflecting on many things, as they enjoy the benefits of a sanitary system unknown to the less fortunate inhabitants of other countries, give never a thought to Sir John Harington.

EXERCISES

1. Why is the opening sentence, with the device of referring to the "old miniature," an effective way of introducing this particular biography?
2. Make a list of the episodes of Harington's career. Is there a pattern to them?
3. Why does Strachey show trivial but likeable aspects of Harington's character through Bungay, the poems to the ladies, and other details? How are these trivialities related to Strachey's irony?
4. Almost all of Strachey's biographies contain not merely incidental ironies but are conceived in essentially ironic terms. Point out incidental ironies in Harington's life, and, if possible, state what you believe to be the over-all irony in and through which Strachey frames his life. Write a paper on this topic.
5. How does Strachey manage simultaneously to depict the life of Harington and the flavor of the era in which he lived?
6. If you were suddenly transported into the Elizabethan world and were expected to think and act like an Elizabethan, what are some of the differences in belief, manners, and dress with which you would be confronted? Write a paper on this subject.

3 | JOSEPH CONRAD

by Bertrand Russell

Bertrand Russell (1872–) has long been an influential figure in mathematics, philosophy, education, and social theory. He is one of the few great philosophers who has written for laymen and has addressed himself to social, moral, and political questions of a practical nature. Russell has always stated his views emphatically and provocatively, and has often evoked sharp controversy. Almost all of his books have been widely read. Some of these are Education and the Social Order, An Outline of Philosophy, History of Western Philosophy, The Principles of Mathematics, Skeptical Essays, Unpopular Essays, *and* Portraits from Memory, *from which the sketch printed below is taken.*

Russell has an admirable sense for the essential and a style which is both simple and informal. In this portrait of Joseph Conrad, Russell is not so much concerned with the events of Conrad's life as with the beliefs and ideas that made up his view of life and that formed the basis of his creative work. He describes his own contacts with Conrad and conveys the attraction that Conrad's integrity and profundity held for him.

I made the acquaintance of Joseph Conrad in September, 1913, through our common friend Lady Ottoline Morrell. I had been for many years an admirer of his books, but should not have ventured to seek acquaintance without an introduction. I travelled down to his house near Ashford in Kent in a state of somewhat anxious expectation. My first impression was one of surprise. He spoke English with a very strong foreign accent, and nothing in his demeanour in any way suggested the sea. He was an aristocratic Polish gentleman to his finger-tips. His feeling for the sea, and for England, was one of romantic love—love from a certain distance, sufficient to leave the romance untarnished. His love for the sea began at a very early age. When he told his parents that he wished for a career as a sailor, they urged him to go into the Austrian navy, but he wanted adventure and tropical seas and strange rivers surrounded by dark forests; and the Austrian navy offered him no scope for these desires. His family were horrified at his seeking a career in the English merchant marine, but his determination was inflexible.

He was, as anyone may see from his books, a very rigid moralist and politically far from sympathetic with revolutionaries. He and I were in most of our opinions by no means in agreement, but in something very fundamental we were extraordinarily at one.

My relation to Joseph Conrad was unlike any other that I have ever had. I saw him seldom, and not over a long period of years. In the out-works of our lives, we were almost strangers, but we shared a certain outlook on human life and human destiny, which from the very first, made a bond of extreme strength. I may perhaps be pardoned for quoting a sentence from a letter that he wrote to me very soon after we had become acquainted. I should feel that modesty forbids the quotation except for the fact that it expresses so exactly what I felt about him. What he expressed and I equally felt was, in his words, "A deep admiring affection which, if you were never to see me again and forgot my existence tomorrow, would be unalterably yours *usque ad finem*."

Of all that he had written I admired most the terrible story called *The Heart of Darkness*, in which a rather weak idealist is driven mad by horror of the tropical forest and loneliness among savages. This story expresses, I think, most completely his philosophy of life. I felt, though I do not know whether he would have accepted such an image, that he thought of civilized and morally tolerable human life as a dangerous walk on a thin crust of barely cooled lava which at any moment might break and let the unwary sink into fiery depths. He was very conscious of the various forms of passionate madness to which men are prone, and it was this that gave him such a profound belief in the importance of discipline. His point of view, one might perhaps say, was the antithesis of Rousseau's: "Man is born in chains, but he can become free." He becomes free, so I believe Conrad would have said, not by letting loose his impulses, not by being casual and uncontrolled, but by subduing wayward impulse to a dominant purpose.

He was not much interested in political systems, though he had some strong political *feelings*. The strongest of these were love of England and hatred of Russia, of which both are expressed in *The Secret Agent:* and the hatred of Russia, both Czarist and revolutionary, is set forth with great power in *Under Western Eyes.* His dislike of Russia was that which was traditional in Poland. It went so far that he would not allow merit to either Tolstoy or Dostoievsky. Turgeniev, he told me once, was the only Russian novelist he admired.

Except for love of England and hatred of Russia, politics did not much concern him. What interested him was the individual human soul faced with the indifference of nature, and often with the hostility of man, and subject to inner struggles with passions both good and bad that led towards destruction. Tragedies of loneliness occupied a great part of his thought and feeling. One of his most typical stories is *Typhoon.* In this story the Captain, who is a simple soul, pulls his ship through by unshakable courage and grim determination. When the storm is over, he writes a long letter to his wife, telling about it. In his account his own part is, to him, perfectly simple. He has merely performed his Captain's duty as, of course, anyone would expect. But the reader, through his narrative, becomes aware of all that he has done and dared and endured. The letter, before he sends it off, is read surreptitiously by his steward, but is never read by anyone else at all because his wife finds it boring and throws it away unread.

The two things that seem most to occupy Conrad's imagination are loneliness and fear of what is strange. *An Outcast of the Islands* like *The Heart of Darkness* is concerned with fear of what is strange. Both come together in the extraordinarily moving story called *Amy Foster.* In this story a South-Slav peasant, on his way to America, is the sole survivor of the wreck of his ship, and is cast away in a Kentish village. All the village fears and ill-treats him, except Amy Foster, a dull, plain girl who brings him bread when he is starving and finally marries him. But she, too, when, in fever, her husband reverts to his native language, is seized with a fear of his strangeness, snatches up their child and abandons him. He dies alone and hopeless. I have wondered at times how much of this man's loneliness Conrad had felt among the English and had suppressed by a stern effort of will.

Conrad's point of view was far from modern. In the modern world there are two philosophies: the one, which stems from Rousseau, and sweeps aside discipline as unnecessary; the other, which finds its fullest expression in totalitarianism, which thinks of discipline as essentially imposed from without. Conrad adhered to the older tradition, that discipline should come from within. He despised indiscipline, and hated discipline that was merely external.

In all this I found myself closely in agreement with him. At our very first meeting, we talked with continually increasing intimacy. We seemed to sink through layer after layer of what was superficial, till gradually both reached the central fire. It was an experience unlike any other that I have known. We looked into each other's eyes, half appalled and half intoxicated to find ourselves together in such a region. The emotion was as intense as passionate love, and at the same time all-embracing. I came away bewildered, and hardly able to find my way among ordinary affairs.

I saw nothing of Conrad during the war or after it until my return from China in 1921. When my first son was born in that year I wished Conrad to be as nearly his godfather as was possible without a formal ceremony. I wrote to Conrad saying: "I wish, with your permission, to call my son John Conrad. My father was called John, my grandfather was called John, and my great-grandfather was called John; and Conrad is a name in which I see merits." He accepted the position and duly presented my son with the cup which is usual on such occasions.

I did not see much of him, as I lived most of the year in Cornwall, and his health was failing. But I had some charming letters from him, especially one about my book on China. He wrote: "I have always liked the Chinese, even those that tried to kill me (and some other people) in the yard of a private house in Chantabun, even (but not so much) the fellow who stole all my money one night in Bankok, but brushed and folded my clothes neatly for me to dress in the morning, before vanishing into the depths of Siam. I also received many kindnesses at the hands of various Chinese. This with the addition of an evening's conversation with the secretary of His Excellency Tseng on the verandah of an hotel and a perfunctory study of a poem, "The Heathen Chinee" is all I know about Chinese. But after reading your extremely interesting view of the Chinese Problem I take a gloomy view of the future of their country." He went on to say that my views of the future of China "strike a chill into one's soul", the more so, he said, as I pinned my hopes on international socialism— "The sort of thing", he commented, "to which I cannot attach any sort of definite meaning. I have never been able to find in any man's book or any man's talk anything convincing enough to stand up for a moment against my deep-seated sense of fatality governing this man-inhabited world." He went on to say that although man has taken to flying, "he doesn't fly like an eagle, he flies like a beetle. And you must have noticed how ugly, ridiculous and fatuous is the flight of a beetle." In these pessimistic remarks, I felt that he was showing a deeper wisdom than I had shown in my somewhat artificial hopes for a happy issue in China. It must be said that so far events have proved him right.

This letter was my last contact with him. I never again saw him to speak to. Once I saw him across the street, in earnest conversation with a man I did not know, standing outside the door of what had been my grandmother's house, but after her death had become the Arts Club. I did not like to interrupt what seemed a serious conversation, and I went away. When he died, shortly afterwards, I was sorry I had not been bolder. The house is gone, demolished by Hitler. Conrad, I suppose is in process of being forgotten. But his intense and passionate nobility shines in my memory like a star seen from the bottom of a well. I wish I could make his light shine for others as it shone for me.

EXERCISES

1. Russell makes relatively few observations about Conrad, but these few stick in the mind and help us to see and understand Conrad. Is there a moral in this for the writer of a biographical sketch?
2. What does this biography reveal about the biographer? In bringing himself into this sketch of Conrad, how does Russell avoid overshadowing Conrad?
3. What are the advantages and dangers of this kind of biography, one in which the biographer is himself involved?
4. For the most part, Russell talks about "feelings"—the feelings he and Conrad shared, Conrad's political feelings, Russell's feelings about Conrad's works. Does he successfully convey his ideas on these abstract matters?
5. Discuss the differences in Russell's and Strachey's techniques. What are some of the differences in their aims?
6. Select a man whose ideas or example have impressed or influenced you and write a biographical sketch of this kind.

4 VIRGINIA WOOLF

by Christopher Isherwood

Christopher Isherwood (1904–) was born in England. He attended Cambridge. Isherwood spent six years as a private tutor in Berlin and there gathered much of the material he later used in his novels and short stories, particularly in Goodbye to Berlin. *John Van Druten's stage adaptation of two stories from the latter collection,* I Am a Camera, *won the New York Drama Critics' Award. Other works by Isherwood are* Prater Violet, The Condor and the Cow, *and* The World in the Evening. *Since 1939, Isherwood has been living in the United States, working mostly in Hollywood; he was naturalized in 1946.*

In his sketch of Virginia Woolf, Isherwood shows her in conversation with members of her intellectual and literary circle. To use terms employed by Henry James, Isherwood does not report his memories of Mrs. Woolf and her friends, he renders *and* dramatizes *them. He re-creates her cultural milieu (Bloomsbury) and presents a series of impressions of her as hostess, conversationalist, and friend.*

Virginia Woolf is dead—and thousands of people, far outside the immediate circle of her friends and colleagues, will be sorry, will feel the loss of a great and original talent to our literature. For she was famous, surprisingly famous when one considers that she was what is called "a writer's writer." Her genius was intensely feminine and personal—private, almost. To read one of her books was (if you liked it) to receive a letter from her, addressed specially to you. But this, perhaps, was just the secret of her appeal.

As everybody knows, Mrs. Woolf was a prominent member of what journalists used to call "The Bloomsbury Group"—which included Lytton Strachey, Vanessa Bell, Duncan Grant, E. M. Forster, Arthur Waley, Desmond MacCarthy and Maynard Keynes. Actually, the "Group" wasn't a group at all, in the self-conscious sense, but a kind of clan; one of those "natural" families which form themselves without the assistance of parents, uncles and aunts, simply because a few sensitive and imaginative people became aware of belonging to each other, and wish to be frequently in each other's company. It follows, of course, that these brothers and sisters under the skin find it convenient to settle in the same neighborhood—Bloomsbury, in this case. It is a district just behind and beyond the

British Museum. Its three large squares, Gordon, Bedford and Tavistock, have something of the dignity and atmosphere of Cambridge college courts.

Open *To the Lighthouse*, *The Common Reader*, or *The Waves*, read a couple of pages with appreciation, and you have become already a distant relative of the Bloomsbury Family. You can enter the inner sanctum, the Woolf drawing-room, and nobody will rise to greet you—for you are one of the party. "Oh, come in," says Virginia, with that gracious informality which is so inimitably aristocratic, "you know everybody, don't you? We were just talking about Charles Tansley. . . . Poor Charles—such a prig. . . . Imagine what he said the other day . . ." And so, scarcely aware, we float into our story.

The Bloomsbury Family held together by consanguinity of talent. That you could express yourself artistically, through the medium of writing, or painting, or music, was taken for granted. This was the real business of life: it would have been indecent, almost, to refer to it. Artistic integrity was the family religion; and, in its best days, it could proudly boast that it didn't harbor a single prostitute, potboiler or hack. Nevertheless, one must live. Some of the brothers and sisters had very odd hobbies. Keynes, for example, whose brilliant descriptive pen could touch in an unforgettable and merciless portrait of Clemenceau on the margin, as it were, of an economic report to the Versailles treaty-makers—Keynes actually descended into that sordid jungle, the City, and emerged a wealthy man! And Virginia—the exquisite, cloistered Virginia—became a publisher. True, the thing happened by gradual stages. It began as a sort of William Morris handicraft—with Leonard and Virginia working their own press, and Virginia's delicate fingers, one supposes, getting black with printer's ink. But all this was ancient history, and the hand-press was stowed away in the cellar under dust-sheets, before the day in the early 'thirties when I first walked timidly up the steps of the house in Tavistock Square.

It is usually easy to describe strangers. Yet, although I didn't meet Virginia more than half a dozen times, I find it nearly impossible to write anything about her which will carry the breath of life. Which century did she belong to? Which generation? You couldn't tell: she simply defied analysis. At the time of our first meeting, she was, I now realize, an elderly lady, yet she seemed, in some mysterious way, to be very much older and very much younger than her age. I could never decide whether she reminded me of my grandmother as a young Victorian girl, or of my great-grandmother—if she had taken some rejuvenating drug and lived a hundred and twenty years, to become the brilliant leader of an intensely modern Georgian *salon*.

One remembers, first of all, those wonderful, forlorn eyes; the slim, erect, high-shouldered figure, strangely tense, as if always on the alert for some distant sound; the hair folded back from the egg-shell fragility of the temples; the small, beautifully-cut face, like a Tennysonian cameo—Mariana, or The Lady of Shalott. Yes, that's the impression one would like to convey—an unhappy, high-born lady in a ballad, a fairy-story princess under a spell, slightly remote from the rest of us, a profile seen against the dying light, hands dropped helplessly in the lap, a shocking, momentary glimpse of intense grief.

What rubbish! We are at the tea table. Virginia is sparkling with gaiety, delicate malice and gossip—the gossip which is the style of her books and which made her the best hostess in London: listening to her, we missed appointments, forgot love affairs, stayed on and on into the small hours, when we had to be hinted, gently but firmly, out of the house. This time, the guest of honor is a famous novelist, whose substantial income proves that Art, after all, can really pay. He is modest enough—but Virginia, with sadistic curiosity, which is like the teasing of an elder sister, drags it all out of him: how much the New York publishers gave, how much the movie people, and what the King said, and the Crown Prince of Sweden—she has no mercy. And then, when it is all over, "You know, Jeremy," she tells him, smiling almost tenderly, "you remind me of a very beautiful prize-winning cow. . . ." "A cow, Virginia . . . ?" The novelist gulps but grins bravely at me; determined to show he can take it. "Yes . . . a very, very fine cow. You go out into the world, and win all sorts of prizes, but gradually your coat gets covered with burs, and so you have to come back again into your field. And in the middle of the field is a rough old stone post, and you rub yourself against it to get the burs off. Don't you think, Leonard . . ." She looks across at her husband, "that that's our real mission in life? We're Jeremy's old stone scratching post."

What else is there to say about her? Critics will place her among the four greatest English women writers. Friends will remember her beauty, her uniqueness, her charm. I am very proud to have known her. Was she the bewitched princess, or the wicked little girl at the tea party—or both, or neither? I can't tell. In any case she was, as the Spaniards say, "very rare," and this world was no place for her. I am happy to think that she is free of it, before everything she loved has been quite smashed. If I wanted an epitaph for her, taken from her own writings I should choose this:

"It was done; it was finished. Yes, she thought, laying down her brush in extreme fatigue, I have had my vision."

EXERCISES

1. Does the reader imagine that he both sees and hears Mrs. Woolf? If so, how has Isherwood managed to give the reader these impressions?

2. Does Isherwood want the reader to feel that the Bloomsbury Group was snobbish or that it insisted that intellectual and artistic achievements be of a very high order? Is there a real distinction here?

3. Is Isherwood concerned with Virginia Woolf as a writer or as a person?

4. How does the opening of the sketch—"Virginia Woolf is dead"—set the tone for the sketch? What does he mean when he says, "This world was no place for her"?

5. Compare this with Russell's portrait of Conrad. Both are personal impressions rather than factual biographies, yet there is a difference in technique. What is this difference?

6. Clive Bell, one of Virginia Woolf's close friends, says she was "most rare." Presumably each of us has met someone who seems out of the ordinary. Write a biographical sketch of such a person. Before you begin, decide on what the person's special quality is and on ways in which you can render or dramatize this quality.

5 THE LEGEND OF DYLAN THOMAS

Time

Time *is a very influential magazine in the realm of the arts and literature as well as in politics. While the mass audience may like the lively and colorful tone which has come to be known as* Time-style, *many well-educated readers consider it brash, and even more, condemn the misrepresentation and superficial treatment of the subject which they feel results from the effort of* Time *writers to maintain the style.*

The selection reprinted here is an account of the life and death of the Welsh poet Dylan Thomas. It is typical of the Time *approach to biography in the selection of "highlights" and in the manner of their telling. While this is supposedly a review of stories and letters by Dylan Thomas, not much space is devoted to his actual work. In addition to those mentioned in this piece, Thomas' published works include:* Twenty-five Poems, The Map of Love, The World I Breathe, *and* Portrait of the Artist as a Young Dog.

Modern poetry often seems a pretty dreary cocktail party. In a quiet corner, of course, perches the agèd eagle, T. S. Eliot, 66, still far and away the No. 1 living poet of the 20th century, sipping his extra-dry sherry of resignation. His old white magic still works, but it no longer holds any surprises. Eliot's lesser poetic cousins—Auden, Spender, Stevens—sip the highballs that somehow fail to intoxicate, that are diluted by too much intellectual ice. There are such grand old but long-familiar individualists as Martini-clever e. e. cummings (with lemon peel) and hard-cider-happy Robert Frost. The younger men frantically mix their drinks, from opaque Bloody Marys to phony-bucolic applejack. Mostly they are reduced to talking to each other.

But one strikingly different figure dominates the whole party: a thick little man, in a dirty, rumpled suit, with tousled hair on a bulging gnome's head, who is swigging boilermakers. He is also roaring out stories, laughing, pinching the girls, charming all who push into range of his eloquence.

For 18 months the picture of this guest has existed only in memory, for Dylan Thomas died in Manhattan in the fall of 1953, at 39. But he is still the life of the party.

The Return of Joy

His 90 poems, collected in a single volume in 1953, have gone through a spectacular seven printings. Records of his booming readings have become bestsellers (TIME, May 2). Now more scraps of Thomas' vivid prose have been put together and issued in a single volume called *Adventures in the Skin Trade and Other Stories*, and his letters are finding their way into print. Dylan Thomas is more alive today than any living poet now writing verse.

The reasons are not hard to find. Thomas returned to poetry what people used to expect of it: joy. His work was sometimes tortured and anguished. It could be obscure—not obscure in a deliberate, cultish manner, but in the sense than an excess of color can produce darkness. But far the larger part of his verse is ebullient, drenched with sight and sound, rich in haunting new language fed from old and sparkling springs.

There is another reason for Dylan Thomas' soaring popularity. Not only his verse but his life fitted in with what people always secretly expect of poets. It was boisterous, dissolute, sometimes repellent, often appealing, both tragic and gay: a mixture easily labeled "romantic." As much as his work, his life—and death—contributed to the burgeoning Dylan Thomas legend.

This death was a drama whose details are still being hotly debated. In its sordidness it recalled, among other sad and disorderly exits, the death of Edgar Allan Poe.* But it proves something about Dylan Thomas, and about the typical kibitzers of greatness who flocked to him. The hangers-on

* An excessive drinker, on and off, for years, Poe was found in a Baltimore tavern on election day in 1849. He was taken unconscious to the hospital, and died, at the age of 40, after three days of violent delirium.

are still fighting, figuratively, over his body. Some stick to the story that Thomas died of a cerebral injury caused by a fall at a drinking party. Another group hints that Thomas was fatally dosed with morphine by a doctor whom a rival clique had summoned to treat the poet's alcoholic miseries. Dame Edith Sitwell, rising disdainfully over such partisan bickering, has said that Thomas died of an infection caught when he scratched an eyeball on a rose thorn.

Like Louis Armstrong

The facts are somewhat different. The New York City medical examiner's record shows that he died of acute and chronic alcoholism, complicated by pneumonia. An attending physician called it "alcoholic insult to the brain." When Thomas arrived in the U.S. for his last visit in October 1953, he planned to go to Hollywood and write an opera with Igor Stravinsky. But first he stopped in New York to make some money by repeating his enormously successful readings of his "play for voices." *Under Milk Wood*, at Manhattan's Y.M.H.A. Poetry Center. He was adrift in the baffling city, childishly delighted by its riches but really not caring what happened to him. That week Thomas called an old friend and said: "I'm tired of all the goddam writers around here. Why don't you give me a party with no writers, only beautiful women?" Late that Saturday night, after the party, Thomas showed up at his favorite tavern, the White Horse, a dark-paneled, homey bar on the western outskirts of Greenwich Village. His eyes were glazed, bloodshot, heavy-lidded. Some pals bought him drinks, and he downed three or four boilermakers in 15 minutes. Later, he went on to another bar, then retired to his hotel room for a warm beer and whisky nightcap with a friend.

Three days and several parties later, New York *Times* Critic Harvey Breit telephoned him at his hotel. "He seemed bad," Breit recalls. "I wanted to say, 'You sound as though from the tomb.' I didn't. I heard myself say instead: 'You sound like Louis Armstrong.' " That afternoon a girl assistant from the Poetry Center went to visit Thomas, who was in bad shape. Towards evening his doctor came and gave him a sedative, and left. The last words his visitor remembers were those of any man who is ill, questions like: "What time is it?"

Around midnight Thomas suddenly went into coma. An ambulance rushed him to nearby St. Vincent's Hospital. During the next few days distraught poets, painters, sculptors and assorted hangers-on crowded into the hospital lobby, sometimes 40 deep. Thomas' wife Caitlin flew in from London, proved so distraught herself that she had to be put temporarily into a hospital at Astoria, L.I. That is where she was when Dylan Thomas died, without regaining consciousness.

The Way from Wales

Dylan Thomas had lurched straight for his fate, trusting in the survival of his poetry, which he had once called statements made on the way to the grave.

For Thomas, the way began in the Welsh seaport of Swansea. He grew up the son of a genteel, ineffectual little schoolmaster who had thrown away the declamatory, bardic Welsh heritage in favor of English-language conformity. But Dylan absorbed all the Celtic mysteries and humors. At 16 he quit school and for a year tried reporting for a Swansea newspaper. "A penguin in a duckpond," said an old staffer.

Having won a poetry contest in 1933, he headed for the capital. He did not exactly wow T. S. Eliot and the polite publishers, but he could not be ignored. Tousled, pink-cheeked and tweedbare, he slept on friends' floors, jumped in bed with friends' wives, won a reputation as a pub orator with a golden voice and an infinite capacity for beer.

"He stood at the bar, this little, thick man with the gooseberry eyes starting out of his head," a friend recalls, "telling wonderful stories and a crowd gathering around him." For a while he and another down-and-outer lived on a porridge made from oats bought by the half-sack from a stable-supply dealer. When there was no one left to touch for a quid, he would retreat to Swansea, where he would sit in the Kardomah café and hold the customers spellbound with tales of London ("As I was saying to Sacheverell . . ."). In London he spun the legend that he was a country boy. Actually, Thomas, who has written pastorales as convincing and sweet as a haystack, probably never shot a bird, rode a horse, caught a fish. If he ever made hay, it was in mighty desultory fashion.

"I'm an Exploiter."

While Thomas was yarning and clowning, he kept sternly to his poet's vocation. When he worked on his lines, crosshatching, chiseling and chivvying for the right word, a bottle might stand untouched all day at his elbow. Says British Critic John Davenport of these years: "After some terrible drunk, he would come to, somewhere out in the country. Utterly exhausted, nervous, there he would be, suddenly stuttering, diffident, fumbling in his pocket—'I don't know if you'd mind—of course you haven't the time'—and dragging out a poem for you to read. There he was, with his dirty, curly hair, probably wearing someone else's trousers, those nail-bitten fingers as if they were stretched for a five-pound note—then he produced some beautiful thing like this."

Shortly before the war, Dylan met and married Caitlin Macnamara, daughter of a bankrupt Irish landed gentleman. They were, says a poetic friend, "two wild ones," living wherever they could, either in squalor or with friends. "Lack of money still pours in," wrote the moody family man during a spell at his mother-in-law's. He once said that his lifelong ambition was "living off a rich woman," and women often helped him.

"Dylan," said the late Poet Norman Cameron, "you're in danger of being widely regarded as a sponge." Replied Thomas indignantly: "I'm not a sponge. I'm an exploiter."

Reprobate Innocent

He began to get assignments writing and reading for the BBC. He also wrote documentary films, though producers sometimes had to lock him in a hotel room to wring a finished script out of him. People loved him as a sort of raffish reproach to the world of respectability, a reprobate innocent. He got away with almost anything. The story goes that as an honored guest for an Oxford poetry society which served only select wines, Thomas asked for a jug of beer at the outset, cheerfully poured each successive vintage wine into the same jug and mixed it up with his teaspoon.

Between London pub rounds, he lived in Laugharne, a silted-up old South Wales cockle port, bright with pink-washed cottages, near where he used to visit his grandfather as a boy. Life at Laugharne seemed to suit him. He played with his three children, visited his parents, who lived in the same village, cut his daily beer intake to ten pints. "It's lovely, on the sea," he said. "You can spit right into the sea from our window, and we frequently do—all the time, in fact. I potter in the morning. I'm a very good potterer. I shop, I go to the village, and speak to people. It's a short street, and it takes hours to get from one end to the other. I stop at the pub and get back for lunch. In the afternoon there's nothing to do, so I work."

About Danny Boy

The Thomas legend will be enhanced by the three chapters from *Adventures in the Skin Trade,* and the 20 stories published with them. Many a poet, when he writes prose, sounds as stodgy as a beached carp, but Thomas easily swam through prose, with a flashing of fins and a show of unexpected twists that could have made him famous as a prose writer if he had never so much as rhymed hell and seashell. Some of the stories sing of the same Welsh town he saluted in *Under Milk Wood;* others are rambling, obscurely symbolic excursions into weirder regions. In *Skin Trade* it was Thomas' sardonic intention to tell how a youngster from the provinces lands in London, much as he himself did. Before the boy sets out for the big city, he daydreams about what it will be like. He sees himself knocking at a rooming house and an Irish girl appearing at the door. "Good morning, madam, have you a cheap room?" asks the boy. "Cheaper than sunlight to you, Danny Boy," says the girl. "Has it got bugs?" "All over the walls, praise be to God." "I'll take it."

But twelve hours after his actual arrival (according to Thomas' plan for the book), the boy was to be arrested in the raw at a railway station—"a kind of Strip-Jack-Naked. He's parted with everything, or they've taken it." In the 82 slaphappy and possibly autobiographical pages Thomas finished, the kid slides from one loony scrape to another, encumbered much of the way with a Bass ale bottle that has unaccountably got stuck fast on his finger.

Even knocking out a clowning letter to New York Poet Oscar Williams, Thomas could not help writing vivid prose. On a plane trip back from New York: "It was stormy and dangerous, and only my iron will kept the big bird up; lightning looked wonderful through the little eyeholes in its underbelly; the bar was open all the way from Newfoundland; and the woman next to me was stone-deaf so I spoke to her all the way, more wildly and more wildly as the plane lurched on through dark and lion-thunder and the firewater yelled through my blood like Sioux, and she unheard all my delirium with a smile; and then the Red Indians scalped me; and then it was London; and my iron will brought the bird down safely . . ."

The Dying Light

Of himself Thomas once said: "I am first class of second class." It was no deprecatory assessment—still leaving the top for Shakespeare, Dante, Milton *et al.* He was a wild, generous, flamboyant, unpredictable, panurgent, ribald and thirsty man who loved the company of his fellow human beings. He was also a lonely misanthrope who saw the world and himself with intolerable clarity. After one three-day binge he groaned to a friend: "To be able to tear off my flesh, to get rid of this awful, horrifying skin we have . . ."

He once wrote, melodramatically but perhaps not inaccurately: "I hold a beast, an angel and a madman in me, and my enquiry is as to their working, and my problem is their subjugation and victory, downthrow and upheaval . . ." In the poems that will remain long after the last alcoholic insult to that skin he loathed, there are many victories for the angelic of the three Dylan Thomases:

Do not go gentle into that good night.
Rage, rage against the dying of the light.

EXERCISES

1. Single out words and phrases that seem to you typical of *Time*style.
2. Assuming that there are subjects for which this style is appropriate, does

it seem to you that it is appropriate in describing the life of Thomas? Give reasons for your opinion.

3. Are the opening paragraphs merely "clever" or do they put the poet in a proper perspective? Do metaphors of this sort seem to you appropriate to literary comments or evaluations?

4. The article is entitled "The Legend of Dylan Thomas." Does this mean the *Time* editors do not vouch for the authenticity of the events reported?

5. Rewrite this sketch in your own words.

6 MY MOTHER AND HER RELATIVES

by George Bernard Shaw

George Bernard Shaw (1856–1950) was an institution long before his death. As early as the 1890's, he had established his reputation as a brilliant critic and speaker; by World War I, he was the mythical G. B. S., a mixture of genius and buffoon. His interests were varied: from Socialism and women's rights to spelling-reform, music, and vegetarianism. An Irishman, Shaw constantly poked fun at the English, at their institutions and at their political, social, and moral attitudes. His self-advertisement and sarcasm both shocked and delighted. Though he began his literary career as a novelist, it is as a playwright that he achieved his greatest success. The long list of his plays includes Mrs. Warren's Profession, Caesar and Cleopatra, Candida, Man and Superman, Major Barbara, Pygmalion, *and* St. Joan. *The prefaces to the published versions of many of his plays are almost as famous as the plays themselves. Critics have accussed Shaw of being too didactic to be a successful dramatist; yet for all their emphasis on ideas rather than emotions, his plays perform very well. The wit and charm with which he presents his lectures to society made them palatable.*

Self Sketches *appeared in 1949. The candor with which, in the selection below, Shaw describes his family is unusual for him. While there are relatively few direct references to himself, we can read a great deal between the lines, particularly in the little treatise on the raising and education of children with which he ends this sketch.*

My mother was the daughter of a country gentleman, and was brought up with ruthless strictness to be a paragon of all ladylike virtues and accomplishments by her grand aunt, whom I remember from my very early childhood as a humpbacked old lady with a pretty face, whose deformity seemed to me quaintly proper to her as a beneficent fairy. Had she known the magically favorable impression she made on me, she would perhaps have left me her property; and I now believe I was brought to her in the hope that I should attract her to this extent. But I was a failure. She had brought my mother up to make such a distinguished marriage as would finally wipe out an unmentionable stain on her pedigree; for though on her parents' side her extraction was everything that could be desired, her grandfather was a mysterious master spirit whose birth was so obscure that there was some doubt as to whether he ever had any legal parents at all. Under cover of the name of an employee named Cullen, he had made a fortune by keeping a pawnshop in one of the poorest quarters of Dublin. Meanwhile, by assuming the rank of country gentleman at a "seat" in the County Dublin, he married into a genuine county family.

But still he kept the pawnshop and the pawnshop kept him; consequently my fairy great grand aunt Ellen was resolute that the daughter of her dead sister-in-law should be brought up in an unquestionably ladylike manner. So my mother had a Spartan childhood, and carried the straight-backed stamp of it to her grave. Misfortunes that would have crushed ten untrained women broke on her like waves on granite.

Nature, expelled with a fork, came back again and wrecked the life plans of her fairy aunt. When my mother grew up, she knew thoroughbass as taught by her musicmaster Johann Bernhard Logier (famous in Dublin as the inventor of the chiroplast, a mechanical finger exerciser which set his piano pupils all wrong); she could repeat two of La Fontaine's fables in French with perfect pronunciation; she could carry herself with complete dignity; and she could have worked as a ragpicker without losing her entire conviction that she was a lady, of a species apart from servants and common persons. But she could not housekeep on a small income; she had no notion of the value of money; she detested her grand aunt and regarded all that had been taught her as religion and discipline as tyranny and slavery. Consequently, as she was naturally very humane, she abandoned her own children to the most complete anarchy. Both my parents, as it happened, were utterly uncoercive.

In due time she was floated in Dublin society to get married. Among other persons with whom she came in contact was George Carr Shaw, an apparently harmless gentleman of forty, with a squint and a vein of humor which delighted in anti-climax, and would have made him an appreciative listener for Charles Lamb. He was a member of a large family which spoke of itself as "the Shaws," and got invited, on the strength of a second cousinship, to Bushy Park, the seat of the bachelor Sir Robert Shaw, Bart., as to whom see Burke's *Landed Gentry*. George Carr Shaw seemed very safe company for my carefully guarded mother, because nobody could conceive his having the audacity, the enterprise, nor the means, to marry anybody, even if it could be supposed that his years or his squint could appeal to so well brought-up a female as Miss Lucinda Elizabeth Gurly. He was therefore well spoken of to her by her relatives as a quite eligible person to know in a general social way. They forgot that, having never been taught what marriage really means, nor experienced impecuniosity, she might marry any adventurer without knowing how much she was doing.

Her tragedy came about by external pressure of a sort that nobody could have foreseen.

Her widowed father most unexpectedly married again: this time the penniless daughter of an old friend of his whose bills he had backed with ruinous consequences. The alliance did not please the family of his first wife, especially his brother-in-law, a Kilkenny squire, to whom he owed money, and from whom he concealed his intention to marry again.

Unfortunately my mother innocently let out the secret to her uncle. The consequence was that my grandfather, going out on his wedding morning to buy a pair of gloves for the ceremony, was arrested for debt at the suit of his brother-in-law. One can hardly blame him for being furious. But his fury carried him beyond all reason. He believed that my mother had betrayed him deliberately so as to stop the marriage by his arrest. My mother, who was on a visit to some relatives in Dublin at the time, had to choose between two homes to return to. One was the house of a stepmother and an enraged father. The other was the house of her aunt, which meant the old domestic slavery and tyranny.

It was at this moment that some devil, perhaps commissioned by the Life Force to bring me into the world, prompted my father to propose marriage to Miss Bessie Gurly. She caught at the straw. She had heard that he had a pension of £60 a year; and to her, who had never been allowed to have more than pocket money nor to housekeep, £60 seemed an an enormous and inexhaustible sum. She calmly announced her engagement, dropping the bombshell as unconcernedly as if it were a colored glass ball from her solitaire board. People played solitaire in those days.

Finding it impossible to make her see the gravity of the pecuniary situation, or to induce her to cancel her engagement on such a ground, her people played another card. They told her that George Carr Shaw was a drunkard. She indignantly refused to believe them, reminding them that they had never objected to him before. When they persisted, she went to him straightforwardly and asked him was it true. He assured her most solemnly that he was a convinced and lifelong teetotaller. And she believed him and married him. But it was true. He drank.

Without attempting to defend my father for telling this whopper, I must explain that he really was in principle a convinced teetotaller. Unfortunately it was the horror of his own experience as an occasional dipsomaniac that gave him this conviction, which he was miserably unable to carry into practice.

I can only imagine the hell into which my mother descended when she found out what shabby-genteel poverty with a drunken husband is like. She told me once that when they were honeymooning in Liverpool (of all places) she opened her bridegroom's wardrobe and found it full of empty bottles. In the first shock of the discovery she ran away to the docks to get employed as a stewardess and be taken out of the country. But on the way she was molested by some rough docklanders and had to run back again.

I have elsewhere recorded how, when my father, taking me for a walk, pretended in play to throw me into the canal, he very nearly did it. When we got home I said to my mother as an awful and hardly credible discovery "Mama: I think Papa is drunk." This was too much for her. She replied "When is he anything else?"

It is a rhetorical exaggeration to say that I have never since believed in anything or anybody; but the wrench from my childish faith in my father as perfect and omniscient to the discovery that he was a hypocrite and a dipsomaniac was so sudden and violent that it must have left its mark on me.

Her aunt cut her off ruthlessly in spite of my infant charms. All my mother had from her was an earlier gift of a bundle of I.O.U.s signed by my grandfather. She was innocent enough to let him see them and ask what she should do with them. He promptly put them into the fire. This did not matter, as he would not have paid them anyhow; but he also tried to use a power of appointment under her grandfather's (the pawnbroker's) will to deprive her of any share of his bequests to his grandchildren; and though the Gurly family solicitor rescued some £40 a year for her by absolutely refusing to allow him to do his worst, it left my mother convinced that her father was a vindictive parent, not too scrupulously conscientious in money matters.

Then there was her brother, my maternal Uncle Walter. But he was dissolute, and had offended her once by being savagely violent to her in a fit of temper. He went their father's feckless way as to the property. Everybody had disappointed her, or betrayed her, or tyrannized over her.

She was not at all soured by all this. She never made scenes, never complained, never nagged, never punished nor retaliated nor lost her self-control nor her superiority to spites and tantrums and tempers. She was neither weak nor submissive; but as she never revenged, so also she never forgave. There were no quarrels and consequently no reconciliations. You did a wrong; and you were classed by her as a person who did such wrongs, and tolerated indulgently up to a point. But if at last you drove her to break with you, the breach was permanent: you did not get back again. Among my *Maxims for Revolutionists* there is "Beware of the man who does not return your blow." From my mother I had learned that the wrath on which the sun goes down is negligible compared to the clear vision and criticism that is neither created by anger nor ended with it.

Under all the circumstances it says a great deal for my mother's humanity that she did not hate her children. She did not hate anybody, nor love anybody. The specific maternal passion awoke in her a little for my younger sister, who died at 20; but it did not move her until she lost her, nor then noticeably. She did not concern herself much about us; for she had never been taught that mothering is a science, nor that it matters in the least what children eat or drink: she left all that to servants whose wage was £8 a year and could neither write nor read. She had no sense of the value of her own training, and gave it no credit for its results, which she may have regarded as gifts of nature; but she had a deep sense of its cruelties. As we grew up and had to take care of ourselves unguided, we met life's difficulties by breaking our shins over them, gaining such wisdom as was inevitable by making fools of ourselves. On the whole it was easier for my mother than her aunt's plan; and it was certainly meant to be kinder: in fact it was very much kinder, but not so much so as she thought. Letting a calf stray into every china shop is not the only alternative to goading it along the street. In short, my mother was, from the technical point of view of a modern welfare worker, neither a mother nor a wife, and could be classed only as a Bohemian anarchist with ladylike habits.

My father was impecunious and unsuccessful: he could do nothing that interested her; and he did not shake off his miserable and disgraceful tippling (he did eventually) until it was too late to make any difference in their relations. Had there not been imagination, idealization, the charm of music, the charm of lovely seas and sunsets, and our natural kindliness and gentleness, it is impossible to say what cynical barbarism we might not have grown into.

My mother's salvation came through music. She had a mezzosoprano voice of extraordinary purity of tone; and to cultivate it she took lessons from George John Vandaleur Lee, already well established in Dublin as an orchestral conductor, an organizer of concerts, and a teacher of singing so heterodox and original that he depended for his performances on amateurs trained by himself, and was detested by his professional rivals, whom he disparaged as voice wreckers, as indeed they mostly were. He extended this criticism to doctors, and amazed us by eating brown bread instead of white, and sleeping with the window open, both of which habits I acquired and have practised ever since. His influence in our household, of which he at last became a member, accustomed me to the scepticism as to academic authority which still persists in me.

He not only made my mother sing by a method that preserved her voice perfectly until her death at over eighty but gave her a Cause and a Creed to live for.

Those who know my play *Misalliance*, in which the lover has three fathers, will note that I also had a natural father and two supplementaries, making three varieties for me to study. This widened my outlook very considerably. Natural parents should bear in mind that the more supplementaries their children find, at school or elsewhere, the better they will know that it takes all sorts to make a world. Also that though there is always the risk of being corrupted by bad parents, the natural ones may be—probably ten per cent. of them actually are—the worst of the lot.

Then there was my maternal Uncle Walter. During my boyhood he was a ship's surgeon on the Inman line (now the American), visiting us between voyages. He had been educated at Kilkenny College, in his time the Eton of Ireland. When he was the smallest boy there, and the only one who could squeeze himself out under the locked college gates, he was sent by the elder boys at night into the town to make assignations for them with ladies of the street, his reward being whisky enough to make him insensibly drunk. (He was, by the way, astonished and horrified by the homosexualities of English public schools, and maintained that schools should always be, like Kilkenny College, within reach of women.) From Trinity College in Dublin, his university, he had had to retire to recuperate after excessive dissipation. Then, as his father, always short of money through backing bills for his friends and recklessly mortgaging, could not support him, he qualified as a surgeon and took the Inman job. He could learn subjects for examination and pass them easily enough, and was apparently an efficient medical officer under discipline.

He was a most exhilarating person, because he had, like my mother, though without her dignity, a youthfulness that no dissipation could exhaust, and was robust and fullblooded. His profanity and obscenity in conversation were of Rabelaisian exuberance; and as to the *maxima reverentia* due to my tender years, he had rather less of it, if possible, than Falstaff had for Prince Hal. To the half dozen childish rhymes taught me by my mother he added a stock of unprintable limericks that constituted almost an education in geography. He was always in high spirits, and full of a humor that, though barbarous in its blasphemous indecency, was Scriptural and Shakespearean in the elaboration and fantasy of its literary expression. Being full of the Bible, he quoted the sayings of Jesus as models of facetious repartee. He considered Anthony Trollope's novels the only ones worth reading (in those days they were regarded as daring exposures of the Church!); and his favorite opera was Auber's *Fra Diavolo*. Possibly if he had been cultivated artistically in his childhood, he would have been a man of refined pleasures, and might have done something in literature.

As it was, he was a scoffer and a rake, because no better pleasures had ever been either revealed or denied to him. In spite of his excesses, which were not continuous, being the intermittent debauches of a seafarer on shore, he was an upstanding healthy man until he married an English widow in America and settled as a general practitioner in Leyton, Essex, then a country district on the borders of Epping Forest. His wife tried to make him behave himself according to English lights: to go to church; to consult the feelings and prejudices of his patients; to refrain from the amusement of scandalizing their respectability; or at least to stint himself in the item of uproarious blasphemy. It was quite useless: her protests only added to the zest of his profanities. Nevertheless, he held his own in Leyton county society because he was very amusing, and was perceptibly a gentleman who drove his own horse and had bought his select practice.

Soon, however, east London spread and swallowed up Leyton. The country houses of his patients were demolished and replaced by rows of little brick boxes inhabited by clerks in tall hats supporting families on fifteen shillings a week. The change ruined my uncle. His wife died in disgust and despair, leaving everything she possessed to the relatives of her former husband. His horse was sold; his watch was pawned; his clothes became disgracefully shabby; and when he died, and I inherited his estate, I found that the wages of the one servant who had stuck to him through it all had not been paid for seventeen years. His father had long before mortgaged the estate up to the hilt; and I should have had to repudiate my inheritance of it had it come to me a few years earlier. As it was, I was able to pay off the mortgages, rebuild the wrecked houses, support the poor relations, and restore the estate to solvency. Finally I municipalized it, having to procure an Act of the Dail (the parliament of Eire) to enable me to do so, or anyone else to follow my example.

The children of Bohemian Anarchists are often in such strenuous reaction against their bringing-up that they are the most tyrannically conventional of parents. The problem of how much and when children can be kindly and safely left to their own devices, and how much guided and ordered, is the most difficult part of parental policy. Prince Peter Kropotkin, a comprehensive thinker, far above the average in wisdom and kindliness, said of children "You can only look on." My mother, if she had ever thought about the matter at all, would have said "You can only go your own way and let the children go theirs." But there can be no such rule of thumb. The line between tutelage and freethought varies from individual to individual. Even within the same family one child can do next to nothing until it is told what to do until it adolesces, when it does what everybody else does. Its brother or sister may be so unbiddable that it must either be left to the police as a criminal or allowed its own way as a freethinking genius.

The degrees between these extremes are micrometrical. No child can be governed so completely as to have no will of its own: the task would be too much for any parent. But a child left to do anything it likes at all ages and on all occasions will swallow matches or set the house on fire with them, and refuse to learn the alphabet and the multiplication table. On the whole it is safer to delegate the child's education to a conventional school, as Voltaire's was to the Jesuits, leaving it to react by its own strength, than to risk its having to learn with difficulty in its sixteenth year what it could have been taught easily in its sixth.

Chances must be taken in any case. A child cannot be trained in Europe for a higher rank than that of the Papal Chair. But its trainer may be asked "What sort of Pope? Gregory the Great or Alexander Borgia? Pius IX or Leo XIII?" The aim may be rather to produce a great citizen and civilizer. If so, it will still be a toss-up whether the result will be a Sidney Webb or a Bakunin.

Neither my parents nor my schoolmasters ever asked themselves such questions; and had I not had the rare luck to make money as a born playwright I might now be ending as a tramp. Much that I should have been taught in my nonage I had to teach myself later; and much that I was taught I had to unlearn. So I can only repeat that the frontier between tutelage and freethought is hard to find, and is not, as a law must be, the same for everybody.

Yet there must be law in large families and in all schools. This complicates the problem beyond any cut and dried solution that I can suggest. Schools at present make a worse mess of it than households. As I write I have before me a letter from a clever little girl in an Irish convent school. She proudly gives me a list of her nine simultaneous school classes in different languages and branches of education, the acquirement of each of which would be a whole time job for many months for a budding Newton. Such a curriculum leaves me speechless. Yet it must not be inferred that I am on the side of those who agitate against what they call premature educational pressure. John Stuart Mill was taught the classical dead languages when he was child by his father James Mill. I have heard James denounced as a monster for this by William Morris. But I am not so sure. John himself was not so sure. I am not defending the current assumption in the plutocratic public schools that a man is educated when he can read Latin and solve quadratic equations. Obviously he may be able to do both and remain dangerously ignorant as a citizen. And mostly, when he has been crammed and coached into a university degree on this assumption, he may never again look at a page of Latin or think of it without loathing, nor keep his accounts in any but the simplest arithmetic. Yet I am faced with the flat fact that most of us (including myself) remember only the paradigms we have been taught in our childhood, however deeply we may philosophize in later life. My memory of the multiplication and pence tables I learnt before I was six, and the Latin declensions and conjugations I learnt before I was ten, I still remember in my ninety-second year, whereas my efforts as an adult to memorize similar paradigms in modern languages were so unsuccessful that I advise students of them not to waste time in trying to learn irregular verbs (the Spanish ones, for instance) but to speak them as regular. Spaniards may laugh; but they will understand, which is all that is necessary. When an English child says "I thinked" and "I goed" it is just as well understood as if it said "I thought" and "I went." Pidgin is as useful as the English of Milton, and much more concise. Our craze for standards of correctness, pushed as it is to make any departure from them a punishable moral delinquency, wastes years of our lives. However many ways are open before us we refuse to move until two of them are labelled respectively right and wrong, with the right as difficult as we can make it and the wrong the shortest and easiest.

EXERCISES

1. Write a short essay in which you compare the characters of Conrad and Shaw as revealed in the biographical sketch of the former and the autobiographical one of the latter.
2. Shaw has written very candidly about his family, especially about his mother and father. Does this description of his parents lead you to agree with the reviewer who thought Shaw's childhood experiences caused him to be fearful of emotions and emotional commitments? What, in Shaw's description, might have led the reviewer to conclude this?
3. Shaw is apparently candid and detached in this essay. Is he completely objective? From what viewpoint does he write?
4. What are Shaw's ideas on education? Do you agree with him?
5. *Self Sketches* appeared in 1949. Do you think Shaw would have been able to write this autobiographical sketch as candidly had he written it as a young man?
6. What does Shaw feel about his mother's life?

7 AUTOBIOGRAPHICAL SKETCH
by D. H. Lawrence

D. H. Lawrence (1885–1930) has been hailed by many critics as one of the most gifted writers of his time. In this autobiographical sketch he tells something of his early life. In 1912, he eloped with another man's wife and spent most of his remaining years abroad. He died in Italy after many years of ill health. Lawrence was a prolific writer of novels, short stories, criticism, travel books, and poetry. Among his best-known novels are Sons and Lovers, The Rainbow, Women in Love, *and* Aaron's Rod. *His candid treatment of sex caused a number of his books to be banned, at least for a time;* Lady Chatterley's Lover, *particularly, became notorious. What censors did not perceive was that Lawrence was a deeply moralistic writer.*

In his fiction, Lawrence wrote a consciously poetic style, heavy with imagery. This sketch, written for a newspaper, is informal, colloquial, even slangy—but in spite of the bantering, satirical tone, his self-appraisal is intensely serious. The factual account of the first part of the sketch is merely the setting for the real point: Lawrence's concern with a problem which he felt troubled many people, "Why is there so little contact between myself and the people whom I know? Why has this contact no vital meaning?"

They ask me: "Did you find it very hard to get on and to become a success?" And I have to admit that if I can be said to have got on, and if I can be called a success, then I *did not* find it hard.

I never starved in a garret, nor waited in anguish for the post to bring me an answer from editor or publisher, nor did I struggle in sweat and blood to bring forth mighty works, nor did I ever wake up and find myself famous.

I was a poor boy. I *ought* to have wrestled in the fell clutch of circumstance, and undergone the bludgeonings of chance before I became a writer with a very modest income and a very questionable reputation. But I didn't. It all happened by itself and without any groans from me.

It seems a pity. Because I was undoubtedly a poor boy of the working classes, with no apparent future in front of me. But after all, what am I now?

I was born among the working classes and brought up among them. My father was a collier, and only a collier, nothing praiseworthy about him. He wasn't even respectable, in so far as he got drunk rather frequently, never went near a chapel, and was usually rather rude to his little immediate bosses at the pit.

He practically never had a good stall, all the time he was a butty, because he was always saying tiresome and foolish things about the men just above him in control at the mine. He offended them all, almost on purpose, so how could he expect them to favour him? Yet he grumbled when they didn't.

My mother was, I suppose, superior. She came from town, and belonged really to the lower bourgeoisie. She spoke King's English, without an accent, and never in her life could even imitate a sentence of the dialect which my father spoke, and which we children spoke out of doors.

She wrote a fine Italian hand, and a clever and amusing letter when she felt like it. And as she grew older she read novels again, and got terribly impatient with *Diana of the Crossways* and terribly thrilled by *East Lynne.*

But she was a working man's wife, and nothing else, in her shabby little black bonnet and her shrewd, clear, "different" face. And she was very much respected, just as my father was not respected. Her nature was quick and sensitive, and perhaps really superior. But she was down, right down in the working class, among the mass of poorer collier's wives.

I was a delicate pale brat with a snuffy nose, whom most people treated quite gently as just an ordinary delicate little lad. When I was twelve I got a county council scholarship, twelve pounds a year, and went to Nottingham High School.

After leaving school I was a clerk for three months, then had a very serious pneumonia illness, in my seventeenth year, that damaged my health for life.

A year later I became a school teacher, and after three years' savage teaching of collier lads I went to take the "normal" course in Nottingham University.

As I was glad to leave school, I was glad to leave college. It had meant mere disillusion, instead of the living contact of men. From college I went down to Croydon, near London, to teach in a new elementary school at a hundred pounds a year.

It was while I was at Croydon, when I was twenty-three, that the girl who had been the chief friend of my youth, and who was herself a school teacher in a mining village at home, copied out some of my poems, and without telling me, sent them to the *English Review,* which had just had a glorious rebirth under Ford Maddox Hueffer.

Hueffer was most kind. He printed the poems, and asked me to come and see him. The girl had launched me, so easily, on my literary career, like a princess cutting a thread, launching a ship.

I had been tussling away for four years, getting out *The White Peacock* in inchoate bits, from the underground of my consciousness. I must have written most of it five or six times, but only in intervals, never as a task or a divine labour, or in the groans of parturition.

I would dash at it, do a bit, show it to the girl; she always admired it; then realise afterwards it wasn't what I wanted, and have another dash. But at Croydon I had worked at it fairly steadily, in the evenings after school.

Anyhow, it was done, after four or five years' spasmodic effort. Hueffer asked at once to see the manuscript. He read it immediately, with the greatest cheery sort of kindness and bluff. And in his queer voice, when we were in an omnibus in London, he shouted in my ear: "It's got every fault that the English novel can have."

Just then the English novel was supposed to have so many faults, in comparison with the French, that it was hardly allowed to exist at all. "But," shouted Hueffer in the bus, "you've got GENIUS."

This made me want to laugh, it sounded so comical. In the early days they were always telling me I had got genius, as if to console me for not having their own incomparable advantages.

But Hueffer didn't mean that. I always thought he had a bit of genius himself. Anyhow, he sent the MS. of *The White Peacock* to William Heinemann, who accepted it at once, and made me alter only four little lines whose omission would now make anybody smile. I was to have £50 when the book was published.

Meanwhile Hueffer printed more poems and some stories of mine in the *English Review*, and people read them and told me so, to my embarrassment and anger. I hated being an author, in people's eyes. Especially as I was a teacher.

When I was twenty-five my mother died, and two months later *The White Peacock* was published, but it meant nothing to me. I went on teaching for another year, and then again a bad pneumonia illness intervened. When I got better I did not go back to school. I lived henceforward on my scanty literary earnings.

It is seventeen years since I gave up teaching and started to live an independent life of the pen. I have never starved, and never even felt poor, though my income for the first ten years was not better, and often worse, than it would have been if I had remained an elementary school teacher.

But when one has been born poor a very little money can be enough. Now my father would think I am rich, if nobody else does. And my mother would think I have risen in the world, even if I don't think so.

But something is wrong, either with me or with the world, or with both of us. I have gone far and met many people, of all sorts and conditions, and many whom I have genuinely liked and esteemed.

People, *personally*, have nearly always been friendly. Of critics we will not speak, they are different fauna from people. And I have *wanted* to feel truly friendly with some, at least, of my fellow-men.

Yet I have never quite succeeded. Whether I get on *in* the world is a question; but I certainly don't get on very well *with* the world. And whether I am a worldly success or not I really don't know. But I feel, somehow, not much of a human success.

By which I mean that I don't feel there is any very cordial or fundamental contact between me and society, or me and other people. There is a breach. And my contact is with something that is non-human, non-vocal.

I used to think it had something to do with the oldness and the worn-outness of Europe. Having tried other places, I know that is not so. Europe is, perhaps, the least worn-out of the continents, because it is the most lived in. A place that is lived in lives.

It is since coming back from America that I ask myself seriously: Why is there so little contact between myself and the people whom I know? Why has the contact no vital meaning?

And if I write the question down, and try to write the answer down, it is because I feel it is a question that troubles many men.

The answer, as far as I can see, has something to do with class. Class makes a gulf, across which all the best human flow is lost. It is not exactly the triumph of the middle classes that had made the deadness, but the triumph of the middle-class *thing*.

As a man from the working class, I feel that the middle class cut off some of my vital vibration when I am with them. I admit them charming and educated and good people often enough. *But they just stop some part of me from working*. Some part has to be left out.

Then why don't I live with my working people? Because their vibration is limited in another direction. They are narrow, but still fairly deep and passionate, whereas the middle class is broad and shallow and passionless. Quite passionless. At the best they substitute affection, which is the great middle-class positive emotion.

But the working class is narrow in outlook, in prejudice, and narrow in intelligence. This again makes a prison. One can belong absolutely to no class.

Yet I find, here in Italy, for example, that I live in a certain silent contact with the peasants who work the land of this villa. I am not intimate with them, hardly speak to them save to say good day. And they are not working for me; I am not their *padrone*.

Yet it is they, really, who form my *ambiente*, and it is from them that the human flow comes to me. I don't want to live with them in their cottages; that would be a sort of prison. But I want them to be there, about the place, their lives going on along with mine, and in relation to mine. I don't idealise them. Enough of that folly! It is worse than setting school-children to express themselves in self-conscious twaddle. I don't expect them to make any millennium here on earth, neither now nor in the future. But I want to live near them, because their life still flows.

And now I know, more or less, why I cannot follow in the footsteps even of Barrie or of Wells, who both came from the common people also and are both such a success. Now I know why I cannot rise in the world and become even a little popular and rich.

I cannot make the transfer from my own class into the middle class. I cannot, not for anything in the world, forfeit my passional consciousness and my old blood-affinity with my fellow-men and the animals and the land, for that other thin, spurious mental conceit which is all that is left of the mental consciousness once it has made itself exclusive.

EXERCISES

1. Why was it that Lawrence felt that he could fit neither into the middle nor the lower class? How does he characterize the middle class? In discussing his classlessness, is he objective or subjective?
2. What make this article seem intensely personal? Is the reader interested in a discussion that is so personal? Does Lawrence deal with universals as well?
3. Does he relate his experiences of childhood and early manhood to his feeling of not belonging?
4. Contrast the tone of this essay with that of Shaw's.
5. Write an essay in which you describe your family, your neighborhood, your schooling, and the influence they have had on you.

8 EARLY SUCCESS

by F. Scott Fitzgerald

F. Scott Fitzgerald (1896–1940) outlines his early career in the selection reprinted below. With the publication of This Side of Paradise, *his first novel, and of* Tales of the Jazz Age *and* The Great Gatsby *(page 118), he established himself as the voice of the "lost generation" of the twenties. Later works include* Tender Is the Night *and* The Crack-up, *a posthumously published collection of essays and letters.*

From early college days, Fitzgerald was an admirer of Samuel Butler's Notebooks, *and kept one himself. Some of the notes are ideas for short stories, but most are cleverly wrought sentences and phrases. His concern with technique is reflected in the self-conscious, sophisticated, and sparkling writing in his fiction and essays. But he did not aim at a brilliant style for its own sake; rather, he sought to achieve perceptive and serious writing. In "Early Success" Fitzgerald recalls his youthful literary triumph. He reflects that "The dream had been early realized and the realization carried with it a certain bonus and a certain burden." The tone of this candid autobiographical sketch conveys the mixture of surface gaiety and nervousness that we have come to associate with his era.*

October, 1937

Seventeen years ago this month I quit work or, if you prefer, I retired from business. I was through—let the Street Railway Advertising Company carry along under its own power. I retired, not on my profits, but on my liabilities, which included debts, despair, and a broken engagement and crept home to St. Paul to "finish a novel."

That novel, begun in a training camp late in the war, was my ace in the hole. I had put it aside when I got a job in New York, but I was as constantly aware of it as of the shoe with cardboard in the sole, during all one desolate spring. It was like the fox and goose and the bag of beans. If I stopped working to finish the novel, I lost the girl.

So I struggled on in a business I detested and all the confidence I had garnered at Princeton and in a haughty career as the army's worst aide-de-camp melted gradually away. Lost and forgotten, I walked quickly from certain places—from the pawn shop where one left the field glasses, from prosperous friends whom one met when wearing the suit from before the war—from restaurants after tipping with the last nickel, from busy cheerful offices that were saving the jobs for their own boys from the war.

Even having a first story accepted had not proved very exciting. Dutch Mount and I sat across from each other in a car-card slogan advertising office, and the same mail brought each of us an acceptance from the same magazine—the old *Smart Set.*

"My check was thirty—how much was yours?"

"Thirty-five."

The real blight, however, was that my story had been written in college two years before, and a dozen new ones hadn't even drawn a personal letter. The implication was that I was on the down-grade at twenty-two. I spent the thirty dollars on a magenta feather fan for a girl in Alabama.

My friends who were not in love or who had waiting arrangements with "sensible" girls, braced themselves patiently for a long pull. Not I—I was in love with a whirlwind and I must spin a net big enough to catch it out of my head, a head full of trickling nickles and sliding dimes, the incessant music box of the poor. It couldn't be done like that, so when the girl threw me over I went home and finished my novel. And then, suddenly, everything changed, and this article is about that first wild wind of success and the delicious mist it brings with it. It is a short and precious time—for when the mist rises in a few weeks, or a few months, one finds that the very best is over.

It began to happen in the autumn of 1919 when I was an empty bucket, so mentally blunted with the summer's writing that I'd taken a job repairing car roofs at the Northern Pacific shops. Then the postman rang, and that day I quit work and ran along the streets, stopping automobiles to tell friends and acquaintances about it—my novel *This Side of Paradise* was accepted for publication. That week the postman rang and rang, and I paid off my terrible small debts, bought a suit, and woke up every morning with a world of ineffable toploftiness and promise.

While I waited for the novel to appear, the metamorphosis of amateur into professional began to take place—a sort of stitching together of your whole life into a pattern of work, so that the end of one job is automatically the beginning of another. I had been an amateur before; in October, when I strolled with a girl among the stones of a southern graveyard, I was a professional and my enchantment with certain things that she felt and said was already paced by an anxiety to set them down in a story—it was called *The Ice Palace* and it was published later. Similarly, during Christmas week in St. Paul, there was a night when I had stayed home from two dances to work on a story. Three friends called up during the evening to tell me I had missed some rare doings: a well-known man-about-town had disguised himself as a camel and, with a taxi-driver as the rear half, managed to attend the wrong party. Aghast with myself for not being there, I spent the next day trying to collect the fragments of the story.

"Well, all I can say is it was funny when it happened." "No, I don't know where he got the taxi-man." "You'd have to know him well to understand how funny it was."

In despair I said:

"Well, I can't seem to find out exactly what happened but I'm going to write about it as if it was ten times funnier than anything you've said." So I wrote it, in twenty-two consecutive hours, and wrote it "funny," simply because I was so emphatically told it was funny. *The Camel's Back* was published and still crops up in the humorous anthologies.

With the end of the winter set in another pleasant pumped-dry period, and, while I took a little time off, a fresh picture of life in America began to form before my eyes. The uncertainties of 1919 were over—there seemed little doubt about what was going to happen—America was going on the greatest, gaudiest spree in history and there was going to be plenty to tell about it. The whole golden boom was in the air—its splendid generosities, its outrageous corruptions and the tortuous death struggle of the old America in prohibition. All the stories that came into my head had a touch of disaster in them—the lovely young creatures in my novels went to ruin, the diamond mountains of my short stories blew up, my millionaires were as beautiful and damned as Thomas Hardy's peasants. In life these things hadn't happened yet, but I was pretty sure living wasn't the reckless, careless business these people thought—this generation just younger than me.

For my point of vantage was the dividing line between the two generations, and there I sat—somewhat self-consciously. When my first big mail came in—hundreds and hundreds of letters on a story about a girl who bobbed her hair—it seemed rather absurd that they should come to me about it. On the other hand, for a shy man it was nice to be somebody except oneself again: to be "the Author" as one had been "the Lieutenant." Of course one wasn't really an author any more than one had been an army officer, but nobody seemed to guess behind the false face.

All in three days I got married and the presses were pounding out *This Side of Paradise* like they pound out extras in the movies.

With its publication I had reached a stage of manic depressive insanity. Rage and bliss alternated hour by hour. A lot of people thought it was a fake, and perhaps it was, and a lot of others thought it was a lie, which it was not. In a daze I gave out an interview—I told what a great writer I was and how I'd achieved the heights. Heywood Broun, who was on my trail, simply quoted it with the comment that I seemed to be a very self-satisfied young man, and for some days I was notably poor company. I invited him to lunch and in a kindly way told him that it was too bad he had let his life slide away without accomplishing anything. He had just turned thirty and it was about then that I wrote a line which certain people will not let me forget: "She was a faded but still lovely woman of twenty-seven."

In a daze I told the Scribner Company that I didn't expect my novel to sell more than twenty thousand copies and when the laughter died away I was told that a sale of five thousand was excellent for a first novel. I think it was a week after publication that it passed the twenty thousand mark, but I took myself so seriously that I didn't even think it was funny.

These weeks in the clouds ended abruptly a week later when Princeton turned on the book—not undergraduate Princeton but the black mass of faculty and alumni. There was a kind but reproachful letter from President Hibben, and a room full of classmates who suddenly turned on me with condemnation. We had been part of a rather gay party staged conspicuously in Harvey Firestone's car of robin's-egg blue, and in the course of it I got an accidental black eye trying to stop a fight. This was magnified into an orgy and in spite of a delegation of undergraduates who went to the board of Governors, I was suspended from my club for a couple of months. The *Alumni Weekly* got after my book and only Dean Gauss had a good word to say for me. The unctuousness and hypocrisy of the proceedings was exasperating and for seven years I didn't go to Princeton. Then a magazine asked me for an article about it and when I started to write it, I found I really loved the place and that the experience of one week was a small item in the total budget. But on that day in 1920 most of the joy went out of my success.

But one was now a professional—and the new world couldn't possibly be presented without bumping the old out of the way. One gradually developed a protective hardness against both praise and blame. Too often people liked your things for the wrong reasons or people liked them whose dislike would be a compliment. No decent career was ever founded on a public and one learned to go ahead without precedents and without fear. Counting the bag, I found that in 1919 I had made $800 by writing, that in 1920 I had made $18,000, stories, picture rights and book. My story price had gone from $30 to $1,000. That's a small price to what was paid later in the Boom, but what it sounded like to me couldn't be exaggerated.

The dream had been early realized and the realization carried with it a certain bonus and a certain burden. Premature success gives one an almost mystical conception of destiny as opposed to will power—at its worst the Napoleonic delusion. The man who arrives young believes that he exercises his will because his star is shining. The man who only asserts himself at thirty has a balanced idea of what will power and fate have contributed, the one who gets there at forty is liable to put the emphasis on will alone. This comes out when the storms strike your craft.

The compensation of a very early success is a conviction that life is a romantic matter. In the best sense one stays young. When the primary objects of love and money could be taken for granted and a shaky eminence had lost its fascination, I had fair years to waste, years that I can't honestly regret, in seeking the eternal Carnival by the Sea. Once in the middle twenties I was driving along the High Corniche Road through the twilight with the whole French Riviera twinkling on the sea below. As far ahead as I could see was Monte Carlo, and though it was out of season and there were no Grand Dukes left to gamble and E. Phillips Oppenheim was a fat industrious man in my hotel, who lived in a bathrobe—the very name was so incorrigibly enchanting that I could only stop the car and like the Chinese whisper: "Ah me! Ah me!" It was not Monte Carlo I was looking at. It was back into the mind of the young man with cardboard soles who had walked the streets of New York. I was him again—for an instant I had the good fortune to share his dreams, I who had no more dreams of my own. And there are still times when I creep up on him, surprise him on an autumn morning in New York or a spring night in Carolina when it is so quiet that you can hear a dog barking in the next county. But never again as during that all too short period when he and I were one person, when the fulfilled future and the wistful past were mingled in a single gorgeous moment—when life was literally a dream.

EXERCISES

1. Characterize the tone in which Fitzgerald wrote about his "crack-up."
2. A note of light sarcasm runs through this essay. Give examples of its more obvious appearances. Why is sarcasm appropriate?
3. What indications of success are described? Why are these particular details mentioned? How are they related to the theme?
4. The essay catches the qualities of the golden twenties that Fitzgerald wrote about. Find specific details to illustrate this point.
5. Fitzgerald felt there were advantages as well as disadvantages to early success. What are some of each?
6. Write an essay in which you describe the sort of person you expect to be when you are forty years old.

III | Book Reviews

More than 35,000 books annually flood the English-speaking market. The book review is one of our chief guides to the nature and worth of these books.

Reviews take a great many forms. Generally, they may be categorized as the brief notice, the short review, and the article-review. The brief notice is sometimes less than 100 words. *The New Yorker, Harper's* and many other periodicals use it to good effect. This length does not allow for a detailed account of the reviewer's response to a book, but it does allow for a general statement about the book's contents and value. The following is an example:

Fifteen Modern American Poets. Edited by George P. Elliott. Rinehart. $1.65. A very fine paper-bound anthology of some of the "younger" American poets. It is a judicious selection which gives the reader room for his own appraisal. Bishop, Eberhart, Roethke, Miles, Scott, and Wilbur, among others.[1]

This is mostly factual, but the reviewer does offer some judgment of the editor's choice of selections.

The short review usually summarizes the contents of a book and comments briefly on its quality, with perhaps a reference to the audience toward whom the book is primarily addressed. Well-written reviews of this sort involve both reporting at a high level and criticism, for if the reviewer is to be intelligible, he must capture the essential theme of the book, restate it, and show how well or how poorly the author develops it. Limitations of space, however, preclude any extensive statement of values underlying the reviewer's judgment. The article-review, of, say, 1000 words or more, allows and even demands some indication of the reviewer's critical principles. Some of these reviews achieve the status of literary criticism. Lionel Trilling's review of Riesman's *The Lonely Crowd* is a good example of this kind of review.

[1] Reprinted from *Commonweal.*

Frequently, as suggested above, the reviewer is satisfied when he has told us something about the contents of a book and given a brief judgment of its quality. This is especially true of reviews of books that make no claim to being works of art. A reviewer dealing with a book of poetry, of plays, or fiction, or any book that does make such claims is more likely to speculate on the nature of literary forms and to introduce aesthetic and critical theory in his evaluation of such works.

The method of the reviewer is determined by how he thinks he can best inform his readers about a book. Obviously, reference books, nonfiction, or novels call for different methods of reviewing. A review of a work of non-fiction, one, for instance, on the causes of war, could be confined to an examination of the author's assumptions and conclusions, or to comparing and contrasting the work with others on the same subject. A review of a novel might interpret its symbolism, analyze the characterizations, or examine its style. In writing about a fairly well-known author, a reviewer is likely to mention some of his previous works; obviously this will enable him to talk about the new book in a clearer perspective, to evaluate it in relation either to the author's general achievement or to the achievement of one or more of his books. If the author is not widely known, a reviewer may try to place him for a reader by comparing his work to the work of a well-known author. He may relate the book to other books of its kind: historical novels, mysteries, informal essays, or history for lay readers. He may also relate it to historical traditions or literary traditions: to the "Turner thesis," to the theory of "economic determinism," to the "new biography," or to the conventions common to "Southern fiction." A book belongs to a milieu, to a culture, and sometimes a single sentence will evoke the background necessary to understand it.

Certain audiences have special knowledge; they are well read in a field or may even be contributors to it. Thus, a reviewer for a scholarly journal can assume an informed audience. A reviewer for such magazines as *The Atlantic Monthly*, *American Scholar*, or *The Griffin* can assume an audience interested in literature and serious books. In writing for less knowledgeable audiences, a reviewer need not write "down," but his approach will be simpler, more general. There is a distinction between simple, nontechnical exposition and popularization that falsifies.

Occasionally, creative writers have ridiculed the reviewer and the critic, and in a variety of ways have quoted the old adage, "Those who can, do; those who can't, teach." One reviewer answered this by saying he was not a chicken and couldn't lay an egg but he knew when he ate a bad one. Some reviewers and critics are undoubtedly creative writers *manqué* (lacking). It does not follow that they are wanting in discrimination or are deficient in analytical powers.

Reviewers and critics face occupational hazards. They may pass negative judgments on an author or a book that will prove of enduring value. The reviews in this section of *Maggie: A Girl of the Streets, The Great Gatsby, An American Tragedy, A Farewell to Arms, Soldier's Pay,* and *Grapes of Wrath* were written when these books first appeared and before their authors were established as important writers. Yet these reviewers realized that the books were the work of men of extraordinary talent. In some cases, our hindsight would scarcely let us improve on the perception shown in these reviews. The reviewer, however, cannot be expected to call the turn every time. He is not infallible. But we can, in all fairness, demand that he respect the intentions of the author and try to understand what the author is trying to do. He should not dismiss an author offhand because his style is alien to him, or because the author's view of life is not in keeping with his own, or because the author's erudition makes unusual demands on him. The function of the critic, according to Matthew Arnold, is "a disinterested endeavour to learn and propagate the best that is known and thought in the world."

1 POETS OF THE ENGLISH LANGUAGE

by Robert A. Hume

The following review was written for College English, *a journal read by many English instructors. The reviewer was able to assume that his readers are familiar with similar anthologies and are well read in literary history and criticism. This is a short, practical, to-the-point review aimed at a specific audience.*

Edited by W. H. AUDEN and NORMAN HOLMES PEARSON. 5 vols. ("Viking Portable Library," Nos. 49–53.) Viking Press, 1950. (Vol. I: *Langland to Spencer*; Vol. II: *Marlowe to Marvell;* Vol. III: *Milton to Goldsmith;* Vol. IV: *Blake to Poe;* Vol. V: *Tennyson to Yeats.*) $2.50 each vol.

Anyone aware of English may well be pleased at one more proof that our language, much as we know it now, has been a medium of poetry for better than six hundred years. By the breadth of their selections for *Poets of the English Language,* W. H. Auden and Norman Holmes Pearson have supplied such proof impressively. Nor need they apologize, as they come near to doing, for omitting biographical information other than dates for the 157 named poets represented. Even were all the entries printed anonymously, they would still provide the important thing: what the editors call "the autobiography of the poetical imagination and fancy."

As a practicing artist Auden has shown nothing if not versatility. Now as co-editor he reveals a wide tolerance of varying forms and moods. At his and Pearson's hands, classicists and Romanticists get equal innings, and no school, whether metaphysical or other, wins undue emphasis. The traditional "greats" enjoy the ampler spacings that few readers would deny them; those with lesser but still familiar names are substantially present; and certain little-known poets, rescued only lately from the mufflings of time, become distinct voices. The tendency too often seen in anthologies to clutter a score of pages with tiny cullings from as many writers has been almost consistently avoided. Each volume contains a helpful "Calendar," listing cultural events as well as important poems for the period covered by the text.

In their introductions the editors comment tellingly not only on the methods and themes of the poets from early to recent times but also on the varying social conditions that formed their workshop. These discussions are notable for frequent mastery of phrase and for a wealth of seemingly casual erudition. It is nothing against them that, although clearly written, they will probably mean more to high-brows than to those whom the editors call middle-brows; for, honestly practiced, the criticism of poetry is not a simple art. Poetry itself, however, is for all brows, and it is gratifying to observe again, in these volumes, how handsomely and irrefutably it pleads for the civilizing spirit.

EXERCISES

1. This reviewer has managed to show several ways in which the Auden and Pearson anthology differs from the usual anthology of English and American poetry. What are the points he makes?

2. What remarks of the reviewer show he assumes that his audience has special knowledge?

3. Does the reviewer give concrete instances of the editors' discrimination in selecting the contents of the anthology?

2 EMINENT POST-VICTORIAN

by Aileen Pippett

Mrs. Aileen Pippett, the reviewer of Lytton Strachey: His Mind and Art, *is the author of* The Moth and the Star, *a biographical study of Virginia Woolf and her work. Thus, she could bring a special knowledge of the techniques involved in the biographical-critical approach to her evaluation of Mr. Sanders' achievement. And the fact that Virginia Woolf and Lytton Strachey were very close friends gave the reviewer the advantage of particular familiarity with the subject of the book.*

LYTTON STRACHEY: His Mind and Art. By Charles Richard Sanders. Illustrated. 381 pp. New Haven: Yale University Press. $6.

Virginia Woolf called Lytton Strachey her "dear old serpent." Now, the serpent fascinates but is seldom loved; it excites admiration rather than respect; sluggish and inert, it strikes or retreats with silent swiftness; reputed to be wise, it tempts to folly; in religion and psychology its importance as a symbol is immense. Almost every image conjured up by the word has been applied to Lytton Strachey, by admirers or detractors, but no convincing picture of the whole man has yet appeared.

Charles Richard Sanders, who teaches English at Duke University, helps considerably to make the picture come alive by devoting an eighth of his volume to a biographical sketch with family portraits: the rest is literary criticism. The opening chapter contains so much information about Strachey's unpublished or uncollected writings, and the critical study casts so much light on his character and opinions as well as the fierce controversies which have raged around him, that this book will certainly interest the general reader and provide the student with invaluable source material.

Here we see Lytton as a delicate but merry child in a prosperous Victorian family, busy with his numerous brothers and sisters writing verses and "idioting" little magazines. Spartan routine at one school and savage bullying at another produced a boy who was biddable to the point of timidity, but his marked literary gifts were recognized by teachers when he was 12. At 15 he was convinced he was hideous; at 25 he regarded himself as a failure, uncouth, dejected, lonely. Actually he was surrounded by admirers and friends.

He was 32, and still unknown as a writer, when he was asked to contribute a volume to the popular Home University Library. The interviewing editor found him debilitated, very silent, but not at all diffident. The resulting "Landmarks in French Literature" astonished and delighted everyone but brought him neither the fame nor the money he needed. He went on living in bed-sitting rooms, largely dependent on his mother and friends. The success of "Eminent Victorians" changed all that, and he was able to live and work comfortably in the country.

His mother was sorry when she learned he had "taken up with Queen Victoria," but the public did not agree with her. "Elizabeth and Essex" was less wildly popular. Virginia Woolf, who had outgrown her dependence on his approval but still loved him tenderly, said "His 'Elizabeth' has come between us. We never discuss our work with one another now." Since his death in 1932 he has been assailed, but he cannot be overlooked. B. S. (Before Strachey) biographies have their virtues and A. S. (After Strachey) biographies may have their shortcomings, but he remains a central, epochal figure in twentieth-century literature.

This man with two voices, the squeak when joking and the rich baritone when serious, was often capricious and spiteful, but he was steadfast in friendship. His intellectual honesty evoked admiration; his physical frailty aroused the protective instinct in men and women alike. His charm was irresistible. Mr. Sanders strives to be impartial, but he admits he has succumbed, and, in so doing, he has discovered the delight that awaits all those who come to Strachey's works with an open mind.

EXERCISES

1. What is the special significance of "Eminent Post-Victorian" as the title of this particular review?
2. Does the phrase "dear old serpent" quicken your interest in learning more about Strachey's character? Why or why not?
3. How important is the reviewer's style in awakening or discouraging interest in the book which is reviewed?
4. Does the reviewer's interest in Strachey cause her to lose sight of Sanders' book? Does she seem fair to the book?

3 BLOOMSDAY'S CHILD

Time

This review of a book about James Joyce is written in a less brassy style than is typical of Time *reviews (**see page 65**). Even so, it is self-consciously clever and "cute." Another characteristic of a* Time *review is that it uses the book merely as a pretext for a* Time *article about the book's subject; the book's central meaning, when not totally ignored, is usually distorted and almost invariably trivialized. The effect of a* Time *review is not to invite the reader to examine the book for himself; rather, it provides the* Time *reader—in a painless, flattering, and entertaining fashion—with the feeling that he has "got it cold."*

MY BROTHER'S KEEPER: JAMES JOYCE'S EARLY YEARS (266 pp.)—*Stanislaus Joyce—Viking* ($5).

"Lives of great men all remind us friends will make them less sublime." Thus most literary memoirs might be described, but James Joyce was lucky in his friends: at worst, they merely carved their initials on the giant oak of his literary reputation. He was even luckier in his late brother, Stanislaus. With candor, insight and a remarkable lack of rancor toward the man who arrogantly dubbed him "my whetstone," Stanislaus was content to draw what is easily the best portrait of his legendary brother as a young man.

Though he followed James Joyce to Trieste in 1905 and remained there for nearly a half-century as an English professor, Stanislaus was the invisible man in Joyce's life. In this book, he emerges as the perfect foil. Joyce was mercurial, Stanislaus was phlegmatic. Joyce drank, Stanislaus was abstemious. Joyce was referred to as "Sunny Jim," Stanislaus as "Bile Beans." In the Dublin days with which this memoir begins and ends, one belief surmounted all brotherly differences—the belief that Jim had genius.

Even as a baby, Jim did the star turns at their home in Bray, a seaside village near Dublin. In a morality play staged in the nursery, little Jim wriggled across the floor as the devil, with a rolled-up sheet for a tail, and easily stole the show from Stanislaus' staid Adam and a sister's Eve. It was a pleasant middle-class childhood until Papa Joyce began dragging his brood on an alcoholic long day's journey into night.

Enemies of Life

John Joyce was not born a failure; he achieved it. Competent connoisseurs compared his tenor voice to the best in Europe, yet he never bothered to train it properly. He failed in politics as well as in business. In his early 40s, John Joyce was left with nothing but a pension of £11 a month. He was the father of a dozen children, but he rarely worked again—though he lived to be 83. Drunk or sober, he affected a monocle, but slipped easily into the language of a stevedore. In one drunken fury, John Joyce almost strangled his long-suffering wife. As Mary Joyce lay dying in her 44th year, he besottedly entered her room and blurted: "If you can't get well, die. Die and be damned to you!" Stanislaus lunged at his father but Jim got the old man safely out of the room.

Jim's outward calm during such incidents always puzzled Stanislaus, though he later realized one of its causes: their mother had become a symbol to the great symbol-maker of "the Irishwoman, the accomplice of the Irish Catholic Church, which [James] called the scullery-maid of Christendom." Stanislaus laces his book with anticlerical gibes; the brothers' joint rejection of the Catholic faith culminated in a scene at their dying mother's bedside in which Jim and Stanislaus refused to kneel and pray for her—an episode that Joyce later used in *Ulysses* as the source of Stephen Dedalus' "agenbite of inwit," *i.e.*, remorse.

The Artist as Priest

Schooled by Jesuits from the age of six, Jim was "God-intoxicated," and Stanislaus was keen enough to recognize that Joyce remained God-intoxicated though he changed gods. The work of art became his religious passion. It was this, says Stanislaus, that prompted Jim as a stripling to say to the mature Yeats: "I regret that you are too old to be influenced by me." Argues Stanislaus: "What my brother said, or meant to say . . . was in plain words that Yeats did not hold his head high enough for a poet of his stature, that he made himself too cheap with people who were not worthy to dust his boots."

Stanislaus became indignant when Jim took to boozing and wenching with Oliver St. John Gogarty, the "stately plump Buck Mulligan" of *Ulysses*. Recalls Stanislaus of his brother: "I hated to see him glossy-eyed and slobbery-mouthed." Gogarty confessed to another friend that he wanted "to make Joyce drink in order to break his spirit," and celebrated the occasions of sin with a limerick:

There is a young fellow named Joyce,
Who possesses a sweet tenor voice.
He goes down to the kips [*brothels*]

With a psalm on his lips,
And biddeth the harlots rejoice.

As for himself, says Stanislaus, "I determined to give continence a fair trial." He also generalizes that "women do not interest Irishmen except as streetwalkers or housekeepers."

Ulysses or Madness?

Joyce's junior by nearly three years, Stanislaus makes no unseemly claims for his own influence on his brother during these apprentice years. He does report having arranged the order of the poems in *Chamber Music* and suggested the title. This gives the lie to Gogarty, who claimed that Joyce was inspired by the tinkle of a night pot in a brothel. For Joyce, the incomparable word-distiller, the charm doubtless rested in the title's double meaning.

Had Stanislaus lived to complete his memoir, Editor Richard Ellmann is certain that he would have pressed the claim that he saved his brother from the triple threat of dissipation, dubious friends and inertia. Joyce never admitted the need to be saved from anything, but Jung himself is reported to have said after reading *Ulysses* that Joyce would have gone mad had he not written the book.

Just as Joyce was obsessed by Dublin and needed to get it out of his system, so Stanislaus was obsessed by James Joyce, and this book was his exorcism. With the true Joycean alchemy, he took truths that were ugly, sordid and violent and composed a memoir that is grave and serene. Yet he did not wholly escape his brother. He died in 1955, on June 16—Bloomsday, *i.e.*, the day in the life of Leopold Bloom chronicled in *Ulysses*. It was a day Stanislaus himself annually celebrated with a party.

EXERCISES

1. What is the meaning of the title given this review, "Bloomsday's Child"?
2. Most readers of this review would probably agree that the style is studied. Point out instances of this.
3. Does the review treat Joyce's career with respect?
4. Compare this review to Aileen Pippett's review of *Lytton Strachey: His Mind and Art*. What are the similarities, if any, of the reviewers' techniques? What are the differences?

4 MISS PORTER'S NEW STORIES

by Gertrude Buckman

This review of Miss Porter's short story collection was written for a knowledgeable audience, the readers of the avante garde *periodical,* The Partisan Review. *Since space limitations would make it difficult to treat each of the stories in detail, the reviewer has concentrated on one element, Miss Porter's style. This is further justifiable because Miss Porter's distinction as a short story writer largely rests on the high and special quality of her style.*

THE LEANING TOWER AND OTHER STORIES. *By Katherine Anne Porter. Harcourt, Brace.* $2.50.

It has for a long time been apparent that Katherine Anne Porter consistently writes a luminous prose, of an exactness of choice and suggestiveness of phrasing, which is altogether extraordinary. Miss Porter's work has probably been subjected to the kind of scrutiny that most writers hardly dare to hope for, rarely achieve, and can almost never withstand. That Miss Porter can bear such careful reading proves her much more than simply an excellent stylist. Even at their slightest, even when as in this, her latest collection, she has written stories which at first glance seem to be little more than self-indulgent puffs of nostalgia, she holds so fast to reality, there is so much heart in her accuracy, that the stories spread out beyond the bare meanings of the words and the incidents related, to become authoritative and substantial images of an entire society.

Though there are no stories in this volume as first-rate as her previous best, and the group has none of the unified impact, the impressiveness of the earlier books, her essential qualities of purity and delicacy are again revealed. It is difficult to trace the literary influences that have shaped her writing; whatever of them she has found useful, she has absorbed; there has been a transmutation of elements; she continues to speak in her own voice, clear, straightforward, serene.

Miss Porter moves freely in a number of realms; her sensibility has not impelled her to breathe only in a rarer atmosphere; she is *of* the world, its objects are her familiars, she recognizes them and enjoys them for what they are, knows their place in our lives. Her imaginative power springs from her alert sense of the actual. Though as "feminine" a writer as Virginia Woolf, she could hardly be more different from her in this. She has avoided neither squalor nor evil in their many aspects. To watch the ways of human beings is to witness too many horrors, and Miss Porter has not been afraid to look at anything, nor to tell what she has seen, and a straight categorical account of the betrayals, thefts, murders, hatreds and terrors in her stories would make her out another James Cain. What lifts her every time is love; not love that sentimentalizes corruption, but love that gives her a sad wisdom even as it carries her to joyousness. In the face of ugliness she neither becomes hard nor succumbs to the bald jargon of the amateur analyst. She utilizes her knowledge in the ways of art. Her tone undergoes the subtlest of alterations with her theme; and if she does not shock us it is because she knows how to prepare us. She properly leaves the sensationalism to the lesser artists, herself using a stricter method, which is more admirable even where it does not altogether succeed, and which makes it possible to contemplate a page of her writing, come upon unexpectedly, with a sense of peace.

EXERCISES

1. This reviewer gives special attention to the quality of Katherine Anne Porter's writing. List the characteristics she discusses.
2. Is there any indication of what the themes of the short stories are?
3. Do the reviewer's references to Virginia Woolf and James Cain serve a useful purpose in this review?

5 READER'S CHOICE

by Charles J. Rolo

The group review—a series of short reviews, by the same reviewer, of recently published books—is a regular feature of such publications as The New Yorker *and* Atlantic Monthly. *Of the reviews (part of a group by Charles J. Rolo) reprinted below, two are of novels, one of a play, and the other of a work of non-fiction. They illustrate a number of techniques discussed in the introduction.*

In the review of The Quiet American, *Rolo begins by placing the theme of the novel in the tradition of novels dealing with "American 'innocence' versus European 'experience.'" He then outlines the essentials of the plot and characterization and ends with an evaluation of the over-all effect of the book. In the review of* The Dreyfus Case, *a work of non-fiction, the reviewer assumes that those who will read this review are familiar with the details of the historical episode with which the book deals. He concentrates, therefore, on the author's interpretation of these facts, taking issue with several points. Though brief, all of the reviews give an indication of the contents and quality of the books discussed.*

In 1954, **Graham Greene** was a correspondent in Indo-China, and out of this experience has come a novel distinctly different in character from its two predecessors, in which Roman Catholic doctrine was the heart of the matter. Religion has no central part in ***The Quiet American*** (Viking, $3.50), a tale of war, love, and political intrigue in and around contemporary Saigon. The novel's theme is one which has been primarily associated with American literature—the theme of American "innocence" versus European "experience."

Greene's narrator, Thomas Fowler, is a middle-aged British correspondent. As a husband and as a lover he has deeply hurt the two women he loved; and now, disillusioned with the human condition in general, he has made it his credo to remain "not involved." A pretty, undemanding Annamite mistress protects him from loneliness, and a few nightly pipefuls of opium take the edge off his unhappiness.

The "quiet American," Alden Pyle—a warmly outgoing and earnest idealist—is officially attached to the Economic Aid Mission, but actually is engaged in undercover work. Fowler is exasperated by his innocence but cannot help being touched by him: Pyle is so obviously "a good man."

Even when he falls in love with Fowler's mistress and wishes to marry her, his conduct throughout could not be more high-minded.

Pyle has swallowed as gospel the works of a globe-trotting American newspaper pundit, whose formula for the salvation of Asia from Communism is for his country to set its face against "colonialism" and throw its weight behind a Third Force—leaders who represent "national democracy." Fowler keeps warning Pyle of the danger of trying to apply this tidy thesis to the tortuous realities of Indo-China—"I wish sometimes," he says, "that you had a few bad motives; you might understand a little more about human beings." But Pyle is convinced that he has found his Third Force leader in the person of General Thé, who is fighting both the French and the Communists, and who in fact is no more than a shoddy bandit. And Pyle continues to supply the General with American explosives even after Thé has embarked on a course of senseless terrorism, whose only result is the killing and maiming of Saigon civilians.

All of this is narrated by Fowler in flashbacks. At the novel's opening, Fowler is informed by the police that Pyle has been found murdered; and the story that follows is charged with the mystery and suspense of a whodunit. Greene has achieved this by not playing quite fair with the reader: one finally discovers that the narrator knew the answers all along. But the deception, it seems to me, is justified by the results: *The Quiet American* is a continuously intriguing piece of storytelling.

If Pyle, as many Americans will feel, is a caricature of American "innocence," Fowler is also an uninspiring symbol of European "experience" —Greene cannot be accused of playing favorites. In Fowler's unsparing image of himself and in his somewhat ambivalent feelings about Pyle, Greene has mordantly dramatized a European attitude which we know to be widely representative. He has also brought into vivid relief a universal human problem—the fearful price of innocence—and has shown that behind innocence there lurk unconscious arrogance and a self-righteous streak of moral blindness.

The trouble of one house

When **Eugene O'Neill** died in 1953, he left among his papers several dramas which have never been produced. One of them—an autobiographical play completed in 1941 and entitled ***Long Day's Journey into Night*** (Yale University Press, $3.75)—has now been published in book form. In a note dedicating the script to his third wife, O'Neill describes it as "this play of old sorrow, written in tears and blood."

The setting is the living room of the Tyrones' summer home; and the action takes place on a single day in the year 1912. James Tyrone has been a successful actor for more than forty years and is now a wealthy man;

but the appalling poverty of his childhood has bequeathed to him phobias which make him pathologically stingy. His wife, Mary, has just returned from a sanatorium, where she has taken a cure for dope-addiction. The eldest son is a hard-drinking ne'er-do-well, with a bitter hostility toward his father. The younger son, who has grown up hero-worshiping his brother, has ruined his health bumming around the world; and now he learns he has contracted tuberculosis.

This, roughly, is the situation set forth in the first two acts. The last two carry us deeper and deeper into the lives of the Tyrones, laying bare the crucial happenings that have shaped them, the hurts they have inflicted on each other, the resentments and ambitions they have concealed, and the self-deceptions they have cherished. When the final curtain falls on a scene of utter desolation, O'Neill's unsparing exposure of his characters has brought with it understanding and pity.

The emotional phrasing of the drama—with its abrupt, surely handled switches from bitterness to affection; from strained amiability to impatience, jeering sarcasm, and remorse; from drunken garrulousness to searing confession—is continuously varied in tone and generally convincing. The play's major weakness is one which has often bedeviled would-be tragedy in modern dress. The protagonists—being not only devoid of heroic attributes but even lacking in ordinary dignity and strength—fail to arouse, as tragedy should, admiration and terror: all one can feel for them is pity. *Long Day's Journey into Night* has the power of a somber and dramatically unfolded case history. It lacks what O'Neill referred to as "the transfiguring nobility of tragedy."

Cause célèbre

The Dreyfus Case (Reynal, $5.00) by **Guy Chapman,** a British historian—the second book on that *cause célèbre* to appear within six months—is unusual in that it challenges the alleged Dreyfusard "legend" which "has passed into history." That Dreyfus was of course innocent and that he was the victim of cruel injustice—this much Mr. Chapman fully recognizes. But regarding other aspects of the case, he arrives at the following verdicts: There is more to be said for the War Office than has generally been admitted. There are really no villains and no heroes in the drama. Anti-Semitism played little or no part in Dreyfus's arrest and conviction, and later was "no more than accessory" in the affair. There was no "plot" on the part of the high military authorities to prevent Dreyfus's innocence from being established.

Now, all of these contentions are shown to be resoundingly false—and by Mr. Chapman's own richly detailed exposition of the record. His documentation—as distinct from his interpretations—substantially corroborates the generally accepted views about the case and, if anything, heightens one's sense of the infamy of the fanatical anti-Dreyfusards.

On one crucial issue, however, even the factual presentation is seriously at fault. Perhaps the most important aspect of the Dreyfus case was that it provided a rallying ground for the various reactionary elements that were not reconciled to the republican form of government; and it led to a frenzied intensification of their maneuvers to undermine the republican regime. The point is beyond controversy, since the extreme rightists were only too eager to broadcast their objectives. But Chapman chooses to deny that there was any serious movement to bring about a *coup d'état*, and he omits much of the evidence which conflicts with this thesis.

The crux of the matter is that Chapman, though no extremist, is authoritarian in sentiment. The political consequences of the Dreyfusard victory—the separation of Church and State and the democratic reforms applied to the Army, which represented a long overdue implementation of republican principles—are regarded by Chapman as calamitous. (Here too, however, he partially refutes himself by noting that the Church, after being freed from the State, revivified itself and grew stronger.) It is apparent that Chapman is in sympathy with those anti-Dreyfusards who, while acknowledging Dreyfus's innocence, saw the issue at stake as an agonizing conflict between justice to the individual and a "higher" principle, the principle of order—that mystical abstraction which is always being invoked by the authoritarian mind. The real issue was a conflict between justice to the individual and *what one body of opinion alleged to be* the interests of national security—an issue that is very much alive again today.

It would be difficult to write a dull book about the Dreyfus case, and this Mr. Chapman has not done; but he has written a curiously perverse one. He consistently denigrates the men who fought to establish the truth, and he proffers excuses for those who resorted to any and every means to establish and perpetuate a lie. His apologia for the latter is that they were merely men of "narrow loyalties" seeking to serve what they believed to be the best interests of the Army and the country. It is an argument which—as the post-war protestations of crime-laden Nazis have so vividly illustrated—can be employed to excuse any sort of villainy.

The "money world"

Keep the Aspidistra Flying (Harcourt, Brace, $3.75) is an early (1936) novel by the late **George Orwell**, which is now being published in this country for the first time. Its hero, Gordon Comstock, is a young poet who has grown up in shabby-genteel poverty; and as a product of the middle class, he has found his lack of money a source of endless humiliation.

Convinced that the "money world" and its code are a disgusting swindle, Gordon has resigned from his job in an advertising agency and has sought to descend into the world of the down-and-outs, where keeping up appearances no longer matters. But two years in the lower depths, and a crisis with his sweetheart, make him realize that he has been a self-righteous prig, and that his revolt against money has been a revolt against life itself. And the story comes to a happy ending as Gordon begins to recognize, with a certain tenderness, the stubborn virtues of his class, whose symbol of respectability is the humble aspidistra on the window sill.

The novel is rather static for the first hundred pages and is marred by the hero's cloying self-pity. Its interest lies partly in the fact that much of Comstock's story is Orwell's autobiography. It is notable, too, for Orwell's savage satire of the "money world," and for the force and precision with which he describes the whole dingy expanse of British lower-middle class life in the 1930s. As in everything Orwell wrote, there is a burning integrity which gives the novel, despite the drabness of its material, a considerable poignancy. Admirers of Orwell's work should find the book well worth their attention.

EXERCISES

1. A reviewer should give his readers sufficient information about the contents and the quality of a book to enable them to decide whether they want to read the book. Is Rolo successful in doing this? Show how he succeeds or fails.
2. Give examples of some of the techniques Rolo uses to "place" the books he reviews for his readers.
3. Compare the review of either *The Quiet American* or *Keep the Aspidistra Flying*, both novels, with the review of *The Dreyfus Case*, a work of non-fiction. What differences, if any, are there in the reviewer's approach to these different kinds of books?
4. Select several books you have recently read and write a "group review" modelled on Rolo's method.

6 "INNER-DIRECTED" AND "OTHER-DIRECTED"

by Lionel Trilling

After reading The Lonely Crowd, *the reviewer, Lionel Trilling, felt that here was a book of importance and interest not only to professional social scientists but also to intelligent laymen. Because it demands close and thoughtful attention, the reviewer restates the book's thesis in his own words and contributes illustrations from his own experience as well as differences of opinion on certain points. The review, thereby, takes on a vitality and significance of its own. It is a fine example of a serious, long review.*

Lionel Trilling, a professor of English at Columbia University, has achieved considerable eminence as a literary critic. He is a frequent contributor of stories and essays to various periodicals and the author of, among other books, The Liberal Imagination, *a collection of essays, and a novel,* The Middle of the Journey.

David Riesman's *The Lonely Crowd* seems to me one of the most important books about America to have been published in recent times. And quite apart from the particularity of its subject, it is one of the most interesting books I have ever read.

This is very large praise, and as I write it I find myself wondering whether I may not be overstating the case for this sociological study in order to counteract the antagonisms to the social sciences which I know to be pretty common among people who like literature very much. But I do not think I am saying more than I mean. My opinion was formed before I ever thought of writing about Mr. Riesman's book and I have tested it by more than one reading.

Yet since I have raised the question of the literary suspiciousness of the social sciences, especially sociology, it might be well to take it specifically into account in connection with *The Lonely Crowd*.

One reason for this suspiciousness is that sociology tends to use a kind of language which must arouse antagonism in people who are at all sensitive to language. This is not because the language of sociology is scientific but because it is often pseudo-scientific and jargonistic and has the effect of giving a false value to ideas that are simple and platitudinous. To any such charge *The Lonely Crowd* is certainly not liable. Mr. Riesman uses two terms that some might boggle at—he speaks of people as being "inner-directed" and "other-directed." But I do not know how else he could denominate the two categories of character that are essential to his thought. In general the book is precisely a work of literature in the old comprehensive sense of the word according to which Hume's essays are literature, or Gibbon's history, or Tocqueville's *Democracy in America.*

Another objection is that sociology is likely to be tendentious without admitting it is, and that it proceeds on unexamined assumptions while insisting that it is wholly objective. But we can count on Mr. Riesman's objectivity because he admits his subjectivity and the hypothetical nature of his enterprise. He is under no illusion of scientific neutrality. He admires certain human qualities and makes no bones about wanting them to be influential in our national life.

Then it is said, and with justice, that sociology often gives the appearance of denying personal autonomy. What is more, much sociological investigation has for its avowed aim the discovery of how to manipulate human behavior in clandestine ways. But Mr. Riesman's book is as far as it can be from denying the possibility of autonomy without denying the inescapable limits of civilized society. Its whole effort, indeed, is directed toward the affirmation of the possibility of autonomy.

People of literary inclinations, I believe, have a natural jealousy of sociology because it seems to be in process of taking over from literature one of literature's most characteristic functions, the investigation and criticism of morals and manners. Yet it is but fair to remark that sociology has preempted only what literature has voluntarily surrendered. Twenty years ago, when the Lynds produced their famous study, *Middletown,* it was possible to say that with all their staff and paraphernalia they had not really told us more about American life than we had learned from a solitary insightful observer, which is what some sociologists call a novelist—they had done no more than confirm *Babbitt* by statistics. Since that time, however, few novelists have added anything genuinely new to our knowledge of American life. But the sociologists have, and Mr. Riesman, writing with a sense of social actuality which Scott Fitzgerald might have envied, does literature a service by suggesting to the novelists that there are new and wonderfully arable social fields for them to till.

The research from which *The Lonely Crowd* developed began as an investigation of the social causes of political attitudes, specifically that of apathy to politics. The book does not consist of conclusions drawn from this research but was written in the course of the still continuing enterprise as the hypothesis on which the research might proceed. In its simplest form this hypothesis consists of the statement that there has been a change in the character of the American people, that where once men whose character was "inner-directed" were dominant in our culture, the tendency is now toward the dominance of men of "other-directed" character. Inner-directed persons are those who internalize adult authority, most notably the ideals and demands of their parents. Other-directed persons are those whose character is formed chiefly by their contemporaries and peers, the formation beginning as soon as they enter social life in play or at school.

Something of the nature of the inner-directed man may be understood from the phrase which, in the nineteenth century, he so often made his motto—"*Ad astra per aspera,*" through difficulties to the seemingly unattainable heights. The old tag might also be translated, "To the heights by means of asperity," for a kind of asperity marks the dealings of the inner-directed man with the world, his fellow-men, and himself. The man of business as well as the scientific or artistic genius, or the religious leader, or the philosopher, were all at one in their submission to inner-direction. The belief that energy, self-control, and self-reverence would achieve miracles was held not only by the dullest spirits of the age but also by the noblest. We must think of the Alger books as being the expression not merely of a strenuous philistinism but of a general culture in which strenuousness was valued in all walks of life. There was a connection between the passions of a Bounderby and a Beethoven.

In America, even as far back as Tocqueville's visit, there was always a tendency for inner-direction to be modified by what Tocqueville regarded as an extravagant awareness of the opinion of others. Emerson believed that this tendency constituted a prime threat to the American spirit and he never wearied of warning his countrymen that Self Reliance—his name for inner-direction—was sadly on the wane. Yet in nineteenth century America the "hardness of the material" still called for a large measure of inner-direction—there were still frontiers to be conquered, social forms to be imposed or broken, technology to be established. It was still useful to idealize "faith," the belief that one's personal vision was right no matter how the world mocked it. School children were assiduously taught in their readers that the heroic man was one who followed his gleam, and that society as a whole was likely to be stupid, retrograde, and cowardly, as witness its treatment of Columbus. And in the poem that every child learned, it was right of Columbus, and not arrogant or undemocratic of him, to say, "Sail on! Sail on!" when his men begged him to turn back. To be "misunderstood," to be alone with one's rightness and virtue, was the stuff of the dreams of youth.

But in the early years of the twentieth century—around 1920, Mr. Riesman believes—the inner-directed character began to lose its ascendancy. The hard, resistant materiality of the world no longer supplied the goal and validated the hard, strenuous will of inner-directed people. Children were less impelled to establish the old parental authority within themselves—parents were less certain of how to establish it in their children and of whether it ought to be established at all. It was by no means clear that the old standards applied to the new kind of work. For in the degree that work had less to do with *things*, it had more to do with *people*. In Mr. Riesman's phrase, the interest shifted from the hardness of the material to the softness of the personnel, and the arts of personality, by which one could manipulate one's fellows or win valuable approval from them, became more important to more people than the direct force of the will exerted upon material difficulties. And children increasingly formed their characters according to the demands of their playmates and schoolmates, equipping themselves with a quick, unconscious sensitivity to the judgment of others—they became increasingly other-directed.

The evidence of this new means of character-formation is manifest in every discussion of juvenile or adolescent social behavior, in which it is always taken for granted that parents are virtually helpless before the power of the child-society. And indeed this power is supported and rationalized by the family and the school, which, on theories of normality and adjustment, second the anxious antagonism which the child-society directs upon any show of difference. For the group life of contemporary children achieves its particular kind of democracy by suppressing special interests and abilities (except in athletics) and by prohibiting the display of vanity or ambition. Even before the child is ready for sociability, his life in literature has prepared him for social adjustment and conformity. *Scuffy the Tugboat* instructs him in the dangers of the Columbus principle, while *Tootle the Engine* leads him to believe that he must not fail to be like all the other little engines and never leave the track to stray into green fields, like a horse.

The ideal of behavior which is indigenous to the social life of the modern child is the model and perhaps the mold of the ideal of adults, at least of the middle class. We are coming to be a civilization in which overt ambition, aggression, and competition are at a discount. Not, of course, that the sources of natural aggression are drying up or that people no longer seek prestige. But self-aggrandizement takes new forms as the ideals of other-direction become increasingly compelling. Overt ambition gives way to what Mr. Riesman calls antagonistic co-operation, which implies affability, blandness, a lively sensitivity to the opinion of the group, the suppression of asperity. Social differences must be minimized as far as possible. Wealth must depreciate itself, and must seek to express itself not in symbols of power but in fineness of taste. Food is ordered less for the old-fashioned virtues of substantiality and abundance, than for the new charms of elegance and artistry—but in this limited space it is impossible to follow Mr. Riesman in the fascinating detail of his description of the cultural changes which other-direction is instituting.

The general opinion is not likely to be in accord with Mr. Riesman—the general opinion is that our culture is marked by an especially fierce and open competitiveness, an unmasked aggressiveness, a crude assertiveness. This is the received idea of a great deal of our literature and of our progressive social thought. It is the pious certainty of Europe, constituting, one sometimes feels, the larger part of the European social and political thought of the moment. And Mr. Riesman's students at the University of Chicago tell him that American life resembles the grim, paranoid Dobu culture or the competitive conspicuously-consuming Kwakiutl culture—none ever finds any resemblance to the peaceable, co-operative Pueblo Indians, although *all* of them wish they could.

I am sure that it is Mr. Riesman who is in the right of the matter. My own experience in teaching confirms his, one incident in particular. For some time I had been increasingly aware that my students had no very great admiration for Stendhal's *The Red and the Black*, gave it nothing like the response that it had had from my college generation. Then one day a whole class, almost all its members gifted men, agreed in saying that they were bored by Julien Sorel and didn't like him. Bored by Julien Sorel! But didn't he, I asked, represent their own desires for preeminence, their own natural young ambition? They snubbed me with their answer and fixed between themselves and me the great gulf of the generations: they did not, they said, understand ambition of Julien's self-referring kind; what they wanted was a decent, socially useful co-operative work to do. I felt like an aging Machiavelli among the massed secretariat of the U.N.

Young men of this kind certainly do not represent anything like the full development of the other-directed character which Mr. Riesman describes. It is even possible that their rejection of the extreme inner-direction of Julien Sorel is not so much in favor of other-direction as of the "autonomous" character which Mr. Riesman proposes as the possible optimum of our culture. More likely, however, they represent a compromise between inner-direction and other-direction. As such they make a spectacle which in many ways is very attractive.

But the tendency of other-direction does not stop with the character of these young men. And the consequences of its fuller development are disquieting. Mr. Riesman remarks that he has found it almost impossible to make a comparison of the two forms of character-direction without making inner-direction seem the more attractive of the two. I don't agree with Mr. Riesman that the preference is a mere prejudice which we must guard against. Granting all that is to be said against the tendency of inner-direction to cut itself off from what is warm and personal, granting too all that may be said for what other-direction does to refine leisure and consumption, it is still inner-direction that must seem the more fully human, even in its excess. Mr. Riesman himself seems to be saying something of this sort when, in speaking of the autonomous character, he remarks that the inner-directed character more closely resembles it than does the other-directed, and that, indeed, it is easier for inner-directed people to approach actual autonomy.

It is in any case true, on Mr. Riesman's showing, that the political life is far more likely to be healthy in a culture in which inner-direction is dominant. The exacerbated sense of others, of oneself in relation to others, does not, it seems, make for the sense of the polity. On the contrary—other-direction is concomittant with a sense of powerlessness in political matters, and this impotence masks itself in many ways, often as hatred of or contempt for politics. This in turn is easily rationalized into a desire for meta-politics, for a perfect and absolute form of government which shall make impossible the conflict of wills of actual politics.

And the apathy which marks our political life lies as a threat beneath all the life of other-direction. Social approval and the desire for it are not love, nor even friendship, nor even community. The life of leisure, of fun, of narcissism, of right choice among the articles of consumption, of sex as the "last frontier" of adventure, of bland adjustment—this life is at every moment susceptible to the cankering boredom which lies beneath its surface.

This is not, I must make clear, the note on which Mr. Riesman ends. It is one of his decisive intellectual virtues that he has no love for the opiate of pessimism. He is not charmed by apocalyptic visions. It is not the end of a culture that he has undertaken to describe but a moment in its history.

EXERCISES

1. Trilling, in his own way, explains the difference between the "inner-directed" and the "other-directed" man. Write several paragraphs establishing the distinction in your own words.
2. What are the dangers, as discussed in this review, in being conventional and "other-directed"? Develop your own views on this subject.
3. Discuss the reasons the reviewer gives for the suspicion with which many literary men regard most sociologists.
4. What distinguishes this review from the preceding ones?

7 CAPITAL

The New York Times
May 1, 1887

When this review of Capital *was written in 1887, that book had already gained some status as the "Bible of the Working Class." The reviewer treats it with respect, acknowledging Marx's erudition (though he doubts whether that erudition had been properly assimilated) and "the brilliant manner in which the actual wrongs of the laboring classes are exposed." But he does take issue with the vehemence of Marx's attack on capitalism and concludes that while Marx may not explicitly encourage bloodshed as necessary for the amelioration of the suffering of the lower classes, "the means he proposes point to that inevitable conclusion." Considering when the review was written, the reviewer's political insight stands up remarkably well.*

As in the review of Maggie *(**page 116**), the style and choice of language reflect a more formal mode of writing than is found today. Certain phrases date the review, for instance, the reference to Marx's race as "Oriental," where today one would say Jewish. However, the attributing of Marx's vindictive attack on capitalism to personal frustration and persecution reveals a psychological approach which is amazingly modern.*

A famous fable, reputed Aesopian and not quoted as often as it deserves, is the one in which the lion takes to task the sculptor for making man invariably triumph over the king of beasts. "If," said Leo, "we only held the chisels, it is quite a different state of things we would represent." These volumes, with others written by Marx, have been called by his followers the "Bible of the Working Classes." Before Marx wrote, they insist, it was only the capitalist's side which was extolled. Now at last justice is done to the working-man.

If political economy be for the best of us a science by no means easy to understand, *Capital*, to appreciate it properly, requires, in many parts, the closest attention. As in Laplace's *Mecanique Celeste*, so in one page of Marx there is material enough for a cogitation of hours. At once the vast erudition of the author is discernible. There are apparently very few things in this world he has not read and absorbed. Whether he digested them properly may be doubted. From Honore de Balzac he jumps to Jeremy

Bentham; from Condillac to Cherborillier; from Greg to Gladstone; and Liebig and Luther, Malthus and Macaulay, Mill, Mirabeau, Thomas Moore, Nasmith and Niebuhr are all found personified in the text.

The life history of Marx was one of personal trouble. Driven from post to pillar, hounded, harassed, harried, is there any wonder that he lost his temper? There was, too, the temperament of his race. Through long oppression in Germany he returned to his original Oriental vindictiveness. Karl Marx had no friendly feeling toward the world in general, and, seeking about for something to smite, he took capital as a subject and lived only to belabor it. All that his learning could do—for he had a vast and complicated erudition—was to twist with ingenuity that rope of sophistry by which he believed he could strangle capital. What, then, might become arguments in favor of his doctrines, or at least incline toward the discussion of them, have been distasteful by the personal acridity of the man himself. Conspicuous above all is his contempt for Germany, at least bureaucratic Germany. Karl Marx may in one hand hold a bludgeon and belabor his opponents with it, but it must be remembered that he was a finished and a precise writer when he wanted to be, and could wield a very sharp and brilliant rapier. If "to give work to the unemployed" was that to which Marx devoted his life, he preached rebellion to the laws which have heretofore governed civilized man.

In the preface to the second edition the author rails at the ignorance then existing in Germany in regard to political economy. "It had to be imported from England and France as a ready-made article. Its German professors remained schoolboys. The theoretical expression of a foreign reality was turned in their hands into a collection of dogmas, interpreted by them in terms of the petty trading world among them, and therefore misinterpreted." This was written in 1873. Before 1848 Marx seemed to think that what he calls "capitalist production" had but little existence in Germany, but after that came "the full bloom of speculation and swindling." Marx must have been singularly sensitive to criticism, for he writes of "the mealy-mouthed babblers of German vulgar economy who fell foul of the style of my book." If he was not understood at home, he says the reason for it was that "Germans remained mere school-boys, imitators and followers, petty retailers and hawkers in the service of the great foreign wholesale concern." "Have at you," cries Karl Marx, and listen you shall, "you mushroom upstarts of the new holy Prusso-German Empire." It is very bad language this very wonderful man uses, but then he quotes many a chapter and verse of Martin Luther, where he shows that the great reformer could screech and scold with any German of his day, past or present.

The fault of a special kind advanced against Marx of his using a symbolism to prove economic abstractions we think no crime. To appreciate him, to understand him, these symbols must be mastered. From them he deduces some of the most important of his theories. In Marx is not to be found the solemn dignity of a Mill nor the placidity of a Wayland nor the accurate uniformity of a Ricardo. If he is anything, Karl Marx is a man in a towering rage. His paragraphs are replete with kicks and cuffs. He wants to slap your face if you are a bourgeois; to smash your skull if you are a capitalist. He is a militant political economist. He may not encourage the spilling of blood to effect the ends he desires; but the means he proposes point to that inevitable conclusion. "Capital is that dead labor that, vampire like, only lives by sucking living labor, and lives the more the more labor it sucks."

If much is bad in this new remarkable book we have commented upon, it is most powerful in the brilliant manner in which the actual wrongs of the laboring classes are exposed. To understand the whole working of the factory acts in England, its entire progress cannot be better studied than in this work. Marx has mastered the whole subject in its most minute details. That horrible system of serfdom which wrecked human lives, that made beasts of men, brutes of women, that kept thousands in a condition worse tenfold than slaves, is ruthlessly exposed. Here Karl Marx rises to his highest pitch. He does not indulge in sarcasm. He is conscious that no word of his could make the picture he draws so clearly more hideous.

EXERCISES

1. Did this reviewer of Marx's *Capital* take a disinterested view of the book?
2. What is the author's view of Marx the man, the theorizer?
3. Would a reviewer today be in a better position to evaluate *Capital?*
4. Select examples of usage and phrases which "date" this review.

8 MAGGIE, A GIRL OF THE STREETS

The New York Times May 31, 1896

It is said that when the publisher Richard Gilder rejected Maggie: A Girl of the Streets, *Stephen Crane asked him, "You mean it is too honest?" and Gilder replied, "Yes, too honest." Both the public and publishers of the 1890's considered taboo many subjects which are now discussed freely. However, thanks to Crane's success with* The Red Badge of Courage, Maggie *was also published.*

This review appeared in The New York Times *in 1896. Implicit in the reviewer's general approach and tone is the squeamishness of many of his contemporaries toward such sordid subjects as Maggie's experiences. But to justify the portrayal of such horrors, he refers to the book's importance as a social document and as a stimulus to those interested in reforming these conditions (see the concluding paragraph). The style, the choice of language, as well as the tone of the review are more formal than they would be in a current review.*

Mr. Crane took out a copyright on this story in 1893, or about two years before he acquired fame as the author of *The Red Badge of Courage,* and a new copyright was taken out this year, which indicates revisions. But we are informed from the best source that the story has never been actually published before, even in serial form. That Mr. Crane had written a story with this title was, however, known—at least to a limited circle. This fact will scarcely detract from the interest with which the story will now be received. On the contrary, it is likely to add to that interest. Whether or not Mr. Crane in 1893 found difficulty in securing a publisher, it will now seem hardly credible to readers that he went long in pursuit of one.

The story is a sad one. Not one gleam of light or of humor falls across its sombre pages. Not only is it a story of a girl of the street—one, however, who was far better than her environment—but a story of the lowest, most vicious tenement-house life. Save for this girl, there is not a character in the book who does not drink, curse, and fight. She alone was free from vices of those sorts, and after she had fallen such was the unconsciousness with which she fell that she never dreamed she was bad. From a home in which drink and blasphemy were constantly indulged in by her father and mother, she had gone to live with a man who seemed to her a hero of the tenements, but who, as a matter of course, was a man of another sort.

Mr. Crane pictures Maggie's home with colors now lurid and now black, but always with the hand of an artist. And the various stages of her career, until in despair at being neglected she, we are led to believe, commits suicide by jumping into the river, are shown with such vivid and terrible accuracy as to make one believe they are photographic. Mr. Crane cannot have seen all that he describes, and yet the reader feels that he must have seen it all. This, perhaps, is the highest praise one can give the book. Mr. Crane is a master of slum slang. His dialogues are surprisingly effective and natural. The talk Pete indulges in while intoxicated makes one see in his mind's eye the very figure of the loathsome beast for the loss of whom Maggie died. But Mr. Crane is, perhaps, as happy in some of his descriptive phrases. Here are examples:

> The little boy ran to the halls shrieking like a monk in an earthquake.
>
> He could appear to strut even while sitting still, and he showed that he was a lion of lordly characteristics by the air with which he spat.

Mr. Crane's story should be read for the fidelity with which it portrays a life that is potent on this island, along with the life of the best of us. It is a powerful portrayal, and, if somber and repellent, none the less true, none the less freighted with appeal to those who are able to assist in righting wrongs.

EXERCISES

1. What aspects of the book and of the author's approach does this review discuss?
2. Remembering the purpose of a book review, would you consider this a successful one? State the reasons for your evaluation of this review.
3. What evidence is there that the reviewer was fearful of calling a spade a spade?

9 THE GREAT GATSBY

The Times Literary Supplement
February 18, 1926

Although he was already well known in America, F. Scott Fitzgerald was a new author for this English reviewer. To place the hero of The Great Gatsby *for his readers, the reviewer compared him to the heroes of Conrad's novels, with which he assumed they would be familiar. He understood quite well what Fitzgerald was trying to do. While he could not know that* The Great Gatsby *would become something of a classic and a significant work for those concerned with explaining the "American character," he recognized that as a work of fiction it was very fine, "undoubtedly a work of art and of great promise."*

Mr. F. Scott Fitzgerald, author of *The Great Gatsby*, is a young American novelist whose work has not hitherto reached England. We understand that with his previous novels, one of which had a university setting, he has won a large amount of popularity in his own country, and that the present novel, his latest, is an effort in a rather different direction from that of ordinary American popular fiction. However this may be, *The Great Gatsby* is undoubtedly a work of art and of great promise. Mr. Fitzgerald has grasped the economical construction of a story, and his power of telling conciseness enables him, without being obscure, to compass a great deal in a short space. He uses words like living things, instead of like dead counters.

Gatz, or Gatsby, is a Conradian hero—one of those beings, like Almayer or the hero of *Heart of Darkness*, who is lifted above all the evil that he does or seeks, above all the dirty trails which shoddy souls leave over the world, and above all the tragedy or destruction in which he finally sinks, by some great elemental loyalty to a dream which, in a different world, would have been beautiful. Mr. Fitzgerald has imagined a son of broken-down and shiftless farm folk who, in his youth, found a platonic conception of himself and "invented just the sort of Jay Gatsby that a seventeen-year-old boy would be likely to invent, and to this conception he was faithful to the end." His dream-universe of "ineffable gaudiness," realized partially by five years of secretaryship to a dissolute old millionaire, is enriched by an experience of love, when as a young officer, a month of Daisy

Buchanan had given him an almost superhuman ecstasy. Daisy, then unmarried, belonged to his dream-universe of beauty, money and ease; penniless Gatsby, having illicitly entered it in the disguise of uniform, comes back after brilliant service in the war to find himself still outside it and Daisy married. By the mouth of Mr. Carraway, who is related to Daisy and visits her home on Long Island, is told what Gatsby did in order to enter into his dream again. All passes in one summer. Gatsby, wealthy through lending himself to nameless corruptions, keeps open house upon the shore of West Egg, because the green light of the Buchanans' dock, on the opposite shore of East Egg, twinkles to him in the darkness. All the lavish show of drunken vulgarity is simply kept up to bring that green light nearer. Through Carraway Gatsby meets Daisy again—the weak, shallow creature who loves only by moments—and their meeting, which culminates in Daisy's weeping over Gatsby's exhibition of multitudinous shirts in his wardrobe, is an admirable piece of writing. And so Gatsby, steadfast in all his corruption, becomes involved in the life of Daisy Buchanan and her sensual savage of a husband Tom, whose typical outing with his mistress, the wife of a seedy garage-keeper, throws a queer light on the manners of New York. Tragedy is not long in coming, for Tom suspects Gatsby, and on the amazing afternoon when Gatsby tells him to his face that Daisy no longer loves him, it is Daisy's tawdriness that brings the dream to the ground with a crash. Daisy, having shattered Gatsby's life, can do no more than wrap him finally in death and dishonour. Mr. Fitzgerald finely maintains, besides his hard, sardonic realism, the necessary emotional intensity, but we must admit that it needs perhaps an excess of intensity to buoy up the really very unpleasant characters of this story.

EXERCISES

1. Many critics have said that *The Great Gatsby* is peculiarly an American novel. What evidence is there for this in the reviewer's summary of the action and of Gatsby's character?
2. The reviewer retells the plot. Does he do more than this?
3. Compare this review to the review of *Maggie: A Girl of the Streets.* Discuss similarities and differences in the techniques of the two reviewers.
4. Can you find any awkward sentences in this review?

10 AN AMERICAN TRAGEDY

The Times Literary Supplement
October 7, 1926

Dreiser has always been a difficult writer to evaluate. His work is marred by many aesthetic lapses, awkward sentences, and touches of naïveté. But his novels carry a sense of reality, they are peopled by memorable characters, and are philosophically engaging. This reviewer perceived both Dreiser's strengths and weaknesses. It is perhaps ironic that while the reviewer attributed the popular preference for An American Tragedy *to Dreiser's previous works to the "sensationalism flattering to the public taste at the moment" (1926), that novel continues as Dreiser's best-known and probably most widely read novel.*

Mr. Theodore Dreiser's is an interesting case. He has written half a dozen very, very long novels, all of which have been highly praised by American critics. Until the publication of his most recent book, however, he was not widely read. It is not difficult to account for popular indifference to his work. He is without pretence of any kind and he builds in a tremendously solid fashion; but his buildings are unlovely. No novelist has greater scorn for appearances and the arts of attraction. Mr. Dreiser has imagination and refinement in plenty, but his manner of saying what he wants to say can be as uncouth, as slipshod and bungling as the ramblings of an illiterate person. In short, for all his sincerity and power of analysis, he is hard to read. Now published as the first volume in an English uniform edition of his novels, *An American Tragedy* is the novel which has won remarkable favour with the reading public in America during the last few months. Why it should have made a greater appeal than *The Financier*, or *The Genius*, or the comparatively short *Jennie Gerhardt* we cannot tell, unless it is simply that it contains elements of sensationalism flattering to public taste at the moment. At any rate, it has the same trying qualities as the rest of Mr. Dreiser's fiction. But it also has in a marked degree his sprawling strength.

That strength—of observation and of purpose—allows us to overlook many faults in him. *An American Tragedy* is a whale of a novel—there are more than 800 pages of close print in the book. Roughly speaking, its theme is the interaction of a religious and an industrial environment on character. When we are first introduced to Clyde Griffiths, he is a boy of twelve, living with his parents in Kansas City. His father is a feckless itinerant preacher who compels his children to help him with his missionary labours. Clyde feels no religious emotion, is bored by having to sing hymns at street corners, and grows ashamed of his social inferiority and devoted to material things. At the first opportunity he gets a job at a cheap drug store, eventually exchanging the work of an "assistant to a soda water clerk" for that of a "bell-hop" at a large, dubious hotel. An ambitious, selfish but moderately decent boy, he enjoys the use of money, kisses several girls, and entertains hopes of prosperity. A tragic escapade in the company of friends hurries him off to Chicago, where he again finds employment as a "bell-hop," and where he again takes to kissing girls. At the age of twenty or so he meets an uncle who has a shirt and collar factory in Lycurgus. He gets a job in the factory, makes full use of his ambiguous position, gets liked for his good looks, and begins to cherish the usual social ambitions. He falls in love with Roberta, a factory girl, and seduces her. But the high-stepping Soudra Finchley attracts his attention, and he falls for her. When Roberta tells him she is going to have a baby his longing for fortune and high society receives a shock. Threatened with her pitiful entreaties, afraid of being exposed and of losing his golden opportunity, and burying his head in Soudra's trailing cloud, he plays with the desperate thought of murdering Roberta. The planning of the murder inevitably brings Raskolnikov to one's mind. Mr. Dreiser undoubtedly makes a tense dramatic business of Clyde's probings and tortured vacillations, but he can put nothing heroic into his hero's desire to save his skin. Roberta dies by drowning; but, although Clyde has decided on the murder, it is by an accident that the boat capsizes. The trial follows. Mr. Dreiser describes it all in enormous detail. Then the execution. We are spared nothing. Mr. Dreiser makes it clear that the lights go out in the prison "as an idiotic or thoughtless result of having one electric system to supply the death voltage and the incandescence." And finally we get a brief picture of the Griffiths in San Francisco. On the windows of the Mission Hall are written "God is Love" and "How Long Since You Wrote to Mother?"

It is a strange book, painstaking, honest, full of pity for human weaknesses, thoughtful and moving—and awkward. When Mr. Dreiser writes, for instance, of the "anomalies of psychic and social reflex and motivation" he inspires little attention. But the things like Clyde's aching curiosity about the dreadful little Hortense, his ingenuous adoration of Soudra's cocksureness, his queer humility and distrust of himself, his very zest for living—these, however badly expressed, are real and disturbing. And their cumulative effect does a great deal to justify Mr. Dreiser's plodding, graceless manner.

EXERCISES

1. What is the difference between the *theme* and the *plot* of a novel?

2. Does this reviewer's analysis of plot take him beyond the theme of *An American Tragedy?* Should it?

3. Do you think the reviewer was "handicapped" in giving a fair appraisal of the book because he was not an American? Justify your answer by reference to the review.

11 SOLDIER'S PAY

The Times Literary Supplement July 3, 1930

Faulkner's Soldier's Pay *was, like some of the novels of Hemingway and Dos Passos, a "lost generation novel." It was also related to the art for art's sake tradition of the 1890's. The English reviewer of this book did not make these connections but concentrated, rather, on conveying to his readers a sense of the novel's action and of Faulkner's style. He could not, of course, know that this author would, in 1950, be awarded the Nobel Prize for literature. But he caught the sense of poetry which pervades Faulkner's writing and which encompassed both the beauty and the ugliness pictured in this novel of post World War I disillusionment.*

We must pay tribute to an English publisher's enterprise in introducing the work of a young American novelist who, as Mr. Richard Hughes says in his preface, is "not only unknown in England but practically unknown in America, also . . . He is a Southerner from Mississippi; and young, prolific and unsuccessful." Mr. William Faulkner, author of *Soldier's Pay*—a tragedy of soldiers returned from the War—has a fertile invention, a power of illustrating and differentiating character, a force in depicting both tragic and comic incident and a nostalgic sense of the poetry which can suffuse even so crude and fleshy a scene as he presents here in Charlestown, Georgia. This sense and what it suffuses may well be illustrated from the last lines of the novel, where two stricken but resigned men—the old Rector who has buried his son and Joe Gilligan who had not gained the love he waited for so patiently—stand listening to the singing in a Negro church:—

Feed Thy Sheep, O Jesus. The voices rose full and soft. There was no organ: no organ was needed, as above the harmonic passion of bass and baritone soared a clear soprano of women's voices like a flight of gold and heavenly birds. They stood together in the dust, the rector in his shapeless black, and Gilligan in his new hard serge, listening, seeing the shabby church become beautiful with mellow longing, passionate and sad. Then the singing died, fading away along the mooned land inevitable with to-morrow and sweat, with sex and death and damnation; and they turned townward under the moon, feeling dust in their shoes.

Comparing this passage with the brilliant opening scene of drunken soldiers going South in a Pullman car, with the incursions into the story of the lustful satyr Januarius Jones, the sick ravings of George Farr after the body of the virgin who had willed him to seduce her, and the admirable scene of the dance that Mr. Hughes rightly compares to the last act of *The Silver Tassie*, one sees why Mr. Faulkner so heavily stresses the "sweat, with sex and death and damnation" that, to our mind, overburden his story.

This, in its main outlines, tells how the resourceful Joe Gilligan, a homeless, common man with a heart of gold, Julian Lowe, a young air cadet who had had no time to win his wings, and Margaret Powers, young war-widow, are brought together in the train by the helplessness of a countryman, Donald Mahon, an ex-officer in the British Air Force, who has been discharged from hospital with a lost memory, a hopelessly stricken body, and a hideous scar on his forehead. The hearts of both Gilligan and Margaret have been drained of so much in the war-years that a passionate protection of the helpless one is the highest emotion they can rise to. Julian Lowe, being but a boy with an unspoiled heart, is quickly sent home to his mother by Margaret, and the story is punctuated by his pathetic letters from San Francisco assuring her that he is waiting to make a home and marry her. Meanwhile, Joe and Margaret carry the helpless, almost blind Donald to the small, sleepy Charlestown where an amiably philosophic Rector is cherishing the memory of a beloved son, presumed dead, and the flighty sensual Cecily Saunders, Donald's fiancée, is already carrying on with another.

The characters pursue or flee from one another in a farandole of desire or repulsion, with the unspeakable Jones preying on them all. Crude desires, simple passions, loyalties and hatreds, and harsh ironies dominate the dance, sometimes expressed in choric interlude from the hidden voices in the hearts. Death and departure end the turmoil; and Joe Gilligan, whose Margaret's heart had been too dead to take him in, is left learning from the Rector that truth is unbearable, yet time steals even agony away. There is much ugliness as well as much beauty in this book.

EXERCISES

1. This reviewer obviously recognized that Faulkner was a writer of very considerable ability. Does he, however, pass the sort of judgment on the book that would tell a reader whether *Soldier's Pay* is a truly important novel?

2. Why did the reviewer include this quotation from the book? Does it fulfill its purpose?

3. Gertrude Stein coined the phrase "the lost generation" which has been used to describe many post-World War I novels. While the reviewer makes no direct reference to the book's relation to "lost generation literature" does the review itself imply such a connection?

12 A FAREWELL TO ARMS

The Times Literary Supplement November 28, 1929

This English review of A Farewell to Arms *begins with the paradoxical statement that Hemingway's theme, approach, and style are not what the British would consider "typically American" but that nevertheless Hemingway is "distinctly and absolutely American." The reviewer's failure to explain this paradox is definitely a weakness and leaves readers wondering what he means. But he does characterize Hemingway's style effectively, and mentions events, scenes, and characters from the book which give the reader a good impression of what it is all about. Though he takes issue with "Hemingway's pessimism" without really discussing it he concedes that in spite of it Hemingway is an original and gifted writer.* A Farewell to Arms *remains one of Hemingway's finest achievements as a novelist.*

Mr. Ernest Hemingway's *A Farewell to Arms* is a novel of great power. Though it adds one to the now many novels of war, it is unlike any other, for Mr. Hemingway's method and outlook are entirely his own. Though his mental processes, his language and his subject-matter are not what we in England should call "typically American," he is one of the few writers in the English language who is distinctively and absolutely American. To everything British he is foreign, and the British, though he likes them, are foreign to him. Nobody but an American could have his staccato style, his particular turn of dialogue, his power of rejecting everything that is extraneous to his keen but selective vision, his dismal animation, his unrationalized pessimism. It is always the same mind, the same man—one who finds no comfort but in vivid circumstance and pleasure of the senses—who tells the story: he tells it to himself, either in long passages of terse dialogue or in direct reflections of his own retina, hardly ever stopping to register a mental comment.

Here, at all events, he has found a theme more suited to him than any before. The events—ambulance work on the Isonzo, the bursting of a trench-mortar shell in a dug-out, a wound, hospital in Milan, return to the front, the great retreat after Caporetto, escape from shooting by the "Battle Police" at the Tagliamento and a further escape at night in a boat from Stresa over the Swiss frontier—are episodes in a world-agony, not merely the adventures of Bohemians; the characters depicted, with a masterly handling of dialogue (particularly the Italian surgeon Rinaldi), are more interesting than the drunkards of *Fiesta;*[1] the love of Henry and Catherine Barkley, the English nurse, is rendered with an extraordinarily intense simplicity; and the peculiar hopelessness of Mr. Hemingway's humour finds an ideal scope in the contrasts and contradictions of war. The actual scenes of war are biting and brilliant: they are so vivid and yet effortless that it is hard to believe one is reading fiction. Mr. Hemingway's description of the retreating army—the blocking of the roads, the effort of the American Lieutenant Henry and his three mechanics to get a motor-ambulance along, their failure when it is bogged in the mud, their flight on foot, the lost morale of the stragglers, the ruthless shooting of senior officers, as they are singled out from the ruck crossing the Tagliamento, the American's plunge into the river and his journey in a gun-truck to Milan—has a note of complete authenticity, and singularly corroborates a similar description in Riccardo Bacchelli's novel *La Città degli Amanti*. Yet, in these nearly identical descriptions, there is an abyss between the two mentalities. The American, completely disillusioned, understands both the patriotism of an Italian officer and the innate opposition to war of an Italian soldier. The undisciplined talk of Henry's drivers is as masterly as that which reveals the Southern scepticism of Rinaldi, the faith of the chaplain or the patriotism of his comrade Gino. Yet, while he understands, he accepts nothing. His only comments are to the effect that any glorification of life is false.

So drink deep and go a-whoring while you may is the very plainly illustrated motto, and love truly, as Henry and Catherine loved, if you can; but the world will get you in the end, as it got Catherine, who died in childbirth with her child at Lausanne, leaving Henry with nothing, on a rainy night. The frankly sensual love-relation between Henry and Catherine is remarkable, not for any loftiness, but for its beautiful precision.

[1] Published in America as *The Sun Also Rises*.

Catherine is a stupid girl, with nothing but love and great courage to recommend her. Henry made love to her at first as a game, but when he came back wounded to Milan he fell passionately in love. In the simple, almost foolish, exchanges of their conversation is built up a picture of a union that transcended difference, of a Phoenix and Turtle on the fleshly plane. The view of Catherine is purely a man's view, but as such it is unfalteringly delineated. After their happy days in Switzerland the end is unbelievably painful, for no horror of that tragic maternity is left to the imagination. And with that death and Henry walking back to the hotel in the rain this gripping story ends abruptly, leaving all its pain raw. Mr. Hemingway's pessimism is his own affair: we can only recognize that it animates an extremely talented and original artist.

EXERCISES

1. Did the reviewer recognize that he was discussing a novel that would come to be considered a masterpiece?
2. There has been a great deal of discussion of "the Hemingway style." What does the phrase mean to you? In answering the question, what help can you get from the review? (See also p. 247)
3. Compare this review to the review of *Soldier's Pay*. Which gives you a better idea of the content and quality of the book reviewed? Why?

13 THE GRAPES OF WRATH

The Times Literary Supplement
September 9, 1939

To restate the theme and evaluate the quality of a lengthy novel in a short review presents a considerable challenge to the reviewer. He must be both economical and clear. This reviewer of The Grapes of Wrath *grasped Steinbeck's intent and central theme and gave a sense of the author's skill as a novelist. But even in following a good review, the reader must remain watchful, for what did the reviewer mean when he described the second part of Steinbeck's "twofold theme" as being "concerned with the tyranny over all classes of economic laws that were framed only to record certain movements and not, in fact, to be the pretext for compelling them"?*

Mr. John Steinbeck's new novel is a campaign, and Mammon is the enemy. While lesser American writers complacently recall their country's past, Mr. Steinbeck is anxiously in touch with its present. He, too, describes an exodus to the West, but this is made in ramshackle motor-cars instead of lumbering wagons. Here there are no battles to bring glory, and at the end the land of promise is a bitter disappointment. There, sure enough, are the farms and orchards and well-watered lands, but others are in possession of them. Yet this the travellers expected: all they hoped for was work; and the indecent exploitation of their necessity to work is shown with cold and precise justice. Mr. Steinbeck's theme, indeed, is two-fold. One part of it is the endurance of the common people in conditions of great hardship; and the other is concerned with the tyranny over all classes of economic laws that were framed only to record certain movements and not, in fact, to be the pretext for compelling them.

At their most wretched, Mr. Steinbeck's people have the refuge of memory and humour, and in their recollections of past raciness we are enabled to see the superior colour and variety of a society in which the owners lived on their land, worked it themselves and measured their prosperity directly against its prosperity. There is, besides, the tedium inseparable from any long work pledged to a single idea; but here the tedium is at its lowest. Against such falling off as there is may be set those passages in which the author makes still more transparent the barrier between his mind and our own. We know his mind now for an original one. He has passages in this book that restate the idea of the interlude in *To the Lighthouse* in terms of another country; but his just understanding of character, the candour and forcefulness of his dialogue and his mastery of climaxes are all his own and inimitable.

EXERCISES

1. The reviewer of *The Grapes of Wrath* says that Steinbeck has an "original" mind. Does he offer any evidence for this statement?
2. Write an essay in which you set forth what you consider to be the characteristics of a good book review. How does this review measure up to your requirements?
3. Select one of the books that has been discussed in this section and write your own review of it.

IV | Arguing a Thesis

Argumentation is often found mixed with other forms of discourse—as part of narrative, description, and particularly exposition. For instance, a newspaper reporter writing an article on a city's parks could organize his exposition of the facts in such a way that by implication the city administration is either praised or criticized. Yet ostensibly the article is a factual account, not an argument. An overt argument, on the other hand, clearly aims to convince and persuade. It states a proposition or thesis and sets out to demonstrate its truth. The method of argumentation as a mode of discourse is to present facts and interpretations of them in such a logical and rhetorically effective way that the listener is led to an inescapable conclusion.

The very statement of an argument presupposes that an opposing position has been or could be stated. This position could be diametrically opposed—or it could be a qualification, a partially different point of view. In this section, Peter Viereck claims that American intellectuals are more inclined to totalitarianism than any other group in America, while Richard Rovere emphatically denies that this is so. In the debate between J. Donald Adams and John Sisk, Adams claims that some words are inherently ugly or beautiful while Sisk replies that this is irrelevant, that the beauty or ugliness of words depends on the context in which they are found. In the first example, Viereck's thesis is *rejected* by Rovere; in the second Adams' thesis is *qualified* by Sisk.

In organizing an argument, the speaker or writer presumably studies all the evidence he can marshal and makes an inference which he states in the form of a proposition or thesis. In presenting his argument he states the evidence on which his thesis rests. However, many arguments arise casually and are conducted on the basis of opinion rather than intensive research and study of evidence. For example, Mr. Adams' first essay was written as an informal reflection on words: his tone became firmer, his logic more rigorous, and his resort to illustrations more marked in the second essay in which he answered Sisk's challenge.

The debate on the influence of American literature abroad also points up some important aspects of argumentation. Each of the contributors adds a new dimension to the debate. Father Bruckberger asks for a more "positive" literature which more truly reflects the affirmative aspects of American life than does the work of many contemporary American writers. His main concern is with the falsely negative picture that this critical literature gives foreigners of life in the United States. The editor of *Life* makes a similar plea. Robert Penn Warren, however, points out that a critical literature is in the long run more constructive, and therefore more affirmative than a complacent one. Mrs. Meyers provides a new perspective by considering the problem in relation to her own experiences in teaching American literature abroad. As these different views are presented, certain facts are seen in new relations to others. While in some debates the debaters become so violent that they are concerned only with overpowering the opponent, here the authors seem to be honestly searching out the implications of their arguments not for the purpose of scoring a point but in an effort to discover the truth.

Evidence is factual by definition, but different kinds of evidence carry different weights because certain facts are more easily demonstrable than others. Our interpretation of facts is a different matter. Thus, a distinction must be made between a demonstrable fact such as, "the temperature is now 32°F." and our speculation as to the effect that this fact is likely to have on, say, the purchase of fur coats. Arguments about government subsidies to farmers will deal to some extent with demonstrable facts, for example, income, acreage, yield per acre, and to some extent with "value judgments," as to the fairness or morality of such subsidies. The fair debater will make quite clear which of his arguments are factual and which represent opinion and personal interpretation.

The conscientious debater will also give a fair appraisal of his opponent's position, stating it in such a way that his opponent can say, "Yes, that is what I believe." He will try to come to grips with his opponent's thesis and anticipate the arguments which will be used against his own position. He may, in many cases, acknowledge the validity of some of his opponent's individual points but show that these do not really damage his own case.

Invalid and sometimes dishonest techniques of arguing have been catalogued by logicians. One of the most common is called an *ad hominem* argument, an argument directed against an adversary rather than against what he has said. A listing of a few others will help us to recognize them when used and to avoid them ourselves.

(1) *False analogy*. Example: Students are not barred from college because they are poor athletes; therefore athletes should not be barred from college because they are poor students. (2) *Begging the question*. Example: Since this legislator has a good voting record in general, we should question neither his motives nor his judgment in this particular case. (3) *Non sequitur*. Example: Because the Democrats (or Republicans) took office, two European governments have greatly increased the number of Communists in their parliaments. (4) *Appeal to prejudice*. Example: The governor was decorated for bravery during his wartime service; therefore there can be no question as to his integrity.

There are, of course, many other faulty techniques. The writer who respects his own thesis will try to avoid all of them, for they will only damage, not strengthen his case.

A | Words by Themselves or in Context

J. Donald Adams, UGLY WORDS

John Sisk, SOUND AND SENSE OF WORDS

J. Donald Adams, MORE ON UGLY WORDS

Mr. Adams, in his first essay, writes that he finds individual words beautiful or ugly and that this is related to their sound or to their capacity for evoking pleasant or unpleasant sensations. Mr. Sisk replies that words in isolation may be beautiful or ugly but that this is irrelevant, that in the final analysis their beauty or ugliness depends on the context in which they are found. Mr. Adams answers this by conceding some of Sisk's points but concludes that even if the context is important, individual words are worth considering in themselves.

Mr. Sisk is really not so much concerned with Adams' thesis about words in isolation as he is with denying the theory that it is poetic diction, the use of "poetic words," which makes poetry possible. He maintains that a poetic context can give beauty to the most trite or "ugly" word. Thus, one thesis can beget another.

1 UGLY WORDS

by J. Donald Adams

J. Donald Adams (1891–   ) was born in New York and educated at Harvard. He taught briefly at the University of Washington and then worked as a newspaper reporter and editorial writer. In 1924, he became assistant editor of New York Times Books, *and the following year, editor, a position he held until 1943. Since then he has contributed a weekly column to* The New York Times Book Review *entitled "Speaking of Books." Mr. Adams has edited several anthologies and has written two critical volumes,* The Shape of Books to Come *and* Literary Frontiers.

Some time ago, in response to a query, I gave over this column to a discussion of what might be considered the most beautiful line in the English language. The other day, reading Eric Barnes' moving biography of Edward Sheldon, *The Man Who Lived Twice,* I came upon a passage in which Mr. Barnes tells how Sheldon, in company with his oculist, Dr. Doherty, once amused himself by conjuring up "the most hideous words in the English language." Together, they concluded that no such list would be complete without the inclusion of "intelligentsia," "funeral parlor," "housewife," and "galluses."

For the most part, these seem to me relatively inoffensive words. "Intelligentsia," to be sure, carries with it a faint tinge of snobbishness, and is, to my mind, definitely unprecise in its connotations, in view of the fact that intelligence and education are by no means interchangeable terms. To call it hideous, however, strikes me as exaggerated. In fact, none of the words which Ned Sheldon and his medical friend found so obnoxious seems to me acutely distasteful, with the exception of "funeral parlor," which carries nice-nellieism to the nth degree. I find nothing to recommend the use, now so prevalent, of the phrase "funeral home," which is unquestionably one of the ultimates in verbal absurdity. It now disfigures the streets of every American town and city. "Housewife," on the other hand, while by no means a glamorous or exciting word, is in my estimate an honest and inoffensive one. And "galluses," I think, wears a humorous and stoutly homespun air. It has a lot more flavor than "suspenders"; as for "braces," that strikes me as a merely inaccurate word.

Even though I cannot subscribe to Sheldon's verbal antipathetics, I am grateful to him for channeling my thoughts, however briefly, in this direction. Unfortunately, for my purpose, some of the most hideous words in the English language cannot be printed in a newspaper, but let's see what can be scared up that falls within the bounds of permitted usage.

Suppose we stop to consider what the qualities are that justify the adjective "hideous" as applied to that decidedly living organism, the word. Those qualities must vary considerably in kind and degree, depending upon the temperament and tastes, the susceptibilities of the person exposed to them. In my own case, I should place first on the list of such qualities, that of disagreeable sound. None of Sheldon's strong aversions seem to me indictable for that reason. All his hated words come smoothly to the tongue, nor do they grate upon the ear. They are not beautiful, or even pretty; they are innocuous so far as euphony goes, though the hissing of "galluses" is no asset. And "intelligentsia," as a matter of fact, has a rather rippling sound. The other quality which merits the application of hideous is the power of a word to evoke disgusting or otherwise extremely repellent sensations.

What nominations, then, might we make of words truly deserving the designation hideous, leaving out of account such words as are offensive to many readers? This narrows our choice, of course, but it should be possible to find a few which are hideous without inducing queasiness. The choice could be more easily made if the words could be taken from certain of the American Indian tongues—beautiful as some Indian words and names are—or from German. *Schrecklichkeit*, for example, or, for that matter, pleasant as its connotations are, *gesundheit*. Even French, the aristocrat of languages, yields a few such distasteful words. *Crépuscule* beloved though it is by many poets, when adopted into English as the adjective "crepuscular," certainly makes a bid for election.

For a mildly hideous word, there is "polygamous." Attractive as it may be in its connotations, it is surely not auditorily entrancing. "Pneumococcus" is a likely candidate, as are other words denoting those pestiferous small organisms which make continual war on us. A special niche might be reserved for words like "mortician" and "beautician," and another special compartment for such verbal contraptions as "snaggle-toothed."

A little worse, I think, than these, is a word that stands for loveliness —"pulchritudinous." If you were Marilyn Monroe and did not know English very well, and someone called you that, would you think you were being complimented? Then there is a word which, not so many years ago, enjoyed a brief vogue among book reviewers, and which has always seemed to me to reach the summit of clumsiness. I refer to "adumbrate," meaning to sketch an outline in a shadowy way. (Now the great vogue word is, and has been for some time, "perceptive," to which no exception can be taken, save on the grounds of overuse.)

"Pococurantism" is to me a definitely hideous word. I had never seen it until I began leafing over the dictionary in search of horrible examples. I doubt that it is ever used, like a lot of other top-heavy Latinities, but it means the attitude or behavior characteristic of a person who may be more briefly and euphoniously described as a trifler. I leave you to compile a list salted to your own taste.

EXERCISES

1. What does Mr. Adams mean by "nice-nellieism"?
2. Mr. Adams believes that the sound of a word separate from its meaning can be "hideous." Make a list of nonsense words, then ask yourself whether they sound hideous or beautiful. What conclusion would you draw?
3. One may find *Agnes* an unpleasant name but *Agnus dei* (lamb of God) pleasant, or one may find *ain't* unpleasant but *quaint* pleasant. Does this affect Mr. Adams' thesis about unpleasant sounds?
4. Mr. Adams uses the expression "special niche" for words. Does "niche" seem to you the best possible word here?

2 SOUND AND SENSE OF WORDS

by John P. Sisk

John Sisk (1914–) was educated at Gonzaga University and at the University of Washington. He has been on the staff of Gonzaga since 1938. A frequent contributor to magazines, Mr. Sisk's interests range from English literature of the Renaissance to the literature of our day. One of his best known essays is a commentary on the pastoral hero in American literature.

Critic J. Donald Adams devoted his New York *Times Book Review* column for September 30, 1956 to a discussion of hideous words, submitting as examples "polygamous," "pneumococcus," "mortician," "beautician," "pulchritudinous" and "pococurantism." These words and others failed to meet his requirements for verbal beauty: either they had a disagreeable sound, did not come smoothly to the tongue, or they evoked "disgusting or otherwise repellent sensations."

This sounds like the literary small-talk one ought to allow a critic to indulge himself in every now and then. But is it small-talk? Words are so important that one ought to pay close attention to all theorizing about them. Mr. Adams' speculations, I suggest, are founded on questionable assumptions that are shared by a great number of people who also believe that they love words and literature. These assumptions about the functions of words are involved with some unfortunate beliefs about all fine writing, and especially about poetry.

One of these assumptions is that the beauty or hideousness of a word can be found in the word itself, isolated or abstracted from any context. This is a dictionary approach to language.

In a dictionary words have an artificial, if very useful, kind of existence. Only in a secondary sense does a word "mean" in a dictionary, or in any other state of isolation. A dictionary definition can be a useful tool for clarifying words in contexts, but, like a prose comment on a poem, it is still best thought of as a clue to a semantic problem that must ultimately be worked out *in situ*. Just as an ecologist has nothing to do with organisms isolated from their biologic environments, so as normal users of language we have nothing to do with isolated words. All communication is done with words in contexts, even where, for instance in conversation, words are apparently used singly. For context is not only other words; it is also time, place, circumstance, accompanying gesture, anticipated response and so on.

Similarly, the beauty in organized language is not so much the result of putting beautiful words together as it is putting words together beautifully—into Eliot's "complete consort dancing together." It is irrelevant to ask whether the words so organized are beautiful when taken singly. The gestalt formula, that the whole is greater than the sum of the parts, is the right one here. The beauty of a pattern of words is ecological, the property of words in a pattern, not a sum of beautiful verbal moments.

How Does "Orcs" Sound?

Mr. Adams' first requirement for a beautiful word—that it have an agreeable sound, come smoothly to the tongue—may work well enough if one is playing parlor games with words as words, but it is useless when applied to words in contexts. What, for instance, would Mr. Adams say about "orcs" (a variety of whales)? Taken by itself, this belch-like monosyllable is hardly lovely. But hear it in the wonderful passage from Book XI of *Paradise Lost:*

. . . then shall this Mount
Of Paradise by might of waves be moved . . .
Down the great River to the Op'ning Gulf,
And there take root an Island salt and bare,
The haunt of Seals and Orcs, and sea-mews' clang.

Equally useless is Mr. Adams' second requirement, the power of a word to evoke pleasant or beautiful sensations. Granted that the isolated word (provided that isolation is possible) may evoke some kind of sensation, still the sensations, or images, that concern us primarily are those evoked by words in patterns. If you test isolated words according to their power to evoke pleasant sensations, you are not only likely to be hopelessly subjective, but you will find out little about their real evocative potential. If Mr. Adams objects to "pulchritudinous" on this score, he might very well object to "polyphiloprogenitive," yet it goes very well in Mr. Eliot's "Sunday Morning Service":

Polyphiloprogenitive
The sapient sutlers of the word . . .

Or Mr. Adams might reasonably say that a word like "illimitable" is too abstract to evoke any kind of sensation—or at any rate a pleasant one. Yet Coleridge, surely a hard man to take a stand against, admired it immensely in Cullen Bryant's lines:

The desert and illimitable air—
Lone wandering, but not lost.

And aren't "incarnadine" and "multitudinous" perfect examples of the "top-heavy Latinities" Mr. Adams abhors? I wonder if he finds them so abhorrent in *Macbeth:*

No, this my hand will rather
The multitudinous seas incarnadine,
Making the green one red.

So Mr. Adams may think he is considering the beauty or hideousness of words taken singly, but what he is really considering is words in partial, vaguely specified or purely personal contexts, from which he is no more able to tear them than anyone else. His assumption, however, is that he has got them loose and that something like definitive statements about their potentialities for contexts can be made about them in this disengaged condition. Thus he can say that there is a faint tinge of snobbishness in "intelligentsia," when the snobbishness is only in contexts he is most familiar with, or has elected to favor—which are by no means all possible contexts.

Perhaps it is best to say that, unless it is unambiguously mimetic, the completely isolated word has only phonic properties—is a pattern, more or less attractive, of certain vowels, consonants and syllabic pauses. From this point of view certainly not all words would be equally beautiful to the ideally sensitive ear. But the problem would be to hear words in one's own language this way, completely separated from all sense and context. One might as well try to be ideally objective about himself.

However, I don't wish to be too hard on Mr. Adams, since most of us talk this way about words every now and then. Admittedly, too, much that has been said or written about individual words has had the effect of making others use them more carefully and effectively in contexts. Perhaps it is just as easy to think and talk about words out of contexts as it is hard to use them that way. And not everyone who so thinks or talks about them has the tastes in poetry that seem to be implied.

Any "Poetic" Words?

Nevertheless, there is a connection between this attitude toward words and the always popular theory that poetry ought to be written with words that are in themselves "poetic"—that it ought to draw upon a special "poetic" vocabulary and should be guided by certain established pleasant combinations of these words. Such poetry is, of course, relatively easy to read and appreciate: as a matter of fact, the reader is predisposed to have a poetic reaction to it, since it draws upon a vocabulary that has a long association with poetic contexts. Consequently, good poetry becomes identified with poetry that places no great strain on the reader: does not shock him with unseemly words, distract him with strange rhythms or spoil his pleasure with too many ideas.

This sounds a great deal like the neo-classical dream of a literary language set apart, much as a precious antique is put out of reach of uncouth fingers, and it points to the "common sense" kind of anti-intellectualism that Arthur Lovejoy finds in the 18th century. However, modern lovers of "poetic" poetry generally find themselves most at home with poetry written in the romantic tradition. It is such a vocabulary and the use made of it that is most often in mind when these people complain that modern poetry lacks verbal beauty. Had they read Wordsworth when he was first published, they would have objected to him in the same terms.

An important factor in this establishing of certain words as in themselves poetic is the instinctive tendency, observable in individuals or periods, to "fix" permanently at least the literary part of the language, so that what is conceived to be poetry can continue to be written. This tendency is in part the expression of a natural fear of time and change, and is one reason why we clutch the dictionary as convulsively as we do—as if it were the only thing that stood between us and semantic chaos.

So far as this tendency is successful it both protects and restricts the range of appreciation. If nothing opposed it the result would be a completely formalized and artificial poetry, comfortably immunized from the new and the unexpected. But it is always being opposed, and periodically the opposition takes dramatic shape: a Donne, a Wordsworth or an Eliot refuses to believe that words can be "fixed," however beautifully.

Words and Hucksters

Corollary to the belief that the beauty of language can be seen in words taken singly is the conviction that the corruption of language is most apparent in the connotative abuse of words—for instance in advertising. Countless once fine words, the argument goes, have been spoiled for poets because the ad-man has inflated them hopelessly out of shape or impregnated them with the garlic of huckstering.

The fear is exaggerated. With this statement, though, I intend no comfort to Madison Avenue, which even in its systolic phase of the soft sell is no less semantically irresponsible than it was before. No doubt advertising has had its effect on language, and has so appropriated certain words that temporarily at least some writers tend to avoid them; and surely anyone concerned about language ought to resist this and all such corruptive forces. But if you will check through any anthology of modern poetry (for instançe, Rhinehart's splendid *Fifteen Modern American Poets*) you will see how many of the presumably corrupted words are just as poetically usable as ever.

The paradox, then, is that good poetry is not made out of beautiful words: out of beautiful words you make bad poetry and perfume ads. Yet the effect of good poetry is to make words beautiful by associating them with the beauty of their contexts. The magic then seems to be a permanent property of the words themselves, ensuring poetic effects to subsequent users. A real poet knows this is not true. The better other poets write, the harder it will be for him. There are no magic, ready-made words. He must, as Eliot puts it in *Four Quartets*, begin all over again his "raid on the inarticulate/With shabby equipment always deteriorating."

EXERCISES

1. What does Mr. Sisk mean by a dictionary approach to words?
2. What does he mean by "gestalt formula"?
3. Explain why the word *orc* as an isolated word has a different sound and a different effect than it has in the context of Milton's lines.
4. Mr. Sisk would undoubtedly say that any word properly used in a context can be beautiful. Presumably Mr. Adams would disagree. Which position seems the more reasonable?

3 | MORE ON UGLY WORDS

by J. Donald Adams

Some time ago in this column I amused myself by discussing hideous words. Now, in an article published in *America* for February 9, I find myself taken rather solemnly to task for having ventured to suggest that the ugliness or beauty of a word counts for much, outside the context in which it is placed. Prof. John P. Sisk of Gonzaga University in Spokane, Wash., thinks that my speculations were "founded on questionable assumptions that are shared by a great number of people who also believe that they love words and literature. * * * One of these assumptions is that the beauty or hideousness of a word can be found in the word itself, isolated or abstracted from any context. This is a dictionary approach to language."

Professor Sisk says he doesn't wish to be too hard on me, "since most of us talk this way about words every now and then." If we do, I think it is with more justification than he seems willing to allow. Far be it from me to quarrel with Professor Sisk when he remarks that "all communication is done with words in contexts," or that "the beauty in organized language is not so much the result of putting beautiful words together as it is putting words together beautifully." But I disagree strongly when he adds that "it is irrelevant to ask whether the words so organized are beautiful when taken singly." Certainly the whole is greater than the sum of the parts, but the parts are in themselves of great importance. Each is capable of contributing to or detracting from the total effect.

Let me use a simple illustration—one which I used once before in a discussion of beautiful words. In the Twenty-third Psalm, which I am sure Professor Sisk would grant as an instance of words which were put beautifully together, we come to the sentence, "He leadeth me beside the still waters." If you substitute "quiet" for "still," I submit that the loveliness of the phrase is seriously impaired. Not merely because the use of "quiet" makes for a less harmonious combination of sounds, but also because to my ear, at least, "still" is the more suggestive word. The liquid quality of the "l's" with which the word ends reinforces the meaning, while the sharpness of "quiet" takes something away. Is it irrelevant to pause for choice between the two words?

And does it not follow, then, that the effect of a word upon the ear—

pleasing or otherwise—cannot be confined, as Professor Sisk would have it, to "playing parlor games with words as words," and that the beauty resident in a word's sound is not, as he contends it is, "useless when applied to words in contexts"?

Because I contend that many words do have a character of their own, independent of context, Professor Sisk concludes I must assume that unattractive sounding words are to be avoided, and proceeds to link my belief in their individual character with "the always popular theory that poetry ought to be written with words that are in themselves 'poetic'—that it ought to draw upon a special 'poetic' vocabulary and should be guided by certain established pleasant combinations of these words."

These two attitudes—belief in the individual character of words and belief in a "poetic" vocabulary—do not necessarily join. Certainly I do not subscribe to the latter, much as I believe in the first. Professor Sisk in the course of his article refers to Coleridge as "a hard man to take a stand against." Surely, then, he will allow me to quote the definitions of good prose and poetry offered by Coleridge: the one, "proper words in their proper places"; the other, "the most proper words in their proper places." I do not repeat them because, good as they are, I think they are completely satisfying, but because they throw a little light on the matters under discussion. Certainly, in the words I quoted from the Twenty-third Psalm, "quiet" would be a proper word in the proper place; "still" the most proper word in its proper place.

Professor Sisk expresses skepticism about the power of a word to evoke pleasant or beautiful sensations. "Granted," he says, "that the isolated word (provided that isolation is possible) may evoke some kind of sensation, still the sensation, or images, that concern us primarily are those evoked by words in patterns. If you test isolated words according to their power to evoke pleasant sensations, you are not only likely to be hopelessly subjective, but you will find out little about their real evocative potential." But the fact that the sensation produced by a word may be subjective in origin does not alter the potentiality of its impact. Why must the sensations or images evoked by words in a pattern be those that concern us primarily? And cannot our reaction to words in a pattern be fully as subjective as our reaction to a single, isolated word?

To anyone who doubts the possession of character by individual words, or the power resident in them, issuing from themselves, I would recommend an evening's browsing in Ivor Brown's series of word anthologies. True, we have eventually and unavoidably to deal with words in their context, but there is much to be gained by consideration of them by and for themselves.

EXERCISES

1. Mr. Adams says the word *still* in "He leadeth me beside the still waters" is more appropriate than *quiet* would be. Does this reenforce his argument about the beauty of words in isolation or does it reenforce Mr. Sisk's about beauty in context? To complicate your understanding of the problem, consider Keats' line

Thou still unravished bride of quietness

We might rewrite this to read

Thou yet unravished bride of stillness

Which is the better line? Is it the individual word or the word-in-context that most determines its beauty?

2. Which of the authors of these articles presents a more convincing case? Analyze the arguments of each to justify your answer.

B | The American Intellectual and Totalitarianism

Peter Viereck, "BLOODY-MINDED PROFESSORS": The Anti-Social Role of Some Intellectuals

Richard H. Rovere, "BLOODY-MINDED PROFESSORS?"

The background to this controversy must be sought in the decade of the depression preceding World War II as well as in the period of the "cold war" beginning in the latter part of the 1940's. Following the "Crash" of 1929, a small percentage of Americans became Communists or fellow-travelers as a reaction to the economic and social distress which they felt reflected the breakdown of the capitalist system. During the war, when Russia and the United States fought together as allies, the climate of opinion toward Russia was generally favorable. With the war over, Russia and the United States emerged as the two dominant world powers. Their wartime friendship deteriorated rapidly as Russia moved to extend her sphere of influence in Europe and Asia. Against the background of growing hostility some Americans became increasingly concerned over the danger to the United States represented by Communists and Communist sympathizers within the country. During the early 1950's, many charges were heard that Communists held responsible positions in government and education, and congressional investigations, in which Senator Joseph McCarthy figured prominently, were begun. Many state legislatures demanded loyalty oaths from their employees, particularly teachers. "Intellectuals" bore the brunt of the attack. Since then it has become rather clear that the alarm was considerably greater than was warranted by the facts.

Peter Viereck's article claims that not only are American intellectuals susceptible to totalitarianism (particularly Communism), but that they are more so than any other group in America. Viereck maintains that

American intellectuals have been divorced from the mainstream of American life and as a consequence they have buttressed their own self-respect by sneering at the basic and stable forms of American life. They have given their allegiance, instead, he claims, to European culture and ideology, particularly Communism. Viereck launches into a vehement diatribe against the political naïveté of these intellectuals and accuses them of having done great harm. Not until the end of the article does he concede that this is not true of "all American intellectuals," and that many of them have performed great service and carried out their role with good judgment and dignity.

Richard Rovere, replying to Viereck's attack, maintains that while some American intellectuals were attracted by Communism in the 1930's and 1940's, the majority of the genuine intellectuals changed their position in the face of evidence that Russian Communism represented all the evils of totalitarianism. He answers various of Viereck's specific accusations, and counters Viereck's thesis by charging that there are other groups which are more prone than intellectuals to fall prey to undemocratic ideologies and that these groups have as much, if not more, effective political power.

1 "BLOODY-MINDED PROFESSORS": THE ANTI-SOCIAL ROLE OF SOME INTELLECTUALS

by Peter Viereck

Peter Viereck (1916–) is a poet and Profesor of European and Russian History at Mount Holyoke. He took his B.A., M.A., and Ph.D., at Harvard, and spent some time studying at Christ Church, Oxford. He served with the U.S. Army in Africa and Italy. Mr. Viereck has been a visiting lecturer at a number of colleges and most recently was a Fulbright Professor of History in Florence. In 1948, he won a Poetry Magazine *award and in 1949, the Pulitzer Prize for poetry. His books include* Metapolitics: From the Romantics to the Rise of Hitler, Terror and Decorum: Poems, Conservatism Revisited: The Revolt Against Revolt, *and* A Walk on the Moss: Pastoral and Lyric Poems.

The power of vested interests is usually exaggerated when compared with the gradual encroachment of ideas. . . . Indeed the world is ruled by little else. . . . Madmen in authority, who hear voices in the air, are distilling their frenzy from some academic scribbler of a few years back.

—*John Maynard Keynes*

If we liberals were right on certain single aspects of the Russian Revolution, we were wrong, disgracefully wrong, on the question as a whole. We were wrong because, in our . . . vision of a new world springing from the womb of this Russian experiment, we permitted ourselves to condone wrongs that we knew must be wrongs.—John Haynes Holmes, America's leading liberal clergyman, 1939 (after the Hitler-Stalin pact).

In one of his breathtakingly apt phrases, Winston Churchill called the communists and their sympathizers *not* a gang of ruthless and bloody-minded gangsters but "a gang of ruthless and bloody-minded professors." The phase is apt because Churchill has spotted a central problem of our century: the strike of the middle-class intellectuals,[1] their reluctance to conserve the very heritage that protects from Russia their freedom and their security.

I wish more of my fellow "professors" would analyze the reasons for their (*our*) soft spot—in addition to spending so much of their leisure deploring loyalty oaths for professors. Such oaths I consider asinine and potentially dangerous. But we will fight them more effectively, and protect more effectively our indispensable academic freedom, by analyzing objectively why intellectuals are more susceptible to the totalitarian lure than any other group in America—only a small minority of them, of course, but proportionately a larger minority than of such other groups as farmers, businessmen, and manual workers. Why? The question cannot be fully answered here, but a few neglected aspects of it can be analyzed.

I

In America, fellow-traveling has never been a working-class movement or a spontaneous people's movement. American pro-communism, and even much of European communism, is a spontaneous movement only among

[1] If writing elsewhere, there might be the danger of playing into wrong hands by criticizing the anti-social rather than the social role of the literary intellectuals. But any forum on their role in the pages of *Confluence* is hardly destined for readers of the *Chicago Tribune*. The act of making such criticisms in *Confluence*, a pro-intellectual international quarterly under the auspices of Harvard University, may assume anti-thought-control, anti-standardization, anti-McCarthyism, and defense of dissent automatically as part of our common reverence for freedom. In such a context of *inter nos*, a criticism of intellectuals—that is, drastic self-criticism—may contribute more to stimulate our free and friendly debates than one more complacent list of the more valuable social functions of intellectuals and one more righteous denunciation (necessary in other forums but hardly here) of "witch-hunts."

the intellectuals of the upper middle class. It arises among that section of them which is psychologically—*not* economically—discontented and self-outlawed. That these, in turn, with their educational leadership, may set a mass movement in motion under certain unusual economic conditions, is another and later matter.

To be sure, the very abstractness of the intellectual tends to make him withdraw from society. But the intellectual's neutral aloofness from his society can change imperceptibly into unconscious hostility. This happens almost automatically in a society that does not appreciate his ideas as much as its electric dishwashers. The alienation of the introvert is nothing new either; the symbolism of Socrates, executed by his own unappreciative society, has always had a suspicious fascination for intellectuals in all ages. Hell hath no fury like an intellectual scorned; the semi-Stalinist fellow-traveling sometimes found in America's largest-circulating liberal weekly, and also in England's, is one way of saying: "I'm not fired, I quit."

Ancestor of this attitude was the nineteenth-century distrust between Paris and *Les Provinces,* that duel between the farm and the café or between the counting-house and the salon; this theme runs through the most influential nineteenth-century French novels (Balzac, Flaubert, Stendhal). American artistic circles know amazingly little of their own co-operative, compromise-minded, and relatively classless society. They naturally know best the society they have studied best: the society portrayed in the French and other novels that composed their own youthful *éducation sentimentale.* This is a society seen through the colored glasses of a literary (at first nonpolitical) anti-bourgeois crusade. In the Roman holiday of the bourgeois arena the intellectual is alternately the martyr and the lion. And there is more than one kind of lion. Among literary intellectuals, the lion of the barricades (re-read Wagner's and Baudelaire's fascinating and parallel accounts of their revolutionary role in 1848) may be the salon-lion *manqué* or not yet arrived.

The baitee becomes the baiter; the sissies of the Right Bank become *les fauves* ("the wild beasts") on the Left Bank. How many American intellectuals, knowing little of their own country, still identify themselves with the victims of bourgeois misunderstanding in Joyce's *Portrait of the Artist as a Young Man* and Flaubert's *Madame Bovary!* Sinclair Lewis's *Main Street* is merely the twentieth-century American version of this nineteenth-century European duel. The young Werther of our time is the self-pitying intellectual "crucified" upon some bourgeois philistine's "cross of gold." Through political and economic radicalism the crucified esthete, "L'Albatros" of Baudelaire, can get revenge against the cross of gold. The romantic-esthetic pose of the introverted stare ("yon Cassius hath a lean and hungry look") can make heads roll in the sand of bloodthirsty politics. "Such men are dangerous," as Caesar knew.

So far as this is a human duel, a psychological and noneconomic one, it has an esthetic root. But an economic root is added readily by the insecurities of the business cycle, with the underpaid professors and ununionized white-collar workers crushed between the millstones of both kinds of bigness: Big business and big trade unions. In the impersonal hustle and bustle of modern industrialism, the intellectual gets rudely pushed about as a barely-tolerated court jester. Without being allowed even the court privileges and indulgently applauded impertinences of the medieval jester.

Then one day, in his humiliation, he discovers Marxism. Purely by accident and yet somehow inevitably. Suddenly everything makes sense again, or seems to: in a jungle of blind commercialism, he again finds a purpose for society; for himself, he finds at last a more dignified role than court jester or court prostitute. Precisely because he understands not one word of Marx's materialistic economic jargon, this nonspiritual church comes to him as a spiritual salvation, a Damascus vision, a reason for going on living. In American and western Europe, Marxism provides a vast political "system" to canalize and seemingly "explain scientifically" the nonpolitical, psychological resentments of Werther, Emma Bovary, the Artist-as-a-Young-Man, and our own poor Carol Kennicott of *Main Street*, America's homespun version of the "sensitive" hero.

Political Marxism, plus the bourgeois-baiting, nonpolitical novel, plus the self-pitying Socrates-hemlock identification, plus genuine social wrongs (and not even the best society attainable by mortals will eliminate all occasions for Tennyson's "Cursed be the social wants")—this quadruple combination won't turn the Western intellectual into a Communist—party membership requires too Calvinistic, almost too bourgeois, a discipline—but it does turn him into the familiar blend of an "aristocratic" snob in art and a fellow-traveling "progressive" in politics. If you are not lucky enough to be endowed with Baudelaire's bitter eyes and resentful chin, then as second best this familiar blend will enable you to strike the twin poses of dandy and stormy petrel at your publisher's cocktail party for buttered-up book reviewers.

Every artist steeped in the magnificent French literature of the last century—that is to say, every typical American literary intellectual—will see that this snob-plus-progressive pose is neither new nor indigenous. Open at random Stendhal, for example, and you find in his autobiographical *Vie de Henri Brulard:*

> I had, and still have, the most aristocratic of tastes. I would do everything in my power to ensure the happiness of the masses. But I think I'd rather spend a fortnight of every month in prison than have to live with shopkeepers. . . . My family were the most aristocratic people in the town. This meant I became a fanatic republican on the spot.

The American middlewest was the scene of the most influential Lewis novels. This has made it today—in part unfairly, merely as a literary convenience—the accepted international symbol of the babbittry once represented by the French provinces of Flaubert and Balzac. The love-hate relationship between our middlewest and its tormented rebel-artists is worth a separate book in itself: Hart Crane ("I could not pull the arrows from my side"), Pound (finding civilization "a bitch gone in the teeth"), Henry Miller, and the others.

Sitting in a Paris café, writing the following lines, you find, typically, not a New York city slicker but the thoroughly midwestern—practically cornfed—Henry Miller: "All my life I felt a great kinship with the madman and the criminal . . . Civilization is rotten . . . Release the instinctive vitality of the primitive." This stale romantic pose, which equips every Sauk Center and Kalamazoo with its drugstore Lucifer and its crackerbox Prometheus Unbound as innately as with its "Y" and its Chamber of Commerce, was harmless enough for years. Then suddenly it got catapulted by October, 1929, into politics, where the old *New Masses* became its residuary legatee. At first the legacy amusingly embarrassed the lucky heir, for the Communist party takes a dim view of bohemianism.

At heart nonpolitical (except in the unusual context of that terrible economic depression), this pose was struck so much better—that is, with profounder insight—by Charles Baudelaire when it was not yet stale. In the revolution of 1848, gun in hand, he leapt joyously into the anti-bourgeois side of the barricades, later explaining: "What was the nature of my intoxication in 1848? Thirst for revenge. Natural delight in destruction. A literary intoxication, the memories of books I had read . . . the dandy's . . . opposition and revolt." This great poet was temporarily drawn to the barricades not by political theory nor economic suffering but by esthetic "thirst for revenge" against France's proto-middlewest and its hucksters-in-embryo.

On the surface, America's literary defenders of Hiss, Coplon, Fuchs, and the eleven convicted Communist leaders have motives more plausible, less romantic. On the surface, the motives are all pure reason and civil liberties, not Miller's "kinship with the madman and the criminal" nor Baudelaire's "natural delight in destruction." But this libertarian surface plausibility evaporates in many (not all) cases when you consider two ignored facts. (1) Communist civil liberties are less impaired in America today than ever in our history; contrast the lawless Palmer raids of the 1920's with the long, fair, painstakingly lawful trials of Hiss, Coplon, and the eleven. Even though communism is murdering Americans in Korea and jailing them illegally in Europe, not one communist inside America—not one—has been deprived of habeas corpus, due process of law, his own legal aid, unlimited free speech in his *Daily Worker.* (2) Most of these same intellectuals did not protest when thousands of innocent Japanese-Americans during the war had their civil liberties impaired incomparably more than any communist today.

These two facts justify the following speculation: to what extent, within the infinite complexity of human motives, are the intellectual defenders of the "persecuted communists" excited not by their civil-liberties rationalization but by a sneaking sympathy with any kind of conspiracy against their hated *booboisie?* Beneath the seemingly detached defense of "communist rights," or of the analogous fascist "martyr" Pound, there often lurks a savage joy at the thought that a conspiracy against "rotten civilization"—against the bourgeois "bitch gone in the teeth"—will release Miller's "vitality of the primitive" and Baudelaire's "revenge and revolt." These speculations concern only a minority; they do not concern the genuine civil-libertarian defender of communist civic rights, a defense perfectly tenable so long as it defends only communist civil liberties and not communist conspiracies. But the minority motivated by the above savage joy happens to include many leading figures in the intellectual and artistic world; this offers priceless psychological clues to the otherwise inexplicable totalitarianism of many writers and the communism or treason of such world-famous scientists as Pontecorvo, Fuchs, and Joliot-Curie.

The proper rebuttal to this savage joy is not to defend an indefensible burgher stodginess or huckster crassness. Unnecessary! Nor are pompous orations on "God Bless America" needed. All you need point out is this: the mean and prosaic qualities which are *rightly* resented in burghers by the literary intellectuals are found ten thousand times more in the mean and prosaic bureaucracy of that dowdiest slum on earth, the U.S.S.R.

Fortunately, newer and younger writers are starting to see American capitalism as it really is—a relatively democratized mixed economy—and not according to catchy false analogies with the 1789 tradition of class struggle in France or with the predatory, class-line capitalism which socialists *rightly* denounced in America and Europe in the early nineteenth century. No poltroonish conformism! I am not saying: stop attacking America's many faults. They are in many ways greater than Europe's. But they are a different kind of faults. They need to be attacked—and studied —in their own context, not that of either French cafés or Russian samovars.

By his French or Russian analogies, the American intellectual has added an artificial and unjustified alienation to that natural and justified alienation which native commercialism has already created. The American context lacks any class-conscious proletarians. It cannot be subjected, without violence to truth, to the "radical" (actually highly conventional) analysis of Marxist clichés. Not "boosting" of America nor a censorship of dissent but more self-knowledge and more knowledge of America is my suggestion for what ails the American literary world.

II

History honors the intellectuals true to their ethical function as society's warning-signals of conscience. But to indict those who betray their ethical function is no "revolt against reason." It is the restoration of reason.

The majority of American intellectuals have little to be ashamed of. Repetition of the slander that most New Dealers and liberal intellectuals were Reds makes it no less contemptible. That guilt falls only on a small minority of intellectuals. Unfortunately that minority was disastrously influential. Unless there really used to be a Pink Terror of social pressure (among fashionable literary circles) in favor of fellow-traveler conformism, Bertrand Russell would not have confirmed that "he lost more friends by his criticism of Soviet terror than by his absolute pacifism during a war in which his country was locked in a battle of life and death with Germany."[2] In other words, in pseudo-liberal intellectual circles (in contrast with the nonintellectual "outer world") it was safer to attack your own free country in wartime than to criticize a certain sacred foreign country for its despotism.

The inroads of pro-communism among intellectuals are many, many times more influential than its often exaggerated political inroads or the feeble electoral campaigns of the tiny Party itself. Merely one example among many: consider the cultural damage—I am thinking of good books rejected as well as bad books published—that could be done by the presence of Angus Cameron until 1951 in one of our finest publishing firms. He put the priceless imprimatur of *respectability* on the pro-communist books published under him by communist propagandists like Howard Fast, Albert Kahn, and others.

With the characteristic hatred of literary Stalinoids for genuine democratic socialists (a hatred more frenzied and frothing than any they expend on fascists), Cameron also was among those who after the war prevented Little, Brown from publishing George Orwell's anticommunist satire, *Animal Farm*. Some 18 to 20 publishers, almost all the leading ones, turned down the best anti-Soviet satire of our time. In view of its wit, its readability, its salability, and its democratic outlook, the most likely motive for these rejections is the brilliantly successful infiltration (then, not now) of Stalinoid sympathizers in the book world: the world that does more

[2] Julien Steinberg, Editor, *Verdict of Three Decades* (New York: Duell, Sloan, and Pearce, 1950), p. 612.

than Congress to mold the attitude of literary Americans toward Russia and foreign policy. The fact that the book finally did get published and with triumphant éclat—in the end serious literature does triumph—cautions us not to exaggerate Stalinoid infiltrations paranoically. But not to overlook them schizophrenically either. The mentality revealed by this attempt to prevent American readers from freely hearing Orwell's free speech about despotism, made Arthur Schlesinger, Jr. cancel his contract with Little, Brown,[3] writing them:

> Each day increases my sense of shame at ever having been associated with your house. I would never have signed up in 1939 if one of your leading members had been an active pro-Nazi, and I have no intention of being published by Little, Brown today when one of your leading members (Angus Cameron) is taking an active part in opposing the democratic effort to check the spread of Soviet totalitarianism.

During those incredible years when Cameron was publishing the communist propaganda of Albert Kahn in an excellent old firm and was organizing his branch of the communist-controlled Progressive party, Alger Hiss was helping to draw up the agenda for Yalta, superintending the San Francisco Conference, directing the Carnegie Peace Foundation, and serving as special assistant to the Director of the Office of Far Eastern Affairs in the State Department. Until recently, even to notice such facts was considered hysterical. That this should have been so considered is the same disgrace as the earlier indifference of Americans to the Nazi danger.[4]

III

In 1945, Elmo Roper took a poll on whether America should offer still greater concessions to Communist Russia. Roper classified the responses

[3] Be it stressed that today Little, Brown is a wholly admirable firm, publishing admirable books without any more Angus Camerons to purge it of freedom-loving Orwells and genuine liberals and democratic socialists.

[4] At the same time, remember that in the 1930's many anti-fascist idealists seemed fellow-travelers merely because they felt (mistakenly but honestly) that only communism opposed a Munich appeasement policy and because they were justifiably disgusted with that kind of capitalist who used to say, "Better Hitler than Leon Blum." Such anti-fascist idealists should not be retroactively slandered as "Reds" today, provided they passed the key test of left-wing decency by ceasing to fellow-travel when the 1939 pact revealed Stalin as merely a Soviet version of totalitarianism and its Nazis. Of course, this is what communism was all along from 1917 on; clearer heads knew this long before the pact, having studied the Moscow trials, the slave labor, and the deliberate starving of peasants in the 1930's. But this does not allow us indiscriminately to impugn the high motive of those who, though less informed about Russia than some of us before 1939, rendered priceless aid and self-sacrifice to the anti-Nazi cause. Today, needless to say, there is no such extenuating circumstance for "softness" toward the Soviet as there was in the shameful Munich year of 1938. Today the Soviet is not the seeming alternative to fascism but *is* fascism incarnate.

according to the education and income of those who replied. A sharp split in American opinion was revealed. Workers and low-income groups distrusted Russia and opposed concessions. Rich Americans, whom Marx would call the bourgeoisie, trusted Russia and wanted still further American concessions. Roper classified these answers not only by wealth but by intellectuality and by knowledge of Russian and world affairs. The uneducated and the nonintellectual, in Roper's words of 1945, "were much less aware of the necessity of cooperation with Russia and much more inclined to charge Russia with dark and sinister intentions . . . Those who knew something about Russia gave broad, balanced opinions—critical on some scores and laudatory on others, but with the balance leaning strongly towards friendly understandings."

In 1946, a Gallup poll asked: "Do you believe Russia is trying to build herself up to a ruling power, or just building up protection against being attacked in another war?" Again answers were classified by education and income. The most optimistic replies came from "the professional and business group." They split almost 50-50 on this question. The most pessimistic replies came from what Gallup called the uneducated "manual workers." Sixty per cent of these "oppressed proletarians" predicted —in contrast with experts and professors—that Russia aimed for world power and expansion.

In other words, the main obstacle to understanding that communists are communists (not good neighbors, not agrarian reformers) was the possession of education, intellect, or great wealth. No wonder one editor made the following comment on all this in 1952: "To predict accurately in 1945 that Russia would act as Russia has acted, you had to be as dumb and poorly informed as an ox."

The misinterpretation of Soviet world-conquest by the best-educated non-oxen of the west did not merely affect the realm of abstract theory. It affected the course of actual history. To what extent it did so cannot be accurately assessed. Here we enter the imponderable realm of the indirect influence exerted by "intellectual atmosphere"—in this case, a trust-Russia atmosphere. One assessment of the historical results of this atmosphere has been formulated by Norman Angell, a Nobel Peace Prize winner. He can hardly be called an imperialist warmonger, or un-liberal, or anti-intellectual. His assessment of the trust-Russia atmosphere among our un-proletarian, upper-middle-class liberals probably exaggerates its concrete territorial or military influences and consequences. But he does offer a real insight into at least the spirit of what was happening:

We defeated Hitler in a second war for democracy and then (against all the counsels of the "imperialist" Churchill) insisted upon a strategy which left the military domination of those states to Stalin, largely *because liberals and leftists* in both Britain and the United States believed Stalin and what he stood for to be so much more democratic than Churchill and what that "Tory imperialist" stood for.[5]

To Angell's insufficiently qualified comment, you must add: Stalin could have and probably would have taken Eastern Europe militarily (though hardly Manchuria) *even without Yalta.* But the issue is not what he would have taken anyway. The issue is why we gave the seal of Western moral approval to what would otherwise have been an open act of highway robbery? Confronted by such an open act, without the Yalta moral sugar-coating, our public opinion—which hampered resistance to Russian aggression till 1947—would at least have hardened earlier, achieving thereby the humanitarian gain of saving countless victims from Soviet torture. This would have also permitted rearmament and a Truman doctrine and an Atlantic pact many months earlier, instead of having to undergo that fatal delay of unilateral disarmament—until Churchill's Fulton speech and Stalin's own actions brought Stalin's Western dupes back to their senses. Back from the Popular Front illusion.

That illusion may be defined as the view that communists are merely misguided, overhasty liberals, moving in the same general "forward-looking" and "antifascist" direction as the rest of us. This illusion views communists as a problem of "civil liberties for non-conformists," instead of as a murderous Red army of invasion on behalf of a Russian fascist ruling class. This illusion made well-groomed and plausible-sounding maniacs of precisely the highest intellectual liberal circles.

If you have forgotten the prevalence of this illusion—so I wrote in an *Atlantic Monthly* article of April, 1940, and so I repeat again—then simply read the list of 165 (allegedly 400) prominent liberal intellectuals, not the worst but the best elements of our culture, who in August, 1939, signed a disgraceful procommunist manifesto. This denounced "the fantastic falsehood that the fascist states and Soviet Russia equally menace the democratic way"; it called "Soviet and Fascist policies diametrically opposed" and called Russia the great "bulwark" of peace. To repeat the list of signers now, in part the elite of the world of liberal weaklies, would embarrass some honest men who subsequently changed their minds for the better. Suffice it to recall again in 1952, as my article originally did in 1940, one tragi-comic coincidence: this manifesto was featured in *The Nation* the very week of the Hitler-Stalin pact!

Originating in the thirties, the Popular Front illusion provided during 1944–47 the moral sugar-coating to Russia's aggressions. Thereby the Popular Front illusion has dealt a blow to peace and liberty, and likewise to lucid reasoning, of still unassessed proportions. Just possibly it will turn out to be the most anti-social act ever committed in the history of

[5] Norman Angell, *The New Leader*, May 26, 1952, p. 11.

mankind by any comparably decent and well-intentioned intelligentsia.

Today intellectuals are admirably rejecting these misconceptions, so far as foreign policy toward aggression in Korea goes. But they have still not rejected (as shown by their refusal to despise Hiss as much as they would Quisling) the most successful communist hoax ever perpetrated: the confusion of criminal deeds with free thought, the confusion of communist military conspiracy with the sacred cause of civil liberties. One can only echo and underline the phrase, "So grave and urgent that a man breaks out in a cold sweat," in the following comment on this whole problem by John Dos Passos:

> A living organism that fails to react to danger is sick or dying. The questions raised in the mind by the moral lynching of Whittaker Chambers by the right-thinking people of this country are so grave and urgent that a man breaks out in a cold sweat to think of them. Can it be that the "liberals" who control communications in the press and the radio and the schools and the colleges . . . refuse, in the light of all the evidence, to recognize the existence of a conspiracy of assassins, bent on the destruction of the right-thinking liberals, as much as on the destruction of the rest of us? The day that this mystery becomes clear, the day when this strange delusion is swept out of the public mind, that day we will be able to go to bed secure in the thought that, if the United States is doomed by forces of history too great for us to overcome, at least we will go down fighting.[6]

IV

I may be accused of joining the standardizers of American thought, the group which sees in conformism a badge of good faith. But that American thought is getting too standardized is by now a standard observation. Too often this observation is misused in order to defame—as "standardizers"—those who exercise their free speech to criticize Western parrotings of the Stalinoid intellectual clichés. May we not call this defamation the McCarthyism of the left?

The dangerous increase in standardizing is undeniable. But its cause is not the lawful prosecution of the law-breaking members of the conspiratorial CP. The cause in part is the mechanizing trend of a mass society, with mass production also of thought capsules. This being so, an independent-minded protest against standardized thinking should perhaps start against that one group who ought to know better. Ought to know better because by education they at least—namely the liberal intellectuals—are relatively free from the mass magazines and mass movies and mass culture. To re-examine their unconscious standardizing should not be construed as "attacking" liberal intellectuals. On the contrary, to scrape the

[6] *Saturday Review*, May 24, 1952.

barnacles off a good boat is never considered an attack on it. Except by the barnacles. There is this difference between the slot-machine banality of the old conservatives and that of the new liberals: the latter is less conscious, less apparent. And therefore more tempting for those intellectual circles that would never be tempted in the first place by the rusty, creaking old conservative slot machine.

Yet when all is said and done, the shame of the Western intellectual is outweighed by his glory. Discriminate criticism of him be resisted. May we not close, on a more positive note, with a plea for the restoration of haloes?

"The virtue of this article . . ." (I hear said of an article loosely calling most intellectuals Reds) ". . . is that it strips intellectuals of their haloes." "The virtue of this book" (I hear said of a best seller calling academic freedom "a myth") "is that it reminds professors they are living on the businessman's wages." But I don't care to see intellectuals stripped of their haloes, even those I most disagree with. This is not for the obvious subjective reason. It is, rather, because I don't care for Karl Marx. Therefore, I do not cherish attitudes like the above two quotations on "haloes" and "businessman's wages." For they seem to justify one of Marx's unfair allegations: "The bourgeoisie has robbed of their haloes various occupations hitherto regarded with awe and veneration. Doctor, lawyer, priest, poet, and scientist have become its wage-laborers."

Academic freedom is not a "myth." Intellectuals are indeed worthy of "awe and veneration." I wish more intellectuals would have the pride to stand up and assert, and re-assert without apology, the glory of their function. They are "wage-laborers" not of bourgeois politicians nor of socialist politicians but of truth and conscience.

Even a totally wrong-headed intellectual still wears a disheveled kind of halo, in the same way that an unfrocked priest still has some kind of link with the apostolic succession. If I did not have so high a view of the intellectual's function, I would not bother being so distressed and angry about the treason of the literary fellow-travelers. Their unforgivable sin is that they, at least, should know better. Nobody expects some miserable yellow-press columnist or some idiotic, intellectual-baiting backwoods-reactionary to know any better. Therefore, morally you should feel just a bit less distressed or angry about the latter, "for they know not what they do."

Here is the modern version of "the sin against the Holy Ghost": when an intellectual fails to remain serieux; when he sullies the miracle of human intelligence and the privilege of his educational advantages to become a highbrow demagogue, an intelligent charlatan, like Ilya Ehrenburg, Herr Doktor Goebbels, or that communist propagandist, the Dean of Canterbury. The job of intellect is not to serve Big Business. The job of intellect is not to serve Big Labor or its trade unions. If anything (let's be arrogant about it) the job of business and the job of labor in America is to serve intellect—on the condition that intellect serves and ennobles the nation as a whole. Intellect serves and ennobles whenever it searches for more truth and more beauty, in its unpretentious, impractical, haloed kind of way.

EXERCISES

1. Is the title of Mr. Viereck's article designed to arouse strong feelings? To whom does it refer?
2. Early in his essay, Mr. Viereck asserts that "intellectuals are more susceptible to the totalitarian lure than any other group in America. . . ." What does he mean by "totalitarian"? Does he offer evidence for this assertion?
3. Putting Mr. Viereck's article out of mind for the time being, explain why the term "intellectual" is difficult to define? Do all intellectuals vote for the same party? Do they all come from the same economic level? Are they all interested in the arts? To what group does Mr. Viereck seem to be referring?
4. In the introduction to this section, we referred to several unfair techniques of argument: false analogy, begging the question, *non-sequitur*, appeal to prejudice, and weighted words. Does Mr. Viereck employ any of these?

2 "BLOODY-MINDED PROFESSORS?"

by Richard H. Rovere

Richard H. Rovere (1915–   ) took his A.B. at Bard College, Columbia University. He has been a staff writer for The New Yorker *since 1944. For a short period he was chief book critic for* Harper's *and he is a frequent contributor to* The New York Times *and other publications. He is the author of* Howe and Hummel: Their True and Scandalous History, *and co-author with Arthur Schlesinger, Jr., of* The General and the President *(1951).*

In an article in the September issue of *Confluence*, Peter Viereck accepts pretty much at face value the notion that intellectuals must bear the basic responsibility for political aberrations and tyrannies. He calls his article "Bloody-Minded Professors," explaining the phrase as a "breathtakingly apt" one which he borrowed from Winston Churchill, who understood that it is the pedagogue rather than the hoodlum or the untutored fanatic who characterizes the Communist movement.

This seems to me, like so much of the rest of Mr. Viereck's article, a large and dangerous oversimplification. There is obviously some truth in it, but not, I think, very much. Mr. Viereck would have us believe that a direct cause of the death of freedom in many parts of the world is the affinity a certain number of Western intellectuals had for Communism in the thirties and forties: "The misinterpretation of Soviet world-conquest by the best-educated non-oxen of the west did not merely affect the realm of abstract theory. It affected the course of actual history." Just how it affected the course of history, he does not quite explain, and he concedes that Stalin could have taken what he wanted in Eastern Europe without the approval or helpful indifference of American intellectuals. But he seems to think that this was not the case with Manchuria, and he argues that American resistance to Soviet aggression would have stiffened far earlier if it had not been for the sapping of morale on the part of intellectuals whose own morale had been sapped by Stalinism.

I should like to deal in detail with certain of Mr. Viereck's points, but I wish to point out that in doing so I have no desire either to justify intellectuals who supported Communism in the thirties or forties or to argue that what intellectuals say or do has no bearing on the course of events. The American intellectuals who turned to Communism damaged their country and the free society of which it is an important part because they damaged themselves and because they poured bilge into our common culture. I do not believe that they delayed the formulation of the Truman Doctrine or the Marshall Plan or the North Atlantic Treaty, which is Mr. Viereck's astonishing contention. I say this not because I underestimate their importance but because I estimate more highly than Mr. Viereck does such factors as the world's great weariness at the end of the last war and the strategic advantage which Russia's Eastern and Western frontiers placed at Stalin's disposal. In general, though, my interest in disputing Mr. Viereck is an interest in keeping the record straight.

I

Mr. Viereck asserts that "intellectuals are more susceptible to the totalitarian lure than any other group in America."

This is at most half true. Although many American intellectuals were Stalinists, in the thirties as well as the forties, there was a large difference between the quality of minds attracted in those two periods, and I think it entirely reasonable to say that it was only in the earlier decade that any substantial number of really first-class people, people who truly represented the intellectual community, were under Communist influence. Those who remained in the Communist movement after the Soviet-Nazi pact or who entered it during the war period were for the most part intellectuals *manqué*—climbers from Hollywood, conscience-stricken press agents and advertising writers, people whose intellectual pretensions outran their performances.

The distinction I have in mind is made, though with reference to a far larger field of inquiry, by Eric Hoffer in *The True Believer*. "Whence come the fanatics?" Hoffer asks, answering, "Mostly from the ranks of the non-creative men of words. The most significant division of men of words is between those who can find fulfillment in creative work and those who cannot. The creative man of words, no matter how bitterly he may criticize and deride the existing order is actually attached to the present. His passion is to reform and not to destroy." And Hoffer goes on to point out that it is the uncreative sort who cling to their roles as True Believers long after the others know there is nothing left to believe in. It was men of this type, barren and bitter, who continued to lend themselves to Communism in the forties, and who, in somewhat diminished numbers, do so today. They represent nothing but their own inadequacies.

In all fairness, it must be recognized that in the thirties there were at least two totalitarian lures. The one that at the time posed the greater, or at least the more direct and immediate, threat to human liberty, had no intellectual following at all in this country. On the contrary, American intellectuals, almost to a man, abhorred fascism, and if many of them lent themselves to a tyranny quite as evil, it was in large measure their loathing of fascism that led them to do so. I do not say that this justified or exonerated them; many crimes are really functions of our virtue, and often these are the most hideous of our crimes. But the fact remains that it was precisely when Communism appeared to be in militant opposition to totalitarianism that it attracted American intellectuals; the point at which they abandoned it was as a rule the point at which they discovered its totalitarian nature. If Mr. Viereck is looking for the group most susceptible to totalitarian lures, I think he would do better to look elsewhere —toward the business community, perhaps, and toward certain religious groups.

There is, of course, a kind of self-hatred among intellectuals that leads some of them to align themselves with organized social hatred. One could see some of this at work in the Communism of the thirties (as one can see it at work today when James Burnham makes allies of demagogues like Senator McCarthy) but I do not think it was the significant aspect of that movement, and I feel certain that Mr. Viereck is doing an injustice both to the truth and to the community of which he is so distinguished a member when he implies that it was.

II

Mr. Viereck acknowledges several times that Communism is no longer much of a force among American intellectuals, but he insists that "they have still not rejected . . . the most successful communist hoax ever perpetrated: the confusion of criminal deeds with free thought. . . ." And he speaks of "the literary defenders of Hiss, Coplon, Fuchs, and the eleven convicted Communist leaders" as though there exists some school or sizable bloc of writers that can be thus characterized.

Now to the best of my knowledge these people have no "literary defenders." Outside the Communist press, which isn't literary and very often isn't even literate, there have been no defenses of any of them in their roles as Communist agents. I think that Mr. Viereck is confusing disapproval of the Smith Act under which the eleven Communists were convicted with admiration for their politics. In this he is very wrong. I happen myself to believe that the eleven were in fact convicted for what I would describe as a malevolent exercise of free speech and thought. But this does not make me one of their defenders, nor does it mean that I am confusing thoughts with deeds. Though I recognize the difficulty of making these distinctions, I rather think the confusion is on the side of the Smith Act.

I think, too, that Mr. Viereck is confusing disbelief in Hiss's guilt, which was widespread before the trial and persists in certain quarters today, with sympathy for the actions of which Hiss was accused and for which—putting aside the technicality of his conviction for perjury rather than for espionage—he is today in prison. Before the conviction of Alger Hiss, and to some extent after it, a number of American intellectuals, in the company of many non-intellectuals, refused to believe that Hiss was guilty as charged, and many of these people were, as John Dos Passos wrote in a passage cited by Mr. Viereck, parties to "the moral lynching of Whittaker Chambers." As one of those who felt from the start that Chambers was telling the essential truth and that Hiss was not, I agree with Mr. Dos Passos that the revealed inability of these people even to entertain the thought that Hiss might be guilty was shocking. For what most of them, knowing Hiss not as a man but merely as the symbol of a certain segment of American life, were really demonstrating, when they showed their hatred of Chambers and their disinclination to hear his story, was that they were smug in their own values and that their values got in the way of their understanding of evil.

But their inability to *believe* that Hiss could be a spy was a very different thing from *defending* him as a spy, and it is the kind of difference I am distressed to see Mr. Viereck ignoring. It was not because these people sympathized with Communist agents that they sympathized with Hiss; they sympathized with him because they thought he had been unjustly accused of being so loathsome a thing—and accused, as it happened, by a man who owned up to having been one. Their sin was a kind of spiritual pride. They felt that Hiss's virtue was as secure as their own because Hiss happened to be peculiarly one of their own. They saw Chambers not as an anti-Communist but as a Communist apostate, and it was as much his having once been a Communist as his current state of apostasy that turned them against him before they had weighed his testimony. A lot of people were taken in by a hoax in the Hiss case, but the hoax, I think, was that the things Hiss seemed to symbolize—the middle class, Harvard, Oliver Wendell Holmes, old-line law offices, soap, the Carnegie Foundation, and, above all, success—put him above reproach. It was not the destructive, revolutionary instincts that came prematurely to Hiss's defense but the bourgeois instincts.

III

In attempting to establish the high incidence of Communism among American intellectuals and to demonstrate Communist power, Mr. Viereck cites the fact that "Some 18 to 20 publishers, almost all the leading ones, turned down the best anti-Soviet satire of our time," which he identifies, rightly, I think, as George Orwell's *Animal Farm*. He goes on to say that "the most likely motive for these rejections" was the "brilliantly successful infiltration (then, not now) of Stalinoid sympathizers in the book world."

Mr. Viereck mentions precisely one instance in which Communist sympathy was unquestionably the explanation for the book's rejection. And I suppose it may have had something to do with its rejection by certain other publishers. (It was eventually published by Harcourt, Brace & Company and given immense circulation.) But I do not for one instant believe that it explained the action of the majority. I have a very vivid recollection of being told of the rejection of the book by the editor of a well-known publishing house, a man who to my knowledge regarded himself as a staunch anti-Communist. Indeed, one celebrated American writer had taken his work to this very editor because he suspected that his former publisher was under Communist influence. This paragon among editors boasted to me that while he personally enjoyed Orwell's book, he felt that it was distinctly in the national interest not to publish it at the time it was offered to him. He misconstrued the national interest, he misconstrued his responsibility as a publisher, he misconstrued democratic culture in general. But he was not and never had been a Communist or fellow traveler, and the instincts that were at work in his case, as in the case of so many who took the side of Alger Hiss, were profoundly bourgeois ones.

Mr. Viereck, constructing a whole new theory of the psychology of Communist intellectuals, tells us that their attitudes toward the United States grew out of their absorption in "nineteenth-century French novels." "They naturally know best the society they have studied best. . . . This is a society seen through the colored glasses of a literary (at first non-political) anti-bourgeois crusade." He goes on to speak of the "familiar blend of an 'aristocratic' snob in art and a fellow-traveling 'progressive' in politics," and he associates the attitudes of Henry Miller and Ezra Pound with those of the typical Communist intellectual.

Nothing, it seems to me, could be wider of the mark. The American intellectuals who fell hardest for Communism were men not of aristocratic tastes in art but of tastes at once conventional and execrable. Many of them, of course, had no literary tastes of any sort. The reading matter of Communists was the dreariest kind of journalism. If they read poetry at all, it was likely to be Whittier and Carl Sandburg, not Rimbaud and Ezra Pound. They read Jack London, not Flaubert, and even London was on the strong side for them. How Mr. Viereck can possibly associate aristocratic tastes with Communists and fellow travelers is beyond me, particularly when he seems so well aware of the fact that the cultural tone they set in the thirties—and there can be little doubt that they did set the cultural tone of that period—was deplorable because it was metallic and strident. Communist culture was not aristocratic; it was cheap and vulgar and corny.

Historically, the fact is that aristocratic tastes were a protection against the Communist fallacy. It was the people under the kind of influence Mr. Viereck describes who had least to do with Communism, and who, when they did become involved, made the earliest departures, while those with the minds of accountants lingered on. Compare the political record of Edmund Wilson with that of Howard Fast! I realize that Mr. Viereck could cite the arresting case of Whittaker Chambers, but if we are going to keep the record straight we must realize that Chambers was a special case. He became a Communist at a time when there were very few intellectuals in the movement. The big influx came in the thirties, at a time when Communism represented itself as a far less revolutionary doctrine than in Chambers's day and when it appeared to many as a reliable enemy of fascism. How bitterly they were mistaken most of them now know, and I should not be surprised if some of them have been aided in finding their error by those great French novels which Mr. Viereck seems to be saying led them to the heresy in the first place.

IV

There is unquestionably a great deal to be said, a very great deal more than I have attempted to say here, about the affair that many American intellectuals had with Communism in the thirties and forties. I am sure Mr. Viereck himself can contribute to our understanding of the whole melancholy affair. But I think that in this instance the very onesidedness of his argument contributes to our misunderstanding. By oversimplifying the issue he obscures one of the most important aspects of the totalitarian menace, that power has its own logic, and that in many of its manifestations totalitarianism is characterized not so much by its dependence on intellectuals as by its very anti-intellectualism, by the struggle for power at any price. Mr. Viereck prefaces the article with the observation of the late John Maynard Keynes that "Madmen in authority, who hear voices in the air, are distilling their frenzy from some academic scribbler of a few years back." But Lord Keynes's remark applies to some demagogues and not to others. The Communist movement owes a clear and heavy debt to intellectuals, but how about the fascist movement? One could, of course, draw up a list of Hitler's and Mussolini's obligations, certain of which would be to Marx and Lenin, but I doubt very much if the prophets of fascism were in any real sense necessary to the movement. Hitler and Mussolini were themselves scribblers, and even if I am wrong in suspecting that they distilled most of their own frenzies, their ideas were simple enough and rude enough to have been generated in their own rude minds in the event that this had been necessary. ("The statesman is an easy man/He tells his lies by rote"—Yeats.)

And if a writer or a professor stands at the shoulder of every madman in authority, where are the mentors of a man like Senator McCarthy? Regrettably, Senator McCarthy comes by a certain amount of the misinformation he spreads through people who qualify or once qualified as intellectuals, but what few ideas he has appear to be strictly his own. The case of Stalin is also instructive. Stalin has recently composed an essay—the eagerness of tyrants to *be* scribblers is quite a phenomenon in itself—that is full of political ideas and analyses, but these, apparently, do not grow out of any reasonable or even unreasonable reading of the sacred texts of Marxism. They seem to grow, on the contrary, directly from the strategic requirements of the situation in which he finds himself at the moment. And this, I think, is where tyrants get most of their ideas. They may plagiarize their betters out of vanity; they may conceal the evils they propose in the language of philosophy; they may indeed be greatly aided by ideas and may manipulate them to secure advantages of power. But, by and large, power has its own logic, which is well within the grasp of even the most sluggish of intellects, and it is a misreading of history to suppose that because some disasters have been abetted by *la trahison des clercs,* all disasters can be understood by some doctrine of *cherchez le clerc.*

EXERCISES

1. Mr. Rovere deals with several of Viereck's assertions. List these assertions, then restate what Rovere says about each.
2. Is Mr. Rovere more precise in identifying the sort of person who became Communists than Viereck is?
3. Does Mr. Rovere give any evidence for his assertion that the "business community" and "certain religious groups" prefer totalitarianism to democracy? Are the phrases "business community" and "certain religious groups" loose definitions?
4. Which article, Viereck's or Rovere's, would be easier to outline? Is there any connection between the ease with which an article can be outlined and its cogency?

C | American Literature and Its Influence Abroad

Fr. Raymond L. Bruckberger, O.P., FRENCH FICTION AND AMERICAN REALITY

Life, WANTED: AN AMERICAN NOVEL

Robert Penn Warren, A LESSON READ IN AMERICAN BOOKS

Ruth Nelson Myers, NOTES ON READING AMERICAN LITERATURE ABROAD

Taken together these articles show that different points of view can contribute much to a thoughtful discussion of a serious problem. Father Bruckberger, in the first article, regrets that contemporary American writers have done nothing to correct the harsh and negative image of America that Frenchmen have gotten from French writers of the nineteenth century. But while he asks for a more affirmative American literature he admits that "the honor of a true literature lies in that it never allows itself to be domesticated to the level of propaganda." He thus poses what Robert Penn Warren later calls "a vexed and vexing" question. The *Life* editorial also asks for a more affirmative American literature. While the editor upholds the value of a literature which reflects its period and praises *The Great Gatsby* and *The Grapes of Wrath* for having done so, he maintains that contemporary writers continue to write critically of our time as though we were still living during the depression, that they overlook the positive and hopeful aspects of American life.

Robert Penn Warren answers both Father Bruckberger and *Life*. He points to the paradox that in the long run "the literature that is most truly and profoundly critical is always the most profoundly affirmative." The strength of a democracy, of America, is precisely that it can afford self-criticism. Mrs. Myers, commenting on all three articles, remarks that in one respect they are all based on a mistaken assumption: namely, that foreigners gain their image of America from American literature. Referring to her personal experience in teaching American literature abroad, she maintains that the foreign view of America is largely based on newspaper stories, on American movies and music, and on such magazines as *Life*.

1 FRENCH FICTION AND AMERICAN REALITY

by Fr. Raymond Leopold Bruckberger, O.P.

Raymond Leopold Bruckberger (1907–) is a French Dominican. He has been called "perhaps the most uncloistered priest since Richelieu." During World War II, Father Bruckberger fought with the Resistance. An American serving with General LeClerc's Free French Infantry describes encountering Father Bruckberger in Paris in August 1944.[1] *He was to have met members of the underground at an appointed rendezvous. Instead, he found three strangers, one a priest "in full clerical costume. He was crouched at a window, firing a machine pistol at the Nazi troops and Petain militiamen in the street below." It was Father Bruckberger. Earlier he had served with the Foreign Legion and a group of Commandos. He was twice awarded the Croix de guerre. But Father Bruckberger's wide European reputation rests on his intellectual achievements. He has been editor of* Le Cheval de Troie, *and is best known as the author of* The Seven Miracles of Gubbio *and* One Sky to Share. *In recent years, Father Bruckberger has lived and traveled in the United States; he plans to write a large-scale book on American life and culture.*

Young people do not have the same amusements in every country. Sports do not have the same importance in France as in America—unless we consider literature as a sport and unless reading novels might advantageously

[1] *Harper's Magazine*, February, 1956.

replace attendance at baseball games. Poe and Melville do not have the same avid following in America as Balzac and Stendhal do in France. We should rather need to compare Balzac and Stendhal with the New York Yankees or the Brooklyn Dodgers. In France, the young read Balzac and Stendhal as eagerly as their American counterparts follow the world series on television. Baseball is after all an innocent diversion which harms nobody. The same thing cannot always be said of literature and novels. One of the greatest present obstacles to Franco-American understanding is possibly the tradition of the French novel.

French writers have always been keenly interested in America. For a long time, from Montaigne to Chateaubriand, they wrote of her with affectionate enthusiasm. But from Stendhal's day to the present time a different current has been all-powerful in French literature, a current of increasing scorn. Certainly, there is also a current of sympathetic interest for America, but it is infinitely less powerful and it is borne on names with infinitely less prestige.

In "The Charterhouse of Parma," published in 1839, there is the following brief conversation:

> Fabrice spoke of going to New York, of becoming a citizen and a soldier in America. . . .
>
> " 'You are making a grave mistake. You will not find a war, and you will tumble once more into a life of frivolity, only this time without elegance, or music, or romance,' answered the Duchess. 'Believe me, for you as for me, life in America would be a sad thing.'
>
> "She explained the worship of the almighty dollar and the respect one must show to ordinary artisans, who make all decisions by means of their votes."

Little reflection is needed to understand why Stendhal did not love America. His essentially aristocratic concept of life was completely opposed to American democracy. Besides, his purely egoistic preoccupation with heroism and hedonistic pleasure—heroism being another kind of pleasure, the most delectable of all—is far from the American ideal, which is essentially altruistic and which emphasizes virtue to the point of puritanism. If we must make a choice between America and Stendhal, let us choose America, as more human and more free, even though we must admit that she lacks the touch of elegance. And let us not regret the choice.

At about the same time, from a source of French literature whose concept was totally different, appeared a new and extremely severe condemnation of America. At the end of "The Village Rector," one of Balzac's characters just returned from America speaks these untender words:

> If I had remained another day in that horrible New York, or in the United States, where there is neither hope, nor faith, nor charity, I should have died

without being sick. The air I breathed gave me a pain in my chest; the food ceased to nourish me. I was dying although I seemed full of life and health. My suffering ceased as soon as I set foot on the vessel. I thought I was in France. . . .

Life in America was a sad thing. It offered none of the keen pleasures dear to the heroes of Stendhal. And then Balzac painted that life as horrible from the standpoint of the life of the soul, asking what could possibly be of further interest in America, "that land of money and selfishness, where souls are cold."

We can put to one side the question of the rule of the dollar that both Balzac and Stendhal enjoyed criticizing so sharply. Actually, man is man wherever you find him. It would be astonishing not to find, in America as elsewhere, men who passionately love money for its own sake. Still, there are those who find it annoying to think that in the last few years the frontiers of the dollar kingdom have been extended beyond the frontiers of the United States as far as Western Europe. But anyone who is well acquainted with both the French and Americans will make no bones about admitting that generally speaking the Frenchman is infinitely more avaricious than the American. French literature itself bears witness.

What is more serious is the depiction of America as a land of selfishness, a land without virtue. Some civilizations, like those of the Renaissance, were founded on the ideal of enjoyment. Others, like those of Sparta and ancient republican Rome, were based on virtue. Stendhal says that American society offers no enjoyment, Balzac that it offers no virtue. Such a society is therefore not civilized at all. Such a society is pure barbarism; and that men should stifle in it is not surprising. That is the picture of America that a young Frenchman may paint for himself as he reads two of the greatest French novelists.

In the twentieth century the caricature was to be pushed still further. To the scorn already inspired by America, a great contemporary novelist has added terror and a kind of consecrated horror. In 1931, thirteen years after the end of World War I, Bernanos wrote at the end of his "La Grande Peur des Bien-Pensants":

At the rate the world is going, it will not be long before giant planes shall have dropped bombs weighing a thousand kilograms, as if they were flowers. . . . And people will say of our war, of our famous war to end war: "Those were the good old days." And, my lads, after the one or two ton bomb, you will see something else, you will see something worse. You will find out what a certain kind of Peace is like. Not the peace that Lenin dimly saw as he lay dying, one eye open, the other closed, on his cot in the depths of his hideous mansard in the Kremlin. The peace that you will see may even now exist in the imagination of some little Yankee bootblack, half Anglo-Saxon, half Jew, a marmot with a rat's head, with Heaven knows what taint from a Negro ancestor hiding in his infuriated marrow; the future Steel King, Rubber King, Oil King; the Trustee of Trusts; the future master of a standardized planet, the god that the universe awaits, the god of a godless universe.

Then Bernanos, still addressing the youth of France, adds this frenzied prophecy, this battle cry, this call to the anti-American crusade:

> Between that Yankee emperor of the future, that god with horn rims and gold teeth, and his long coveted prey, the immense and fragile universe, there lies nothing now but the rampart of your hearts. . . .

We may still shrug and pass on. But neither Stendhal nor Balzac nor Bernanos were Communists. Quite the contrary. They were not pulling chestnuts out of the fire for Soviet propaganda against America; they believed what they wrote. They are read and reread by the youth in France, which absorbs not only their genius but their prejudices; which considers them not only masters of style but masters of thought. One may certainly say that the injustice of their accusations is manifest, and that it can be excused—if it can be—only because none of the three had even set foot on the territory of the United States.

Nevertheless, their accusations are still alive and are still making a profound impression. They help us to understand the panic that shook Western Europe at the news that America, after the atom bomb, possessed in the hydrogen bomb a weapon of unimaginable destruction. On this point, at least, Bernanos' prophecy was not false. Coming as it did twenty-four years before the event, it is of extraordinary force. But it is clear that his prophecy is not likely to reassure the French or to produce a favorable climate for American leadership in Western Europe.

Actually, what I have quoted shows to what extent American leadership has gone astray since the end of the war because of its blithe ignorance of the real feelings of Europe about America. How has American leadership principally expressed itself? By massive financial aid, which has only confirmed Europeans in their simplistic notion that America is the kingdom of the dollar god. And by a crushing military potential, supported earlier by the atom bomb and now by the hydrogen bomb, which has only confirmed Europeans in their no less simplistic notion that the destiny of our planet is henceforth at the mercy of the caprice of a barbarian race which possesses neither virtue nor humanity, and which lacks, besides, any sense whatever of the divine. Why would they not be terrified of a destructive omnipotence given into the hands of a people "without elegance, or music or romance"—"with neither faith, nor hope, nor charity," a people dreaming a future domination of "a godless universe"?

It is possible to dismiss such words as nothing more than outbursts from men who wrote fiction. Unfortunately, novelists in France have an unequaled power over opinion. In the time of Stendhal and Balzac, Tocqueville was writing his admirable book on American democracy. Tocqueville is hardly read at all in France. Stendhal is still a best seller, as are Balzac and Bernanos. To counter-balance such influence as theirs, we need other novels and other novelists, closer to America and more appreciative of her. It is true that Giraudoux and Blaise Cendrars, who have both visited the United States, have done something in the right direction.

But it is the honor and the responsibility of American novelists, above all, to make their country better known and loved. The times seem favorable. In the last twenty years, the great American novels have become best sellers in France, read as much as and sometimes more than French novels. Alas, what has happened is that those novels have only confirmed the shabby conception that the French already have of America. How many of the French are today basing their judgment of American society on "The Grapes of Wrath" and "The Air Conditioned Nightmare"?

Don't misunderstand me, I do not reproach American novelists for having written books that sometimes give a cruel vision of America. The honor of a true literature lies in that it never allows itself to be domesticated to the level of propaganda. The mission of a true literature has always been to create and sustain a great quarrel within the national conscience. I am only pointing out a fact. The French find in their own literature a terribly denunciatory image of America. What has happened is that some of the great American novelists widely read in France have accentuated the impression instead of correcting it.

At this point rises the question of the novelist's responsibility to his own country and the status of his country in the world. Is it right that the great flowering of the American novel should hamper rather than promote America's leadership of the free world? In general, contemporary French novelists clearly understand that they have a responsibility toward their country. Bernanos, Montherland, Mauriac, Malraux, Sartre, Camus, have all taken political positions and have supported them in their books. In a general way, American novelists are much more reserved. Perhaps it is they who are right from the standpoint of a pure literary function; but their foreign public, which reads them assiduously, remains, by their neglect of responsibility, in the same errors, the same prejudices, the same calumnies against America, in a time when it is extremely important that America be known and loved for what she really is.

America is not simply a blind financial and military power, as she is represented. If her leadership is not to fail, it must be founded on the higher values that she possesses in profusion. These things must some day be said to the world. And who can say them better than those Americans who have already gained by means of their admirable novels, a hearing in the world?

EXERCISES

1. Does Father Bruckberger agree with those French authors who find America vulgar and lacking in culture? Does he agree that Americans are more concerned with the dollar and with materialistic pursuits than Frenchmen are?
2. Look up the following: Balzac, Stendhal, Mauriac, Malraux, Sartre, and Camus in *Cassell's Encyclopedia of World Literature* (Funk and Wagnalls) or in some other reference work. If your French is good enough, look them up in *Petit Larousse.*
3. Is the title of the present article, "French Fiction and American Reality" a good title? What are your reasons?
4. What is Father Bruckberger's opinion about the stature of the modern American novel? What function does he see it playing for the American mind and conscience? And what function does he see it playing in the formation of French opinion about Americans and their capacity for world leadership?
5. Does Father Bruckberger suggest that American novelists should write a different sort of novel, one that would have a better effect as propaganda? Or is he suggesting that our novelists write propaganda pamphlets? Or does he leave the reader in doubt about which sort of writing he is asking for?
6. Look up the word *egalitarian* in your dictionary. Does Father Bruckberger imply that America is more egalitarian than France, at least nineteenth-century France?

2 WANTED: AN AMERICAN NOVEL

by the Editor of Life Magazine

Life Magazine, *with its sister magazines,* Time *and* Fortune, *is extremely influential. This editorial was written shortly after the publication of* The Man in the Gray Flannel Suit, *a novel which for a time figured prominently on the best-seller list. Taking this book as a starting point, the editorial goes on to plead for an "affirmative" literature.*

Sloan Wilson, a young writer whose first novel (*The Man in the Gray Flannel Suit*) is moving up best-seller lists, recently made a statement in defense of his book's happy ending which is worth repeating: "The world's treated me awfully well," he said, "and I guess it's crept into my work. . . . These are, we forget, pretty good times. Yet too many novelists are still writing as if we were back in the Depression years."

Wilson put his finger on a strange contradiction. Ours is the most powerful nation in the world. It has had a decade of unparalleled prosperity. It has gone further than any other society in the history of man toward creating a truly classless society. Yet it is still producing a literature which sounds sometimes as if it were written by an unemployed homosexual living in a packing-box shanty on the city dump while awaiting admission to the county poorhouse.

This is doubly strange because past American eras have produced art which faithfully mirrored their times; *The Great Gatsby* still speaks eloquently of Prohibition's frauds and deceits, *Main Street* of the high tide of provincial self-satisfaction, *The Grapes of Wrath* with a just anger for the unnecessary humiliations of Depression, while *Look Homeward, Angel* may well speak for a timeless America. But who speaks for America today? One might argue, with some plausibility, that the fearful indecisions of an atomic age keep a representative literature from being born, but when has life ever been secure? Atomic fear or not, the incredible accomplishments of our day are surely the raw stuff of saga.

Wilson's uneven book may be flimsy art but it is at least affirmative. Happily there are a few other signs of a trend away from degeneracy and negation. For example, Lionel Shapiro's *Sixth of June*, though it revolves about a triangle, is not resolved by adultery. Herman Wouk's *Marjorie Morningstar* is a mutiny, says *Time*, against "three decades of U.S. fiction dominated by skeptical criticism, sexual emancipation, social protest and psychoanaltyical sermonizing." Wouk's book even endorses premarital chastity. And there is visible in other work what Critic Maxwell Geismar calls "a return to the security of a religious universe."

A change is needed. Nobody wants Pollyanna literature. Poets have always had what Robert Frost admits is "a vested interest in human misery"; agony begets art. Maybe art mistrusts prosperity. But at least the breeches-busting Paul Bunyan of the U.S. today seems to deserve better literature than the papaya-smelly, overripe school of the Truman Copotes, or the obscenity-obsessed school of "new realism" exemplified by a parade of war novels which mostly read like the diary of a professional grievance collector with a dirty mind and total recall. James Gould Cozzens' *Guard of Honor* was one of the few military novels that rang true with dignity. In most of the others the enemy is not the one shooting at us but our own officers and Army.

Europeans are already prejudiced against America by savage animadversions in their own classics against our "vulgar" democracy ("If I had remained another day in that horrible . . . United States, where there is neither hope nor faith, nor charity," wrote Balzac, "I should have died without being sick"). Small wonder that our own selfdepreciation helps them enlarge the evil image to that which France's Michel Mohrt describes in his new study of American novels: "a hypocritical society based on the power of money, racial prejudice, sexual taboos. Exile, alcohol, suicide seem the only escape." Such a onetime exile, Henry (*Tropic of Cancer*) Miller, puts it more savagely in the current *Chicago Review*. The American seen through the eyes of our leading writers, he asserts, is "a digit in machine-made formulas . . . he has neither face nor name but is shuffled about like the victim of a soulless society on an electronic chessboard operated by a dummy hidden in the cells of a publisher's diseased brain. . . ." The writing, he adds, "reeks of embalming fluid."

It is understandable that American groups which feel the most isolated should produce the most anguished writing, and that so much of it should come from the South. Its ante bellum slave society was in some ways similar to the feudal Russian system whose injustices and tensions produced a Dostoevski and a Tolstoi. William Faulkner has a patent kinship with Dostoevski and his preoccupation with guilt. But Faulkner, for all his enormous gifts, can be searched in vain for that quality of redemption, through love and brotherhood, which always shines amid Dostoevski's horrors. It shines also amid the worst havoc of Tolstoi's overturned world (Moscow, too, was burned, even if not by Sherman).

To find this redeeming quality of spiritual purpose today's reader must turn not to novels but to nonfiction like Russell Davenport's *The Dignity of Man* or to the British book, *The Conquest of Everest*. That conquest held a deeper meaning than the achievement. The European Hillary and the Asian Tenzing are a hopeful symbol for a wider brotherhood yet to be achieved. Their final triumph expresses the unquenchable reaching of man's soul for a truth higher than reality, for a good better than himself, the qualities which modern literature so often deny. In every healthy man there is a wisdom deeper than his conscious mind, reaching beyond memory to the primeval rivers, a yea-saying to the goodness and joy of life. This is what is most missing from our hothouse literature—the joy of life itself.

EXERCISES

1. Write either an editorial in agreement or disagreement with the *Life* editorial or a letter to the editor, saying why you agree or disagree with the *Life* editorial.

2. Identify *The Great Gatsby, Main Street, The Grapes of Wrath,* and *Look Homeward Angel.* On the basis of reviews and other references (or your having read the novels), would you say these are "affirmative" books? Are they also critical?

3. Examine the *Book Review Digest* to see what sort of reviews were given to Shapiro's *Sixth of June* and Wouk's *Marjorie Morningstar.* Does it seem likely that either of these books will be of lasting literary interest?

3 A LESSON READ IN AMERICAN BOOKS

by Robert Penn Warren

Robert Penn Warren (1905–) was born in Kentucky and attended Vanderbilt University. He was part of the group that contributed to a "little magazine," The Fugitive *and later gained a national reputation as "the Agrarians." With Cleanth Brooks, Warren edited* The Southern Review *and collaborated on a number or texts widely used in colleges and universities. Warren has earned a high place in American literature as a critic, poet, and novelist. His books include* All the King's Men, World Enough and Time, Brother to Dragons, *and* Promises.

Once upon a time there was a nation, which we shall call X. At the time of which we write this nation stood at a moment of great power and great promise. A few generations earlier it had concluded a long and bloody civil war to achieve unity. More recently, in that unity, it had won a crashing victory over foreign foes. It had undergone, and was undergoing, a social revolution; there was unparalleled prosperity, a relaxing of old sanctions and prejudices, a widening of opportunity for all classes, great rewards for energy and intelligence. Its flag was on strange seas; its power was felt in the world. It was, even, producing a famous literature.

But—and here is the strange thing in that moment of energy and optimism—a large part, the most famous part, of that literature exhibited violence, degradation and despair as part of the human condition: Tales of the old time of the civil war, tales of lust and horror, brother pimping for sister, father lusting for daughter, a head of the state doting on a fair youth, an old man's eyes plucked out, another old man killed in his sleep, friendship betrayed, obligations foregone, good men cursing the gods, and the whole scene drenched in blood. Foreigners encountering this literature might well conclude that the Land of X was peopled by degenerates sadly lacking in taste, manners and principle.

This is England, Elizabethan England, that we are talking about, and not the United States in this year of Our Lord and the Great Prosperity. But *mutatis mutandis,* and with proper recognition of the fact that we can scarcely claim a William Shakespeare, only John Fords and John

Websters, we can talk about the United States in this connection, and join in conversation with Father Bruckberger, who has lately appeared in these pages, and with the editorial writer of *Life Magazine* for September 12.

These writers are concerned, as we must all be concerned, with America's image in the eyes of the world. "Is it right," asks Father Bruckberger, a sympathetic Frenchman visiting our shores, "that the great flowering of the American novel should hamper . . . America's leadership of the free world?" And the editorial writer in *Life*: "Europeans are already prejudiced against America by savage animadversions in their own classics against our 'vulgar' democracy. . . . Small wonder that our own self-depreciation helps them enlarge the evil image. . . ."

These two quotations raise a question, vexed and vexing, a question already old, no doubt, when the Greeks worried about it: how should esthetic value be related to prudential considerations? Presumably some of our literature has esthetic value (Father Bruckberger handsomely calls it a "flowering"), but it confirms some Europeans in their inherited low opinion of America, the country of "the almighty dollar," and of "respect to ordinary artisans," as Stendhal puts it, and the "land of money and selfishness, where souls are cold," as Balzac puts it. What do we do, then, when esthetic value is in conflict, or in apparent conflict, with political values?

Father Bruckberger does not undertake to answer this for us. On the one hand, he says that the "honor" of a literature is that it creates and sustains "a great quarrel within the national consciousness." But on the other hand, he bewails the effect abroad of this very quarrel within our national consciousness. Certainly, he is too informed to attempt to resolve the difficulty along the lines laid down by the editorial writer in *Life*, who, with certain ritualistic reservations, says that because America is now enjoying a boom, our literature should be optimistic, and applauds the current success of "The Man in the Gray Flannel Suit" because, though "flimsy art," it is "at least affirmative."

In fact, the editorial writer of *Life* takes as his golden text a quotation from Sloan Wilson, the author of "The Man in the Gray Flannel Suit": "The world's treated me awfully well, and I guess it's crept into my work. . . . These are, we forget, pretty good times. Yet too many novelists are still writing as if we were back in the Depression years."

Though I have not yet read "The Man in the Gray Flannel Suit," I should venture to doubt that the world is going to treat its author quite as well as it has treated Ernest Hemingway, William Faulkner, Theodore Dreiser, Sinclair Lewis, T. S. Eliot, Robert Frost, and quite a few other American writers who never found such a ready equation between bank balance and philosophy. What is really at stake in this is a question of freedom. If the creative act is of any value it is, in its special way, an act of freedom. It is, of course, conditioned by a thousand factors, but study of its conditions—economic, biologic, or whatever—has yet to reveal the secret of how that new intuition, the truly created object whose newness is the mark of freedom, comes to be. But Mr. Wilson, and presumably the approving editorial writer in *Life*, would deny this freedom, would, in fact, go even farther than Karl Marx in asserting the economic determinism of literature. If you are not making dough, you will not be a booster. Literature is a reflex of the stock market.

The philosopers of the Age of Conformism grant, however, that criticism was once all right, long back. As the *Life* editorial puts it: " 'The Great Gatsby' still speaks eloquently of Prohibition's frauds and deceits, 'Main Street' of the high tide of provincial self-satisfaction, 'The Grapes of Wrath' with a just anger for the unnecessary humiliations of Depression. . . ." But criticism isn't all right in this day and time, for there is nothing really wrong now to be criticized, and anybody who is critical, who isn't "affirmative," is a fool or knave, a traitor or a sexual deviant, or a failure. May we not, however, in some chill hour between dark and dawn, have the thought that our own age may—just possibly—have its own frauds and deceits, deeper and more ambiguous than those anatomized in "The Great Gatsby," that though this is not the age of provincial self-satisfaction, it may be the age of national self-righteousness and require a sharper scalpel than even "Main Street," and that Divine Providence has given no written guarantee that it will not rebuke the smuggery of the Great Boom?

I do not think that the novel has yet been written to anatomize adequately this moment of our history, and I share the distaste of the editorial writer in *Life* for some of the works he alludes to, but the "American novel" which we should call for would not be less, but more, critical than those now current. At the same time I should hope that the literature to come will be more "affirmative," to use the word of the editorial. But the paradox here is that the literature that is most truly and profoundly critical is always the most profoundly affirmative.

In so far as a literature struggles to engage the deep, inner issues of life, the more will that literature be critical—the more, that is, will it engender impatience with the compromises, the ennui, the materialism, the self-deception, the complacency, and the secret, unnamable despairs that mark so much of ordinary life. Such a critical literature is at the same time affirmative because it affirms the will and courage to engage life at fundamental levels: the rock, if struck hard enough, will give forth the living waters.

The editorial in *Life* would not, I suppose, find these kinds of affirmation significant. He is concerned with doctrine, more or less explicitly put. But sometimes, even when doctrine is explicitly put, he has not, cannot, or does not, read it. Faulkner, he says, "for all his enormous gifts, can be searched in vain for that quality of redemption, through love and brotherhood, which always shines amid Dostoevsky's horrors." That very redemption, and its cost, is a recurrent theme of Faulkner's work. There is, for example, "The Bear," with old Ike's vision of man's place in creation: God created man to hold suzerainty over the earth in His name, "not to hold for himself and his descendants' inviolable title forever, generation after generation, to the oblongs and squares of the earth, but to hold the earth mutual and intact in the communal anonymity of brotherhood, and all the fee He asked was pity and humility and sufferance and endurance and the sweat of his face for bread."

But let us go back where we started: the bad political impression which some of our literature presumably gives abroad. What are we to do? If we can't get writers to write the kind of literature we think useful for foreign consumption—if there really isn't such a thing as literature to specification—what then?

The answer is, I think, simple—and appalling. We must trust in our humility, and in our strength.

We must trust in our humility, because only by humility, the recognition that we have not fulfilled our best possibilities, can we hope to fulfill those possibilities. Some day, far-called, our navies may melt away, and on that day we may need the wisdom of ultimate humility. Meanwhile, in our moment of strength we hope that our strength is more than a historical accident, an index of the weakness of others. We hope that it has a moral grounding. But if that hope is to be more than a hope, it must be subjected to the test of conscience, and literature is one of the voices of our national conscience, however faltering and defective that voice may sometimes be. We must rebuke our hubris, not out of fear, but from love of a truth that we hope is within us.

We must trust in our strength, because only the strong can afford the luxury of radical self-criticism. Only if we believe in our strength can we take the risks of our full political and cultural development, with all the disintegrative and paradoxical possibilities in that dialectic. We should trust our strength, because America has a secret weapon, if we choose to use it: the weapon of not having a secret. It is the weapon of radical self-criticism—radical in the non-political and literal sense of the word. There was an old name for this, a name not often now used in this connection. That name was democracy.

So much for ourselves. But what of those poor foreigners who are so readily deceived by our literature? Are they, in the long run, quite so trapped in their prejudice, quite so incapable of the imaginative act, as Father Bruckberger seems to think? If so, why do they find our literature so fascinating, and why do they honor it? Can it be that, in a measure, they find in it a vital image of man, and some comment on his condition? Do they find in it, in the very fact of its existence, some mark of freedom?

I shall tell a story. A little while after the war in Europe I became acquainted with a young Italian who, in the first year of the war, as an officer in the Fascist Army, had deserted and taken to the mountains, to fight on our side. I once asked him what led him to this drastic step. He replied that American novelists had converted him. How, I asked. "Well," he said, "the Fascists used to let us read American fiction because it gave, they thought, a picture of a decadent America. They thought it was good propaganda for fascism to let us read Dreiser, Faulkner, Sinclair Lewis. But you know, it suddenly occurred to me that if democracy could allow that kind of criticism of itself, it must be very strong and good. So I took to the mountains."

EXERCISES

1. What is the meaning of the title, "A Lesson Read in American Books"?
2. What country did Warren seem to be talking about in his first two paragraphs? Would you call this opening a rhetorical device? Does it seem to you to be an effective opening? Why?
3. Warren employs a number of ironic phrases. Point out some of them. Does this cause you to feel that Warren is "sarcastic"? Or would you say his ironies give a firmer intellectual tone to his writing?
4. In what part of your dictionary will you find the phrase "mutatis mutandis"? What does it mean?
5. Does Warren believe that we cannot do anything about the misunderstandings caused by our novels when they are read abroad? Does he believe that all foreign readers misunderstand us because of our fiction? If not, does he have any suggestions about minimizing the misunderstanding that does occur?
6. What does Mr. Warren mean by the "economic determinism" of literature? Does he say that a writer's economic position has nothing whatsoever to do with his attitudes? Does he say it can have something to do with his attitudes, but that it is not the sole factor?
7. Which of the arguments you have read, the *Life* editorial, Father Bruckberger's article, or Mr. Warren's article, seems to you to be most cogently argued? Give your reasons.

4 | NOTES ON READING AMERICAN LITERATURE ABROAD

by Ruth N. Myers

Mrs. Ruth Nelson Myers (1905–) was born in Texas and received degrees from the University of Texas, the University of Oregon, and Columbia University. Mrs. Myers has worked in a number of libraries including the Yale University library and the New York Public Library. She is currently teaching at New Haven State Teachers College. In 1950–51, she was a Fulbright lecturer at Pierce College in Athens and in 1955–56, exchange professor at Hiroshima University in Japan. Mrs. Myers has published poetry in a number of magazines and was awarded the Yale Cook Poetry Prize for 1943–44.

Why don't Americans write nice, cheerful novels, plays and poems that reflect "the American way of life"? Why are current American novels full of insanity, violence, depravity, lust, and degradation when life in America is on the whole, if not sane and tame entirely, at least rather far from the distortions presented in American literature? The question which has often been asked by teachers and librarians making up reading lists and worrying about the effect of current literature on the young, has recently been raised again in *Life*, in the *Saturday Review*, in *Harper's*, and in *The New York Times Book Review.*

The cause of the present concern is now international. What will the rest of the world think of America if they judge us by what goes on in our novels, plays, and poems? How can the rest of the world trust and form alliance with or look for leadership from a nation such as we appear to be, not in the pages of unsympathetic visitors, but as we reveal ourselves in our own literature? *Life* says in effect that our literature may be bad for American prestige abroad and our writers ought to be more cheerful, more American, and above all concerned with the image of the United States in the eyes of the world.

One can imagine Mr. Dulles' embarrassment in the scene we are about to imagine. Mr. Dulles is standing on a brink before the eyes of the world. He is about to arbitrate some delicate and crucial matter when there is a commotion, and the eyes of the world are focused on the noisy entrance of this confused troup—Popeye, Maggie, Lonnie, Anna Christie, Sister Carrie, Blanche DuBois, Studs Lonigan, the characters from *Death of a Salesman, Winesburg, Ohio,* and *Tobacco Road,* who march around a prickly pear rattling a few dry bones. Babbitt gives every one a big smile and an American flag to wave while they all sing "America I love You," words by e e cummings. Quick fadeout as Nick Adams rushes on shouting, "Boys, I've made a separate peace."

For a number of years, first as a librarian and then as a teacher of undergraduate courses in Book Selection and in twentieth-century literature, I too have been concerned when the question of esthetic values in conflict with political values, or moral values, or religious values, or local values has raised its complex head—which was just about every day. In addition, on two occasions I have had the opportunity of reading American literature with foreign students, five years ago as a Fulbright teacher in Greece and this year as an exchange professor at Hiroshima University.

From this experience, I should like to agree in part with Robert Penn Warren's article (*NYTBR,* 11 Dec. 1955), disagree a little here and there, and try to indicate why the whole matter, much more complex than the length or purpose of Mr. Warren's article allowed him to indicate, is far from hopeless.

My first point is rather negative but important. Perhaps unfortunately, our writers do not have as much influence on foreign opinion as many believe, or wish, them to have. News from the U. S. as reported in the local papers, what other Asians say about us, the movies, our music, sports, comics, the radio, and especially the advertisements in any of our magazines and the pictures in *Life,* all have much greater influence than our literature, i.e., reach a wider and less sophisticated audience, and reach it emotionally and very quickly. What is reported as going on at a trial in Mississippi or on the Alabama campus has an immediate impact that makes that of *Native Son* or *Tobacco Road* seem practically nonexistent. Our music and sports are much admired and copied; our movies are popular but not understood. As one of my best students told me, "I do not understand the movies, but I go to learn the English and the strange love." Certainly, the picture of American life as pieced together by the Greek girls from the advertisements in our magazines was ridiculous and misleading; and if *Life* is really concerned about American prestige abroad, some of its own pictorial shenanigans might well give them pause.

My second point I do not expect to be believed, and I still find it very shocking. Many students do not know whether a writer is an American or an Englishman. Frequently the books in English in a school or college library are shelved together (there are always many more English authors and publications than American), the departments are called English language and literature, and the courses present English and American works together; so *Life* really has an international job on its hands and will have to talk our English cousins into presenting the American way of life in the interest of American prestige abroad.

Moreover, many of the students do not have a clear idea of the period or date of any author. To a certain extent this is true of undergraduates in the United States, but the situation is further complicated abroad by translation dates or edition dates which the student accepts as the date of composition. Any recent gloom or glee is mixed and diluted by writers from the past who are mistaken for modern or current.

Actually, in some ways the older the literature, the easier and therefore the more popular it is with some students. The big, formal words and archaic expressions are rather well set forth in the dictionaries; the slang, the ellipses, the informal usage that so much of our current writing makes use of are not treated as well in the dictionaries and are practically impossible for the student to master. In addition, in Japan there is a feeling and veneration for antiquity—the older the writer the better. So many graduate students write theses on Chaucer, Spenser, or the minor Elizabethans. Of course, our modern literature may be read in translation, but I have reason to believe many of the translations are rather strange.

But enough of this. Let us suppose that our student can read, and that he knows his writer's nationality and date. His task is still difficult and the result is uncertain.

Mr. Warren tells a story of a young fascist officer who was converted to our side by reading American novels (Dreiser, Faulkner, Lewis) since it occurred to him that "if democracy could allow that kind of criticism of itself, it must be very strong and good."

I believe this story. It touches me and gives me hope. It also reminds me of some other stories which are also true. Five years ago the favorite reading of the average Greek girl in my class was *Little Lord Fauntleroy, Uncle Tom's Cabin,* and translations of any novel by Ouida or Jules Verne. With this group I was assigned to read the short stories in the Modern Library collection. The only story they liked was "The Apple Tree," but they liked it very much, and it comforts me now to think that they think kindly of some American literature because of that fine American writer, John Galsworthy. Of course, we read several Hemingway stories and on the final examination, one of many optional questions was to discuss violence in Hemingway. One answer went: a story by Hemingway is a work of art; a work of art can have no violence; therefore, there is no violence in a Hemingway story.

An Armenian student read *The Grapes of Wrath* and a report on the American Public Library, published by the ALA. Both distressed her deeply. I discovered that reality to her was always judged 20–50% worse than what was stated in any book, fiction or non-fiction. If ALA said that

42% of the people in the United States had inadequate library service, then contrary to her previous opinion, there must be practically no library service in America; and most of the U. S. must be starving with the Okies.

In Japan I have worked with young men and women, juniors and seniors in the university, and again I have read modern short stories. No matter what we read, many of the students find fate, destiny, and nihilism. They find fate, destiny, nihilism so frequently and often in such unlikely places that I find fate, destiny, and nihilism in the eye of the beholder. Fate, destiny, and nihilism are also found in the notes of the Japanese editions of American literature text-books, and it is very difficult to get a Japanese student to question the notes of a text-book.

So, I would not count too heavily on having a foreign student "find in it [American literature] a vital image of man, and some comment on his condition . . . some mark of freedom. . . ." I would rather expect him to bring some critical formula, some personal experience, or some vague longing from the emotional climate of his class or society to bear where they were irrelevant or misleading. I could only be certain that I could not tell in advance what his reaction would be.

Just consider for a moment how much of our literature is Christian and how much of it concerns romantic love. Neither has validity in Japan, which is Buddhist if anything, and where marriages are still arranged. In a conversation class we were talking about the movie "East of Eden" which every one had found confusing. Two or three knew who Adam was, but no one knew who Cain and Abel were. I am now used to American students' not knowing who Ahab was, but I still believe the undergraduate at home would know Cain and Abel. Certainly, no tag, no allusion, no echo of the King James Version gives meaning to what is read in Japan. Or consider the differences in poetic and dramatic form between Japanese and American literature—or rather don't, or we'll never get on with this. But the chances for error of fact, taste, experience, and judgment are great in reading any foreign literature and the differences between Occident and Orient multiply the hazards.

Nevertheless, several of the Greek girls knew what literature was about. Probably Mr. Warren's young Italian did; several of my Japanese students do too. Not many, but there are a few—probably about the same proportion anywhere—who have sensitivity and responsiveness, who can understand, can grasp the meaning of the whole story and experience it aesthetically. This is, I believe, partly a matter of temperament and partly a matter of training. I do not think it has anything to do with democracy, with being a Japanese, with being an American, with the color of one's skin or one's political beliefs, although I have tried to show how these may keep one from understanding literature.

Moreover, the critics are quite correct in saying that most current American literature is not American, does not reflect the American way or the American character. It is a great art nevertheless, and a Senate investigation is not yet in order. It is, I believe, the beginning of a new world literature, and the few good students are citizens of that world.

Art has always been involved in making the individual or specific become the general or universal. For a long time the individual or specific and the national were practically synonymous: Athens, Rome, Florence, Venice were local habitations which were also national. After some of the countries became unified and too big, the artists used various classes of society for a "home land," specializing in upper class, middle class, the village, the cathedral towns, etc. Some later tried living in an ideological country, but the air was a bit dry and the soil not rich enough. The Irish have fared very well because their green island stayed small and individual.

The Americans, as transplanted Englishmen, Frenchmen, or whatever, at first fared rather badly as literary artists. It was partly as Cooper guessed that they needed a past, but even more they needed roots, perhaps a set of chains to dance in, certainly a feeling of belonging, of being at home. A hundred years ago we had a fine harvest, and then we began to have difficulty. Whitman was determined to be American and went around frantically clucking and calling the names of classes and masses, of rivers and mountains and towns, trying to get used to them, trying to make them his. Mark Twain took it a little more easily and succeeded in being the last great American writer; even he is sometimes called a local colorist. Henry James was intermittently very American, and it is logical that his characters in contact and conflict with European manners should be very much alive now that America is a world power and we are all so aware of the interplay of cultures. Of course, we have had writers who have written American books—i.e., have caught much of the American character in individual stories or books: Willa Cather several times, Thornton Wilder in *The Skin of Our Teeth* and partly in *Our Town*, Tennessee Williams in *Camino Real*, Ogden Nash. The examples may be a bit personal but the general idea is sound.

But after Mark Twain, no writers succeeded in being wholly American, because the country got too big and varied for any one heart to hold; and so we had a lot of local color writers, many of whom were very good. We have continued to have local-colorists who have become so very good indeed that they shoot right up to universal heights from the Mississippi mud and make no stop at a station called U. S. A. When any American other than a Southerner reads Faulkner, he reads him on a universal not on a national level.

All of this has coincided with a double movement throughout the world involving intense nationalism and internationalism. Seventy-seven countries are now in the U. N., many of them new and small. They will be producing a national literature before too long.

For better or worse, American art seems to have moved beyond this. To be sure, there *is* something very real that can be called "The American Character." It exists in the pages of the sociologists and to varying degrees in each American. For your amusement here is "The American Character" as recently compiled by one of my classes after they had been pushed unmercifully to go beyond "big and rich." None of it comes from the stories they had been studying. Some of them had read Commager and Mead; they did not know about Riesman. The American is good-natured, generous, gregarious, anti-authoritarian, "democratic and equalitarian by conviction if not by practice," hard-working, lucky, more intelligent than he seems, intensely practical and pragmatic, materialistic, ingenious, experimental, impatient, too honest, naive, unfamiliar with evil and fear (at least the Oriental versions of these), often informal or vulgar (this was not defined or discussed); his thinking is quantitative, his social consciousness is highly developed, but he is too individualistic and self-confident; he is humanitarian rather than religious (some thought him too religious); he is sure he is right; and above all he is optimistic.

The chief trouble with this list is that the generalizing has already been done. It may indicate something about national character, but it is certainly not art, even if you were to dress it in gray flannel or if you give it the glamor of Hollywood.

The virtue of literature is not that it is national or shows national character but that it does say something vital about the human situation in a way that gives pleasure. Much American literature, both old and new, does this. One may read it at home or abroad with pride. It's going to be all right, *Life* and *The New York Times Book Review*. It's going to be all right. Don't worry so. It's un-American.

EXERCISES

1. List the reasons Mrs. Myers gives in developing her thesis that American books have much less influence in creating a picture of American life for those abroad than do other factors.
2. Characterize the tone of Mrs. Myers' article.

V Creating a Unified Impression

Good writing, whether in the form of an essay, a story or a poem, creates a unified impression. The author's intention, his theme, permeates the piece—if not explicitly, at least implicitly. To achieve this, the writer must be clear about his intention, about what he wants to say. He must not lose his theme in a maze of irrelevancies, and if he digresses, he must do so consciously and with a purpose, returning to the central theme.

Theme is not identical with subject. Subject matter is the material discussed or described; theme is the writer's attitude toward the subject, his understanding and interpretation of it. Many writers have written about the same subject, for instance, about love, but they have differed in what they have said about it. The subject of Joseph Warren Beach's essay, "The Dirty Street," is the dirt and disorder that prevails in certain European cities. His theme is that there is a certain instinct for disorder that serves the "spirit of Life." F. Scott Fitzgerald, in the letters to his daughter, touches on several subjects. But whether he is teasing her, or talking about books, the underlying theme is the need to develop a set of worthwhile values.

Theme is the core of any piece of writing, no matter what mode of discourse the writer uses, exposition, argumentation, description, or narration. It is useful to distinguish these though they rarely appear in pure form. However, depending on the author's purpose, one form of discourse usually predominates within a piece. Exposition is used to convey information, either factual or interpretive, or both. For instance, "The Comic Strip in American Life" is primarily expository, though the author also introduces argumentation. Its theme is that there are significant clues to American life and values in our comic strips.

Argumentation, as we have seen in the preceding section, aims to convince and persuade by logic and cogency and often by an appeal to emotion. The theme is the writer's thesis, and is usually stated both at the beginning and end of the argument, while every point within the argument is meant to reinforce the central thesis.

Effective description appeals to the senses, and aims at allowing the reader to perceive something with the immediacy of direct experience, to see its color, shape, and life. The unifying function of theme is particularly important in description. This is well illustrated in William Faulkner's "Impressions of Japan." The series of scattered vignettes of Japanese life that Faulkner presents are bound together by his underlying intent, to show that the surface differences between Japanese and American life and customs are transcended by the common bonds of humanity. While mainly descriptive, this essay also includes narration.

Narration is the description of a sequence of events. It is usually concerned not only with surface action, with showing how one event passes into another, but also with explaining or at least hinting at the causes of this movement. The success of narration, as of other modes of discourse, depends on the author's ability to sustain his theme. Stephen Crane achieves this with great art in his "The Wreck of the *Commodore*," in which his narration of a series of events is bound together by the theme of the different reactions of individuals within a group toward a common disaster.

In the analysis of writing, pervasiveness of theme is referred to as unity. Of importance in the creation of a unified impression is the achievement of a predominating tone—an intellectual and emotional resonance which permeates the composition. The Perrin essay has a predominant tone of light humor, the Edman, an air of knowledgeability, the Faulkner, one of quiet reflectiveness.

But the achievement of unity is not all that is needed for an effective composition. Two other principles of organization, coherence and emphasis are of great importance. Coherence signifies the orderly and logical arrangement of the different elements which make up any composition. Each phase of the composition must develop logically into the next. It is possible for an account to have a high degree of unity but a lack of coherence. For instance, an accident victim might well give a unified account of what happened, but might, in the excitement, confuse the order of events—so that the listener or reader would have a unified impression of the person's reactions to the event but no clear understanding of how it actually happened.

A composition might, however, be both unified and coherent and still fail of its purpose because of improper emphasis. It is through his use of emphasis, the highlighting of some ideas and events and the subordination of others, that the writer establishes the significant elements of his theme, placing some in the foreground, some in the background. In effect it is through a skillful use of emphasis that he can most tellingly manifest his intention.

In evaluating a composition, whatever its form, all of the factors discussed should be kept in mind. There is the distinction between subject and theme. The effective writer is one who has clearly worked out his theme and knows what he wants to say. There are the four modes of discourse: exposition, argumentation, description, and narration. The writer selects that mode most suited to his purpose, often using more than one. In organizing his composition, he must strive to achieve unity and coherence and make dramatic use of emphasis. None of these qualities exists in and by itself; each has to be seen in relation to the other. The measure of a good writer is his control of all these elements and his ability to keep them in a proper relationship to each other.

1 LETTERS TO HIS DAUGHTER

by F. Scott Fitzgerald

F. Scott Fitzgerald (for biographical note see page 85) wrote these letters to his daughter. Casual as they are, they reveal the qualities which made him a skillful and effective writer. Though these letters were written at wide intervals and deal with a number of subjects, there is an underlying emphasis on the importance of developing solid and lasting values, of distinguishing between the superficial and the genuine. Remembering Fitzgerald's autobiographical essay (page 85), we can appreciate his concern to have his daughter profit from his own experience.

August 8, 1933
La Paix, Rodgers' Forge,
Towson, Maryland

Dear Pie:

I feel very strongly about you doing duty. Would you give me a little more documentation about your reading in French? I am glad you are happy—but I never believe much in happiness. I never believe in misery either. Those are things you see on the stage or the screen or the printed page, they never really happen to you in life.

All I believe in in life is the rewards for virtue (according to your talents) and the *punishments* for not fulfilling your duties, which are doubly costly. If there is such a volume in the camp library, will you ask Mrs. Tyson to let you look up a sonnet of Shakespeare's in which the line occurs *Lilies that fester smell far worse than weeds.*

Have had no thoughts today, life seems composed of getting up a *Saturday Evening Post* story. I think of you, and always pleasantly; but if you call me "Pappy" again I am going to take the White Cat out and beat his bottom *hard, six times for every time you are impertinent.* Do you react to that?

I will arrange the camp bill.

Half-wit, I will conclude. Things to worry about:

Worry about courage
Worry about cleanliness
Worry about efficiency
Worry about horsemanship . . .

Things not to worry about:

Don't worry about popular opinion
Don't worry about dolls
Don't worry about the past
Don't worry about the future
Don't worry about growing up
Don't worry about anybody getting ahead of you
Don't worry about triumph

Don't worry about failure unless it comes through your own fault

Don't worry about mosquitoes
Don't worry about flies
Don't worry about insects in general
Don't worry about parents
Don't worry about boys
Don't worry about disappointments
Don't worry about pleasures
Don't worry about satisfactions

Things to think about:

What am I really aiming at?

How good am I really in comparison to my contemporaries in regard to:

(a) Scholarship
(b) Do I really understand about people and am I able to get along with them?

(c) Am I trying to make my body a useful instrument or am I neglecting it?

With dearest love,

Autumn, 1937

I shall somehow manage not to appear in a taxicab on Thanksgiving and thus disgrace you before all those "nice" girls. Isn't it somewhat old-fashioned to describe girls in expensive backgrounds as "nice?" I will bet two-thirds of the girls at Miss Walker's School have at least one grandparent that peddled old leather in the slums of New York, Chicago, or London, and if I thought you were accepting the standards of the cosmopolitan rich, I would much rather have you in a Southern school, where scholastic standards are not so high and the word "nice" is not debased to such a ludicrous extent. I have seen the whole racket, and if there is any more disastrous road than that from Park Avenue to the Rue de la Paix and back again, I don't know it.

They are homeless people, ashamed of being American, unable to master the culture of another country; ashamed, usually, of their husbands, wives, grandparents, and unable to bring up descendants of whom they could be proud, even if they had the nerve to bear them, ashamed of each other yet leaning on each other's weakness, a menace to the social order in which they live—oh, why should I go on? You know how I feel about such things. If I come up and find you gone Park Avenue, you will have to explain me away as a Georgia cracker or a Chicago killer. God help Park Avenue.

July 7, 1938

I am certainly glad that you're up and around, and sorry that your selection of Post-Flaubertian realism depressed you. I certainly wouldn't begin Henry James with *The Portrait of a Lady*, which is in his "late second manner" and full of mannerisms. Why don't you read *Roderick Hudson* or *Daisy Miller* first? *Lord Jim* is a great book—the first third at least and the conception, though it got lost a little bit in the law-courts of Calcutta or wherever it was. I wonder if you know why it is good? *Sister Carrie*, almost the first piece of American realism, is damn good and is as easy reading as a True Confession.

Summer, 1939

I want to have you out here for part of the summer. I have a nice cottage in the country, but very *far* out in the country, and utterly inaccessible if one doesn't drive well. Whether a piano here would be practical or not I don't know (remember how I felt about radio) but all that might be arranged if the personal equation were not doubtful (a situation for which for the moment I take full blame). Since I stopped picture work three months ago, I have been through not only a T.B. flare-up but also a nervous breakdown of such severity that for a time it threatened to paralyze both arms—or to quote the doctor: "The Good Lord tapped you on the shoulder." While I am running no fever above 99, I don't know what this return to picture work is going to do, and when and if my health blows up, you know what a poor family man I am. . . .

I am of course not drinking and haven't been for a long time, but any illness is liable to have a certain toxic effect on the system and you may find me depressing, over-nervous about small things and dogmatic—all these qualities more intensified than you have previously experienced them in me. Beyond this I am working very hard and the last thing I want at the end of the day is a problem, while, as it is natural at your age, what you want at the end of the day is excitement. I tell you all this because lately we had planned so many meetings with anticipation and they have turned out to be flops. Perhaps forewarned will be forearmed. . . .

If the experiment proves upsetting, I will have no further choice than to pack you off East somewhere again, but there are several friends here whom you could visit for a time if we failed to make a satisfactory household. So the trip will be worthwhile. Also I am more of a solitary than I have ever been, but I don't think that will worry you, because you had your dosages of motion picture stars on two other trips. To describe how humorless I feel about life at this point you have simply to read the Tarkington story called *Sinful Dadda Little* in the *Post* issue of July 22 (still current I believe), and remember that I read it without a particle of amusement, but with a complete disgust at *Dadda* for not drowning the two debutantes, at the end.

EXERCISES

1. Write a paragraph or two in which you explain the values Fitzgerald wanted his daughter to accept. Give evidence.
2. Recalling Fitzgerald's autobiographical article, "Early Success," can you suggest why he wrote the kind of letters he did to his daughter?
3. Write a letter to a friend or relative in which you discuss some of the things that have happened to you thus far in college, and in doing so explain what these things mean to you.
4. Compare the style of these letters to that of "Early Success." Is it essentially the same or is it different? Illustrate.

2 IMPRESSIONS OF JAPAN
by William Faulkner

William Faulkner (1897–) is among the most notable literary figures of the twentieth century. Although his novels and short stories are set in the Deep South, their appeal is universal. In 1950, he was awarded the Nobel Prize for literature. While some critics recognized Faulkner as a major writer with the publication of The Sound and the Fury *in 1929, general acclaim was slower in coming.* Sanctuary *was widely read, largely because of its sensational and violent theme.* As I Lay Dying *is considered by some as his most successful experimental novel and* Light in August *as his most powerful and moving work. In addition to other novels, Faulkner has published several collections of short stories and poetry.*

The sketch reprinted here was written during Faulkner's lecture tour of Japan in 1955. The brief, rich descriptions of landscape, faces, and dress, are woven together by Faulkner's theme, the common bond of humanity which allows him as an American to transcend the obvious differences between two worlds.

The engines are long since throttled back; the overcast sinks slowly upward with no semblance whatever of speed until suddenly you see the aircraft's shadow scudding the cottony hillocks; and now speed has returned again, aircraft and shadow now rushing toward one another as toward one mutual headlong destruction.

To break through the overcast and fling that shadow once more down, upon an island. It looks like land, like any other air-found landfall, yet you know it is an island, almost as if you saw both seabound flanks of it at the same instant, like a transparent slide; an island more miraculously found in the waste of water than Wake or Guam even, since here is a civilization, an ordered and ancient homogeny of the human race.

It is visible and audible, spoken and written too: a communication between man and man because human speaks it; you hear and see them. But to this one western ear and eye it means nothing because it resembles nothing which that western eye remembers; there is nothing to measure it against, nothing for memory and habit to say, "Why, this looks like the word for house or home or happiness"; not even just cryptic but acrostic too, as though the splashed symbols of the characters held not mere communication but something urgent and important beyond just information, promising toward some ultimate wisdom or knowledge containing the secret of man's salvation. But then no more, because there is nothing for western memory to measure it against; so not the mind to listen but only the ear to hear that chirrup and skitter of syllables like the cries of birds in the mouths of children, like music in the mouths of women and young girls.

The faces: Van Gogh and Manet would have loved them: that of the pilgrim with staff and pack and dusty with walking, mounting the stairs toward the Temple in the early sunlight; the Temple lay-brother or perhaps servant, his gown tucked about his thighs, squatting in the gate of the compound before beginning, or perhaps having already set it into motion, the day; that of the old woman vending peanuts beneath the gate for tourists to feed the pigeons with: a face worn with living and remembering, as though not one life had been long enough but rather every separate breath had been needed to etch into it all those fine and myriad lines; a face durable and now even a comfort to her, as if it had by now blotted up whatever had ever ached or sorrowed behind it, leaving it free now of the anguishes and the griefs and the enduring: here is one anyway who never read Faulkner and neither knows nor cares why he came to Japan nor gives one single damn what he thinks of Ernest Hemingway.

He is much too busy to have time to bother about whether he is happy or not, quite dirty, perhaps five years old, pastless and apparently immune even from parents, playing in the gutter with the stub of a cigarette.

The bowl of mountains containing the lake is as full of hard rapid air as the mouth of a wind-tunnel; for some time now we have been thinking that maybe it is already too late to take a reef in the mainsail: yet there it is. It is only a skiff yet to the western eye it is as invincibly and irrevocably alien as a Chinese junk, driven by a battered U.S. made outboard engine and containing a woman in a kimono beneath an open paper parasol such as would have excited no comment in a sunny reach of the English Thames, as fragile and invulnerable in the center of that hard blue bowl of wind as a butterfly in the eye of a typhoon.

The geisha's mass of blueblack lacquered hair encloses the painted face like a helmet, surmounts, crowns the slender body's ordered and ritual posturing like a grenadier's bearskin busby, too heavy in appearance for that slender throat to bear, the painted fixed expressionless face immobile and immune also above the studied posturing: yet behind that painted and lifeless mask is something quick and alive and elfin: or more than elfin: puckish: or more than puckish even: sardonic and quizzical, a gift for comedy, and more: for burlesque and caricature: for a sly and vicious revenge on the race of men.

Kimono. It covers her from throat to ankles; with a gesture as feminine as the placing of a flower or as female as the cradling of a child, the hands themselves can be concealed into the sleeves until there remains one unbroken chalice-shape of modesty proclaiming her feminity where nudity would merely parade her mammalian femaleness. A modesty which flaunts its own immodestness like the crimson rose tossed by no more than one white flick of hand, from the balcony window—modesty, than which there is nothing more immodest and which therefore is a woman's dearest possession; she should defend it with her life.

Loyalty. In her western clothes, blouse and skirt, she is merely one dumpy and nondescript young woman though in kimono at the deft balanced rapid tripping glide she too comes into her own share of that national heritage of feminine magic. Though she has more than that; she partakes of her share of that other quality which women have in this land which was not given them by what they have on: loyalty, constancy, fidelity, not for, but at least one hopes not without, reward. She does not speak my language nor I hers, yet in two days she knows my countryman's habit of waking soon after first light so that each morning when I open my eyes a coffee tray is already on the balcony table; she knows I like a fresh room to breakfast in when I return from walking, and it is so: the room done for the day and the table set and the morning paper ready; she asks without words why I have no clothes to be laundered today, and without words asks permission to sew the buttons and darn the socks; she calls me wise man and teacher, who am neither, when speaking of me to others; she is proud to have me for her client and, I hope, pleased that I try to deserve that pride and match with courtesy that loyalty. There is a lot of loose loyalty in this land. Even a little of it is too valuable to be ignored. I would wish that all of it were deserved or at least appreciated as I have tried to do.

This is the same rice paddy which I know back home in Arkansas and Mississippi and Louisiana, where it replaces now and then the cotton. This one is merely a little smaller and a little more fiercely cultivated, right up to the single row of beans which line the very edge of the irrigation canals, the work here done by hand where in my country machines do it since we have more machines than we have people; nature is the same: only the economy is different.

And the names are the same names too: Jonathan and Winesap and Delicious; the heavy August foliage is blue gray with the same spray which we use. But there the resemblance ceases: every single apple enclosed in this twist of paper until that whole tree to this western eye becomes significant and festive and ceremonial like the symbolical tree of the western rite of Christmas. Only it is more significant here: where in the West there is one small often artificial tree to a family, wrested from the living dirt to be decked in ritual tinsel and then to die as though the tree were not the protagonist of a rite but the victim of a sacrifice, here not one tree to a family but every tree of all is dressed and decked to proclaim and salute older gods than Christ: Demeter and Ceres.

Briefer and faster now, toward the journey's nearing end: goldenrod, as evocative of dust and autumn and hay fever as ever in Mississippi, against a tall bamboo fence.

The scenery is beautiful but the faces are better still.

The swift supple narrow grace with which the young girl bows and in that same one glowing motion recovers, tougher through very tenderness than the rigid culture which bent her as is the willow bough itself to the hard gust which can never do more than sway it.

The tools they use evoke the ones Noah must have built his ark with, yet the framework of the house seems to rise and stand without nails in the fitted joints nor even the need for nails, as if here were a magic, an art in the simple building of man's habitations which our western ancestors seemed to have lost somewhere when they moved.

And always the water, the sound, the plash and drip of it, as if here were a people making constant oblation to water as some peoples do to what they call their luck.

So kind the people that with three words the guest can go anywhere and live: Gohan;[1] Sake:[2] Arrigato.[3] And one more word:

Tomorrow now the aircraft lightens, a moment more and the wheels will wrench free of the ground, already dragging its shadow back toward the overcast before the wheels are even tucked up, into the overcast and then through it, the land, the island gone now which memory will always know though eye no longer remembers. Sayonara.[4]

EXERCISES

1. Re-examine the opening and closing paragraphs. You will see that Faulkner opens and closes his discussion of Japan as though a curtain rose on a play and after an appropriate length of time, dropped. What is the psychological effect of this?

2. One may notice cinematic qualities in this essay. Could the essay be satisfactorily adapted for a travelogue? Why, or why not?

3. In the introduction, we mentioned several important qualities which contribute to the creation of a unified impression. Analyze this article and show how it has or lacks these qualities.

[1] Food, or cooked rice.
[2] A rice wine.
[3] Thank you.
[4] Good-bye.

3 THE DIRTY STREET

by Joseph Warren Beach

Joseph Warren Beach (1880–1957) received his B.A. from the University of Minnesota and his doctorate from Harvard. While the major part of his teaching career was spent at the University of Minnesota, he also taught at other universities, including Harvard, Johns Hopkins, and the Sorbonne. Professor Beach was among the first American scholars to write critical studies of novelists and poets, concerning himself especially with their techniques. Among these studies are The Comic Spirit in George Meredith *and* The Method of Henry James. *His book* The Twentieth Century Novel *helped formulate the critical method now widely used in the teaching of fiction. He published a number of other works, including a novel and two volumes of poetry.*

In this informal essay, the author muses over the differences between the Teutonic and Latin temperaments as reflected in the insistence of the one on the values of cleanliness and order and the indifference of the other to these very same things. He searches for the values that are implicit in this disregard for dirt and disorder—and finds some.

Sunday morning I walked down the dirty street. It may have been Rome and it may have been Naples. I am sure it was not Geneva, Lyons, or Columbus, Ohio. I had some errand, but I promptly forgot it. Better streets were black with decent bourgeois coming from Mass, but the dirty street was violet and green with the woolen shawls of women who had come out to buy provisions for the Sunday dinner. And it was further enlivened by their families, who had all brought their curiosities or their mischief into the street. The boys were throwing copper coins on the pavement to hear them jingle, or to see whether they would come up heads or tails. The little shops were all open, as they must be perforce where so many of them seemed to be the abiding-place of the shopkeeper, and his social club. And moreover the street was lined with carts and booths dispensing oranges and fresh vegetables. Within three blocks there were two hurdy-gurdies going, and five blind fiddlers in one concert lined against the wall. And no one in the dirty street declined to drop a coin in the cup for them. The place was full of a pleasant confusion. The pavement was muddy and stained with dishwater from more than one doorway. And the air was laden with what Aspasia calls the bad smells of Italian streets. And yet the people seemed happy, and I'm sure that I was happy, and almost forgot to bring home my pocketful of oranges.

Aspasia is sorry for the dirty street, and thinks something ought to be done about it. She thinks it ought to be cleaned up. But what if the street likes to be dirty? Cleanliness and order are, I suppose, esthetic instincts in their way; but they do not seem to be primary instincts with the Latins of the South as they are with the Teutons of the North. The Latins seem to lay greater stress on the sensuous elements of beauty. Perhaps they like animation better than order, and smells better than cleanliness. Perhaps they like their smells. I like them, and I bless the mild climate and the easy notions of hygiene that fill the streets of Naples with the fragrance of green things. Dogs know their masters by their smells; why may not men know, and love, their homes by the same happy sensuous means? And who is to be the judge in such a matter?

Perhaps in Dirty Street they look upon disorder as a time-saving device. The Philadelphia woman who washes down her front steps every morning has subtracted that much from the time available for other purposes. And so with anyone who is forever engaged in setting things to rights. The philosopher bids us consider the true ends of existence. For himself the philosopher chooses the contemplative life. The citizens of Dirty Street may be regarded in the light of humble Platos, who spend their time by choice in contemplation and peripatetic discussion. They certainly seem to have plenty of leisure for standing around, and it is a business in which they take great satisfaction. Aspasia considers that there are many obvious ways in which these poor people, by the application of thought and energy, might better their condition; and civilization itself, she considers, since the days of Prometheus, is one grand process of bettering human conditions. She likes to see people getting somewhere. But I say to her: You people who are forever so anxious to be getting somewhere—is it that you aren't happy where you are?

Or perhaps they have a feeling like that of our friend Vacaresco, with regard to restaurants and cafés. He is a Roumanian who, for love of art, has made his home in France, and whom we came to know while he was making an esthetic pilgrimage to Rome. I know not by what ignoble manual work he had scraped together the sum of two hundred and fifty dollars—to use our measure of value—which he counted upon to support him in leisure for a term of years while he lived the life of the spirit. We were first introduced to him by common friends—fellows of the brush and chisel—when we had come together in the same picture gallery. And we asked them all to take tea with us of an afternoon at Faraglia's, in the Piazza Venezia. But Vacaresco wouldn't come to tea in the Piazza

Venezia. There was nothing surly about him, but he simply didn't turn up with "the boys." And he wouldn't come to dinner at the Pensione Boos. He didn't like the sound of a boarding-house that was lodged, however humbly, in a *palazzo!*

When we went to dine with "the boys" in a back street near the Pantheon, our Roumanian was there. He seemed glad enough to see us, and he was the life of our gay party. Well, we had a very good dinner; we learned to eat spaghetti; and we spent a most rational evening in high discourse. But Aspasia wanted to know, in strict privacy, why they couldn't serve just as good a dinner, and why we couldn't spend as rational an evening, in some place where they sweep the floor. Is not the life of the spirit consistent with the introduction of modern improvements?

Well, my dear Aspasia, I must say that I have great sympathy with the Vacaresco point of view, and I wish I could make clear to you the grounds of reason in it. Modern improvements represent for you a feeling of the spirit from the bonds of matter. For you they represent a saving of energy; vacuum cleaners, electric washing-machines, model kitchenettes: things undreamed of in the philosophy of Dirty Street. And to us they suggest so pitiful a waste of energy! We think of cities and races wholly given over to modern improvements, pushing up the scale of living, turning luxuries into necessities, so busy saving time that they have no leisure, so passionate in the pursuit of comfort that they have no pleasure in life. Have you not seen them at Nice or Atlantic City? They have spent their youth and strength, and made their money; and now they have come to spend it in the city of pleasure, on the Board Walk or the Promenade des Anglais, and they look in vain for any real value to be got in exchange for their coin. Vacaresco will not come to Faraglia's for tea because he feels there the commercial spirit of competition, with the silly expensive music that goes into the bill, the expensive clothes of the young men, the cold eyes of *pescecani* estimating the cost of your outfit. He thinks of the American family that spends, getting from Cherbourg to New York, more than the sum that he has saved from years of hard work for a little term of freedom.

Oh, I know what searching things you would have to say on your side if we let you have your say. (I myself must have steam-heated lodgings in Italy, or I should never live to sing the praises of Dirty Street.) Oh yes, you would say, we are all the same in our hearts. We all love luxury, rich and poor alike, Bohemians and *bons bourgeois*, and when we sneer at the *pescecani*, it is half envy on our parts. Well, let it be so. It may be that we know our weakness, and that we instinctively hate a world in which every glance is an entanglement. The serious young artist affects to despise the night life of Paris; he wants to make his money last, and get his work done, and come back to his folks respecting himself in his heart. He may be lying about the night life of Paris, but it is a pious lie. And the way he feels about the poor old dirty Café du Dôme is the way we feel about the clean and bright and orderly places of the earth. We're really afraid we might fall a victim to their seductions, and in the fleshpots of Egypt forget the Land of Canaan. We want to walk softly, to keep on the shady side of the street, to avoid comparisons, and avoid distractions. This is no doubt a dreadful confession of weakness. *Mais que voulez-vous?* We make no pretensions to heroism. We are no Edisons, no Savonarolas. We are poor hermits taking to the desert to escape the temptations of the world. And we have no ambition, like that misguided monk of Anatole France, to grapple with the great worldling, Thaïs, in hopes of converting her to the spiritual life.

But after all, it is perhaps at bottom no affair of reason, but something instinctive and obscure. There is something nostalgic in our sentimental attraction to Dirty Street, and something superstitious. We do not wish to lift our heads too high, for fear of attracting the attention of the gods. That is the way, I fancy, that Dirty Street feels about its own case. There is a comfortable security in being humble. The wheel of Fortune, forever turning, can have no terrors for the modest sybarites of Dirty Street; it may conceivably lift them high, but it cannot cast them down. These old-world gentry are no doubt completer philosophers than we, being of so old a civilization. In their obscurity they have outlived so much greatness; they have survived so many catastrophes. They have but to look on smoking Vesuvius and shrug their shoulders. They have but to look on the Column of Trajan, or the Arch of Constantine.

In the evening I passed through Dirty Street at the hour of the lighting of lamps. Black-faced men were carrying in coal in sacks. At the corner the boys were gathered around the cows with their cups to receive their portion of warm milk direct from the maker. All objects and acts referred to the primary necessities of life, and that, in our day, is an esthetic asset for any street. Religion was much in evidence, itself perhaps the most primary of necessities after the stilling of hunger. There was one Madonna nobly enshrined with fluted pillars, and lights, and pots of geranium. The shoemaker had adorned his cave with the traditional grotto of the Holy Family, and it glowed with candles and electric globes. My most Protestant friends call it idolatry, but I had no feeling but that of envy for those who are able to worship, if they do worship, at such domestic shrines.

Every house had the Madonna on some table or dresser, as one saw at a glance through the open door. For most of the houses opened directly on the street, and the living-room was continuous with the sidewalk, the women nursing their babies or putting up their hair in serene disregard of who passed by. Sometimes there were cooking operations going on, and always there were beds, plenty of beds, capacious bedsteads of brass —there was that much in the way of modern improvements. There was rather too much furniture in these rooms for what Aspasia calls order. But they made attractive pictures in the light of the few candles at the feet of the Madonnas. In the streets there was little light, and the big star that I call Venus winked benignly over the roof tops.

Aspasia says I am romantic on the subject of Dirty Street. And it may be. But what does it mean to be romantic, and why must it be a term of reproach? When we speak of the Romantic movement in literature, we have in mind a reaction of human nature against too much order. And it may well be that there is a normal human instinct for disorder as well as that other normal instinct for order, and that an excess of either condition is bound to provoke rebellion. A contemporary Italian critic has a very interesting theory about the working of the spirit of Life, as he calls that creative force which Bergson's calls the *Élan Vital.* Life, he says, in its perpetual free movement of creation, is continually producing forms to express its meaning and vitality; and, once produced, these forms continually tend to solidify, to harden, and intrench themselves against change and innovation; and so, instead of expressing Life, they simply hinder it, since it is the essence of the spirit of Life to be forever creating new forms to express its ever-changing and evolving self. A queer theory, is it not, to flourish alongside of the political doctrine of *Fascismo* and the Big Stick, of a system of government which implies the establishment and maintenance of order by compulsion? But singularly like to Carlyle's idea of the eternal tailor forever reclothed, and Carlyle would have been the first to hail Mussolini as the God-sent hero.

I have no desire now to dwell on the paradoxes of philosophy, but merely to let the philosophers remind us how order itself may become a nuisance and a weariness. It is probably for this reason that people brought up in too orderly a fashion are so liable to go to the dogs; that ministers' sons are the devil's grandsons; that they are so often but three generations from shirt sleeves to shirt sleeves. Have we not in Dirty Street stumbled upon the secret of so many of Time's revenges? Historians have long been trying to explain the fall of the Roman Empire. Has it never occurred to them to suggest that the Roman Empire fell because it was tired of holding itself upright? Perhaps the Romans were tired of so much order, and simply called in the Goths and Longobards to give them a little much-desired confusion.

EXERCISES

1. What is the viewpoint of the narrator? What does he say or imply about (a) Aspasia, (b) orderly existence, (c) the romantic approach, (d) modern government, (e) mechanized culture, (f) the human need for disorder.
2. This essay could be called a paradoxical exercise. Write a paragraph in which you explain why this is so.

3. Do the descriptive passages add to the forcefulness of the argument?
4. Account for the indefiniteness of location in the opening paragraph.
5. Make a list of the allusions in this essay. Identify as many of them as you can. Would the essay be more or less interesting if there were fewer allusions?
6. Write an essay on one of the following topics:

   Americans are too conscious of soap
   There is too much uniformity (or too little uniformity) in suburbia
   The sort of house I'd like to own
   Small Town, USA

4 THE WRECK OF THE COMMODORE

by Stephen Crane

Stephen Crane (1871–1900) was born in New Jersey and spent much of his earlier life in upstate New York. He attended Syracuse University and worked for the Herald *and* Tribune *in New York City. His best-known work is* The Red Badge of Courage, *a novel about the Civil War;* Maggie: a Girl of the Streets *(see page 116) is one of the first American novels in the naturalist tradition. Crane wrote many short stories. "The Open Boat" is one of the most widely read. It is based on the adventure Crane recounted in the newspaper story reprinted here, from the New York Press, January 7, 1897, page 1.*

JACKSONVILLE, FLA., Jan. 6.—It was the afternoon of New Year's. The Commodore lay at her dock in Jacksonville and negro stevedores processioned steadily toward her with box after box of ammunition and bundle after bundle of rifles. Her hatch, like the mouth of a monster, engulfed them. It might have been the feeding time of some legendary creature of the sea. It was in broad daylight and the crowd of gleeful Cubans on the pier did not forbear to sing the strange patriotic ballads of their island.

Everything was perfectly open. The Commodore was cleared with a cargo of arms and munition for Cuba. There was none of that extreme modesty about the proceeding which had marked previous departures of the famous tug. She loaded up as placidly as if she was going to carry oranges to New York, instead of Remingtons to Cuba. Down the river, furthermore, the revenue cutter Boutwell, the old isosceles triangle that protects United States interests in the St. John's, lay at anchor, with no sign of excitement aboard her.

Exchanging Farewells

On the decks of the Commodore there were exchanges of farewells in two languages. Many of the men who were to sail upon her had many intimates in the old Southern town, and we who had left our friends in the remote North received our first touch of melancholy on witnessing these strenuous and earnest goodbys.

It seems, however, that there was more difficulty at the custom house. The officers of the ship and the Cuban leaders were detained there until a mournful twilight settled upon the St. John's, and through a heavy fog the lights of Jacksonville blinked dimly. Then at last the Commodore swung clear of the dock, amid a tumult of goodbys. As she turned her bow toward the distant sea the Cubans ashore cheered and cheered. In response the Commodore gave three long blasts of her whistle, which even to this time impressed me with their sadness. Somehow, they sounded as wails.

Then at last we began to feel like filibusters. I don't suppose that the most stolid brain could contrive to believe that there is not a mere trifle of danger in filibustering, and so as we watched the lights of Jacksonville swing past us and heard the regular thump, thump, thump of the engines we did considerable reflecting.

But I am sure that there were no hifalutin emotions visible upon any of the faces which fronted the speeding shore. In fact, from cook's boy to captain, we were all enveloped in a gentle satisfaction and cheerfulness. But less than two miles from Jacksonville, this atrocious fog caused the pilot to ram the bow of the Commodore hard upon the mud and in this ignominious position we were compelled to stay until daybreak.

Help from the Boutwell

It was to all of us more than a physical calamity. We were now no longer filibusters. We were men on a ship stuck in the mud. A certain mental somersault was made once more necessary.

But word had been sent to Jacksonville to the captain of the revenue cutter Boutwell, and Captain Kilgore turned out promptly and generously fired up his old triangle, and came at full speed to our assistance. She dragged us out of the mud, and again we headed for the mouth of the river. The revenue cutter pounded along a half mile astern of us, to make sure that we did not take on board at some place along the river men for the Cuban army.

This was the early morning of New Year's Day, and the fine golden southern sunlight fell full upon the river. It flashed over the ancient Boutwell, until her white sides gleamed like pearl, and her rigging was spun into little threads of gold.

Cheers greeted the old Commodore from passing ship and from the shore. It was a cheerful, almost merry, beginning to our voyage. At Mayport, however, we changed our river pilot for a man who could take her to open sea, and again the Commodore was beached. The Boutwell was fussing around us in her venerable way, and, upon seeing our predicament, she came again to assist us, but this time, with engines reversed, the Commodore dragged herself away from the grip of the sand and again headed for the open sea.

The captain of the revenue cutter grew curious. He hailed the Commodore: "Are you fellows going to sea to-day?"

Captain Murphy of the Commodore called back: "Yes, sir."

And then as the whistle of the Commodore saluted him, Captain Kilgore doffed his cap and said: "Well, gentlemen, I hope you have a pleasant cruise," and this was our last word from shore.

When the Commodore came to enormous rollers that flee over the bar a certain light-heartedness departed from the ship's company.

Sleep Impossible

As darkness came upon the waters, the Commodore was a broad, flaming path of blue and silver phosphorescence, and as her stout bow lunged at the great black waves she threw flashing, roaring cascades to either side. And all that was to be heard was the rhythmical and mighty pounding of the engines. Being an inexperienced filibuster, the writer had undergone considerable mental excitement since the starting of the ship, and in consequence he had not yet been to sleep and so I went to the first mate's bunk to indulge myself in all the physical delights of holding one's-self in bed. Every time the ship lurched I expected to be fired through a bulkhead, and it was neither amusing nor instructive to see in the dim light a certain accursed valise aiming itself at the top of my stomach with every lurch of the vessel.

The Cook is Hopeful

The cook was asleep on a bench in the galley. He is of a portly and noble exterior, and by means of a checker board he had himself wedged on this bench in such a manner the motion of the ship would be unable to dislodge him. He woke as I entered the galley and delivered himself of some dolorous sentiments: "God," he said in the course of his observations, "I don't feel right about this ship, somehow. It strikes me that something is going to happen to us. I don't know what it is, but the old ship is going to get it in the neck, I think."

"Well, how about the men on board of her?" said I. "Are any of us going to get out, prophet?"

"Yes," said the cook. "Sometimes I have these damned feelings come over me, and they are always right, and it seems to me, somehow, that you and I will both get and meet again somewhere, down at Coney Island, perhaps, or some place like that."

One Man Has Enough

Finding it impossible to sleep, I went back to the pilot house. An old seaman, Tom Smith, from Charleston, was then at the wheel. In the darkness I could not see Tom's face, except at those times when he leaned forward to scan the compass and the dim light from the box came upon his weatherbeaten features.

"Well, Tom," said I, "how do you like filibustering?"

He said, "I think I am about through with it. I've been in a number of these expeditions and the pay is good, but I think if I ever get back safe this time I will cut it."

I sat down in the corner of the pilot house and almost went to sleep. In the meantime the captain came on duty and he was standing near me when the chief engineer rushed up the stairs and cried hurriedly to the captain that there was something wrong in the engine room. He and the captain departed swiftly.

I was drowsing there in my corner when the captain returned, and, going to the door of the little room directly back of the pilot house, he cried to the Cuban leader:

"Say, can't you get those fellows to work? I can't talk their language and I can't get them started. Come on and get them going."

Helps in the Fireroom

The Cuban leader turned to me and said: "Go help in the fireroom. They are going to bail with buckets."

The engine room, by the way, represented a scene at this time taken from the middle kitchen of hades. In the first place, it was insufferably warm, and the lights burned faintly in a way to cause mystic and grewsome shadows. There was a quantity of soapish sea water swirling and sweeping and swishing among machinery that roared and banged and clattered and steamed, and, in the second place, it was a devil of a ways down below.

Here I first came to know a certain young oiler named Billy Higgins. He was sloshing around this inferno filling buckets with water and passing them to a chain of men that extended up the ship's side. Afterward we got orders to change our point of attack on water and to operate through a little door on the windward side of the ship that led into the engine room.

No Panic on Board

During this time there was much talk of pumps out of order and many other statements of a mechanical kind, which I did not altogether comprehend but understood to mean that there was a general and sudden ruin in the engine room.

There was no particular agitation at this time, and even later there was never a panic on board the Commodore. The party of men who worked with Higgins and me at this time were all Cubans, and we were under the direction of the Cuban leaders. Presently we were ordered again to the afterhold, and there was some hesitation about going into the abominable fireroom again, but Higgins dashed down the companionway with a bucket.

Lowering Boats

The heat and hard work in the fireroom affected me and I was obliged to come on deck again. Going forward, I heard as I went talk of lowering the boats. Near the corner of the galley the mate was talking with a man.

"Why don't you send up a rocket?" said this unknown man. And the mate replied: "What the hell do we want to send up a rocket for? The ship is all right."

Returning with a little rubber and cloth overcoat, I saw the first boat about to be lowered. A certain man was the first person in this first boat, and they were handing him in a valise about as large as a hotel. I had not entirely recovered from astonishment and pleasure in witnessing this noble deed when I saw another valise go to him.

Human Hog Appears

This valise was not perhaps so large as a hotel, but it was a big valise anyhow. Afterward there went to him something which looked to me like an overcoat.

Seeing the chief engineer leaning out of his little window, I remarked to him:

"What do you think of that blank, blank, blank?"

"Oh, he's a bird," said the old chief.

It was now that was heard the order to get away the lifeboat, which was stowed on top of the deckhouse. The deckhouse was a mighty slippery place, and with each roll of the ship, the men there thought themselves likely to take headers into the deadly black sea.

Higgins was on top of the deckhouse, and, with the first mate and two colored stokers, we wrestled with that boat, which, I am willing to swear, weighed as much as a Broadway cable car. She might have been spiked to the deck. We could have pushed a little brick schoolhouse along a corduroy road as easily as we could have moved this boat. But the first mate got a tackle to her from a leeward davit, and on the deck below the captain corralled enough men to make an impression upon the boat.

We were ordered to cease hauling then, and in this lull the cook of the ship came to me and said: "What are you going to do?"

I told him my plans, and he said:

"Well, my God, that's what I am going to do."

A *Whistle of Despair*

Now the whistle of the Commodore had been turned loose, and if there ever was a voice of despair and death, it was in the voice of this whistle. It had gained a new tone. It was as if its throat was already choked by the water, and this cry on the sea at night, with a wind blowing the spray over the ship, and the waves roaring over the bow, and swirling white along the decks, was to each of us probably a song of man's end.

It was now that the first mate showed a sign of losing his grip. To us who were trying in all stages of competence and experience to launch the lifeboat he raged in all terms of fiery satire and hammerlike abuse. But the boat moved at last and swung down toward the water.

Afterward, when I went aft, I saw the captain standing, with his arm in a sling, holding on to a stay with his one good hand and directing the launching of the boat. He gave me a five-gallon jug of water to hold, and asked me what I was going to do. I told him what I thought was about the proper thing, and he told me then that the cook had the same idea, and ordered me to go forward and be ready to launch the ten-foot dingy.

In the Ten-Foot Dingy

I remember well that he turned then to swear at a colored stoker who was prowling around, done up in life preservers until he looked like a feather bed. I went forward with my five-gallon jug of water, and when the captain came we launched the dingy, and they put me over the side to fend her off from the ship with an oar.

They handed me down the water jug, and then the cook came into the boat, and we sat there in the darkness, wondering why, by all our hopes of future happiness, the captain was so long in coming over to the side and ordering us away from the doomed ship.

The captain was waiting for the other boat to go. Finally he hailed in the darkness: "Are you all right, Mr. Graines?"

The first mate answered: "All right, sir."

"Shove off, then," cried the captain.

The captain was just about to swing over the rail when a dark form came forward and a voice said: "Captain, I go with you."

The captain answered: "Yes, Billy; get in."

Higgins Last to Leave Ship

It was Billy Higgins, the oiler. Billy dropped into the boat and a moment later the captain followed, bringing with him an end of about forty yards of lead line. The other end was attached to the rail of the ship.

As we swung back to leeward the captain said: "Boys, we will stay right near the ship till she goes down."

This cheerful information, of course, filled us all with glee. The line kept us headed properly into the wind, and as we rode over the monstrous waves we saw upon each rise the swaying lights of the dying Commodore.

When came the gray shade of dawn, the form of the Commodore grew slowly clear to us as our little ten-foot boat rose over each swell. She was floating with such an air of buoyancy that we laughed when we had time, and said "What a gag it would be on those other fellows if she didn't sink at all."

But later we saw men aboard of her, and later still they began to hail us.

Helping Their Mates

I had forgot to mention that previously we had loosened the end of the lead line and dropped much further to leeward. The men on board were a mystery to us, of course, as we had seen all the boats leave the ship. We rowed back to the ship, but did not approach too near, because we were four men in a ten-foot boat, and we knew that the touch of a hand on our gunwale would assuredly swamp us.

The first mate cried out from the ship that the third boat had foundered alongside. He cried that they had made rafts, and wished us to tow them.

The captain said, "All right."

Their rafts were floating astern. "Jump in!" cried the captain, but there was a singular and most harrowing hesitation. There were five white men and two negroes. This scene in the gray light of morning impressed one as would a view into some place where ghosts move slowly. These seven men on the stern of the sinking Commodore were silent. Save the words of the mate to the captain there was no talk. Here was death, but here also was a most singular and indefinable kind of fortitude.

Four men, I remember, clambered over the railing and stood there watching the cold, steely sheen of the sweeping waves.

"Jump," cried the captain again.

The old chief engineer first obeyed the order. He landed on the outside raft and the captain told him how to grip the raft and he obeyed as promptly and as docilely as a scholar in riding school.

The Mate's Mad Plunge

A stoker followed him, and then the first mate threw his hands over his head and plunged into the sea. He had no life belt and for my part, even when he did this horrible thing, I somehow felt that I could see in the expression of his hands, and in the very toss of his head, as he leaped thus to death, that it was rage, rage, rage unspeakable that was in his heart all the time.

And then I saw Tom Smith, the man who was going to quit filibustering after this expedition, jump to a raft and turn his face toward us. On board the Commodore three men strode, still in silence and with their faces turned toward us. One man had his arms folded and was leaning against the deckhouse. His feet were crossed, so that the toe of his left foot pointed downward. There they stood gazing at us, and neither from the deck nor from the rafts was a voice raised. Still was there this silence.

Tried to Tow the Rafts

The colored stoker on the first raft threw us a line and we began to tow. Of course, we perfectly understood the absolute impossibility of any such thing; our dingy was within six inches of the water's edge, there was an enormous sea running, and I knew that under the circumstances a tugboat would have no light task in moving these rafts.

But we tried it, and would have continued to try it indefinitely, but that something critical came to pass. I was at an oar and so faced the rafts. The cook controlled the line. Suddenly the boat began to go backward and then we saw this negro on the first raft pulling on the line hand over hand and drawing us to him.

He had turned into a demon. He was wild—wild as a tiger. He was crouched on this raft and ready to spring. Every muscle of him seemed to be turned into an elastic spring. His eyes were almost white. His face was the face of a lost man reaching upward, and we knew that the weight of his hand on our gunwale doomed us.

The Commodore Sinks

The cook let go of the line. We rowed around to see if we could not get a line from the chief engineer, and all this time, mind you, there were no shrieks, no groans, but silence, silence and silence, and then the Commodore sank.

She lurched to windward, then swung afar back, righted and dove into the sea, and the rafts were suddenly swallowed by this frightful maw of the ocean. And then by the men on the ten-foot dingy were words said that were still not words—something far beyond words.

The lighthouse of Mosquito Inlet stuck up above the horizon like the point of a pin. We turned our dingy toward the shore.

The history of life in an open boat for thirty hours would no doubt be instructive for the young, but none is to be told here and now. For my part I would prefer to tell the story at once, because from it would shine the splendid manhood of Captain Edward Murphy and of William Higgins, the oiler, but let it suffice at this time to say that when we were swamped in the surf and making the best of our way toward the shore the captain gave orders amid the wildness of the breakers as clearly as if he had been on the quarter deck of a battleship.

John Kitchell of Daytona came running down the beach, and as he ran the air was filled with clothes. If he had pulled a single lever and undressed, even as the fire horses harness, he could not seem to me to have stripped with more speed. He dashed into the water and dragged the cook. Then he went after the captain, but the captain sent him to me, and then it was that he saw Billy Higgins lying with his forehead on sand that was clear of the water, and he was dead.

EXERCISES

1. Is this a more subjective account of the sinking of a vessel than one would be likely to find in a current newspaper story? What is meant by an objective as opposed to a subjective account?
2. Characterize the tone of Crane's writing in this article.
3. What happened to the rafts? Does Crane say? Does his treatment of this part of his narrative or rather his failure to treat this part injure its unity?

5 | THE COMIC STRIP IN AMERICAN LIFE

The Times Literary Supplement
September 17, 1954

This article, by an anonymous contributor to the London Times Literary Supplement, *presents an Englishman's sympathetic though rather patronizing view of American life as mirrored in American comic strips. He maintains that our comic strips express, if often unconsciously, "many of the chief characteristics of the nation—or at least that part of it approximating most closely to the urban Middle West, that has come to be accepted as standard America." Among aspects of American life he finds reflected in comic strips are love of money, love of children, love of new experiences, and a desire to be on the side of virtue. But he does conclude that the "American Way of Life, like the American comic strip, brings happiness to many, and no great evil."*

The Americans are the most earnest of peoples, and have a fervent faith in the respectability of folk-lore. Thus they tend to clothe in misty feyness anything from Apache war dances to boogie-woogie, and any derelict Kentucky hillsman humming to himself as he shears the goats is likely to find himself hailed as an authentic Elizabethan relic. Any popular manifestation can achieve respectability by the metamorphosis to a "native culture." A prime and pleasant example of the attitude is to be found at the farming village of Crystal City in southern Texas: for there in the middle of the square, painted in gay colours, surrounded by well-trimmed lawns, honoured by all, stands a life-sized figure of Popeye the Sailorman, one of the most venerable personalities of the American cartoon.

The comic strip of the American daily Press long ago achieved the status of a folk movement, and it is perfectly acceptable, in almost any company, to admit that you follow the fortunes of Dick Tracy or Steve Canyon. Indeed, the strips do have honourable popular origins. They first appeared in more or less their present form in the 1860s, when a tremendous flow of immigrants was arriving from Europe, and for many poor strangers who spoke no English they served as an introduction to

American ways of thought and life. (They also, incidentally, ended the great era of American political cartooning—the era of Keppler and *Puck*; for as the "funnies" gained ever wider popularity, so more and more of the most skilful newspaper artists turned to their production. To this day the standard of skill of the comic strip is generally higher than that of the political cartoon.)

The early strips thus reflected many facets of American living, and it is perhaps not fanciful to suggest that they still express, often unconsciously, many of the chief characteristics of the nation—or at least that part of it approximating most closely to the urban Middle West, that has come to be accepted as standard America. The diversity of the United States is still immense, in custom as in country; but that unpleasant alleged "norm" called the American Way of Life—drug stores and dating, profit motives and women's clubs—is spreading relentlessly, and has about it a deadening and intolerant sameness. We may trace its traits and prejudices closely in the world of the strip cartoon.

For example, the visitor to a Middle West manufacturing town is almost sure to notice the predominance of women. This is a powerfully matriarchal society. In the home the self-possessed, well-read, relatively leisured housewife has innumerable advantages over her generally plodding husband; in civic affairs the women's organizations, from opera societies to church clubs, are always potent; and in politics such groups as the League of Women Voters have much influence. In any family party dining out a woman is likely to pay the restaurant bill. In economic affairs the purchasing power of the housewife is all important, and the whole structure of American commercial life is designed largely to satisfy the demands of women.

This maternalism is accurately portrayed (without bitterness) in the strip cartoons. A favourite situation is that of Dad and Junior slipping away from the women for a weekend's fishing, pursued by admonitions about warm underwear. Dagwood, in Chic Young's admirable cartoon *Blondie*, is always getting into trouble from his wife for stealing a sandwich from the kitchen or muddying the hall floor. "We are going visiting to-day," announces the dictatorial wife in *Bringing Up Father*: and Father puts his hat on. Women are often ignorant in the strip cartoons, often drive their cars foolishly or make inane remarks; but they are always in command.

Many such episodes concern a wife's desire for a mink coat, the supreme American symbol of opulence; for the American has never lost his respect for wealth, however acquired, and still passionately enjoys the office-boy-to-millionaire saga. A man is judged by the make of his car, and there is scarcely a club or a hotel in the nation that will exclude any rich man from its custom. If you have money, you are consequently esteemed (only in certain parts of the country, outside the cartoon standard, does birth assume an equally absurd importance). Christine Jorgensen achieved celebrity a year or two ago by a change of sex; to-day she is chiefly notable for earning $5,000 a week in the night clubs. If it makes money, almost anything is respectable.

Sometimes the awe of wealth assumes a positively mystical quality, and this is best expressed in the strip cartoons by the figure of the tycoon in *Little Orphan Annie.* He is a shadowy, ethereal figure, surrounded by servants of vaguely Oriental origin, at once exhausted and uplifted by the endless struggles of international finance; the telephones on his desk muffled-looking, his yacht always moored in quiet backwaters, his language always kindly, his associates loyal to the death. His is a god-like image, benevolent and aloof, like a thousand dollar bill. But Mr. Warbucks (for such is his unlikely name) belongs exclusively to the world of Rockefeller Centres and J. P. Morgans. Extreme wealth of a more homely kind is represented in the cartoons by another personality: the sort of millionaire who prints a nickname on his visiting card. He is popular for a variety of *noblesse oblige* which requires him to slap inferiors on the back and call his juniors by their Christian names. He is cheerfully, if not garishly, dressed (one such man who recently appeared in *Dick Tracy* was wearing a yellow suit). He is the kind of millionaire most Americans would like to be; still a regular fellow, in spite of it all, and still a real scream at the Elks.

They are scarcely caricatures, these portraits, for it is undeniable that under the pressures of the system most standard Americans, within their respective sections of society, are very much alike. Even in the far west the hardy eccentrics are disappearing, and the chambers of commerce are taking over. Few of the old crusading editors are still complaining, the Mississippi pilots work by radar. Indeed, the strip cartoons generally decline to admit that there is any America at all outside their chosen "norm." There has rarely appeared in a cartoon narrative a poor white's cabin from the southern states, squalid and crumbling and ridden with cockroaches; nor, for that matter, a trim little Maryland farm with its jolly housewife hanging out the washing. The American home of the strip cartoon is that of Dixie Dugan and her family in a famous series: it is a weatherboard house with a small garden running down to the street, with a mailbox by the gate, a hammock for Dad to swing in by the porch, and indubitably a refrigerator and a television set inside. For the comic strip, as for the Voice of America, this is the U.S.A.

When somebody appears who is not a complete American, by these rigid standards, he is generally regarded as a figure of fun. More than one cartoon deals with hill-billy folk, the men heavily covered with tangled beards, the women wearing poke bonnets and smoking pipes. They talk in the quaintest of dialects and live in mountain shacks. One strip deals with an immigrant family still not totally Americanized, and demonstrates their origins by spelling English words in the German manner. When Englishmen turn up (often as a subject of ambition for socially conscious mothers) they speak with a wildly exaggerated drawl and generally wear dinner-jackets.

Perhaps allied with its maternalism, perhaps stemming from the heritage of the frontier, is America's overwhelming love of children. It is a pleasant experience to walk with a small boy along an American street, and to find both men and women enthralled and delighted by the very presence of a child. American children must be the most violently loved on earth. As a result, some of the happiest and best of the comic strips are those that deal with children. Generally, in art as in life, the protagonists in these adventures are freckled, tousled, slightly spoiled boys, or small girls of precocious tendencies. It is an odd fact that American children, in spite of their pioneering background, are closely home-bound in their enterprises. Sail along the Mississippi for a month and you will scarcely see a Huck Finn playing along its banks (if you do, he is in rags and lives in a shanty-boat, and may even be a half-caste; and is therefore outside the cartoon pale). Young Americans will play daringly and imaginatively in their own backyard, but they seldom venture into the woods. So, in the strips, Mom is never far away, and the place is warm with security. Two situations often recur. Boys are depicted selling soft drinks for cash, thus displaying an early and commendable instinct for profit. Girls are for ever interrupting their elder sisters' moments of courtship with remarks that sometimes seem to show an astonishingly early onset of puberty.

An agreeable American trait is a ceaseless greed for knowledge and experience, even vicarious experience. In the United States lecturers are often thanked with the words, "Thank you for sharing this experience with us": wording that sometimes softens the impact of an apparently totally insensible audience. Anything that will increase knowledge of any kind, any new sensation or point of view or reaction, is eagerly accepted. Discussion groups prosper, and newspapers are read more thoroughly, in general, than they are in England. The importance of keeping up with current events, even through somebody else's distorted vision, is demonstrated by the terrifying success of commentators and news digests.

To satisfy these worthy yearnings, strip cartoons often assume what might be called a documentary character, associating a fictional episode with a genuine background. A character in the cartoon, *Joe Palooka*, for instance, has recently been climbing the mountain K2 (described, on unnamed authority, as being "probably higher than Mount Everest"); a choice of setting that happily coincides with a sudden American interest in alpinism. Dick Tracy's adventures are often accompanied by authentic "tips for crime-stoppers." The doings of the space rockets, while they appeal to a decidedly space-conscious American youth, also interest those many thousands of adult Americans who view the cosmos with a certain dark foreboding. One cartoon of highly educational leanings is liable to devote a whole day's pictures (without fair warning) to the habits of the red-crested quail. It is commendable for a cartoon, like a box of bricks, to be "educational." So it should be if (as one of the greatest of Americans said) education is the highest duty of government. It is easy to be too glib about the American strip cartoon, to scoff too unkindly at its naivety, to correlate it only with the failings that are obviously prominent in American society. To-day, in almost every field of American activity, the spread of numbing conformity is being challenged by men of taste, talent and integrity. If there can be said to be one distinct class of Americans different from others, yet scattered throughout the continent, it is that body of people dubbed by its enemies "the intellectuals"; people of every political conviction, of every shade of background, but educated, honest and (above all) reasonable. To this growing section of the population most commercial offerings must now make some appeal; and there are signs that even the strip cartoon is maturing.

For years the genius of Walt Disney has been exerted in the comic strips, both through Disney characters like Donald Duck and Goofy, and through the efforts of many plagiarists. His own cartoons are nearly always good and gay. In another kind, Mr. Walt Kelly has devised an animal character named Pogo, an opossum living in the Florida Everglades, whose activities often give rise to a witty strain of political satire, besides involving some enchanting animal friends. Dennis the Menace is an agreeably annoying small boy whose parents are distinctly outside the Women's Club mould. Even in the strip cartoons, symbols of enveloping Americanism, there are signs that the United States will never be entirely standardized.

Nor, indeed, within the presently accepted pattern, are the vices of the newspaper strip cartoon really very vicious. The so-called "comic books," sold separately and irregularly, often contain material of nauseating fancy, but the Press cartoons are usually innocuous enough. Now and again there is an unpleasantly violent scene, now and again a little too much sex (and the extreme comedy of sexual relations is accepted even by the *New Yorker*); but all in all they deal in fairly straightforward adventure and the lives of fairly decent people: and the cops generally win.

In as much as they reflect materialism, contempt for the individualist, cloying sentiment and parochialism, they do no more than express general American tendencies; and however much the foreigner may dislike such trends, whatever pride he may take in his own national superiorities, he must in fairness admit that the American Way of Life, like the American comic strip, brings happiness to many, and no great evil. In any case, as the Chicago bartender said to his disgruntled customer, "If ya don't like the saloon, why doncha go fishing?"

EXERCISES

1. This article (written by an Englishman) on American *mores* as reflected in the comic strips might well strike an American reader both as perceptive and amusingly wrong-headed. Make a list of the observations the writer has made about American life. With which of these do you agree, with which do you disagree, and with which of them would you agree if the statement were properly modified?
2. Select a newspaper cartoon with which you are fairly well acquainted and write a theme in which you interpret what it "says" to the American reader. These questions may help you in working up ideas for the theme: Why do you read the cartoon? With what aspect of American life is it concerned? Is it satiric in intent? Would you show it to a foreigner in order to help him understand American life?
3. Is it fair to discuss Americans in terms of their comic strips? What other popular mass media would furnish candid commentary on American taste, intellect, and ambition?

6 FORMER STUDENTS

by Irwin Edman

Irwin Edman (for biographical note see page 23) here reflects on some of his former students, on what has happened to them since they left college, on their attitudes to their former teachers and to what they have been taught. His main point is that the teacher "lives in what has happened to the minds of his students, and in what they remember of things infinitely greater than themselves or than himself."

Once at a gathering in New York various people were mentioned who in diverse ways had begun to make their young presence felt in the world. One had written a play; another had become a psycho-analyst; still another a distinguished literary critic; one a radical editor; still another a foreign correspondent; and one even "the Iron Man" of big-league baseball. Every once in a while I found myself murmuring with not greatly concealed pride: "He is a former student of mine." Finally, a rather bored young lady looked at me pointedly. "Tell me," she asked, "was Chaliapin a former student of yours?"

I have since tried, not very successfully, to refrain from muttering proudly when the brighter young minds among contemporaries are mentioned: "Former student of mine!" For I cannot pretend to have taught any of them their present accomplishments. They did not learn playwriting, psychiatry, literary criticism, foreign correspondence, or baseball from me. And if I were honest, I should have to claim as former students of mine the hundreds of boring and unpleasant people, the failure and the complacent, successful nonentities, the rakes and the time-servers, whom I had the opportunity once to lecture to and whose quiz papers I once read. There are ten thousand former students of mine, I have calculated, roaming about the world. That does not include half a dozen, including some of the best, I have outlived. It does include hundreds I have forgotten and doubtless hundreds who have forgotten me. I met one of the latter once. It was at a club in New York. He was a little drunk, and he looked at me vaguely. He seemed to recall that he had seen me somewhere. A light dawned.

"I greatly enjoyed that course of yours in—in history."

"Mathematics," I corrected him gently.

"That's it," he said, "mathematics. You made calculus interesting, I must say."

"No," I said, "it was the theory of functions." I thought I might as well be credited with something even more majestic that I knew nothing about.

I must admit former students generally do better than that, and they greet a former teacher with a touching sense that once long ago they did get something from him. Sometimes it is nothing more than a joke, used to illustrate something they have completely forgotten. But the joke remains, and probably the theory it was meant to illustrate is dated by now, anyway. Sometimes they surprise you by remembering a quite incidental remark. Occasionally it is good enough for you to wish you could be sure you *had* said it and they had not heard it from some other professor—a professor of calculus, for instance. Or they remember some trick of gesture you had, or the way you suddenly, for emphasis, write a single word on the blackboard, or the mordant things you try to say to listeners, cruelties invariably regarded as merely gently whimsical. Or they even remember ideas that, being the first time they had heard them, made a great impression. They are ideas, often, about which by this time you have changed your mind, or lost faith in. One former student told me he had still the notebook he kept in the first year I taught anybody. He promises not to use it for blackmail against me. He insists that I misspelt Malebranche on the blackboard and, as a result, he has misspelt it almost automatically ever since.

Among the students one does remember, there is a tendency to remember them as they were, as, with notebooks before them, they sat as young men of nineteen or twenty in your classroom, or talked with you in your office. I find it hard to realize that time passes, or to realize that though freshmen and sophomores always look the same each year, they don't look the same (though they often are) ten years or fifteen years later. Meeting some of them after a lapse of years, one wonders what has happened to them, or whether one could ever have taught them anything, or where they can have learned all they seem to have found out about books and life, or how they could, who had once been so eager and bright, be so stodgy now.

I have had them look at me, too, in obvious wonder that they could ever have believed I could teach them anything and, once or twice, frankly express resentment at what they had learned.

I often wonder what students remember of a "former teacher," and can judge of their memories only by my own. But I wonder, too, what it is that one teaches them; how much difference a teacher can make. The psycho-analysts assure us these days that the great damage we call education is done largely in the first six years of a child's life, and that a teacher can do less and less fundamentally to the mind and character of a pupil after that as he passes from grade school to college. I hope that is so. It appears to relieve many of us of great responsibilities. The freshman comes with a kind of fatal predestination; he is what he is, and a course of a seminar cannot make any very great difference. I realize how momentary a tangent any teaching is upon a student's psyche, or his mental equipment.

Yet it is something, and something for which students, doubtless with justice, are not grateful.

"Teaching," Santayana writes in *Character and Opinion in the United States*, "is a delightful paternal art, and especially teaching intelligent and warm-hearted youngsters, as most American collegians are; but it is an art like acting, where the performance, often rehearsed, must be adapted to an audience hearing it only once. The speaker must make concessions to their impatience, their taste, their capacity, their prejudices, their ultimate good; he must neither bore nor perplex nor demoralize them. His thoughts must be such as can flow daily, and be set down in notes; they must come when the bell rings and stop appropriately when the bell rings a second time. The best that is in him, as Mephistopheles says in *Faust*, he dare not tell them; and as the substance of this possession is spiritual, to withhold is often to lose it."

What boredom, perplexity, and demoralization do one's students remember! I once caught a glimpse of what it was. I ran into a former student at a week-end in the country. I had known him fairly well and, even before I knew him, had noticed, as had some colleagues, the sharp, critical eye which he fixed upon one during a lecture. There are always half a dozen students in a class in whose presence one would not willingly be boring or stupid or inaccurate. When one is so unwillingly, one sees the immediate register of disappointment (or is it fulfilled expectation?) in their eyes. S—— had been one of those.

The conversation had been general and desultory. At the end of the evening he came into my room. He sat down on a chair and looked at me sharply. He seemed older than I remembered him, but he had always seemed grown up. He had, I had heard, various reasons for discouragement, both personal and professional, since he had left college. At one point some years ago he had suddenly turned up and asked if I couldn't think of a good reason for his not committing suicide, since he was about to do so. My reasons were not too good, but they seemed good enough. He was here still, not much happier apparently.

"Look here," he said, "I have been wanting to tell you for some years that your former students have a lot to hold against you, especially the good ones, those who got what you gave them."

"What harm did I do?" I asked, weakly. "I am in a worse case than Socrates. At least he could boast at his trial that none of his former students—those whom he was supposed to have corrupted—had appeared to testify against him. But here you come yourself, saying I have done you irreparable damage. Really, a course in the Philosophy of Art can't do that much harm to anyone, not even to those who get an A."

"Yes it can, and did," he insisted, "and I'm not the only one who was damaged, and you're not the only one who did the damage, though you did a great deal. You taught me and a good many others to think that contemplation, detachment, eternal things, that Truth, Goodness, and Beauty, were the proper preoccupations for a young man in this world. Well, that isn't the kind of world we are living in, and you gave us a profound sense of unreality. It's taken me years to get over it and I'm not quite over it yet. But Freud and Marx have helped me, and I wish I had found out about them sooner. I must admit I first heard about them from you, but you didn't sound as if you thought them as important as Plato or Santayana. You made me live beyond my intellectual income; you made me set store by a lot of things that had no more relation to the moving things in the world and to the lives of men than backgammon or Venetian brocades. I admit you woke me up to a few beautiful things and moving ideas, but it was a fool's Paradise. I've reversed the usual order and gone through Purgatory since."

"Well, you've found a new Paradise of your own—the revolution—haven't you?"

"Call it that, but it's one of the forces going on in the world; it isn't the lost causes of sweetness and light."

I tried to say something about the lost causes being the only enduring ones; but S—— suddenly softened a little. "It was a pleasant enough trance while it lasted," he said.

"I'm sorry the coming to was so bad," I said.

Former students are not often so bitter, I must admit. They are frequently almost embarrassing in their assertion that you awakened them to think, or to think clearly, or to feel qualities in things and ideas and people they had never perceived before. They can be incredibly kind, even or especially when they think they are being objective and just. For it is difficult to distinguish the persons from the things they communicate, and many a teacher gets a certain glamour in a student's memory because the teacher is associated with that student's first encounter with Plato or Shakespeare, Bach or Phidias. A teacher dealing with great things cannot help sometimes seeming—if only to the undistinguishing young—to be their voice or their oracle; and to a very young mind, if only for a short time, the teacher is confused with the things taught. This may, indeed, be very bad for the teacher, who, in the mirror of his student's generosity, makes something like the same identification, too. His colleagues will correct him, and many of his unbemused students would, too, given the opportunity. For even the luckiest teacher dealing with students avid for ideas will have a good many who look at him as if they dared him to teach them anything. I met one of that category once. He looked at me curiously. "I never could understand," he said, "why you thought philosophy interesting. And yet you seemed to do so. I was quite struck with that fact. That's the only thing I remember from the course."

It should really be a most discouraging fact (I am convinced it is a fact, in any case) that there is nothing much one does for the good student, and nothing very much that one can do for the poor one. In the case of the brilliant successes among former students of mine, I am convinced they were in essence as sophomores what they are now. If they are now learned men, they were already on the road to learning in their sophomore year. One of my former pupils can lay claim now to an erudition that I shall never have. But he was an erudite sophomore, and a little disturbing to an instructor in his first year of teaching. Another, though he is wiser about the world now, was wiser then than I shall ever be about it, and wrote almost as clearly and well then as he does now. The campus politicians are now real politicians, some of them, and not only in the field of politics. Sometimes there are apparent changes: the æsthetes become hard-boiled or disillusioned; the sentimentalists, cynics. But even in those cases the change is not always a real one.

Now that I have been teaching more than twenty years and have thus seen five generations—a college generation being four years—of college students, former students seem to return. I do not mean that they come back in the flesh as one did recently with his ten-year-old child to the campus; I mean one recognizes in the sophomore or junior there in the first row a replica of some predecessor not so very different of classes long ago. If I had known fewer students I should have been readier to predict what will become of them. It is easy enough with the run of the mill, though even with them, so rapidly is our world changing, it is not so easy as it used to be. There are not so many fathers' businesses to go into; the typical pre-lawyer may not find an office to be a lawyer in; the young snob and richling may find the world in which he can be both of those things vanishing under his feet. It is not easy even with the "originals," who also, for a teacher long in harness, fall into types. How was I to guess—how would anyone have guessed—that the editor of the best college humorous magazine in ten years, neatly ironic, merrily sceptical, and amusedly disillusioned, would turn into an uncompromising revolutionary, the Washington correspondent of the *Daily Worker?* How was one to suspect that the playboy whose life was bounded by fraternities and dances and drinking would be sobered by something or other into becoming a diligent professional classical scholar—a pedantic one at that? How could I have dreamed (though I might have done so) that the withering cynic of his class, whose god was Swift, should have become a mystical and fanatical rabbi?

I suspect that in each of these cases, had I been wiser or known my student better, I should not have had much occasion for surprise. There is much one does not find out about students, since it is natural that a teacher does rather more of the talking. And there is a lot one would never find out from the way in which students talk to a teacher.

There is only one thing by which I continue, with a foolish and persistent naïveté, to be surprised. I expect, somehow, that a student ten years after college will still have the brightness and enthusiasm, the disinterested love of ideas, and the impersonal passion for them that some develop during their undergraduate days. Time and again I have run into them, and wondered what the world has done to them that that passionate detachment should have gone. I know some of the things, brutal or familiar enough to the point almost of banality: a family, the struggle for a living, a disillusion with the status of contemplation in the nightmare of a violent world. But it is not revolution or disillusion that surprises me; both are intelligible. It is the death-in-life that assails the spirits of young men who had been alive when I knew them in college. A fierce hate, a transcendent revolutionary contempt for ideas, especially traditional ones, a revolt against the academy; all these things are not dismaying. They are symptoms that life is not dead and that spirit lives in some form, however tortured or fantastic or unprecedented. It is when spirit is utterly dead, when the one-time eager youth becomes precociously middle-aged, that one feels above all that education is a failure. One awakened something for a short time. But did one? Perhaps I have, like a good many teachers, flattered myself. It was not we who awakened them; it was the season of their lives, and the things and ideas which, despite us, for a moment—if only for a moment—stirred them. There are times when, if one thought about former students too much, one could not go on teaching. For the teacher meeting his former students is reminded of the fact that Plato long ago pointed out in the *Republic*. It is not what the teacher but what the world teaches them that will in the long run count, and what they can learn from the latter comes from habits fixed soon after birth and temperaments fixed long before it. There are just a few things a teacher can do, and that only for the sensitive and the spirited. He can initiate enthusiasms, clear paths, and inculcate discipline. He can communicate a passion and a method; no more. His most serious triumph as a teacher is the paradoxical one of having his students, while he is teaching them and perhaps afterwards, forget him in the absorption of the tradition or the inquiry of which he is the transient voice. Lucky for him if later his students feel his voice was just. As in the playing of music, it is the music, not the musician, that is ultimate. And in the art of teaching, it is what is taught that counts, not the teacher. It is a great tribute to an artist to say that he plays Beethoven or Bach, and puts nothing between them and his audience. But in so doing he becomes one with both the composer and the listener. In the listener's memory he anonymously shares the composer's immortality. The teacher, too, is best remembered who is thus forgotten. He lives in what has happened to the minds of his students, and in what they remember of things infinitely greater than themselves or than himself. They will remember, perhaps, that once in a way, in the midst of the routine of the classroom, it was something not himself that spoke, something not themselves that listened. The teacher may well be content to be otherwise forgotten, or to live in something grown to ripeness in his students that he, however minutely, helped bring to birth. There are many students thus come to fruition whom I should be proud to have say: "He was my teacher." There is no other immortality a teacher can have.

EXERCISES

1. Edman's style has a certain edge that in part may be the result of his appreciating the paradoxical and the ironic. Point to sentences or to anecdotes that give evidence of this.

2. Write a paragraph in which you state what Edman feels it is possible for a teacher to give a student and what it is impossible for him to give.

3. Write an essay on one of the following:

The mannerisms of a former teacher of mine

The library is the best teacher on the campus

How one can distinguish good teaching from bad

4. Does this article create a unified impression? If so, how? If not, why?

7 THE NIGHTINGALE SONG

by Noel Perrin

Noel Perrin (1927–) was educated at Exeter and Woodberry schools and at Williams College and Duke University. He did graduate work at Cambridge University and is now on the staff at Woman's College, University of North Carolina. "The Nightingale Song" is a humorous account of an adventure in research. Mr. Perrin describes his efforts to establish the actual sound of the nightingale's song so that he could vindicate his claim that T. S. Eliot "shows rare accuracy in his description of nature."

In Madingley Wood, near Cambridge, England, there is a grove famous for nightingales. Nettles grow thick under the trees there, and the nettles attract the nightingales—just why, nobody is quite sure, though last year my supervisor at Cambridge, where I was then doing graduate work in English, said it was because the nightingales want to sting themselves. In the Middle Ages, he pointed out, nightingales were constantly impaling themselves on thorns; they believed that the pain made them sing better. Modern nightingales, too degenerate for the thorn technique, try to encourage their melody with nettles.

One night last May, a careful observer might have seen me in the Wood, standing under a large copper-beech tree, near a patch of nettles. I was waiting to hear the nightingales sing, and I was standing because an English wood is nearly always too wet to sit down in. It wasn't just some idle love of birds that had drawn me there. It was my duty as an American citizen. I had just written a paper on the poetry of T. S. Eliot, and, among other things, I'd remarked that, for a modern poet, Eliot shows rare accuracy in his descriptions of nature.

"Bosh!" my supervisor had said when he returned the paper to me. "What about Eliot's *nightingales*? ' "Jug Jug" to dirty ears,' he quotes them in 'The Waste Land.' 'Jug Jug' to *tin* ears, perhaps. No nightingale ever made the noise 'Jug Jug' in his life, and so much for Mr. Eliot's rare accuracy. He'd better leave English birds to English poets."

My pride of country was aroused. As soon as I left the supervisor's rooms, I rushed to my college library and took down an enormous "Dictionary of Birds." It was no help at all. "The song of the European or English nightingale (*Luscinia megarhyncha*) is indescribable," wrote the author evasively. Well, at least Eliot had done better than *that*. But to uphold the honor of American poetry, so must I. I decided to go and actually hear the bird for myself.

By eight o'clock that same evening, I had walked the four miles out to Madingley and was standing under my tree, listening hard. By eight-thirty, I had heard nothing but a lovesick crow. There was no use hoping for nightingales while he was around, so I sat down (getting my pants wet instantly) and returned to the literary approach. What *English* poets, I asked myself, had committed themselves on the voice of the nightingale?

Shakespeare was the obvious one to start with, but I could come up with nothing better than Bottom's boast "I will roar you as 'twere any nightingale." Bottom's ears were obviously the wrong sort for hearing nightingales, so I passed on to Shelley. Once I'd realized that the skylark was the only bird he ever wrote an ode to, I tried Keats. Of course! In "Ode to a Nightingale," Keats must have given the bird the best description it has ever had. What does Keats say? Well, as far as I could remember, Keats says that nightingales sing of summer in full-throated ease and that the time to hear them is at midnight.

It seemed a long while to wait.

When I got back to Cambridge, at about two o'clock, I was soaking wet from the hard rain that had started at twelve-thirty. My hands ached from nettle stings, and my shoes were full of mud. I was through relying on Keats for bird lore; midnight had passed without a sound. And I had made no progress toward the vindication of American poetry.

In the morning, my roommate asked me what on earth I'd done to my hands, and I told him the whole story. "Oh, well, it wouldn't have mattered if you had heard a nightingale," he said cheerfully. "Still be your word against the supervisor's, wouldn't it? Besides, the old boy is right. Nightingales don't go 'Jug Jug,' they go 'tsoo tsoo.' See Edward Thomas on this."

So I saw Edward Thomas. I went back to my college library and looked up his collected poems. "Tsoo," his nightingales cry. The sub-librarian heard me cursing softly and came over to me. I told *him* the whole story. "But Mr. Eliot's quite right," he said. "Nightingales do have a note that sounds very much like 'Jug Jug.' Beautiful it is, sir. I think you'll find it quoted in Samuel Taylor Coleridge—'The Nightingale, A Conversation Poem,' from 'Lyrical Ballads.' That should satisfy your supervisor, sir."

I carried "A Conversation Poem" with me to my next supervision, and pointed out the lines to my supervisor. He read them aloud:

"And murmurs musical and swift jug jug,
And one low piping sound more sweet than
all—

Well, Perrin, true enough," he said easily. "But the 'Jug Jug' counts for no more than the preliminary cough of a Wagnerian tenor. That 'low piping sound' is the real *song* of the nightingale. It's as if Eliot had announced that he was going to describe a violin concerto and then had written, 'The violins tune up, "Squeak Squeak" to dirty ears.' "

Two days later, I went to Oxford for the weekend and attended a literary tea. After the third cup, I found myself telling the whole story to my host, a sympathetic don of Lincoln College. He rubbed his hands with pleasure. "What curious nightingales you have at Cambridge," he said. "All that tuning up. Your birds must suffer from sore throats, like your lecturers. A healthy, normal nightingale—the one that lives in my garden, for example—doesn't need to warm up. He just opens his beak and starts singing. And 'Jug Jug' is an integral part of what he sings. If I were you," he concluded, pouring me a fourth cup of tea, "I should look at John Lyly's 'The Songs of Birds,' from 'Campaspe,' the edition of 1584. Then I'd have a word with my supervisor."

I couldn't wait until I got back to Cambridge to speak to my supervisor. That same night, I posted him a card from Oxford. It read:

Jug, Jug, Jug, Jug, tereu shee cryes,
And still her woes at Midnight rise.
—J. Lyly

When I returned to Cambridge on Monday, there was a note waiting for me.

Dear Perrin [my supervisor had written]: I didn't realize you were so serious about nightingales. I fear you are leaning on a feeble reed in John Lyly, however. His bird cries are pure literary artifice, and not even original.

Look up the Latin version of the Greek myth of Philomela, who was turned into a nightingale, and of King Tereus, who was responsible. Then tell me if you still believe in Lyly's "tereu"s—or in his "Jug, Jug"s.

Underneath, he had inscribed the following:

Every thing did banish moan
Save the nightingale alone.
She, poor bird, as all forlorn,
Leaned her breast up-till a thorn,
And there sung the dolefull'st ditty,
That to hear it was great pity.
Fie, fie, fie, now would she cry,
Teru, teru, by and by,
That to hear her so complain
Scarce I could from tears refrain.
—Richard Barnfield (1574–1627)

I was still smarting from this blow when a fresh note came on Tuesday.

Dear Perrin [it began]: I've been doing a little research on literary references to the nightingale, myself. There weren't many major poets rash enough to try to reproduce his characteristic song. But there was one: Lord Tennyson.

Unlike your Mr. Eliot, Tennyson *does* have an extraordinary accurate ear. I quote from a minor poem of his called "The Grandmother":

The moon like a rick on fire was rising
over the dale,
And whit, whit, whit, in the bush beside
me chirrupt the nightingale.

The next morning, I presented myself at the Cambridge University Library precisely at nine-thirty, opening time. About eleven, I emerged from its bowels, grimy to the elbows from handling old books, and bearing a sheet of paper. On it were written these words from a poem titled "To Mistress Isabel Pennell," by the reasonably major poet John Skelton:

To hear this nightingale
Among the birdes smale
Warbeling in the vale,
Dug, dug,
Jug, jug,
Good year and good luck,
With chuck, chuck, chuck,
chuck.

In the entrance hall, I ran into my supervisor. He, too, was grimy and had a slip of paper. Silently we exchanged. "Walther von der Vogelweide," his said. "Early German minnesinger. From 'Unter den Linden':

Near the woods, down in the vale,
Tandaradi!
Sweetly sang the nightingale."

My supervisor spoke first. "Perrin, suppose you meet me at Madingley pub at eight," he said. "It's going to be a long evening. We might as well start with a pint of beer."

EXERCISES

1. Write three paragraphs in which you treat the unity, the coherence, and the emphasis of this essay.
2. This essay is written in a mocking tone. Give illustrations of this.

8 HERE IS NEW YORK

by E. B. White

E. B. White (1899–   ) was born at Mt. Vernon, New York, took his B.A. at Cornell (1921), and worked as a reporter. For a good many years he has been a contributor to the New Yorker Magazine, *writing editorials and humorous sketches. From 1938 to 1943, he wrote a column for* Harper's Magazine. *Among his best known books are* Is Sex Necessary? *(with James Thurber),* Every Day is Saturday, One Man's Meat, *and* The Second Tree from the Corner.

"Here is New York" successfully captures the reactions of a perceptive and imaginative person to living in New York. "The city is like poetry: it compresses all life, all races and breeds, into a small island and adds music and the accompaniment of internal engines. The island of Manhattan is without doubt the greatest human concentrate on earth, the poem whose magic is comprehensible to millions of permanent residents but whose full meaning will always remain illusive." White gives statistics and objective descriptions but weaves them together with his own experiences to pay a very personal tribute to the city.

A look into the soul
of an international capital

On any person who desires such queer prizes, New York will bestow the gift of loneliness and the gift of privacy. It is this largess that accounts for the presence within the city's walls of a considerable section of the population; for the residents of Manhattan are to a large extent strangers who have pulled up stakes somewhere and come to town, seeking sanctuary or fulfillment or some greater or lesser grail. The capacity to make such dubious gifts is a mysterious quality of New York. It can destroy an individual, or it can fulfill him, depending a good deal on luck. No one should come to New York to live unless he is willing to be lucky.

New York is the concentrate of art and commerce and sport and religion and entertainment and finance, bringing to a single compact arena the gladiator, the evangelist, the promoter, the actor, the trader, and the merchant. It carries on its lapel the unexpungeable odor of the long past, so that no matter where you sit in New York you feel the vibrations of great times and tall deeds, of queer people and events and undertakings. I am sitting at the moment in a stifling hotel room in 90-degree heat, halfway down an air shaft, in midtown. No air moves in or out of the room, yet I am curiously affected by emanations from the immediate surroundings. I am twenty-two blocks from where Rudolph Valentino lay in state, eight blocks from where Nathan Hale was executed, five blocks from the publisher's office where Ernest Hemingway hit Max Eastman on the nose, four miles from where Walt Whitman sat sweating out editorials for the *Brooklyn Eagle*, thirty-four blocks from the street Willa Cather lived in when she came to New York to write books about Nebraska, one block from where Marceline used to clown on the boards of the Hippodrome, thirty-six blocks from the spot where the historian Joe Gould kicked a radio to pieces in full view of the public, thirteen blocks from where Harry Thaw shot Stanford White, five blocks from where I used to usher at the Metropolitan Opera, and only a hundred and twelve blocks from the spot where Clarence Day the Elder [1] was washed of his sins in the Church of the Epiphany (I could continue this list indefinitely); and for that matter I am probably occupying the very room that any number of exalted and somewise memorable characters sat in, some of them on hot, breathless afternoons, lonely and private and full of their own sense of emanations from without.

[1] Rudolf Valentino, who died in 1925, was a popular star in the early days of films. Nathan Hale was an American patriot executed by the British as a spy in the American Revolution. Hemingway had a critical and personal difference of opinion with the writer and poet Max Eastman. Walt Whitman, the poet, was for a time on the staff of the newspaper *The Brooklyn Eagle*. Willa Cather was one of America's most important and popular novelists. The Hippodrome, where the clown and impersonator Marceline appeared, has since been torn down. Joe Gould is a famous Greenwich Village literary character. Harry Thaw, in 1906, killed the architect Stanford White, who, Thaw believed, had succeeded in winning the affections of Thaw's wife. Clarence Day was a distinguished New York citizen who was made the hero of the book *God and My Father*, and later of the successful play *Life with Father*, by his son Clarence Day, Jr. The delayed baptism of the elder Day was a central episode of the play.

When I went down to lunch a few minutes ago I noticed that the man sitting next to me (about eighteen inches away along the wall) was Fred Stone, the actor. The eighteen inches were both the connection and the separation that New York provides for its inhabitants. My only connection with Fred Stone was that I saw him in *The Wizard of Oz* [2] around the beginning of the century. But our waiter felt the same stimulus from being close to a man from Oz, and after Mr. Stone left the room the waiter told me that when he (the waiter) was a young man just arrived in this country and before he could understand a word of English, he had taken his girl for their first theater date to *The Wizard of Oz*. It was a wonderful show, the waiter recalled—a man of straw, a man of tin. Wonderful! (And still only eighteen inches away.) "Mr. Stone is a very hearty eater," said the waiter thoughtfully, content with this fragile participation in destiny, this link with Oz.

New York blends the gift of privacy with the excitement of participation; and better than most dense communities it succeeds in insulating the individual (if he wants it, and almost everybody wants or needs it) against all enormous and violent and wonderful events that are taking place every minute. Since I have been sitting in this miasmic air shaft, a good many rather splashy events have occurred in town. A man shot and killed his wife in a fit of jealousy. It caused no stir outside his block and got only small mention in the papers. I did not attend. Since my arrival, the greatest air show ever staged in all the world took place in town. I didn't attend and neither did most of the eight million other inhabitants, although they say there was quite a crowd. I didn't even hear any planes except a couple of west-bound commercial airliners that habitually use this air shaft to fly over. The biggest ocean-going ships on the North Atlantic arrived and departed. I didn't notice them and neither did most other New Yorkers. I am told this is the greatest seaport in the world, with six hundred and fifty miles of water front, and ships calling here from many exotic lands, but the only boat I've happened to notice since my arrival was a small sloop tacking out of the East River night before last on the ebb tide when I was walking across the Brooklyn Bridge. I heard the liner *Queen Mary* blow one midnight, though, and the sound carried the whole history of departure and longing and loss. The Lions [3] have been in convention. I've seen not one Lion. A friend of mine saw one and told me about him. (He was lame, and was wearing a bolero.) At the ballgrounds and horse parks the greatest sporting spectacles have been enacted. I saw no ballplayer, no race horse. The governor came to town. I heard the siren scream of his motorcycle police escort, but that was all

[2] A play based on a well-known American book of fantasy for children.

[3] The International Association of Lions Clubs, a fraternal order with branches in most American towns.

there was to that—an eighteen-inch margin again. A man was killed by a falling cornice. I was not a party to the tragedy, and again the inches counted heavily.

I mention these merely to show that New York is peculiarly constructed to absorb almost anything that comes along (whether a thousand-foot liner out of the East or a twenty-thousand-man convention out of the West) without inflicting the event on its inhabitants; so that every event is, in a sense, optional, and the inhabitant is in the happy position of being able to choose his spectacle and so conserve his soul. In most metropolises, small and large, the choice is often not with the individual at all. He is thrown to the Lions. The Lions are overwhelming; the event is unavoidable. A cornice falls, and it hits every citizen on the head, every last man in town. I sometimes think that the only event that hits every New Yorker on the head is the annual St. Patrick's Day parade, which is fairly penetrating—the Irish are a hard race to tune out, there are 500,000 of them in residence, and they have the police force right in the family.

The quality in New York that insulates its inhabitants from life may simply weaken them as individuals. Perhaps it is healthier to live in a community where, when a cornice falls, you feel the blow; where, when the governor passes, you see at any rate his hat.

I am not defending New York in this regard. Many of its settlers are probably here merely to escape, not face, reality. But whatever it means, it is a rather rare gift, and I believe it has a positive effect on the creative capacities of New Yorkers—for creation is in part merely the business of forgoing the great and small distractions.

Although New York often imparts a feeling of great forlorness or forsakenness, it seldom seems dead or unresourceful; and you always feel that either by shifting your location ten blocks or by reducing your fortune by five dollars you can experience rejuvenation. Many people who have no real independence of spirit depend on the city's tremendous variety and sources of excitement for spiritual sustenance and maintenance of morale. In the country there are a few chances of sudden rejuvenation —a shift in weather, perhaps, or something arriving in the mail. But in New York the chances are endless. I think that although many persons are here from some excess of spirit (which caused them to break away from their small town), some, too, are here from a deficiency of spirit, who find in New York a protection, or an easy substitution.

There are roughly three New Yorks. There is, first, the New York of the man or woman who was born here, who takes the city for granted and accepts its size and its turbulence as natural and inevitable. Second, there is the New York of the commuter—the city that is devoured by locusts each day and spat out each night. Third, there is the New York of the person who was born somewhere else and came to New York in quest of something. Of these three trembling cities the greatest is the last—the city of final destination, the city that is a goal. It is this third city that accounts for New York's high-strung disposition, its poetical deportment, its dedication to the arts, and its incomparable achievements. Commuters give the city its tidal restlessness; natives give it solidity and continuity; but the settlers give it passion. And whether it is a farmer arriving from Italy to set up a small grocery store in a slum, or a young girl arriving from a small town in Mississippi to escape the indignity of being observed by her neighbors, or a boy arriving from the Corn Belt with a manuscript in his suitcase and a pain in his heart, it makes no difference: each embraces New York with the intense excitement of first love, each absorbs New York with the fresh eyes of an adventurer, each generates heat and light to dwarf the Consolidated Edison Company.[4]

The commuter is the queerest bird of all. The suburb he inhabits has no essential vitality of its own and is a mere roost where he comes at day's end to go to sleep. Except in rare cases, the man who lives in Mamaroneck or Little Neck or Teaneck, and works in New York, discovers nothing much about the city except the time of arrival and departure of trains and buses, and the path to a quick lunch. He is desk-bound, and has never, idly roaming in the gloaming, stumbled suddenly on Belvedere Tower in the Park, seen the ramparts rise sheer from the water of the pond, and the boys along the shore fishing for minnows, girls stretched out negligently on the shelves of the rocks; he has never come suddenly on anything at all in New York as a loiterer, because he has had no time between trains. He has fished in Manhattan's wallet and dug out coins, but he has never listened to Manhattan's breathing, never awakened to its morning, never dropped off to sleep in its night. About 400,000 men and women come charging onto the Island each week-day morning, out of the mouth of tubes and tunnels. Not many among them have ever spent a drowsy afternoon in the great rustling oaken silence of the reading room of the Public Library, with the book elevator (like an old water wheel) spewing out books onto the trays. They tend their furnaces in Westchester and in Jersey, but have never seen the furnaces of the Bowery, the fires that burn in oil drums on zero winter nights. They may work in the financial district downtown and never see the extravagant plantings of Rockefeller Center—the daffodils and grape hyacinths and birches and the flags trimmed to the wind on a fine morning in spring. Or they may work in a midtown office and may let a whole year swing round without sighting Governor's Island from the sea wall. The commuter dies with tremendous mileage to his credit, but he is no rover. His entrances and exits are more

[4] The Consolidated Edison Company supplies power for New York City.

devious than those in a prairie-dog village; and he calmly plays bridge while his train is buried in the mud at the bottom of the East River. The Long Island Rail Road alone carried forty million commuters last year; but many of them were the same fellow retracing his steps.

The terrain of New York is such that a resident sometimes travels farther, in the end, than a commuter. The journey of the composer Irving Berlin from Cherry Street in the lower East Side to an apartment uptown was through an alley and was only three or four miles in length; but it was like going three times around the world.

A poem compresses much in a small space and adds music, thus heightening its meaning. The city is like poetry: it compresses all life, all races and breeds, into a small island and adds music and the accompaniment of internal engines. The island of Manhattan is without any doubt the greatest human concentrate on earth, the poem whose magic is comprehensible to millions of permanent residents but whose full meaning will always remain illusive. At the feet of the tallest and plushiest offices lie the crummiest slums. The genteel mysteries housed in the Riverside Church are only a few blocks from the voodoo charms of Harlem. The merchant princes, riding to Wall Street in their limousines down the East River Drive, pass within a few hundred yards of the gypsy kings; but the princes do not know they are passing kings, and the kings are not up yet anyway—they live a more leisurely life than the princes and get drunk more consistently.

New York is nothing like Paris; it is nothing like London; and it is not Spokane multiplied by sixty, or Detroit multiplied by four. It is by all odds the loftiest of cities. It even managed to reach the highest point in the sky at the lowest moment of the depression. The Empire State Building shot twelve hundred and fifty feet into the air when it was madness to put out as much as six inchs of new growth. (The building has a mooring mast that no dirigible has ever tied to; it employs a man to flush toilets in slack times; it has been hit by an airplane in a fog, struck countless times by lightning, and been jumped off of by so many unhappy people that pedestrians instinctively quicken step when passing Fifth Avenue and 34th Street.)

Manhattan has been compelled to expand skyward because of the absence of any other direction in which to grow. This, more than any other thing, is responsible for its physical majesty. It is to the nation what the white church spire is to the village—the visible symbol of aspiration and faith, the white plume saying that the way is up. The summer traveler swings in over Hell Gate Bridge and from the window of his sleeping car as it glides above the pigeon lofts and back yards of Queens looks southwest to where the morning light first strikes the steel peaks of mid-town, and he sees its upward thrust unmistakable: the great walls and towers rising, the smoke rising, the heat not yet rising, the hopes and ferments of so many awakening millions rising—this vigorous spear that presses heaven hard.

It is a miracle that New York works at all. The whole thing is implausible. Every time the residents brush their teeth, millions of gallons of water must be drawn from the Catskill mountains and the hills of Westchester. When a young man in Manhattan writes a letter to his girl in Brooklyn, the love message gets blown to her through a pneumatic tube—*pfft*—just like that. The subterranean system of telephone cables, power lines, steam pipes, gas mains, and sewer pipes is reason enough to abandon the island to the gods and the weevils. Every time an incision is made in the pavement, the noisy surgeons expose ganglia that are tangled beyond belief. By rights New York should have destroyed itself long ago, from panic or fire or rioting or failure of some vital supply line in its circulatory system or from some deep labyrinthine short circuit. Long ago the city should have experienced an insoluble traffic snarl at some impossible bottleneck. It should have perished of hunger when food lines failed for a few days. It should have been wiped out by a plague starting in its slums or carried in by ships' rats. It should have been overwhelmed by the sea that licks at it on every side. The workers in its myriad cells should have succumbed to nerves, from the fearful pall of smoke-fog that drifts over every few days from Jersey, blotting out all light at noon and leaving the high offices suspended, men groping and depressed, and the sense of world's end. It should have been touched in the head by the August heat and gone off its rocker.

Mass hysteria is a terrible force, yet New Yorkers seem always to escape it by some tiny margin: they sit in stalled subways without claustrophobia, they extricate themselves from panic situations by some lucky wisecrack, they meet confusion and congestion with patience and grit—a sort of perpetual muddling through. Every facility is inadequate—the hospitals and schools and playgrounds are overcrowded, the express highways are feverish, the unimproved highways and bridges are bottlenecks; there is not enough air and not enough light, and there is usually too much heat or too little. But the city makes up for its hazards and its deficiencies by supplying its citizens with massive doses of a supplementary vitamin—the sense of belonging to something unique, cosmopolitan, mighty, and unparalleled.

To an outlander a stay in New York can be and often is a series of small embarrassments and discomforts and disappointments: not understanding the waiter, not being able to distinguish between a sucker joint and a friendly saloon, riding the wrong subway, being slapped down by a bus driver for asking an innocent question, enduring sleepless nights when the street noises fill the bedroom. Tourists make for New York, particularly in summertime—they swarm all over the Statue of Liberty (where many a resident of the town has never set foot), they invade the Automat,[5] visit radio studios, St. Patrick's Cathedral, and they window shop. Mostly they have a pretty good time. But sometimes in New York you run across the disillusioned—a young couple who are obviously visitors, newlyweds perhaps, for whom the bright dream has vanished. The place has been too much for them; they sit languishing in a cheap restaurant over a speechless meal.

The oft-quoted thumbnail sketch of New York is, of course: "It's a wonderful place, but I'd hate to live there." I have an idea that people from villages and small towns, people accustomed to the convenience and the friendliness of neighborhood over-the-fence living, are unaware that life in New York follows the neighborhood pattern. The city is literally a composite of tens of thousands of tiny neighborhood units. There are, of course, the big districts and big units: Chelsea and Murray Hill and Gramercy (which are residential units), Harlem (a racial unit), Greenwich Village (a unit dedicated to the arts and other matters), and there is Radio City (a commercial development), Peter Cooper Village (a housing unit), the Medical Center (a sickness unit) and many other sections each of which has some distinguishing characteristic. But the curious thing about New York is that each large geographical unit is composed of countless small neighborhoods. Each neighborhood is virtually self-sufficient. Usually it is no more than two or three blocks long and a couple of blocks wide. Each area is a city within a city within a city. Thus, no matter where you live in New York, you will find within a block or two a grocery store, a barbershop, a newsstand and shoeshine shack, an ice-coal-and-wood cellar (where you write your order on a pad outside as you walk by), a dry cleaner, a laundry, a delicatessen (beer and sandwiches delivered at any hour to your door), a flower shop, an undertaker's parlor, a movie house, a radio-repair shop, a stationer, a haberdasher, a tailor, a drugstore, a garage, a tearoom, a saloon, a hardware store, a liquor store, a shoe-repair shop. Every block or two, in most residential sections of New York, is a little main street. A man starts for work in the morning and before he has gone two hundred yards he has completed half a dozen missions: bought a paper, left a pair of shoes to be soled, picked up a pack of cigarettes, ordered a bottle of whisky to be dispatched in the opposite direction against his home-coming, written a message to the unseen forces of the wood cellar, and notified the dry cleaner that a pair of trousers awaits call. Homeward bound eight hours later, he buys a bunch of pussy willows, a Mazda bulb, a drink, a shine—all between the

[5] One of a chain of low-priced, self-service restaurants where food is obtained by inserting coins in slots.

corner where he steps off the bus and his apartment. So complete is each neighborhood, and so strong the sense of neighborhood, that many a New Yorker spends a lifetime within the confines of an area smaller than a country village. Let him walk two blocks from his corner and he is in a strange land and will feel uneasy till he gets back.

Storekeepers are particularly conscious of neighborhood boundary lines. A woman friend of mine moved recently from one apartment to another, a distance of three blocks. When she turned up, the day after the move, at the same grocer's that she had patronized for years, the proprietor was in ecstasy—almost in tears—at seeing her. "I was afraid," he said, "now that you've moved away I wouldn't be seeing you any more." To him, *away* was three blocks, or about seven hundred and fifty feet.

I am, at the moment of writing this, living not as a neighborhood man in New York but as a transient, or vagrant, in from the country for a few days. Summertime is a good time to re-examine New York and to receive again the gift of privacy, the jewel of loneliness. In summer the city contains (except for tourists) only die-hards and authentic characters. No casual, spotty dwellers are around, only the real article. And the town has a somewhat relaxed air, and one can lie in a loincloth, gasping and remembering things.

I've been remembering what it felt like as a young man to live in the same town with giants. When I first arrived in New York my personal giants were a dozen or so columnists and critics and poets whose names appeared regularly in the papers. I burned with a low steady fever just because I was on the same island with Don Marquis, Heywood Broun, Christopher Morley, Franklin P. Adams, Robert C. Benchley, Frank Sullivan, Dorothy Parker, Alexander Woollcott, Ring Lardner, and Stephen Vincent Benét.[6] I would hang around the corner of Chambers Street and Broadway, thinking: "Somewhere in that building is the typewriter that archy the cockroach [7] jumps on at night." New York hardly gave me a living at that period, but it sustained me. I used to walk quickly past the house in West 13th Street between Sixth and Seventh where Franklin P. Adams lived, and the block seemed to tremble under my feet—the way Park Avenue trembles when a train leaves Grand Central. This excitation (nearness of giants) is a continuing thing. The city is always full of young worshipful beginners—young actors, young aspiring poets, ballerinas, painters, reporters, singers—each depending on his own brand of tonic to stay alive, each with his own stable of giants.

New York provides not only a continuing excitation but also a spectacle that is continuing. I wander around, re-examining this spectacle, hoping

[6] American writers prominent in the 1920's and 30's.
[7] The hero of books by Don Marquis. (The cockroach was unable to type capital letters.)

that I can put it on paper. It is Saturday, toward the end of the afternoon. I turn through West 48th Street. From the open windows of the drum and saxaphone parlors come the listless sounds of musical instruction, monstrous insect noises in the brooding field of summer. The Cort Theater is disgorging its matinee audience. Suddenly the whole block is filled with the mighty voice of a street singer. He approaches, looking for an audience, a large, cheerful Negro with grand-opera contours, strolling with head thrown back, filling the canyon with uninhibited song. He carries a long cane as his sole prop, and is tidily but casually dressed—slacks, seersucker jacket, a book showing in his pocket.

This is perfect artistic timing; the audience from the Cort, where Sartre's *The Respectful Prostitute* is playing,[8] has just received a lesson in race relations and is in a mood to improve the condition of the black race as speedily as possible. Coins (mostly quarters) rattle to the street, and a few minutes of minstrelsy improves the condition of one Negro by about eight dollars. If he does as well as this at every performance, he has a living right there. New York is the city of opportunity, they say. Even the mounted cop, clumping along on his nag a few minutes later, scans the gutter carefully for dropped silver, like a bird watching for spilt grain.

It is seven o'clock and I re-examine an ex-speakeasy in East 53rd Street, with dinner in mind. A thin crowd, a summer-night buzz of fans interrupted by an occasional drink being shaken at the small bar. It is dark in here (the proprietor sees no reason for boosting his light bill just because liquor laws have changed). How dark, how pleasing; and how miraculously beautiful the murals showing Italian lake scenes—probably executed by a cousin of the owner. The owner himself mixes. The fans intone the prayer for cool salvation. From the next booth drifts the conversation of radio executives; from the green salad comes the little taste of garlic. Behind me (eighteen inches again) a young intellectual is trying to persuade a girl to come live with him and be his love. She has her guard up, but he is extremely reasonable, careful not to overplay his hand. A combination of intellectual companionship and sexuality is what they have to offer each other, he feels. In the mirror over the bar I can see the ritual of the second drink. Then he has to go the men's room and she has to go to the ladies' room, and when they return, the argument has lost its tone. And the fan takes over again, and the heat and the relaxed air and the memory of so many good little dinners in so many good little illegal places, with the theme of love, the sound of ventilation, the brief medicinal illusion of gin.

Another hot night I stop off at the Goldman Band concert in the Mall in Central Park. The people seated on the benches fanned out in front of the band shell are attentive, appreciative. In the trees the night wind stirs,

[8] In 1948, when this essay first appeared.

bringing the leaves to life, endowing them with speech; the electric lights illuminate the green branches from the under side, translating them into a new language. Overhead a plane passes dreamily, its running lights winking. On the bench directly in front of me, a boy sits with his arm around his girl; they are proud of each other and are swathed in music. The cornetist steps forward for a solo, begins, "Drink to me only with thine eyes . . ." In the wide, warm night the horn is startlingly pure and magical. Then from the North River another horn solo begins—the *Queen Mary* announcing her intentions. She is not on key; she is a half tone off. The trumpeter in the bandstand never flinches. The horns quarrel savagely, but no one minds having the intimation of travel injected into the pledge of love. "I leave," sobs Mary. "And I will pledge with mine," sighs the trumpeter. Along the asphalt paths strollers pass to and fro; they behave considerately, respecting the musical atmosphere. Popsicles [9] are moving well. In the warm grass beyond the fence, forms wriggle in the shadows, and the skirts of the girls approaching on the Mall are ballooned by the breeze, and their bare shoulders catch the lamplight. "Drink to me only with thine eyes." It is a magical occasion, and it's all free.

On week ends in summer the town empties. I visit my office on a Saturday afternoon. No phone rings, no one feeds the hungry IN-baskets, no one disturbs the papers; it is a building of the dead, a time of awesome suspension. The whole city is honeycombed with abandoned cells—a jail that has been effectively broken. Occasionally from somewhere in the building a night bell rings, summoning the elevator—a special fire alarm ring. This is the pit of loneliness, in an office on a summer Saturday. I stand at the window and look down at the batteries and batteries of offices across the way, recalling how the thing looks in winter twilight when everything is going full blast, every cell lighted, and how you can see in pantomime the puppets fumbling with their slips of paper (but you don't hear the rustle), see them pick up their phone (but you don't hear the ring), see the noiseless, ceaseless moving about of so many passers of pieces of paper: New York, the capital of memoranda, in touch with Calcutta, in touch with Reykjavik, and always fooling with something.

In the café of the Lafayette, the regulars sit and talk. It is busy yet peaceful. Nursing a drink, I stare through the west windows at the Manufacturers Trust Company and at the red brick fronts on the north side of Ninth Street, watching the red turning slowly to purple as the light dwindles. Brick buildings have a way of turning color at the end of the day, the way a red rose turns bluish as it wilts. The café is a sanctuary. The waiters are ageless and they change not. Nothing has been modernized. Notre Dame stands guard in its travel poster. The coffee is strong and full of chicory, and good.

[9] Sherbet frozen on a stick.

Walk the Bowery under the elevated railway at night and all you feel is a sort of cold guilt. Touched for a dime, you try to drop the coin and not touch the hand, because the hand is dirty; you try to avoid the glance, because the glance accuses. This is not so much personal menace as universal—the cold menace of unresolved human suffering and poverty and the advanced stages of the disease alcoholism. On a summer night the drunks sleep in the open. The sidewalk is a free bed, and there are no lice. Pedestrians step along and over and around the still forms as though walking on a battlefield among the dead. In doorways, on the steps of the savings bank, the bums lie sleeping it off. Standing sentinel at each sleeper's head is the empty bottle from which he drained his release. Wedged in the crook of his arm is the paper bag containing his things. The glib barker on the sight-seeing bus tells his passengers that this is the "street of lost souls," but the Bowery does not think of itself as lost; it meets its peculiar problem in its own way—plenty of gin mills, plenty of flophouses, plenty of indifference, and always, at the end of the line, Bellevue Hospital.

A block or two east and the atmosphere changes sharply. In the slums are poverty and bad housing, but with them the reassuring sobriety and safety of family life. I head east along Rivington. All is cheerful and filthy and crowded. Small shops overflow onto the sidewalk, leaving only half the normal width for passers-by. In the candid light from unshaded bulbs gleam watermelons and lingerie. Families have fled the hot rooms upstairs and have found relief on the pavement. They sit on orange crates, smoking, relaxed, congenial. This is the nightly garden party of the vast Lower East Side—and on the whole they are more agreeable-looking hot-weather groups than some you see in bright canvas deck chairs on green lawns in country circumstances. It is folksy here with the smell of warm flesh and squashed fruit and fly-bitten filth in the gutter, and cooking.

At the corner of Lewis, in the playground behind the wire fence, an open-air dance is going on—some sort of neighborhood affair, probably designed to combat delinquency. Women push baby carriages in and out among the dancers, as though to exhibit what dancing leads to at last. Overhead, like banners decorating a cotillion hall, stream the pants and bras from the pulley lines. The music stops, and a beautiful Italian girl takes a brush from her handbag and stands under the street lamp brushing her long blue-black hair till it shines. The cop in the patrol car watches sullenly.

The Consolidated Edison Company says there are eight million people in the five boroughs of New York, and the company is in a position to know. As in every dense community, virtually all races, all religions, all nationalities are represented. Population figures are shifty—they change almost as fast as one can break them down. It is safe to say that about two million of New York's eight million are Jews—roughly one in four. Among this two million who are Jewish are, of course, a great many nationalities —Russian, German, Polish, Rumanian, Austrian, a long list. The Urban League of Greater New York estimates that the number of Negroes in New York is about 700,000. Of these, about 500,000 live in Harlem, a district that extends northward from 110th Street. The Negro population has increased rapidly in the last few years. There are half again as many Negroes in New York today as there were in 1940. There are about 230,000 Puerto Ricans living in New York. There are half a million Irish, half a million Germans. There are 900,000 Russians, 150,000 English, 400,000 Poles, and there are quantities of Finns and Czechs and Swedes and Danes and Norwegians and Latvians and Belgians and Welsh and Greeks, and even Dutch, who have been here from away back. It is very hard to say how many Chinese there are. Officially there are 12,000 but there are many Chinese who are in New York illegally and who don't like census takers.[10]

The collision and the intermingling of these millions of foreign-born people representing so many races, creeds, and nationalities make New York a permanent exhibit of the phenomenon of one world. The citizens of New York are tolerant not only from disposition but from necessity. The city has to be tolerant, otherwise it would explode in a radio-active cloud of hate and rancor and bigotry. If the people were to depart even briefly from the peace of cosmopolitan intercourse, the town would blow up higher than a kite. In New York smolders every race problem there is, but the noticeable thing is not the problem but the inviolate truce. Harlem is a city in itself, and being a city Harlem symbolizes segregation; yet Negro life in New York lacks the more conspicuous elements of Jim Crowism. Negroes ride subways and buses on terms of equality with whites, but they have not yet found the same equality in hotels and restaurants. Professionally, Negroes get on well in the theater, in music, in art, and in literature; but in many fields of employment the going is tough. The Jim Crow principle lives chiefly in the housing rules and customs. Private owners of dwellings legally can, and do, exclude Negroes. Under a recent city ordinance, however, apartment buildings that are financed with public moneys or that receive any tax exemption must accept tenants without regard to race, color, or religion.

To a New Yorker the city is both changeless and changing. In many respects it neither looks nor feels the way it did twenty-five years ago. The elevated railways have been pulled down, all but the Third Avenue.

[10] All these figures are as of 1948. There are now approximately 750,000 Negroes and 376,000 Puerto Ricans in the city.

An old-timer walking up Sixth past the Jefferson Market jail misses the railroad, misses its sound, its spotted shade, its little aerial stations, and the tremor of the thing. Broadway has changed in aspect. It used to have a discernible bony structure beneath its loud bright surface; but the signs are so enormous now, the buildings and shops and hotels have largely disappeared under the neon lights and letters and the frozen-custard façade. Broadway is a custard street with no frame supporting it. In Greenwich Village the light is thinning: big apartments have come in, bordering Washington Square, and the bars are mirrored and chromed. But there are still in the Village the lingering traces of poesy, Mexican glass, hammered brass, batik, lamps made of whisky bottles, first novels made of fresh memories—the old Village with its alleys and ratty one-room rents catering to the erratic needs of those whose hearts are young and gay.

Grand Central Terminal has become honky-tonk, with its extra-dimensional advertising displays and its tendency to adopt the tactics of a travel broker. I practically lived in Grand Central at one period (it has all the conveniences and I had no other place to stay) and the great hall seemed to me one of the more inspiring interiors in New York, until advertisements for Lastex and Coca-Cola got into the temple.

All over town the great mansions are in decline. Schwab's house facing the Hudson on Riverside is gone. Morgan's house on Madison Avenue is a church administration office. What was once the Fahnestock house is now Random House. Rich men nowadays don't live in houses; they live in the attics of big apartment buildings and plant trees on the setbacks, hundreds of feet above the street.

There are fewer newspapers than there used to be, thanks somewhat to the late Frank Munsey.[11] One misses the *Globe*, the *Mail*, the *Herald*; and to many a New Yorker life has never seemed the same since the *World* took the count.

Police now ride in radio prowl cars instead of gumshoeing around the block swinging their sticks. A ride in the subway costs ten cents, and the seats are apt to be dark green instead of straw yellow. Men go to saloons to gaze at televised events instead of to think long thoughts. It is all very disconcerting. Even parades have changed some. The last triumphal military procession in Manhattan simply filled the city with an ominous and terrible rumble of heavy tanks.

The slums are gradually giving way to the lofty housing projects—high in stature, high in purpose, low in rent. There are a couple of dozens of these new developments scattered around; each is a city in itself (one of them in the Bronx accommodates twelve thousand families), sky acreage hitherto untilled, lifting people far above the street, standardizing their

[11] An American publisher who successfully set the pattern for combining newspapers.

sanitary life, giving them some place to sit other than an orange crate. Federal money, state money, city money, and private money have flowed into these projects. Banks and insurance companies are in back of some of them. Architects have turned the buildings slightly on their bases, to catch more light. In some of them, rents are as low as eight dollars a month a room. Thousands of new units are still needed and will eventually be built, but New York never quite catches up with itself, is never in equilibrium. In flush times the population mushrooms and the new dwellings sprout from the rock. Come bad times and the population scatters and the lofts are abandoned and the landlord withers and dies.

New York has changed in tempo and in temper during the years I have known it. There is greater tension, increased irritability. You encounter it in many places, in many faces. The normal frustrations of modern life are here multiplied and amplified—a single run of a crosstown bus contains, for the driver, enough frustration and annoyance to carry him over the edge of sanity: the traffic light that changes always an instant too soon, the passenger that bangs on the shut door, the truck that blocks the only opening, the coin that slips to the floor, the question asked at the wrong moment. There is greater tension and there is greater speed. Taxis roll faster than they rolled ten years ago—and they were rolling fast then. Hackmen used to drive with verve; now they sometimes seem to drive with desperation, toward the ultimate tip. On the West Side Highway, approaching the city, the motorist is swept along in a trance—a sort of fever of inescapable motion, goaded from behind, hemmed in on either side, a mere chip in a millrace.

The city has never been so uncomfortable, so crowded, so tense. Money has been plentiful and New York has responded. Restaurants are hard to get into; businessmen stand in line for a Schrafft's luncheon as meekly as idle men used to stand in soup lines. (Prosperity creates its bread lines, the same as depression.) The lunch hour in Manhattan has been shoved ahead half an hour, to 12:00 or 12:30, in the hopes of beating the crowd to a table. Everyone is a little emptier at quitting time than he used to be. Apartments are festooned with No Vacancy signs. There is standing-room-only in Fifth Avenue buses, which once reserved a seat for every paying guest. The old double-deckers are disappearing—people don't ride just for the fun of it any more.

At certain hours on certain days it is almost impossible to find an empty taxi and there is a great deal of chasing around after them. You grab a handle and open the door, and find that some other citizen is entering from the other side. Doormen grow rich blowing their whistles for cabs; and some doormen belong to no door at all—merely wander about through the streets, opening cabs for people as they happen to find them. By comparison with other less hectic days, the city is uncomfortable and inconvenient; but New Yorkers temperamentally do not crave comfort and convenience—if they did they would live elsewhere.

The subtlest change in New York is something people don't speak much about but that is in everyone's mind. The city, for the first time in its long history, is destructible. A single flight of planes no bigger than a wedge of geese can quickly end this island fantasy, burn the towers, crumble the bridges, turn the underground passages into lethal chambers, cremate the millions. The intimation of mortality is part of New York now: in the sound of jets overhead, in the black headlines of the latest edition.

All dwellers in cities must live with the stubborn fact of annihilation; in New York the fact is somewhat more concentrated because of the concentration of the city itself, and because, of all targets, New York has a certain clear priority. In the mind of whatever perverted dreamer might loose the lightning, New York must hold a steady, irresistible charm.

It used to be that the Statue of Liberty was the signpost that proclaimed New York and translated it for all the world. Today Liberty shares the role with Death. Along the East River, from the razed slaughterhouses of Turtle Bay, as though in a race with the spectral flight of planes, men are carving out the permanent headquarters of the United Nations—the greatest housing project of them all. In its stride, New York takes on one more interior city, to shelter, this time, all governments, and to clear the slum called war. New York is not a capital city—it is not a national capital or a state capital. But it is by way of becoming the capital of the world. The Secretariat Building, a marble and glass cigar box set on end, is already a familiar landmark. Forty-seventh Street has been widened and traffic will soon flow in a new tunnel under First Avenue. Once again the city will absorb, almost without showing any sign of it, a congress of visitors. It has already shown itself capable of stashing away the United Nations—a great many of the delegates have been around town during the past couple of years, and the citizenry has hardly caught a glimpse of their coattails or their black Homburgs.

This race—this race between the destroying planes and the struggling Parliament of Man—it sticks in all our heads. The city at last perfectly illustrates both the universal dilemma and the general solution, this riddle in steel and stone is at once the perfect target and the perfect demonstration of nonviolence, of racial brotherhood, this lofty target scraping the skies and meeting the destroying planes halfway, home of all people and all nations, capital of everything, housing the deliberations by which the planes are to be stayed and their errand forestalled.

A block or two west of the new City of Man in Turtle Bay there is an old willow tree that presides over an interior garden. It is a battered tree, long suffering and much climbed, held together by strands of wire but beloved of those who know it. In a way it symbolizes the city: life under difficulties, growth against odds, sap-rise in the midst of concrete, and the steady reaching for the sun. Whenever I look at it nowadays, and feel the cold shadow of the planes, I think: "This must be saved, this particular thing, this very tree." If it were to go, all would go—this city, this mischievous and marvelous monument which not to look upon would be like death.

EXERCISES

1. Outline the topics White develops. What theme unifies or helps to unify them?
2. White introduces colloquial phrases—"the queerest bird," "off his rocker," etc.—into otherwise dignified and even consciously poetic prose. Make a list of such phrases. Do they injure the tone of his essay or complicate the tone?
3. Compare this essay to Faulkner's. Do the two authors use any similar techniques?
4. If you have lived in New York City or visited there, write an essay about your reactions to it. If you have not, write an essay about your reactions to another city.

VI Naturalness and Pretentiousness in Writing

We are all familiar with the maxim "style is the man," implying that a writer's beliefs and attitudes, his sophistication and subtlety, indeed, both his good and bad qualities are revealed in his style. This belief in the uniquely personal quality of a writer's style is reflected in references to Henry James' style, or to that of Joseph Conrad. Less familiar is the comment "style is the subject." This suggests that a given subject invites, even demands, a style appropriate to itself. Neither "style is the man" nor "style is the subject" is exclusively and wholly true. Certainly a great deal about the "man" will be revealed in his treatment of a subject. At the same time, the writer strives to adapt his style so that it most effectively expresses his theme and communicates his intention. Furthermore, he will keep in mind his audience, the place, and the occasion, and this too will influence his style.

When we talk of naturalness and pretentiousness in writing, the crucial criterion is that of appropriateness. Whether the style of a composition is appropriate can be judged by its effectiveness in conveying the writer's theme. If he means to be ironic or humorous, lyrical or serious, his style should communicate his intention and his meaning to his readers. For instance, if he wants to write lyrically about young love, he will probably fail if he uses long and involved sentences and ponderous diction. However, if he wants to clarify a highly abstruse philosophical point for his colleagues, his exposition will suffer if he confines himself to monosyllables and does not avail himself of technical terms that convey subtle distinctions.

Pretentiousness in writing usually reflects a failure of the writer's sense of the appropriate. Often, it manifests itself in unnecessarily pompous diction and elaborate construction. It would be wrong, however, to confuse ornateness with pretentiousness. Some of the finest English stylists have written very complex and elaborate prose, as you will see in Section VIII, without writing pretentiously. The style appears natural to the theme, appropriate to the occasion, and effectively and elegantly communicates the author's intention. But when Carl Van Vechten in *The Tattooed Countess* describes his heroine as "piguid" and a baby carriage as "carious and otiose" the result is affected and pretentious prose.

A form of pretentiousness common in contemporary expository prose is the unnecessary use of terminology and the corruption of genuine professional terminology into jargon. We live in a period of specialized bodies of knowledge, each having its own terminology. This is true of literary criticism and philosophy and of the natural and the social sciences. Specialists in each field know the history and meaning of its terminology and for them it becomes a kind of shorthand, a way of categorizing and sorting complex ideas. But as Malcolm Cowley and Sheridan Baker show in their articles, legitimate terminology can easily become jargon which is used to hide a lack of originality or even meaning behind a façade of authoritative sounding words.

George Orwell, in his essay, points to insincerity, to a deliberate desire to mislead, as a frequent cause of pretentious writing in the field of politics. He shows that euphemistic abstractions are used to conceal unpleasant truths. For instance, the deportation of thousands of people, herded into camps and moved far from their homes, is called "a transfer of population." Orwell labels this "inflated writing." It might be said that not only politics, but many "big" subjects tempt writers to this form of pretentious writing. Religion, nationalism, eulogies, and the "finer" emotions invite vague and abstract language.

Unfortunately, honesty and sincerity alone cannot always keep a writer from sounding pretentious or inflated. Theodore Dreiser was a sincere writer but his style, as Lionel Trilling and others have pointed out, is sometimes arty, bookish in the bad sense. Trilling says: "He is full of flowers of rhetoric and shines like paste gems; at hundreds of points his diction is not only genteel but fancy. It is he who speaks of 'a scene more distingué than this' or of a woman 'artistic in form and feature' . . . ."

There is, also, the problem of stereotyped phrasing, of clichés. In one sense of the word, the cliché is "natural." It comes spontaneously into one's head, like the saliva to the mouth of one of Pavlov's dogs. Requiring almost no thought, it is the enemy of originality. It denies a subject its potential fullness of thought and of grace, and prevents a writer from developing his special quality, his own style.

1 ERNEST HEMINGWAY

by Harvey Breit

Harvey Breit (1913–) formerly assistant editor of The New York Times Book Review, *enjoyed a wide following for his weekly page "In and Out of Books." A native New Yorker, Mr. Breit began to devote himself seriously to writing during the depression while living in New Mexico. He has contributed to many magazines, including* Poetry *and* Partisan Review, *and is the author of* There Falls Tom Fool, *a volume of poetry, and of* Writers Observed, *a collection of biographical sketches of writers based on interviews with them.*

The following is an account of an interview with Ernest Hemingway, who provided both the questions and the answers. Famous as the author of such novels as A Farewell to Arms *(see page 124) and* For Whom the Bell Tolls, *as well as of many short stories, Hemingway is particularly noted for his portrayal of action—of war, bull fighting, hunting, and fishing. His staccato dialogue, short and simple sentences, colloquial diction, and detached, direct narrative are very distinctive, and have been widely imitated. In his introductory paragraph, Mr. Breit reproduces some of the characteristics of the "Hemingway style."*

This week Mr. Ernest Hemingway is the news truly. Not only the literary news. Like Earl Sande booting home a Derby winner, or Johnny Vander Meer pitching two no-hitters in succession, or the Manassa Mauler battering big Jess Willard, a book by Papa is front page news. This fact creates certain misunderstandings. Mr. Hemingway seems to be in the news more than he actually is only because each time he makes his move it starts talk. This is not his fault, and the people who think of Mr. Hemingway as a chap who likes moving into the spotlight are not less than dead wrong. As a matter of record, it would be difficult to find a writer who lives more privately, minding his own business and cultivating his own garden (in the best Voltairean sense of the phrase).

Well here we are too, just as meddlesome as the rest. Mr. Hemingway writes a small, fine novel, *The Old Man and the Sea,* and instead of letting him be, and being happy about it, we're after him—and there is no discharge from the war. True, we went after him equivocally, ridden by a guilt sufficient to prevent us from asking questions. We merely asked him for a statement, or a number of statements, on whatever was occupying him at the time. Pro and gallant that he is, Mr. Hemingway kicked through with a set of answers to a set of questions that he himself devised. Without further ado, then, here is Mr. Hemingway answering Mr. Hemingway:

Q. How do you feel, Mr. H.?

A. Very well, thank you.

Q. What are your plans?

A. To take a vacation, if I have any money left after taxes, and then go back to work.

Q. Where would you like to take your vacation?

A. Either out West or in Europe.

Q. Do you enjoy writing, Mr. H.?

A. Very much. But if you do it as well as you can each day, it is tiring.

Q. Do you mind talking about it?

A. I do not believe in talking about it and I try to avoid talking about it. If I have to talk about a book that I have written it destroys the pleasure I have from writing it. If the writing is any good everything there is to say has been conveyed to the reader.

Q. What about fishing?

A. I have enjoyed it ever since I can remember. But I do not enjoy talking about it except to professional fishermen. One of the reasons I quit fishing at Bimini was to avoid the nightly post mortems of the anglers. Another was because the big fish caught were wasted. No fish caught in Cuba is wasted.

Q. Do you spend much time on the sea?

A. In twenty years of my life probably half of it has been spent on the sea.

Q. Can you work while at sea?

A. Perhaps better than anywhere else. My boat, The Pilar,[1] has no radio, no telephone and, since the war, no radio communications of any kind. You can anchor in the lee of some bay in the Gulf Stream and write on a writing board with no intrusions and you have no excuses if you fail to work well.

Q. Does your wife like the sea?

A. She loves it very much. She has never been seasick and she loves to swim and fish, all kinds of fishing, and to watch the stars at night.

[1] The name of the blasphemous and noblehearted matriarch of *For Whom the Bell Tolls.*

Q. Do you have a happy life, Mr. Hemingway?

A. I have never heard a happy life defined. I have always been happy when I am working. If I cannot work I usually do something bad and have remorse and then my conscience makes me work. A conscience tells truths that are as uncomfortable as those a compass sometimes shows. Personally I am happy when I work hard and love someone. Since I have done both these things now for a long time I would say I have a happy life. Times have always been bad. But Walter Raleigh wrote very well the night before he climbed the steps to the scaffold erected in the Old Palace yard of Westminster. I see no reason now not to write well because the times are bad both for those who write and those who read.

September 7, 1952

EXERCISES

1. Does the idiom employed in the first two paragraphs strike you as unusual? Single out phrases that seem typical of the "Hemingway style."
2. Hemingway's style has had a considerable influence on twentieth-century American prose, especially in fiction. Hemingway himself once said he had taught a generation to write. We have said that style is influenced by the subject, the occasion, and the quality of the writer's mind. Write a short paper in which you consider these three things in relation to anyone's undertaking to write like Hemingway.
3. Write a paragraph in which you consider the naturalness (or if you wish, the pretentiousness) of Hemingway's style.

2 SCHOLARLY STYLE, OR THE LACK THEREOF

by Sheridan Baker

Sheridan Baker (1918–) was born in Santa Rosa, California, and educated at the University of California, Berkeley. He is now a member of the English department at the University of Michigan. The editor of The Papers of the Michigan Academy of Science, Arts, and Letters, *Mr. Baker has also published poetry and articles in many magazines.*

In "Scholarly Style or the Lack Thereof," Mr. Baker analyzes some of the common failings of scholarly and scientific writing today. He examines certain clumsy constructions and pretentious vocabulary frequently found in poor writing in the natural and social sciences. He concludes with a list of seven suggestions for those who wish to write clear and lucid prose.

Teachers and scholars are constantly picking at faulty writing. Indeed, instructors in English do little else. But the writing of the college professor himself, I think, could stand one more attack, though I repeat much said before. Recently, as I was getting together a volume from different scientific and scholarly fields, several things from freshman handbooks and articles on composition came home.[1] Regardless of person or field, I saw, writing always fails in the same way. Words should count, they should make sense, and the great enemy of counting sensibly is wordiness. I saw also that behind the professor's wordiness lay a failure of attitude, a mistaken stance encouraged by both our scientific and our pedantic selves.

We mistake, I think, how scholarship should look and sound in public. Picture a young man in a rusty cutaway and striped pants, a celluloid collar and flowing tie, face serious, eyes glazed, gesticulating with his gloves, mumbling long words while no one at the party pays him the slightest attention. Or perhaps he is dapper, nose-in-the-air, full of jargon and wind. Picture either one and you will have some idea of the way a great many scholars attempt to address their readers. Both have the wrong attitude. Our scientific temper has made our syntax ponderous, and our dignity strings out long words like so much bunting.

Now, both scholar and scientist owe first allegiance to the scientific method. Whether he works with books or social behavior or metallic salts, the researcher collects his facts, weighs them, and shapes from probability an hypothesis about the truth. But the scientific attitude has nevertheless, I think, done much to load our sentences with nouns, and to teach us the passive voice.

Because the scientist, social or natural, prefers *things* to *qualities*, he prefers nouns to adjectives. Indeed, whenever he can, he makes qualities into things by building nouns around them. He will write *Spanish-type* instead of *Spanish*. He will write *in size* instead of *long*. He will always say *of a peculiar order* when he means *peculiar*, and *of an indefinite nature* when he means *indefinite*, and *of great importance* when he means *important*. He will encumber prepositions with nouns, apparently because this makes the preposition more substantial, less like a disembodied process. He will say *in order to* rather than *to*, and *by means of* rather than *by*. Where *and* or *with* would serve, he writes *in relation to*. When he wants to add a phrase, he will select the relative pronoun—usually *which*—rather than the adjective or participle: "a subject *which was* popular a decade ago" rather than "a subject popular a decade ago."

The trouble with this is its density—more words, less light, and almost

[1] I am especially indebted to George Orwell, "Politics and the English Language," in *Shooting an Elephant* (New York: Harcourt, Brace and Co., 1950), pp. 77–92, and to Robert C. Waddell, *Grammar and Style* (New York: Dryden Press, 1951).

no movement. The *ofs* and the *whiches* have thrown our prose into a hundred-years' sleep. Here is a piece typically respectable and drowsy:

Many biological journals, especially those *which* regularly publish new scientific names, now state in each issue the exact date *of* publication *of* the preceding issue. In dealing with journals *which* do not follow this practice, or with volumes *which* are issued individually, the biologist often needs *to* resort *to* indexes . . . *in order to* determine the actual date *of* publication *of* a particular name.

By eliminating *ofs* and the nouns they bring, by changing *which*-phrases into participles, and nouns into verbs, we can cut this passage almost to half without touching the sense:

Many biological journals, especially those regularly *publishing* new scientific names, now give the date of each preceding issue. With journals not *following* this practice, and with some books, the biologist must turn to indexes . . . *to date* a particular name.

Our heavy preference for nouns, moreover, leads to a habit worse than any indulgence in *whiches* and *ofs:* we modify nouns by nouns instead of by adjectives. The social sciences here sin more than most. Working with intangibles, the social scientist seems urged to stiffen his nouns with nouns, and the reader can separate main thought from modifier only after initiation. "Child sex education" stands for "the sexual education of children," I think, unless it stands for "educating someone about the sex of children." Is sex educational, or is education sexual? The noun-habit often carries us completely away from what words mean, and keeps us there by elevated sound alone. And even if by habit we learn to read these constructions, they remain lumpy and unattractive: *body consciousness, human body function, significance level, sign situation, population theory, art ability, teacher grades, nature-nurture evidence.* If we can't drop one of the nouns or find its related adjective, the only cure is homeopathic—a cautious shot of *ofs.*

II

Our scientific taste prefers not only the solid noun but the impersonal passive voice—an opiate which cancels responsibility, hides identity, and numbs the reader. And our adherence to officialdom and groups strengthens the preference.

We have almost forgotten that the simple English sentence, the basis of good writing, moves. It moves from *subject* through *verb* to *object:* "Smith laid the cornerstone on April 1." But because we must sound important, because the institution must be bigger than Smith, we write "the cornerstone was laid on April 1," and the human being vanishes from the earth. The doer and the writer both—all traces of individuality

—disappear behind elongated verbs. Men don't do things, things merely are done; stones move into place, whole campuses emerge from the ground, regulations crystallize overhead. Committees always write this way—and the ecological effect on scholarly writing is deadly. "It was moved that a conference would be held," the secretary writes, to avoid pinning the rap on anybody.

Unfortunately, we like this. We use the passive voice at every opportunity, even with nothing to hide and no one to protect. The passive voice seems dignified and authoritative, and, for all this, it makes our writing dreary with extra *ises, beens* and *bys.* It overruns every scholarly field:

Public concern *has also been given* a tremendous impetus *by* the findings of the Hoover Commission in the federal government, and "little Hoover" commissions to survey the organizational structure and functions of many state governments *have been established.* [In the federal government, the findings of the Hoover Commission have also greatly stimulated public concern, and many states have established "little Hoover" commissions to survey their governments.]

The algal mats *are made up of* the interwoven filaments of several genera. [The interwoven filaments of several genera make up these algal mats.]

Many of the remedies *would probably be shown to be* "faith cures." [Many of the remedies are probably "faith cures."]

In this way less developed countries *can be enabled* to participate in the higher production system of the Western World. [These programs can help backward countries to Western productivity.]

Anxiety and emotional conflict *are lessened* when latency sets in. The total personality *is oriented* in a repressive, inhibitory fashion so as to maintain the barriers, and what Freud has called "psychic dams," against psychological impulses. [When latency sets in, anxiety and emotional conflict subside. The personality inhibits itself, maintaining its barriers—Freud's "psychic dams"—against psychosexual impulses.]

The passive voice, simply in its wordiness, is unclear; but, eliminating the real subject of the verb, as it does, it is intrinsically unclear also. An essay, getting started, will state, "it was demonstrated," and one can only guess as to whether the writer or his rivals had done the demonstrating.

The passive voice is the natural voice of science. Not only officialdom but scientific objectivity tempts us to it. It sounds dispassionate and impersonal; it stops time and holds life still so we can catalogue it. (Flowers never grow in this dry land; they "are found.") Perhaps scientific German has had something to with it. At any rate, since the scientist describes what *is,* since our dignity demands *is laid* instead of *laid, is* becomes almost our only verb. All of us, following first the natural and then the social scientist, define, partition, arrange categories, and cement our writing into blocks with an equals-sign our only predication.

Is so besets us—we are so willing to sit back on our *ises*—that we not only replace active with passive voice, but active verbs with sedentary ones. We can almost see the roadblocks—separated by a narrow *was*, inverted to look passive—in this opening sentence:

Typical of the rationalism of the eighteenth century was a view of prose fiction which developed during the middle decades.

After a little blasting, we might get on into the essay, leaving something like this behind:

A new view of prose fiction, typically rational, developed in the middle decades of the eighteenth century.

To make matters worse, we spread our *is*ms by handing out *exists* and *existences* at every opportunity. We write "this association is not known to exist," not "this association is unknown." And we like to carry phrases around in a stretcher that looks like this: "There is——which." *It* may substitute for *there. That* or *who* may substitute for *which*. But they are all equally wordy: "Moreover, *there is* one class of worker *which* never seeks regular employment." If we drop the italicized words, nothing diminishes but clumsiness.

III

If we straighten out our syntax, however, we are still left with the ornate vocabulary we think proper to scholarship. Vocabulary is a matter of tone. Tone is a matter of attitude. All our *ofs*, our *whiches*, our passives, our clumps of substantives—all rise from the same source as our vocabulary: the pompous and circumstantial attitude so common to our scholarly, scientific pages. Official anonymity is in our ears. We wish to be modest and objective. We want to impress other zoologists, psychologists, economists, and literary men by writing like them. And the result is an inky, back-bay fog. We should work like scholars and scientists, but we should write like writers. We should take our subjects seriously but ourselves with grains of salt, with the knowledge that we are all sinners, all wordy, and all—whether courtly or pontifical—too fond of big Latin words.

Two scientific fishermen have compared numbers of bass in the pond to numbers in the basket, and have watched imported bass survive in mixed company. Their article begins:

Of the many things which influence angling success, the size of population of the species sought must be a prime factor. In order to gain information on the relationship between population and yield to fishermen in a fishery based mainly on large mouth bass, *Micropterus salmoides* (Lacépède), we have experimented. . . .

The trouble with this is not *Micropterus salmoides*. Technical Latin words are precise and useful. The trouble lies in *influence, success, population, factor, information, relationship, population,* and the ambiguous *yield to*—all slushing along together through the weedy connectives. Does your subject seem mundane or trival? Then give it a Latin diploma and it will graduate into elegant dullness. Actually, this article soon begins to read quite well. After a Latin period or two the writers get down to ponds and fish; they leave the academic procession and get out their waders. If we traded our Latin words for Anglo-Saxon ones wherever we could make a bargain, and long words for short ones; if we wrote *find* for *determine, see* for *inquire, watch* for *observe, book* for *volume;* if we banished all words containing *tion,* and then let not more than three sneak back into any one paragraph, our writing would be clearer. Subjects needing Latin technicalities should insist the more stoutly on short English words for the writing in between.

But the social sciences—especially sociology and psychology—unblessed with Latin genera, are in a bad way. They must make their own terms as they go, and few men have Freud's command of words. Some words, like *schizophrenia* and *psychosomatic,* describe what they represent; *ego* and *id* are clear enough. But, for the most part, poor writers have endowed psychology with a technical vocabulary that would put even Solomon on the couch. We hear of *reaction fixation,* of *reaction to action. Factors, aspects,* and *situations* are *functions* of every sentence, and a word like *motivation* takes on private meanings which force the writer to new definitions. *Affect* changes into a noun and affects the sanity of everyone trying to write effectively.

Language is public property that must not be rough-hewn to private ends. A real knowledge of Latin might save us from this—a real understanding of what a word means at the root. But we are not Latinists; we are merely Latinate. Always looking for an exact scientific language, we never write with an alert and delighted sense that words have more than one meaning, that our sentences can strike harmonics and still be precise. Beware of the writer who must define his terms, I say. He may be unable to use language, as it runs, to express his meaning, and—whatever his motivation—the result is pomposity. He is Humpty Dumpty, the original egghead, making words say what he wants them to mean instead of meaning what he wants to say. He is either evading the toil of finding the right word, or defining the obvious:

Let us agree to use the word *signal* as an abbreviation for the phrase "the simplest kind of sign." (This agrees fairly well with the customary meaning of the word "signal.")

A definer of words is usually a bad writer. The man, above, who had to get his signals straight, a semanticist, by the way, grinds out about three parts sawdust to every one of meat. In the following excerpt, the italics are his; the brackets, mine. Read the sentence first as it was written; then read it again, omitting the bracketed words:

> The moral of such examples is that *all intelligent criticism* [*of any instance*] *of language* [*in use*] *must begin with understanding* [*of*] *the motives* [*and purposes*] *of the speaker* [*in that situation.*]

Here, each of the bracketed phrases is already implied in the others. Attempting to be precise, our writer has only clouded his meaning. We have reached our last infirmity of scientific mind. Naturally the speaker would be "in that situation"; naturally a sampling of language would be "an instance" of language "in use." And even if *motives* are not *purposes*, the difference is too small to dawdle over. His next sentence deserves some kind of immortality. He means "muddy language causes trouble":

> Unfortunately, the type of case that causes trouble in practice is that in which the kind of use made of language is not transparently clear. . . .

IV

Clearly, it is hard to be transparent. Writing is hard. Even divinity has found it necessary to write in the middle of the night with great commotion. Writing is probably more than half of the researcher's job, as anyone will testify who has found himself hunting up one more fact, and running one more test, postponing the awful hour when he must face the mystery of the word, to gather his thoughts and to communicate. It is a matter of finding first the right attitude, and then the right words—and no more. If we have little to say, we will be pompous, we will write in the passive voice, we will throw phrases in the air like dust.

But if you have something to say and still sound tumid, we can work out our salvation. Here are some suggestions:

1. Economize. Think of explaining what you have to say clearly, simply and pleasantly to a small mixed group of intelligent people.
2. Never use a long word when you can find a short one, or a Latin word when you can find a good Old English one.
3. Suspect yourself of wordiness whenever you see an *of*, a *which* or a *that*. Inspect all areas surrounding any form of *to be*. Never use *exist*.
4. Resolve not to use the passive voice. Simply fly in the face of convention and begin your sentences with "I" or "we" or "the writer."
5. Take pains to avoid modifying a noun with a noun.
6. Make sure that each word really makes sense. No one who had inspected the meaning of his words could have written: "Every seat in the auditorium was filled to capacity."

7. Beware of the metaphor. It is the spirit of good prose. It gives the reader a picture, a glimpse of what the subject really looks like to the writer. But it is dangerous, can easily get tangled and insistent, the more so when it almost works: don't have a violent explosion pave the way for a new growth.

The important thing is, I think, to pick up each sentence in turn, asking ourselves if we can possibly make it shorter. This done, clarity will come of itself, and with it the peculiar pleasure of having wrestled—the struggle itself will be agony—with the written word, and written well. We may even live in a style in which we never dreamed we could become accustomed.

EXERCISES

1. Mr. Baker says that participles and verbs give prose "movement." What does he mean by this? Illustrate.
2. Look up the term *etymology* in the explanatory notes in your dictionary. What are the most common sources of modern English words, that is, from what languages have they been borrowed?
3. What does Baker mean by saying, "Tone is a matter of attitude."
4. The editor of your text has generally used "We believe" or "We ought" rather than "I believe" or "I ought." Which seems to you preferable? Give your reasons.
5. Should the list of rules given at the end of Mr. Baker's article be taken with a grain of salt or should they be taken literally? State the reasons for your opinion.

3 SOCIOLOGICAL HABIT PATTERNS IN LINGUISTIC TRANSMOGRIFICATION

by Malcolm Cowley

Malcolm Cowley (1898–) was educated at Harvard and at the University of Montpelier in France. In the 1920's, he lived for a time in Paris, a member of the group of American expatriate writers including Ernest Hemingway and Gertrude Stein. He described this experience in Exile's Return. *From 1929 to 1944, he was associate editor of* The New Republic. *Cowley also wrote* The Literary Situation, *a collection of critical essays, and edited two important anthologies,* After the Genteel Tradition *and* Books That Changed Our Minds. The Portable Faulkner, *edited by him, contributed greatly to the reestablishment of William Faulkner's reputation, appearing as it did at a time when all of Faulkner's books had gone out of print.*

In this article, Mr. Cowley takes to task those sociologists who have become so engrossed with jargon that they can no longer express themselves in clear and simple English. He maintains that this resort to "professional slang" often conceals a lack of insight and original thought.

I have a friend who started as a poet and then decided to take a postgraduate degree in sociology. For his doctoral dissertation he combined his two interests by writing on the social psychology of poets. He had visited poets by the dozen, asking each of them a graded series of questions, and his conclusions from the interviews were modest and useful, though reported in what seemed to me a barbarous jargon. After reading the dissertation I wrote and scolded him. "You have such a fine sense of the poet's craft," I said, "that you shouldn't have allowed the sociologists to seduce you into writing their professional slang—or at least that's my judgemental response to your role selection."

My friend didn't write to defend himself; he waited until we met again. Then dropping his voice, he said: "I knew my dissertation was badly written, but I had to get my degree. If I had written it in English, Professor Blank"—he mentioned a rather distinguished name—"would have rejected it. He would have said it was merely belletristic."

From that time I began to study the verbal folkways of the sociologists. I read what they call "the literature." A few sociologists write the best English they are capable of writing, and I suspect that they are the best men in the field. There is no mystery about them. If they go wrong, their mistakes can be seen and corrected. Others, however—and a vast majority—write in a language that has to be learned almost like Esperanto. It has a private vocabulary which, in addition to strictly sociological terms, includes new words for the commonest actions, feelings, and circumstances. It has the beginnings of a new grammar and syntax, much inferior to English grammar in force and precision. So far as it has an effect on standard English, the effect is largely pernicious.

Sometimes it misleads the sociologists themselves, by making them think they are profoundly scientific at points where they are merely verbose. I can illustrate by trying a simple exercise in translation, that is, by expressing an idea first in English and then seeing what it looks like in the language of sociology.

An example that comes to hand is the central idea of an article by Norman E. Green, printed in the February, 1956, issue of the *American Sociological Review*. In English, his argument read as follows:

> Rich people live in big houses set farther apart than those of poor people. By looking at an aerial photograph of any American city, we can distinguish the richer from the poorer neighborhoods.

I won't have to labor over a sociological expression of the same idea, because Mr. Green has saved me the trouble. Here is part of his contribution to comparative linguistics. "In effect, it was hypothesized," he says—a sociologist must never say "I assumed," much less "I guessed"—"that certain physical data categories including housing types and densities, land use characteristics, and ecological location"—not just "location," mind you, but "ecological location," which is almost equivalent to locational location—"constitute a scalable content area. This could be called a continuum of residential desirability. Likewise, it was hypothesized that several social data categories, describing the same census tracts, and referring generally to the social stratification system of the city, would also be scalable. This scale could be called a continuum of socio-economic status. Thirdly, it was hypothesized that there would be a high positive correlation between the scale types on each continuum."

Here, after ninety-four words, Mr. Green is stating, or concealing, an assumption with which most laymen would have started, that rich people live in good neighborhoods. He is now almost ready for his deduction, or snapper:

> This relationship would define certain linkages between the social and physical structure of the city. It would also provide a precise definition of the

commonalities among several spatial distributions. By the same token, the correlation between the residential desirability scale and the continuum of socio-economic status would provide an estimate of the predictive value of aerial photographic data relative to the social ecology of the city.

Mr. Green has used 160 words—counting "socio-economic" as only one —to express an idea that a layman would have stated in thirty-three. As a matter of fact, he has used many more than 160 words, since the whole article is an elaboration of this one thesis. Whatever may be the virtues of the sociological style—or Socspeak, as George Orwell might have called it—it is not specifically designed to save ink and paper. Let us briefly examine some of its other characteristics.

Fuzzing Up the Obvious

A layman's first impression of sociological prose, as compared with English prose, is that it contains a very large proportion of abstract words, most of them built on Greek or Latin roots. Often—as in the example just quoted—they are used to inflate or transmogrify a meaning that could be clearly expressed in shorter words surviving from King Alfred's time.

These Old English or Anglo-Saxon words are in number less than one-tenth of the entries in the largest dictionaries. But they are the names of everyday objects, attributes, and actions, and they are also the pronouns, the auxilliary verbs, and most of the prepositions and conjunctions, so that they form the grammatical structure of the language. The result is that most novelists use six Anglo-Saxon words for every one derived from French, Latin, or Greek, and that is probably close to the percentage that would be found in spoken English.

For comparison or contrast, I counted derivations in the passage quoted from the *American Sociological Review*, which is a typical example of "the literature." No less than forty-nine per cent of Mr Green's prose consists of words from foreign or classical languages. By this standard of measurement, his article is more abstruse than most textbooks of advanced chemistry and higher mathematics, which are said to contain only forty per cent of such words.

In addition to being abstruse, the language of the sociologists is also rich in neologisms. Apparently they like nothing better than inventing a word, deforming a word, or using a technical word in a strange context. Among their favorite nouns are "ambit," "extensity" (for "extent"), "scapegoating," "socializee," "ethnicity," "directionality," "cathexis," "affect" (for 'feeling"), "maturation" (for both "maturing" and "maturity"), and "commonalities" (for "points in common"). Among their favorite adjectives are "processual," "prestigeful," and "insightful"—which last is insightful to murder—and perhaps their favorite adverb is "minimally," which seems to mean "in some measure." Their maximal pleasure seems to lie in making new combinations of nouns and adjectives and nouns used as adjectives, until the reader feels that he is picking his way through a field of huge boulders, lost among "universalistic-specific achievement patterns" and "complementary role-expectation-sanction systems," as he struggles vainly toward "ego-integrative action orientation," guided only by "orientation to improvement of the gratification-deprivation balance of the actor"—which last is Professor Talcott Parsons's rather involved way of saying "the pleasure principle."

But Professor Parsons, head of the Sociology Department at Harvard, is not the only delinquent recidivist, convicted time and again of corrupting the language. Among sociologists in general there is a criminal fondness for using complicated terms when there are simple ones available. A child says "Do it again," a teacher says "Repeat the exercise," but the sociologist says "It was determined to replicate the investigation." Instead of saying two things are alike or similar, as a layman would do, the sociologist describes them in being either isomorphic or homologous. Instead of saying that they are different, he calls them allotropic. Every form of leadership or influence is called a hegemony.

A sociologist never cuts anything in half or divides it in two like a layman. Instead he dichotomizes it, bifurcates it, subjects it to a process of binary fission, or restructures it in a dyadic conformation—around polar foci.

The New Grammar

So far I have been dealing with the vocabulary of sociologists, but their private language has a grammar too, and one that should be the subject of intensive research by the staff of a very well-endowed foundation. I have space to mention only a few of its more striking features.

The first of these is the preponderance of nouns over all the other parts of speech. Nouns are used in hyphenated pairs or dyads, and sometimes in triads, tetrads, and pentads. Nouns are used as adjectives without change of form, and they are often used as verbs, with or without the suffix "ize." The sociological language is gritty with nouns, like sanded sugar.

On the other hand, it is poor in pronouns. The singular pronoun of the first person has entirely disappeared, except in case histories, for the sociologist never comes forward as "I." Sometimes he refers to himself as "the author" or "the investigator," or as "many sociologists," or even as "the best sociologists," when he is advancing a debatable opinion. On rare occasions he calls himself "we," like Queen Elizabeth speaking from the throne, but he usually avoids any personal form and writes as if he were a force of nature.

The second-personal pronoun has also disappeared, for the sociologist pretends to be speaking not to living persons but merely for the record. Masculine and feminine pronouns of the third person are used with parsimony, and most sociologists prefer to say "the subject," or "X——," or "the interviewee," where a layman would use the simple "he" or "she." As for the neuter pronoun of the third person, it survives chiefly as the impersonal subject of a passive verb. "It was hypothesized," we read, or "It was found to be the case." Found by *whom?*

The neglect and debasement of the verb is another striking feature of "the literature." The sociologist likes to reduce a transitive verb to an intransitive, so that he speaks of people's adapting, adjusting, transferring, relating, and identifying, with no more of a grammatical object than if they were coming or going. He seldom uses transitive verbs of action, like "break," "injure," "help," and "adore." Instead he uses verbs of relation, verbs which imply that one series of nouns and adjectives, used as the compound subject of a sentence, is larger or smaller than, dominant over, subordinate to, causative of, or resultant from another series of nouns and adjectives.

Considering this degradation of the verb, I have wondered how one of Julius Caesar's boasts could be translated into Socspeak. What Caesar wrote was "*Veni, vidi, vici*"—only three words, all of them verbs. The English translation is in six words: "I came, I saw, I conquered," and three of the words are first-personal pronouns, which the sociologist is taught to avoid. I suspect that he would have to write: "Upon the advent of the investigator, his hegemony became minimally coextensive with the areal unit rendered visible by his successive displacements in space."

The whole sad situation leads me to dream of a vast allegorical painting called "The Triumph of the Nouns." It would depict a chariot of victory drawn by the other conquered parts of speech—the adverbs and adjectives still robust, if yoked and harnessed; the prepositions bloated and pale; the conjunctions tortured; the pronouns reduced to sexless skeletons; the verbs dichotomized and feebly tottering—while behind them, arrogant, overfed, roseate, spilling over the triumphal car, would be the company of nouns in Roman togas and Greek chitons, adorned with laurel branches and flowering hegemonies.

EXERCISES

1. What was Mr. Cowley's purpose in choosing the title he did for this article? Suggest other titles.

2. What are some of the characteristics of "sociological jargon" according to Mr. Cowley?

3. Does Mr. Cowley object to jargon purely on aesthetic grounds? What reasons does he give for his opposition to jargon?

4. Jargon in one form or another has undoubtedly always existed in the English and American languages, but its use seems particularly marked in our own era. List several reasons for the proliferation of jargon in the twentieth century and then write an essay on "Jargon, A Mark of Our Era."

4 | AMERICAN PROSE TODAY

by Geoffrey Moore

Geoffrey Moore (1918–) is an English critic who has had experience in government and television as well as in teaching. Mr. Moore taught at several American universities and is now Lecturer in American Literature at the University of Manchester. He edited The Penguin Book of Modern American Verse, *and has contributed to both American and British literary journals and magazines. He writes regularly for the* Times Literary Supplement.

"In American Prose Today," Mr. Moore examines several passages of American expository prose—historical, critical, "official," and journalistic. In the course of his analysis he makes some interesting comparisons between British and American prose. He concludes that while the "independence and vigor" characteristic of American life "may produce good novels and stories" it does not seem "to make a good climate for expositional prose."

It is a natural, simple, and unaffected speech that I love, so written as it is spoken, and such upon the paper as it is in the mouth, a pithy, sinewy, full, strong, compendious and material speech, not so delicate and affected as vehement and piercing. . . .

Florio's *Montaigne*

"We have really everything in common with America—except, of course, the language." Oscar Wilde's witticism still has some truth, although, like mother-of-pearl, it changes colour according to the angle of view. It is true that some British readers have, or pretend to have, difficulty with some American writing. Different terms for the same thing can sometimes be puzzling; unfamiliar idioms, reference to objects or institutions unknown in England, and a slicker, wilder sense of humour even more so. Fashionables, particularly literary fashionables, affect remarks like "I couldn't quite follow all the jokes—that peculiar dialect, is it *Bronx?*" (see G. S. Fraser, "The Aesthete and the Senationalist," *Partisan Review*, April, 1955). And there are even a dogged few of the Old Guard who cry "Beaver!" whenever they recognise an Americanism, and send a fiery letter to their favourite fourpenny. However, the majority of the English are by now hopelessly lost. It's not merely that "O.K." is widely used among the working-class and lower-middle-class and that errand boys and young clerks say "I don't get you" and "I haven't seen him in years." But—oh, more horrible still—even our distinguished worthies use American words and phrases, and in their written style, moreover. H. W. Horwill once made a list, including "proposition," "up against" (it), "disgruntled," and "out to" (increase efficiency) which had been used by such unimpeachably British personages as Sir Winston Churchill, the Archbishop of York, Sir Michael Sadler, and Sir William Holdsworth. In fact, the process has gone so far that even those purists who would rather die than be discovered committing an Americanism unconsciously use words of American origin in normal usage. Leafing through a dictionary of American English, one finds, on almost every page, words which are now commonly accepted in England as English—"in the neighbourhood of" (say, a million pounds), "landslide" (for the English "landslip"), "to take a cut" (in wages). Even "boarding-house," "business man," "graveyard," "law-abiding," overcoat," and "telegram" are American importations; and there are a great many more, some of them now abandoned in their country of origin.

The influence of American usages, most of them new, but some from an English older than that now current in Britain, may be put to detailed proof by reference to the dictionary of Sir William Craigie and Professor Hulbert and that of Professor M. M. Mathews, and, among numerous other books, to H. L. Mencken's cocksure but massively documented *The American Language* and its *Supplements*. But most readers would, I think, be willing to accept, without proof, the statement that, in certain respects, American English has a dynamic which British English no longer possesses. It can be found in that popular and picturesque style common to detective stories and Hollywood movies (so popular in fact that English writers like Peter Cheyney and James Hadley Chase have worked hard to supply a pastiche of it). It can be found in the vivid American phrases of each new generation, from "what makes him tick" and "to blow one's top" to "out of this world" and "strictly from hunger" (when I was at school it was "Sez you")—embarrassing clichés already, of course, but nonetheless vivid. It can be found more pervasively, however, in less sensational words which, for over a hundred and fifty years, have been forcing their way into general Anglo-American usage—words like "belittle," "demoralizing," and "lengthy."

But, say we accept these facts, what do they tell us? Merely that a great new nation, in an expanding and optimistic frame of mind, has been striking out in all directions, coining new words and phrases, and using accepted ones in new contexts. It is, after all, only what we might have expected. What is more interesting is to inquire whether this great new nation has by now developed a distinctive prose, expressive of its spirit. We do not quarrel these days about whether there is not an American literature. There plainly is, and we can point to its various aspects and analyse, within reason, its characteristics. But is there such a thing as an American prose? I refer here to nonfiction, the prose of exposition, the ordinary literary means of communication.

The sophist might answer: Yes, American prose is prose written by Americans. But, we persist: Is it different from English prose, and, if so, how? Or, alternatively: Is there "an American style"? The answer might be that there are a number of American styles and that they owe their nature to the circumstances of American development. Not merely racial, or religious, or social differences, but, as Mr. Wallace Stevens once said, physical ones too, have made the attitude of the people different, and the attitude of a people is reflected in its prose. Add to this the spirit which founded the United States, the early struggles, the theocratic art-banishing society of New England, the early establishment of a unique kind of democracy, the distrust of aristocratic virtues (elegance, propriety, mannered grace, intellect) and the acceptance of brotherhood-become-chumminess, and you have a taste of the brew which might be expected to make American prose different from British. From the first, the American moved about a lot and so, despite the difference in accent between, say, South Carolina and New Hampshire, usage was sufficiently standard that he could be understood in any part of the country. In England, however, as Mr. Harold Whitehall has pointed out, the inhabitants of, for example, Howden in Yorkshire used to find it very difficult to understand the inhabitants of Dewsbury, forty miles away. And so, largely on the basis of aristocratic speech, Britain developed a *lingua franca*, Received Standard English, the rules of which could be laid down and accepted as gospel. H. W. Fowler could write a *Modern English Usage*, but no American ever either dared to write, or felt the necessity of writing, a *Modern American Usage*. Mr. Horwill, an Englishman, did, of course, produce one, but that was for the aid of the British. However, there seems, by this time, to have developed a generally accepted and, as it were, legitimate body of American usage which can be called Standard without fear of offending Americans' own susceptibilities. At least I take it to be so and, with this in mind, I should like to examine various examples of modern "expositional" American prose in an effort to discover whether they have the "independence and vigour" which, in 1954, *The Times Literary Supplement* found so marked in American creative writing. Although this will involve commenting on usage, I do not propose to single out American usages which are now perfectly acceptable in Britain.

Political Prose

My purpose was to sketch the genesis and set in some crude historical perspective the present troubled world scene, and then to attempt to defrost a tiny segment of the opaque window through which we see others and others see us—and to do it briefly, having listened to many lectures myself!

This is from the foreword to Adlai Stevenson's *Call to Greatness*, Two things are immediately noticeable: first, the modest tone, and, second, the use of an original figure of speech which has been drawn naturally and unaffectedly from American experience. Almost all Americans, except those who live in the extreme Southern states, find it necessary at some time during the winter to "defrost," either manually or by aid of a device built into their cars, a driving window which has been made opaque by frost or frozen snow. The style might be described as "literary" (e.g., "genesis," "present troubled world scene"), yet it gives an impression of ease. It has the ring of sincerity and makes us feel that we can trust a man who is at once so unpretentious and yet so quietly convinced that he can clarify our vision of world affairs.

Having come to the above conclusion about this passage, I was surprised, on re-reading it, to find that it is actually ungrammatical. I say "surprised" since, as a teacher, my eye is, if anything over-alert to such things. The fault is in the first line, in which, to make grammatical sense, there should be an "of" after "genesis." It gives a very awkward ring to the sentence, however, and the writer, being American, was led to reject it. An Englishman would probably either have put it in or re-worded the sentence. It is, I think, a good example of how even the most educated and highly literate of Americans have, when they feel like it, a cavalier attitude toward the niceties of grammar. I have noticed that in the *non solum, sed etiam* construction, for example, Americans rarely put in the "also."

Historical Prose

(a) *As the sectional tension increased, the sense of irrepressible differences, long buried in the national consciousness, began to burst into the clear. The growing pressure on the North had finally persuaded many Northerners that the slavery system embodied a fundamental threat to free society.*

(b) *August gave way to September, September to October, and the clamor grew increasingly furious. Jackson men paraded the streets in the glare of torches, singing campaign songs, carrying hickory poles, gathering around huge bonfires blazing high into the night.*

These two extracts are both from Arthur M. Schlesinger, Jr.'s *The Age of Jackson.* Together they make a point better than one alone, and that point is that the methods and the vocabulary of the journalist have invaded the writing of history. (cf., *Time,* April 22, 1955, "Warm in the April sunshine, London's upper-crust horseplayers crowded the club enclosure at Kempton Park Race Track. Peeresses in Dior tweeds appraised each other. . . ." etc.) The tone is different. *Time's* is not merely colourful; it is impertinent. Mr. Schlesinger is not writing sensationally, he is merely trying to "bring the scene to life." Although he is in no sense perverting the facts, he is nonetheless "popularising" history. And since he is not merely a famous historian, but also an academic one, approved of academically, the method is worth remarking on. It is not entirely new. Strachey was, of course, a populariser and, so to pick an example from a number of others, was Philip Guedalla; but the texture of these English writers was finer grained, more glittering. Mr. Schlesinger's style, although it is not bad, is without flair, bouncy yet workaday ("as sectional tension increased," "embodied a fundamental threat"), with an occasional, rather disconcerting vernacular phrase (e.g., "into the clear"). It is the style of a man who has not thought much about language. The four parts of Mr. Schlesinger's first sentence create four different effects. The first gives us the sense of *pulling,* the second of energy contained under *pressure,* like steam in a kettle, the third *buries* this steam kettle, the fourth allows it to "burst into the clear" which seems superficially to fit with the idea of "irrepressible differences," but is vaguely disconcerting until we realize that the stress is on "into the clear," which is a hunting term. There is, in other words, a confusion of different kinds of language. This is for me a most interesting discovery, since I did not pick Mr. Schlesinger invidiously, but in a spirit of enquiry, knowing him to be one of the most outstanding of the younger American historians.

Critical Prose

(a) *Such an art when it pretends to measure life is essentially vicarious; it is a substitute for something that never was—like a tin soldier, or Peter Pan. It has all the flourish of life and every sentimental sincerity. Taken for what it is, it is charming and even instructive. Taken solemnly, as it is meant to be, the distortion by which it exists is too much for it, and it seems a kind of baby-talk.*

(b) . . . *aesthetic value has been defined as conformity to or expression of a culture. This is the side of formism most prevalent today. A work of art has aesthetic value in proportion as it gives expression to its age. This definition tends to run over into a culture relativism very congenial to contemporary art historians, and in marked contrast to the universality of aesthetic values emphasized in the first formulation of aesthetic value for formism above as representation of the universal.*

(c) *There is nothing to do different from what we already do: if poets write poems and readers read them, each as best they can—if they try to live not as soldiers or voters or intellectuals or economic men, but as human beings—they are doing all that can be done. But to expect them (by, say, reciting one-syllable poems over the radio) to bring back that Yesterday in which people stood on chairs to look at Lord Tennyson, is to believe that General Motors can bring back "the tradition of craftmanship" by giving, as it does, prizes to Boy Scouts for their scale-models of Napoleonic coaches; to believe that the manners of the past can be restored by encouraging country-people to say* Grüss Gott *or* Howdy, stranger *to the tourists they meet along summer lanes.*

The first extract is from R. P. Blackmur's essay on the verse of E. E. Cummings in *The Double Agent;* the second is from Stephen C. Pepper's *The Basis of Criticism in the Arts;* and the third from Randall Jarrell's *Poetry and the Age.* The field of criticism in the United States is so rich that I should have preferred to take at least two or three more examples —from Edmund Wilson, say, or Van Wyck Brooks, or the late F. O. Matthiessen. However, these three samples do at least reveal three important aspects of American criticism. The second passage is of the kind which is so often the target for British writers—jargon criticism. I could have quoted more extreme examples (from Kenneth Burke, for instance) for there is a great deal of this kind of thing, particularly in academic or semi-academic writing, of which there is so much more in the United States than anywhere else. I think of it sometimes as a Germanic derivation. "The side of formism," "cultural relativism," and the garbled mumble of the end of the final sentence—this is the antithesis of clarity. Perhaps it is the result of Coleridge's example; he learnt from Germany too. Perhaps it is the overseriousness and earnestness of the American commentator. Perhaps it is a little of the unconscious desire to blind the vulgar with science. Perhaps it is an attempt to order a frighteningly vast world of thought and feeling. Perhaps it is—as Marius Bewley suggested of Kenneth Burke—that these "methodological" critics have developed their jargon and their unreadable style in order to isolate them "against the shock of the work of art itself." But, whatever the reason, the effect is both exasperating and perturbing.

The Blackmur passage, on the other hand, is a good illustration of what we mean when we say that someone's writing "has style." The language is both elegant and precise, the manner judicious but not portentous, flavored by just the right amount of everyday reference ("tin soldier, or Peter Pan" and "baby-talk"). It is the writing of an acute sensibility. We cannot help feeling the force of the conviction behind the sentiments, not only because of what they say but because of the manner of their expression. The language is faintly Jamesian, ("all the flourish of life and every sentimental sincerity"). The final effect is of a man who respects literature too much to make it merely a stamping-ground for pseudo-scientific theories.

Mr. Jarrell, in his conversational ease, his common sense and his liveliness, is representative of the younger generation of American critics. He will not allow his individual perception and spirit to be subdued by the acceptances of academic style and theory. His is a style of wit and irony, which can sometimes approach the self-consciously brilliant but is anchored to earth (and this is why it is so effective for most readers) by the essential rightness of the sentiments. The style is more noticeably idiosyncratic than Mr. Blackmur's. It is perceptive, impressionistic, and opinionated. But in the last resort it obtains its effect by laying the cards on the table and saying, as it were, "Now, after all. . . ." Only a man with a wide cultural background and a sureness of judgement based on good taste can afford to do this. Finally, the style achieves a vividness and concreteness by reference to manners and institutions well known in American life.

Humorous Prose

(a) *I have a lot of other notes jotted down about why I hate women, but I seem to have lost them all, except one. That one is to the effect that I hate women because, while they never lose old snapshots or anything of that sort, they invariably lose one glove. I believe that I have never gone anywhere with any women in my whole life who did not lose one glove. I have searched for single gloves under tables in crowded restaurants and under the feet of people in darkened movie theatres. I have spent some part of every day or night hunting for a woman's glove. If there were no other reason in the world for hating women, that one would be enough. In fact, you can leave all the others out.*

(b) *I first heard pure Slurvian fluently spoken by a co-worker of mine who told me that his closest friend was a man named Hard (Howard). Hard was once in an automobile accident, his car, unfortunately, cliding with another, causing Hard's wife, Dorthy, who was with him, to claps. Dorthy didn't have much stamina but was a sweet women—sweet as surp.*

The first passage is from James Thurber's *Let Your Mind Alone!*, the second is from John Davenport's "Slurvian Self-Taught." They seem to me to show two sides of American humour, both driving perhaps from the frontier tradition. Despite its urbanity, the Thurber piece is in the tradition of Mark Twain, the father of the American natural style and one of the first to use the device of exaggeration (the "tall tale") successfully as a literary mode. As Mark Twain in his descriptive passages and essays used the simple, common "conversational" style and idiom of his day, so Mr. Thurber uses the natural "conversational" style of our day. I perhaps ought to explain what I mean by "conversational." By this I understand the vernacular of the ordinary educated person translated into literature (notice the direct "I," and "in my whole life"). While, therefore, it is "a conversational style," it is not exactly as it would be in spontaneous speech. "Invariably," for example, and "I have" would sound a little mannered if actually spoken by one friend to another. Actual speech usage would be too clumsy for a writer whose effects are as subtly obtained as Mr. Thurber's. The humour, which I find irresistible, arises from exaggerating a fairly common situation. The writer is half-serious, half-joking, and the hit-on-the-funny-bone effect is helped by the direct and simple language, and by the masterly sense of timing. The last sentence is both a parting shot and an ending which gathers up the whole of the essay.

The second extract is deadpan, and achieves its effect by being written as if it were a sort of anecdotal reminiscence by a professional investigator of linguistics. This level is allowed to merge into the level of overt humour, as in the last sentence of the passage quoted. It could not, I feel, have been written by anyone but an American, because no one but an American could have the knowledge of and feeling for the vernacular (slurred or otherwise) which this writer displays. The sense of timing which both writers exploit so magnificently seem to be a part of the American temperament (to ask why arouses some interesting anthropological and sociological speculations). It is displayed outside literature by such comedians as Jack Benny and Fred Allen. The former, particularly, builds easily on the natural cadences of American speech, in which there runs a faint but constant undercurrent of humour.

Journalistic Prose

In a democratic country, in which almost everyone can read and in which everyone is supposed to have equal opportunities for education, or for anything else, one might expect to find a "typical" or "representative" American style, in the kind of publication which is read by the majority. According to figures taken from the polls of the Princeton Institute of Public Opinion and Mr. J. K. Wood's *Magazines of the United States*, although only approximately 20 per cent of Americans read books at all, 83 per cent regularly read newspapers and magazines.

1. Newspapers

(a) *Secretary of Agriculture Ezra Taft Benson has called on western Kansas farmers to begin a day of "prayer and supplication to ask God in heaven to send rain." Well, that's one way of stopping the good Kansas dirt from blowing over to Russia. It's certainly not the best way. The secretary has made a tour; he's impressed. But first and foremost the secretary is a politician, not a conservationist. It will take a little more than politics to keep that western Kansas dirt on the ground.*

This passage from a student newspaper editorial seems clear and direct —"conversational," "natural," in fact, yet not altogether or ingenuously so. The tone is cocky. "Secretary of Agriculture Ezra Taft Benson" is borrowed from *Time's* style, which was presumably invented to give the impression that everybody's time, including *Time's*, was limited. Yet the saving of one three-letter word and two commas is not worth the ungracefulness of the usage. One feels that the writer is breathing down one's neck. A cliché slips in ("first and foremost"). "Impressed" gives one a feeling of inadequately describing Mr. Benson's possible reactions. Noticeable American usages are "called on," which has a Town Meeting ring, and "politician," which in England means someone in politics but in the United States is a bad word.

(b) *Reed's number one problem is working capital. So in order to get money for equipment and to meet his payroll until he gets to rolling, he is incorporating the business and plans to sell stock. The telephone switchboard will be installed soon and within the next few weeks he plans to have a grand opening.*

This is from an article in the *St. Louis Post-Dispatch,* and is subcolloquial. It reads like a cross between the vernacular and the language of radio copy-writers—more the latter. Few in conversation talk about their "number one" problem, but writers of "commercials" do. "Meet his payroll" and "get to rolling" are examples of those vivid coinages which arise out of a forceful expanding society in which the tone of general prose is set by the majority, who have no ear for subtlety of language. They are designed to give an impressionistic picture to people whose range of communication, understanding, and imagination is narrow. This kind of prose does not work through the intelligence but through the emotions. The repetition of "get" and "plan" emphasizes the narrowness of the vocabulary. Within its limits it is a most effective kind of communication, and sufficiently hard-punching to penetrate the dullest mind capable of reading words on a page. It is an example of American pragmatism. It is probably inevitable in a democratic society in which the mass media have superseded the printed page as the chief means of communication. It reflects the speech and the habits of mind of the majority of people and it would be sentimental, ineffectual, and entirely unrealistic (not to say reactionary) for one to regret that this particular form of speech ever invaded prose. But one does.

(c) *The **Pakistan** grain storage contract presents a flagrant case of official negligence and mismanagement. Any monkey business with government con-*

tracts can and should be a matter of public concern. So we have this relatively small item of grain elevators grown into a national story.

(d) *For the present, and with all due consideration of both Soviet aims and motivations, it appears as if the Soviets are prepared to give ground at least in part and at least at one point—Austria. After stalling and sabotaging the Austrian treaty in more than 260 treaty meetings stretching over nearly a decade, they have now reached agreement with Austria on the terms of liberation which, barring new Soviet demands, the West is likely to accept.*

These two passages are from editorials, the first in the *Kansas City Star* for May 4, 1955, the second from *The New York Times* for May 2, 1955. The most noticeable thing about the first is the way in which it combines an elevated and judicious style with colloquialisms. "Presents a flagrant case" in the first passage consorts oddly with "monkey business." The grave "can and should be a matter of public concern" is immediately followed by the colloquial "So we have this . . . ," as one might say, to a friend, "So we have this fellow (or car, or problem) on our hands." This lack of taste, of consistency of tone, of feeling for what is appropriate in the context may arise from the comparative lack of literary training in American, particularly Middle Western, schools. *The New York Times* passage is a much better piece of writing and much more of a piece. It is much less "literary' than a leader in the London *Times* would be, but more pompous. To some extent, "stalling," which is vivid and vernacular, conflicts with the high editorial style ("all due consideration").

2. Magazines

(a) *The only comment on the American economy that can be made with perfect assurance is that nobody really understands it. On the whole, this is a good thing. An economy capable of being thoroughly understood would probably prove treacherous. Of course, there are always a few professionals who like to believe that they understand the American economy, and these people turn up at Congressional hearings to explain why the market acts the way it does, but it is quite obvious that they are just groping their way along, the same as everybody else.*

This is from the editorial page of *The New Yorker* entitled "Talk of the Town," the nearest thing to the essay one can find in the United States today. It is highly intelligent and professionally polished, yet intimate and engaging in its manner. The man who wrote this passage did have an ear, and he did have taste. The short second sentence picks up an echo both of the New York Yiddish colloquialism "This is a good thing?" and the British (*1066 and All That*) "a Good Thing," and yet is simply effective without these probably unintended connotations. The third sentence is disarming. It is as sensitively balanced as a line of verse. "Treacherous" strikes one as being just the right word; no other will do. It is meaningful, connotative, and funny, yet not fancy. "Of course," "these people," and "the same as everybody else" keep the level down, an important thing in a milieu in which ceremony or over-refinement are quickly smelled out. This kind of prose mirrors the most attractive kind of American personality, that of a man who is polite but not deferential, droll, easy in manner, and responsive.

(b) *Barsov went. At his own request, the U.S. authorities flew him to Linz. "Are you sure you want to go back?" they asked him at the end. He was.*

The Soviets had a propaganda bonanza in Barsov; they pointed to him as an example of what happens to those who desert the Soviets and trust the West.

This quotation from an article in the *Reader's Digest* is an example of "bright" snappy journalism. The clipped style ("Barsov went," "He was.") probably owes something to the Walter Winchell manner of radio reporting. The American slang word "bonanza" (a rich strike) is a good choice since it adds, like a raccoon's tail to a streamlined car, a human touch to prose which is in danger of becoming cold through its professional terseness. This prose is tailored for "modern people" who, after a day in the office or the factory, believe that the best way to relax is by not mentally taxing themselves. It has, therefore, a "cat on the mat" simplicity and clarity, otherwise a number of readers (who knows how many?) would consider themselves too tired even to try to grasp its import. This kind of prose must also have a reasonable quota of direct speech and be sharply paragraphed, for unrelieved indirect speech and normal paragraphing would be too dull and difficult to lure the fickle attention of the new kind of reader. Such devices are, of course, used in other publications too, both inside and outside the United States. In Britain, for example, the *Daily Express*, which is much influenced by the fashions of the United States, is an extreme example of bright journalism.

Mention of the *Reader's Digest* brings up the matter of condensing and rewriting which is practiced in a much more open, thoroughgoing, and ruthless way in the United States than anywhere else, mainly in the interests of efficient marketing. Morally, the practice is highly questionable, but I will confine myself to its effect on prose in magazines. It is said that the *Reader's Digest* not only condenses articles and novels already published, but that to a considerable extent it commissions articles, has them rewritten to exactly the right style and length, and then, by agreement, places them in selected magazines, so that it will seem in any given month that there is a choice from the nation's periodicals. In the case of *The New Yorker*, a magazine of a different breed, I have also often heard the complaint that articles and even stories pass through the editorial mill to such an extent that some are completely rewritten. How much this is true I have no way of telling since the workings of *The New Yorker* are clothed in comparative mystery. I judge that it is probably exaggerated, owing to the nature of the contributors, for one thing. Where an ordinary working journalist might have few misgivings about having his prose tampered with, the respected critics and writers whose work appears in *The New Yorker* might be expected to have more to say. At any rate, there is a noticeable difference, as might be expected, between the style of a book-piece by Anthony West, or Edmund Wilson, and an article on television by Philip Hamburger, or between a short story by Eudora Welty and one by John Cheever. Whatever editing there is is probably not only less extreme but different in kind from that of the *Reader's Digest*. *Reader's Digest* prose is excellent up to a point —clear, uninvolved and pithy; but it is no vehicle for conveying ideas of any subtlety. Nuances of language it will not bear; that is not its purpose. Subtle, imaginative language and original figures of speech—if they are ever present in the contributions—must be smoothed into prose which can be easily grasped by the meanest intelligence. The magazine must be an efficient machine, and it is. But a steady diet of its prose has the same effect on the mind as a steady diet of pap on the teeth. *The New Yorker*, on the other hand, communicates at a level of intelligence and imagination which is probably higher than that of any other general magazine written in English. Both the *Reader's Digest* and *The New Yorker* probably have an ideal reader in mind, but they are very different kinds of people. The *Reader's Digest* aims at the Everyman of the Twentieth Century, the lowest common denominator of reader. Given that purpose the *Reader's Digest* editors do an extremely efficient job. Considering the editorial policy of maximum human interest and maximum optimism, the success with which the editors manipulate their material this side of sentimentality is extraordinary. What is important in this comparison, however, is, I believe, the difference in intention. The editors of the *Reader's Digest* seem, like the writers for *Time*, to be working in a region below their own natural range. The editors of *The New Yorker*, on the other hand, seem to be aiming at men and women like themselves. It is this, I imagine, which is responsible for the difference in tone, depth, and degree of idiosyncracy between the prose of the two magazines.

(c) *The speaker rustled his notes, clinked a pocketful of keys and stared at the ceiling while he fumbled for words. Then his wife's voice cut through the jangle: "Put your keys down, honey." Meekly, irascible Columnist Westbrook Pegler obeyed. For once the foaming temper was in check. Mellow with memory, onetime Sportswriter Pegler had turned out for the Tucson, Ariz. Press Club dinner, greeting the new baseball season.*

Peg. . . .

This passage is, of course, from *Time* (April 11, 1955). The formula is familiar and highly successful: first, the dramatic opening, the deliberate holding back of the name. Who can this Milquetoast be? To our surprise, it is none other than irascible Columnist Westbrook Pegler, who, having been introduced in a cloud of unknowing, soon becomes, in the democratic fashion, our friend, "Peg." This richly staged introduction, as designing as an advertiser's banquet, achieves its purpose admirably, again within the imaginative scope and vocabulary of the lowest common denominator of readers, although the level is, one suspects, rather higher than that of the *Reader's Digest.* It is the most lavish example so far of the presentation of factual material in an emotional way. It was prophesied by Tocqueville as a concomitant of the Age of Democracy. Everyone can read, but few can or want to read properly. Even to say "properly" is suspect in this time of the triumph of the mindless. Must democracy inevitably lead to the relaxing of standards and pandering to increasingly jaded palates? It is a nice question. The "average reader" cannot be expected to use his brain because he wants "relaxation" after his day's work, or because he has no time to spare, or because he wasn't taught properly in High School. So the writers of *Time* labour (and they probably have some fun doing it, too) to present him with ever more brightly written and attractively presented material. If they did not, their public would go off and read *Newsweek,* no doubt.

Advertising Prose

(a) *Yes, only Viceroy has this filter composed of 20,000 tiny filter traps. You cannot obtain the same filtering action in* any other cigarette. . . . *That's why more college men and women smoke Viceroys than any other filter cigarette.* . . .

This passage, taken from an advertisement by the makers of Viceroy cigarettes in a student newspaper, is typical of nationwide current advertising technique for cigarettes, and of the kind of prose used in such advertisements.

The copywriters have apparently now reached their nadir, for they are using the same formula in print as on the radio. Perhaps this is significant in terms of the relationship of speech to literature in the United States, but I doubt it. The method is one of insidious hammering, as if with a little rubber hammer which the torturer wields tirelessly, so that, in the end, one's whole body is in tune with the nagging rhythmic blows. Four (at least four) things are constant: first, the meaningless and tiresome "yes," worn like a charm to scare away the advertising man's bogey (lack of smoothness, lack of a "friendly" yet authoritative, selling ring); second, the appeal to "science"; third, the "You cannot . . . in *any other cigarette*" (which varies in some cases to "No other cigarette made . . . etc.); and, fourth, the repetition on the same, though slightly modulated note ("That's why . . . than any other filter smoke"). Writers on the traditional ballad tell us that their anonymous authors used the device of "incremental repetition" in order that a rhythmic, memorable pattern might be retained in the minds of an audience which lived in an oral tradition. Here is incremental repetition today, serving other ends in another society.

WHY SWELTER? JUST A TWIST OF THE WRIST CHANGES HOT MISERY . . . TO COOL COMFORT!

LIVE AND WORK IN G-E "COMFORT-CONDITIONED AIR"!

Simply dial out swelter with this great new General Electric Room Air Conditioner! You can sleep dry and cool tonight *in G-E "Comfort-Conditioned Air"—air that*'s always *cool, dry and filtered to reduce dust, dirt and pollen.*

WHY NOT CALL ON YOUR GENERAL ELECTRIC DEALER NOW?

The most noticeable thing about this passage, which is taken from an advertisement in *Life,* is its colourful and highly sensory use of language. This, coupled with the exclamatory style, creates an effect of pseudo-momentousness. Nothing more, possibly, in the way of emotive effect, could have been crammed into the headline. The advertising copywriters are, as I believe Mr. Hayakawa once pointed out, the folk-poets of modern commercial civilisation. They know all the tricks of language that a poet or a story writer knows, but they put them to the service, not of art, but of commercial persuasion. As Tocqueville said, "Democracy not only infuses a taste for letters among the trading classes, but introduces a trading spirit into literature." The writer of this copy ("Just a Twist of the Wrist") had an ear for the fundamental rhythms of the English language, a language which naturally and easily falls into patterns of rhyme, alliteration and onomatopoeia. These are patterns which can be found as easily in literature as in ordinary speech, from "A faire felde ful of folke / Fonde I there bytwene," of William Langland to "The breezes blew, the white foam flew, / The furrow follow'd free" of Coleridge, from Cockney rhyming slang to the "What's cookin', good-lookin' " of the American high school boy.

"Dial it out" is another example of verbal ingenuity devoted to the end of persuading. The effect is concentrated and dramatic. One can see oneself just dialling away "swelter," (i.e. the state of sweltering) by that "twist of the wrist." The use of "swelter" here, incidentally, is an interesting illustration of the extreme grammatical flexibility of the English language in communicating sensations, and also of the streamlining tendency of American English.

Another interesting convention is "Comfort-Conditioned Air." Perhaps the copywriter, like Fleming with his moulds, made the discovery by sheer accident. At any rate, it seems to be a reversal of the familiar "Air-Conditioned Comfort." And the wonder of it is that it means something. The poet, fiddling with words, struck rich ore (a bonanza). The effect of it was so heady that when he came to compose the whole line he made the very air, now "cool, dry and filtered," the property of General Electric. What kind of air have you there, Mr. Jones? I have G.E. Comfort-Conditioned Air in here, Mr. Smith.

One last point calls for mention and that is the use of "great," which, second to "beautiful," seems to be the most overworked word in the English language. If this air-conditioner is "great," what then was the invention of the aeroplane or the propounding of the Theory of Relativity?

I trust that my own tone, in commenting on these these examples, has not at times seemed like those of the Reverend John Witherspoon. The Reverend John's is mild in comparison with later British commentators who were apt to report on the misuse of language in the United States with shouts of glee, thus arousing the animosity and eventually the triumphant counter-cries of H. L. Mencken. A pre-Revolutionary (immigrant) American, the Reverend John hoped for a specifically American style, to be watched over by some "center of learning and politeness." In the meantime he thought it his duty to point out the various misuses of the English language in America, which he listed under the headings of: (1) Americanisms, (2) vulgarisms in England and America, (3) vulgarisms in America alone, (4) local phrases or terms, (5) common blunders arising from ignorance, (6) cant phrases, (7) personal blunders, and (8) technical terms introduced into the language.

On subjects like America and Prose one's mind cannot be made a blank. One has impressions, and my impression, before examining the samples I have chosen, was that in spite of some obvious examples of excessive rhetoric, of ineptness in handling words, of crudeness, of a peculiarly American kind of inflation, American prose as a whole had more naturalness than the English and at its best a transparent sincerity and simplicity worthy of American ideals. I did not, however, choose my quotations to prove this point. I threw my net as wide as I could, examined the pieces as objectively as possible, and relied on my findings to provide me with some conclusions which might or might not prove what I had previously accepted.

I find, on the whole, that my preconceptions are borne out only in so far as the best topical commentary, the best political writing, the best criticism and, above all, the best humorous writing is concerned. Elsewhere, there are great variations. Of course, the reader might object that he could have chosen a whole set of other samples which would alter the emphasis, or alternatively, that the quotations were far too short for judgment. This might be true, but short of conducting a statistical survey I do not see what else could be done. Perhaps, before our time runs out, one of the great Foundations will have provided funds for such an enterprise. But since language cannot be gauged like physical reactions, and the value of the comments depends on the taste of the investigator, it would be a difficult task. In the meantime, and in the light of my own crude sampling, I offer, diffidently, some general conclusions.

In the first place, it seems to me that American "expositional prose" is much weaker than American creative prose. Only in the case of people of acute sensibility, at the highest level, do we find a kind of prose which, by its tasteful natural diction, its use of figures drawn from American life, and its ease of manner can be held up as an example of the use of English which is both good and distinctively American. The American temperament seems better fitted to explore the creative possibilities of language, and one can find all kinds of examples to support this from the ebullience but relative crudeness of Thomas Wolfe to the fine-grained yet almost overwhelmingly rhetorical "immediacy" of William Faulkner. In the hands of the modern American short story writer, particularly, American prose is both beautiful and exciting to read. Life leaps from the page: sights, colours, smells, all the multifarious aspects of common and uncommon human existence make an impact which British creative prose rarely achieves. But the cultural climate of the United States in the 20th century has apparently not been conducive to the development of a widespread and distinctively American instrument for conveying facts, ideas, and comment at the general level. Feelings and emotions get in the way, for one thing. There is too commonly an inability to express a logical sequence of thought with "ease, grace, precision," what I have called "having no ear" for the English language. One reason for this lies, I am sure, in the deep-seated American feeling that "style" is something ornamental, part of a way of life that is variously called "British" or "aristocratic." It does not matter that the reaction, which is an emotional one, is understandable. What matters is that it is bad for American prose. To quote Sir Arthur Quiller-Couch again:

> The editor of a mining paper in Denver, U.S.A., boldly the other day laid down this law, that niceties of language were mere "frills": all a man needed was "to get there," that is, to say what he wished in his own way. But just here . . . lies the mischief. You will not get there by hammering away on your own untutored impulse. You must first be your own reader, chiselling out the thought definitely for yourself: and, after that, must carve out the intaglio more

sharply and neatly, if you would impress its image accurately upon the wax of other men's minds.

But there is another reason, I believe, for the comparative lack of literary ability in all but the exceptional in the United States and this lies in the tendency to "educate for life" and to relegate literature to an inferior place. A questionnaire sent out in 1949 for *Harper's Magazine* by Norman Lewis revealed what Mr. Lewis called a "linguistic liberalism" among those people in the United States who "use the English language as a direct means of earning a livelihood." This meant accepting such expressions as "His work is different *than* mine," "I encountered *less* difficulties than I had expected" (attributed to Mr. Arthur Schlesinger, Jr.), and "The reason I'm worried is *because* I think she's ill." If we substitute "sloppy English" for "linguistic liberalism" we are, I think, nearer the mark. Yet, as against ninety-three American College Professors of English who rejected the first expression, there were sixty-two who accepted it as worthy of currency in educated speech. Forty-nine out of the one hundred and fifty-five even accepted the barbarous second example, and the astounding total of eighty-nine out of one hundred and fifty-five the third. This perhaps partly explains why college students' essays are such examples of bad prose. But what is far more perturbing than uneducated usage in educated exposition is the sheer muddle of the language, the lack of an ability, in the college group, to express ideas lucidly and coherently. Yet even those who seem on the page to be semi-literate morons can make good sense when they speak, be ready in comment, even advance ideas. One's conclusion cannot but be that American conditions, educational and otherwise, have militated against clear and graceful literary expression. Yet Abraham Lincoln, that self-educated man, could express himself simply, cogently, and with style. Could he have learnt it had he grown up in America today? Where would he find models? Well, he could find them for one thing in Mr. Stevenson's prose, or Mr. Thurber's. He could read *The New Yorker*, or the *Atlantic*, or *Harper's*. The compilers of college textbooks of exposition certainly seem to strive to put good examples of prose before their readers. One wonders what the 40 per cent of college professors of English who say "His work is different *than* mine" do with them. Point out their queer usage perhaps?

It seems, then, that "independence and vigour," which the United States has in abundance, may produce good novels and stories but does not make a good climate for expositional prose which, unlike creative writing, touches everybody. In fact, the outstanding exceptions which I have noted would be classified by some as outside the mainstream of American culture. It almost seems as if there were, as Disraeli said of 19th century English society, "two nations" in America, but instead of these two nations being the rich and the poor they are the educated and the uneducated, the literate and the semi-literate. One remembers some of Tocqueville's prophecies:

> The most common expedient employed by democratic nations to make an innovation in language consists in giving some unwonted meaning to an expression already in use. This method is very simple, prompt, and convenient; no learning is required to use it aright, and ignorance itself rather facilitates the practice; but that practice is most dangerous to the language.

There will always, I feel, be Americans to whom these practices will be abhorrent. They will uphold the standards of American prose to the end. But to whom will they make their communication, except to each other?

All this raises, no doubt, most interesting questions, some as basic as one could wish for, such as: Does literacy matter? It is true that one can be intelligent without being literate. But Western Civilisation is build upon such principles and traditions as demand literacy. To deny it is to deny Western Civilisation as an idea and to prepare the way for barbarism. Yet some years ago a Californian professor seriously suggested, not merely that the oral might eventually entirely supersede the written communication, but that it was a good thing that it should do so. Perhaps in the end it will be so. Perhaps the triumph of the mass media and the encouragement of "speech" rather than literature in schools has started a tide which cannot be turned. And what, when it is upon them, will the publishers and manufacturers of typewriters do then, poor things? If they are, like the rest of us, still here, that is.

EXERCISES

1. Check the meaning of the following words in your dictionary, then write a series of sentences using each: idioms; pastiche, sophist, *lingua franca*, genesis, cadences, hackles, incremental, nadir, insidious.

2. In the final sentence of his section on "Political Prose," Mr. Moore claims that most Americans rarely use the "also" in the *non solum . . . sed etiam* (not only . . . but also) construction. Do you agree?

3. Is Mr. Moore on sound ground when he says that Mr. Stevenson's first sentence (see page 265) should have included an "of" after "genesis"? Look up *elliptical* in your dictionary and relate the definition of it to this question.

4. Mr. Moore objects to the following usages (see page 278): "His work is different *than* mine"; "I encountered *less* difficulties than I had expected"; "The reason I'm worried is *because* I think she's ill."

Why does he object—in what way do these examples differ from "correct" usage? What conclusions do you draw from the fact that a large number of professors in American colleges accepted the above examples "as worthy of currency in educated speech"?

5. "Advertising Prose," according to Mr. Moore, invariably uses four devices. What are they? Write a two-minute radio commercial for "Shade-grown Coffee."

6. Write a short essay giving your views on one or more types of American Prose, e.g., political, historical, magazine, etc., discussed by Mr. Moore.

5 POLITICS AND THE ENGLISH LANGUAGE

by George Orwell

George Orwell (pseudonym of Eric Blair; 1903–1950) wrote several novels including Keep the Aspidistra Flying, Coming Up for Air *and* Burmese Days; *autobiographical books including* Homage to Catalonia; *and political satires.* Animal Farm, *a satire on Communist hierarchies, and* Nineteen Eighty-four, *a frightening projection of life in a totalitarian state, are probably the most widely read of his books. A fearless and critical writer, Orwell was a liberal who was willing to face and expose the prejudices he recognized in himself and his fellow liberals.*

Orwell looked on writing as a very serious enterprise which places great responsibility on the writer. He described his own experience in writing "as a horrible, exhausting struggle, like a long bout of some painful illness." In his political satires, Orwell graphically illustrated the dangers of propaganda. "Politics and the English Language" reflects this concern about the distortion of truth by a misuse of language. It is a plea for the precise and honest use of language as "an instrument for expressing and not for concealing or preventing thought."

Most people who bother with the matter at all would admit that the English language is in a bad way, but it is generally assumed that we cannot by conscious action do anything about it. Our civilization is decadent, and our language—so the argument runs—must inevitably share in the general collapse. It follows that any struggle against the abuse of language is a sentimental archaism, like preferring candles to electric light or hansom cabs to aeroplanes. Underneath this lies the half-conscious belief that language is a natural growth and not an instrument which we shape for our own purposes.

Now, it is clear that the decline of a language must ultimately have political and economic causes: it is not due simply to the bad influence of this or that individual writer. But an effect can become a cause, reinforcing the original cause and producing the same effect in an intensified form, and so on indefinitely. A man may take to drink because he feels himself to be a failure, and then fail all the more completely because he drinks. It is rather the same thing that is happening to the English language. It becomes ugly and inaccurate because our thoughts are foolish, but the slovenliness of our language makes it easier for us to have foolish thoughts. The point is that the process is reversible. Modern English, especially written English, is full of bad habits which spread by imitation and which can be avoided if one is willing to take the necessary trouble. If one gets rid of these habits one can think more clearly, and to think clearly is a necessary first step towards political regeneration: so that the fight against bad English is not frivolous and is not the exclusive concern of professional writers. I will come back to this presently, and I hope that by that time the meaning of what I have said here will have become clearer. Meanwhile, here are five specimens of the English language as it is now habitually written.

These five passages have not been picked out because they are especially bad—I could have quoted far worse if I had chosen—but because they illustrate various of the mental vices from which we now suffer. They are a little below the average, but are fairly representative samples. I number them so that I can refer back to them when necessary:

(1) I am not, indeed, sure whether it is not true to say that the Milton who once seemed not unlike a seventeenth-century Shelley had not become, out of an experience even more bitter in each year, more alien (*sic*) to the founder of that Jesuit sect which nothing could induce him to tolerate.

PROFESSOR HAROLD LASKI (Essay in *Freedom of Expression*).

(2) Above all, we cannot play ducks and drakes with a native battery of idioms which prescribes such egregious collocations of vocables as the Basic *put up with* for *tolerate* or *put at a loss* for *bewilder*.

PROFESSOR LANCELOT HOGBEN (*Interglossa*).

(3) On the one side we have the free personality: by definition it is not neurotic, for it has neither conflict nor dream. Its desires, such as they are, are transparent, for they are just what institutional approval keeps in the forefront of consciousness; another institutional pattern would alter their number and intensity; there is little in them that is natural, irreducible, or culturally dangerous. But *on the other side*, the social bond itself is nothing but the mutual reflection of these self-secure integrities. Recall the definition of love. Is not this

the very picture of a small academic? Where is there a place in this hall of mirrors for either personality or fraternity?

Essay on psychology in *Politics* (New York).

(4) All the "best people" from the gentlemen's clubs, and all the frantic fascist captains, united in common hatred of Socialism and bestial horror of the rising tide of the mass revolutionary movement, have turned to acts of provocation, to foul incendiarism, to medieval legends of poisoned wells, to legalize their own destruction of proletarian organizations, and rouse the agitated petty-bourgeoisie to chauvinistic fervour on behalf of the fight against the revolutionary way out of the crisis.

Communist pamphlet.

(5) If a new spirit *is* to be infused into this old country, there is one thorny and contentious reform which must be tackled, and that is the humanization and galvanization of the B.B.C. Timidity here will bespeak canker and atrophy of the soul. The heart of Britain may be sound and of strong beat, for instance, but the British lion's roar at present is like that of Bottom in Shakespeare's *Midsummer Night's Dream*—as gentle as any sucking dove. A virile new Britain cannot continue indefinitely to be traduced in the eyes, or rather ears, of the world by the effete languors of Langham Place, brazenly masquerading as "standard English." When the Voice of Britain is heard at nine o'clock, better far and infinitely less ludicrous to hear aitches honestly dropped than the present priggish, inflated, inhibited, school-ma'amish arch braying of blameless bashful mewing maidens!

Letter in *Tribune*.

Each of these passages has faults of its own, but, quite apart from avoidable ugliness, two qualities are common to all of them. The first is staleness of imagery: the other is lack of precision. The writer either has a meaning and cannot express it, or he inadvertently says something else, or he is almost indifferent as to whether his words mean anything or not. This mixture of vagueness and sheer incompetence is the most marked characteristic of modern English prose, and especially of any kind of political writing. As soon as certain topics are raised, the concrete melts into the abstract and no one seems able to think of turns of speech that are not hackneyed: prose consists less and less of *words* chosen for the sake of their meaning, and more and more of *phrases* tacked together like the sections of a prefabricated hen-house. I list below, with notes and examples, various of the tricks by means of which the work of prose-construction is habitually dodged:

Dying metaphors. A newly invented metaphor assists thought by evoking a visual image, while on the other hand a metaphor which is technically "dead" (e.g. *iron resolution*) has in effect reverted to being an ordinary word and can generally be used without loss of vividness. But in between these two classes there is a huge dump of worn-out metaphors which have lost all evocative power and are merely used because they save people the trouble of inventing phrases for themselves. Examples are: *Ring the changes on, take up the cudgels for, toe the line, ride roughshod over, stand shoulder to shoulder with, play into the hands of, no axe to grind, grist to the mill, fishing in troubled waters, on the order of the day, Achilles' heel, swan song, hotbed.* Many of these are used without knowledge of their meaning (what is a "rift," for instance?), and incompatible metaphors are frequently mixed, a sure sign that the writer is not interested in what he is saying. Some metaphors now current have been twisted out of their original meaning without those who use them even being aware of the fact. For example, *toe the line* is sometimes written *tow the line.* Another example is *the hammer and the anvil,* now always used with the implication that the anvil gets the worst of it. In real life it is always the anvil that breaks the hammer, never the other way about: a writer who stopped to think what he was saying would be aware of this, and would avoid perverting the original phrase.

Operators, or *verbal false limbs.* These save the trouble of picking out appropriate verbs and nouns, and at the same time pad each sentence with extra syllables which give it an appearance of symmetry. Characteristic phrases are: *render inoperative, militate against, prove unacceptable, make contact with, be subjected to, give rise to, give grounds for, have the effect of, play a leading part* (*role*) *in, make itself felt, take effect, exhibit a tendency to, serve the purpose of, etc., etc.* The keynote is the elimination of simple verbs. Instead of being a single word, such as *break, stop, spoil, mend, kill,* a verb becomes a *phrase,* made up of a noun or adjective tacked on to some general-purposes verb such as *prove, serve, form, play, render.* In addition, the passive voice is wherever possible used in preference to the active, and noun constructions are used instead of gerunds (*by examination of* instead of *by examining*). The range of verbs is further cut down by means of the *-ize* and *de-* formations, and banal statements are given an appearance of profundity by means of the *not un-* formation. Simple conjunctions and prepositions are replaced by such phrases as *with respect to, having regard to, the fact that, by dint of, in view of, in the interests of, on the hypothesis that;* and the ends of sentences are saved from anti-climax by such resounding commonplaces as *greatly to be desired, cannot be left out of account, a development to be expected in the near future, deserving of serious consideration, brought to a satisfactory conclusion,* and so on and so forth.

Pretentious diction. Words like *phenomenon, element, individual* (as noun), *objective, categorical, effective, virtual, basic, primary, promote, constitute, exhibit, exploit, utilize, eliminate, liquidate,* are used to dress up simple statement and give an air of scientific impartiality to biased judgments. Adjectives like *epoch-making, epic, historic, unforgettable, triumphant, age-old, inevitable, inexorable, veritable,* are used to dignify the sordid processes of international politics, while writing that aims at glorifying war usually takes on an archaic colour, its characteristic words being: *realm, throne, chariot, mailed fist, trident, sword, shield, buckler, banner, jackboot, clarion.* Foreign words and expressions such as *cul de sac, ancien régime, deus ex machina, mutatis mutandis, status quo, gleichschaltung, weltanschauung,* are used to give an air of culture and elegance. Except for the useful abbreviations *i.e., e.g.,* and *etc.,* there is no real need for any of the hundreds of foreign phrases now current in English. Bad writers, and especially scientific, political and sociological writers, are nearly always haunted by the notion that Latin or Greek words are grander than Saxon ones, and unnecessary words like *expedite, ameliorate, predict, extraneous, deracinated, clandestine, subaqueous* and hundreds of others constantly gain ground from their Anglo-Saxon opposite numbers.[1] The jargon peculiar to Marxist writing (*hyena, hangman, cannibal, petty bourgeois, these gentry, lacquey, flunkey, mad dog, White Guard,* etc.) consists largely of words and phrases translated from Russian, German or French; but the normal way of coining a new word is to use a Latin or Greek root with the appropriate affix and, where necessary, the -ize formation. It is often easier to make up words of this kind (*deregionalize, impermissible, extramarital, non-fragmentatory* and so forth) than to think up the English words that will cover one's meaning. The result, in general, is an increase in slovenliness and vagueness.

Meaningless words. In certain kinds of writing, particularly in art criticism and literary criticism, it is normal to come across long passages which are almost completely lacking in meaning.[2] Words like *romantic, plastic, values, human, dead, sentimental, natural, vitality,* as used in art criticism, are strictly meaningless, in the sense that they not only do not point to any discoverable object, but are hardly even expected to do so by the reader. When one critic writes, "The outstanding feature of Mr. X's work is its living quality," while another writes, "The immediately striking thing about Mr. X's work is its peculiar deadness," the reader accepts this as a simple difference of opinion. If words like *black* and *white* were involved, instead of the jargon words *dead* and *living,* he would

[1] An interesting illustration of this is the way in which the English flower names which were in use till very recently are being ousted by Greek ones, *snapdragons* becoming *antirrhinum, forget-me-not* becoming *myosotis,* etc. It is hard to see any practical reason for this change of fashion: it is probably due to an instinctive turning-away from the more homely word and a vague feeling that the Greek word is scientific.

[2] Example: "Comfort's catholicity of perception and image, strangely Whitmanesque in range, almost the exact opposite in aesthetic compulsion, continues to evoke that trembling atmospheric accumulative hinting at a cruel, an inexorably serene timelessness . . . Wrey Gardiner scores by aiming at simple bulleyes with precision. Only they are not so simple, and through this contented sadness runs more than the surface bittersweet of resignation." (*Poetry Quarterly.*)

see at once that language was being used in an improper way. Many political words are similarly abused. The word *Fascism* has now no meaning except in so far as it signifies "something not desirable." The words *democracy, socialism, freedom, patriotic, realistic, justice,* have each of them several different meanings which cannot be reconciled with one another. In the case of a word like *democracy,* not only is there no agreed definition, but the attempt to make one is resisted from all sides. It is almost universally felt that when we call a country democratic we are praising it: consequently the defenders of every kind of régime claim that it is a democracy, and fear that they might have to stop using the word if it were tied down to any one meaning. Words of this kind are often used in a consciously dishonest way. That is, the person who uses them has his own private definition, but allows his hearer to think he means something quite different. Statements like *Marshal Pétain was a true patriot, The Soviet Press is the freest in the world, The Catholic Church is opposed to persecution,* are almost always made with intent to deceive. Other words used in variable meanings, in most cases more or less dishonestly, are: *class, totalitarian, science, progressive, reactionary, bourgeois, equality.*

Now that I have made this catalogue of swindles and perversions, let me give another example of the kind of writing that they lead to. This time it must of its nature be an imaginary one. I am going to translate a passage of good English into modern English of the worst sort. Here is a well-known verse from *Ecclesiastes:*

> I returned, and saw under the sun, that the race is not to the swift, nor the battle to the strong, neither yet bread to the wise, nor yet riches to men of understanding, nor yet favour to men of skill; but time and chance happeneth to them all.

Here it is in modern English:

> Objective consideration of contemporary phenomena compels the conclusion that success or failure in competitive activities exhibits no tendency to be commensurate with innate capacity, but that a considerable element of the unpredictable must invariably be taken into account.

This is a parody, but not a very gross one. Exhibit (3), above, for instance, contains several patches of the same kind of English. It will be seen that I have not made a full translation. The beginning and ending of the sentence follow the original meaning fairly closely, but in the middle the concrete illustrations—race, battle, bread—dissolve into the vague phrase "success or failure in competitive activities." This had to be so, because no modern writer of the kind I am discussing—no one capable of using phrases like "objective consideration of contemporary phenomena"

—would ever tabulate his thoughts in that precise and detailed way. The whole tendency of modern prose is away from concreteness. Now analyse these two sentences a little more closely. The first contains 49 words but only 60 syllables, and all its words are those of everyday life. The second contains 38 words of 90 syllables: 18 of its words are from Latin roots, and one from Greek. The first sentence contains six vivid images, and only one phrase ("time and chance") that could be called vague. The second contains not a single fresh, arresting phrase, and in spite of its 90 syllables it gives only a shortened version of the meaning contained in the first. Yet without a doubt it is the second kind of sentence that is gaining ground in modern English. I do not want to exaggerate. This kind of writing is not yet universal, and outcrops of simplicity will occur here and there in the worst-written page. Still, if you or I were told to write a few lines on the uncertainty of human fortunes, we should probably come much nearer to my imaginary sentence than to the one from *Ecclesiastes.*

As I have tried to show, modern writing at its worst does not consist in picking out words for the sake of their meaning and inventing images in order to make the meaning clearer. It consists in gumming together long strips of words which have already been set in order by someone else, and making the results presentable by sheer humbug. The attraction of this way of writing is that it is easy. It is easier—even quicker, once you have the habit—to say *In my opinion it is a not unjustifiable assumption that* than to say *I think.* If you use ready-made phrases, you not only don't have to hunt about for words; you also don't have to bother with the rhythms of your sentences, since these phrases are generally so arranged as to be more or less euphonious. When you are composing in a hurry—when you are dictating to a stenographer, for instance, or making a public speech—it is natural to fall into a pretentious, Latinized style. Tags like *a consideration which we should do well to bear in mind* or *a conclusion to which all of us would readily assent* will save many a sentence from coming down with a bump. By using stale metaphors, similes and idioms, you save much mental effort, at the cost of leaving your meaning vague, not only for your reader but for yourself. This is the significance of mixed metaphors. The sole aim of a metaphor is to call up a visual image. When these images clash—as in *The Fascist octopus has sung its swan song, the jackboot is thrown into the melting pot*—it can be taken as certain that the writer is not seeing a mental image of the objects he is naming; in other words he is not really thinking. Look again at the examples I gave at the beginning of this essay. Professor Laski (1) uses five negatives in 53 words. One of these is superfluous, making nonsense of the whole passage, and in addition there is the slip *alien* for akin, making further nonsense, and several avoidable pieces of clumsiness which increase the general vagueness. Professor Hogben (2) plays ducks and drakes with a battery which is able to write prescriptions, and, while disapproving of the everyday phrase *put up with,* is unwilling to look *egregious* up in the dictionary and see what it means. If (3) one takes an uncharitable attitude towards it, it is simply meaningless: probably one could work out its intended meaning by reading the whole of the article in which it occurs. In (4), the writer knows more or less what he wants to say, but an accumulation of stale phrases chokes him like tea leaves blocking a sink. In (5), words and meaning have almost parted company. People who write in this manner usually have a general emotional meaning—they dislike one thing and want to express solidarity with another—but they are not interested in the detail of what they are saying. A scrupulous writer, in every sentence that he writes, will ask himself at least four questions, thus: What am I trying to say? What words will express it? What image or idiom will make it clearer? Is this image fresh enough to have an effect? And he will probably ask himself two more: Could I put it more shortly? Have I said anything that is avoidably ugly? But you are not obliged to go to all this trouble. You can shirk it by simply throwing your mind open and letting the ready-made phrases come crowding in. They will construct your sentences for you—even think your thoughts for you, to a certain extent—and at need they will perform the important service of partially concealing your meaning even from yourself. It is at this point that the special connection between politics and the debasement of language becomes clear.

In our time it is broadly true that political writing is bad writing. Where it is not true, it will generally be found that the writer is some kind of rebel, expressing his private opinions and not a "party line." Orthodoxy, of whatever colour, seems to demand a lifeless, imitative style. The political dialects to be found in pamphlets, leading articles, manifestoes, White Papers and the speeches of under-secretaries do, of course, vary from party to party, but they are all alike in that one almost never finds in them a fresh, vivid, home-made turn of speech. When one watches some tired hack on the platform mechanically repeating the familiar phrases—*bestial atrocities, iron heel, bloodstained tyranny, free peoples of the world, stand shoulder to shoulder*—one often has a curious feeling that one is not watching a live human being but some kind of dummy: a feeling which suddenly becomes stronger at moments when the light catches the speaker's spectacles and turns them into blank discs which seem to have no eyes behind them. And this is not altogether fanciful. A speaker who uses that kind of phraseology has gone some distance towards turning himself into a machine. The appropriate noises are coming out of his larynx, but his brain is not involved as it would be if he were choosing his words for himself. If the speech he is making is one that he is accustomed to make over and over again, he may be almost unconscious of what he is saying, as one is when one utters the responses in church. And this reduced state of consciousness, if not indispensable, is at any rate favourable to political conformity.

In our time, political speech and writing are largely the defence of the indefensible. Things like the continuance of British rule in India, the Russian purges and deportations, the dropping of the atom bombs on Japan, can indeed be defended, but only by arguments which are too brutal for most people to face, and which do not square with the professed aims of political parties. Thus political language has to consist largely of euphemism, question-begging and sheer cloudy vagueness. Defenceless villages are bombarded from the air, the inhabitants driven out into the countryside, the cattle machine-gunned, the huts set on fire with incendiary bullets: this is called *pacification*. Millions of peasants are robbed of their farms and sent trudging along the roads with no more than they can carry: this is called *transfer of population* or *rectification of frontiers*. People are imprisoned for years without trial, or shot in the back of the neck or sent to die of scurvy in Arctic lumber camps: this is called *elimination of unreliable elements*. Such phraseology is needed if one wants to name things without calling up mental pictures of them. Consider for instance some comfortable English professor defending Russian totalitarianism. He cannot say outright, "I believe in killing off your opponents when you can get good results by doing so." Probably, therefore, he will say something like this:

> While freely conceding that the Soviet régime exhibits certain features which the humanitarian may be inclined to deplore, we must, I think, agree that a certain curtailment of the right to political opposition is an unavoidable concomitant of transitional periods, and that the rigours which the Russian people have been called upon to undergo have been amply justified in the sphere of concrete achievement.

The inflated style is itself a kind of euphemism. A mass of Latin words falls upon the facts like soft snow, blurring the outlines and covering up all the details. The great enemy of clear language is insincerity. When there is a gap between one's real and one's declared aims, one turns as it were instinctively to long words and exhausted idioms, like a cuttlefish squirting out ink. In our age there is no such thing as "keeping out of politics." All issues are political issues, and politics itself is a mass of lies, evasions, folly, hatred and schizophrenia. When the general atmosphere is bad, language must suffer. I should expect to find—this is a guess which I have not sufficient knowledge to verify—that the German, Russian and Italian languages have all deteriorated in the last ten or fifteen years, as a result of dictatorship.

But if thought corrupts language, language can also corrupt thought. A bad usage can spread by tradition and imitation, even among people who should and do know better. The debased language that I have been discussing is in some ways very convenient. Phrases like *a not unjustifiable assumption, leaves much to be desired, would serve no good purpose, a consideration which we should do well to bear in mind,* are a continuous temptation, a packet of aspirins always at one's elbow. Look back through this essay, and for certain you will find that I have again and again committed the very faults I am protesting against. By this morning's post I have received a pamphlet dealing with conditions in Germany. The author tells me that he "felt impelled" to write it. I open it at random, and here is almost the first sentence that I see: "(The Allies) have an opportunity not only of achieving a radical transformation of Germany's social and political structure in such a way as to avoid a nationalistic reaction in Germany itself, but at the same time of laying the foundations of a co-operative and unified Europe." You see, he "feels impelled" to write—feels, presumably, that he has something new to say—and yet his words, like cavalry horses answering the bugle, group themselves automatically into the familiar dreary pattern. This invasion of one's mind by ready-made phrases (*lay the foundations, achieve a radical transformation*) can only be prevented if one is constantly on guard against them, and every such phrase anaesthetizes a portion of one's brain.

I said earlier that the decadence of our language is probably curable. Those who deny this would argue, if they produced an argument at all, that language merely reflects existing social condition, and that we cannot influence its development by any direct tinkering with words and constructions. So far as the general tone or spirit of a language goes, this may be true, but it is not true in detail. Silly words and expressions have often disappeared, not through any evolutionary process but owing to the conscious action of a minority. Two recent examples were *explore every avenue* and *leave no stone unturned,* which were killed by the jeers of a few journalists. There is a long list of flyblown metaphors which could similarly be got rid of if enough people would interest themselves in the job; and it should also be possible to laugh the *not un*-formation out of existence,[3] to reduce the amount of Latin and Greek in the average sentence, to drive out foreign phrases and strayed scientific words, and, in general, to make pretentiousness unfashionable. But all these are minor points. The defence of the English language implies more than this, and perhaps it is best to start by saying what it does *not* imply.

To begin with, it has nothing to do with archaism, with the salvaging of obsolete words and turns of speech, or with the setting-up of a "standard

[3] One can cure oneself of the *not un-* formation by memorizing this sentence: *A not unblack dog was chasing a not unsmall rabbit across a not ungreen field.*

English" which must never be departed from. On the contrary, it is especially concerned with the scrapping of every word or idiom which has outworn its usefulness. It has nothing to do with correct grammar and syntax, which are of no importance so long as one makes one's meaning clear, or with the avoidance of Americanisms, or with having what is called a "good prose style." On the other hand it is not concerned with fake simplicity and the attempt to make written English colloquial. Nor does it even imply in every case preferring the Saxon word to the Latin one, though it does imply using the fewest and shortest words that will cover one's meaning. What is above all needed is to let the meaning choose the word, and not the other way about. In prose, the worst thing one can do with words is to surrender to them. When you think of a concrete object, you think wordlessly, and then, if you want to describe the thing you have been visualizing, you probably hunt about till you find the exact words that seem to fit it. When you think of something abstract you are more inclined to use words from the start, and unless you make a conscious effort to prevent it, the existing dialect will come rushing in and do the job for you, at the expense of blurring or even changing your meaning. Probably it is better to put off using words as long as possible and get one's meaning as clear as one can through pictures or sensations. Afterwards one can choose—not simply *accept*—the phrases that will best cover the meaning, and then switch round and decide what impression one's words are likely to make on another person. This last effort of the mind cuts out all stale or mixed images, all prefabricated phrases, needless repetitions, and humbug and vagueness generally. But one can often be in doubt about the effect of a word or a phrase, and one needs rules that one can rely on when instinct fails. I think the following rules will cover most cases:

(i) Never use a metaphor, simile or other figure of speech which you are used to seeing in print.

(ii) Never use a long word where a short one will do.

(iii) If it is possible to cut a word out, always cut it out.

(iv) Never use the passive where you can use the active.

(v) Never use a foreign phrase, a scientific word or a jargon word if you can think of an everyday English equivalent.

(vi) Break any of these rules sooner than say anything outright barbarous.

These rules sound elementary, and so they are, but they demand a deep change of attitude in anyone who has grown used to writing in the style now fashionable. One could keep all of them and still write bad English, but one could not write the kind of stuff that I quoted in those five specimens at the beginning of this article.

I have not here been considering the literary use of language, but merely language as an instrument for expressing and not for concealing or preventing thought. Stuart Chase and others have come near to claiming that all abstract words are meaningless, and have used this as a pretext for advocating a kind of political quietism. Since you don't know what Fascism is, how can you struggle against Fascism? One need not swallow such absurdities as this, but one ought to recognize that the present political chaos is connected with the decay of language, and that one can probably bring about some improvement by starting at the verbal end. If you simplify your English, you are freed from the worst follies of orthodoxy. You cannot speak any of the necessary dialects, and when you make a stupid remark its stupidity will be obvious, even to yourself. Political language—and with variations this is true of all political parties, from Conservatives to Anarchists—is designed to make lies sound truthful and murder respectable, and to give an appearance of solidity to pure wind. One cannot change this all in a moment, but one can at least change one's own habits, and from time to time one can even, if one jeers loudly enough, send some worn-out and useless phrase—some *jackboot, Achilles' heel, hotbed, melting pot, acid test, veritable inferno* or other lump of verbal refuse—into the dustbin where it belongs.

EXERCISES

1. Orwell maintains that the English language is in decline. What reasons does he give? Are they sufficient to prove his assertion?
2. If you agree with Orwell can you give additional reasons to support his claim? If you disagree, how would you answer his claims?
3. Read carefully the five passages Orwell quotes. Rewrite them to read more simply and clearly.
4. Why is Orwell so strongly opposed to abstractions?
5. Compare Orwell's advice to writers with Baker's (who acknowledged his debt to Orwell's article). Which is the more arbitrary?

6 THE CLICHÉ EXPERT TESTIFIES ON BASEBALL

by Frank Sullivan

Frank Sullivan (1892–) a resident of Saratoga Springs, New York, has published hundreds of articles, many of which have been collected in book form. Among these books are Innocent Bystanding, Broccoli and Old Lace, In One Ear, *and* A Pearl in Every Oyster. *One of Sullivan's most successful creations is the character of Dr. Arbuthnot, authority on clichés favored by experts on such subjects as baseball, theater reviewing, politics, and polite conversation about the weather.*

The article reprinted below misses few of the phrases familiar to all who follow the sports columns and radio and television commentaries on baseball. In this context the cliché is amusing. Considered more seriously, it can be recognized as a barrier to precise expression and communication. Indeed, George Orwell (page 289) sees the cliché as a threat to clear thought and calls it "a continuous temptation, a packet of aspirins always at one's elbow."

Q—Mr. Arbuthnot, you state that your grandmother has passed away and you would like to have the afternoon off to go to her funeral.

A—That is correct.

Q—You are an expert in the clichés of baseball—right?

A—I pride myself on being well versed in the stereotypes of our national pastime.

Q—Well, we'll test you. Who plays baseball?

A—Big-league baseball is customarily played by brilliant outfielders, veteran hurlers, powerful sluggers, knuckle-ball artists, towering first basemen, key moundsmen, fleet base runners, ace southpaws, scrappy little shortstops, sensational war vets, ex-college stars, relief artists, rifle-armed twirlers, dependable mainstays, doughty right-handers, streamlined backstops, power-hitting batsmen, redoubtable infielders, erstwhile Dodgers, veteran sparkplugs, sterling moundsmen, aging twirlers, and rookie sensations.

Q—What other names are rookie sensations known by?

A—They are also known as aspiring rookies, sensational newcomers, promising freshmen, ex-sandlotters, highly touted striplings, and youngsters who will bear watching.

Q—What's the manager of a baseball team called?

A—A veteran pilot. Or youthful pilot. But he doesn't manage the team.

Q—No? What does he do?

A—He guides its destinies.

Q—How?

A—By the use of managerial strategy.

Q—Mr. Arbuthnot, please describe the average major-league-baseball athlete.

A—Well he comes in three sizes, or types. The first type is tall, slim, lean, towering, rangy, huge, husky, big, strapping, sturdy, handsome, powerful, lanky, rawboned, and rugged.

Q—Quite a hunk of athlete.

A—Well, those are the adjectives usage requires for the description of the Type One, or Ted Williams, ballplayer.

Q—What is Type Two like?

A—He is chunky or stocky—that is to say, Yogi Berra.

Q—And the third?

A—The third type is elongated and does not walk. He is Ol' Satchmo, or Satchel Paige.

Q—What do you mean Satchmo doesn't walk?

A—Not in the sports pages, he doesn't. He ambles.

Q—You mentioned a hurler, Mr. Arbuthnot. What is a hurler?

A—A hurler is a twirler.

Q—Well, what is a twirler?

A—A twirler is a flinger, a tosser. He's a moundsman.

Q—Moundsman?

A—Yes. He officiates on the mound. When the veteran pilot tells a hurler he is to twirl on a given day, that is a mound assignment, and the hurler who has been told to twirl is the mound nominee for that game.

Q—You mean he pitches?

A—That is right. You have cut the Gordian knot.

Q—What's the pitcher for the other team called?

A—He is the mound adversary, or mound opponent, of the mound nominee. That makes them rival hurlers, or twirlers. They face each other and have a mound duel, or pitchers' battle.

Q—Who wins?

A—The mound victor wins, and as a result he is a mound ace, or ace moundsman. He excels on the mound, or stars on it. He and the other moundsmen on his team are the mound corps.

Q—What happens to the mound nominee who loses the mound duel?

A—He is driven off the mound.

Q—What do you mean by that?

A—He's yanked. He's knocked out of the box.

Q—What's the box?

A—The box is the mound.

Q—I see. Why does the losing moundsman lose?

A—Because he issued, grants, yields, allows, or permits too many hits or walks, or both.

Q—A bit on the freehanded side, eh? Where does the mound victor go if he pitches the entire game?

A—He goes all the way.

Q—And how does the mound adversary who has been knocked out of the box explain his being driven off the mound?

A—He says, "I had trouble with my control," or "My curve wasn't working," or "I just didn't have anything today."

Q—What happens if a mound ace issues, grants, yields, allows, or permits too many hits and walks?

A—In that case, sooner or later, rumors are rife. Either that or they are rampant.

Q—Rife where?

A—In the front office.

Q—What's that?

A—That's the place where baseball's biggies—also known as baseball moguls—do their asking.

Q—What do they ask for?

A—Waivers on erratic southpaw.

Q—What are these baseball biggies further known as?

A—They are known as the Shrewd Mahatma or as Horace Stoneham, but if they wear their shirt open at the neck they are known as Bill Veeck.

Q—What do baseball biggies do when they are not asking for waivers?

A—They count the gate receipts, buy promising rookies, sell aging twirlers, and stand loyally by Manager Durocher.

Q—And what does Manager Durocher do?

A—He guides the destinies of the Giants and precipitates arguments with the men in blue.

Q—What men in blue?

A—The umpires, or arbiters.

Q—What kind of arguments does Durocher precipitate?

A—Heated arguments.

Q—And the men in blue do what to him and other players who precipitate heated arguments?

A—They send, relegate, banish, or thumb them to the showers.

Q—Mr. Arbuthnot, how do you, as a cliché expert, refer to first base?

A—First base is the initial sack.

Q—And second base?

A—The keystone sack.

Q—What's third base called?

A—The hot corner. The first inning is the initial frame, and an inning without runs is a scoreless stanza.

Q—What is one run known as?

A—A lone run, but four runs are known as a quartet of tallies.

Q—What is a baseball?

A—The pill, the horsehide, the old apple, or the sphere.

Q—And what's a bat?

A—The bat is the willow, or the wagon tongue, or the piece of lumber. In the hands of a mighty batsman, it is the mighty bludgeon.

Q—What does a mighty batsman do?

A—He amasses runs. He connects with the old apple. He raps 'em out and he pounds 'em out. He belts 'em and he clouts 'em.

Q—Clouts what?

A—Circuit clouts.

Q—What are they?

A—Home runs. Know what the mighty batsman does to the mighty bludgeon?

Q—No. What?

A—He wields it. Know what kind of orgies he fancies?

Q—What kind?

A—Batting orgies. Slugfests. That's why his team pins.

Q—Pins what?

A—All its hopes on him.

Q—Mr. Arbuthnot, what is a runner guilty of when he steals home?

A—A plate theft.

Q—And how many kinds of baseball games are there?

A—Five main classifications: scheduled tussles, crucial contests, pivotal games, drab frays, and arc-light tussles.

Q—And what does the team that wins—

A—Sir, a baseball team never wins. It scores a victory, or gains one, or chalks one up. Or it snatches.

Q—Snatches what?

A—Victory from the jaws of defeat.

Q—How?

A—By a ninth-inning rally.

Q—I see. Well, what do the teams that chalk up victories do to the teams that lose?

A—They nip, top, wallop, trounce, rout, down, subdue, smash, drub, paste, trip, crush, curb, whitewash, erase, bop, slam, batter, check, hammer, pop, wham, clout, and blank the visitors. Or they zero them.

Q—Gracious sakes! Now I know why ballplayers are old at thirty-five.

A—Oh, that isn't the half of it. They do other things to the visitors.

Q—Is it possible?

A—Certainly. They jolt them, or deal them a jolt. They also halt, sock, thump, larrup, vanquish, flatten, scalp, shellac, blast, slaughter, K.O., mow down, topple, whack, pound, rap, sink, baffle, thwart, foil, maul, and nick.

Q—Do the losers do anything at all to the victors?

A—Yes. They bow to the victors. And they taste.

Q—Taste what?

A—Defeat. They trail. They take a drubbing, pasting, or shellacking. They are in the cellar.

Q—What about the victors?

A—They loom as flag contenders. They're in the first division.

Q—Mr. Arbuthnot, what is the first sign of spring?

A—Well, a robin, of course.

Q—Yes, but I'm thinking of our subject here. How about when the ballplayers go south for spring training?

A—Ballplayers don't go south for spring training.

Q—Why, they do!

A—They do *not*. They wend their way southward.

Q—Oh, I see. Well, do all ballplayers wend their way southward?

A—No. One remains at home.

Q—Who is he?

A—The lone hold out.

Q—Why does the lone holdout remain at home?

A—He refuses to ink pact.

Q—What do you mean by that?

A—He won't affix his Hancock to his contract.

Q—Why not?

A—He demands a pay hike, or salary boost.

Q—From Whom?

A—From baseball's biggies.

Q—And what do baseball's biggies do to the lone holdout?

A—They attempt to lure him back into the fold.

Q—How?

A—By offering him new contract.

Q—What does lone holdout do then?

A—He weighs offer. If he doesn't like it, he balks at terms. If he does like it, he inks pact and and gets pay hike.

Q—How much pay hike?

A—An undisclosed amount in excess of.

Q—That makes him what?

A—One of the highest-paid baseball stars in the annals of the game, barring Ruth.

Q—What if baseball's biggies won't give lone holdout pay hike?

A—In that case, loneholdout takes pay cut, old salary, or job in filling station in home town.

Q—Now, when baseball players reach the spring training camp and put on their uniforms—

A—May I correct you again, sir? Baseball players do not put on uniforms. They don them.

Q—I see. What for?

A—For a practice session or strenuous workout.

Q—And why must they have a strenuous workout?

A—Because they must shed the winter's accumulation of excess avoirdupois.

Q—You mean they must lose weight?

A—You put it in a nutshell. They must be streamlined, so they plunge.

Q—Plunge into what?

A—Into serious training.

Q—Can't get into serious training except by plunging, eh?

A—No. Protocol requires that they plunge. Training season gets under way in Grapefruit and Citrus Leagues. Casey Stengel bars night life.

Q—Mr. Arbuthnot, what is the opening game of the season called?

A—Let me see-e-e. It's on the tip of my tongue. Isn't that aggravating? Ah, I have it—the opener! At the opener, fifty-two thousand two hundred and ninety-three fans watch Giants bow to Dodgers.

Q—What do those fifty-two thousand two hundred and ninety-three fans constitute?

A—They constitute fandom.

Q—And how do they get into the ballpark?

A—They click through the turnstiles.

Q—Now then, Mr. Arbuthnot, the climax of the baseball season is the World Series, is it not?

A—That's right.

Q—And what is the World Series called?

A—It's the fall classic, or crucial contest, also known as the fray, the epic struggle, and the Homeric struggle. It is part of the American scene, like ham and eggs or pumpkin pie. It's a colorful event.

Q—What is it packed with?

A—Thrills, Drama.

Q—What kind of drama?

A—Sheer or tense.

Q—Why does it have to be packed with thrills and drama?

A—Because if it isn't, it becomes drab fray.

Q—Where does the fall classic take place?

A—In a vast municipal stadium or huge ballpark.

Q—And the city in which the fall classic is held is what?

A—The city is baseball mad.

Q—And the hotels?

A—The hotels are jammed. Rooms are at a premium.

Q—Tickets, also, I presume.

A—Tickets? If you mean the cards of admission to the fall classic, they are referred to as elusive Series ducats, and they *are* at a premium, though I would prefer to say that they are scarcer than the proverbial hen's teeth.

Q—Who attends the Series?

A—A milling throng, or great outpouring of fans.

Q—What does the great outpouring of fans do?

A—It storms the portals and, of course, clicks through the turnstiles.

Q—Causing what?

A—Causing attendance records to go by the board. Stands fill early.

Q—What else does the crowd do?

A—It yells itself hoarse. Pent-up emotions are released. It rides the men in blue.

Q—What makes a baseball biggie unhappy on the morning of a Series tussle?

A—Leaden skies.

Q—Who is to blame for leaden skies?

A—A character known to the scribes as Jupiter Pluvius, or Jupe.

Q—What does rain dampen?

A—The ardor of the fans.

Q—If the weather clears, who gets credit for that?

A—Another character, known as Old Sol.

Q—Now, the team that wins the Series—

A—Again, I'm sorry to correct you, sir. A team does not win a Series. It wraps it up. It clinches it.

Q—Well, then what?

A—Then the newly crowned champions repair to their locker room.

Q—What reigns in that locker room?

A—Pandemonium, bedlam, and joy.

Q—Expressed how?

A—By lifting youthful pilot, or his equivalent, to the shoulders of his teammates.

Q—In the locker room of the losers, what is as thick as a day in—I mean so thick you could cut it with a knife?

A—Gloom. The losers are devoid.

Q—Devoid of what?

A—Animation.

Q—Why?

A—Because they came apart at the seams in the pivotal tussle.

Q—What happens to the newly crowned champions later?

A—They are hailed, acclaimed, and feted. They receive mighty ovations, boisterous demonstrations, and thunderous welcomes.

Q—And when those are over?

A—They split the Series purse and go hunting.

Q—Mr. Arbuthnot, if a powerful slugger or mighty batsman wields a mighty bludgeon to such effect that he piles up a record number of circuit clouts, what does that make him?

A—That is very apt to make him most valuable player of the year.

Q—And that?

A—That makes the kids of America look up to him as their hero.

Q—If most valuable player of the year continues the batting orgies that make the kids of America worship him, what then?

A—Then he becomes one of Baseball's Immortals. He is enshrined in Baseball's Hall of Fame.

Q—And after that?

A—Someday he retires and becomes veteran scout, or veteran coach, or veteran pilot. Or sports broadcaster.

Q—And then?

A—Well, eventually a memorial plaque is unveiled to him at the opener.

Q—Thank you, Mr. Arbuthnot. You have been most helpful. I won't detain you any longer, and I hope your grandmother's funeral this afternoon is a tense drama packed with thrills.

A—Thanks a lot. Goodbye now.

Q—Hold on a moment, Mr. Arbuthnot. Just for my own curiosity—couldn't you have said "thanks" and "goodbye" and let it go at that, without adding that "lot" and "now" malarkey?

A—I could have, but it would have cost me my title as a cliché expert.

EXERCISES

1. How does a cliché become a cliché? Why?

2. From your daily newspaper cut out a sports column, a review of a film or play, or a news report and underline all the clichés you can find. Rewrite the item substituting your own words for the clichés.

3. In the introduction to this section we suggested that certain subjects seem to invite inflated language. Graduation addresses, testimonial speeches, etc., often sound pretentious and are studded with clichés. Can you give reasons why this should be so?

4. Write a dialogue on one of the following: Murder in a Love Nest; What My Alma Mater Means to Me; A New Dramatic Star is Born.

VII The English Language

We depend on language to express and communicate our needs, feelings, ideas, and attitudes. Most of our thinking (some say all of it) is in words. There have been attempts to correlate intelligence and language ability, and to establish correlations between a man's vocabulary, or his speaking or writing ability, and his earning power. Language is inextricably woven into the fabric of our lives. It is therefore not surprising that social scientists, psychologists, philosophers, anthropologists, and sociologists, as well as linguists, are concerned with the origin, development, and structure of language.

Because of this interest in language, scholars, editors, and laymen are constantly debating what is happening to our language. Some express alarm at the departure—in usage and grammar—from traditional standards of "correctness." Others affirm that language is a living and therefore constantly changing instrument which has to adapt itself to a constantly changing world. Their yardstick is not traditional prescription but common usage. Between those who mourn the loss of standards and precision, and those who hail flexibility, there are many who deplore some changes and approve others.

Linguists, through their study of changes in pronunciation, grammar, and vocabulary, have been able to tell us a great deal about the history of our language. Charlton Laird's article, reviewing the development of English from early times through the Norman Conquest, shows some of the manifold influences at work in its growth and change. Change is influenced by many factors, among them, invasions, geographical isolation, political and social pressures, scientific discoveries. It is often difficult to assess precisely what, how, when, and why certain changes take place. A study of all available documents, however, has enabled linguists to reconstruct the general development of the language from Anglo-Saxon through Middle English to Modern English.

Thus we know that Anglo-Saxon was a more inflected language than Modern English (with word endings denoting grammatical relationships such as subject and object, while in Modern English, word order performs this function). Yet certain characteristics of Anglo-Saxon are strongly marked in Modern English, for example, the actor-action pattern in sentence structure (by 1100 A.D., it was used 50 per cent of the time).

The man ran hard
The building doused its lights
Destruction promised to come

Modern English of course also uses the passive voice, though probably more frequently in the written than the spoken language. But many students of style (see Cowley, p. 257, and Baker, p. 249) deplore what they consider an excessive use of the passive. They claim that the actor-action pattern is part of the spirit of our language. Certainly it is more vigorous.

To the modern reader, the language of *Beowulf*, of the Anglo-Saxon *Chronicles,* or of King Alfred's translations of the Venerable Bede appears as a foreign language. But Middle English, the language of Chaucer, brings us close to Modern English. For instance:

I sleep never on the Mount of Pernaso
Ne lerned Marcus Tullius Cithero

Toward the end of the fourteenth century, Midland, the dialect spoken in London, Oxford, and Cambridge, and thus used in government and education, began to assert itself as the dominant dialect of the three groups, Southern, Midland, and Northern. Chaucer wrote in Midland, as did Wycliff, translator of the Bible. Even more significant was its use by Caxton, the first English printer. Of Malory's *Morte D'Arthur,* published by Caxton in 1485, Stuart Robinson writes that it is "thoroughly representative of the standardization as well as the simplicity and flexibility that the language has attained in the late Middle English times." The publication of *Morte D'Arthur* antedated Shakespeare by just about a century.

Yet, as we implied earlier, it would be a mistake to take the term "standardization" too strictly. While a basic pattern had been established, the "flexibility" which Robinson notes allowed for continuing changes, both in England and America. With colonization, English became subject to new influences. Although there never has been a time when something written in England had to be translated for Americans, or vice versa, there are differences in vocabulary and especially in intonation and pronunciation. Three of the articles in this section—Pyles' on pronunciation, Shain's on idioms, and Mencken's on slang—examine American usage and make some comparisons with English usage. The development of American English has become a study in itself.

1 ENGLISH: HIS SISTERS AND HIS COUSINS AND HIS AUNTS

by Charlton Laird

Charlton Laird (1901–) studied at the University of Iowa and at Stanford University. Now chairman of the English department at the University of Nevada, he is the author of several books, including Synonyms and Antonyms, The World Through Literature, *and* The Miracle of Language.

"English: His Sisters and His Cousins and His Aunts," is a humorous account of influences on the English language from the coming of the Angles and Saxons through the Norman Conquest. Mr. Laird shows, among other things, that the influence of the Norman invasion on the development of the English language was considerably less than is commonly supposed. "Little Athelwold's daddy, if he had to sue his neighbour, may have sued him in French, and he prayed to the Virgin Mary in Latin; but when he spanked little Athelwold he spanked him in Anglo-Saxon, and the evidence that he did is all over the language."

"Who sees things grow from their origin," Aristotle says, "will have the most advantageous view of them." No arch-Methuselah has seen language grow from its origin, but we have now glimpsed the origin and growth of English and its sister languages from Indo-European. Without this fundamental understanding—that English is one of a family of languages and partakes of the qualities of that family—no one can ask significant questions about the background of our speech. But now we can propound some of the most searching questions. Let us try to do so.

What is the nature of the English language, and how did it acquire this nature?

This question is too large to answer all at once, but we can start on it by breaking it down a bit. Pretty clearly English, like most languages, is made up of symbols for meaning (words), and some method of putting these words together so that they convey enlarged meaning (grammar). Of these two, the words are the more obvious; everybody is aware of words, whereas much grammar is unconscious. Accordingly let us start with words, and ask ourselves where our words came from—later we can ask how they came to be what they are today.

. . . If English came from Anglo-Saxon, and Anglo-Saxon came from Indo-European, at least part of our vocabulary must descend to us from Indo-European through Anglo-Saxon. How much of it, and which parts of it? To start an answer, one might start counting the words in ordinary prose, dividing them into those which came from Anglo-Saxon and those which did not. On the assumption that the stuff you are now reading is ordinary prose, the next paragraph will be printed with *as* for *Anglo-Saxon* over the words which come from that language, and *o* for *other* over the remaining words.

as as as o as o o as as o o as
There is, of course, a preliminary question. Did the Anglo-Saxons get
as o as as o o as as o as as o o
all their words from Indo-European, or did they have some secret cache
as as as as o as o o o as as
of words from which they could surreptitiously augment their word stock?
o as o as as as as o as as as o
Presenting the evidence for an answer would require our going into Anglo-
o as as o as as as as o as as o as as o
Saxon as a language, and that, at the moment, we are scarcely in a posi-
as as as o as as as as as o as o
tion to do. But fortunately the answer is not in dispute. The Angles
as as o as as o o o o as
and the Saxons came from relatively isolated Germanic peoples. Having
as as o as o o o as as & o? as as as o as
been in contact with Roman traders, they had picked up a few Latin words.
as o as as as o as o o as as
All their neighbors spoke some derivative of Indo-European, and from
o as o o as as as as as as as as as
them the Anglo-Saxons borrowed a few more words. Thus even the borrowed
as as o o as as o o as as o o
words in Anglo-Saxon came from Indo-European, but the important fact
as as as as as as o o as & o? as
is that although speakers of West Germanic acquired scattered words
as as as as as o as o as as as as o o
here and there, the great bulk of their word stock came to them directly
as o o as as as o o as as o
from Proto-Germanic, and most of Proto-Germanic came from Indo-
o
European.

We are now ready to look at the paragraph above. The first result is obvious; the *as*'s predominate. That is, in this passage more words come from Anglo-Saxon than from all other sources combined. The subject matter influences these results a little; had the subject been *pterodactyls* instead of *words*, the *pterodactyls* would have been marked *o*. On the other hand, had the subject been *farm grains and animals*, there would have been still more words marked *as*. The linguistic habits of the writer make some difference, also. The writer could have changed *would require our going* to *would necessitate going*, and thus drop out one *as* word. Or he could have written *we should have to go*, and thus drop out one *o* word. But he could not have changed the result much if he had tried, because of the nature of the words themselves.

A little study of this passage will reveal the reason. The bulk of the words marked *o* fall into a few categories. They are learned words, like *Proto-Germanic* and language; they are qualifying words, like *fortunately*, *relatively*, *surreptitiously*; they are the sort of words used in sophisticated discussion, like *preliminary*, *question*, *derivative*, and *dispute*. The words marked *as* include the bulk of the common names for things, like *word* and *neighbor*; the words for customary actions, like *go* and *speak*; the words which have little meaning in themselves, but which are essential to any coherent use of the language, like *a*, *the*, *of*, *from*, *get*, *do*, *had*, *there*. In short, most of the common words of the language come from Anglo-Saxon; most of the words not from Anglo-Saxon are comparatively uncommon. There are exceptions, of course. *They*, *their*, and *them* are the most striking exceptions; there are special circumstances accounting for them to which we shall return. Some borrowed words, like *question*, have become relatively common. But the exceptions are obviously exceptions; the core of functioning English vocabulary is Anglo-Saxon vocabulary.

Just to keep the record straight, we might remind ourselves that counting words in a piece of prose is not the only plausible check of vocabulary. We might, for instance, count a page in a dictionary. Were we to do so, we should get another answer, but we might postpone that test until we have followed further the Anglo-Saxons and the linguistic habits they brought with them.

We have already observed that the somewhat barbaric farmers who came to the island of Britain in the fifth and sixth centuries were a mixture of West Germanic-speaking lowlanders, mostly Angles and Saxons. Strictly speaking their language was not Anglo-Saxon and no such language existed; there were only Anglian dialects, Saxon dialects, and other Germanic dialects, which have descended with variations until this day. But Anglo-Saxon is a convenient term; not everybody knows what it means, but nobody confuses it with anything else, as they do its synonym, *Old English*. "Oh, I just love those Old English novels," an acquaintance of mine gushed, in speaking of Thomas Hardy. At least, nobody thinks

Thomas Hardy wrote Anglo-Saxon. Roughly, then, the Hengist and Horsa of the Venerable Bede and all their rude pirate friends spoke what we may call Anglo-Saxon.

They continued to speak it for some hundreds of years, disturbed by nothing more than a few obstreperous Celts and one another's battle-axes. It took them a century or so to drive out or to pacify the Celts. Some of these Celts died in battle; others took sanctuary on convenient islands, Ireland and the Isle of Man, for instance. Some fled to the continent and founded a colony in what is now Brittany—named, presumably, from the British immigrants. But probably most of them stayed on the island of Britain. Those who could not live with the Germans fled to the mountains of Scotland and Wales where the invaders were not disposed to follow. The invaders were farmers, and wooded mountains are not farming country; besides, it is often unhealthy to go among mountains if somebody on top of the mountain does not like you.

Many Celts stayed where they were, reduced to subsidiary or servile positions under the invaders. Apparently the Germans were not shockingly hard on them, provided they would surrender anything the Germans wanted, especially the best farming land. The Celtic graveyards of the period are in villages up on the hilltops, connected by the ancient Celtic trackways. Down in the rich valleys are the Germanic graveyards. In defense of the invaders one should add, perhaps, that the Celts had not bothered with that land; it was covered with oak trees, which were hard to get rid of, and the Celts had not taken much to farming anyhow. But whether they were treated badly or not, the Celts did not love their Germanic fellow Indo-Europeans. In fact, they seem to have hated them so much that although the Celts had become Roman Christians they took no chances of seeing any Germans in the Christian heaven. They declined to convert them to Christianity, thereby dooming them expeditiously to hell.

So the invading Germans fought a slow war of conquest with the native Celts, and continued fighting small dynastic wars among themselves after they had subdued the natives. They settled down and became natives themselves, and soon an ancestor of the English language was the native speech. In all this, they absorbed no Celtic religion. Many Celtic names for places survive, mostly old Celtic roots with Latin endings, now changed beyond all ready recognition; for instance, *Eboracum* became *York*, and *Caer Luguvalium* became *Carlisle.* But you can search for hours through a dictionary without finding any other sort of word which the Anglo-Saxons in the valleys got from the Celts on the hilltops or the Celtic servants in the kitchen. A few Celtic words we have. A few words for place names have become common nouns, *down* for *hill*, for instance. Later we acquired Celtic words with Celtic goods. We borrowed Celtic *whisky*, and corrupted the Celtic word for it, *usquebaugh* (water of life), but all that happened long after. The early Celts had no whisky to lend. The explanation for the meager Celtic influence upon English supposedly is that the invaders conquered slowly, keeping their own ranks intact, taking new land only when they needed it; hence there were never a few conquering Germans surrounded by large numbers of native Celts. The Celts who stayed had to learn Anglo-Saxon; the Germans never bothered to learn Celtic. The experience of the white people in what became the United States is somewhat analogous; since on the whole the whites drove the Indians before them, and kept the Indians in a servile position and few in number when the two peoples mixed, relatively few Indian words except place names have found their way into standard English. Many of our Indian words date from the day when a small number of white trappers or traders lived in a predominantly Indian culture. That seemingly did not happen in Britain; any German who found himself in a predominantly Celtic culture did not live long.

Thus the Angles and the Saxons, their friends and their dialects, became established in England. Christianity eventually found its way to them in spite of the native Celts, partly from Ireland and partly from the Continent. Several relatively large political areas, or kingdoms, took something like shape on the island. To the north and east were Northumbria and Mercia, mainly Anglian areas; to the south and west were various divisions of Saxons; at the extreme southeast tip were the descendants of the Jutes—whoever they were. They were apparently the first comers among the Germanic people. The Venerable Bede, with a handy etymological guess, said they came from Jutland, but we now know they did not. The best guess seems to be that they were professional soldiers—that is, professional international robbers; anyhow, their descendants lived mostly in what is now Kent. This was the situation when some strong-minded relatives of the Germanic invaders came to visit. They announced their arrival by sacking the Abbey of Lindisfarne late in the eighth century, and not until about the year 900 did the Anglo-Saxons have reason to hope they had stopped coming.

These guests . . . came mainly from Norway and Denmark and they brought with them techniques which the intrepid northern sailors had worked out. They possessed long, open boats, pushed by crude sails or manned with long oars. If the oarsmen were hardy enough, these boats could be taken across the Atlantic Ocean. And they were, for the oarsmen were hardy. The combination of boats and boatmen constituted the best navy in Europe. It constituted, also, a threat to the very existence of the civilization of western Europe, for once again offense had advanced faster than defense, and civilization appeared helpless before the onslaughts of the Nordic seafarers.

They had a tactic. A few boats with a few hundred armed men would sail into a harbor or row up a river—the shallow draft of the boats permitted entry, especially at high tide, into many rivers. The men would land to murder, rape, burn, or do what they pleased; mainly, of course, they wanted to rob, but other inconveniences usually attended the robbing. Before the residents could muster a fighting force, the marauders had filled their boats with plunder and were gone, ready to sail into another harbor or up another river and repeat the process.

Against this attack Europe had little defense. The Vikings overran Ireland, they pillaged all over France, they sacked in Spain and the Mediterranean areas. For a time they held most of England. They swept in from the north and east, butchering and plundering. Men hid in the woods, eating what they could find, and there were no virgins in the land. How all this was stopped is not to be told here. Partly, of course, it stopped because the North ran out of excess Vikings, for in spite of their prowess, Vikings tended to die suddenly. In England the Norsemen were stopped partly because King Alfred built a better navy than they had. On the Continent the feudal system, based upon the fortress, deterred the Vikings, or Creek Men, by providing a refuge near the creek. It was a long, complicated, bloody business. But we are concerned with linguistics, not with bloodletting.

By the end of the ninth century, King Alfred and his West Saxons had stopped the Vikings in England. By beating them in battle, by outsmarting them in geopolitics, by converting them to Christianity and threatening them with the terrors of hell, he got them to agree, sporadically, to stop looting and settle down. They had come in such great numbers that they could not be driven out. They were mostly Danes and, like the Anglo-Saxons, they were mostly farmers who wanted land. The habitable parts of the island of Britain—the outlying areas harbored only wolves, Welshmen, and Scotsmen, who did not count—were divided along a line running roughly from modern London to modern Liverpool, which just happened to be about the line between the Anglian-speaking and the Saxon-speaking groups. The area to the northeast of this line became Danelaw, the country in which the law of the Danes was the law of the land, the country in which the Vikings could do as they pleased; the areas to the southwest remained Saxon.

This line is the line of cleavage of British dialects until this day. To the south and west are forms descending from the Saxon dialects. To the north and east the forms descend from Anglian, as these have been altered, corrupted, and augmented with influence from Old Norse. Most medieval works composed in the north can be recognized at once, not only by grammatical differences, but also by the Norse words in the vocabulary. Many of these words have been lost in Modern English or are preserved only in certain dialects not now considered standard English, which has descended mainly from the dialect of London (*bushy* in southern England can be *bosky* in the north), but to see how Viking influence upon vocabulary has persisted, one has only to look at a map of Britain. In Anglo-Saxon a common word for an inhabited place was *tun,* which in modern English can appear as *town, ton, don, dun,* and the like. A corresponding word in Old Norse is *ham.* A glance at the map will show that southern and western areas are seeded with *Wimbledon, Brighton, Taunton, Swindon.* In the occasional occurrences of *ham* in the south as in *Hampton, Southhampton, ham* is presumably the Anglo-Saxon word for *home,* or a similar word meaning "meadow" or "river land," which did not come from Old Norse. To the north are *Nottingham, Birmingham, Durham,* and *Bullingham,* and in a truly Danish area, *North Ham, South Ham,* and *West Ham* surround *Ham.*

In this manner the Vikings left a lasting imprint upon the language of Britain, partly because so many of them stayed, and stayed clustered in their own little groups, partly because they were so important—after all, King Canute was the King of Denmark before he was King of England —and partly because the languages of the invaders and the invaded were so similar that subsequent inhabitants of Britain did not always know whether they were talking North Germanic Old Norse or West Germanic Anglo-Saxon. Nor do we always know. For instance, most dictionaries say that the origin of our word *gutter* was Old French *goutiere,* from a word meaning "a drop" (Modern French *goutte*), which has certainly given us English *gout.* But it could also have come from an Old Norse word. When Robert Mannyng of Brunne wrote:

> He toke the gate and went thru the gate

he means to say that a man walked along the path (Old Norse *gata*) and went through the gate (Anglo-Saxon *gaet*). We should note, furthermore, that the nominative masculine form of the word gata in Old Norse ended in *r,* that is, *gatr,* and that if Robert Mannyng had been trying to write this sound he would probably have written *gater* or *gutter,* just as we do. Did the Old Norse word for path, *gatr,* become the path along the side of the street, where, when there was water, the water ran? Or did the Old French *goutiere,* a trough to catch the drops from the eaves, become a place for water to run along a road as well as a way for water to run along a house? The answer is not easy. Often we do not know whether we are speaking Old Norse or not.

The most spectacular borrowing from Old Norse is probably that to be found in the Modern English plural third person pronoun. The Anglo-Saxon pronouns *hie, hiera, heom, hie* became so corrupted that they were readily confused with singulars (the nominative plural became *he,* identical with the masculine singular; the possessive became *her*, identical with the feminine singular; the dative and accusative merged and became *hem*, identical with a variant spelling of *him*). When this happened, speakers of Middle English gradually adopted the Old Norse plural pronoun, which has given us our *they, their, them.*

No sooner had the Angles and Saxons learned to live more or less at ease with their obstreperous relatives from the North, than more relatives arrived, beginning in the summer of 1066. These, too, were Vikings, but they had been living in France and had become sophisticated. Or somewhat sophisticated. They had not been tractable folk when they arrived. They had harried widely and laid siege to Paris. They finally agreed to being bought off, accepting a large chunk of France on the promise of keeping other Vikings out of that country. The story is that when their leader was asked to kiss the French king's foot in sign of fealty he picked it up so high the king went over backward. After they settled in France these reformed Vikings learned to talk French of a sort, greedily acquired the advantages of western European culture, and proceeded to set up a Norman empire which was eventually to stretch from Scotland to Sicily. They took advantage of some dynastic changes on the neighboring island of Britain—their home was just across the channel from England in what is still called Normandy—moved in rapidly, defeated a hastily gathered army near Hastings, and established themselves, under William the Conqueror, as rulers of the country.

The victors acted like the winners in a political election. There was little raping or pillaging. Anybody who accepted the results of the hustings at Hastings was allowed to go about his business. Many an Englishman probably did not notice the change much more than many a Democrat does when the Republicans come in. Of course the winners appropriated all of the best jobs, including the important posts in the church and in education, which was part of the church, as well as in government. Norman Frenchmen became the governors, the administrators, the preachers, the teachers, the big landowners, and the like. These people used French, and forced those who dealt with them to use French—or rather, the Scandinavianized French which we call Anglo-Norman. Meanwhile, intellectual matters were in the hands of the Universal Church, which wrote and even spoke Latin. English, as a written language, almost disappeared.

Anyone examining the preserved writings of this time and making up his mind solely on bulk and importance of written work, would inevitably conclude that the English people must thereafter have spoken French or Latin or some kind of mixture of them. Letters were written in French, cases at law were conducted in French, sermons were delivered in French, handbooks of agriculture and conduct were written in French, stories were told in French. Meanwhile, learned disquisitions were conducted in

Latin, the schools were based upon Latin, and great international works like Geoffrey of Monmouth's *History of the Kings of Britain,* which was known and venerated all over Europe, were written in Latin. Only stray pieces of script have been preserved from that time of anything that stems from Anglo-Saxon, and these, like Lawman's *Brut,* were even then little known.

But what happened? English survived to become again the official language of England, and all the works written in French or Latin, if they any longer had an importance, had to be translated into Middle English. Obviously most Englishmen must have gone right on talking Anglo-Saxon while they wrote French. Or at least their wives went on talking Anglo-Saxon, and little Athelwold learned Anglo-Saxon as he learned to toddle. Little Athelwold's daddy, if he had to sue his neighbor, may have sued him in French, and he prayed to the Virgin Mary in Latin; but when he spanked little Athelwold he spanked him in Anglo-Saxon, and the evidence that he did is all over the language. The words *bottom, buttocks, butt,* and *rump* are all from Germanic roots, along with some other terms now considered vulgar.

Furthermore, the impact of the Norman French upon the English language was much slighter than is commonly supposed. A very large percentage of the words in any dictionary came into English from Latin or Greek, and many of them by way of French. The natural assumption has been that William the Conqueror and his Normans brought these words along with him. The argument—or the presumption, for supposed truth was long taken for granted—ran somewhat as follows: English vocabulary is heavily French; the Normans conquered England; the Normans spoke French; *ergo* the conquering Normans forced their French vocabulary upon the English people. This assumption is written into many conventional reference works and assumed in most of the others. The most interesting fact about it is that it is not true.

Doubtless the Normans would have been glad to fasten their language on the country. Within limits they tried to. But they were too few, and they were too remote from English life. After a while everybody forgot who had been Normans and who had been Anglo-Saxons, and most people did not care. But meanwhile, little Athelwold had been whopped in Anglo-Saxon, and he learned the language with a sense of intimacy which he never acquired for French. Anyhow, only relatively few Englishmen ever learned French, even Anglo-Norman. Educated people did, of course, but not many people were educated.

This sounds like theorizing. How can we know that French vocabulary in English does not come mainly and directly from the Norman Conquest? In several ways, but here are two.

Comparatively few French words were borrowed into English during

Anglo-Norman times, and the great bulk of them were borrowed after French ceased to be spoken as a native language in England. For instance, the following is a tabulation of about a thousand words selected objectively, and arranged by the half century of their first appearance in English, so far as the word is recorded in the *New English Dictionary*. The *New English Dictionary* (1928), in its revised re-issue (1933) called the *Oxford English Dictionary*, is the monumental thirteen-volume work which is the standard authority for the history of English words.

The study was begun many years ago by the distinguished Danish grammarian, Otto Jespersen, and concluded by Professor Albert C. Baugh of the University of Pennsylvania. These men would be the first to point out that the figures cannot be taken at their face value. By these figures, less than one per cent (9 out of 1000 words) were borrowed from French into English during the first 134 years of Norman occupancy. This is obviously not correct. Part of the paucity of Anglo-Norman words results, surely, from the scarcity of written Middle English from that period.

Date of first appearance in English	*Number of words*	*Date of first appearance in English*	*Number of words*
1050	2	1451–1500	90
1051–1100	0	1501–1550	62
1101–1150	2	1551–1600	95
1151–1200	7	1601–1650	61
1201–1250	35	1651–1700	37
1251–1300	99	1701–1750	33
1301–1350	108	1751–1800	26
1351–1400	198	1801–1850	46
1401–1450	74	1851–1900	25

Furthermore, the results of the *New English Dictionary*, though they reveal a mine of information, are far from complete. The *Middle English Dictionary* now being published will certainly increase this percentage somewhat. But even after all possible qualifications, exceptions, probably errors, and the like have been allowed for, the basic fact remains obvious. The bulk of French words appeared in the English language long after Anglo-Norman was no longer spoken as a native tongue.

Now for the second piece of evidence, which perhaps need not be labored, the more because the evidence requires going into grammatical forms. The words which were borrowed appear mostly in the dialect of the French of Paris, not in the dialect of Normandy, the home of the conquerors. Evidence for a statement like this must inevitably be detailed, but the following may provide an index which is roughly reliable. Anyone who knows Modern French recognizes most of the French words at once. These French words are recognizable because they come mostly from the French of Paris, and standard Modern French also stems from the French of Paris. Words which came into English from Anglo-Norman are often not readily recognizable as French. For instance, our word *carrefour,* a square or crossroads, comes to us from something like standard Old French. But the main intersection in the old town of Oxford, England, is called Carfax, somewhat to the wonder of some local people who associate the word by folk etymology with *car tracks,* although there are no car tracks there. The explanation is that this place name preserves the Anglo-Norman form, sometimes spelled *carfoukes,* from Medieval Latin *quadrifurcus,* having four forks. And so it goes. The bulk of the French words which we use today did not come into English in Anglo-Norman times, and when they did come, they came in a form the Normans in England would never have used—the whole of France laughed at the way those Hrolf-come-lately Norsemen tried to talk French. Only the exceptions, like *Carfax,* are Anglo-Norman.

The Norman Conquest ended the direct invasions of the English language by military means. The effects of both the Viking and Norman invasions, as invasions, were meager in language, much more meager than most people suppose. The Viking invasion eventually affected the language, not because the Danes invaded, but because so many of them settled down. The Norman Conquest had great indirect effect, because Normans cemented English connections with the Continent; the invasion was followed by a flow of Continental goods and fashions, and these eventually brought their words along with them. But the evidence in England as elsewhere is that conquest alone seldom influences language very much. Language is too fundamental, too much rooted in childhood, in the family, in eating and sleeping and making a living, ever to be directly influenced much by war. Language grows from life, not from death.

Most of the relatives of English have remained peacefully at home, minding their own meanings. If they have come to English speech, they have done so through the ordinary channels of interlingual exchange. To understand their impact upon our language we must become acquainted with the concept of cognates. The word means "born together," and it refers specifically to words which have descended in various languages from a common parent. Naturally, any word in English which has descended through Anglo-Saxon from Indo-European is likely to have sisters, cousins, and aunts scattered over a fair share of the civilized world. Any of tens of thousands of examples would suffice, but let us take the word *mother.*

This word certainly occurred in Indo-European, supposedly in a form something like mater. If so, Latin has preserved it intact. The Greek *meter* is not much different, nor is the Celtic *maither*—Celtic is etymologically close to Latin. Sanskrit has *matar;* Slavic, *mati* and *mote.* The Proto-Germanic form must have been something like *modor,* judging from the occurrence of the word in Old High German, Plattdeutsch, and Old Norse; German *Mutter* and English *mother* develop from Old High German *mouter* and Anglo-Saxon *modor* respectively. Thus, modern equivalents of mother like French *mère,* German *Mutter,* and Spanish *madre* are cognates, distant cousins which have all descended from old great-grandmother Indo-European, each through its own line of descent by the various aunts and uncles.

Sometimes the cousins go visiting, in entirely peaceful ways. *Maternal* obviously comes from mater, and thus an English-speaking mother can have either of two cognate forms applied to her; she may be *maternal* from the Latin or *motherly* from the English. The synonyms *matriarchy* and *Mutterrecht* are cognates from Greek and German respectively. *Maiden* and *matron,* though to a degree antonyms, can probably be traced to the same root. Our dictionaries and our language are scattered with the cousins, the second cousins, the third, eighth and tenth cousins of English, many of them readily recognizable, but many of them obscure to all but the experts. They are numerous, so numerous that most of the English vocabulary which has not come directly from Indo-European by way of Anglo-Saxon has come indirectly from Indo-European by way of some more or less distant relative. English is deeply indebted to its far-flung linguistic family.

EXERCISES

1. Write three or four sentences on a topic of your own choice, then look up each word in a dictionary to see what its origin is.
2. Outline the history of English, beginning with Indo-European as it is given in Mr. Laird's article.
3. What are cognates? List several examples.
4. What proof does Mr. Laird give that "the impact of the Norman French upon the English language was much slighter than is commonly supposed"?

2 AMERICAN PRONUNCIATION

by Thomas Pyles

Thomas Pyles (1905–) is a member of the English department at the University of Florida. He studied at the universities of Maryland and Chicago, at Cambridge and Johns Hopkins. Mr. Pyles has published many articles and reviews and is the author of Words and Ways of American English, *from which our selection is taken.*

In "American Pronunciation," Mr. Pyles makes many comparisons between English and American speech. He examines the influences of tradition and of spelling on pronunciation and concludes that while Americans pride themselves on the daring and independence of American speech, they are more bound by "standards" of correctness than they realize.

Although Americans are still conscious of the very apparent differences between British pronunciation and their own manner of speaking, they have grown increasingly tolerant of British speech. Yet many of us can remember a time, no longer than twenty-five or thirty years ago, when standard British English—that type of English pronunciation called variously Received Standard, Received Pronunciation, and Southern British English—was commonly regarded in this country as somewhat affected, not to say downright effeminate. Now, however, we have become so accustomed to it in the talking films and on the radio—both of them agencies which, with all their artistic shortcomings, have certainly mitigated American linguistic provincialism—that we take it very much in our stride. Sometimes we even regard this type of British English with a sort of sneaking admiration, for there is a widespread notion among Americans, many of whom suffer from a sort of national linguistic inferiority complex, that even uneducated English people speak better than we do, whatever "speaking better" means.

Differences between American and British pronunciation are far more subtle and elusive than mere variation in the treatment of certain speech sounds such as the postvocalic *r* or in the pronunciation of individual shibboleth words like *schedule, lieutenant, laboratory,* and *clerk.* More sharply distinctive, if less often noted, is intonation. Actually the English pronunciation of an overwhelming majority of individual words does not differ markedly from the American—a fact frequently overlooked by the lay observer, who is looking only for differences; even the Englishman's supposedly characteristic pronunciation of the sound indicated by *a* in words of the *path, glass, staff* type, his slightly rounded vowels in words like *stop, God, clock,* and his treatment of post-vocalic *r* do not differ, as a matter of fact, from the practice of many Americans—for instance, eastern New Englanders, who may have every one of these characteristics. An Iowan or a Nebraskan with a fair ear for speech sounds can learn to pronounce broad *a* in those words in which the speaker of standard British English has this sound in distinction to the flat *a* heard in most varieties of American speech; he can, with assiduous practice, learn to omit *r* before consonant sounds or when it is final; he may even acquire the "flapped" *r* between vowels to be heard in the Englishman's pronunciation of *America, very, sorry,* and the like; he can remember to say *shedule* (for *schedule*), *diction'ry, labórat'ry, leftenant, eevolution,* and to rime *mobile* and *fertile* with *mile;* he can, in fact, acquire all the characteristics of British pronunciation so far as individual speech sounds go. But, unless he is sufficiently acute to be able to counterfeit British intonation convincingly, he will deceive no one who has ever listened discerningly to genuine British speech.

For, though the words may be the same, the music is strikingly different. And it is this fact primarily which makes British speech sometimes quite difficult for the American to understand, just as the distinctive intonation of American English sometimes baffles the Englishman. Of course, real unintelligibility is seldom involved any more; it would be more accurate merely to say that the foreign flavor of British speech to the American and of American speech to the Englishman is due largely to these differences in intonation, or pitch variation in speech. In singing, where the stresses and the tune are set by the composer, what is called an "accent" is hardly noticeable, so that to determine whether a singer is English or American is sometimes not possible. Singers in English dance bands sing Tin Pan Alley creations in what often seems to the American listener to be perfectly good American English. Usually they are not trying to do so. Conversely, there is little or nothing that incontrovertibly indicates the American origin of most of our native singers of popular songs of the sentimental or impassioned variety, though their regional and social origins are evident enough when they indulge in supposedly witty chit-chat with masters of ceremonies and announcers. If the singer has learned to omit preconsonantal and final *r's* and to pronounce broad *a*—tricks which even untrained vocalists often acquire—then the chances of identifying him by nationality become practically infinitesimal.

There are, of course, regional, local, and even social variations in intonation within both American and British English. The speech tune of a Bostonian is different from that of a Chicagoan, even somewhat different from that of a New Yorker; similarly, the intonation patterns of Liverpool or Manchester are not precisely those of London. But these are slight as compared with those intonational variations which unmistakably mark off the speech of the American from that of the Englishman—variations so noticeable as sometimes to cause mutual irritation, though fortunately this is much less frequent nowadays than formerly.

The tempo of speech is more or less an individual matter, depending to a large extent upon the intellectual make-up of the speaker and to some extent upon his familiarity with what he happens to be talking about: a person of a slow, deliberative habit of mind is likely to phrase his thoughts in a slow and deliberative manner; the man of volatile temperament whose mind functions rapidly, though not necessarily profoundly, is likely to speak rapidly. Both probably speak more rapidly than normally when excited either by external circumstances or by keen interest in the subject they are discussing. It is also doubtless true that when a speaker is talking about what he likes to talk about—presumably also what he knows something about—he is likely to speak somewhat more rapidly than when his interest in his subject is only mild and his knowledge of it uncertain. It is, nevertheless, widely believed in this country that Englishmen speak more rapidly (in "clipped tones," of course) than Americans. It is most likely that nationality has nothing to do with the tempo of speech; the Britisher seems to be "rattling away" at a terrific rate because his speech is in some respects—principally in intonation—strange to us. There is also a widespread American belief that Southerners speak more slowly than Yankees: the truth would seem to be that some of them do and some of them don't. Much has been made of the Southern "drawl," but the quality described by the word has been attributed and the word itself applied to the speech of New Englanders, as, for example, when Noah Webster in his *Dissertations* enjoined the New England "yeoman" to improve his "drawling nasal manner of speaking."

Along with the "drawl," which certainly must denote a slow speech tempo, whatever else it may mean, the American "twang" has frequently been commented upon. It is difficult to know precisely what characteristic of American speech this word describes. Probably it originally denoted nasality, but frequently it seems to have a much more inclusive meaning. In any case, it is certain that most Englishmen, and many Americans as well, believe that American speech is excessively nasal—in fact, that Americans "talk through their noses." There is some slight justification for the notion, particularly in Midwestern and Western speech, and there was doubtless even more in former times in all sections of the country. But the meaning of terms like *drawl* and *twang* is sometimes very difficult to pin down.

Similarly, British English is often referred to, usually with approval, as "clipped," which is not much less vague than the American "drawl" and "twang," though it seems clear that "clipping" is sometimes conceived of as the antithesis of "drawling." Sometimes *crisp* is also used as descriptive of British speech; apparently it denotes the same qualities as *clipped.* These terms, unsatisfactory as they are because of their subjectivity, nevertheless do mean something, or at any rate have meant something. Perhaps the "clipped" quality of British speech to American ears is due to the Englishman's pronunciation of *t* between vowels (as in *water, butter, later*) as a voiceless dental stop, in contrast to the widespread American pronunciation of this sound as something very like a *d.* It is likely, too, that the "flapped" *r* between vowel sounds used by some speakers of British English plays some part in the American impression of British speech as "clipped" or "crisp." But this is a rather slight justification for so sweeping a description as is implied by the words. Perhaps the Englishman's strong (from an American point of view, frequently excessive) stressing of accented syllables, occasionally at the expense of unaccented syllables, as in his pronunciation of such words as *library* and *medicine* as *lybry* and *medsin,* gives a "clipped" effect to some hearers. It is possible, too, that his preference for a short ĭ sound in the second syllable of *telegraph, telephone, animal,* and the like, in all of which American English prefers the so-called "murmur" vowel indicated by the symbol ə (schwa) in the alphabet of the International Phonetic Association, has something to do with this impression of "clippedness." But all such subjective terminology, let it be said again, is really quite unsatisfactory for the description of speech.

No one with the ability to hear, however, can doubt that American intonation, as compared with British, tends to be monotonous (the word is of course used here only in the sense "having a narrow pitch range"). It is on the whole more deliberate, and frequently seems intent upon giving to each syllable what is thought to be its proper value, in contrast to British English, with its marked risings and fallings, its stronger stresses, and its consequent scanting (from the American point of view) of unstressed syllables, as in a word like *extraordinary,* in which the Englishman stresses the *-or-* and seems to be taking the rest in a sort of running jump.

This American tendency to give what is apparently felt to be its due regard to each and every syllable may well be a survival of older British usage. It has been suggested, indeed, that the deliberate and measured articulation of American English, as well as the nasalization which is still to some extent characteristic of it may originally have been a Puritan affectation. There is some reason to believe that, along with speaking "i' the nose," the English Puritans of the seventeenth century cultivated a singsong manner of speaking which was doubtless thought, by themselves at least, to give an impression of superior piety. Nicholas Cresswell, an Englishman who spent some time in this country in the 1770s, referred to an indescribable "whining cadence" which characterized the speech of New Englanders of that day; it was the sole local peculiarity which he observed in American speech and may well have been a survival of older usage among the English Puritans. Webster, who certainly did not in the least disapprove of the development of Puritanism which flourished in his day, must have had no suspicion of any such origin, for he speaks disapprovingly in his *Dissertations* of "that drawling, whining cant that distinguishes a certain class of people." He is obviously referring to a type of pronunciation current in his native western New England.

The Puritan origin of American intonation is an attractive theory, and one wishes that it were capable of proof. It has also been pointed out that our intonation resembles that of the north of England much more closely than that of the more fashionable type of English spoken in the south of England, which is frequently thought of in this country, quite mistakenly, as being the speech of all England. It is not likely that Captain Marryat's explanation of American intonation was ever widely accepted in this country: "the Americans dwell upon their words when they speak —a custom arising, I presume, from their cautious, calculating habits; and they have always more or less of a nasal twang." When the gallant sailor-novelist asked an American lady why she drawled, she replied in a burst of not altogether uncommendable linguistic patriotism, "Well, I'd drawl all the way from Maine to Georgia, rather than clip my words as you English people do."

It was long ago noted that Americans talked "by the book." Perhaps occasional statements in the eighteenth century to the effect that the educated colonists used "better" English than those who stayed at home may indicate nothing more than that American pronunciation even in those days tended to follow spelling. It is likely that most of the commentators were also favorably impressed by the comparative uniformity of American English. Some of them, in fact, mention it. But, aside from this notable uniformity, one wonders what other objective standard they might have had, the state of linguistic knowledge being what it was in their day. Perhaps they were favorably impressed by a type of articulation which seemed to them superior in its clarity because it conformed to written language.

There can be no doubt that to the American school tradition must be attributed some of the dubious credit (dubious from a historical and aesthetic point of view, at any rate) for the deliberate articulation of American English. Unquestionably much of it survives, as has been suggested previously, from earlier British practice, particularly that of the northern part of England and the lowlands of Scotland. Deliberate, monotonous speech may result from factors other than the attempt to follow a written standard: but the consciousness of such a standard may well bring with it an overcareful and overprecise manner of speech which a great many speakers no doubt think of as somehow "purer" and more "correct" than the more volatile, dashing, and devil-may-care usage of a society based upon hereditary aristocracy. And it might indeed be argued that it is more truly democratic to follow a written standard than to imitate in servile fashion the usage of those who speak according to an ancient tradition, for with a written standard "good" speech is within the reach of even the commonest man.

It is likely indeed that the long and widespread use of Noah Webster's *Spelling Book* in its myriad editions, with its emphasis upon syllabication and its injunction to the pupil to give to each syllable its "true value," has tended to check any tendency in America towards such rakish pronunciations as the Englishman's *litracha* (*literature*), *medsin*, and *ikstrawnry* (*extraordinary*). In any event, educated American pronunciation, while lacking tonal and accentual variety, has gained somewhat in clarity and distinctness. The American actually says "How do you do?" not "Howjado?" or "Jado?" He never pronounces *immediate* as *immejit*, as many British speakers do; rather, he seems to be treating each syllable of the word with loving care. He may even scorn to say anything so seemingly careless as *ejacate* (*educate*), and take especial pains to say *ed-you-cate*, as I have heard speakers do.

Nevertheless, pronunciations based upon spelling, when these involve a change in the traditional pronunciation of a word in popular use, are a pretty sure indication not only of a spiritual arrogance which it is difficult to admire in the abstract but also of an ignorance of the relationship between writing and language. Persons who do not understand this relationship are likely to conclude that, inasmuch as *forehead* is so spelled and means "the fore part of the head," it should be spoken as *fore head*—a conclusion which involves the assumption that all previous speakers who have pronounced the word *forid* were speaking incorrectly. Such assumptions must necessarily be common to those who set themselves to speak better than their fellows.

Now when people lack an oral tradition for the pronunciation of a given word, they certainly cannot be blamed if they pronounce that word as the spelling seems to indicate it should be pronounced. In such a case spelling is our only guide. And this is the procedure regularly followed when we come upon learned polysyllables which we mentally pronounce in the course of our reading—words which we never actually speak, but which, if we did, we should pronounce as spelled. There is absolutely no reason why Americans should have an oral tradition governing the pronunciation of such words as *Cholmondeley*, *Beaulieu*, and *retch* (pronounced in British English *Chumley, Bewley,* and *reech*), since these are not words in common use in America. But consciously to change the pronunciation of a word one has used since first learning to talk—words like *often* and *forehead*—is quite another matter. These are words for which we once possessed a tradition. The abandonment of that tradition, where it has been abandoned, was due in the beginning to a habit of mind which seems to be particularly common in America. This is not of course to suggest that writing has not played a part in the development of all languages which have been reduced to writing; here, as elsewhere, we are concerned with a matter of degree.

Regarding themselves as the rightful custodians of linguistic propriety, and sincerely convinced that "their" language was rapidly deteriorating in America, British observers have for years descanted upon what seemed to them to be the "barbarity" of American English. Although there have been a few outstanding exceptions, most of these commentators have been quite honestly of the opinion that, because on the one hand it has lost some of the older traditions of British English and on the other hand has failed to acquire some of the more recent ones, American English is a corrupt and degenerate language. It should be said that the severest strictures have come from men with little or no consciousness of the fact of linguistic development, men to whom the idea never occurred that American English might be expected to develop somewhat differently from British English.

But there is, as has been observed, another side to the picture. Although we may lack a tradition for the pronunciation of such words as *Glamis* and *Majoribanks* and *St. John* (as *glahmz, marchbanks,* and *sinjun* respectively), we have acquired a tradition of our own—a highly literate tradition inculcated by generations of schoolmasters and schoolmarms, part of whose stock in trade is knowing how the language should be spoken and written. Ironically enough, though the schoolteacher is thought to be in possession of the arcana of linguistic elegance, he is actually little regarded in other lines of endeavor: his opinions in matters of English usage are sought and deferred to as "authoritative" by business and professional men whose attitude towards him in other circumstances would inevitably be patronizing. But the fact remains that the influence of the schools must ever be reckoned with in any examination of the English of America, for the layman has complete and unadulterated confidence in the supposed sources of linguistic information which teachers are thought to be in possession of—sources in which he has infinitely more faith than he has in his own observation of the actual usage of those who speak the language. It is an ironical fact that in this great democratic nation, authority, not usage, has come to be the guiding principle of language for practically all Americans who have ever been to school. Even though he may be deemed a babe in the wood in regard to the affairs of practical life, it is widely, practically universally, held that in the matter of linguistic propriety ("correct English"), "teacher knows best."

Educated American English is thus by no means free and easy-going, daring and independent, as it is flattering to our patriotism to believe; it is if anything overcareful and precise, indeed almost "prissy" in its concern for what are thought of as standards. Such pronunciations as *obey, possessed,* and *occasion* with the vowel of the first syllable pronounced as *oh* (instead of the "murmur vowel") and *efficient* and *effective* with the first syllable as *ee,* though not unknown in a certain type of British oratory, indicate what would seem to most speakers of British English an unnecessary and uncalled-for precision in language. Some American students of speech, it must be said, would consider such pronunciations instances of semiliterate formal usage. Nevertheless, a good many pronunciations cited by Professor J. S. Kenyon in his valuable "Cultural Levels and Functional Varieties of English" (*College English,* October, 1948) as semiliterate formal—*sun day* for *Sunday* instead of the *sundy* more usual in cultivated speech, *president* with the final syllable clearly pronounced as *dent, coalumbia* for *Columbia*—are by no means unusual in the speech of those who have gone through college and even graduate school. There can be little question that the attitude towards language which has given birth to such artificialities has made considerably more headway in this country than in England.

Spelling pronunciations must certainly be regarded as, among other things, clearly indicative of a subservience to the linguistic attitudes and standards inculcated by the schools. As has been shown elsewhere, although such pronunciations are gaining ground somewhat in British English, they are of particularly frequent occurrence in American English. So little is traditional pronunciation regarded when it seems to depart from what is indicated by spelling that words like *parliament* (a fancy spelling for a word of Old French origin, spelled *parlement* in that language and in Middle English) and *comptroller* (an equally flashy Latinized spelling of *controller*) are frequently pronounced as spelled by highly literate and even by distinguished people. The spelling pronunciation of the latter word is, in fact, so common that one wonders why it is not recorded in the dictionaries, though none which I have consulted indicates any other pronunciation than *controller. Comp-troller* is, however, in no sense an ignorant pronunciation, linguistically naïve though it may be; it is in fact the usual pronunciation on many university campuses of the title of an important financial officer.

It is doubtless true that American English lacks a tradition for the pronunciation of *Anthony,* a name which was not often bestowed upon

American males until the comparatively recent craze for supposedly swank "British" Christian names, like *Stephen, Peter, Michael,* etc., in this country. The traditional pronunciation *antony* (whence the nickname *Tony*), still current in England, is so rare in America that one wonders why the dictionaries bother to record it as an American pronunciation. Even *Mark Antony* is frequently pronounced by the educated, if not the highly cultivated, with medial *-th-*. Now in the lack of any tradition in regard to the pronunciation of this word, to pronounce it as spelled is a perfectly reasonable and natural thing to do. Both *author* and *anthem* contain the same fancy spelling of *t*, and in both these words the standard pronunciation has had the *th* sound in British and American English for a very long time. A similar misinterpretation of spelling is evidenced in the pronunciation of *Waltham, Eltham, Gotham* and the like, in which the suffixal force of *-ham* (as in *Buckingham, Birmingham*) was at one time felt; in time, however, the *t* and the *h* were mistakenly regarded as occurring in the same syllable, with the consequence that the words came to be pronounced with the medial consonant sound of *Luther*. The pronunciations *waltum* and *eltum* (with loss of *h* due to lack of stress on the final syllable) survive in British use, though pronunciations with medial *-th-*, originally blunders, are widely current as variants. Only *got 'em* is current for the town of *Gotham* in Nottinghamshire—a pronunciation never hard from Americans when they employ the word as a nickname for New York City.

Pride, born of a misguided attitude towards spelling—an attitude most likely to thrive in a period of widespread partial literacy—must be held responsible for changing the pronunciation of common, everyday words like *often,* for which a traditional pronunciation *offen* has long been current. Pronunciation of this word with *-t-* is to be heard in British English, it must be noted, and is presumably in perfectly good standing; it is recorded as a variant in both Daniel Jones's *English Pronouncing Dictionary* and H. C. Wyld's *Universal Dictionary*. Probably it is by now so frequent in both England and America that a long-forgotten novelist's social "typing" of a character by having another character remark of her that "she is the sort of person who pronounces the *t* in often" would have no point for many readers. Although American dictionaries do not record this variant (with one exception, which states it to be "not uncommon among the educated speakers in some sections"), there can be no doubt that it is in fairly wide use all over the country, and that only the conservatism of dictionaries has prevented its being more of a matter of record than it is. When the Duke of Windsor, as Prince of Wales, used the pronunciation in a public address, the London *Times* is said to have attributed it to the influence of the American "set" with which he was consorting, and predicted dolefully that it was only a question of time before he would be wearing a hard straw hat (a "boater"), white flannel trousers, and a blue jacket—a combination considered very natty in America at that time. There can be no doubt, however, that the faction to the extreme linguistic right have fought a losing battle in this instance. *Often* with the *t* sounded is now quite literally the "King's English," if the usage of two kings is a sufficient hallmark; for George VI quite audibly pronounced the *t* in his broadcast speech to the Empire on Christmas Day, 1950.

Another spelling pronunciation already alluded to, *forehead* with *-h-* and evenly distributed stress on both syllables, is listed as a variant in all American dictionaries. It has gained ground at a great rate and is probably more common in current educated American speech, excluding perhaps that of the very highly cultivated and cosmopolitan, than *farid* or *forid.* Daniel Jones did not record the spelling pronunciation of this word until his seventh edition (London, 1945), in which he indicated that it was still rare; Wyld in 1932 called it "vulgar or modern."

Instances of the American faith in spelling as a guide to "correct" pronunciation might be multiplied, but only a few more must suffice. *Worsted* "yarn" is a word so familiar and homely that one would suppose that it would have an excellent chance of retaining its traditional pronunciation *woostid* (the *oo* as in *foot*), as indeed it has among the illiterate and the highly cultivated, whose usage coincides more often than most schoolmasters like to admit. In the great middle ground between these two extremes, however, a spelling pronunciation is widely current which is identical with that of the past tense of *to worst,* with which it has of course no etymological connection. Professor Kenyon in his *American Pronunciation* (10th ed., Ann Arbor, 1950) points out that a good many British place names also occur in America, frequently with pronunciation according to the spelling; he cites such pronunciation for *Greenwich* and *Thames* (British *grinidge* or *grenidge* and *temz*) in Connecticut, *Walthamstow* (British *waltumstow*) and *Edinburgh* (British *edinbruh* or *edinburruh*) in Massachusetts. To these he might have added *Windham* as *wind ham* (British *windum*) in Vermont (but *Durham* in North Carolina preserves the traditional pronunciation) and *Delhi* (not English in origin, of course, though of English transmission and pronounced *delly* by the English) in New York, which residents of that state pronounce *dell high.* The first syllable, and sometimes the second as well, of *Berkshire,* the name of the hills in western Massachusetts, is pronounced in America as the spelling seems to us to indicate; the same is true of the first syllable of *Berkeley,* the name of the city in California. Both these place names are of English origin, and the English use *bark* as the first syllable in both. But the tendency to pronounce according to spelling is by no means confined to America, as we have seen, even though it may have reached extremes here: the English themselves now pronounce the first syllable of *Berkhamsted* (or *Berkhampstead* in a variant spelling) as *burk*, although *bark* is used, according to Daniel Jones, "by some residents, especially members of county families," i.e., the landed gentry. *Worcester* in Massachusetts has retained both its traditional spelling and pronunciation, as has *Worcester* County in Maryland, but residents of the town in Ohio of the same name must have found the discrepancy between spelling and pronunciation intolerable; rather than change the pronunciation, however, they changed the spelling to *Wooster*, which must have made everyone concerned very happy. *Hartford* in Connecticut shows a similar spelling change with the same motivation; *Hartford*, a county in Maryland, has by its respelling preserved another traditional pronunciation of the name of the county seat of *Hertfordshire* in England, the first syllable of which is either *har-* or *hart-*. Other instances of the triumph of traditional pronunciation achieved by respelling are *Barclay*, *Darby*, *Clark*, and *Carr*, from earlier *Berkeley*, *Derby*, *Clerk*, and *Kerr* (or *Ker*).

It is likely that spelling with doubled final consonant has something to do with the American tendency to stress strongly the final syllables of proper names which have initial stress in British English, for instance, *Ríddell*, *Púrcell*, *Párnell*, and *Bárnett*, though *Riddéll* and *Purcéll* occur as variants of the first two. Judging from a close examination of Jones's *English Pronouncing Dictionary*, the same tendency is gaining ground in England. *Littell*, formerly pronounced *little*, is now given final stress by the English, precisely as in American usage (Jones does not even record the older pronunciation as a variant) and *Liddell* is about equally divided between *liddle* and *liddéll*. *Russell* and *Mitchell* have only initial stress in both British and American, despite their spellings.

The usual American pronunciation of *Bernard*, *Gerard*, and *Maurice* with final stress is probably due to modern French influence. *Gerárd* occurs only occasionally in British English; the word is usually stressed on the first syllable, a pronunciation so rare in America, if indeed it is current at all, that the *New Yorker*'s theatrical reviewer found it necessary to explain it to his readers: "the hero of this anecdote, Gerard (pronounced 'Jerd'), is a younger brother of the Duke of Bristol" (November 4, 1950). American final stress in *Gerald* would be analogous to *Gerard*, but is never heard. In British English *Maurice* and *Morris* are homophones, but *mo-réece* (or *muh-réece*) is the most usual American pronunciation of *Maurice*, which is thus differentiated from *Morris*. Such pronunciation, which must be comparatively recent in origin, presumably began as a pedantic affectation born of the desire to indicate the speaker's recognition of the French spelling and his superior knowledge of the phonology of the French language, but it is by now so well established in this country as to be heard from comparatively unaffected speakers. For some reason, final stress is judged rather swank in American English, and in many circles to pronounce the cited names in the usual modest British fashion would be considered as somewhat lacking in "tone."

Before passing on to the national and regional characteristics of American pronounciation, we might well consider a few more aspects of that emotional and intellectual attitude toward language which is most widely current in America. It is not surprising that, with our love of authority in such matters, we should revere the dictionary as we do—just "the dictionary," though there are actually a number of dictionaries of varying degrees of reliability. To be sure, the cultured Englishman also uses the dictionary for ascertaining the meanings of words which are strange to him, but inasmuch as he is likely to regard the English language as *his* language, it would probably not occur to him to try to find out from a book how he "ought" to pronounce words he has always pronounced or heard pronounced by people of good standing. On the other hand, the American of comparable economic, cultural, and social status is quite likely to assume, because he has been so well indoctrinated with the belief that teachers, lexicographers, and compilers of lists of words "usually mispronounced" know best, that the chances are against his saying much of anything correctly on his own, and to desire the authority, not of usage, in which he has been taught to have no real faith, but of the dictionary. Even if conscious of the fact that there are a number of dictionaries, he is not likely to have made a comparative investigation, and hence is not aware that there is a certain amount of disagreement among them as to what constitutes "good" pronunciation. In general, it should be said, lexicographers nowadays do not consider themselves linguistic lawgivers. Professor W. Cabell Greet stated an enlightened attitude in his prefatory remarks on pronunciation in the *American College Dictionary* when he wrote, "Without seeking to impair any citizen's right to be his own professor of English, we look for what is national, contemporary, and reputable." Usually the modern lexicographer is content to record what, according to his observation, is "national, contemporary, and reputable" and to recommend only by implication. Even the best of our modern dictionaries are not infallible in the accuracy of their recordings of actual usage; but they are compiled by honest and expertly trained men, and, though it is easy to pick a few flaws, the wonder is really that there are not more, considering the magnitude of the task of preparing such a work. Nevertheless, there is evidence that lexicographers do sometimes turn a deaf ear to "national, contemporary, and reputable usage" and assume a directive function, as when a leading dictionary records *abdómen* and *ay-éerial* as "first choice" or "preferred" pronunciations of *abdomen* and *aerial*. One wonders, also, why curiosities like the practically archaic variant pronunciation of *oboe* as *oh boy* should be allowed to take up precious space. Actually, there is some cause for rejoicing in the fact that the leading modern dictionaries now record first the pronunciation riming with *hobo* and that no longer can "holier than thou" speakers claim that *oleomargarine* "must" be pronounced with a hard *g* because the much more usual pronunciation with soft *g* is "not in the dictionary." But the popular attitude is still reflected in the opinion of many that these pronunciations were "incorrect" up to the time of their being recorded by "the dictionary."

It may seem contradictory that, with our reverence for "the dictionary," more of us do not use such dictionary pronunciations as have been cited. It is probable that some speakers would like to do so, being convinced that stressing the second syllable of *abdomen* and pronouncing *aerial* with four syllables is "more correct," but simply lack the courage; it is also probable that many do not know that these are "recommended" pronunciations, not having "looked up" the words in question. In addition, many persons have never really learned to interpret accurately the diacritical markings, respellings, and phonetic symbols used by the dictionaries to indicate pronunciation and hence are not aware of some of the discrepancies between recommended and actual usage. Authority cannot, of course, wholly inhibit linguistic change; it can only slow it up, and it has done so with amazing effectiveness.

In one respect, however, the schools have superseded the authority of the dictionary, namely, in the treatment of words (including personal and place names) of foreign origin which have been long established in English contexts. The older tradition of Anglicization still followed for the most part by the dictionaries has been almost completely lost in American English. It is not simply, as Professor Greet has said in *World Words* (New York, 1944), a pronouncing dictionary prepared to assist announcers and other speakers of the Columbia Broadcasting System, that "our bright people are more interested in the present international world than in the traditions of English"; quite aside from any world-consciousness, most of our "bright people" have had a smattering—seldom more—of foreign languages at school.

It is fairly obvious that an attitude of mind has developed concomitantly with the teaching of the modern foreign languages—the teaching of the "reformed" or "classical" pronunciation of Latin, with its un-English vowels, has doubtless contributed—in regard to the pronunciation of words of foreign origin, when that origin is recognized. This attitude expresses itself in the attempt to pronounce such words according to the phonetic system of the language from which they have been borrowed, insofar as that system is known to the speaker. To do so has come, indeed, to be felt as a sort of linguistic obligation. The effect on certain words having behind them a long tradition of Anglicization has been marked in

American English to a somewhat greater extent than in British English—though in British English also the tradition of Anglicization exemplified in the older pronunciation of *Calais,* which rimed with *malice,* is to a large extent lost. Though *Callis* is still used by a few old-fashioned British speakers, the usual British pronunciation now rimes with *Sal lay* or with *Sally;* in American English, except as the name of Calais, Maine, which is still pronounced in the old way, it invariably rimes with *allay*—the stress on the final syllable indicating in American English consciousness of French origin, as also in *ballet, café, chagrin,* etc., all usually spoken with initial stress in British English. The notion that French words should be spoken with strong final stress is part of the American school tradition and may, incidentally, be tied up with the tendency, previously treated, to give final stress to English names in *-ell* and *-ett* like Purcell and Barnett, which resemble French feminines in *-elle* and *-ette,* for instance *pucelle* and *lunette.*

By now every American who ever went to high school is aware of the fact that in languages other than English the letter *a* has the approximate value that it has in *father.* This is an elementary fact that almost any linguistic booby, who may of course be quite bright in other departments, is able to master and, moreover, to remember. A good many new pronunciations are attributable to this notion that *a* whenever it occurs in any word of recognizable foreign origin, no matter how long it has been a part of the English word stock, ought to be pronounced as *ah.* In any case, pronounciation of such words as *dilettante* and *Dante* with broad *a* is certainly due to the influence of the schools, though such a modification of older English speech habits would probably not have made quite so much headway as it has without the abetment of that overweening desire to be "correct" which is so prominent a characteristic of educated American English.

This new broad *a* (new as far as English is concerned) occurs principally in words whose foreign origin is plainly recognizable—not as a rule in the more familiar Renaissance borrowings like *balcony, cameo, stanza*—and is frequently to be heard from speakers who take pride in their linguistic Americanism and who would never affect the broad vowel in such words as *bath, master,* and *staff.* It is of increasingly frequent occurrence in words which have entered English by way of the modern foreign languages, but which have nevertheless a long tradition of Anglicization behind them. It is quite true that current fashion prescribes for foreign words of more recent adoption, like *ersatz* and *camouflage,* and particularly proper names, like *Goethe* and *Clemenceau,* pronunciation according to the sound system of the language of origin; consequently people are much concerned to know how such words "ought" to be pronounced. When the exact foreign pronunciation of such words is not known to the speaker, it is deemed sufficient to pronounce in a markedly un-English fashion. Thus, a radio commentator confronted with the name (or *nom de guerre*) *Stalin* may choose, if he has had a little German, to pronounce the first syllable *shtah-*, as in German, and heavily stress the last syllable as in American school-French.

The phenomenon with which we are here concerned is essentially a confusion of the older tradition, exemplified in *Cicero, Montaigne,* and *Cervantes* (though *Cervantes* is coming increasingly to have a Spanish or at any rate a pseudo-Spanish pronunciation), with the newer tendency—a confusion which frequently results in new pronunciations for foreign words of long standing in English. Such words as a general rule are rather more likely to lose their Anglicized pronunciations in American usage than in British: this is true of *Marseilles, Versailles,* and *Lyons,* previously pronounced *marsails, versails,* and *lions,* but now given the supposed French pronunciations *marsáy* or *marsáyuh, vairsígh* or *vairsíghuh,* and *lee-ón* (the last frequently with nasalized vowel). *Prague* (for Czech *Praha*) formerly rimed with *Craig,* but this pronunciation has been supplanted by *prahg.* For a while during World War II, radio speakers took considerable pride in saying *Praha,* but the more sensible of them eventually gave it up. Italian proper names are likely to undergo a sort of Italianization even when their English forms differ from the Italian—for instance *Milan* (Italian *Milano*), which in a very frequent American pronunciation has a strongly accented final syllable with broad (or "Italian") *a.* It is true that the dictionaries without exception fail to record this pronunciation, but it is nevertheless in wide use among educated speakers and is no doubt considered rather elegant. The first pronounciation recorded by dictionaries, with the second syllable accented but riming with *fan,* is probably somewhat less frequent than the pseudo-foreign one—in fact, in many educated, if not sophisticated, circles it would be considered somewhat lacking in polish. The other recorded pronunciation, which rimes with *Dillon,* is probably as rare in American usage as the pronunciation of *Seville* with initial accent (thus riming with *devil*)—a pronunciation which is, incidentally, recorded as American by the dictionaries, though I have never heard it from any American speaker. *Milan* as the name of towns in Michigan, Missouri, and Tennessee is quite unpretentiously pronounced to rime with *smilin'*.

One familiar with the older tradition but unacquainted with the current American trend might well suppose that a name so well established in educated usage as that of the foremost Italian poet would rime with *panty.* This pronunciation of *Dante* is indeed the only one recorded in British usage by Daniel Jones; it is likely, therefore, that it is heavily predominant in England. As for American usage, the fancier pronunciation with "Italian" *a* is certainly just as heavily predominant. The distinction between English *-y* and Italian *-e* is too subtle for most American ears, and hardly worth bothering with, inasmuch as the speaker may so easily experience a warm glow of satisfaction in his supposed linguistic *savoir faire* by pronouncing *Dante* as *dahnty;* he has made it abundantly clear that he jolly well knows his way around in the Italian language, having met all practical requirements by the mere substitution of the Italian vowel in the first syllable. It should be noted, however, that the use of Italian *a* in *Dante,* as well as in other words from Italian, such as *dilettante* (frequently pronounced without final *-e,* probably under the impression that the word is French and analogical with *debutante*), *andante, canto,* and *regatta,* is a conscious elaboration of natural English speech, born of a desire to speak "correctly" which in America has taken precedence of a long tradition of cultivated English usage. To pronounce these obviously un-English words and those which follow as if they were English seems somehow amateurish to us; and it is noteworthy that in speech as in sports the amateur approach has little appeal for Americans, who desire above all to be experts.

The traditional English pronunciation of *Don Quixote* as *don quicksoat* or *quicksut* is about as archaic in American English as the pronunciation of *Don Juan* which rimes with *new one* (used in American English, usually somewhat apologetically, only as the title of Byron's poem). To say *don quicksoat* is to give occasion for winces of pain at one's crudeness in most American circles; the "educated" pronunciation is predominatingly *keehṓty* (sometimes *keehṓtay*), which is thought to be purest Castilian. It is perhaps just as well that there is no general awareness of the fact that when Cervantes composed his masterpiece the Spanish value of *x* was the sound usually indicated in English by *sh;* otherwise many "correct" speakers would undoubtedly try very hard to say *keeshoty.*

In a large group of words and phrases of Latin origin, American English has probably gone somewhat farther than British English in what R. W. Chapman in his note "Latin in English" has called "the attempt to foist 'correct' B.C. pronunciation of . . . Latin on a modern vernacular" (*Notes and Queries,* December 13, 1947). As Dr. Chapman points out, the absurdity reaches a climax in the reversal of the final vowels in *alumni* and *alumnae;* "for the faction of the Left call the girls *aloomnigh* or *alumnigh,* and the faction of the Right call the boys just that (or *alumny*), so that a vital distinction is blurred or obliterated." As a result of the teaching of the "reformed" (or "classical" or "Roman") pronunciation of Latin, with seldom a word of instruction in the traditional English method, there prevails in America, and to a lesser extent in England, which has a somewhat better established tradition for the English pronunciation of Latin than we have, an uncertainty in the pronunciation of Latin learned words, phrases, and proper names. The thing has in fact gone so far that many speakers hesitate to employ such words or phrases for fear that their pronunciation will not be understood or that it will invite suspicion of their learning. For a while there was a period of transition, during which one was practically forced to have two pronunciations of Latin, one—the "classical"—for the partially educated and academically hidebound, and one—the traditional English—for the truly cultured and sophisticated. It is evident, however, from the number of "classical" pronunciations current in British English as recorded by Daniel Jones—and he is recording a type of spech which is from the American point of view highly sophisticated—that even on this level there is now considerable wavering. But, as far as American usage is concerned, the speaker is always safer to use the "waynee, weedee, weekee" type of Latin pronunciation taught in the schools; for this supposed "correct" pronunciation has, in this country at least, almost completely superseded the traditions of the past still embalmed in the dictionaries. *Sigh-ny quay non* (the "dictionary pronunciation" of *sine qua non*) is quite as archaic in American English nowadays as *don quicksoat* for *Don Quixote*. Even the familiar *per se* is nowadays more often *pur say* (or even *pair say*) than traditional *pur see*. The old tradition has gone down in ignominious defeat at the hands of a supposedly more proper standard of pronunciation taught in the schools, and it may be only a question of time before *Julius Caesar* will be *Yulius Kysar*. As a consequence, Latin has become for the first time in a good many centuries a dead language even among the learned. The fact that the English tradition has been only incompletely lost in some words has resulted in hybrid pronunciations like *ultimatum* with the unrounded English *u* of *but* in the first syllable and Latin *ah* instead of the traditional English *ay* in the third syllable. *Alma mater* is now usually "Latinized," that is, pronounced *ahlma mahter*, though the hybrid pronunciation *alma mahter* is very frequent. Of the dictionaries of British English, none records any pronunciation save the traditional English (*alma mayter*), a pronunciation which is also, quite misleadingly, given first place in practically all American dictionaries. The phrase is, of course, of much less frequent occurrence in England than in America.

To summarize, then, we are hardly justified in characterizing educated American pronunciation, the speech of our average "effective citizens," excluding the few who have given up in despair of ever achieving the very high standard set by those whom we have chosen to be our authorities, as bold, daring, and independent. Although its traditions are not invariably those of the mother country, it has acquired very real traditions of its own, based not upon usage, but upon authority—the authority of the written word as this is interpreted by the schools. Nothing could be less true of present American English than Captain Marryat's sneer of more than a century ago, when he declared that "every one appears to be independent, and pronounces just as he pleases." American pronunciation has become a carefully schooled and regimented type of pronunciation, sometimes even overcareful from the British point of view; it is on the whole as true to its standards, based as these are upon theoretic and academic criteria, as British English is to its older traditions of usage based upon social custom. The notion that American English is "sloppy" has little basis in fact, particularly on the educated level; and uneducated American speech is certainly no sloppier than uneducated British speech. Except for the American propensity for "tall talk," which is stylistic rather than linguistic in nature, admiration for frontiersmen and cowboys has probably had little or no effect upon the speech of Americans beyond their teens.

EXERCISES

1. What does Mr. Pyles mean by British and American *intonation?*
2. Does Mr. Pyles consider tempo in speech to be a regional or a national matter?
3. Do you pronounce the *t* in *often,* the *a* in *Sunday,* or the *h* in forehead? What are the recent developments in American pronunciation with regard to these words?
4. List ten words that the English pronounce differently from Americans. Indicate the nature of the differences. For the American pronunciation you may want to refer to John S. Kenyon and Thomas A. Knott, *A Pronouncing Dictionary of American English,* G. and C. Merriam, 1953.
5. What does Mr. Pyles think about basing pronunciation on the spelling of a word?
6. What proof does Mr. Pyles give that "the notion that American English is 'sloppy' has little basis in fact, particularly on the educated level"?

3 AMERICAN AND BRITISH ENGLISH

by Charles Shair

Charles Shain (1915–) studied at Princeton and King's College, Cambridge. Mr. Shain is a member of the English department at Carleton College, and has contributed articles to Modern Language Notes, New England Quarterly, *the* American Quarterly, *and other journals. In 1952–1953, he was a Fulbright Research Scholar at Birbeck College, University of London, and gave a number of lectures in England and on the Continent. The selection printed here is an address he read before a Belgian audience.*

In "American and British English," Mr. Shain makes a number of interesting points. He shows that certain idioms, for example, the British "to stand for Parliament" and the American "to run for Congress," reflect a difference not only in usage but also in attitudes toward decorum and propriety. He concludes that language is not merely a means of communication—it is also "the expression of the mores of a society, a kind of moving and changing image of its culture."

It is perhaps a greater privilege than you suspect for an American to be asked to talk about the English language just out of earshot of England. Or perhaps I am not out of earshot. If there is an Englishman present, he may want to speak to me later in private, or to rise after I have finished to express his dissent with some of the things I have been saying. But there is one enviable aspect of the Anglo-American language situation that citizens of both countries would agree on. Our common language provides us with endless matter for conversation. We are perhaps the only people in the world who have a subject to move on to immediately after we have finished talking about the weather.

Not that the language we share is as neutral a subject as the weather. But we have learned to be increasingly polite to one another about our two versions of English. The respect shown the American language in Britain has been in the past a good barometer of Anglo-American storms and calms. The way Americans speak or write gets its varying status from the political, economic or military repute that America stands in at any one time. And it is quite natural and human that this should be so.

Nowadays, in my experience, it is only after the first or second hour of a language discussion that our two national prides begin to warm up and polite laughter begins to hide sharp edges of meaning or hurt feelings.

For language is, of course, more than just a means of communication. It is the expression of the mores of a society, a kind of moving and changing image of its culture. Any national language—especially the spoken language—always carries a hum and buzz of implications which are often more significant and interesting than the bare facts being communicated. For example one learns something about the history of social forces in England and America when he knows that what in American is called a "white-collar job" is in England called a "black-coat job"; what in American is called a "business suit" in England is called a "lounge suit"; what in Wall Street is called "*playing* the stock market" is in the City of London called "*gambling* on the stock exchange"; what an American would call "riding the party band-wagon" an Englishman might express more decorously as "attaching oneself to the winning side." During the war, the British armed forces had a pamphlet distributed to them for the guidance of its members in dealing with American servicemen. Women in the British services were told not to be shocked if a G.I. opened a conversation with "Hi-ya Baby." In Iowa, the pamphlet explained, that it was equivalent to "Lovely day, isn't it?" During the past winter I have heard two English politicians illustrate the differences between the democratic processes in England and America by pointing out that in England "we stand for Parliament" while in America "you run for Congress."

These complicated, and often comic, differences between the two languages—if I may now begin to refer to them as two languages—has of course attracted the attention of wits. It was Oscar Wilde who first expressed the paradox that the greatest barrier between the English and the Americans was that they spoke the same language. *The Manchester Guardian*, a while back, looked forward to the day (perhaps with its tongue in its cheek) when Britain and America will understand one another perfectly because they will have agreed that they do *not* speak the same language. The favorite illustration used to prove this paradox nowadays is a story from the last volume of Mr. Churchill's history of the war. There he tells how a British proposal at a war-time conference to "table" an urgent paper led to a "long and even acrimonious argument" with the Americans. "To table" in British Parliamentary English means to act upon a paper or motion immediately. In America it means postponing all discussion to a later date.

Meanwhile in both countries the linguistic purists—or, to speak less invidiously, those people who have a concern for high standards of English—are worried because the English language recognizes no central authority. Among them, I believe, are people who would envy your linguistic situation in Belgium, that is, the relation between the French of Brussels and Antwerp and the best French of Paris. (Or perhaps I am wrong in this.) Recently in London I found a small book on "Belgicismes." It was called "Ne dites pas . . . Dites. . . ." No one would dare to write a guide with such a title for Americans today—though attempts of this kind were made during the last century. There is no such animal as Academic English; we English-speaking people have no equivalent to "comme on fait en France." The English language has been in a state of chaos ever since it was born, and it has caused only misery among those who have tried to order it and make it as logical a language as French.

See what has been the destiny of the language of the British Isles. In the middle of the 16th century it began to emigrate into the remotest parts of the world, until now it is spoken by more people than have ever been able to talk together before. Some two hundred million people now speak English. Nearly seven tenths of them live in the United States. Another tenth live in British dominions or parts of the British Commonwealth which have come under strong American influence. It looks as if the original British English will continue to be reinforced or, if you like, corrupted by American English for many years to come. Americanisms had already begun to creep into British English over a century ago when the predominance of the Mother Country in wealth, population and prestige was secure and most Americans were reverentially colonial in their attitude toward British culture. Now in the middle of the twentieth century the balance of linguistic power is upset beyond all redress.

What are the basic differences between British and American English? If you have most of your experiences of English through reading, you may say the differences are not very many. And in a general way you would be right. Recently a handbook was published in London for the guidance of English publishers who always "anglicize" American books before they issue them in English editions. The list of necessary changes in vocabulary, idiom and syntax occupied less than ninety small pages. To the non-English speaking person, differences in spelling, I suppose, are most noticeable. Whenever American spelling is "simpler" than English, it is nearly always due to the influence of one man, the American linguistic nationalist of the late eighteenth century, Noah Webster.

Like the Biblical Noah, Noah Webster was a kind of original and left a permanent mark on all the Americans who came after him. His influence derives especially from a spelling book he prepared for American schools and families, which eventually sold eighty million copies. (His royalty was less than a cent a copy but the book kept him in comfort for the rest of his life.) Webster's spelling book changed most of the British words which ended in *our* to *or* (humor, honor, labor, etc.); other words which came into English from the French and ended in *re,* he changed to *er* (center and theater); he simplified other words derived from French into closer conformity with English analogies (mask for masque, check for cheque, meaning a bank draft); and he tidied up the spelling of many other words which we still spell differently from the English like *tire, wagon, program, traveler, plow, jail,* and many others.

But there are greater differences in vocabulary than the recent handbook I spoke of would lead you to believe. It isn't nearly complete. If you have been a visitor to both England and America you will know how the difference in the language of train and automobile travel can tax your patience and your resources. As some Belgians say (according to my book of Belgicismes) "Nous etions *sur* le tram" and the Parisians say "*dans* le tramway" so we Americans get *on* and *off* a train, and the British get *into* and *out of* it. There are different words in America for the English *tram, railway, guard, engine-driver, carriage, compartment, van, luggage, goods train, plough* (which we call a *cow-catcher*) and even *booking office* and *single* and *return* ticket. Somehow we still manage to use one another's trains. An equal number of differences occur in naming the parts of that vehicle which in England is a *motor* or *motor* car, and in America is an *automobile,* or more frequently in recent years, a *car.* The British words which an American woman must learn in order to keep house in England, my wife has discovered this year to be legion. There are different English words for such staple articles in an American kitchen and larder as *corn, string beans, lima beans, crackers, biscuits, molasses, raisins, pie, apple sauce, pitcher, bowl, bureau, window shade, kerosene, garbage, can, faucet, dishpan,* and that eternal domestic process known in America as "doing the dishes" which the English call "washing up." As some of you disagree with the French as to *quartier* and *appartement,* so we disagree with the British as to *apartment,* our word, and *flat,* theirs. As some of you must learn to say 'des bonbons" instead of "des boules," so we must learn when we come to England, to find our way through a world of *sweets, sweetmeats, boiled sweets, desserts, cakes* and *toffees,* all of which bear different names on our side of the Atlantic.

We can generalize a little about the ways in which the American people made their separate vocabulary. Obviously many innovations resulted from experiences on the new continent. Americans got *prairie, canoe, hickory, skunk, moose, portage, bayou* and *levee* from the Indian and French frontier. From the New York Dutch we took words like *scow* and *boss* (this latter probably from our democratic scruples, to avoid saying master: the British adopted it later). From the Palatinate Germans who settled in Pennsylvania we took *noodle, pretzel* and *sauerkraut.* The first colonists had to invent new words for new things, like *foothill, watershed, blizzard, mass-meeting, garter snake.* Many words which sounded later to English ears like Americanisms had actually come over on the Mayflower with the first immigrants: *mad,* for the British *angry, guess* for the British *suppose, fall* for the British *autumn,* and others. Another Mayflower-transplanted archaism was the British word *sick,* which the British in a prudish moment in their history, chose to think of as a nasty word, meaning *to vomit,* and substituted the more genteel word *ill.* Fifteen years ago an American friend of mine got sick with appendicitis and had to go *to the hospital* (as an American would say; *to hospital* as an Englishman would say). He spent an uncomfortable first night and in the morning a nurse came to him and asked him if he had been sick. This, to him, nonsensical question he ascribed to the unfeeling nature of the whole British people, and he wanted to crawl right out of bed and go home to America. In the last fifteen years, I notice, the so-called Americanism *sick* has established itself in England again, and the English, perhaps unfortunately, have lost the useful distinction between being ill and being sick.

Because America was an isolated land for many years, the American vocabulary has a good many archaisms, and today American dictionary makers are rather proud of collecting them. There are some nice words among them (or at least they seem pleasant to us; your taste in words may be different) for instance, *to whittle, to hustle, green horn, flapjack, chore* (which the British still have in char-woman), *jeans* and *homespun.*

But many of these vocabulary differences appear more frequently in the spoken language than in the literary or reader's language. It is the differences between spoken English and spoken American which chiefly, I suppose, attract your attention. To speak first of the two systems of pronunciation. The guardians of a pure English in the British Isles began to throw up their hands as the influence of imported American silent movies came to be felt in the early '20's. But when American talkies flooded the movie palaces in England after 1929, these people gave in to dark despair. But, of course, American talkies haven't brought the pronunciation of British and American English any more closely together.

The greatest differences in the two spoken languages is that though we may roughly speak the same words, we don't speak them to the same tune. If by British English is meant the sounds made by educated London and the B.B.C. you probably know that its tone has greater variety of pitch, greater speed, more variety of tempo and uses more breath than the more deliberate level tone of American speech. Another difference between the spoken languages of each country that a stranger traveling through them for the first time would remark is the surprising uniformity of accent in America, compared to the varying accents in the British Isles. A stranger might travel two thousand miles in America and hear more uniformity in the spoken language than he would hear in one hundred or even twenty miles in England. You probably know of the differences that exist in the spoken English of northern and southern England, and Scotland, Ireland and Wales, and how differently English can sound in the mouths of the countryman and the factory worker and the public school graduate. In America there are of course differences between the educated and uneducated speaker, but in general there are only three different dialects: the speech of New England, the speech of the southern states east of the Mississippi, and the speech which is usually called General American and is spoken by the remaining two thirds of the people who live on the remaining four fifths of the land.

These different American dialects have their origins in the early history of the country. The emigration from Britain to America which formed the sounds of modern American took place between the early 17th and late 18th centuries. Two other significant periods of emigration followed. In the first half of the 19th century great numbers of Irish and Germans settled in America. Between the American Civil War and modern times many emigrants have come from the Scandinavian countries, from Southern Europe and from the Slavic countries. But the sounds of American English were formed by the first wave of settlers: the influence of the later emigrants, many of them non-English speaking, has been quite small. Of the original settlers in New England and the Southern states, most came from the south of England. They brought with them a broad *a* and a soft or non-existent *r* from, chiefly, the rural English spoken in 17th and 18th century southern England. To the middle states, New York, Pennsylvania, New Jersey, the colonists came largely from the north of England, from Scotland and northern Ireland, and because they were the most active settlers in developing the western frontiers, their speech spread most widely and became the General American speech I described.

The other forces making for a uniform American speech have been our universal free education, the lack of sharp class differences in our society, and the mingling of people from all sections of the country in the growing West. It has been said that it is unusual to find an adult American living in the place in which he was born. This is an obvious exaggeration, but it is true that we still change our place of abode very easily and often. This diffusion of the spoken American language has not existed for a long enough time to permit pronounced dialectical differences to occur among the two thirds of the Americans who speak the same way. Some day we may have several more distinct regional forms of speech. But the standardizing influence of radio, television, the movies, and the quick and easy methods of travel may continue to keep American speech fairly uniform for a long time to come.

But to return to the differences between the sounds of British English and American English. The chief differences result from the fact that American, in its comparative isolation across the Atlantic, has not followed step by step the many changes that have occurred in British English since the middle of the 18th century. American is in many respects archaic in its sounds. The broad *a* (which you hear in the British dance and ask) had existed in rural English, but Dr. Johnson, the 18th century dictionary-maker, complained of it as a new-fangled pronunciation brought from Italy by traveling Englishmen. It became fashionable in England but not in General American. When Americans say "gat," "nat" and "shap" instead of *got, not* and *shop,* we are again speaking in a way that was fashionable in the England of Charles II. When we say, "Having *gotten* a loaf of bread from the shop, the boy *ate* it," an Englishman says, "Having *got* a loaf of bread from the shop, the boy *et* it," we are speaking an older English but not therefore, to many English ears, a more respectable one. To many Englishmen today our language still sounds harsh, nasal and vulgar. But things have improved since the middle of the 19th century when one popular English novelist wrote in a novel which described Americans:

> How I would like to convey to the many excellent and admirable Americans who utter their clearheaded thoughts through their noses, and startle away the attentions of their English listeners by strange accents and odd quantities, how fatal to real success in society such peculiarities are and ever will be. When Americans will condescend, like the Russians for instance, to have English tutors, English governesses, and English servants to attend upon their children, then they will speak English as well as the Russians do, but not till then.

Last month the London Evening Standard published an article on British and American English by the distinguished British historian, Sir Harold Nicolson. In large black letters his words were headlined: "I say the Americans speak better English than we do."

American English speech sounds, it seems obvious to me, will have very little influence on English pronunciation in the future, despite the movies and the many thousands of Americans who infest the British Isles in the form of airmen and visitors. But unfortunately, given any one culture's ability to misunderstand another and to moralize upon the differences between them, many Americans will probably go on thinking that the educated British accent is affected and supercilious. And many Englishmen will go on thinking that the Americans (and Canadians) speak only a vulgar and lazy misrepresentation of recognized English words. Americans will still continue to wince at an English actor's version of the American accent on the stage of the B.B.C., and some Americans will still try to acquire an English accent too quickly. I heard one this winter who, after six months in England, had gotten confused to the extent of saying *lomb chops* and *table lomps.* A case that deserves more sympathy is that of a young son of an English friend of mine. He was born while his family were living in Chicago, and the boy learned to speak there. Now at the age of eight, he is back again in his homeland, and knows that he must learn the English sounds as quickly as he can, in order to avoid the scorn of his school-mates. He was discovered recently by his father reading the British radio programs out loud for practice, but he had fallen at the first hurdle. He was pronouncing the early morning program "Massed Brass Bands": *mahssed brahss bahnds.*

On the lower levels of language, in the wonderful realm of slang, both Englishman and American quickly gets beyond his depth in the other man's country. But the flow of popular and easily-learned slang has been mainly eastward across the Atlantic. Americans have nothing to help them toward an understanding of British slang comparable to the American movies in England. Beyond this, an American is not being just a super-patriot when he takes pride in the fact that almost from the beginning of America as a nation our colloquial language has had a graphic descriptive vigor which many Englishmen have found attractive. Many others have of course deplored the inroads that American slang has made in England. But what these Gloomy Gusses don't pause to notice is that the English people have the advantage (which they use) of selecting what they like from the American slang which comes wafting across the ocean. The rubbish among it soon perishes just as bad slang disappears very rapidly in any country.

The resistance against American slang was quite effective in England until after the American Civil War. Then our professional funny men like Mark Twain broke down the barriers with their English lectures and books. The movies and the last war's G.I.'s continued the flood, and now it seems to penetrate everywhere. In a *New Statesman and Nation,* not a pro-American journal, I ran into these: "The prevailing idiom of Mr. Eliot's verse is dead-pan." "He is one of the backroom boys." "For crying out loud." Even rather dignified writers who protested against the importation of American slang early in the century used it, perhaps unconsciously. Sir Arthur Quiller-Couch used *rubber-neck;* John Masefield, *to cough up* (meaning to pay money reluctantly). The House of Commons, a Member of Parliament recently reported, had heard these expressions, *to pass the buck* (meaning to pass on blame); a *backslider* (a person who defaults from his position out of cowardice); *to deliver the goods* (to make a success of something, usually against odds); "you're telling me" (which has no translation except the rough one which means you're right and I know it).

The English, I hasten to add, have a very good way with slang themselves, and most Americans take great delight in learning their way into it when they are on an English visit. But the pressure of numbers and the high-powered American entertainment, song-writing and comic-book industries keep the tide of slang flowing all one way.

I should conclude, perhaps, with some special notices and warnings for the innocent bystander, the unfortunate non-English-speaking person who would like to find his way through this linguistic journal without losing his shirt or his dignity. The nomenclature for *underclothing* (or *underwear* as we usually say) and of those various pieces of elastic with which most of us hold up our stockings or our trousers is full of pitfalls and embarrassments. Perhaps all a novice can hope to do is to retire with a kindly looking shop assistant and communicate by means of gestures. An Englishman who is getting ready for an American visit must be warned that when his American hostess, bidding him goodnight on a cold winter's night, asks "Would you like a *comforter?*" she means an eiderdown bed-covering and not one of those India rubber objects that babies suck on. To call your hostess's house or face in England *homely* is to compliment it. To do so in America would be to invite social disaster.

The word O.K. must now be regarded as not only universal but respectable. Lord Beaverbrook at the Moscow Conference of 1941 in replying to Stalin's interpreter that Britain would promise to furnish a long list of war materials said "O.K." Mr. Harriman, the American delegate, said "Agreed." O.K. is probably the most successful of all Americanisms. The first Americans captured by the Japanese in the Philippines found that every Japanese prison guard knew it. Our Moslem allies in North Africa knew it before the English and Americans arrived. During the Spanish Civil War, American soldiers found Spanish children using it instead of "Salud." On my first Sunday in London I asked a Cockney boy in the City of London for a street direction. My ear wasn't yet well enough tuned to his accent and the only word I understood was his last one when I thanked him. He replied, "Okey-dokey."

But surely the note to end on is not the differences between the two versions of English but the remarkable fact of their interdependence and mutual assistance. Americans borrow British words like *tabloid, bungalow, cop,* and (from the last war) *commando, alert, quisling, paratrooper,* and their fine R.A.F. slang. If we ever knew these words were first British, we have soon forgotten it and made them our own. Not many people in England know or care that these words were American inventions, *highbrow, overcoat, reliable, belittle, telephone, telegram, typewriter.* Since I was last in England fifteen years ago, *radio, subway* and *movies* have moved across the Atlantic and largely displaced *wireless, underground* and *cinema,* and no one in England seems to mind very much. Perhaps people on this side of the Atlantic are more ready to accept the fact that the so-called Americanization of Britain, and even of Europe, is only the return wave of the original Europization of America. And therefore we can take heart, if and when we need to, that many important words like *liberty*, *justice* and *fraternity* have common meanings, not only between Britain and America, but wherever an historical and humane vocabulary of Europe is to be found.

EXERCISES

1. Find out whatever you can about Noah Webster, then write a brief account of his influence on American English.

2. Make a list of fifteen English and American words that are spelled differently.

3. Write a three hundred word book review of one of the following: Bergen Evans and Cornelia Evans, *A Dictionary of Contemporary American Usage*, Random House, 1957; Mitford M. Matthews, *A Dictionary of Americanisms*, University of Chicago Press, 1951; Albert H. Marckwardt, *American English*, Oxford University Press, 1958; or H. L. Mencken, *The American Language*, Alfred A. Knopf, 1936.

4. After reading Mr. Shain's article what do you think of Oscar Wilde's statement that the greatest barrier between the English and Americans is that they speak the same language? State your reasons for agreeing or disagreeing with Wilde.

4 THE NATURE OF SLANG

by H. L. Mencken

H. L. Mencken (1880–1956) was at the height of his popularity as a literary and social critic in the 1920's as editor first of Smart Set *and later of* The American Mercury *(which he founded with George Jean Nathan). A bitter critic of what he considered traditional American illusions about democracy and society, Mencken satirized American provincialism and vulgarity. But his most enduring influence has been through his book* The American Language*—a massive work of scholarship which, unlike most scholarly books, was written with such wit and liveliness that it reached a large, popular audience and established the subject as an exciting one worthy of serious interest.*

"The Nature of Slang" explores the origin of many English and American slang words and phrases. Mencken shows how slang enriches the language: for it originates "in the effort of ingenious individuals to make the language more pungent and picturesque."

Slang is defined by the Oxford Dictionary as "language of a highly colloquial type, considered as below the level of standard educated speech, and consisting either of new words or of current words employed in some special sense." The origin of the word is unknown. Ernest Weekley, in his "Etymological Dictionary of Modern English," 1921, suggests that it may have some relation to the verb *to sling,* and cites two Norwegian dialect words, based upon the cognate verb *slenge* or *slengje,* that appear to be its brothers: *slengjeord,* a neologism, and *slengjenamn,* a nickname. But he is not sure, so he adds the note that "some regard it as an argotic perversion of the French *langue,* language." A German philologian, O. Ritter, believes that it may be derived, not from *langue,* but from *language* itself, most probably by a combination of blending and shortening, as in *thieve(s' lang)uage, beggar(s' lang)uage,* and so on.[1] "Webster's New International," 1934, follows somewhat haltingly after Weekly. The Oxford Dictionary, 1919, evades the question by dismissing *slang* as "a word of cant origin, the ultimate source of which is not apparent." When it first appeared in English, about the middle of the Eighteenth Century,[2] it was employed as a synonym of *cant,* and so designated "the special vocabulary used by any set of persons of a low or disreputable character"; and half a century later it began to be used interchangeably with *argot,* which means the vocabulary special to any group, trade or profession. But during the past fifty years the three terms have tended to be more or less clearly distinguished. The jargon of criminals is both a kind of slang and a kind of argot, but it is best described as *cant,* a word derived from the Latin *cantus,* and going back, in its present sense, to *c.* 1540. One of the principal aims of cant is to make what is said unintelligible to persons outside the group, a purpose that is absent from most forms of argot and slang. Argot often includes slang, as when a circus man calls his patrons *suckers* and speaks of refunding money to one full of complaints as *squaring the beef,* but when he calls the circus grounds the *lot* and the manager's quarters the *white wagon,* he is simply using the special language of his trade, and it is quite as respectable as the argot of lawyers or diplomats. The essence of slang is that it is of general dispersion, but still stands outside the accepted canon of the language. It is, says George H. McKnight,[3] "a form of colloquial speech created in a spirit of defiance and aiming at freshness and novelty. . . . Its figures are consciously farfetched and are inten-

[1] *Archiv für das Studium der neueren Sprachen,* Vol. CXVI, 1906. I am indebted for the reference to Concerning the Etymology of *Slang,* by Fr. Klaeber, *American Speech,* April, 1926. The process is not unfamiliar in English: *tawdry,* from *Saint Audrey,* offers an example.

[2] It has since appeared in German, French and Swedish, as is shown by the titles of Deutsches Slang, by Arnold Genthe; Strassburg, 1892; Le Slang, by J. Manchon; Paris, 1923; and Stockholmska Slang, by W. P. Uhrström; Stockholm, 1911.

[3] English Words and Their Background; New York, 1923, p. 43.

tionally drawn from the most ignoble of sources. Closely akin to profanity in its spirit, its aim is to shock." Among the impulses leading to its invention, adds Henry Bradley,[4] "the two more important seem to be the desire to secure increased vivacity and the desire to secure increased sense of intimacy in the use of language." "It seldom attempts," says the London *Times*, "to supply deficiencies in conventional language; its object is nearly always to provide a new and different way of saying what can be perfectly well said without it."[5] What chiefly lies behind it is simply a kind of linguistic exuberance, an excess of word-making energy. It relates itself to the standard language a great deal as dancing relates itself to music. But there is also something else. The best slang is not only ingenious and amusing; it also embodies a kind of social criticism. It not only provides new names for a series of everyday concepts, some new and some old; it also says something about them. "Words which produce the slang effect," observes Frank K. Sechrist,[6] "arouse associations which are incongruous or incompatible with those of customary thinking."

Everyone, including even the metaphysician in his study and the eremite in his cell, has a large vocabulary of slang, but the vocabulary of the vulgar is likely to be larger than that of the cultured, and it is harder worked. Its content may be divided into two categories: (*a*) old words, whether used singly or in combination, that have been put to new uses, usually metaphorical, and (*b*) new words that have not yet been admitted to the standard vocabulary. Examples of the first type are *rubberneck*, for a gaping and prying person, and *iceberg*, for a cold woman; examples

[4] *Art.* Slang, Encyclopaedia Britannica, 14 ed.; New York, 1929.

[5] American Slang (leading article), May 11, 1931. Many other definitions of *slang* are quoted in What is Slang? by H. F. Reves, *American Speech*, Jan., 1926. A few by literati may be added. "Slang," said Carl Sandburg, "is language that takes off its coat, spits on its hands, and gets to work." "Slang," said Victor Hugo, "is a dressing-room in which language, having an evil deed to prepare, puts on a disguise." "Slang," said Ambrose Bierce, "is the speech of him who robs the literary garbage-carts on their way to the dumps." Emerson and Whitman were its partisans. "What can describe the folly and emptiness of scolding," asked the former (Journals, 1840), "like the word *jawing?*" "Slang," said Whitman, "is the wholesome fermentation or eructation of those processes eternally active in language, by which the froth and specks are thrown up, mostly to pass away, though occasionally to settle and permanently crystalize." (Slang in America, 1885.) And again: "These words out to be collected—the bad words as well as the good. Many of these bad words are fine." (An American Primer, *c.* 1856.)

[6] The Psychology of Unconventional Language, *Pedagogical Seminary*, Dec., 1913, p. 443. "Our feeling and reactions to slang words," continues Sechrist, "may be due to the word as such, to the use it is put to, to the individual using it, to the group using it, to the thing tabooed to which it applies, or to the context in which it is found. . . . Unconventional language keeps close to the objective world of things. It keeps oriented to the sense of touch, contact, pressure, preferring a language material which is ultimately verifiable by the most realistic sense." This last, I fear, is somewhat dubious. See also An Investigation of the Function and Use of Slang, by A. H. Melville, *Pedagogical Seminary*, March, 1912; and La Psychologie de l'argot, by Raoul de La Grasserie, *Revue Philosophique* (Paris), Vol. LX, 1905.

of the second are *hoosegow, flimflam, blurb, bazoo* and *blah*. There is a constant movement of slang terms into accepted usage. *Nice*, as an adjective of all work, signifying anything satisfactory, was once in slang use only, and the purists denounced it,[7] but today no one would question "a *nice* day," "a *nice* time," or "a *nice* hotel." The French word *tête* has been a sound name for the human head for many centuries, but its origin was in *testa*, meaning a pot, a favorite slang word of the soldiers of the decaying Roman Empire, exactly analogous to our *block, nut* and *bean*. The verb-phrase *to hold up* is now perfectly good American, but so recently as 1901 the late Brander Matthews was sneering at it as slang. In the same way many other verb-phrases, *e.g., to cave in, to fill the bill* and *to fly off the handle*, once viewed askance, have gradually worked their way to a relatively high level of the standard speech. On some indeterminate tomorrow *to stick up* and *to take for a ride* may follow them. "Even the greatest purist," says Robert Lynd, "does not object today to the inclusion of the word *bogus* in a literary English vocabulary, though a hundred years ago *bogus* was an American slang word meaning an apparatus for coining false money. *Carpetbagger* and *bunkum* are other American slang words that have naturalized themselves in English speech, and *mob* is an example of English slang that was once as vulgar as *incog* or *photo*." [8] Sometimes a word comes in below the salt, gradually wins respectability, and then drops to the level of slang, and is worked to death. An example is offered by *strenuous*. It was first used by John Marston, the dramatist, in 1599, and apparently he invented it, as he invented *puffy, chilblained, spurious* and *clumsy*. As strange as it may seem to us today, all these words were frowned on by the purists of the time as uncouth and vulgar, and Ben Jonson attacked them with violence in his "Poetaster," written in 1601. In particular, Ben was upset by *strenuous*. But it made its way despite him, and during the next three centuries it was used by a multitude of impeccable authors, including Milton, Swift, Burke, Hazlitt, and Macaulay. And then Theodore Roosevelt invented and announced the Strenuous Life, the adjective struck the American fancy and passed into slang, and in a little while it was so horribly threadbare that all persons of careful speech sickened of it, and to this day it bears the ridiculous connotation that hangs about most slang, and is seldom used seriously.

All neologisms, of course, are not slang. At about the time the word *hoosegow*, derived from the Spanish, came into American slang use, the word *rodeo*, also Spanish, came into the standard vocabulary. The dis-

[7] It came in about 1765. During the early Eighteenth Century *elegant* was commonly used, and in Shakespeare's day the favorite was *fine*. *Nice* has had many rivals, *e.g., ripping* and *topping* in England, and *grand* and *swell* in America, but it hangs on.

[8] The King's English and the Prince's American, *Living Age*, March 15, 1928.

tinction between the two is not hard to make out. *Hoosegow* was really not needed. We had plenty of words to designate a jail, and they were old and good words. *Hoosegow* came in simply because there was something arresting and outlandish about it—and the users of slang have a great liking for pungent novelties. *Rodeo*, on the other hand, designated something for which there was no other word in American—something, indeed, of which the generality of Americans had just become aware—and so it was accepted at once. Many neologisms have been the deliberate inventions of quite serious men, *e.g.*, *gas*, *kodak*, *vaseline*. *Scientist* was concocted in 1840 by William Whewell, professor of moral theology and casuistical divinity at Cambridge. *Ampere* was proposed solemnly by the Electric Congress which met in Paris in 1881, and was taken into all civilized languages instantly. *Radio* was suggested for wireless telegrams by an international convention held in Berlin in 1906, and was extended to wireless broadcasts in the United States about 1920, though the English prefer *wireless* in the latter sense. But such words as these were never slang; they came into general and respectable use at once, along with *argon*, *x-ray*, *carburetor*, *stratosphere*, *bacillus*, and many another of the sort. These words were all sorely needed; it was impossible to convey the ideas behind them without them, save by clumsy circumlocutions. It is one of the functions of slang, also, to serve a short cut, but it is seldom if ever really necessary. Instead, as W. D. Whitney once said, it is only a wanton product of "the exuberance of mental activity, and the natural delight of language-making." [9] This mental activity, of course, is the function of a relatively small class. "The unconscious genius of the people," said Paul Shorey, "no more invents slang than it invents epics. It is coined in the sweat of their brow by smart writers who, as they would say, are *out for the coin*." [10] Or, if not out for the coin, then at least out for notice, *kudos*, admiration, or maybe simply for satisfaction of the "natural delight of language-making." Some of the best slang emerges from the argot of college students, but everyone who has observed the process of its gestation knows that the general run of students have nothing to do with the matter, save maybe to provide an eager welcome for the novelties set before them. College slang is actually made by the campus wits, just as general slang is made by the wits of the newspapers and theaters. The idea of calling an engagement-ring a *handcuff* did not occur to the young gentlemen of Harvard by mass inspiration; it occurred

[9] The Life and Growth of Language; New York, 1897, p. 113.

[10] The American Language, in Academy Papers; New York, 1925, p. 149. Henry Bradley says (*Art.* Slang, Encyclopaedia Britannica, 14th ed.; 1929) that "slang develops most freely in groups with a strong realization of group activity and interest, and groups without this interest, *e.g.*, farmers, rarely invent slang terms."

to a certain definite one of them, probably after long and deliberate cogitation, and he gave it to the rest and to his country.

Toward the end of 1933 W. J. Funk of the Funk and Wagnalls Company, publishers of the Standard Dictionary and the *Literary Digest*, undertook to supply the newspapers with the names of the ten most fecund makers of the American slang then current. He nominated T. A. (Tad) Dorgan, the cartoonist; Sime Silverman, editor of the theatrical weekly, *Variety;* Gene Buck, the song writer; Damon Runyon, the sports writer; Walter Winchell and Arthur (Bugs) Baer, newspaper columnists; George Ade. Ring Lardner and Gelett Burgess.[11] He should have added Jack Conway and Johnny O'Connor of the staff of *Variety;* James Gleason, author of "Is Zat So?"; Rube Goldberg, the cartoonist; Johnny Stanley and Johnny Lyman, Broadway figures; Wilson Mizner and Milt Gross. Conway, who died in 1928, is credited with the invention of *palooka* (a third-rater), *belly-laugh, Arab* (for Jew), S.A. (sex appeal), *high-hat, pushover, boloney* (for buncombe, later adopted by Alfred E. Smith), *headache* (wife), and the verbs *to scram, to click* (meaning to succeed), and *to laugh that off.*[12] Winchell, if he did not actually invent *whoopee,* at least gave it the popularity it enjoyed, *c.* 1930.[13] He is also the father of *Chicagorilla, Joosh* (for Jewish), *pash* (for passion) and *shafts* (for legs), and he has devised a great many nonce words and phrases, some of them euphemistic and others far from it, *e.g.*, for married: *welded,*

[11] Mr. Funk added my own name to the list, but this, apparently, was only a fraternal courtesy, for I have never devised anything properly describable as slang, save maybe *booboisie*. This was a deliberate invention. One evening in February, 1922, Ernest Boyd and I were the guests of Harry C. Black at his home in Baltimore. We fell to talking of the paucity of words to describe the victims of the Depression then current, and decided to remedy it. So we put together a list of about fifty terms, and on Feb. 15 I published it in the Baltimore *Evening Sun*. It included *boobariat, booberati, boobarian, boobomaniac, boobuli* and *booboisie*. Only *booboisie,* which happened to be one of my contributions, caught on. A bit later I added *Homo boobus*, and Boyd, who is learned in the tongues, corrected it to *Homo boobiens*. This also had its day, but its use was confined to the *intelligentsia,* and it was hardly slang. Even *booboisie* lies rather outside the bounds.

[12] Conway's coinages are listed by Walter Winchell in Your Broadway and Mine, New York *Graphic,* Oct. 4, 1928, and in A Primer of Broadway Slang, *Vanity Fair,* Nov., 1927. On December 29, 1926, under the title of Why I Write Slang, Conway contributed a very shrewd article to *Variety*. In it he differentiated clearly between the cant of criminals, which is unintelligible to the general, and what he called Broadway slang. The latter differs from the former, he said, "as much as Bostonese from hog Latin."

[13] Lexicographical explorers have found *whoopee* in a cowboy song published by John A. Lomax in 1910, in Kipling's Loot (Barrack-Room Ballads), 1892, and in Mark Twain's A Tramp Abroad, 1880. *Whoope* was common in the English literature of the Fifteenth, Sixteenth and Seventeenth Centuries, but it was probably only our *whoop* with a silent final *e*. Said Winchell in the New York *Mirror*, Jan. 17, 1935: "They contend *whoopee* is older than Shakespeare. Well, all right. I never claimed it, anyhow. But let 'em take *makin' whoopee* from me and look out!"

sealed, lohengrined, merged and *middle-aisled*; for divorced: *Reno-vated*; for contemplating divorce: *telling it to a judge, soured, curdled, in husband trouble, this-and-that-way,* and *on the verge*; for in love: *on the merge, on fire, uh-huh, that way, cupiding, Adam-and-Eveing,* and *man-and-womaning it*; for expecting young: *infanticipating, baby-bound* and *storked.* I add a few other characteristic specimens of his art: *go-ghetto, debutramp, phffft, foofff* (a pest), *Wildeman* (a homosexual), *heheheh* (a mocking laugh), Hard-Times Square (Times Square), *blessed-event* (the birth of young), *the Hardened Artery* (Broadway), *radiodor* (a radio announcer), *moom-pitcher* (moving picture), *girl-mad, Park Rowgue* (a newspaper reporter) and *intelligentlemen.* Most of these, of course, had only their brief days, but a few promise to survive. Dorgan, who died in 1929, was the begetter of *apple-sauce, twenty-three, skiddoo,*[14] *ball-and-chain* (for wife), *cake-eater, dumb Dora, dumbell* (for stupid person), *nobody home,* and *you said it.* He also gave the world, "Yes, we have no bananas," though he did not write the song, and he seems to have originated *the cat's pajamas,* which was followed by a long series of similar superlatives.[15] The sports writers, of course, are all assiduous makers of slang, and many of their inventions are taken into the general vocabulary. Thus, those who specialize in boxing have contributed, in recent years, *kayo, cauliflower-ear, prelim, shadow-boxing, slug-fest, title-holder, punch-drunk,*[16] *brother-act, punk, to side-step* and *to go the limit;*[17] those

[14] Dorgan's claims to both *twenty-three* and its brother *skiddoo* have been disputed. An editorial in the Louisville *Times,* May 9, 1929, credits Frank Parker Stockbridge with the theory that *twenty-three* was launched by The Only Way, a dramatization of Dickens's Tale of Two Cities, presented by Henry Miller in New York in 1899. In the last act an old woman counted the victims of the guillotine, and Sydney Carton was the twenty-third. According to Stockbridge, her solemn "Twenty-three!" was borrowed by Broadway, and quickly became popular. He says *skiddoo,* derived from *skedaddle,* was "added for the enlightenment of any who hadn't seen the play."

[15] See Tad Dorgan is Dead, by W. L. Werner, *American Speech,* Aug., 1929. *The flea's eyebrows, the bee's knees, the snake's hips* and *the canary's tusks* will be recalled. A writer in *Liberty,* quoted in *American Speech, Feb.,* 1927, p. 258, says that Dorgan also helped to popularize *hard-boiled,* the invention of Jack Doyle, keeper of a billiard academy in New York.

[16] For a learned discourse on the pathological meaning of this term see *Punch Drunk,* by Harrison S. Martland, *Journal of the American Medical Association,* Oct. 13, 1928. In severe cases "there may develop a peculiar tilting of the head, a marked dragging of one or both legs, a staggering, propulsive gait with facial characteristics of the parkinsonian syndrome, or a backward swaying of the body, tremors, vertigo and deafness." Some of the synonyms are *cuckoo, goofy, cutting paper-dolls* and *slug-nutty.*

[17] See Jargon of Fistiana, by Robert E. Creighton, *American Speech,* Oct., 1933, and Color Stuff, by Harold E. Rockwell, the same, Oct., 1927. William Henry Nugent, in The Sports Section, *American Mercury,* March, 1929, says that the father of them all was Pierce Egan, who established *Pierce Egan's Life in London and Sporting Guide* in 1824. A year earlier Egan printed a revised edition of Francis Grose's Classical Dictionary of the Vulgar Tongues, 1785. In it appeared *to stall off, cheese it, to trim* (in the sense of to swindle), *to pony up, squealer, sucker, yellow-belly,* and many other locutions still in use.

who cover baseball have made many additions to the list of baseball terms given in Chapter V;[18] and those who follow the golf tournaments have given currency to *birdie, fore, par, bunker, divot, fairway, to tee off, stance,* and *onesome, twosome, threesome* and so on—some of them received into the standard speech, but the majority lingering in the twilight of slang.[19]

George Philip Krapp attempts to distinguish between slang and sound idiom by setting up the doctrine that the former is "more expressive than the situation demands." "It is," he says, "a kind of hyperesthesia in the use of language. *To laugh in your sleeve* is idiom because it arises out of a natural situation; it is a metaphor derived from the picture of one raising his sleeve to his face to hide a smile, a metaphor which arose naturally enough in early periods when sleeves were long and flowing; but *to talk through your hat* is slang, not only because it is new, but also because it is a grotesque exaggeration of the truth."[20] The theory, unluckily, is combated by many plain facts. *To hand it to him, to get away with it* and even *to hand him a lemon* are certainly not metaphors that transcend the practicable and probable, and yet all are undoubtedly slang. On the other hand, there is palpable exaggeration in such phrases as "he is not worth the powder it would take to kill him," in such adjectives as *breakbone* (fever), and in such compounds as *fire-eater,* and yet it would be absurd to dismiss them as slang. Between *blockhead* and *bonehead* there is little to choose, but the former is sound English, whereas the latter is American slang. So with many familiar similes, *e.g., like greased lightning, as scarce as hen's teeth:* they are grotesque hyperboles, but hardly slang.

The true distinction, in so far as any distinction exists at all, is that indicated by Whitney, Bradley, Sechrist and McKnight. Slang originates in the effort of ingenious individuals to make the language more pungent and picturesque—to increase the store of terse and striking words, to

[18] See Baseball Slang, by V. Samuels, *American Speech,* Feb., 1927, p. 255. Hugh Fullerton, one of the rev. elders of the fraternity, says that the first baseball reports to be adorned with neologisms, *e.g., south-paw, initial-sack, grass-cutter, shut-out* and *circus-play,* were written by Charlie Seymour of the Chicago *Inter-Ocean* and Lennie Washburn of the Chicago *Herald* during the 80's. Some years ago the Chicago *Record-Herald,* apparently alarmed by the extravagant fancy of its baseball reporters, asked its readers if they would prefer a return to plain English. Such of them as were literate enough to send in their votes were almost unanimously against a change. As one of them said, "One is nearer the park when Schulte *slams the pill* than when he merely *hits the ball.*" For the argot of baseball players, as opposed to the slang of sports writers, see Baseball Terminology, by Henry J. Heck, *American Speech,* April, 1930.

[19] See Golf Gab, by Anne Angel, *American Speech,* Sept., 1926. In 1934 Willis Stork, a student of Dr. Louise Pound at the University of Nebraska, prepared a paper on The Jargon of the Sports Writers, mainly confined to an examination of the sports pages of two Lincoln, Neb., papers, the *State Journal* and the *Star* from July 1, 1933 to July 15, 1934. So far it has not been published. See also Our Golf Lingo Peeves the British, *Literary Digest,* April 11, 1931.

[20] Modern English; New York, 1910, p. 211.

widen the boundaries of metaphor, and to provide a vocabulary for new shades of difference in meaning. As Dr. Otto Jespersen has pointed out,[21] this is also the aim of poets (as, indeed, it is of prose writers), but they are restrained by consideration of taste and decorum, and also, not infrequently, by historical or logical considerations. The maker of slang is under no such limitations: he is free to confect his neologism by any process that can be grasped by his customers, and out of any materials available, whether native or foreign. He may adopt any of the traditional devices of metaphor. Making an attribute do duty for the whole gives him *stiff* for corpse, *flat-foot* for policeman, *smoke-eater* for fireman, *skirt* for woman, *lunger* for consumptive, and *yes-man* for sycophant. Hidden resemblances give him *morgue* for a newspaper's file of clippings, *bean* for head, and *sinker* for a doughnut. The substitution of far-fetched figures for literal description gives him *glad-rags* for fine clothing, *bonehead* for ignoramus, *booze-foundry* for saloon, and *cart-wheel* for dollar, and the contrary resort to a brutal literalness gives him *kill-joy*, *low-life* and *hand-out*. He makes abbreviations with a free hand—*beaut* for beauty, *gas* for gasoline, and so on. He makes bold avail of composition, as in *attaboy* and *whatdyecallem*, and of onomatopoeia, as in *biff*, *zowie*, *honky-tonk* and *wow*. He enriches the ancient counters of speech with picturesque synonyms, as in *guy*, *gink*, *duck*, *bird* and *bozo* for fellow. He transfers proper names to common usage, as in *ostermoor* for mattress, and then sometimes gives them remote figurative significances, as in *ostermoors* for whiskers. Above all, he enriches the vocabulary of action with many new verbs and verb-phrases, *e.g.*, *to burp*, *to neck*, *to gang*, *to frame up*, *to hit the pipe*, *to give him the works*, and so on. If, by the fortunes that condition language-making, his neologism acquires a special and limited meaning, not served by any existing locution, it enters into sound idiom and is presently wholly legitimatized; if, on the contrary, it is adopted by the populace as a counter-word and employed with such banal imitativeness that it soon loses any definite significance whatever, then it remains slang and is avoided by the finical. An example of the former process is afforded by *tommy-rot*. It first appeared as English school-boy slang, but its obvious utility soon brought it into good usage. In one of Jerome K. Jerome's books, "Paul Kelver," there is the following dialogue:

> "The wonderful songs that nobody ever sings, the wonderful pictures that nobody ever paints, and all the rest of it. It's *tommy-rot!*"
> "I wish you wouldn't use slang."
> "Well, you know what I mean. What is the proper word? Give it to me."
> "I suppose you mean *cant*."

[21] Language: Its Nature, Development and Origin; London, 1922, p. 300. G. K. Chesterton said pretty much the same thing in The Defendant; London, 1901; "All slang is metaphor, and all metaphor is poetry."

"No, I don't. *Cant* is something that you don't believe in yourself.[22] It's *tommy-rot;* there isn't any other word."

Nor were there any other words for *hubbub, fireworks, foppish, fretful, sportive, dog-weary, to bump* and *to dwindle* in Shakespeare's time; he adopted and dignified them because they met genuine needs.[23] Nor was there any other satisfactory word for *graft* when it came in, nor for *rowdy,* nor for *boom,* nor for *joy-ride,* nor for *slacker,* nor for *trust-buster.* Such words often retain a humorous quality; they are used satirically and hence appear but seldom in wholly serious discourse. But they have standing in the language nevertheless, and only a prig would hesitate to use them as George Saintsbury used *the best of the bunch* and *joke-smith.* So recently as 1929 the Encyclopaedia Britannica listed *boot-legger, speakeasy, dry, wet, crook, fake, fizzle, hike, hobo, poppycock, racketeer* and O.K. as American slang terms, but today most of them are in perfectly good usage. What would one call a racketeer if *racketeer* were actually forbidden? It would take a phrase of four or five words at least, and they would certainly not express the idea clearly.[24]

On the other hand, many an apt and ingenious neologism, by falling too quickly into the gaping maw of the proletariat, is spoiled forthwith and forever. Once it becomes, in Oliver Wendell Holmes's phrase, "a cheap generic term, a substitute for differentiated specific expressions," it quickly acquires such flatness that the fastidious flee it as a plague. The case of *strenuous* I have already mentioned. One recalls, too, many capital verb-phrases, thus ruined by unintelligent appreciation, *e.g., to freeze on to, to have the goods, to cut no ice, to fall for,* and *to get by;* and some excellent substantives, *e.g., dope* and *dub,* and compounds, *e.g., come-on* and *easy-mark,* and simple verbs, *e.g., to neck* and *to vamp.* These are all quite as sound in structure as the great majority of our most familiar words and phrases—*to cut no ice,* for example, is certainly as good as *to butter no parsnips*—, but their adoption by the ignorant and their endless use and misuse in all sorts of situations have left them tattered

[22] This sense of the word, of course, is to be differentiated sharply from the philological sense of a more or less secret jargon.

[23] A long list of his contributions to the vocabulary, including a number borrowed from the slang of his time, is to be found in Modern English in the Making, by George H. McKnight; New York, 1928, p. 188 *ff.*

[24] In 1932–33 Dr. Walter Barnes of the New York University set four of his associates to canvassing 100 college, high-school and elementary teachers on the subject of slang. They were asked to scrutinize a list of 432 slang terms, and to estimate them as acceptable, trite and forceless, doubtful, or offensive. Those chosen as most acceptable were *pep, fake, stiff upper lip, double-cross* and *booster.* All these, in ordinary discourse, are nearly if not quite irreplaceable. Others high on the list were *speakeasy, bone-dry, broke, fan, go-getter, snappy, to make the grade, pull* (in the sense of influence), *come-back, frame-up, racket, give-away, cinch* and *to turn down.* The results of the inquiry were issued in mimeograph as Studies in Current Colloquial Usage; New York, 1933.

and obnoxious, and soon or late they will probably go the way, as Brander Matthews once said, of all the other "temporary phrases which spring up, one scarcely knows how, and flourish unaccountably for a few months, and then disappear forever, leaving no sign." Matthews was wrong in two particulars here. They do not arrive by any mysterious parthenogenesis, but come from sources which, in many cases, may be determined. And they last, alas, a good deal more than a month. *Shoo-fly* afflicted the American people for four or five years, and "I *don't* think," *aber nit, over the left, good night* and *oh yeah* were scarcely less long-lived.[25] There are, indeed, slang terms that have survived for centuries, never dropping quite out of use and yet never attaining to good usage. Among verbs, *to do* for to cheat has been traced to 1789, *to frisk* for to search to 1781, *to grease* for to bribe to 1557, and *to blow* for to boast to *c.* 1400.[26] Among nouns, *gas* for empty talk has been traced to 1847, *jug* for prison to 1834, *lip* for insolence to 1821, *sap* for fool to 1815, *murphy* for potato to 1811, *racket* to 1785, *bread-basket* for stomach to 1753, *hush-money* to 1709, *hick* to 1690, *gold-mine* for profitable venture to 1664, *grub* for food to 1659, *rot-gut* to 1597 and *bones* for dice to *c.* 1386. Among the adjectives, *lousy* in the sense of inferior goes back to 1690; when it burst into American slang in 1910 or thereabout it was already more than two centuries old. *Booze* has never got into Standard English, but it was known to slang in the first years of the Fourteenth Century. When *nuts* in the sense revealed by "Chicago was *nuts* for the Giants" came into popularity in the United States *c.* 1920, it was treated by most of the newspaper commentators on current slang as a neologism, but in truth it had been used in precisely the same sense by R. H. Dana, Jr., in "Two Years Before the Mast," 1840, and by Mark Twain in "Following the Equator," 1897.[27] Sometimes an old slang word suddenly acquires a new meaning. An example is offered by *to chisel.* In the sense of to cheat, as in "He *chiseled* me out of $3," it goes back to the first years of the Nineteenth Century, but with the advent of the N.R.A., in the late

[25] The life of such a word or phrase seems to depend, at least to some extent, upon its logical content. When it is sheer silliness the populace quickly tires of it. Thus "Ah there, my size, I'll steal you," "Where did you get that hat?", "How'd you like to be the ice-man?", "Would you for fifty cents?", "Let her go, Gallegher," "So's your old man" and their congeners were all short-lived. Many such vacuities have a faintly obscene significance. It is their function to conceal the speaker's lack of a logical retort by raising a snicker. Those of rather more sense and appositeness, *e.g.*, "Tell your troubles to a policeman," "How do you get that way?", "Where do you get that stuff?", "I'll say so" and "You said a mouthful," seem to last longer. In 1932 a Bridgeport, Conn., high-school teacher, Miss Julia Farnam, told the Bridgeport *Post* on returning from a visit to England that she had met there "the daughter of an earl" who thought "You said a mouthful" "the cleverest expression she ever heard." (*Post*, Oct. 3.)

[26] These and the following examples are taken from The Age of Slang, by J. Louis Kuethe, *Baltimore Evening Sun*, July 3, 1934.

[27] For this I am indebted to Mr. James D. Hart of Cambridge, Mass.

Summer of 1933, it took on the new meaning of to evade compliance with the law by concealment or stealth. It has been credited to Franklin D. Roosevelt, but I believe that its true father was General Hugh S. Johnson, J.D.

With the possible exception of the French, the Americans now produce more slang than any other people, and put it to heavier use in their daily affairs. But they entered upon its concoction relatively late, and down to the second decade of the Nineteenth Century they were content to take their supply from England. American slang, says George Philip Krapp, "is the child of the new nationalism, the new spirit of joyous adventure that entered American life after the close of the War of 1812." [28] There was, during the colonial and early republican periods, a great production of neologisms, as we have seen in Chapter III, but very little of it was properly describable as slang. I find *to boost*, defined as to raise up, to lift up, to exalt, in the glossary appended to David Humphreys's "The Yankey in England," 1815,[29] but all the other slang terms listed, *e.g.*, *duds* for clothes, *spunk* for courage, and *uppish*, are in Francis Grose's "Classical Dictionary of the Vulgar Tongue," published in London thirty years before. The Rev. John Witherspoon's denunciation of slang in "The Druid," 1781, is a denunciation of English slang, though he is discussing the speech habits of Americans. But with the great movement into the West, following the War of 1812, the American vulgate came into its own, and soon the men of the ever-receding frontier were pouring out a copious stream of neologisms, many of them showing the audacious fancy of true slang. When these novelties penetrated to the East they produced a sort of linguistic shock, and the finicky were as much upset by the "tall talk" in which they were embodied as English pedants are today by the slang of Hollywood.[30] That some of them were extremely extravagant is a fact: I need point only to *blustiferous*, *clamjamphrie*, *conbobberation*, *helliferocious*, *mollagausauger*, *peedoodles*, *ripsniptiously*, *slangwhanger*, *sockdolager*, *to exflunctify*, *to flummuck*, *to giraffe*, *to hornswoggle*, *to obflisticate*, and *to puckerstopple*.[31] Most of these, of course, had their brief days and then disappeared, but there were others that got into the common vocabulary and still survive, *e.g.*, *blizzard*, *to hornswoggle*, *sockdolager* and *rambunctious*, the last-named the final step in a process which began with *robustious* and ran through *rumbustious* and *rambustious* in England before Americans took a hand in it. With them came many verb-phrases, *e.g.*, *to pick a crow with*, *to cut one's*

[28] Is American English Archaic? *Southwest Review*, Summer, 1927, p. 302.

[29] The first example in the Supplement to the Oxford Dictionary is from John Neal's Brother Jonathan, 1825.

[30] Specimens of this tall talk are given in Chapter IV, Section 1.

[31] For these examples I am indebted to M. M. Mathews, who prints a longer list in The Beginnings of American English; Chicago, 1931, pp. 114–15.

eye-teeth, to go the whole hog. This "tall talk," despite the horror of the delicate, was a great success in the East, and its salient practitioners—for example, David Crockett—were popular heroes. Its example encouraged the production of like neologisms everywhere, and by 1840 the use of slang was very widespread. It is to those days before the Civil War that we owe many of the colorful American terms for strong drink, still current, *e.g., panther-sweat, nose-paint, red-eye, corn-juice, forty-rod, mountain-dew, coffin-varnish, bust-head, stagger-soup, tonsil-paint, squirrel-whiskey* and so on, and for drunk, *e.g., boiled, canned, cock-eyed, frazzled, fried, oiled, ossified, pifflicated, pie-eyed, plastered, snozzled, stewed, stuccoed, tanked, woozy.*[32] "Perhaps the most striking difference between British and American slang," says Krapp,[33] "is that the former is more largely merely a matter of the use of queer-sounding words, like *bally* and *swank*, whereas American slang suggests vivid images and pictures." This was hardly true in the heyday of "tall talk," but that it is true now is revealed by a comparison of current English and American college slang. The vocabulary of Oxford and Cambridge seems inordinately obvious and banal to an American undergraduate. At Oxford it is made up in large part of a series of childish perversions of common and proper nouns, effected by adding *-er* or inserting *gg*. Thus, breakfast becomes *brekker*, collection becomes *collecker*, the Queen Street Cinema becomes the *Queener*, St. John's becomes *Jaggers* and the Prince of Wales becomes the *Pragger-Wagger*. The rest of the vocabulary is equally feeble. To match the magnificent American *lounge-lizard* the best the Oxonians can achieve is a *bit of a lad*, and in place of the multitudinous American synonyms for *girl*,[34] there are only *bint* (Arabic for *woman*) and a few other such flabby terms.[35]

[32] For a much longer list see Slang Synonyms for *Drunk*, by Manuel Prenner, *American Speech*, Dec., 1928.

[33] The English Language in America; New York, 1925, Vol. I, p. 114.

[34] There is a list of them in English Words and Their Background, by George H. McKnight; New York, 1923, p. 61.

[35] I am indebted here to Mr. Hiram D. Blauvelt. The literature dealing with American college slang begins with A Collection of College Words and Customs, by B. H. Hall; Cambridge, Mass., 1851. Its contents are summarized in College Slang of a Century Ago, by Joseph C. Smith, *Delta Kappa Epsilon Quarterly*, May, 1933. For the slang in vogue at the beginning of the present century see College Words and Phrases, by Eugene H. Babbitt, *Dialect Notes*, Vol. II, Pt. I, 1900, a very valuable compilation. For later periods see College Slang, by M. C. McPhee, *American Speech*, Dec., 1927, and College Abbreviations, by W. E. Schultz, the same, Feb., 1930. There are many monographs on the slang of definite colleges, for example: College Slang Words and Phrases From Bryn Mawr College, by Howard J. Savage, *Dialect Notes*, Vol. V, Pt. V, 1922; Colgate University Slang, by J. A. Russell, *American Speech*, Feb., 1930; A Babylonish Cruise [Girard College], by Carroll H. Frey, *Steel and Garnet*, Dec., 1922; Johns Hopkins Jargon, by J. Louis Kuethe, *American Speech*, June, 1932; Kansas University Slang, by Carl Pingry and Vance Randolph, the same, Feb., 1928; Midshipman Jargon, by Mary B. Peterson, the same, Aug., 1928; Negro Slang in Lincoln University, by Hugh Sebastian, the same, Dec., 1934; University of Missouri Slang, by Virginia Carter, the same, Feb., 1931; Slang at Smith, by M. L. Farrand, *Delineator*, Oct., 1920; Stanford Expressions,

All college slang, of course, borrows heavily from the general slang vocabulary. For example, *chicken*, which designated a young girl on most American campuses until 1921 or thereabouts,[36] was used by Steele in 1711, and, in the form of *no chicken*, by Swift in 1720.

EXERCISES

1. What are the meanings of the following: *philology, jargon, neologism* and *cant?* Write sentences using each of these words.
2. Write a definition of slang as the term is used by Mencken.
3. Does Mencken use slang himself except as illustrations?
4. List ten or more slang expressions you used in high school. Which of these seem out of date? Why? Which, if any, do you think you are likely to continue to use? Why?

---

by W. R. Morse, *American Speech*, March, 1927; Stanfordiana, by John A. Shidler and R. M. Clarke, Jr., the same, Feb., 1932; More Stanford Expressions, by John A. Shidler, the same, Aug., 1932; and College Slang Words and Phrases From Western Reserve University, *Dialect Notes*, Vol. IV, Pt. III, 1915.

[36] I take the date from Slang Today and Yesterday, by Eric Partridge; 2nd ed.; London, 1935, p. 429. Partridge says that it was displaced, at least for a time, by the English *flapper*.

VIII | Traditions of English and American Prose

Each man speaks with his own voice and writes with his own style. When we talk of the prose of this or that century we sometimes forget that Carlyle, Pater, Mark Twain, and Henry James were all Victorians but differed considerably from each other in style. But given the individual quality of style, it is still possible to speak of a tradition of prose and of strains within that tradition: for periods do have certain literary fashions, intellectual trends, explicit or implicit rules, usages, and idioms which are reflected in style. When we speak of the heritage of English and American prose we mean that writing which embodies both the spirit of an era and the excellence of individual writers.

Literature handbooks refer to types of English prose in terms derived from the classical tradition: Euphuistic, Arcadian, Senecan,[1] Ciceronian, Attic, and so on. Such categories can be useful up to a point. But we must remember, first, that we rarely find examples of prose which are

[1] Many students of English prose maintain that the two principal literary styles during the Renaissance were the Senecan (from the Latin writer Seneca) and the Ciceronian (from the Latin writer Cicero). The essays by Bacon and Browne are examples of the Senecan style—abrupt, allusive, and pithy. The Ciceronian style is more copious, rhythmical, and studied, as in this sentence from Sir Philip Sidney's "An Apologie for Poetrie":

And truely, even Plato, whosoever considereth shall find that in the body of his work, though the inside and strength were Philosophy, the skinne as it were and beautie, depended most of Poetry.

pure instances of one type and, second, that these classifications account for only part and not all of the characteristics of any given piece of prose. For example, the essays by Bacon and Browne in this section are both written in the Senecan style, yet they are markedly different from each other.

Speaking of style in more general terms, Somerset Maugham, in "Writing Prose," distinguishes two main streams in English prose: the "rich ornate" and the "simple lucid." In the Sermon on the Mount, from the King James Version of the Bible (1611), we have an example of the "rich ornate," here embodied in pithy, allusive, and aphoristic sentences. The essays by Bacon (1561–1626), Browne (1605–82), and Milton (1608–74), in their individual ways also fall within the "rich ornate" tradition, as does that of Walter Pater, a nineteenth-century writer. Swift's "A Modest Proposal" (1729) exemplifies the "simple lucid" strain at its best.

Because style must be appropriate to theme, it is bound to reflect to some extent the intellectual climate of a period. The development of the spirit and method of scientific inquiry has been a major influence on the thought and writing of post-Renaissance man. In his *History of the Royal Society* (1667), Bishop Sprat wrote that the Society—many members of which were literary men—had

> exacted from all their members a close, naked, natural way of speaking, positive expressions, clear senses, a native easiness, bringing all things as near the Mathematical plainness as they can, and preferring the language of Artizans, Countrymen, and Merchants, before that of Wits and Scholars.

This was a plea for naturalness, an attack on affectation and pretentiousness. The emphasis on precision and a "native easiness" has persisted in our tradition. However, it has not followed that all writers of a scientific bend of mind have attained a style marked by "Mathematical plainness," any more than it has followed that those concerned with elegance and art in literature have always written with felicitous grace.

Historians have called the eighteenth century the "Age of Reason." And we find that writers of that period—Defoe, Addison, Swift, and Benjamin Franklin—reflected many of the values of the "Age of Reason" in their style; they tried to achieve clarity, coherence, and decorum in their writing. Unlike the Senecan style of the earlier period, the eighteenth-century style has an air of careful deliberation.

The nineteenth century produced a rich variety of English and American prose stylists writing both fiction and non-fiction. There was both open and latent controversy between those who, in philosophical terms, aligned themselves on the side of Science and those who aligned themselves on the side of Art. A careful study of nineteenth-century prose might show how a writer's allegiance to one or the other side in this controversy affected his manner of writing. Such an analysis would have to be both complex and subtle. But we may venture the generalization that the proponents of art for art's sake tended to write in what Maugham calls the "rich ornate" style to a greater degree than those who took the side of Science. But whichever side of the controversy they upheld, the nineteenth-century writers of stature approached writing with profound respect for the craft. Thomas Huxley, among the outstanding writers on scientific matters, was not only a fine prose stylist, but is considered by some to have been a finer stylist than Walter Pater whose work epitomizes the art for art's sake movement.

In "Recent Prose," Robert Graves and Alan Hodge remark that there is a greater multiplicity and variety in twentieth-century prose than in that of any other period. Certainly there have been many conscious experiments with style, as in the writing of James Joyce and Gertrude Stein, to mention two extreme examples. The style of contemporary writers—though often complex—is on the whole less consciously ornate and rhetorical than that of past writers. Both in England and America, the trend has been to straightforward, direct, and unadorned writing.

In earlier sections, there has been some discussion of the differences between English and American prose. It is not easy to make clear distinctions. Particularly in the eighteenth and nineteenth centuries, many American as well as English writers thought of American literature as an extension of English literature. But there was a tendency in American writing, as in speech, to break away from fixed usages and formal requirements of English writing. For example, Emerson did not feel obliged to follow the usual rules for organizing a lecture or essay. In *The Green Hills of Africa,* Ernest Hemingway claims that all modern American prose stems from Mark Twain's *The Adventures of Huckleberry Finn.* In this book, Twain's style is direct, simple, idiomatic, and indebted to folk speech. Hemingway's own style shows Twain's influence, but it would be a great exaggeration to maintain that *all* modern American prose is likewise indebted to Twain. Furthermore, Twain's own expository writing is consciously literary and rhetorical. For a literary style it is rather breezy, but it is not folksy.

In his essay, Maugham recounts his own efforts to develop a fine style. After trying to write first like Pater and then like Swift, he concluded that he must write like himself, that writing "is a delicate art that must be painfully acquired." We present this anthology of English and American prose not to encourage students to write like Milton, Swift, or Henry James, but to show that the finest writers in all periods have looked upon writing as an art and have approached it with respect and painstaking care.

1 WRITING PROSE

by W. Somerset Maugham

William Somerset Maugham (1874–) has long enjoyed a wide audience for his many short stories and novels. Of Human Bondage, *one of his early novels, is considered his best. It was adapted for the screen as were* The Moon and Sixpence *(based on the life of Paul Gauguin),* Christmas Holiday, *and* The Razor's Edge, *as well as several of his short stories. In 1938, Maugham published his autobiography,* The Summing Up, *from which the following is an excerpt.*

"Writing Prose" is divided into two sections. In the first, Maugham discusses handbook rules and academic attitudes toward writing. In the second, he gives a survey of what he considers the two major lines in English and American writing—the "rich ornate" and the "simple lucid." Laced with references to his own experience in writing and to his personal preferences and dislikes, this essay provides an informal introduction to the anthology that follows.

I have never had more than two English lessons in my life, for though I wrote essays at school, I do not remember that I ever received any instruction on how to put sentences together. The two lessons I have had were given me so late in life that I am afraid I cannot hope greatly to profit by them. The first was only a few years ago. I was spending some weeks in London and had engaged as temporary secretary a young woman. She was shy, rather pretty, and absorbed in a love affair with a married man. I had written a book called *Cakes and Ale*, and, the typescript arriving one Saturday morning, I asked her if she would be good enough to take it home and correct it over the week-end. I meant her only to make a note of mistakes in spelling that the typist might have made and point out errors occasioned by a handwriting that is not always easy to decipher. But she was a conscientious young person and she took me more literally than I intended. When she brought back the typescript on Monday morning it was accompanied by four foolscap sheets of corrections. I must confess that at the first glance I was a trifle vexed; but then I thought that it would be silly of me not to profit, if I could, by the trouble she had taken and so sat me down to examine them. I suppose the young woman had taken a course at a secretarial college and she had gone through my novel in the same methodical way as her masters had gone through her essays. The remarks that filled the four neat pages of foolscap were incisive and severe. I could not but surmise that the professor of English at the secretarial college did not mince matters. He took a marked line, there could be no doubt about that; and he did not allow that there might be two opinions about anything. His apt pupil would have nothing to do with a preposition at the end of a sentence. A mark of exclamation betokened her disapproval of a colloquial phrase. She had a feeling that you must not use the same word twice on a page and she was ready every time with a synonym to put in its place. If I had indulged myself in the luxury of a sentence of ten lines, she wrote: "Clarify this. Better break it up into two or more periods." When I had availed myself of the pleasant pause that is indicated by a semicolon, she noted: "A full stop"; and if I had ventured upon a colon she remarked stingingly: "Obsolete." But the harshest stroke of all was her comment on what I thought was rather a good joke: "Are you sure of your facts?" Taking it all in all I am bound to conclude that the professor at her college would not have given me very high marks.

The second lesson I had was given me by a don, both intelligent and charming, who happened to be staying with me when I was myself correcting the typescript of another book. He was good enough to offer to read it. I hesitated, because I knew that he judged from a standpoint of excellence that is hard to attain; and though I was aware that he had a profound knowledge of Elizabethan literature, his inordinate admiration for *Esther Waters* made me doubtful of his discernment in the productions of our own day: no one could attach so great a value to that work who had an intimate knowledge of the French novel during the nineteenth century. But I was anxious to make my book as good as I could and I hoped to benefit by his criticisms. They were in point of fact lenient. They interested me peculiarly because I inferred that this was the way in which he dealt with the compositions of undergraduates. My don had, I think, a natural gift for language, which it has been his business to cultivate; his taste appeared to me faultless. I was much struck by his insistence on the force of individual words. He liked the stronger word rather than the euphonious. To give an example, I had written that a statue would be placed in a certain square and he suggested that I should write: the statue will stand. I had not done that because my ear was offended by the alliteration. I noticed also that he had a feeling that words should be used not only to balance a sentence but to balance an idea. This is sound, for an idea may lose its effect if it is delivered abruptly; but it is a matter of delicacy, since it may well lead to verbiage. Here a knowledge of stage dialogue should help. An actor will sometimes say to an author: "Couldn't you give me a word or two more in this speech? It seems to take away all the point of my line if I have nothing else to say." As I listened to my don's remarks I could not but think how much better I should write now if in my youth I had had the advantage of such sensible, broad-minded and kindly advice.

As it is, I have had to teach myself. I have looked at the stories I wrote when I was very young in order to discover what natural aptitude I had, my original stock-in-trade, before I developed it by taking thought. The manner had a superciliousness that perhaps my years excused and an irascibility that was a defect of nature; but I am speaking now only of the way in which I expressed myself. It seems to me that I had a natural lucidity and a knack for writing easy dialogue.

When Henry Arthur Jones, then a well-known playwright, read my first novel, he told a friend that in due course I should be one of the most successful dramatists of the day. I suppose he saw in it directness and an effective way of presenting a scene that suggested a sense of the theater. My language was commonplace, my vocabulary limited, my grammar shaky, and my phrases hackneyed. But to write was an instinct that seemed as natural to me as to breathe, and I did not stop to consider if I wrote well or badly. It was not till some years later that it dawned upon me that it was a delicate art that must be painfully acquired. The discovery was forced upon me by the difficulty I found in getting my meaning down on paper. I wrote dialogue fluently, but when it came to a page of description I found myself entangled in all sorts of quandaries. I would struggle for a couple of hours over two or three sentences that I could in no way manage to straighten out. I made up my mind to teach myself how to write. Unfortunately I had no one to help me. I made many mistakes. If I had had someone to guide me like the charming don of whom I spoke just now, I might have been saved much time. Such a one might have told me that such gifts as I had lay in one direction and that they must be cultivated in that direction; it was useless to try to do something for which I had no aptitude. But at that time a florid prose was admired. Richness of texture was sought by means of a jeweled phrase and sentences stiff with exotic epithets; the ideal was a brocade so heavy with gold that it stood up by itself. The intelligent young read Walter Pater with enthusiasm. My common sense suggested to me that it was anemic stuff; behind those elaborate, gracious periods I was conscious of a tired, wan personality. I was young, lusty, and energetic; I wanted fresh air, action, violence, and I found it hard to breathe that dead, heavily scented atmosphere and sit in those hushed rooms in which it was indecorous to speak above a whisper. But I would not listen to my common sense. I persuaded myself that this was the height of culture and turned a scornful shoulder on the outside world where men shouted and swore, played the fool, wenched and got drunk. I read *Intentions* and *The Picture of Dorian Gray.* I was intoxicated by the color and rareness of the fantastic words that thickly stud the pages of *Salome.* Shocked by the poverty of my own vocabulary, I went to the British Museum with pencil and paper and noted down the names of curious jewels, the Byzantine hues of old enamels, the sensual feel of textiles, and made elaborate sentences to bring them in. Fortunately I could never find an opportunity to use them and they lie there yet in an old notebook ready for anyone who has a mind to write nonsense. It was generally thought then that the Authorized Version of the Bible was the greatest piece of prose that the English language has produced. I read it diligently, especially the Song of Solomon, jotting down for future use turns of phrase that struck me and making lists of unusual or beautiful words. I studied Jeremy Taylor's *Holy Dying.* In order to assimilate his style I copied out passages and then tried to write them down from memory.

The first fruit of this labor was a little book about Andalusia called *The Land of the Blessed Virgin.* I had occasion to read parts of it the other day. I know Andalusia a great deal better now than I knew it then, and I have changed my mind about a good many things of which I wrote. Since it has continued in America to have a small sale, it occurred to me that it might be worth while to revise it. I soon saw that this was impossible. The book was written by someone I have completely forgotten. It bored me to distraction. But what I am concerned with is the prose, for it was as an exercise in style that I wrote it. It is wistful, allusive, and elaborate. It has neither ease nor spontaneity. It smells of hothouse plants and Sunday dinner like the air in the greenhouse that leads out of the dining-room of a big house in Bayswater. There are a great many melodious adjectives. The vocabulary is sentimental. It does not remind one of an Italian brocade, with its rich pattern of gold, but of a curtain material designed by Burne-Jones and reproduced by Morris.

I do not know whether it was a subconscious feeling that this sort of writing was contrary to my bent or a naturally methodical cast of mind that led me then to turn my attention to the writers of the Augustan Period. The prose of Swift enchanted me. I made up my mind that this was the perfect way to write and I started to work on him in the same way as I had done with Jeremy Taylor. I chose *The Tale of a Tub.* It is said that when the Dean re-read it in his old age he cried: "What genius I had then!" To my mind his genius was better shown in other works. It is a tiresome allegory and the irony is facile. But the style is admirable. I cannot imagine that English can be better written. Here are no flowery periods, fantastic turns of phrase or high-flown images. It is a civilized prose, natural, discreet, and pointed. There is no attempt to surprise by an extravagant vocabulary. It looks as though Swift made do with the first word that came to hand, but since he had an acute and logical brain it was always the right one, and he put it in the right place. The strength and balance of his sentences are due to an exquisite taste. As I had done before I copied passages and then tried to write them out again from memory. I tried altering words or the order in which they were set. I found that the only possible words were those Swift had used and that the order in which he had placed them was the only possible order. It is an impeccable prose.

But perfection has one grave defect: it is apt to be dull. Swift's prose is like a French canal, bordered with poplars, that runs through a gracious and undulating country. Its tranquil charm fills you with satisfaction, but it neither excites the emotions nor stimulates the imagination. You go on and on and presently you are a trifle bored. So, much as you may admire Swift's wonderful lucidity, his terseness, his naturalness, his lack of affectation, you find your attention wandering after a while unless his matter peculiarly interests you. I think if I had my time over again I would give to the prose of Dryden the close study I gave to that of Swift. I did not come across it till I had lost the inclination to take so much pains. The prose of Dryden is delicious. It has not the perfection of Swift nor the easy elegance of Addison, but it has a springtime gaiety, a conversational ease, a blithe spontaneousness that are enchanting. Dryden was a very good poet, but it is not the general opinion that he had a lyrical quality; it is strange that it is just this that sings in his softly sparkling prose. Prose had never been written in England like that before; it has seldom been written like that since. Dryden flourished at a happy moment. He had in his bones the sonorous periods and the baroque massiveness of Jacobean language and under the influence of the nimble and well-bred felicity that he learnt from the French he turned it into an instrument that was fit not only for solemn themes but also to express the light thought of the passing moment. He was the first of the rococo artists. If Swift reminds you of a French canal Dryden recalls an English river winding its cheerful way round hills, through quietly busy towns and by nestling villages, pausing now in a noble reach and then running powerfully through a woodland country. It is alive, varied, windswept; and it has the pleasant open-air smell of England.

The work I did was certainly very good for me. I began to write better; I did not write well. I wrote stiffly and self-consciously. I tried to get a pattern into my sentences, but did not see that the pattern was evident. I took care how I placed my words, but did not reflect that an order that was natural at the beginning of the eighteenth century was most unnatural at the beginning of ours. My attempt to write in the manner of Swift made it impossible for me to achieve the effect of inevitable rightness that was just what I so much admired in him. I then wrote a number of plays and ceased to occupy myself with anything but dialogue. It was not till five years had passed that I set out again to write a novel. By then I no longer had any ambition to be a stylist; I put aside all thought of fine writing. I wanted to write without any frills of language, in as bare and unaffected a manner as I could. I had so much to say that I could afford to waste no words. I wanted merely to set down the facts. I began with the impossible aim of using no adjectives at all. I thought that if you could find the exact term a qualifying epithet could be dispensed with. As I saw it in my mind's eye my book would have the appearance of an immensely long telegram in which for economy's sake you had left out every word that was not necessary to make the sense clear. I have not read it since I corrected the proofs and do not know how near I came to doing what I tried. My impression is that it is written at least more naturally than anything I had written before; but I am sure that it is often slipshod and I daresay there are in it a good many mistakes in grammar.

Since then I have written many other books; and though ceasing my methodical study of the old masters (for though the spirit is willing, the flesh is weak), I have continued with increasing assiduity to try to write better. I discovered my limitations and it seemed to me that the only sensible thing was to aim at what excellence I could within them. I knew that I had no lyrical quality. I had a small vocabulary and no efforts that I could make to enlarge it much availed me. I had little gift of metaphor; the original and striking simile seldom occurred to me. Poetic flights and the great imaginative sweep were beyond my powers. I could admire them in others as I could admire their far-fetched tropes and the unusual but suggestive language in which they clothed their thoughts, but my own invention never presented me with such embellishments; and I was tired of trying to do what did not come easily to me. On the other hand, I had an acute power of observation and it seemed to me that I could see a great many things that other people missed. I could put down in clear terms what I saw. I had a logical sense, and if no great feeling for the richness and strangeness of words, at all events a lively appreciation of their sound. I knew that I should never write as well as I could wish, but I thought with pains I could arrive at writing as well as my natural defects allowed. On taking thought it seemed to me that I must aim at lucidity, simplicity and euphony. I have put these three qualities in the order of the importance I assigned to them.

I have never had much patience with the writers who claim from the reader an effort to understand their meaning. You have only to go to the great philosophers to see that it is possible to express with lucidity the most subtle reflections. You may find it difficult to understand the thought of Hume, and if you have no philosophical training its implications will doubtless escape you; but no one with any education at all can fail to understand exactly what the meaning of each sentence is. Few people have written English with more grace than Berkeley. There are two sorts of obscurity that you find in writers. One is due to negligence and the other to willfulness. People often write obscurely because they have never taken the trouble to learn to write clearly. This sort of obscurity you find too often in modern philosophers, in men of science, and even in literary critics. Here it is indeed strange. You would have thought that men who passed their lives in the study of the great masters of literature would be sufficiently sensitive to the beauty of language to write if not beautifully at least with perspicuity. Yet you will find in their works sentence after sentence that you must read twice to discover the sense. Often you can only guess at it, for the writers have evidently not said what they intended.

Another cause of obscurity is that the writer is himself not quite sure of his meaning. He has a vague impression of what he wants to say, but has not, either from lack of mental power or from laziness, exactly formulated it in his mind and it is natural enough that he should not find a precise expression for a confused idea. This is due largely to the fact that many writers think, not before, but as they write. The pen originates the thought. The disadvantage of this, and indeed it is a danger against which the author must be always on his guard, is that there is a sort of magic in the written word. The idea acquires substance by taking on a visible nature, and then stands in the way of its own clarification. But this sort of obscurity merges very easily into the willful. Some writers who do not think clearly are inclined to suppose that their thoughts have a significance greater than at first sight appears. It is flattering to believe that they are too profound to be expressed so clearly that all who run may read, and very naturally it does not occur to such writers that the fault is with their own minds which have not the faculty of precise reflection. Here again the magic of the written word obtains. It is very easy to persuade oneself that a phrase that one does not quite understand may mean a great deal more than one realizes. From this there is only a little way to go to fall into the habit of setting down one's impressions in all their original vagueness. Fools can always be found to discover a hidden sense in them. There is another form of willful obscurity that masquerades as aristocratic exclusiveness. The author wraps his meaning in mystery so that the vulgar shall not participate in it. His soul is a secret garden into which the elect may penetrate only after overcoming a number of perilous obstacles. But this kind of obscurity is not only pretentious; it is shortsighted. For time plays it an odd trick. If the sense is meager, time reduces it to a meaningless verbiage that no one thinks of reading. This is the fate that has befallen the lucubrations of those French writers who were seduced by the example of Guillaume Apollinaire. But occasionally it throws a sharp cold light on what had seemed profound and thus discloses the fact that these contortions of language disguised very commonplace notions. There are few of Mallarmé's poems now that are not clear; one cannot fail to notice that his thought singularly lacked originality. Some of his phrases were beautiful; the materials of his verse were the poetic platitudes of his day.

Simplicity is not such an obvious merit as lucidity. I have aimed at it because I have no gift for richness. Within limits I admire richness in others, though I find it difficult to digest in quantity. I can read one page of Ruskin with delight, but twenty only with weariness. The rolling period, the stately epithet, the noun rich in poetic associations, the subordinate clauses that give the sentence weight and magnificence, the grandeur like that of wave following wave in the open sea; there is no doubt that in all this there is something inspiring. Words thus strung together fall on the ear like music. The appeal is sensuous rather than intellectual, and the beauty of the sound leads you easily to conclude that you need not bother about the meaning. But words are tyrannical things, they exist for their meanings, and if you will not pay attention to these, you cannot pay attention at all. Your mind wanders. This kind of writing demands a subject that will suit it. It is surely out of place to write in the grand style of inconsiderable things. No one wrote in this manner with greater success than Sir Thomas Browne, but even he did not always escape this pitfall. In the last chapter of *Hydriotaphia* the matter, which is the destiny of man, wonderfully fits the baroque splendor of the language, and here the Norwich doctor produced a piece of prose that has never been surpassed in our literature; but when he describes the finding of his urns in the same splendid manner the effect (at least to my taste) is less happy.

But if richness needs gifts with which everyone is not endowed, simplicity by no means comes by nature. To achieve it needs rigid discipline. So far as I know ours is the only language in which it has been found necessary to give a name to the piece of prose which is described as the purple patch; it would not have been necessary to do so unless it were characteristic. English prose is elaborate rather than simple. It was not always so. Nothing could be more racy, straightforward and alive than the prose of Shakespeare; but it must be remembered that this was dialogue written to be spoken. We do not know how he would have written if like Corneille he had composed prefaces to his plays. It may be that they would have been as euphuistic as the letters of Queen Elizabeth. But earlier prose, the prose of Sir Thomas More, for instance, is neither ponderous, flowery nor oratorical. It smacks of the English soil. To my mind King James's Bible has been a very harmful influence on English prose. I am not so stupid as to deny its great beauty. It is majestical. But the Bible is an oriental book. Its alien imagery has nothing to do with us. Those hyperboles, those luscious metaphors, are foreign to our genius. I cannot but think that not the least of the misfortunes that the Secession from Rome brought upon the spiritual life of our country is that this work for so long a period became the daily, and with many the only, reading of our people. Those rhythms, that powerful vocabulary, that grandiloquence, became part and parcel of the national sensibility. The plain, honest English speech was overwhelmed with ornament. Blunt Englishmen twisted their tongues to speak like Hebrew prophets. There was evidently something in the English temper to which this was congenial, perhaps a native lack of precision in thought, perhaps a naive delight in fine words for their own sake, an innate eccentricity and love of embroidery, I do not know; but the fact remains that ever since, English prose has had to struggle against the tendency to luxuriance. When from time to time the spirit of the language has reasserted itself, as it did with Dryden and the writers of Queen Anne, it was only to be submerged once more by the pomposities of Gibbon and Dr. Johnson. When English prose recovered simplicity with Hazlitt, the Shelley of the letters, and Charles Lamb at his best, it lost it again with De Quincey, Carlyle, Meredith, and Walter Pater. It is obvious that the grand style is more striking than the plain. Indeed many people think that a style that does not attract notice is not style. They will admire Walter Pater's, but will read an essay by Matthew Arnold without giving a moment's attention to the elegance, distinction and sobriety with which he set down what he had to say.

The dictum that the style is the man is well known. It is one of those aphorisms that say too much to mean a great deal. Where is the man in Goethe, in his birdlike lyrics or in his clumsy prose? And Hazlitt? But I suppose that if a man has a confused mind he will write in a confused way, if his temper is capricious his prose will be fantastical, and if he has a quick, darting intelligence that is reminded by the matter in hand of a hundred things, he will, unless he has great self-control, load his pages with metaphor and simile. There is a great difference between the magniloquence of the Jacobean writers, who were intoxicated with the new wealth that had lately been brought into the language, and the turgidity of Gibbon and Dr. Johnson, who were the victims of bad theories. I can read every word that Dr. Johnson wrote with delight, for he had good sense, charm and wit. No one could have written better if he had not willfully set himself to write in the grand style. He knew good English when he saw it. No critic has praised Dryden's prose more aptly. He said of him that he appeared to have no art other than that of expressing with clearness what he thought with vigor. And one of his *Lives* he finished with the words: "Whoever wishes to attain an English style, familiar but not coarse, and elegant but not ostentatious, must give his days and nights to the volumes of Addison." But when he himself sat down to write, it was with a very different aim. He mistook the orotund for the dignified. He had not the good breeding to see that simplicity and naturalness are the truest marks of distinction.

Whether you ascribe importance to euphony, the last of the three characteristics that I mentioned, must depend on the sensitiveness of your ear. A great many readers, and many admirable writers, are devoid of this quality. Poets as we know have always made a great use of alliteration. They are persuaded that the repetition of a sound gives an effect of beauty. I do not think it does so in prose. It seems to me that in prose alliteration should be used only for a special reason; when used by accident it falls on the ear very disagreeably. But its accidental use is so common that one can only suppose that the sound of it is not universally offensive. Many writers without distress will put two rhyming words together, join a monstrous long adjective to a monstrous long noun, or between the end of one word and the beginning of another have a conjunction of consonants that almost breaks your jaw. These are trivial and obvious instances. I mention them only to prove that if careful writers can do such things, it is only because they have no ear. Words have weight, sound, and appearance; it is only by considering these that you can write a sentence that is good to look at and good to listen to.

If you could write lucidly, simply, euphoniously and yet with liveliness you would write perfectly: you would write like Voltaire. And yet we know how fatal the pursuit of liveliness may be: it may result in the tiresome acrobatics of Meredith. Macaulay and Carlyle were in their different ways arresting; but at the heavy cost of naturalness. Their flashy effects distract the mind. They destroy their persuasiveness; you would not believe a man was very intent on plowing a furrow if he carried a hoop with him and jumped through it at every other step. A good style should show no sign of effort. What is written should seem a happy accident. I think no one in France now writes more admirably than Colette, and such is the ease of her expression that you cannot bring yourself to believe that she takes any trouble over it. I am told that there are pianists who have a natural technique so that they can play in a manner that most executants can achieve only as the result of unremitting toil, and I am willing to believe that there are writers who are equally fortunate. Among them I was much inclined to place Colette. I asked her. I was exceedingly surprised to hear that she wrote everything over and over again. She told me that she would often spend a whole morning working upon a single page. But it does not matter how one gets the effect of ease. For my part, if I get it at all, it is only by strenuous effort. Nature seldom provides me with the word, the turn of phrase, that is appropriate without being far-fetched or commonplace.

I have read that Anatole France tried to use only the constructions and the vocabulary of the writers of the seventeenth century whom he so greatly admired. I do not know if it is true. If so, it may explain why there is some lack of vitality in his beautiful and simple French. But simplicity is false when you do not say a thing that you should say because you cannot say it in a certain way. One should write in the manner of one's period. The language is alive and constantly changing; to try to write like the authors of a distant past can only give rise to artificiality. I should not hesitate to use the common phrases of the day, knowing that their vogue was ephemeral, or slang, though aware that in ten years it might be incomprehensible, if they gave vividness and actuality. If the style has a classical form it can support the discreet use of a phraseology that has only a local and temporary aptness. I would sooner a writer were vulgar than mincing; for life is vulgar, and it is life he seeks.

I think that we English authors have much to learn from our fellow authors in America. For American writing has escaped the tyranny of King James's Bible and American writers have been less affected by the old masters whose mode of writing is part of our culture. They have formed their style, unconsciously perhaps, more directly from the living speech that surrounds them; and at its best it has a directness, a vitality, and a drive that give our more urbane manner an air of languor. It has been an advantage to American writers, many of whom at one time or another have been reporters, that their journalism has been written in a more trenchant, nervous, graphic English than ours. For we read the newspaper as our ancestors read the Bible. Not without profit either; for the newspaper, especially when it is of the popular sort, offers us a part of experience that we writers cannot afford to miss. It is raw material straight from the knacker's yard, and we are stupid if we turn up our noses because it smells of blood and sweat. We cannot, however willingly we would, escape the influence of this workaday prose. But the journalism of a period has very much the same style; it might all have been written by the same hand; it is impersonal. It is well to counteract its effect by reading of another kind. One can do this only by keeping constantly in touch with the writing of an age not too remote from one's own. So can one have a standard by which to test one's own style and an ideal which in one's modern way one can aim at. For my part the two writers I have found most useful to study for this purpose are Hazlitt and Cardinal Newman. I would try to imitate neither. Hazlitt can be unduly rhetorical; and sometimes his decoration is as fussy as Victorian Gothic. Newman can be a trifle flowery. But at their best both are admirable. Time has little touched their style; it is almost contemporary. Hazlitt is vivid, bracing, and energetic; he has strength and liveliness. You feel the man in his phrases, not the mean, querulous, disagreeable man that he appeared to the world that knew him, but the man within of his own ideal vision. (And the man within us is as true in reality as the man, pitiful and halting, of our outward seeming.) Newman had an exquisite grace, music, playful sometimes and sometimes grave, a woodland beauty of phrase, dignity and mellowness. Both wrote with extreme lucidity. Neither is quite as simple as the purest taste demands. Here I think Matthew Arnold excels them. Both had a wonderful balance of phrase and both knew how to write sentences pleasing to the eye. Both had an ear of extreme sensitiveness.

If anyone could combine their merits in the manner of writing of the present day, he would write as well as it is possible for anyone to write.

EXERCISES

1. Maugham makes a good case for the lucid, direct style. Can you make as good a case for the rhetorical or "grand" style? In answering this question, refer to specific writers and to their subjects.
2. What does Maugham think of American writing?
3. Maugham tried to imitate Swift's prose. What is the value in imitating an established writer's work? What is the danger?

2 *from* THE SERMON ON THE MOUNT

There were several partial translations of the Bible, made from the Latin Vulgate, prior to the fourteenth century. The first major translation was the Wycliffe Bible, completed in 1380. Later versions were prepared by William Tindale (who translated the First Testament from the Greek) in the sixteenth century and Michael Coverdale's Bible, the first complete English Bible to be printed. This included Tindale's translation of the Pentateuch and New Testament and translations from the Vulgate and other versions. The Authorized Version, *which drew heavily on earlier versions, was prepared by a body of scholars working together under the auspices of King James I. The work was completed and published in 1611.*

The Authorized Version of the Bible, *commonly called the King James' Version, is probably the most widely and persistently read book ever published in the English language. Many writers have derived their themes from the Bible—Milton for one—and even more have studied the richness of its diction and the beauty of its style. Countless phrases from the* Authorized Version *have become part of our spoken and written language. Many of these can be found in "The Sermon on the Mount."*

(*Matthew*, 6)

1 Take heed that ye do not your alms before men, to be seen of them: otherwise ye have no reward of your Father which is in heaven.

2 Therefore when thou doest *thine* alms, do not sound a trumpet before thee, as the hypocrites do in the synagogues and in the streets, that they may have glory of men. Verily I say unto you, They have their reward.

3 But when thou doest alms, let not thy left hand know what thy right hand doeth:

4 That thine alms may be in secret: and thy Father which seeth in secret himself shall reward thee openly.

5 ¶ And when thou prayest, thou shalt not be as the hypocrites *are*: for they love to pray standing in the synagogues and in the corners of the streets, that they may be seen of men. Verily I say unto you, They have their reward.

6 But thou, when thou prayest, enter into thy closet, and when thou hast shut thy door, pray to thy Father which is in secret; and thy Father which seeth in secret shall reward thee openly.

7 But when ye pray, use not vain repetitions, as the heathen *do*: for they think that they shall be heard for their much speaking.

8 Be not ye therefore like unto them: for your Father knoweth what things ye have need of, before ye ask him.

9 After this manner therefore pray ye: Our Father which art in heaven, Hallowed be thy name.

10 Thy kingdom come. Thy will be done in earth, as *it is* in heaven.

11 Give us this day our daily bread.

12 And forgive us our debts, as we forgive our debtors.

13 And lead us not into temptation, but deliver us from evil: For thine is the kingdom, and the power, and the glory, for ever. Amen.

14 For if ye forgive men their trespasses, your heavenly Father will also forgive you:

15 But if ye forgive not men their trespasses, neither will your Father forgive your trespasses.

16 ¶ Moreover when ye fast, be not, as the hypocrites, of a sad coun-

tenance: for they disfigure their faces, that they may appear unto men to fast. Verily I say unto you, They have their reward.

17 But thou, when thou fastest, anoint thine head, and wash thy face;

18 That thou appear not unto men to fast, but unto thy Father which is in secret: and thy Father which seeth in secret shall reward thee openly.

19 ¶ Lay not up for yourselves treasures upon earth, where moth and rust doth corrupt, and where thieves break through and steal:

20 But lay up for yourselves treasures in heaven, where neither moth nor rust doth corrupt, and where thieves do not break through nor steal:

21 For where your treasure is, there will your heart be also.

22 The light of the body is the eye: if therefore thine eye be single, thy whole body shall be full of light.

23 But if thine eye be evil, thy whole body shall be full of darkness. If therefore the light that is in thee be darkness, how great *is* that darkness!

24 ¶ No man can serve two masters: for either he will hate the one, and love the other; or else he will hold to the one, and despise the other. Ye cannot serve God and mammon.

25 Therefore I say unto you, Take no thought for your life, what ye shall eat, or what ye shall drink; nor yet for your body, what ye shall put on. Is not the life more than meat, and the body than raiment?

26 Behold the fowls of the air: for they sow not, neither do they reap, nor gather into barns; yet your heavenly Father feedeth them. Are ye not much better than they?

27 Which of you by taking thought can add one cubit unto his stature?

28 And why take ye thought for raiment? Consider the lilies of the field, how they grow; they toil not, neither do they spin:

29 And yet I say unto you, That even Solomon in all his glory was not arrayed like one of these.

30 Wherefore, if God so clothe the grass of the field, which to-day is, and to-morrow is cast into the oven, *shall he* not much more *clothe* you, O ye of little faith?

31 Therefore take no thought, saying, What shall we eat? or, What shall we drink? or, Wherewithal shall we be clothed?

32 (For after all these things do the Gentiles seek:) for your heavenly Father knoweth that ye have need of all these things.

33 But seek ye first the kingdom of God, and his righteousness; and all these things shall be added unto you.

34 Take therefore no thought for the morrow: for the morrow shall take thought for the things of itself. Sufficient unto the day *is* the evil thereof.

EXERCISES

1. E. M. Forster in an essay entitled "English Prose Between 1918 and 1939" says that the English of the "Authorized Version [has] at last become remote from popular English." He quotes the following from a speech by Colonel Oliver Stanley, "Cables and Wireless":

> When the end comes, when victory is won, then history will begin to assess merit. We shall all of us be searching our conscience. . . . We shall be discussing who succeeded and who failed. . . . I have no doubt at all, when we come to discuss the part that "Cable and Wireless" has played, what the verdict of the nation will be—"Well done, thou good and faithful servant."

Mr. Forster says that the quotation from St. Matthew's Gospel (chapter 25, verse 23) obviously did not come from Colonel Stanley's blood, it came from his cliché box. Why does Forster say this?

2. Rewrite one verse of your choice, using a twentieth-century idiom.

3. Read any passage of your choice in the King James Version of the Bible and the same passage in a modern revised version. Which do you prefer? Why?

3 OF LOVE

by Francis Bacon

Sir Francis Bacon (1561–1626) had a many-sided career as a statesman, philosopher, and essayist. He held political office during the reign of Queen Elizabeth and under James I became Lord Chancellor. Charged with bribery and corruption, he confessed his guilt before the House of Lords and was briefly imprisoned in the Tower. After his release he retired from public life. His contributions to philosophy and the pursuit of scientific inquiry stem from Novum Organum *and* Of the Advancement of Learning. *His literary reputation rests on the latter and on his* Essays *and* New Atlantis. New Atlantis *is a fragmentary sketch of a utopian commonwealth; the* Essays *deal with many subjects and are remarkable for their controlled style. Viewing Bacon's achievements and political villainies, Alexander Pope called him "the wisest, brightest, meanest of mankind."*

Bacon wrote in a number of styles, depending on his subject. In Of the Advancement of Learning, *he frequently used loose, descriptive sentences; in the* Essays *he wrote a tight, pithy, allusive style. Many of the sentences from his* Essays *have attained the status of proverbs.*

The stage is more beholding to love, than the life of man. For as to the stage, love is ever matter of comedies, and now and then of tragedies; but in life it doth much mischief; sometimes like a siren, sometimes like a fury. You may observe that amongst all the great and worthy persons (whereof the memory remaineth, either ancient or recent) there is not one that hath been transported to the mad degree of love: which shows that great spirits and great business do keep out this weak passion. You must except nevertheless Marcus Antonius, the half partner of the empire of Rome, and Appius Claudius, the decemvir and lawgiver; whereof the former was indeed a voluptuous man, and inordinate; but the latter was an austere and wise man: and therefore it seems (though rarely) that love can find entrance not only into an open heart, but also into a heart well fortified, if watch be not well kept. It is a poor saying of Epicurus, *Satis magnum alter alteri theatrum sumus;*[1] as if man, made for the contemplation of heaven and all noble objects, should do nothing but kneel before a little idol, and make himself a subject, though not of the mouth (as beasts are), yet of the eye; which was given him for higher purposes. It is a strange thing to note the excess of this passion, and how it braves the nature and value of things, by this; that the speaking in a perpetual hyperbole is comely in nothing but in love. Neither is it merely in the phrase; for whereas it hath been well said that the arch-flatterer, with whom all the petty flatterers have intelligence, is a man's self; certainly the lover is more. For there was never proud man thought so absurdly well of himself as the lover doth of the person loved; and therefore it was well said, *That it is impossible to love and to be wise.* Neither doth this weakness appear to others only, and not to the party loved; but to the loved most of all, except the love be reciproque.[2] For it is a true rule, that love is ever rewarded either with the reciproque or with an inward and secret contempt. By how much the more men ought to beware of this passion, which loseth not only other things, but itself! As for the other losses, the poet's relation doth well figure them: that he that preferred Helena, quitted the gifts of Juno and Pallas. For whosoever esteemeth too much of amorous affection quitteth both riches and wisdom. This passion hath his floods in the very times of weakness; which are great prosperity and great adversity; though this latter hath been less observed: both which times kindle love, and make it more fervent, and therefore show it to be the child of folly. They do best, who if they cannot but admit love, yet make it keep quarter; and sever it wholly from their serious affairs and actions of life; for if it check once with business, it troubleth men's fortunes, and maketh men that they can no ways be true to their own ends. I know not how, but martial men are given to love: I think it

[1] We are for each other a sufficiently large theater.
[2] reciprocal.

is but as they are given to wine; for perils commonly ask to be paid in pleasures. There is in man's nature a secret inclination and motion towards love of others, which if it be not spent upon some one or a few, doth naturally spread itself towards many, and maketh men become humane and charitable; as it is seen sometime in friars. Nuptial love maketh mankind; friendly love perfecteth it; but wanton love corrupteth and embaseth it.

EXERCISES

1. Check the meaning of the term *aphorism*. We suggested that Bacon's style in this essay is aphoristic; point out four or five sentences that you would consider aphoristic.
2. Check on the meaning of the term *allusive*. Show why Bacon's style here is characterized as allusive. Can you think of any twentieth-century writers you have read whose style is allusive?
3. What do you think of Bacon's view of romantic love?

4 *from* HYDRIOTAPHIA, OR URN BURIAL

by Thomas Browne

Sir Thomas Browne (1605–82) a physician by profession, was also a scholar and writer. He studied medicine in England and abroad and opened a practice near Halifax. His literary works include Religio Medici, Urn Burial, *and* The Garden of Cyrus. *An encyclopedic treatise on Common and Vulgar Errors filled with recondite knowledge earned him an international reputation and was translated into several languages.*

Urn Burial, *from which the following brief selection is taken, was inspired by the discovery of some Roman burial urns in Norfolk. Browne began by discussing various modes of burial throughout history and then meditated on the solemnity of death and the vicissitudes of fame. Highly ornate, Latinate in diction, this aspires to the highest reaches of rhetoric, but it is not lacking in humor.*

Of Ambition and Fame

Now since these dead bones have already outlasted the living ones of Methuselah, and in a yard under ground, and thin walls of clay, outworn all the strong and specious buildings above it; and quietly rested under the drums and tramplings of three conquests: what prince can promise such diuturnity unto his relics, or might not gladly say,

Sic ego componi versus in ossa velim? [1]

Time, which antiquates antiquities, and hath an art to make dust of all things, hath yet spared these minor monuments.

In vain we hope to be known by open and visible conservatories, when to be unknown was the means of their continuation, and obscurity their protection. If they died by violent hands, and were thrust into their urns, these bones become considerable, and some old philosophers would honor them, whose souls they conceived most pure, which were thus snatched from their bodies, and to retain a stronger propension unto them; whereas they weariedly left a languishing corpse, and with faint desires of reunion. If they fell by long and aged decay, yet wrapped up in the bundle of time, they fall into indistinction, and make but one blot with infants. If we begin to die when we live, and long life be but a prolongation of death, our life is a sad composition; we live with death, and die not in a moment. How many pulses made up the life of Methuselah, were work for Archimedes: [2] common counters sum up the life of Moses his man. Our days become considerable, like petty sums, by minute accumulations; where numerous fractions make up but small round numbers; and our days of a span long, make not one little finger. . . .

EXERCISES

1. Browne writes in what Maugham calls the ornate style. One of Maugham's points is that this style demands a subject matter worthy of it. Write a paragraph or two in which you justify the appropriateness or criticize the inappropriateness of Browne's style to his subject.
2. What similarities, if any, can you find in Browne's style and that of "The Sermon on the Mount" and Bacon's "Essay on Love"?

[1] Do I wish I were turned into bones?
[2] Greek mathematician.

5 *from* THE AREOPAGITICA

by John Milton

John Milton (1608–74) is famous of course as a major English poet. Educated at Cambridge, he first contemplated the Anglican ministry, but then decided on a secular career. He spent several years in independent study preparing himself to compose something the world "would not willingly let die." Lycidas *(1637) is among the better known of his earlier works—his greatest is* Paradise Lost *(completed around 1663).* Paradise Regained *and* Samson Agonistes *were published together in 1671. Apart from his career as a poet, Milton was politically active in Cromwell's revolt against the Stuarts and held office under the Commonwealth. With the Restoration, he was for a short time imprisoned and lost the major part of his fortune.*

Milton wrote a number of pamphlets on theological and political matters. Two of these, advocating divorce (arising out of an unfortunate personal experience) brought him in conflict with Parliament which wanted to enforce a licensing law that would in effect make possible censorship of printed matter. This led Milton to write a violent attack on censorship—the Areopagitica [1]*—addressed to the Parliament. He showed that censorship through licensing had been the practice of those (the Stuarts) whom the Parliament had overthrown. He pointed to the threat that censorship presents to the advancement of learning and the development of character.*

I deny not but that it is of greatest concernment in the Church and Commonwealth to have a vigilant eye how books demean themselves as well as men; and thereafter to confine, imprison, and do sharpest justice on them as malefactors. For books are not absolutely dead things, but do contain a potency of life in them to be as active as that soul was whose progeny they are; nay, they do preserve as in a vial the purest efficacy and extraction of that living intellect that bred them. I know they are as lively, and as vigorously productive, as those fabulous dragon's teeth; and being sown up and down, may chance to spring up armed men. And yet, on the other hand, unless wariness be used, as good almost kill a man as kill a good book: who kills a man kills a reasonable creature, God's image;

[1] Areopagus refers to the hill of Ares in Athens, the meeting place of the highest judicial tribunal in the city.

but he who destroys a good book, kills reason itself, kills the image of God, as it were, in the eye. Many a man lives a burden to the earth; but a good book is the precious life-blood of a master spirit, embalmed and treasured up on purpose to a life beyond life. 'Tis true, no age can restore a life, whereof perhaps there is no great loss; and revolutions of ages do not oft recover the loss of a rejected truth, for the want of which whole nations fare the worse. We should be wary, therefore, what persecution we raise against the living labors of public men, how we spill that seasoned life of man, preserved and stored up in books; since we see a kind of homicide may be thus committed, sometimes a martyrdom; and if it extend to the whole impression, a kind of massacre, whereof the execution ends not in the slaying of an elemental life, but strikes at that ethereal and fifth essence, the breath of reason itself, slays an immortality rather than a life. . . .

Good and evil we know in the field of this world grow up together almost inseparably; and the knowledge of good is so involved and interwoven with the knowledge of evil, and in so many cunning resemblances hardly to be discerned, that those confused seeds which were imposed upon Psyche as an incessant labor to cull out, and sort asunder, were not more intermixed. It was from out the rind of one apple tasted, that the knowledge of good and evil, as two twins cleaving together, leaped forth into the world. And perhaps this is that doom which Adam fell into of knowing good and evil, that is to say, of knowing good by evil.

As therefore the state of man now is, what wisdom can there be to choose, what continence to forbear without the knowledge of evil? He that can apprehend and consider vice with all her baits and seeming pleasures, and yet abstain, and yet distinguish, and yet prefer that which is truly better, he is the true wayfaring Christian. I cannot praise a fugitive and cloistered virtue, unexercised and unbreathed, that never sallies out and sees her adversary, but slinks out of the race where that immortal garland is to be run for, not without dust and heat. Assuredly we bring not innocence into the world, we bring impurity much rather: that which purifies us is trial, and trial is by what is contrary. That virtue therefore which is but a youngling in the contemplation of evil, and knows not the utmost that vice promises to her followers, and rejects it, is but a blank virtue, not a pure; her whiteness is but an excremental whiteness; which was the reason why our sage and serious poet Spenser, whom I dare be known to think a better teacher than Scotus or Aquinas, describing true temperance under the person of Guion, brings him in with his palmer through the cave of Mammon and the bower of earthly bliss, that he might see and know, and yet abstain.

Since therefore, the knowledge and survey of vice is in this world so necessary to the constituting of human virtue, and the scanning of error to the confirmation of truth, how can we more safely, and with less danger, scout into the regions of sin and falsity, than by reading all manner of tractates and hearing all manner of reason? And this is the benefit which may be had of books promiscuously read. . . .

EXERCISES

1. One of Milton's students has said: "There is no light prose in Milton. It is the prose of a classical humanist. . . ." One of the terms commonly applied to Milton's style, in prose as well as in poetry, is "majestic." How might one justify the term?

2. The "Areopagitica" is commonly looked upon as one of the great documents in the constant fight against censorship. Is the solemnity and complexity of its language a help or hindrance in its influence on the twentieth-century fight for freedom of expression?

3. What arguments does Milton use against anything but the most minor government or church censorship?

6 A MODEST PROPOSAL

by Jonathan Swift

Jonathan Swift (1667–1745) was one of the finest prose writers and satirists in the English language. Ordained as an Anglican minister, he had active political connections with the English Tory leaders and exerted considerable influence through his political pamphlets. In spite of recognition and some success in his career in the Church and as a writer, he also suffered many disappointments both in his professional and personal life. He had a number of unhappy love affairs, the details of which are obscure. One of them, with Esther Johnson (whom he may have secretly married), resulted in his Journal to Stella,[1] *a volume of letters in cryptic language; it includes accounts of his daily life, his friends, and activities. His most famous book,* Gulliver's Travels, *is a powerful and bitter satire on human nature in general and on particular aspects of English politics in his time. Among others of his works are* The Battle of the Books *and* A Tale of a Tub, *also in the satirical vein.*

A Modest Proposal *was written as a protest against economic conditions in Ireland. It reveals Swift's irony at its best—for his passion was expressed in highly controlled, lucid prose admirably suited for argumentation.*

[1] A pseudonym for Esther Johnson.

It is a melancholy object to those who walk through this great town or travel in the country, when they see the streets, the roads, and cabin-doors crowded with beggars of the female sex, followed by three, four, or six children, all in rags, and importuning every passenger for an alms. These mothers instead of being able to work for their honest livelihood, are forced to employ all their time in strolling to beg sustenance for their helpless infants, who, as they grow up, either turn thieves for want of work, or leave their dear native country, to fight for the Pretender in Spain, or sell themselves to the Barbadoes.

I think it is agreed by all parties, that this prodigious number of children in the arms, or on the backs, or at the heels of their mothers, and frequently of their fathers, is in the present deplorable state of the kingdom a very great additional grievance; and therefore whoever could find out a fair, cheap, and easy method of making these children sound and useful members of the common-wealth, would deserve so well of the public as to have his statue set up for a preserver of the nation.

But my intention is very far from being confined to provide only for the children of professed beggars; it is of a much greater extent, and shall take in the whole number of infants at a certain age, who are born of parents in effect as little able to support them, as those who demand our charity in the streets.

As to my own part, having turned my thoughts, for many years, upon this important subject, and maturely weighed the several schemes of other projectors, I have always found them grossly mistaken in their computation. It is true, a child just dropt from its dam, may be supported by her milk for a solar year with little other nourishment, at most not above the value of two shillings, which the mother may certainly get, or the value in scraps, by her lawful occupation of begging; and it is exactly at one year old that I propose to provide for them in such a manner, as, instead of being a charge upon their parents, or the parish, or wanting food and raiment for the rest of their lives, they shall, on the contrary, contribute to the feeding and partly to the clothing of many thousands.

There is likewise another great advantage in my scheme, that it will prevent those voluntary abortions, and that horrid practice of women murdering their bastard children, alas! too frequent among us—sacrificing the poor innocent babes, I doubt, more to avoid the expense than the shame—which would move tears and pity in the most savage and inhuman breast.

The number of souls in this kingdom being usually reckoned one million and a half, of these I calculate there may be about two hundred thousand couple whose wives are breeders; from which number I subtract thirty thousand couples, who are able to maintain their own children, although I apprehend there cannot be so many, under the present distresses of the kingdom; but this being granted, there will remain an hundred and seventy thousand breeders. I again subtract fifty thousand, for those women who miscarry, or whose children die by accident or disease within the year. There only remain an hundred and twenty thousand children of poor parents annually born: The question therefore is, How this number shall be reared, and provided for? which, as I have already said, under the present situation of affairs, is utterly impossible by all the methods hitherto proposed; for we can neither employ them in handicraft or agriculture; we neither build houses, (I mean in the country) nor cultivate land: They can very seldom pick up a livelihood by stealing till they arrive at six years old, except where they are of towardly parts, although, I confess, they learn the rudiments much earlier; during which time they can however be properly looked upon only as probationers; as I have been informed by a principal gentleman in the county of Cavan, who protested to me, that he never knew above one or two instances under the age of six, even in a part of the kingdom so renowned for the quickest proficiency in that art.

I am assured by our merchants, that a boy or a girl before twelve years old, is no saleable commodity, and even when they come to this age, they will not yield above three pounds, or three pounds and half a crown at most, on the exchange; which cannot turn to account either to the parents or kingdom, the charge of nutriment and rags having been at least four times that value.

I shall now therefore humbly propose my own thoughts, which I hope will not be liable to the least objection.

I have been assured by a very knowing American of my acquaintance in London, that a young healthy child well nursed is at a year old a most delicious nourishing and wholesome food, whether stewed, roasted, baked, or boiled; and I make no doubt that it will equally serve in a fricasse, or a ragout.

I do therefore humbly offer it to publick consideration, that of the hundred and twenty thousand children, already computed, twenty thousand may be reserved for breed, whereof only one fourth part to be males; which is more than we allow to sheep, black cattle, or swine, and my reason is, that these children are seldom the fruits of marriage, a circumstance not much regarded by our savages; therefore, one male will be sufficient to serve four females. That the remaining hundred thousand may at a year old be offered in sale to the persons of quality and fortune, through the kingdom, always advising the mother to let them suck plentifully in the last month, so as to render them plump, and fat for a good table. A child will make two dishes at an entertainment for friends, and when the family dines alone, the fore or hind quarter will make a reasonable dish, and seasoned with a little pepper or salt will be very good boiled on the fourth day, especially in winter.

I have reckoned upon a medium, that a child just born will weigh 12 pounds, and in a solar year, if tolerably nursed, encreaseth to 28 pounds.

I grant this food will be somewhat dear, and therefore very proper for landlords, who, as they have already devoured most of the parents seem to have the best title to the children.

Infant's flesh will be in season throughout the year, but more plentiful in March, and a little before and after; for we are told by a grave author, an eminent French physician, that fish being a prolifick dyet, there are more children born in Roman Catholick countries about nine months after Lent, than at any other season; therefore reckoning a year after Lent, the markets will be more glutted than usual, because the number of popish infants, is at least three to one in this kingdom, and therefore it will have one other collateral advantage, by lessening the number of papists among us.

I have already computed the charge of nursing a beggar's child (in which list I reckon all cottagers, labourers, and four fifths of the farmers) to be about two shillings per annum, rags included; and I believe no gentleman would repine to give ten shillings for the carcass of a good fat child, which, as I have said will make four dishes of excellent nutritive meat, when he hath only some particular friend, or his own family to dine with him. Thus the squire will learn to be a good landlord, and grow popular among his tenants; the mother will have eight shillings neat profit, and be fit for work till she produces another child.

Those who are more thrifty (as I must confess the times require) may flay the carcass; the skin of which, artifically dressed, will make admirable gloves for ladies, and summer boots for fine gentlemen.

As to our city of Dublin, shambles may be appointed for this purpose, in the most convenient parts of it, and butchers we may be assured will not be wanting; although I rather recommend buying the children alive, and dressing them hot from the knife, as we do roasting pigs.

A very worthy person, a true lover of his country, and whose virtues I highly esteem, was lately pleased, in discoursing on this matter, to offer a refinement upon my scheme. He said, that many gentlemen of this kingdom, having of late destroyed their deer, he conceived that the want of venison might be well supplied by the bodies of young lads and maidens, not exceeding fourteen years of age, nor under twelve; so great a number of both sexes in every country being now ready to starve, for want of work and service: And these to be disposed of by their parents if alive, or otherwise by their nearest relations. But with due deference to so excellent a friend, and so deserving a patriot, I cannot be altogether in his sentiments; for as to the males, my American acquaintance assured me from frequent experience, that their flesh was generally tough and lean, like that of our schoolboys, by continual exercise, and their taste disagreeable, and to fatten them would not answer the charge. Then as to the females, it would, I think with humble submission, be a loss to the publick, because they soon would become breeders themselves: And besides it is not improbable that some scrupulous people might be apt to censure such a practice (although indeed very unjustly) as a little bordering upon cruelty, which, I confess, hath always been with me the strongest objection against any project, how well soever intended.

But in order to justify my friend, he confessed, that this expedient was put into his head by the famous Psalmanazar, a native of the island Formosa, who came from thence to London, above twenty years ago, and in conversation told my friend, that in his country when any young person happened to be put to death, the executioner sold the carcass to persons of quality, as a prime dainty, and that, in his time, the body of a plump girl of fifteen, who was crucified for an attempt to poison the Emperor, was sold to his Imperial Majesty's prime minister of state, and other great mandarins of the court, in joints from the gibbet, at four hundred crowns. Neither indeed can I deny, that if the same use were made of several plump young girls in this town, who, without one single groat to their fortunes, cannot stir abroad without a chair, and appear at a play-house and assemblies in foreign fineries which they never will pay for; the kingdom would not be the worse.

Some persons of a desponding spirit are in great concern about that vast number of poor people, who are aged, diseased, or maimed, and I have been desired to employ my thoughts what course may be taken, to ease the nation of so grievous an encumbrance. But I am not in the least pain upon that matter, because it is very well known, that they are every day dying, and rotting, by cold, and famine, and filth, and vermin, as fast as can be reasonably expected. And as to the younger labourers, they are now in almost as hopeful a condition. They cannot get work, and consequently pine away for want of nourishment, to a degree, that if at any time they are accidentally hired to common labour, they have not strength to perform it, and thus the country and themselves are happily delivered from the evils to come.

I have too long digressed, and therefore shall return to my subject. I think the advantages by the proposal which I have made are obvious and many, as well as of the highest importance.

For *first*, as I have already observed, it would greatly lessen the number of papists, with whom we are yearly over-run, being the principal breeders of the nation, as well as our most dangerous enemies, and who stay at home on purpose with a design to deliver the kingdom to the Pretender, hoping to take their advantage by the absence of so many good Protestants, who have chosen rather to leave their country, than stay at home, and pay tithes against their conscience to an episcopal curate.

Secondly, the poorer tenants will have something valuable of their own which by law may be made liable to distress, and help to pay their landlord's rent, their corn and cattle being already seized, and money a thing unknown.

Thirdly, whereas the maintenance of an hundred thousand children, from two years old, and upwards, cannot be computed at less than ten shillings a piece per annum, the nation's stock will be thereby increased fifty thousand pounds per annum, besides the profit of a new dish, introduced to the tables of all gentlemen of fortune in the kingdom who have any refinement in taste, and the money will circulate among our selves, the goods being entirely of our own growth and manufacture.

Fourthly, the constant breeders, besides the gain of eight shillings sterling per annum, by the sale of their children, will be rid of the charge of maintaining them after the first year.

Fifthly, this food would likewise bring great custom to taverns, where the vintners will certainly be so prudent as to procure the best receipts for dressing it to perfection; and consequently have their houses frequented by all the fine gentlemen, who justly value themselves upon their knowledge in good eating; and a skilful cook, who understands how to oblige his guests, will contrive to make it as expensive as they please.

Sixthly, this would be a great inducement to marriage, which all wise nations have either encouraged by rewards, or enforced by laws and penalties. It would encrease the care and tenderness of mothers towards their children, when they were sure of a settlement for life to the poor babes, provided in some sort by the publick, to their annual profit instead of expence; we should soon see an honest emulation among the married women, which of them could bring the fattest child to the market. Men would become as fond of their wives during the time of their pregnancy, as they are now of their mares in foal, their cows in calf, or sows when they are ready to farrow, nor offer to beat or kick them (as is too often a practice) for fear of a miscarriage.

Many other advantages might be enumerated. For instance, the addition of some thousand carcasses in our exportation of barreled beef: the propagation of swine's flesh, and improvement in the art of making good bacon, so much wanted among us by the great destruction of pigs, too frequent at our tables, which are no way comparable in taste or magnificence to a well grown, fat yearling child, which roasted whole will make a considerable figure at a Lord Mayor's feast, or any other publick entertainment. But this, and many others, I omit, being studious of brevity.

Supposing that one thousand families in this city, would be constant customers for infant's flesh, besides others who might have it at merry meetings, particularly at weddings and christenings, I compute that Dublin would take off annually about twenty thousand carcasses, and the rest of the kingdom (where probably they will be sold somewhat cheaper) the remaining eighty thousand.

I can think of no one objection, that will possibly be raised against this proposal, unless it should be urged, that the number of people will be thereby much lessened in the kingdom. This I freely own, and 'twas indeed one principal design in offering it to the world. I desire the reader will observe, from the inclemencies of the weather, and the most inevitable prospect of entailing the like, or greater miseries, upon their breed for ever.

I profess in the sincerity of my heart, that I have not the least personal interest in endeavouring to promote this necessary work, having no other motive than the publick good of my country, by advancing our trade, providing for infants, relieving the poor, and giving some pleasure to the rich. I have no children by which I can propose to get a single penny; the youngest being nine years old and my wife past child-bearing.

EXERCISES

1. Maugham admires Swift's prose and says: "It is a civilized prose, natural, discreet and pointed. There is no attempt to surprise by an extravagant vocabulary. It looks as though Swift had made do with the first word that came to hand, but since he had an acute and logical brain it was always the right one, and he put it in the right place." After reading "A Modest Proposal" do you consider Maugham's assessment extravagant or justified? Give your reasons.
2. Some readers of "A Modest Proposal" have taken the piece at face value. Does this denote a failing on the part of Swift or on the part of those readers? Is there always a danger in the use of irony because of the possibility of misinterpretation?
3. Outline Swift's arguments in support of his "Proposal." Recalling the section on "Arguing a Thesis," would you say that his points lead to an "inescapable conclusion"? Is your reaction to his argument influenced by the "unhumanitarian" nature of his proposal?

7 | BOOKS *

by Samuel Johnson

Samuel Johnson (1709–84) was particularly influential in literary circles during his time. He is best known to posterity through the work of his very fine biographer, James Boswell, to whom he owed much of his reputation as a great writer. Johnson studied briefly at Oxford, conducted a private school for two years in Lichfield (his birthplace) and in 1737, arrived in London accompanied by the actor David Garrick. He contributed to The Gentleman's Magazine *and in 1738, published a poem, "London." For seven years he worked on his* Dictionary, *published in 1755. He also wrote a series of short biographies,* Lives of the Poets *and a novel,* Rasselas.

In 1747, Johnson submitted his "Plan" for the Dictionary to Lord Chesterfield, whose patronage he wished to obtain. The latter ignored Johnson's appeal, but, when the Dictionary was about to be published, wrote two favorable notices on it for the World. *Johnson angrily repudiated Chesterfield in the letter which follows. He was a man of learning and solemn dignity—these characteristics are manifest in his style both in the essay on "Books" and in his letter to Chesterfield.*

One of the peculiarities which distinguish the present age is the multiplication of books. Every day brings new advertisements of literary undertakings, and we are flattered with repeated promises of growing wise on easier terms than our progenitors.

How much either happiness or knowledge is advanced by this multitude of authors, it is not very easy to decide. He that teaches us anything which we knew not before, is undoubtedly to be reverenced as a master. He that conveys knowledge by more pleasing ways may very properly be loved as a benefactor; and he that supplies life with innocent amusement will be certainly caressed as a pleasing companion. But few of those who fill the world with books have any pretensions to the hope either of pleasing or instructing. They have often no other task than to lay two books before them, out of which they compile a third, without any new materials of their own, and with very little application of judgment to those which former authors have supplied.

* From *The Idler*, No. 85. Saturday, December 1, 1759.

That all compilations are useless I do not assert. Particles of science are often very widely scattered. Writers of extensive comprehension have incidental remarks upon topics very remote from the principal subject, which are often more valuable than formal treatises, and which yet are not known because they are not promised in the title. He that collects those under proper heads is very laudably employed, for, though he exerts no great abilities in the work, he facilitates the progress of others, and, by making that easy of attainment which is already written, may give some mind, more vigorous or more adventurous than his own, leisure for new thoughts and original designs.

But the collections poured lately from the press have been seldom made at any great expense of time or inquiry, and therefore only serve to distract choice without supplying any real want. It is observed that "a corrupt society has many laws," and I know not whether it is not equally true that an ignorant age has many books. When the treasures of ancient knowledge lie unexamined, and original authors are neglected and forgotten, compilers and plagiaries are encouraged, who give us again what we had before, and grow great by setting before us what our own sloth had hidden from our view.

Yet are not even these writers to be indiscriminately censured and rejected. Truth, like beauty, varies its fashions, and is best recommended by different dresses to different minds; and he that recalls the attention of mankind to any part of learning which time has left behind it may be truly said to advance the literature of his own age. As the manners of nations vary, new topics of persuasion become necessary, and new combinations of imagery are produced; and he that can accommodate himself to the reigning taste may always have readers who perhaps would not have looked upon better performances. To exact of every man who writes that he should say something new would be to reduce authors to a small number; to oblige the most fertile genius to say only what is new would be to contract his volumes to a few pages. Yet surely there ought to be some bounds to repetition. Libraries ought no more to be heaped forever with the same thoughts differently expressed, than with the same books differently decorated.

The good or evil which these secondary writers produce is seldom of any long duration. As they owe their existence to change of fashion, they commonly disappear when a new fashion becomes prevalent. The authors that in any nation last from age to age are few, because there are very few that have any other claim to notice than that they catch hold on present curiosity, and gratify some accidental desire, or produce some temporary conveniency.

But, however the writers of the day may despair of future fame, they ought at least to forbear any present mischief. Though they cannot arrive at eminent heights of excellence, they might keep themselves harmless.

They might take care to inform themselves before they attempt to inform others, and exert the little influence which they have for honest purposes. But such is the present state of our literature, that the ancient sage who thought "a great book a great evil" would now think the multitude of books a multitude of evils. He would consider a bulky writer who engrossed a year, and a swarm of pamphleteers who stole each an hour, as equal wasters of human life, and would make no other difference between them than between a beast of prey and a flight of locusts.

LETTER TO LORD CHESTERFIELD

February 7, 1755.

My Lord,

I have been lately informed, by the proprietor of the World, that two papers, in which my Dictionary is recommended to the publick, were written by your Lordship. To be so distinguished, is an honour, which, being very little accustomed to favours from the great, I know not well how to receive, or in what terms to acknowledge.

When, upon some slight encouragement, I first visited your Lordship, I was overpowered, like the rest of mankind, by the enchantment of your address; and could not forbear to wish that I might boast myself *Le vainqueur du vainqueur de la terre;*—that I might obtain that regard for which I saw the world contending; but I found my attendance so little encouraged, that neither pride nor modesty would suffer me to continue it. When I had once addressed your Lordship in publick, I had exhausted all the art of pleasing which a retired and uncourtly scholar can possess. I had done all that I could; and no man is well pleased to have his all neglected, be it ever so little.

Seven years, my Lord, have now past, since I waited in your outward rooms, or was repulsed from your door; during which time I have been pushing on my work through difficulties, of which it is useless to complain, and have brought it, at last, to the verge of publication, without one act of assistance, one word of encouragement, or one smile of favour. Such treatment I did not expect, for I never had a Patron before.

The shepherd in Virgil grew at last acquainted with Love, and found him a native of the rocks.

Is not a Patron, my Lord, one who looks with unconcern on a man struggling for life in the water, and, when he has reached ground, encumbers him with help? The notice which you have been pleased to take of my labours, had it been early, had been kind; but it has been delayed til I am indifferent, and cannot enjoy it; till I am solitary, and cannot impart it; till I am known, and do not want it. I hope it is no very cynical asperity not to confess obligations where no benefit has been received, or to be unwilling that the Publick should consider me as owing that to a Patron, which Providence has enabled me to do for myself.

Having carried on my work thus far with so little obligation to any favourer of learning, I shall not be disappointed though I should conclude it, if less be possible, with less; for I have been long wakened from that dream of hope, in which I once boasted myself with so much exultation,

My Lord,
Your Lordship's most humble,
Most obedient servant,
Sam. Johnson

EXERCISES

1. Johnson is held by critics and literary historians to have been a great prose stylist, and a number of students have analyzed his prose. The following are considered to be characteristic of his style: (a) a preference for abstract terms; (b) a fondness for polysyllables; (c) arrangement of clauses in parallel or balanced patterns; or (d) the forming of subjects from infinitives or "that" clauses. Write an analysis of "Books" in which you discuss Johnson's style in the light of the four characteristics listed here.

2. Characterize the tone of Johnson's letter to Lord Chesterfield. Can you conceive of a similar situation confronting a contemporary author? If you can, in what ways would his letter differ from Johnson's?

8 *from* THE IDEA OF A UNIVERSITY

by John Henry Newman

John Henry Newman (1801–90) studied at Oxford and was one of the leaders of the Tractarian (Oxford) Movement which sought to revitalize the Church of England. In 1845, Newman joined the Catholic Church and in 1879, was made a Cardinal. For a time he was rector of the new Catholic University in Dublin, a position from which he resigned due to differences with the Irish clergy. However, it was while at Dublin that he delivered the famous lectures later published as The Idea of a University Defined, *from which the following selection is taken. Newman's best-known work is his autobiographical* Apologia Pro Vita Sua, *an explanation of his intellectual position and his conversion. A religious poem,* The Dream of Gerontius, *was set to music by Sir Edward Elgar.*

Newman has been hailed as one of the finest of English prose writers. His prose is facile, supple, and cogent. "A Definition of a Gentleman" is a choice example of his simple and elegant style.

A *Definition of a Gentleman*

Hence it is that it is almost a definition of a gentleman to say he is one who never inflicts pain. This inscription is both refined and, as far as it goes, accurate. He is mainly occupied in merely removing the obstacles which hinder the free and unembarrassed action of those about him; and he concurs with their movements rather than takes the initiative himself. His benefits may be considered as parallel to what are called comforts or conveniences in arrangements of a personal nature: like an easy chair or a good fire, which do their part in dispelling cold and fatigue, though nature provides both means of rest and animal heat without them. The true gentleman in like manner carefully avoids whatever may cause a jar or a jolt in the minds of those with whom he is cast;—all clashing of opinion, or collision of feeling, all restraint, or suspicion, or gloom, or resentment; his great concern being to make every one at their ease and at home. He has his eyes on all his company; he is tender towards the bashful, gentle towards the distant, and merciful towards the absurd; he can recollect to whom he is speaking; he guards against unseasonable allusions, or topics which may irritate; he is seldom prominent in conversation, and never wearisome. He makes light of favours while he does them, and seems to be receiving when he is conferring. He never speaks of himself except when compelled, never defends himself by a mere retort, he has no ears for slander or gossip, is scrupulous in imputing motives to those who interfere with him, and interprets everything for the best. He is never mean or little in his disputes, never takes unfair advantage, never mistakes personalities or sharp sayings for arguments, or insinuates evil which he dare not say out. From a long-sighted prudence, he observes the maxim of the ancient sage, that we should ever conduct ourselves towards our enemy as if he were one day to be our friend. He has too much good sense to be affronted at insults, he is too well employed to remember injuries, and too indolent to bear malice. He is patient, forbearing, and resigned, on philosophical principles; he submits to pain, because it is inevitable, to bereavement, because it is irreparable, and to death, because it is his destiny. If he engages in controversy of any kind, his disciplined intellect preserves him from the blundering discourtesy of better, though less educated minds; who, like blunt weapons, tear and hack instead of cutting clean, who mistake the point in argument, waste their strength on trifles, misconceive their adversary, and leave the question more involved than they find it. He may be right or wrong in his opinion, but he is too clear-headed to be unjust; he is as simple as he is forcible, and as brief as he is decisive. Nowhere shall we find greater candour, consideration, indulgence: he throws himself into the minds of his opponents, he accounts for their mistakes. He knows the weakness of human reason as well as its strength, its province and its limits. If he be an unbeliever, he will be too profound and large-minded to ridicule religion or to act against it; he is too wise to be a dogmatist or fanatic in his infidelity. He respects piety and devotion; he even supports institutions as venerable, beautiful, or useful, to which he does not assent; he honours the ministers of religion, and he is contented to decline its mysteries without assailing or denouncing them. He is a friend of religious toleration, and that, not only because his philosophy has taught him to look on all forms of faith with an impartial eye, but also from the gentleness and effeminacy of feeling, which is the attendant on civilisation.

Not that he may not hold a religion too, in his own way, even when he is not a Christian. In that case his religion is one of imagination and sentiment; it is the embodiment of those ideas of the sublime, majestic, and beautiful, without which there can be no large philosophy. Sometimes he acknowledges the being of God, sometimes he invests an unknown principle or quality with the attributes of perfection. And this deduction of his reason, or creation of his fancy, he makes the occasion of such excellent thoughts, and the starting-point of so varied and systematic a teaching, that he even seems like a disciple of Christianity itself. From the very accuracy and steadiness of his logical powers, he is able to see what sentiments are consistent in those who hold any religious doctrine at all, and he appears to others to feel and to hold a whole circle of theological truths which exist in his mind not otherwise than as a number of deductions.

Such are some of the lineaments of the ethical character, which the cultivated intellect will form, apart from religious principle. They are seen within the pale of the Church and without it, in holy men and in profligate; they form the *beau ideal* of the world; they partly assist and partly distort the development of the Catholic. They may subserve the education of a St. Francis or a Cardinal Pole; they may be the limits of the virtue of a Shaftesbury or a Gibbon. Basil and Julian were fellow-students at the schools of Athens, and one became a saint and doctor of the Church, the other her scoffing and relentless foe. (1852)

EXERCISES

1. One student of English prose style has said that Newman has two great virtues as a stylist, one, his ability to handle difficult subjects clearly and simply,

and, two, a personal, colloquial tone. Write a paragraph in which you characterize (using illustrations) Newman's style.

2. What is there about the conduct of a gentleman as discussed by Newman which could, paradoxically, "partly assist and partly distort the development of the Catholic" or of anyone committed to a strict religious and moral code?

9 *from* THE AUTOBIOGRAPHY

by Thomas Henry Huxley

Thomas Henry Huxley (1825–95) earned his medical degree from the University of London and specialized in marine biology. As one of the chief exponents of Darwin's evolutionary theory, he was nicknamed "Darwin's Bulldog." A prolific writer, he contributed much to awakening popular interest in science. His books include Man's Place in Nature, The Physical Basis of Life, *and* Ethics and Evolution. *He was the grandfather of both Julian and Aldous Huxley.*

The following excerpt is from Huxley's Autobiography. *The style is literary and polished without being ornate or florid.*

The last thing that it would be proper for me to do would be to speak of the work of my life, or to say at the end of the day whether I think I have earned my wages or not. Men are said to be partial judges of themselves. Young men may be, I doubt if old men are. Life seems terribly foreshortened as they look back and the mountain they set themselves to climb in youth turns out to be a mere spur of immeasurably higher ranges when, by failing breath, they reach the top. But if I may speak of the objects I have had more or less definitely in view since I began the ascent of my hillock, they are briefly these: To promote the increase of natural knowledge and to forward the application of scientific methods of investigation to all the problems of life to the best of my ability, in the conviction which has grown with my growth and strengthened with my strength, that there is no alleviation for the sufferings of mankind except veracity of thought and of action, and the resolute facing of the world as it is when the garment of make-believe by which pious hands have hidden its uglier features is stripped off.

It is with this intent that I have subordinated any reasonable, or unreasonable, ambition for scientific fame which I may have permitted myself to entertain to other ends; to the popularization of science; to the development and organization of scientific education; to the endless series of battles and skirmishes over evolution; and to untiring opposition to that ecclesiastical spirit, that clericalism, which in England, as everywhere else, and to whatever denomination it may belong, is the deadly enemy of science.

In striving for the attainment of these objects, I have been but one among many, and I shall be well content to be remembered, or even not remembered, as such. Circumstances, among which I am proud to reckon the devoted kindness of many friends, have led to my occupation of variout prominent positions, among which the Presidency of the Royal Society is the highest. It would be mock modesty on my part, with these and other scientific honors which have been bestowed upon me, to pretend that I have not succeeded in the career which I have followed, rather because I was driven into it than of my own free will; but I am afraid I should not count even these things as marks of success if I could not hope that I had somewhat helped that movement of opinion which has been called the New Reformation.

EXERCISES

1. What does Huxley mean by "New Reformation"?
2. Is there any internal evidence (style or subject matter) that this passage was written by a Victorian?

10 *from* STUDIES IN THE HISTORY OF THE RENAISSANCE

by Walter Horatio Pater

Walter Horatio Pater (1839–94) was educated at Oxford and spent most of his life there as a teacher. He resisted the growing emphasis on scientific thought and upheld the importance of the personal, the idiosyncratic, and the emotional or subjective approach to life. Pater stressed the importance of beauty and formal perfection in art. He was a spokesman for the art for art's sake movement, and in his own work strove for the formal beauty it advocated. Among his best-known works are a collection of essays, Studies in the History of the Renaissance, *a philosophical novel,* Marius the Epicurean, Imaginary Portraits, *and* Appreciations.

Pater's style was subtle, highly refined, and ornate. His sentences are scrupulously and meticulously wrought. But for all his emphasis on emotion, there is something labored, metallic about his writing.

Philosophiren, says Novalis, *ist dephlegmatisiren vivificiren.*[1] The service of philosophy, of speculative culture, towards the human spirit is to rouse, to startle it into sharp and eager observation. Every moment some form grows perfect in hand or face; some tone on the hills or the sea is choicer than the rest; some mood of passion or insight or intellectual excitement is irresistibly real and attractive for us,—for that moment only. Not the fruit of experience, but experience itself, is the end. A counted number of pulses only is given to us of a variegated, dramatic, life. How may we see in them all that is to be seen in them by the finest senses? How shall we pass most swiftly from point to point, and be present always at the focus where the greatest number of vital forces unite in their purest energy?

To burn always with this hard, gemlike flame, to maintain this ecstasy, is success in life. In a sense it might even be said that our failure is to form habits: for, after all, habit is relative to a stereotyped world, and meantime it is only the roughness of the eye that makes any two persons, things, situations, seem alike. While all melts under our feet, we may well catch at any exquisite passion, or any contribution to knowledge that seems by a lifted horizon to set the spirit free for a moment, or any stirring of the senses, strange dyes, strange colors, and curious odors, or work of the artist's hands, or the face of one's friend. Not to discriminate every moment some passionate attitude in those about us, and in the brilliancy of their gifts some tragic dividing of forces on their ways, is, on this short day of frost and sun, to sleep before evening. With this sense of the splendor of our experience and of its awful brevity, gathering all we are into one desperate effort to see and touch, we shall hardly have time to make theories about the things we see and touch. What we have to do is to be forever curiously testing new opinions and courting new impressions, never acquiescing in a facile orthodoxy of Comte, or of Hegel, or of our own. Philosophical theories or ideas, as points of view, instruments of criticism, may help us to gather up what might otherwise pass unregarded by us. "Philosophy is the microscope of thought." The theory or idea or system which requires of us the sacrifice of any part of this experience, in consideration of some interest into which we cannot enter, or some abstract theory we have not identified with ourselves, or what is only conventional, has no real claim upon us.

One of the most beautiful passages in the writings of Rousseau is that

[1] To be a philosopher is to rid oneself of sluggishness, to come to life.

in the sixth book of the *Confessions,* where he describes the awakening in him of the literary sense. An undefinable taint of death had always clung about him, and now in early manhood he believed himself smitten by mortal disease. He asked himself how he might make as much as possible of the interval that remained; and he was not biased by anything in his previous life when he decided that it must be by intellectual excitement, which he found just then in the clear, fresh writings of Voltaire. Well! we are all *condamnés,* as Victor Hugo says: we are all under sentence of death but with a sort of indefinite reprieve—*les hommes sont tous condamnés à mort avec des sursis indéfinis:* we have an interval, and then our place knows us no more. Some spend this interval in listlessness, some in high passions, the wisest, at least among "the children of this world," in art and song. For our one chance lies in expanding that interval, in getting as many pulsations as possible into the given time. Great passions may give us this quickened sense of life, ecstasy and sorrow of love, the various forms of enthusiastic activity, disinterested or otherwise, which come naturally to many of us. Only be sure it is passion—that it does yield you this fruit of a quickened, multiplied consciousness. Of this wisdom, the poetic passion, the desire of beauty, the love of art for art's sake, has most; for art comes to you professing frankly to give nothing but the highest quality to your moments as they pass, and simply for those moments' sake.

EXERCISES

1. Pater is concerned with the difference between what he calls "experience" and generalized, abstract knowledge. What is his point?
2. What is the tone of Pater's style? Illustrate.
3. Is Pater's style more or less emotional than Huxley's? Illustrate.

11 SELF-RELIANCE

by Ralph Waldo Emerson

Ralph Waldo Emerson (1803–82) was born in Boston and educated at Harvard. Ordained as a minister, he resigned over a difference in theology. A tour of Europe brought him the friendship of several eminent English writers, particularly Wordsworth, Coleridge, and Carlyle, who stimulated his interest in German idealism. Under this influence, Emerson, together with a number of New England writers, founded the Transcendental[1] *Club, whose literary paper,* The Dial, *Emerson edited for a short period. Henry Thoreau and Nathaniel Hawthorne were among the members of this Club. Emerson lectured widely on literature and human culture and wrote both essays and poetry. His works include* Essays, Representative Men *(a series of lectures)* Poems, *and* Society and Solitude.

"Self-Reliance" is among the best-known of Emerson's essays. A fine stylist, he is said to have been less concerned with the structure and logic of his essays and lectures than with his style. His writing is poetic, his sentences suggestive.

Trust thyself: every heart vibrates to that iron string. Accept the place the divine providence has found for you, the society of your contemporaries, the connection of events. Great men have always done so, and confided themselves childlike to the genius of their age, betraying their perception that the absolutely trustworthy was seated at their heart, working through their hands, predominating in all their being. And we are now men, and must accept in the highest mind the same transcendent destiny; and not minors and invalids in a protected corner, not cowards fleeing before a revolution, but guides, redeemers and benefactors, obeying the Almighty effort and advancing on Chaos and the Dark.

What pretty oracles nature yields us on this text in the face and behavior of children, babes, and even brutes! That divided and rebel mind, that distrust of a sentiment because our arithmetic has computed the strength and means opposed to our purpose, these have not. Their mind being whole, their eye is as yet unconquered, and when we look in their

[1] The term "transcendental" derives from Emerson's essay ("Nature") on the relation of the soul to nature. His doctrine is based on the philosophy of the German idealists, particularly on Kant's *Critique of Pure Reason.*

faces we are disconcerted. Infancy conforms to nobody; all conform to it; so that one babe commonly makes four or five out of the adults who prattle and play to it. So God has armed youth and puberty and manhood no less with its own piquancy and charm, and made it enviable and gracious and its claims not to be put by, if it will stand by itself. Do not think the youth has no force, because he cannot speak to you and me. Hark! in the next room his voice is sufficiently clear and emphatic. It seems he knows how to speak to his contemporaries. Bashful or bold then, he will know how to make us seniors very unnecessary.

The nonchalance of boys who are sure of a dinner, and would disdain as much as a lord or do or say aught to conciliate one, is the healthy attitude for human nature. A boy is in the parlor what the pit is in the playhouse; independent, irresponsible, looking out from his corner on such people and facts as pass by, he tries and sentences them on their merits, in the swift, summary way of boys, as good, bad, interesting, silly, eloquent, troublesome. He cumbers himself never about consequences, about interests; he gives an independent, genuine verdict. You must court him; he does not court you. But the man is as it were clapped into jail by his consciousness. As soon as he has once acted or spoken with *éclat* he is a committed person, watched by the sympathy or the hatred of hundreds, whose affections must now enter into his account. There is no Lethe for this. Ah, that he could pass again into his neutrality! Who can thus avoid all pledges and, having observed, observe again from the same unaffected, unbiased, unbribable, unaffrighted innocence,—must always be formidable. He would utter opinions on all passing affairs, which being seen to be not private but necessary, would sink like darts into the ear of men and put them in fear.

These are the voices which we hear in solitude, but they grow faint and inaudible as we enter into the world. Society everywhere is in conspiracy against the manhood of every one of its members. Society is a joint-stock company, in which the members agree, for the better securing of his bread to each shareholder, to surrender the liberty and culture of the eater. The virtue in most request is conformity. Self-reliance is its aversion. It loves not realities and creators, but names and customs.

Whoso would be a man, must be a nonconformist. He who would gather immortal palms must not be hindered by the name of goodness, but must explore if it be goodness. Nothing is at last sacred but the integrity of your own mind. Absolve you to yourself, and you shall have the suffrage of the world. I remember an answer which when quite young I was prompted to make to a valued adviser who was wont to importune me with the dear old doctrines of the church. On my saying, "What have I to do with the sacredness of traditions, if I live wholly from within?" my friend suggested,—"But these impulses may be from below, not from above." I replied, "They do not seem to me to be such; but if I am the Devil's child, I will live then from the Devil." No law can be sacred to me but that of my nature. Good and bad are but names very readily transferable to that or this; the only right is what is after my constitution; the only wrong what is against it. A man is to carry himself in the presence of all opposition as if every thing were titular and ephemeral but he. I am ashamed to think how easily we capitulate to badges and names, to large societies and dead institutions. Every decent and well-spoken individual affects and sways me more than is right. I ought to go upright and vital, and speak the rude truth in all ways. If malice and vanity were the coat of philanthropy, shall that pass? If an angry bigot assumes this bountiful cause of Abolition, and comes to me with his last news from Barbadoes, why should I not say to him, "Go love thy infant; love thy wood-chopper; be good-natured and modest; have that grace; and never varnish your hard, uncharitable ambition with this incredible tenderness for black folk a thousand miles off. Thy love afar is spite at home." Rough and graceless would be such greeting, but truth is handsomer than the affectation of love. Your goodness must have some edge to it,—else it is none. The doctrine of hatred must be preached, as the counteraction of the doctrine of love, when that pules and whines. I shun father and mother and wife and brother when my genuis calls me. I would write on the lintels of the door-post, *Whim*. I hope it is somewhat better than whim at last, but we cannot spend the day in explanation. Expect me not to show cause why I seek or why I exclude company. Then again, do not tell me, as a good man did today, of my obligation to put all poor men in good situations. Are they *my* poor? I tell thee, thou foolish philanthropist, that I grudge the dollar, the dime, the cent I give to such men as do not belong to me and to whom I do not belong. There is a class of persons to whom by all spiritual affinity I am bought and sold; for them I will go to prison if need be; but your miscellaneous popular charities; the education at college of fools; the building of meeting-houses to the vain end to which many now stand; alms to sots, and the thousand-fold Relief Societies;—though I confess with shame I sometimes succumb and give the dollar, it is a wicked dollar, which by and by I shall have the manhood to withhold.

philanthropy

Virtues are, in the popular estimate, rather the exception than the rule. There is the man *and* his virtues. Men do what is called a good action, as some piece of courage or charity, much as they would pay a fine in expiation of daily non-appearance on parade. Their works are done as an apology or extenuation of their living in the world,—as invalids and the insane pay a high board. Their virtues are penances. I do not wish to expiate, but to live. My life is for itself and not for a spectacle. I much prefer that it should be of a lower strain, so it be genuine and equal, than that it should be glittering and unsteady. I wish it to be sound and sweet, and not to need diet and bleeding. I ask primary evidence that you are a man, and refuse this appeal from the man to his actions. I know that for myself it makes no difference whether I do or forbear those actions which are reckoned excellent. I cannot consent to pay for a privilege where I have intrinsic right. Few and mean as my gifts may be, I actually am, and do not need for my own assurance or the assurance of my fellows any secondary testimony.

What I must do is all that concerns me, not what the people think. This rule, equally arduous in actual and in intellectual life, may serve for the whole distinction between greatness and meanness. It is the harder because you will always find those who think they know what is your duty better than you know it. It is easy in the world to live after the world's opinion; it is easy in solitude to live after our own; but the great man is he who in the midst of the crowd keeps with perfect sweetness the independence of solitude.

The objection to conforming to usages that have become dead to you is that it scatters your force. It loses your time and blurs the impression of your character. If you maintain a dead church, contribute to a dead Bible-society, vote with a great party either for the government or against it, spread your table like base housekeepers,—under all these screens I have difficulty to detect the precise man you are: and of course so much force is withdrawn from your proper life. But do your work, and I shall know you. Do your work, and you shall reinforce yourself. A man must consider what a blind-man's-buff is this game of conformity. If I know your sect I anticipate your argument. I hear a preacher announce for his text and topic the expediency of one of the institutions of his church. Do I not know beforehand that not possibly can he say a new and spontaneous word? Do I not know that with all this ostentation of examining the grounds of the institution he will do no such thing? Do I not know that he is pledged to himself not to look but at one side, the permitted side, not as a man, but as a parish minister? He is a retained attorney, and these airs of the bench are the emptiest affectation. Well, most men have bound their eyes with one or another handkerchief, and attached themselves to some one of these communities of opinion. This conformity makes them not false in a few particulars, authors of a few lies, but false in all particulars. Their every truth is not quite true. Their two is not the the real two, their four not the real four; so that every word they say chagrins us and we know not where to begin to set them right. Meantime nature is not slow to equip us in the prison-uniform of the party to which we adhere. We come to wear one cut of face and figure, and acquire by degrees the gentlest asinine expression. There is a mortifying experience in particular, which does not fail to wreak itself also in the general history; I mean "the foolish face of praise," the forced smile which we put on in company where we do not feel at ease, in answer to conversation which does not interest us. The muscles, not spontaneously moved but moved by a low usurping willfulness, grow tight about the outline of the face, with the most disagreeable sensation.

For nonconformity the world whips you with its displeasure. And therefore a man must know how to estimate a sour face. The by-standers look askance on him in the public street or in the friend's parlor. If this aversion had its origin in contempt and resistance like his own he might well go home with a sad countenance; but the sour faces of the multitude, like their sweet faces, have no deep cause, but are put on and off as the wind blows and a newspaper directs. Yet is the discontent of the multitude more formidable than that of the senate and the college? It is easy enough for a firm man who knows the world to brook the rage of the cultivated classes. Their rage is decorous and prudent, for they are timid, as being very vulnerable themselves. But when to their feminine rage the indignation of the people is added, when the ignorant and the poor are aroused, when the unintelligent brute force that lies at the bottom of society is made to growl and mow, it needs the habit of magnanimity and religion to treat it godlike as a trifle of no concernment.

The other terror that scares us from self-trust is our consistency; a reverence for our past act or word because the eyes of others have no other data for computing our orbit than our past acts, and we are loth to disappoint them.

But why should you keep your head over your shoulder? Why drag about this corpse of your memory, lest you contradict somewhat you have stated in this or that public place? Suppose you should contradict yourself; what then? It seems to be a rule of wisdom never to rely on your memory alone, scarcely even in acts of pure memory, but to bring the past for judgment into the thousand-eyed present, and live ever in a new day. In your metaphysics you have denied personality to the Deity, yet when the devout motions of the soul come, yield to them heart and life, though they should clothe God with shape and color. Leave your theory, as Joseph his coat in the hand of the harlot, and flee.

A foolish consistency is the hobgoblin of little minds, adored by little statesmen and philosophers and divines. With consistency a great soul has simply nothing to do. He may as well concern himself with his shadow on the wall. Speak what you think now in hard words and tomorrow speak what tomorrow thinks in hard words again, though it contradict everything you said today.—"Ah, so you shall be sure to be misunderstood." Is it so bad then to be misunderstood? Pythagoras was misunderstood, and Socrates, and Jesus, and Luther, and Copernicus, and Galileo, and Newton, and every pure and wise spirit that ever took flesh. To be great is to be misunderstood. . . .

EXERCISES

1. *The Literary History of the United States* (1946) says this about Emerson's style: "The new form which Emerson developed is neither wholly essay nor wholly lecture. Its unit is the carefully wrought sentence. . . . Each contains in crystalline suspension the whole meaning of the essay. . . ." Write a short essay giving your views on this characterization of Emerson's style in relation to "Self-Reliance."

2. Compare Emerson's style to Huxley's and Pater's. Can you find any clear indication that Emerson was an American while the other two writers were English?

3. Is there anything in the content or style of this essay which clearly places Emerson as a nineteenth- rather than a twentieth-century writer?

12 *from* WHAT PAUL BOURGET THINKS OF US *

by Mark Twain

Mark Twain (Samuel L. Clemens; 1835–1910) had a varied career as printer's devil, steamboat pilot, soldier, miner, journalist, and author. Raised in Hannibal, Missouri on the banks of the Mississippi, he retained almost perfect recollection of his childhood and youth there, and drew heavily on these memories for his most famous works, Life on the Mississippi, The Adventures of Tom Sawyer, *and* The Adventures of Huckleberry Finn. *His experiences as a frontier town reporter in Nevada and California yielded many humorous sketches and stories, including "The Celebrated Jumping Frog of Calaveras County," while his observations abroad led to his famous* Innocents Abroad.

Twain is considered by many literary historians as the most typically American of our writers. Certainly at a time when Henry James was writing about America "and with this vast new world, je n'ai que faire" *(see p. 8), Twain found much to say about*

* Published originally in the *North American Review,* CLX: 48–62, 1895. Paul Bourget (1852–1935) was a French novelist who in 1894 recorded his impressions of the United States.

America. When he described things European it was consciously through American eyes, and with a tendency to mock those things on which Europeans most prided themselves. Too, his off-hand, breezy manner can perhaps be considered typically American. The following review eloquently pleads Twain's belief that one can write meaningfully about America only after long and firsthand experience.

. . . A foreigner can photograph the exteriors of a nation, but I think that that is as far as he can get. I think that no foreigner can report its interior—its soul, its life, its speech, its thought. I think that a knowledge of these things is acquirable in only one way—not two or four or six—*absorption;* years and years of unconscious absorption; years and years of intercourse with the life concerned; of living it, indeed; sharing personally in its shames and prides, its joys and griefs, its loves and hates, its prosperities and reverses, its shows and shabbinesses, its deep patriotisms, its whirlwinds of political passion, its adorations—of flag, and heroic dead, and the glory of the national name. Observation? Of what real value is it? One learns peoples through the heart, not the eyes or the intellect.

There is only one expert who is qualified to examine the souls and the life of a people and make a valuable report—the native novelist. This expert is so rare that the most populous country can never have fifteen conspicuously and confessedly competent ones in stock at one time. This native specialist is not qualified to begin work until he has been absorbing during twenty-five years. How much of his competency is derived from conscious "observation"? The amount is so slight that it counts for next to nothing in the equipment. Almost the whole capital of the novelist is the slow accumulation of *un*conscious observation—absorption. The native expert's intentional observation of manners, speech, character, and ways of life can have value, for the native knows what they mean without having to cipher out the meaning. But I should be astonished to see a foreigner get at the right meanings, catch the elusive shades of these subtle things. Even the native novelist becomes a foreigner, with a foreigner's limitations, when he steps from the state whose life is familiar to him into a state whose life he has not lived. Bret Harte got his California and his Californians by unconscious absorption, and put both of them into his tales alive. But when he came from the Pacific to the Atlantic and tried to do Newport life from study—conscious observation—his failure was absolutely monumental. Newport is a disastrous place for the unacclimated observer, evidently.

To return to novel-building. Does the native novelist try to generalize the nation? No, he lays plainly before you the ways and speech and life of a few people grouped in a certain place—his own place—and that is one book. In time he and his brethren will report to you the life and the people of the whole nation—the life of a group in a New England village; in a New York village; in a Texan village; in an Oregon village; in villages in fifty states and territories; then the farm-life in fifty states and territories; a hundred patches of life and groups of people in a dozen widely separated cities. And the Indians will be attended to; and the cowboys; and the gold and silver miners; and the negroes; and the Idiots and Congressmen; and the Irish, the Germans, the Italians, the Swedes, the French, the Chinamen, the Greasers; and the Catholics, the Methodists, the Presbyterians, the Congregationalists, the Baptists, the Spiritualists, the Mormons, the Shakers, the Quakers, the Jews, the Campbellites, the infidels, the Christian Scientists, the Mind-Curists, the Faith-Curists, the Train-robbers, the White Caps, the Moonshiners. And when a thousand able novels have been written, *there* you have the soul of the people, the life of the people, the speech of the people; and not anywhere else can these be had. And the shadings of character, manners, feelings, ambitions, will be infinite.

EXERCISES

1. There are at least two forms of repetition—of phrases and of ideas—in this selection. Point out examples.
2. How does Twain achieve his humor in this selection?
3. Do you find anything particularly "American" about Twain's style?
4. Twain mentions several qualifications that a novelist must have to capture the "souls and life of a people." What are they? Do you agree or disagree? Give your reasons. Would you add any further qualifications to Twain's list?
5. How would you relate this essay to the debate on "American Literature Abroad" in Section IV? What do you think Twain's position would have been in such a debate?

13 | *from* THE ART OF FICTION

by Henry James

Henry James (for biographical note see page 6) is now regarded as one of the most distinguished American novelists. In the following essay he discusses the ways in which a creative writer gathers material for his work and transforms it into art. James was constantly aware of the problems of artistry. His detractors believe this preoccupation caused him to be detached from everyday actuality; some of them find his fiction bloodless. His admirers believe it helped him to make highly refined distinctions, both in character drawing and in the development of his themes. Whatever one feels about his fiction, it is clear that as a critic James made basic distinctions and then shaded his arguments subtly.

. . . It is equally excellent and inconclusive to say that one must write from experience; to our suppositious aspirant such a declaration might savor of mockery. What kind of experience is intended, and where does it begin and end? Experience is never limited, and it is an immense sensibility, a kind of huge spider-web of the finest silken threads suspended in the chamber of consciousness, and catching every air-borne particle in its tissue. It is the very atmosphere of the mind; and when the mind is imaginative—much more when it happens to be that of a man of genius—it takes to itself the faintest hints of life, it converts the very pulses of the air into revelations. The young lady living in a village has only to be a damsel upon whom nothing is lost to make it quite unfair (as it seems to me) to declare to her that she shall have nothing to say about the military. Greater miracles have been seen than that, imagination assisting, she should speak the truth about some of these gentlemen. I remember an English novelist, a woman of genius, telling me that she was much commended for the impression she had managed to give in one of her tales of the nature and way of life of the French Protestant youth. She had been asked where she learned so much about this recondite being, she had been congratulated on her peculiar opportunities. These opportunities consisted in her having once, in Paris, as she ascended a staircase, passed an open door where, in the household of a *pasteur*, some of the young Protestants were seated at table round a finished meal. The glimpse made a picture; it lasted only a moment, but that moment was experience. She had got her direct personal impression, and she turned out her type. She knew what youth was, and what Protestantism; she also had the advantage of having seen what it was to be French, so that she converted these ideas into a concrete image and produced a reality. Above all, however, she was blessed with the faculty which when you give it an inch takes an ell, and which for the artist is a much greater source of strength than any accident of residence or of place in the social scale. The power to guess the unseen from the seen, to trace the implication of things, to judge the whole piece by the pattern, the condition of feeling life in general so completely that you are well on your way to knowing any particular corner of it—this cluster of gifts may almost be said to constitute experience, and they occur in country and in town, and in the most differing stages of education. If experience consists of impressions, it may be said that impressions are experience, just as (have we not seen it?) they are the very air we breathe. Therefore, if I should certainly say to a novice, "Write from experience and from experience only," I should feel that this was rather a tantalizing monition if I were not careful immediately to add, "Try to be one of the people on whom nothing is lost!"

I am far from intending by this to minimize the importance of exactness—of truth of detail. One can speak best from one's own taste, and I may therefore venture to say that the air of reality (solidity of specification) seems to me to be the supreme virtue of a novel—the merit on which all its other merits helplessly and submissively depend. If it be not there they are all as nothing, and if these be there, they owe their effect to the success with which the author has produced the illusion of life. The cultivation of this success, the study of this exquisite process, form, to my taste, the beginning and the end of the art of the novelist. They are his inspiration, his despair, his reward, his torment, his delight. It is here in very truth that he competes with life; it is here that he competes with his brother the painter in *his* attempts to render the look of things, the look that conveys their meaning, to catch the color, the relief, the expression, the surface, the substance of the human spectacle. He cannot possibly take too many [notes], he cannot possibly take enough. All life solicits him, and to "render" the simplest surface, to produce the most momentary illusion, is a very complicated business. But this, I fear, he can never learn in any manual; it is the business of his life. He has to take a great many [notes] in order to select a few, he has to work them up as he can, and even the guides and philosophers who might have most to say to him must leave him alone when it comes to the application of precepts, as we leave the painter in communion with his palette. That his characters "must be clear in outline"—he feels that down to his boots; but how he shall make them so is a secret between his good angel and himself.

It would be absurdly simple if he could be taught that a great deal of "description" would make them so, or that on the contrary the absence of description and the cultivation of dialogue, or the absence of dialogue and the multiplication of "incident," would rescue him from his difficulties. Nothing, for instance, is more possible than that he be of a turn of mind for which this odd, literal opposition of description and dialogue, incident and description, has little meaning and light. People often talk of these things as if they had a kind of internecine distinctness, instead of melting into each other at every breath, and being intimately associated parts of one general effort of expression. I cannot imagine composition existing in a series of blocks, nor conceive, in any novel worth discussing at all, of a passage of description that is not in its intention narrative, a passage of dialogue that is not in its intention descriptive, a touch of truth of any sort that does not partake of the nature of incident, or an incident that derives its interest from any other source than the general and only source of the success of a work of art—that of being illustrative. A novel is a living thing, all one and continuous, like any other organism, and in proportion as it lives will it be found, I think, that in each of the parts there is something of each of the other parts. The critic who over the close texture of a finished work shall pretend to trace a geography of items will mark some frontiers as artificial, I fear, as any that have been known to history. There is an old-fashioned distinction between the novel of character and the novel of incident which must have cost many a smile to the intending fabulist who was keen about his work. It appears to me as little to the point as the equally celebrated distinction between the novel and the romance—to answer as little to any reality. There are bad novels and good novels, as there are bad pictures and good pictures; but that is the only distinction in which I see any meaning, and I can as little imagine speaking of a novel of character as I can imagine speaking of a picture of character. When one says picture one says of character, when one says novel one says of incident, and the terms may be transposed at will. What is character but the determination of incident? What is incident but the illustration of character? What is either a picture or a novel that is not of character? What else do we seek in it and find in it? It is an incident for a woman to stand up with her hand resting on a table and look at you in a certain way; or if it be not an incident I think it will be hard to say what it is. At the same time it is an expression of character. If you say you don't see it (character in *that —allons donc!*), this is exactly what the artist who has reasons of his own for thinking he does see it undertakes to show you. When a young man makes up his mind that he has not faith enough after all to enter the Church as he intended, that is an incident, though you may not hurry to the end of the chapter to see whether perhaps he doesn't change once more. I do not say that these are extraordinary or startling incidents. I do not pretend to estimate the degree of interest proceeding from them, for this will depend upon the skill of the painter. It sounds almost puerile to say that some incidents are intrinsically much more important than others, and I need not take this precaution after having professed my sympathy for the major ones in remarking that the only classification of the novel that I can understand is into that which has life and that which has it not.

Nothing, of course, will ever take the place of the good old fashion of "liking" a work of art or not liking it: the most improved criticism will not abolish that primitive, that ultimate test. . . . As people feel life, so they will feel the art that is most closely related to it. This closeness of relation is what we should never forget in talking of the effort of the novel. Many people speak of it as a factitious, artificial form, a product of ingenuity, the business of which it is to alter and arrange the things that surround us, to translate them into conventional, traditional moulds. This, however, is a view of the matter which carries us but a very short way, condemns the art to an eternal repetition of a few familiar clichés, cuts short its development, and leads us straight up to a dead wall. Catching the very note and trick, the strange irregular rhythm of life, that is the attempt whose strenuous force keeps Fiction upon her feet.

I cannot see what is meant by talking as if there were a part of a novel which is the story and part of it which for mystical reasons is not—unless indeed the distinction be made in a sense in which it is difficult to suppose that any one should attempt to convey anything. "The story," if it represents anything, represents the subject, the idea, the *donnée* of the novel; and there is surely no "school" which urges that a novel should be all treatment and no subject. There must assuredly be something to treat; every school is intimately conscious of that. This sense of the story being the idea, the starting-point, of the novel, is the only one that I see in which it can be spoken of as something different from its organic whole; and since in proportion as the work is successful the idea permeates and penetrates it, informs and animates it, so that every word and every punctuation-point contribute directly to the expression, in that proportion do we lose our sense of the story being a blade which may be drawn more or less out of its sheath. The story and the novel, the idea and the form, are the needle and thread, and I never heard of a guild of tailors who recommended the use of the thread without the needle, or the needle without the thread.

I have left the question of the morality of the novel till the last, and at the last I find I have used up my space. It is a question surrounded with difficulties, as witness the very first that meets us, in the form of a definite question, on the threshold. Vagueness, in such a discussion, is fatal, and what is the meaning of your morality and your conscious moral purpose? Will you not define your terms and explain how (a novel being a picture) a picture can be either moral or immoral? You wish to paint a moral picture or carve a moral statue: will you not tell us how you would set about it? We are discussing the Art of Fiction; questions of art are questions (in the widest sense) of execution; questions of morality are quite another affair, and will you not let us see how it is that you find it so easy to mix them up? . . . There is one point at which the moral sense and the artistic sense lie very near together; that is in the light of the very obvious truth that the deepest quality of a work of art will always be the quality of the mind of the producer. In proportion as that intelligence is fine will the novel, the picture, the statue partake of the substance of beauty and truth. To be constituted of such elements is, to my vision, to have purpose enough. No good novel will ever proceed from a superficial mind; that seems to me an axiom which, for the artist in fiction, will cover all needful moral ground.

EXERCISES

1. Robert Graves and Alan Hodge (see page 410) say that a characteristic of the prose of Henry James is the "carefully contrived parentheses" in his sentences. Can you find examples of such parentheses here?
2. What is James' point about a writer finding *significant* details as opposed to documentation?
3. Compare James' style to Twain's. James and Twain were contemporaries and both were Americans; do you find this reflected in their writing?

14 RECENT PROSE

by Robert Graves and Alan Hodge

Robert Graves (1895–) has been one of the most prolific of twentieth-century authors, as novelist, poet, and critic. He is considered by many as one of the best poets writing in the modernist vein. His novels have been very successful, among them Wife to Mr. Milton, I, Claudius, *and* Claudius the God.

Alan Hodge (1915–) was educated at Oxford and then worked as a journalist. He has collaborated with Graves on two books, The Long Weekend *and* The Reader Over Your Shoulder, *from which the following selection is taken.*

In "Recent Prose," the authors analyze brief passages from books by well-known nineteenth- and twentieth-century writers. They discuss some of the manifold influences reflected in a writer's style. For example, they show how a writer's social attitudes can influence his diction and point of view in presenting a scene or dramatizing an incident; how certain subjects invite a "pictorial" style, while others invite an "analytical" style. They stress that the understanding of a writer's style requires not merely a careful examination of diction, metaphors, and rhetorical devices, but of his underlying purpose and intention.

Middle-class family life was the subject of most early and middle-nineteenth century novels that were not Gothic tales of mystery and horror, or calmer, historical novels of the Sir Walter Scott, Harrison Ainsworth school. Though the novelists often introduced moral teaching and pleas for social reform into their stories, they were chiefly concerned with the delineation of character and the development of plot. This realism was a safeguard against over-elaborate writing, although the plain style was now regarded as 'low' even by the village constable. It was a heavily emotional realism, however, because a new emphasis upon the duty of showing mercy and charity toward the unfortunate had made pathos as highly esteemed as wit had formerly been.

There had been no sudden revolution in England as there had been in France, but successive agitations in favour of particular reforms; and these were usually prompted as much by humanitarian as by political feelings.

The new industrial middle classes were enjoying a prudently guarded opulence, and at the same time, in manufacturing districts there was poverty and misery on a scale that had not been known in England since the Black Death. The middle classes felt collectively, though not individually, responsible for this state of affairs, and from their guilty humanitarianism grew numerous movements for piece-meal social reform and numerous minor philanthropic institutions. The equalitarian arguments that had brought about the French Revolution were used, in a modified form, to bring about such reforms as the abolition of slavery under the British flag; but the feelings which made them possible derived rather from the Christian charity insisted on by the Methodists, and other evangelical reformers of the period, than from equalitarianism.

The severity shown by the new religious spirit against idle and lascivious reading, especially on a Sunday, compelled popular novelists to turn humanitarian; and besides the naturally poor and oppressed, their pity had to take in all those who came to moral or financial grief. The strict and sedate code of behaviour that had supervened on the lax and reckless Regency code was two-sided: public opinion first struck down all who failed to meet their social obligations, then pitied them as they lay bleeding. All personal and social problems were seen through a haze of sympathy, which was, however, not allowed to obscure the harshness of moral censure. Women, children and the poor were weaker vessels, particularly liable to sin and misfortune; when they fell, and were hurried away into charitable quarantine, the blame for their miserable fate was conscientiously laid on the defects of social circumstances.

In Thackeray's novels, pathos is usually an undertone, only occasionally rising to a loud throb, as in this passage from *Vanity Fair*, 1848:

> She was wrapped in a white morning dress, her hair falling on her shoulders and her large eyes fixed and without light. By way of helping on the preparations for the departure, and showing that she too could be useful at a moment so critical, this poor soul had taken up a sash of George's from the drawers whereon it lay and followed him to and fro, with the sash in her hand, looking on mutely while the packing proceeded. She came out and stood leaning at the wall, holding this sash against her bosom, from which the heavy net of crimson dropped like a large stain of blood.

Several devices here raise the tone of the passage from sadness to pathos. 'Large eyes fixed and without light' is a sentimental overstatement; 'mutely' instead of 'silently' carries a further suggestion of suffering; with 'this poor soul' Thackeray enters personally on the scene to intercede for the reader's pity; and in the last sentence the simile of the bloodstain is shocking in its poignancy. Similar devices for moving the emotions of their readers, most of whom lived dull and sheltered lives, were used by all the well-known novelists and magazine writers of this period, including George Eliot, George Borrow, Charles Kingsley, Charles Dickens, and the Americans, Edgar Allan Poe, Nathaniel Hawthorne, Herman Melville, Washington Irving. Dickens's stories are never allowed to tell themselves: he forcibly obtrudes his own emotions, often raising the pitch of the style to hysteria. He also tries to heighten the effect of his pathetic passages by a foil of robust facetiousness; as Elizabethan dramatists had heightened their tragic effects by comic relief. Here is a quotation from his *Old Curiosity Shop*:

She was dead. Dear, patient, gentle, noble Nell was dead. Her little bird—a poor slight thing the pressure of a finger would have crushed—was stirring nimbly in its cage; and the strong heart of its child mistress was mute and motionless for ever.

Where were the traces of her early cares, her sufferings, and fatigues? All gone. Sorrow was dead indeed in her, but peace and perfect happiness were born; imaged in her tranquil beauty and profound repose.

And still her former self lay there, unaltered in this change. Yes. The old fireside had smiled upon that same sweet face; it had passed, like a dream, through haunts of misery and care; at the door of the poor schoolmaster on the summer evening, before the furnace fire on the cold wet night, at the still bedside of the dying boy, there had been the same mild lovely look. So shall we know the angels in their majesty, after death.

The old man held one languid arm in his, and had the small hand tight folded to his breast, for warmth. It was the hand she had stretched out to him with her last smile—the hand that had led him on, through all their wanderings. Ever and anon he pressed it to his lips; then hugged it to his breast again, murmuring that it was warmer now; and, as he said it, he looked, in agony, to those who stood around, as if imploring them to help her.

And here is another passage from the same book, with death treated facetiously:

' "Then we have nothing for it but resignation," said Mr. Brass; "nothing but resignation, and expectation. It would be a comfort to have his body; it would be a dreary comfort."

"Oh, beyond a doubt," assented Mrs. Jiniwin hastily; "if we once had that, we should be quite sure."

"With regard to the descriptive advertisement," said Sampson Brass, taking up his pen. "It is a melancholy pleasure to recall his traits. Respecting his legs now—?"

"Crooked, certainly," said Mrs. Jiniwin.

"Do you think they *were* crooked?" said Brass, in an insinuating tone. "I think I see them now coming up the street very wide apart, in nankeen pantaloons a little shrunk and without straps. Ah! What a vale of tears we live in. Do we say crooked?"

"I think they were a little so," observed Mrs. Quilp with a sob.

"Legs crooked," said Brass, writing as he spoke. "Large head, short body, legs crooked—"

"Very crooked," suggested Mrs. Jiniwin.

"We'll not say very crooked, ma'am," said Brass piously. "Let us not bear hard upon the weaknesses of the deceased. He is gone, ma'am, to where his legs will never come in question.—We will content ourselves with crooked, Mrs. Jiniwin."

"I thought you wanted the truth," said the old lady. "That's all." '

This is melodrama in novel-form. Versions of most of Dickens's novels were staged during his lifetime. He was a natural orator and actor. He seems to have spoken over to himself, under his breath, every sentence that he wrote; and he toured Britain and the United States, giving public readings from his works. This accounts for much of his popularity in Victorian times, when the example set by the Queen popularized domesticity—the father of the family, instead of spending his evenings drinking and singing at the club as his own father had done, was supposed to stay at home and join a family reading circle. In the *Old Curiosity Shop,* as in all Dickens's novels, each chapter begins with an obvious cue to the reader: 'This should be read by Paterfamilias, in his manly, jolly voice,' or 'This is for the gentle, womanly voice of Materfamilias,' or 'Master John may be trusted with this.'

The popular Victorian novel (which was usually published in fortnightly parts, so that no member of a family could read on to the end, ahead of the rest) cannot be judged by modern solo-reading standards: its pictorial qualities, its frequent changes in atmosphere, the crowdedness that now make it such difficult going, explain themselves if it is read aloud dramatically to a roomful of leisured people of various ages in mid-Victorian costume. The practice of home-reading gradually lapsed at the turn of the century, and virtually ended with the First World War.

Pictorial styles were also used by John Ruskin and Walter Pater, who were not novelists but literary preachers and therefore indulged in even greater complexity of language. When Ruskin confined himself to expounding moral or aesthetic theory his style was fairly straightforward, but this was rare: his elaborate word-painting usually crowded out the precepts it was supposed to illustrate. The following sentence, describing the front of St Mark's Cathedral, is taken from the *Stones of Venice,* 1851–1853:

And well may they fall back, for beyond those troops of ordered arches there rises a vision out of the earth, and all the great square seems to have opened out of it in a kind of awe, that we may see it far away;—a multitude of pillars and white domes, clustered into a low pyramid of coloured light, a treasure-heap, it seems, partly of gold, and partly of opal and mother-of-pearl, hollowed beneath into five great vaulted porches, ceiled with fair mosaic, and beset with sculpture of alabaster, clear as amber, and delicate as ivory, sculpture fantastic and involved, of palm leaves and lilies, and grapes and pomegranates, and birds clinging and fluttering among the branches, all twined together into an endless network of buds and plumes; and, in the midst of it, the solemn forms of angels, sceptred, and robed to the feet, and leaning to each other across the gates, their figures indistinct among the gleaming of the golden ground through the leaves beside them, interrupted and dim like the morning light as it faded back among the branches of Eden, when first its gates were angel-guarded long ago.

A luxuriant mass of details is given, but with little sense of relation between them. The majestic sweep of the rhythm carries the reader over the details before he has time to assemble them in his mind. Ruskin himself must have formed a general impression of St Mark's and then carefully studied particulars, but does not here present them in such proportion as to explain his impression. It will be noticed how frequently the word 'among' occurs in the last few lines—birds among the branches, figures among the gleaming gold, light among the branches of Eden—all entrancing items in the decoration, but with no precise or esssential places in it. This is a misrepresentation of the solid design of St Mark's.

Pater was much more Classical in spirit than Ruskin, in the sense that he was clear and not luxuriant, elaborate and not profuse. But he, too, was trying to convey impressions of indescribable feelings: he wanted to catch and record in print the aesthetic *frissons*, or thrills, which he considered the highest rewards of a cultured existence. This could only be done indirectly by suggestion and parable. His novel, *Marius the Epicurean*, is one long historical parable, and his other works purely suggestive sketches.

Just as Ruskin, in a final effort to communicate his impression of St Mark's, makes use of a conceit about dawn breaking in the Garden of Eden, so Pater has recourse to fancy in trying to describe the feelings with which Leonardo da Vinci's *La Gioconda* inspired him. He imagines the mood of the painter on the days that he added the famous smile. The paragraph is taken from *Studies in the History of the Renaissance*, published in 1873; it was written at Oxford, where Pater was a college tutor, at a time when Ruskin was also lecturing there.

On this day truly no mysterious light, no irresistibly leading hand from afar, reached him; only, the peculiarly tranquil influence of its first hour increased steadily upon him in a manner with which, as he conceived, the aspects of the place he was then visiting had something to do. The air there, air supposed to possess the singular property of restoring the whiteness of ivory, was pure and thin. An even veil of lawn-like white cloud had now drawn over the sky; and under its broad, shadowless light every hue and tone of time came out upon the yellow old temples, the elegant pillared circle of the shrine of the pastoral Sybil, the houses seemingly of a piece with the ancient fundamental rock.

Pater calculated the pictorial suggestiveness of each word, subordinating its sense to the emotional, vocal and rhythmical context. He did this more precisely than Ruskin because his emotions had greater precision and he was better able to isolate and analyse them. Nevertheless, the repeated rhythme of 'air there, air' reads somewhat affectedly.

Among the exceptional writers who avoided both the pathetic and the pictorial styles were Anthony Trollope and Samuel Butler. Trollope escaped a formal education because of the poverty of his family; but his mother, author of *Domestic Manners of the Americans,* was a shrewd and vigorous writer and he seems to have learnt much from her. He spent most of his life as a Post Office official and hunting man. He published more than twenty long novels, all dealing with middle-class family life, plainly told and with few emotional digressions. Conversation and pure narrative make up the greater part of them, and there is far less descriptive writing than in most nineteenth-century novels from Sir Walter Scott's onwards. The following is a passage from the first chapter of *Orley Farm,* published in 1862:

> The whole stood in one line fronting on to a large lawn which fell steeply away from the house into an orchard at the bottom. The lawn was cut in terraces, and here and there upon it there stood apple trees of ancient growth; for here had been the garden of the old farmhouse. They were large, straggling trees, such as do not delight the eyes of modern gardeners; but they produced fruit by the bushel, very sweet to the palate, though probably not so perfectly round, and large, and handsome as those which the horticultural skill of the present day requires.

Trollope does not refrain from making general comments—for example, this comment on the modern taste in apples—but they are always short and relevant. He does not draw an elaborate 'atmosphere' out of them; the story distills its own atmosphere as it unfolds. Here he has given a brief and factual setting before breaking into the story proper.

Samuel Butler was not primarily a novelist: most of his works were treatises on art, literature, psychology and science; but he wrote a Utopian fantasy in novel form, *Erewhon,* 1872, and twenty years later a sequel, *Erewhon Revisited,* and one domestic novel, *The Way of All Flesh,* written between 1872 and 1884 but not published until after his death in 1903. He is usually described as a satirist, because these novels expose many of the shams of contemporary life, but his satire is very different from Swift's: it is more analytical and more understanding, less witty, more humorous and more original. His style is plain and unemotional, but sharper than Trollope's because his judgments are less conventionally formed. This is from *The Way of All Flesh:*

> Some people say that their schooldays were the happiest in their lives. They may be right, but I look with suspicion upon those whom I hear saying this. It is hard enough to know whether one is happy or unhappy now, and still harder to

compare the relative happiness or unhappiness of different times of one's life; the utmost that can be said is that we are fairly happy so long as we are not distinctly aware of being miserable. As I was talking with Ernest one day not so long since about this, he said he was so happy now that he was sure he had never been happier, and did not wish to be so, but that Cambridge was the first place where he had ever been consciously and continuously happy.

Butler has not let this piece of analysis get out of hand: his style is equal to it. Excesses and shortcomings in Victorian prose, and in modern prose which derives from it, are usually due to the writer's not knowing just how to reconcile the sense of what he wishes to say with the various literary devices which pride of craftsmanship has impelled him to use. Butler's style is as free from these devices as it is from fanciful emotional colouring. He lived on a small income; published all his books, except *Erewhon,* at a loss; and was generally regarded as a crank because of his refusal to conform with literary and scientific fashions.

Butler died when the twentieth century was just beginning; his own century had bequeathed it no general prose tradition. There were conventions of pathetic writing, of pictorial writing, of ornate historical and political writing, but these were suited only to certain subjects and the achievement of certain effects. Most famous writers of the late nineteenth century had worked out eccentrically individual styles. William Morris revived the mediaeval narrative manner, with a mixture of devices taken from Thomas Malory and the authors of Norse sagas. George Meredith used a complex metaphorical language, the obscure implications of which were a fascinating study for his admirers. There was also the precious and witty style of Oscar Wilde, based on Ruskin and Pater; and, based on French models, the 'sensitive' and lucid style of George Moore. Here is a painfully sensitive passage from George Moore's *Confessions of a Young Man,* 1886:

Then there is a failure—I can do nothing, nothing; my novel I know is worthless; my life is a leaf, it will flutter out of sight. I am weary of everything and wish I were back in Paris. I am weary of reading, there is nothing to read, Flaubert bores me. What nonsense has been talked about him! Impersonal! He is the most personal writer. But his odious pessimism! How weary I am of it, it never ceases, it is lugged in *à tout propos* and the little lyrical phrase with which he winds up every paragraph, how boring it is! Happily, I have "A Rebours" to read, that prodigious book, that beautiful mosaic. Huysmans is quite right, ideas are well enough until you are twenty, afterwards only words are bearable . . . a new idea, what can be more insipid—fit for Members of Parliament. Shall I go to bed? No. I would that I had a volume of Verlaine, or something of Mallarmé's to read—Mallarmé for preference. Huysmans speaks of Mallarmé in "A Rebours," and in hours like these a page of Huysmans is as a dose of opium, a glass of something exquisite and spirituous.

In 1878 the rugged-minded Charles Doughty, a poet and physician, went travelling in the deserts of Arabia, disguising neither his Christian distaste for Moslem superstition nor his English dislike for thievish and temperamental Arabs, and wrote a monumental account of his experiences in *Arabia Deserta*, 1888. He had not gone for adventure or for geographical or ethnological reasons, but (as he later told T. E. Lawrence) to 'redeem English from the slough into which it has fallen since the time of Spenser.' Here is an illustration of the way in which he redeemed English from neologisms:

We journeyed in the beaten path towards Gofar; and after going a mile, "Let us wait, quoth Eyâd, and see if this Merjàn be not coming." At length we saw it was he who approached with a bundle on his head,—he brought temmn and dates, which his sister (wedded in the town) had given him. Eyâd drew out a leathern budget, in which was some victual for the way that he had received from the Mothîf, (without my knowledge): it was but a little barley meal and dates of ill kind, in all to the value of about one shilling. We sat down, Merjàn spread out his good dates, and we breakfasted; thus eating together I hoped they might yet be friendly, though only misfortunes could be before me with such unlucky rafîks. . . .

"Nay," said Eyâd, beginning to swagger, "the returning shall not be as our coming; I will ride myself." I said no more; and cast thus again into the wilderness I must give them line.

And Doughty's contemporary, the complex-minded Henry James, an American with strong English sympathies, invented a new way of teasing the sentence with carefully contrived parentheses that delayed but did not confuse the rhythm as it meandered towards a comfortable close. This is from one of his later novels, *The Golden Bowl*, 1905:

Charlotte throned, as who should say, between her hostess and her host, the whole scene having crystallized as soon as she took her place, to the right quiet lustre; the harmony was not less sustained for being superficial, and the only approach to a break in it was while Amerigo remained standing long enough for his father-in-law, vaguely wondering, to appeal to him, invite or address him, and then, in default of any such word, selected for presentation to the other visitor a plate of *petits fours*. Maggie watched her husband—if it now could be called watching—offer this refreshment; she noted the consummate way—for "consummate" was the term she privately applied—in which Charlotte cleared her acceptance, cleared her impersonal smile, of any betrayal, of any slightest value, of consciousness; and then felt the slow surge of a vision that, at the end of another minute or two, had floated her across the room to where her father stood, looking at a picture, an early Florentine sacred subject, that he had given her on her marriage.

Many more styles were invented as the twentieth century advanced and since there was keen competition among writers as to who should be 'great' and since it was admitted that 'greatness' was achieved only by a highly individual style, new tricks and new devices multiplied. In this plurality of styles little writers grew confused: they imitated one Master after another—Pater, Morris, James, Moore, Wilde—in the hope of suddenly finding themselves great men in their own right. It did not occur to them that unless they had something to say there was no need to write: most of them expected the ritual of writing to produce the subject.

Robert Louis Stevenson in an essay on literary style recommended imitation. He admitted that:

> Whenever I read a book or a passage that particularly pleased me, in which a thing was said or an effect rendered with propriety, in which there was either some conspicuous force or some happy distinction in the style, I must sit down at once and set myself to ape that quality. In these vain bouts, I got some practice in rhythm, in harmony, in construction, and the co-ordination of parts. I have thus played the sedulous ape to Hazlitt, to Lamb, to Wordsworth, to Sir Thomas Browne, to Defoe, to Hawthorne, to Montaigne, to Baudelaire and to Obermann.

The effect of this sedulous imitation was to make Stevenson's works seem rather unreal: the negative virtue of faultlessness in an artificial prose style, especially where the writer's chief object is 'to render an effect,' can be very disagreeable. A reader feels that he is being written at, not written for. Other writers were neither so industrious nor so expert as Stevenson in their imitations of 'The Masters,' and so the Edwardian pudding-stone style began. It is still used by young writers who feel that they cannot be taken seriously until they have read the chief books of ancient and advanced contemporary literature in at least six languages and mastered all the styles and devices. Naturally they do not really read these books, or know the languages; but use crammer-school methods for learning just enough to pass muster. The literary result recalls the old Scottish nonsense story of Sir Gammer Vance who had a famous collection of curiosities and 'lived in a little thumb-bottle just outside his own front door.'

Typical pudding-stone is Sir Arthur Quiller-Couch's style, though he was not a young writer when he adopted it. In his unpretentious popular novels of the 'Eighties and 'Nineties he had been at his best: with simple humorous tales of the West Country and, though avoiding any suspicion of illiteracy, with no thought of setting himself up as an authority on English. He later took up style as a simple evangelist might take up ritual; and was appointed King Edward VII Professor of English Literature at Cambridge University. The following is a quotation from his *On the Art of Writing*, 1916. It is a concoction of styles which the contemporary reader was perhaps expected to taste critically with: 'Ah! a savour of Morris! Ah! a smack of Bunyan! Ah! a touch of Henry James! Ah, oh, ah! a tang, taste, suspicion, whiff, of Burke, Hazlitt, Jeremy Taylor, Washington Irving!'

Seeing that in human discourse, infinitely varied as it is, so much must ever depend on *who* speaks, and to *whom*, in what mood and upon what occasion; and seeing that Literature must needs take account of all manner of writers, audiences, moods, occasions; I hold it a sin against the light to put up a warning against any word that comes to us in the fair way of use and wont (as "wire," for instance, for telegram), even as surely we should warn off hybrids or deliberately pedantic impostors, such as "anti-body" and "picture-drome," and that, generally, it is better to err on the side of liberty than on the side of the censor: since by the manumitting of new words we infuse new blood into a tongue of which (or we have learnt nothing from Shakespeare's audacity) our first pride should be that it is flexible, alive, capable of responding to new demands of man's untiring quest after knowledge and experience.

In this passage we see the first clear signs of the breakdown of prose logic that has become so evident since the end of the First World War. Even in late Victorian times, no person of Sir A. Quiller-Couch's eminence would have dared to publish a sentence so plainly grotesque as 'By the manumitting of new words we infuse new blood into a tongue which is flexible, alive, capable of responding to new demands of man's untiring quest after knowledge and experience.' When the test of translation into Latin is applied, it fails at every point. No Latin orator would have figured new words as slaves to be manumitted: he would have seen them as barbarians applying for citizenship. Nor would he have figured the act of manumission as infusing new blood into anything: he would have put in the step here left out, namely, that after manumission the former slaves would be permitted to marry into their masters' families. Nor would he have mixed metaphor and realism in the phrase 'infuse new blood into a tongue': for blood is usually infused into the veins of the arm or leg and never into a tongue. Nor would he have written of a *tongue* as 'flexible and alive': he would have known that any human tongue, unless its owner happens to be paralysed, poisoned, or frozen stiff, is flexible and alive. He would therefore have avoided the word *lingua* (which means 'tongue' in the senses both of speech and of the organ of speech) and used instead '*modus loquendi*,' a 'manner of speaking.' Nor would he have admitted that a tongue into which new blood has been infused could 'respond to man's demands' as if it were a separate person or animal. Nor would he have mixed his vocabularies—Ennius with Petronius—as is done here: the Elizabethan phrase 'I hold it a sin against the light to put up a warning against any word that comes to us in the fair way of use and wont' mixed with the late-Victorian devotional-scientific phrase 'capable of responding to new demands of man's untiring quest.'

In Victorian times there was a clean separation, in the popular mind, of journalism from literature: journalism was considered vulgar, however well the journalist worked. The favourite debating theme—'Will Kipling *live?*'—was based on a doubt whether anyone whose writing had been formed by journalistic practice could possibly be 'great,' rather than on a doubt of Kipling's integrity as an observer and a moralist. It did not occur to anyone that O. Henry, Kipling's American counterpart, could 'live'; he was a mere reporter of the language of the bar and lodging house and had a prison record. Yet it was felt that Kipling and O. Henry had some quality that Meredith and Henry James lacked; and gradually popular novelists began to simplify their style in imitation. This made a cleavage between popular and literary writers, or, as they became known shortly after the First World War, 'Low-brows and High-brows.' If this had meant a cleavage between the writers who wrote stylistically and those who wrote plainly, it would have been excellent: but journalism then implied grammatical and verbal looseness and, as the influence of American journalism grew, a gradual weakening of logic under self-induced emotional stress. Whether to range oneself with the Low-brows or with the High-brows was a difficult choice.

As the twentieth century advanced, the competition in style became a competition in being modern rather than in being great. Writers in Britain, however, were less affected by the modernist obsession than American writers, especially those who had visited France. Throughout the Victorian era the Americans had looked to Britain to set the literary standard for all departments of writing except the humorous, in which they took the lead under Mark Twain, Artemus Ward, and Gelett Burgess. In other departments they emulated their British contemporaries, and very often surpassed them in grace and clarity of language: for example, Victorian England could not boast of two essayists so judicious and correct as Ralph W. Emerson and James Russell Lowell. But at the end of the First World War the Americans knew themselves to be the strongest and richest nation of the world, and therefore felt that this cultural dependence on Britain derogated from their national dignity. As in the War of Independence, when British political and military influence had to be shaken off, they turned for help to Paris. Paris had for long been the world-centre of literary, philosophical and artistic fashion. American writers, as would-be spokesmen of the most modern country in the world, needed the most modern of styles to express this feeling adequately; naturally, they went to Paris. For ten years Paris teemed with American literary experimentalists—the franc was low, life was free, there was no Prohibition. They returned finally to the United States in 1930, when the Great Depression deprived them of their incomes, having all served their apprenticeships in one or other of the schools of modernist writing.

The most celebrated American writer in Paris was Gertrude Stein. She had settled there several years before the tide of experimentalists flowed, and stayed for several years after it had ebbed—witnessing the defeat of France in 1940. She had been trained as a neurologist and philosopher and her experiments in writing derived from an assumption that Time and Progress, as nineteenth-century scientists and theologians had understood them, were now irrelevant concepts: in the modern world they were replaced by the simple casual relationships which arise out of mere continuous existence. This assumption was given weight by the findings of the new school of relativity-physicists, published after the First World War.

Gertrude Stein's method consisted in turning to a literary purpose the unreasoned relations of words in people's minds and the disconnection and repetition which are normal in modern conversation. She thus abandoned the tradition of orderly prose narrative—the old kind of story about the things that happened to people, arising out of some given situation and in turn giving rise to further happenings and new situations. For the most part her prose was a simple succession and repetition of words, phrases and sentences, without historical beginning or ending and without logical meaning. It was humorous and exciting, to those interested in new uses of words, but difficult to read. Solemn literary critics and newspaper comedians derided it; but in Paris in the 'Twenties she had a great following among the young American émigrés—who learnt from her how to use the simplest words and the most conversational idioms in new rhythmical movements which would give their work a characteristically American pace.

In the 'Thirties, when she had become an accepted literary figure, Gertrude Stein was invited to make important lecture-tours in the United States. She then explained what her 'nonsense' meant. Here is a paragraph from a lecture on *Narration*, delivered in 1934. If it is read over with conversational emphasis it makes plain sense, although the thought is most complicated:

> When I first began writing really just began writing, I was tremendously impressed by anything by everything having a beginning a middle and an ending. I think one naturally is impressed by anything having a beginning a middle and an ending when one is beginning writing and that is a natural thing because when one is emerging from adolescence, which is really when one first begins writing, one feels that one would not have been one emerging from adolescence if there had not been a beginning and a middle and an ending to anything. So paragraphing is a thing that anyone is enjoying and sentences are less fascinating, but then gradually well if you are an American gradually you find that it is not really necessary that anything that everything has a beginning a middle and an ending. . . .

Gertrude Stein solved the logical problem of Time, which she speaks about here, by frequent use of the timeless present participle.

Only one other writer in English carried his experiments in prose so far as Gertrude Stein; and he went in a totally different direction. This was James Joyce, an Irishman, whose Dublin upbringing and Jesuit education provide the constant background to his work. Like the American experimentalists, he spent the greater part of his life on the Continent, in Switzerland, France and Italy. Being out of contact with the mass of his compatriots has always helped the literary innovator. Joyce's first books, *Dubliners* and *Portrait of the Artist as a Young Man,* were straightforward stories in the realistic style of the French-influenced Anglo-Irish school. His next book, *Ulysses,* a long novel describing twenty-four hours in the lives of a group of Dublin people, is made up chiefly of their inconsequential talk and ruminations. Woven into these, by means of word-associations, are recurring Greek and Latin themes—particularly the theme of Ulysses the Wanderer which gives the book its title. *Ulysses* became famous partly because it was banned as obscene by the British and American Customs authorities, partly because it was the most ambitious attempt yet made to use 'the stream of consciousness' in writing: that is, to reveal the private thoughts of characters in all their natural confusion. This manner of writing was founded on psychological researches which had been intended to show that consciousness was a turbid stream of mixed desires and memories: it was thus a psychological assumption rather than a prose style. Many other writers made use of it, with many varying styles.

Ulysses begins in a straightforward manner but soon becomes more complicated, passing, like Harriette Wilson's *Memoirs,* through a series of imitations or parodies of all previous English styles. It is as if Joyce was testing each of them in order and finding all wanting. In his last book, *Finnegan's Wake,* published in 1940, after he had been working on it for fifteen years, he finally invented a comically composite style and language which he could call his own: a super-pudding-stone. In it, ordinary English words are portmanteau'd and deliberately misspelt, others are introduced from many foreign languages, including Hebrew and Sanskrit, and the result is an almost indecipherable system of interlacing puns and verbal associations imposed upon the familiar Irish background. Here is a comparatively easy passage:

What wouldn't I poach—the rent in my riverside my otther shoes, my beavery honest!—for a dace feast of grannom with the finny ones, flashing down the swansway, leaps ahead of the swift mac Eels and the pursewinded carpers, rearin antis rood perches astench of me, or, when I'd like own company best, with the help of a norange and bear, to be reclined by the lasher on my logansome, my g.b.d. in my f.a.c.e., solfanelly in my shellyholders and lov'd latakia the benuvolent, for my nose thrills with jealosomines wilting away to their heart's deelight and the king of sap-timber letting down his humely odours for my consternation, dapping my griffen, burning water in the spearlight, or catching trophies of the king's royal college of sturgeons for to bake pike and pie while, O twined me abower in l'Alouette's Tower, all Adelaide's naughtingerls, juckjucking benighth me, I'd tonic my twittynice Dorian blackbudds off my singasongasongapiccolo to pipe musicall airs on numberous fairyaciodes.

This is a fisherman's idyll spoken by an Irish priest: if it is read aloud, the Irish rhythm can be easily felt, and many familiar Irish properties recognized. If it is studied closely, more and more linguistic detail can be interpreted. This appeals to the reader's vanity of general knowledge and guessing power—'Ah,' he says, 'by the *naughtingerls* he means also *nightingales*—because the German for nightingale is *Nachtigall* and *nachte* is old English for *naughty*, and 'gal' is 'girl,' which in the Middle Ages was also spelt 'gerl'; and *nosethrills* are *nostrils*—the mediaeval spelling was *nosthrils*; and *jealosomines* are *jessamines* because of the old English term *jelsomine* from the Italian *gelsomino*. And *norange* recalls the derivation of 'orange' from the Spanish word *naranja*. And surely '*swansway*,' besides meaning the river Liffey, contains a glancing reference to Proust's long, indolent novel, Englished as *Swann's Way*? And *logansome* is a mixture of *lonesome* and *logan-stone*, or rocking stone. . . . etc., etc. In order to understand the whole book the reader would have to disentangle patiently as much more of the snarled detail as he could (a part depends on private associations of Joyce's); then he would have to put together a new book, working out the relations between the details and trying to see what Joyce intended to signify. No writer could, or need, carry stylistic or linguistic experiment further than this.

When Joyce died, shortly after the publication of this book, it was time for writers in search of literary novelty and complex styles of their own to realize that the game was played out. Joyce had caught 'all the trophies of the king's royal college of sturgeons.' Meanwhile, too, Gertrude Stein had analysed conversational speech, taking it to pieces and gradually building it up again with successive studies of the word, the phrase, the sentence, the paragraph; so there was now little more to be learned about conversation. At last writers were at liberty to use prose for simple prose purposes—and not feel behind the times in doing so.

EXERCISES

1. Make a list of the authors quoted in this article. After the name of each write two or three sentences characterizing the style of that author.
2. What are the most important points that Graves and Hodge make about nineteenth-century writers and writing? About twentieth-century writers and writing?
3. One often hears the statement that Victorian writers were too long-winded to appeal to modern readers. Is this fair? Justify your answer referring to the various Victorian writers represented in this text.

IX Analysis of Imaginative Literature

In the nineteenth century the notion was not uncommon that a work of art is like a delicate flower—examine it too closely and it will lose its scent, wither, and die. Even today some artists, whether writers, painters, or composers, protest the critical analyses of their works, claiming that more often than not their purpose and method are misunderstood and misinterpreted. Eudora Welty, whose "The Reading and Writing of Short Stories" is reprinted here, confesses that she is often baffled by analysis and criticism of her own work. "When I see them [her stories] analyzed—most usually 'reduced to their elements'—sometimes I think, 'This is none of me.' " But we need not throw out the baby with the bathwater. Analyses of works of art *are* sometimes prejudiced, far-fetched, and misleading instead of illuminating, but perceptive and honest analysis can do much to increase our comprehension and enjoyment of a work of art. It is significant that creative writers from Coleridge and Matthew Arnold to Virginia Woolf and T. S. Eliot have through their critical analyses of literature contributed greatly to our appreciation of other writers.

Speaking of the novel—though it is also relevant to other works of art—Elizabeth Bowen distinguishes two central attributes of the artist: his craftsmanship and his imagination. Imagination enables him not only to create but to perceive in a unique way. Sherwood Anderson remarked that: "The life of reality is confused, disorderly, almost always without purpose, whereas in the artist's imaginative life there is a purpose. There is determination to give the tale, the song, the painting Form—to make it true and real to the theme, not to life. . . ." Analysis can lead us to a better understanding of how the artist gives form to the raw and disordered experience of life and through his imagination transforms life into art.

The analysis of a literary work may take a variety of forms—from emphasis on analysis of the work of art "for art's sake" to an approach to the work through the life and time of the author. The study of a work through the life of the author is called the biographical method. In the twentieth century, biographical criticism has tended to be psychological or psychoanalytical; the critic discovers some characteristic psychological bent of the writer—usually traceable to significant events or experiences in the author's childhood—and shows how this is reflected in his writings. Historical criticism relates a work to its cultural milieu, to the politics, religion, and world-view of its period. Marxist criticism, one type of historical criticism, relates the work to the economic class structure of the society from which it comes, and especially to the author's class position.

The analysis of a work of art "for art's sake" uses a variety of formal aesthetic criteria. One type of such criticism, the so-called New Criticism, is extremely rigorous in excluding biographical and historical analysis and in concentrating on the text itself.

Each of these methods, and others we have not mentioned, can help us understand and appreciate works of literature.

Yet, undoubtedly, there are many aspects of any work of art, especially of its total aesthetic effect, that seem to resist analysis. This need not disturb us, for it reveals something significant about the nature of art. A novel, a poem, a play, or, for that matter, a painting or musical composition, has a mode of discourse peculiar to itself, one which defies paraphrasing. There remains always what Eudora Welty calls a mystery, "the mystery of allurement." For a novel or a short story is more than an interesting theme, absorbing characters, the skillful use of an array of techniques, or the statement of a moral truth. It is the creation of a fictional or poetical world which is in many ways different from the real world but which nevertheless intensifies our experience and understanding of that real world.

Significant literature enlarges our understanding of the world, of human relationships, of the human situation. Because it creates a world apart from the disordered flow of daily existence, it can give us an intensified sense of the physical world, of human emotions, and of conflicts. A sensitive and careful reading of good literature can do much to sharpen our own perception and awareness of the world around us.

The selections included here, with the possible exception of "The Art of the Short Story" (the author is anonymous), are contributed by writers who have distinguished themselves in the field of creative literature. Eudora Welty is best known for her short stories; Elizabeth Bowen, for her novels; Archibald MacLeish, for his poetry. Each of them is not only a master of his craft but also is profoundly aware of the peculiar human value of his art.

1 THE READING AND WRITING OF SHORT STORIES

by Eudora Welty

Eudora Welty (1909–) was born in Jackson, Miss. She attended Mississippi State College for Women, Wisconsin, where she took her B.A., and Columbia, where she studied advertising. Some of her earliest stories were published in the Southern Review; *they received a good deal of attention and within a short time her stories were appearing in almost every new collection. With a few recent exceptions, almost all of her stories have a Southern setting and usually exhibit a comic-grotesque view of the world. Her books include* A Curtain of Green (1941), The Wide Net (1943), Delta Wedding (1945), *and* The Bride of the Innisfallen (1955).

In this article she explains that each good story is unique and special. By implication, she disagrees with those who claim that there are five or six or however many story situations and that a knowledge of them enables one to write a good story. She explains that a Hemingway story or an E. M. Forster story lives as a part of the "Hemingway world" or the "Forster world"—that it is not an exact mirroring of the everyday world in which we live. The good writer has perceptions about human relationships and human experiences, he creates a fictional world in which these perceptions live as color and movement and emanate their significance.

Experience teaches us that when we are in the act of writing we are alone and on our own, in a kind of absolute state of Do Not Disturb. And experience tells us further that each story is a specific thing, never a general thing—never. The words in the story we are writing now might as well never have been used before. They all shine; they are never smudged. Stories are *new* things, stories make words new; that is one of their illusions and part of their beauty. And of course the great stories of the world are the ones that seem new to their readers on and on, always new because they keep their power of revealing something.

But although all stories in the throes of being written seem new and although good stories are new and persist, there will always be some characteristics and some functions about them as old as time, as human nature itself, to keep them more or less alike, at least of a family; and there may be other things, undiscovered yet, in the langauge, in technique, in the world's body of knowledge, to change them out of our present recognition. Critics, historians, and scholars deal with these affairs—and keep good track of them—while for us, the practitioners, the writing of stories seems to simmer down—between stories—into some generalities that are worth talking about.

Between stories—yes, that's when we can talk.

I think we write stories in the ultimate hope of communication, but so do we make jelly in that hope. Communication and hope of it are conditions of life itself. Let's take that for granted, and not get sidetracked by excitement. We hope somebody will taste our jelly and eat it with even more pleasure than it deserves and ask for another helping—no more can we hope for in writing a story. Always in the back of our heads and in our hearts are such hopes, and attendant fears that we may fail—we do everything out of the energy of some form of love or desire to please. The writing of a story uses the *power* of this love or hope, of course, and not its simple, surface form such as comes out—rather nicely—in jelly-making.

During the writing of a story, all the energy we have is put to pressure and reaches a changed-over state—so as to act for the sole and concentrated purpose of making our work excellent and to the pattern of some preconceived idea we have of beauty. The diffusion of this energy will, in the long run, prevent our story from communicating, in the degree that it prevents it from being our own.

But the practical problems of the story at hand are, on the whole, minutiae. The little things that plague and absorb us in every story never let up. There, help is possible. And that they are little things explains, possibly, how it is that we can shed such problems so entirely once a story is done. Who remembers afterwards the nuisance of counting the children, or preparing the reader for the murder, or getting the moon in the right part of the sky? They aren't truly important problems, and patience is the answer—time and patience.

To get at general problems we have to go deeper—in fact, the deepest we can go—into the act of writing itself. The whole thing is subjective. All any of us can *know* about writing is what it seems like to us. It's not an imitative process.

Direct connection is all we have with short stories—reading and writing them. It is not ours to note influences, trace histories, and consider trends. We are in the thick of stories by being personally and directly concerned with them. It is from this close, unromantic, perhaps much less sure and much more passionate point of view, that we writers gaze at the art of the short story.

If we learn mostly little things from correction—from critics—do we learn the big things by doing? I think it the only way, but not an infallible way. That is, there is nothing that will guarantee our writing a better story next time than the one we have just finished. Some first stories remain a writer's best work. We work by the story—by the piece. The next story will always be a different thing. There are no two days alike—time moves. There are no two stories alike—*our* time moves. We were in one story and now we are in another—two worlds—and there are many more, though the thought neither helps nor hinders us any in the one where we now struggle.

2

How do we write a story? Our own way. Beyond that, I think it is hard to assign a process to it.

The mind in writing a story is in the throes of imagination, and it is not in the calculations of analysis. There is a Great Divide in the workings of the mind, shedding its energy in two directions: it creates in imagination, and it tears down in analysis. The two ways of working have a great way of worrying the life out of each other. But why can't they both go their ways in peace?

Let's not, to begin with, deny the powers and achievements of good criticism. That would be smug, ignorant, and blind. Story criticism can seem blind itself, when it is ingrown and tedious; on the other hand, it can see things in large wholes and in subtle relationships we should be only stupid not to investigate. It can illuminate even though, in the face of all its achievements, its business is not: to tell *how*. There is the Great Divide.

I feel like saying as a friend, to beginning writers, Don't be unduly worried by the analyses of stories you may see in some textbooks or critical articles. They are brilliant, no doubt useful to their own ends, but should not be alarming, for in a practical sense they just do not bear in a practical way on writing. To use my own case, that being the only one I can rightly speak of, I have been baffled by analysis and criticism of some of my stories. When I see them analyzed—most usually, "reduced to elements"—sometimes I think, "This is none of me." Not that I am too proud to like being reduced, especially; but that I could not remember *starting* with those elements—with anything that I could so label. The fact that a story will reduce to elements, can be analyzed, does not necessarily mean it started with them—certainly not consciously. A story can start with a bird song.

Criticism, or more strictly, analysis, is an impossible way to learn how the story was written. Analysis is a one-way process, and is only good after the event. In the newsreel pictures when the dive is shown in reverse, a swimmer can come back out of the water; the splash is swallowed up, he rises in the air and is safe and dry back on the diving board. But in truth you can't come by way of analysis back to the starting point of inspiration; that's against some law of the universe, it might almost seem. I myself lack a scientific upbringing; I hear the arrow of time exists, and I feel quite certain, by every instinct, so does the arrow of creation.

Readers of Sir Arthur Eddington—who may be enjoyed even by a reader ill-equipped in science if the reader loves good literature—will remember he explains the term "entropy" as *becoming*. Our physical world is ever in the act of becoming, and not its opposite. You can't undo a dive, you can't put Humpty Dumpty together again or restore unshot the arrow to the bow. Mr. Eddington does not bother with the writing of short stories and does not say, but you can't analyze a story back to its beginning and truly find thereby what the story started out to do, what then modified and determined it, and what eventually made it a superior story and not just a good story. A story is not the same thing when it ends that it was when it began. Something happens—the writing of it. It *becomes*. And as a story becomes, I believe we as readers understand by becoming too—by enjoying.

Let's look at some short stories as writers of stories ourselves and people who like them; let's see a little how they are disposed, watch them in their motions, and enjoy them.

Luckily, we shall have none of the problems of *not* enjoying them. Putting a story in its place—we shall escape that. Putting a story in its place when its place has become the important thing means absolutely not giving over to the story. It also means taking oneself with proper seriousness, keeping close watch not to make a fool of oneself, and watching limbs, lest one go out on a few. Enjoying them, we can go out on many a limb. Yet there is really a tougher requirement for enjoying: flexibility and openness of the mind—of the pores, possibly. For heaven forbid we should feel disgrace in seeking understanding by way of pleasure.

We would be sure of this, I believe, if we asked ourselves, How would we wish a story of our own to be understood? By way of delight—by its being purely read, for the first fresh impact and the wonder attached; isn't this the honest answer? It seems to me too that almost the first hope we ever had, when we gave someone a story all fresh and new, was that the story would *read new*. And that's how we should read.

What bliss! Think how often this is denied us. That's why we think of childhood books so lovingly. But hasn't every writer the rightful wish to have his story so read? And isn't this wish implicit in the story itself? By reading secondhandedly, or obediently as taught, or by approaching a story without an open mind, we wrong its very first attribute—its uniqueness, with its sister attribute of freshness. We are getting to be old, jaded readers—instructed, advised readers, victims of summaries and textbooks; and if we write stories as victims of this attitude ourselves, what will happen to us? While we read and while we write, let's forget what we're being forever told and find the fresh world again—of enjoyment and pleasure and the story unspoiled, delighted in or hated for its own sake.

By enjoying, I don't mean to be *easy* on a story. Not all melted, the way William Saroyan at times requests readers to be. I mean only not to bother the story—not interrupt and interpret it on the side as if the conscience were at stake. To see it clear and itself, we must see it objectively.

After all, the constellations, patterns, we are used to seeing in the sky are purely subjective; it is because our combining things, our heroes, existed in the world almost as soon as we did that we were able long ago to see Perseus up there, and not a random scattering of little lights. Let's look at a particular story and see it solitary out in space, not part of some trend. It doesn't matter a bit for the moment who wrote it or when, or what magazine or book it appeared in or got rejected from, or how much or how little money the author got for it or whether he had an agent, or that he received letters in the mail when it was printed, saying, "It is found that your story does not reduce to the elements of a story." We're seeing this story as a little world in space, just as we can isolate one star in the sky by a concentrated vision.

3

The first thing we notice about our story is that we can't really see the solid outlines of it—it seems bathed in something of its own. It is wrapped in an atmosphere. This is what makes it shine, perhaps, as well as what initially obscures its plain, real shape.

We are bearing in mind that the atmosphere in a story may be its chief glory—and for another thing, that it may be giving us an impression altogether contrary to what lies under it. The brightness may be the result of whizzing in a circle. Some action stories fling off the brightest clouds of obscuring and dazzling light, like ours here. Our penetrating look brings us the suspicion finally that this busy object is quite dark within, for all its clouds of speed, those primary colors of red and yellow and blue. It looks like one of Ernest Hemingway's stories, and it is.

Now a story behaves, it goes through motions—that's part of it. Some stories leave a train of light behind them, meteorlike, so that much later than they strike our eye we may see their meaning like an after-effect. These wildly careening stories are in many ways among the most interesting of all—the kind of story sometimes called apocalyptic. I think of Faulkner's stories as being not meteors but comets; in a way still beyond their extravagance and unexpectedness and disregard of the steadier laws of time and space, Faulkner's stores are cometlike in that they do have a wonderful course of their own: they reappear, in their own time they reiterate their meaning, and by reiteration show a whole further story over and beyond their single significance.

If we have thought of Hemingway's stories, then, as being bare and solid as billiard balls, so scrupulously cleaned of adjectives, of every unneeded word as they are, of being plain throughout as a verb in itself is plain, we may come to think twice about it. The atmosphere that cloaks D. H. Lawrence's stories is of sensation, which is a pure but thick cover, a cloak of self-luminous air, but the atmosphere that surrounds Hemingway's stories is just as thick and to some readers less illuminating. Action can be inscrutable, more than sensation can be. It can be just as voluptuous, too, just as vaporous, and much more desperately concealing.

So the first thing we see about a story is its mystery. And in the best stories, we return at the last to see mystery again. Every good story has mystery—not the puzzle kind, but the mystery of allurement. As we understand the story better, it is likely that the mystery does not necessarily decrease; rather it simply grows more beautiful.

Now, of what is this story composed, the one we're sighting? What is the plot, in other words?

E. M. Forster in his book on the novel makes the acute distinction between plot and narrative thread. A story is a "narrative of events arranged in their time-sequence. A plot is also a narrative of events, the emphasis falling on causality." With a plot, instead of keeping on asking, What next? we ask, Why?

Well, in Hemingway's story, which is "Indian Camp," one of his early ones, Nick goes with his father, a doctor, to see a sick Indian woman. She is suffering in labor and the doctor operates on her without an anesthetic. In the bunk above her head, her husband lies with a sore foot. After the operation is over and the child has been successfully born, the husband is found to have slit his throat because he was not able to bear his wife's suffering. Nick asks, "Is dying hard, Daddy?" "No, I think it's pretty easy," his father says.

The story is composed of this—the inability to endure suffering. The wish to die rather than face pain. Is this a red and blue world? I see it as dark as night—Hemingway's world is again and again a world of fear. Of physical cruelty, pain, the giving of pain, and for a counter the inability to receive it except in propriety—one way. In Hemingway there is only one way, you know. It is a fear-ridden world, in which the only exorcisement is ritual—the bullfighter's code, the rules of sport, of warfare. This story is over and over again told with a kind of appetite, gusto; and this paradox of essence and effect is one of the hypnotic and incomparable things about Hemingway—his value and his mystery. His imitators lack both value and mystery. Violence in itself is not a story; there is violence and there is the story, or rather the plot, of violence.

How do we get, in Hemingway, that sense of opaqueness? It is not because the stories are stories of action—for action can be radiant, we know—not because they are bare and clean of adjectives and fuss. (Why are feelings and adjectives supposed to be in themselves any more—or any less—illuminating than action and verbs?) To this reader, Hemingway's stories are opaque because they are moralizing stories. And to be moralizing is to be flat-surfaced—to take up your stand behind a shield. The stories aren't really out in the open at all, the outdoors notwithstanding; the arena functions like an ambush, with the author behind taking pot shots at the reader.

Be stoic. We are taught by Hemingway, who is *instructive* by method, that there is a way we had better be. The world is full of fear and danger, says he. We say, All right—it is that. He says, I give you the ceremony. Better not look any closer, but keep to your places. So braveness and fear, instructions and ceremonial to-do, step in front of reality just as surely as sentimentality can. Our belligerent planet Mars has an unknown and unrevealed heart.

But we have to go on from there. For what comes of it? Part of Hemingway's power comes straight out of this conditioning he imposes on his stories. In San Francisco there's a painting by Goya, who himself used light, action, and morality dramatically, of course. The bull ring and the great tossing wall of spectators are cut in diagonal half by a great shadow of afternoon. There lies the wonder of the painting—the opaque paired with the clear, golden sun; half of the action, with dense, clotting shade. It's like this in Hemingway's plots.

In the same way, one power of Hemingway's famous use of conversation derives from the fact that it's often in translated or broken sentences—a shadow inserted between the direct speakers. It is an obscuring and at the same time a magical touch; it illuminates from the side. It makes us aware of the fact that communication is going on.

As we now picture Hemingway's story, isn't it something like this—not transparent, not radiant from the front; but from the side, from without his story, from a moral source, comes its beam of light; and his story is not radiant, but spotlighted. Don't we feel the kind of excitement from reading his stories that we more usually feel at a play?

4

As we all have observed, plot can throw its weight in any of several ways, varying in their complexity, flexibility, and interest: onto the narrative, or situation; onto the character; onto the interplay of characters; and onto some higher aspects of character, emotional states, and so on, which is where the rules leave off, if they've come with us this far, and the uncharted country begins. Let's look at further stories, still not seeking to evaluate their authors or the stories among others of their authors, but taking them up where we find them as they bring out some aspect or another of plot.

Stephen Crane's "The Bride Comes to Yellow Sky" tells a story of situation; it is a playful story, using two situations, like counters.

Jack Potter, the town marshal of Yellow Sky, has gone to San Anton' and gotten married and is bringing his bride home in a Pullman—the whole errand to be a complete surprise to the town of Yellow Sky. "He knew full well that his marriage was an important thing to his town. It could only be exceeded by the burning of the new hotel."

And in Yellow Sky another situation is building up in matching tempo with the running wheels. A messenger appears in the door of the Weary Gentleman saloon crying "Scratchy Wilson's drunk and has turned loose with both hands." "Immediately a solemn, chapel-like gloom was upon the place. . . . 'Scratchy Wilson is a wonder with a gun, a perfect wonder, and when he goes on the war-trail, we hunt our holes—naturally.' " Scratchy enters town, pistols in both hands. His "cries of ferocious challenge rang against walls of silence. And his boots had red tops with gilded imprints, of the kind beloved in winter by little sledding boys on the hillsides of New England. . . . He walked with the creeping movement of the midnight cat. As it occurred to him, he roared menacing information. . . . The little fingers of each hand played sometimes in a musician's way. . . . The only sounds were his terrible invitations."

All this is delightful to us not only for itself but for its function of play, of assuring our anticipation; the more ferocious Scratchy is, the more we are charmed. Our sense of the fairness, the proportion of things is gratified when he "comfortably fusiladed the windows of his most intimate friend. The man was playing with this town; it was a toy for him." This plot of situation gives us a kind of kinetic pleasure; just as being on a seesaw is pleasant not only for where we are but for where the other person is.

The train arrives, Jack Potter and bride get off, and Jack's emotion-charged meeting with Yellow Sky is due; and Scratchy Wilson turns out to be its protagonist. They come face to face, and Potter, who says, "I ain't got a gun on me, Scratchy," takes only a minute to make up his mind to be shot on his wedding day.

"If you ain't got a gun, why ain't you got a gun?" Scratchy sneers at the marshal. And Potter says, "I ain't got a gun because I've just come from San Anton' with my wife. I'm married." "Married?" asks Scratchy—he has to ask it several times, uncomprehending. "Married?"

"Seemingly for the first time, he saw the drooping, drowning woman at the other man's side. 'No!' he said. He was like a creature allowed a glimpse of another world. . . . 'Is this the lady?'

" 'Yes; this is the lady,' answered Potter.

" 'Well,' said Wilson at last, slowly, 'I s'pose it's all off now.'

". . . He was not a student of chivalry; it was merely that in the presence of this foreign condition he was a simple child of the earlier plains. He picked up his starboard revolver, and, placing both weapons in their holsters, he went away. His feet made funnel-shaped tracks in the heavy sand."

So, in Crane's story, two situations, two forces, gather, meet—or rather are magnetized toward one another, almost—and collide. One is vanquished—the unexpected one—with neatness and absurdity, and the vanquished one exits; all equivalents of comedy.

5

In Katherine Mansfield's "Miss Brill," there are only one character and only one situation. The narrative is simple, Miss Brill's action consists nearly altogether in sitting down; she does nothing but go and sit in the park, return home and sit on her bed in her little room. Yet considerably more of a story is attempted by this lesser to-do than Crane attempted in "Yellow Sky"; its plot is all implication.

"Miss Brill" is set on a stage of delight. "Although it was so brilliantly fine—the blue sky powdered with gold, and great spots of light like white wine splased over the *Jardins Publiques*—Miss Brill was glad that she had decided on her fur. . . . [She] put up her hand and touched her fur. Dear little thing!" We see right off that for Miss Brill delight is a kind of coziness. She sits listening to the band, her Sunday habit, and "Now there came a little flutey bit—very pretty!—a little chain of bright drops. She was sure it would be repeated. It was; she lifted her head and smiled."

Miss Brill has confidence in her world—anticipation: what will happen next? Ah, but she knows. She's delighted but safe. She sees the others from her little perch, her distance—the gay ones and then those on benches: "Miss Brill had often noticed there was something funny about nearly all of *them*. They were odd, silent, nearly all old, and from the way they stared they looked as though they'd just come from dark little rooms or even—even cupboards!" For she hasn't identified herself at all.

The drama is light in this story. There is no collision. Rather the forces meeting in the *Jardins Publiques* have, at the story's end, passed through each other and come out the other side; there has not been a collision, but a change—something much more significant. This is because, though there is one small situation going on, a very large and complex one is implied—the outside world, in fact.

One of the forces in the story is life itself, corresponding to the part of Scratchy Wilson, so to speak. Not violent life—life in the setting of a park on Sunday afternoon in Paris. All it usually does for Miss Brill is promenade stylishly while the band plays, form little tableaux, separate momently into minor, rather darker encounters, and keep in general motion with bright colors and light touches—there are no waving pistols at all, to storm and threaten.

Yet, being life, it does threaten. In what way, at last? Well, how much more deadly to Miss Brill than a flourished pistol is an overheard remark—about *her*. Miss Brill's vision—a vision of love—is brought abruptly face to face with another, ruder vision of love. The boy and girl in love sit down on her bench, but they cannot go on with what they have been saying because of her, though "still soundlessly singing, still with that trembling smile, Miss Brill prepared to listen.

" 'No, not now,' said the girl. 'Not here, I can't.'

" 'But why? Because of that stupid old thing at the end there? . . . Why does she come here at all—who wants her? Why doesn't she keep her silly old mug at home?'

" 'It's her fur which is so funny,' giggled the girl. 'It's exactly like a fried whiting.'

" 'Ah, be off with you!' said the boy in an angry whisper."

So Miss Brill, she who could spare even pity for this world, in her innocence—pity, the spectator's emotion—is defeated. She had allowed herself occasional glimpses of lives not too happy, here in the park, which had moved her to little flutters of sadness. But that too had been coziness—coziness, a remedy visitors seek to take the chill off a strange place with. She hadn't known it wasn't good enough. All through the story she has sat in her "special seat"—another little prop to endurance—and all unknown to her she sat in mortal danger. This is the story. The danger nears, a word is spoken, the blow falls—and Miss Brill retires, ridiculously easy to mow down, as the man with the pistols was easy to stare down in "Yellow Sky," for comedy's sake. But Miss Brill was from the first defenseless and on the losing side, and her defeat is the deeper for it, and one feels sure it is for ever.

6

The plot of a short story in many instances is quite openly a projection of character. In a highly specialized instance, but a good example, the whole series of ghostly events in *The Turn of the Screw* may obviously be taken as a vision—a set of hallucinations of the governess who tells us the story. The story is a manufactured evidence against the leading character, in effect.

Not always does plot project character, even primarily. William Sansom, a young English writer, might be mentioned as one new writer who pays his highest respect to pure idea. Virginia Woolf too was at least as interested in a beam of light as she was in a tantrum.

In outward semblance, many stories have plots in common—which is of no more account than that many people have blue eyes. Plots are, indeed, what we see with. What's seen is what we're interested in.

On some level all stories are stories of search—which isn't surprising at all. From the intense wild penetration of the hunter in "The Bear" by William Faulkner to the gentle Sunday excursion of Katherine Mansfield's "Miss Brill"; from the cruel errand of Nick's father to the Indian camp in Ernest Hemingway's story to the fantasy of soaring into the realm of the poetic imagination in E. M. Forster's "Celestial Omnibus"; from the fireman seeking the seat of the fire in William Sansom's "Fireman Flower" to the Henry James man in "The Jolly Corner" seeking, with infinite pains and wanderings, the image of himself and what he might have been, through the corridors of a haunted house—in any group of stories we might name as they occur to us, the plot is search. It is the ancient Odyssey and the thing that was ancient when first the Odyssey was sung. Joyce's *Ulysses* is the titan modern work on the specific subject, but when Miss Brill sits in the park, we feel an old key try at an old lock again—she too is looking. Our most ancient dreams help to convince us that her timid Sunday afternoon is the adventure of her life, and measure for us her defeat.

Corresponding to the search involved is always the other side of the coin. On one side of James's coin is search, on the other side is blight. Faulkner is concerned with doom and history, Hemingway with career, ritual, and fate—and so on. Along with search go the rise and fall of life, pride and the dust. And Virginia Woolf sees errand and all alike dissolving in a surpassing mystery.

When plot, whatever it does or however it goes, becomes the outward manifestation of the very germ of the story, then it is purest—then the narrative thread is least objectionable, then it is not in the way. When it is identifiable in every motion and progression of its own with the motions and progression of simple revelation, then it is at its highest use. Plot can be made so beautifully to reveal character, reveal atmosphere and the breathing of it, reveal the secrets of hidden, inner (that is, "real") life, that its very unfolding is a joy. It is a subtle satisfaction—that comes from where? Probably it comes from a deep-seated perception we all carry in us of the beauty of organization—of that less strictly definable thing, of form.

Where does form come from—how do you "get it"? My guess is that form is evolved. It is the residue, the thrown-off shape, of the very act of writing, as I look at it. It is the work, its manifestation in addition to the characters, the plot, the sensory impressions—it is the result of these, which comes to more than their mathematical total. It is these plus something more. This something more springs from the whole. It pertains to the essence of the story. From the writer's point of view, we might say that form is somehow connected with the process of the story's work—that form *is* the work. From the reader's point of view, we might say that form is connected with recognition; it is what makes us know, in a story, what we are looking at, what unique thing we are for a length of time intensely contemplating. It does seem that the part of the mind which form speaks to and reaches is the memory.

7

In stories today, form, however acutely and definitely it may be felt, does not necessarily imply a formal structure. It is not accounted for by structure, rather. A story with a "pattern," an exact kind of design, may lack a more compelling over-all quality which we call form. Edgar Allan Poe and other writers whose ultimate aim depended on pattern, on a perfect and dovetailing structure (note the relation to puzzles and to detection and mystery here), might have felt real horror at a story by D. H. Lawrence first of all because of the unmitigated shapelessness of Lawrence's narrative. Lawrence's world of action and conversation is as far from the frozen perfection, the marblelike situations, of Poe as we can imagine; Lawrence's story world is a shambles—a world just let go, like a sketchy housekeeper's un-straightened-up room. More things are important than this dust! Lawrence would say, and he would be as right as the crier of that cry always is.

And what about his characters? Are they real, recognizable, neat men and women? Would you know them if you saw them? Not even, I think, if they began to speak on the street as they speak in the stories, in the very words—they would only appear as deranged people. For the truth seems to be that Lawrence's characters don't really speak their words—not conversationally, not to one another; they are *not* speaking on the street, but are playing like fountains or radiating like the moon or storming like the sea, or their silence is the silence of wicked rocks. It is borne home to us that Lawrence is writing of our human relationships on earth in terms of eternity, and these terms set Lawrence's form.

The author himself appears in authorship in phases like the moon, and sometimes blesses us and sometimes smites us while we stand there under him. But we see that his plots and his characters are alike sacrificed to something; there is something which Lawrence considers as transcending them both. Others besides him have thought that something does. But Lawrence alone, that I have knowledge of now, thinks the transcending thing is found direct through the senses. It is the world of the senses that Lawrence writes in, works in, thinks in, takes as his medium—and if that is strange to us, isn't the loss ours? Through this world he will send his story. It is the plot too; it is his story's reason for being, with sex the channel the senses most deeply, mysteriously, run through, cutting down through layers and centuries and country after country of hypocrisy.

Virginia Woolf presents an interesting variation of this conception; she was an intellectual. Extremely conscious of sex, she was intellectually or philosophically concerned with it. She could make a fantasy of her world, and her people could laugh. But the extreme beauty of her writing is due greatly to one fact, it seems to me: that the imprisonment of life in the word was as much a matter of the senses with her as it was a concern of the intellect. The scent, the gesture, the breath moving from the lips, the sound of the hour striking in the clock, the rippling texture of surface in running water and flowing air—all these things she sought with all her being to apprehend, for they were the palpable shadows and colored reflections of the abstract world of the spirit, the matter that mirrored the reality.

The impressionist dictum at one time that light is the most important actor in the picture can apply to the work of Virginia Woolf; here light does move frequently as a character and on business of its own, from scene to scene, and only itself remains unaffected by cruder and frailer human vision. In one story, "The Searchlight," light is literally the main character.

But it has to be observed that in Mrs. Woolf's stories the beam of light arises not out of the unconscious but out of the conscious being. It is manipulated, like a wand; it touches and discriminates, from here to there, with precise, rather haughty, almost ladylike purpose, to illuminate quite clearly the particular in the abstract world. So near can the sensory come to the philosophic in her stories that the words "breathing," "breath," and the other words which mean this, give us the feeling of a creator ever consciously breathing life into the creation.

While Virginia Woolf uses her senses intellectually, Lawrence uses his intellect sensuously. And while Chekov builds up character, Lawrence breaks down character. These opposites are perpetrated only in one interest, in getting at truth.

D. H. Lawrence is somewhat like the True Princess, who felt beneath forty mattresses that there was a pea under her. Lawrence is as sensitive to falsity as the True Princess was to the pea. And he is just as sure to proclaim the injury.

How can he be so quarrelsome with us while at the same time he is enrapturing us with his extraordinary powers to make us see and feel beauty? But my feeling toward his writing is my feeling toward greatness anywhere. Take it—take it all. It is no laughing matter. It is more pertinent to give in to that beauty of his and better to grit our teeth at his cruelty—for he is cruel—than to laugh at or be annoyed by the shambles he makes of the everyday world.

We all use the everyday world in our stories, and some of us feel inclined or even bound to give it at least a cursory glance and treatment, but Lawrence does not care. He feels no responsibility there at all. He does not care if the mechanics and props of everyday life suffer in his stories from distortion unto absurdity, if his narrative thins and frays away into silliness. Those things aren't what he's concerned with. His plots might remind you of some kind of tropical birds—that are awkward in structure and really impossible-looking when they're on the ground, and then when they take wing and fly, a miracle happens. All that clumsiness and outrageousness is gone; the bird's body becomes astonishingly functional, and iridescent in flight.

8

Wlliam Faulkner carries on a plot of development of a kind which I have not yet discussed. The more we read and write, the more clearly we see how many ways there are of *using material.* Some compile meticulously, adding and subtracting and getting a sum which is a story, and which could be graphed if required; sometimes Henry James, who uses this method, seems to be plotting, all exquisitely, graph after graph of different kinds of blights. Other writers distill material, getting clearer and purer essences as though by some boiling down process—Lawrence, for example. Faulkner seems to set upon his material and divine his stories from it.

The furious speed of Faulkner's stories is one of the marks of a divining writer. His stories seem to race with time, race with the world. You remember—who could forget?—one sentence of 1600 words in "The Bear." How this skyscraper could race—like a dinosaur across the early fields of time—is something to teach us mainly that in the world of our story-making, wonders never cease. But that sentence runs along with a strange time-encompassing quality of seeming all to happen at once; while we are reading we are still hearing the part behind, and the part before is being anticipated by means of its present part. It makes us realize how true it is that prose is a structure, in its every part—the imagination, by instinct or otherwise, is engineered when we write. A sentence can be in as perfect control as a bridge or a church. Not too obviously or too exquisitely perhaps, or the reader might start testing as he goes, which would be fatal to the story.

But the reason Faulkner's unwieldly-looking sentences can race is of course their high organization—a musical organization. And Faulkner is highly organized and his evocation does seem to come out of the place where music comes from. Don't let his turbulence ever blind us; his structure is there—daring structure. To me, above all other present-day story-tellers he is the one ahead of his time—the most astonishingly powered and passionate writer we have. "The Bear" is an apocalyptic story of the end of the wilderness. It ends with the senseless clang on clang of a man idiotically pounding pieces of his broken gun together while, in the isolated gum tree over his head, forty or fifty squirrels are running frantically around. It signifies for one thing the arrival of the machine age and the squealing treadmill. The story encompasses past and future, all the past of the land from the Indian times on to this. It has towering heroic figures, wilderness figures, symbolic figures; and we get the knowledge in every happening of its happening again, over and over—and the marvelous whole world of the wilderness, the whole history of Mississippi.

For in "The Bear" the structure of time is constantly in danger of being ripped away, torn down by the author—the *whole* time bulges at the cracks to get into the present-time of the story. This dilation in time sense and intractability in space sense, the whole blown-up surface of the story, has of itself a kind of looming quality, a portentousness. Like the skin of a balloon, time and space are stretched to hold more, while the story remains in form and function itself.

It is this, most of all, that makes "The Bear" a great deal more than a hunting story. It is a very long story, in five parts, and in Part IV the flimsy partition that keeps the story time apart from whole time flies away entirely. The entire history of the land and a people crowds into a chapter of an expansion, in sentence and paragraph, almost outrageous to the eye alone. Duration of time and extent of space, which always took the accusative case, and were disposed of that way, are let loose now—they are evoked, and tear through the story running backwards and forwards, up and down, into Indian times and the very future, like a pack of beasts from the world's wilderness itself. And this is the beauty of the story. Its self-destruction, self-immolation, is the way it transcends all it might have been had it stayed intact and properly nailed together. There is its wonder.

Sherwood Anderson, it could be said, used this power of expansion in quite another sense in the Winesburg stories—whereby the uneventful and imprisoned life he saw around him became moving and tragic as though another dimension had been added when it passed through his passionate survey—like the same river flowing between deeper walls. In the case of "The Bear," I feel that to Faulkner the escapement of wild time and place must have seemed one *attribute* of the thing he was describing, the lost attribute—just as to Anderson passion was the lost attribute of Winesburg—implicit in it and supplied now, in his stories.

Faulkner in letting time and place out of the box was not being reckless and exhibiting his talents—though what a spectacle they make!—but being true, faithful to his conception of the story at hand. If this alarms many readers, even the very ones most alarmed will have to be the first ones to admit the strict propriety of it.

9

A story's major emphasis may fall on the things that make it up—on character, on plot, on its physical or moral world, in sensory or symbolic form. And perhaps the way this emphasis is let fall may determine the value of the story; may determine not how well it is written, but the worth of its being written.

Of course fashion and the habits of understanding stories at given periods in history may play their parts, unconsciously or willfully. But mainly, I venture to think, the way emphasis falls, the value of a story, is the thing nearest dependent upon the individual and personal factor involved, the writer behind the writing.

The fine story writers seem to be in a sense obstructionists. As if they hold back their own best interests. It's a strange illusion. For if we look to the source of the deepest pleasure we receive from a writer, how surprising it seems that this very source is the quondam obstruction. The fact is, in seeking our source of pleasure we have entered another world again. We are speaking of beauty.

And beauty is not a blatant or promiscuous or obvious quality; indeed at her finest she is somehow associated with obstruction—with reticence of a number of kinds. The beauty of "The Bear" seems tied up intimately with the reluctance to confine the story to its proper time sequence and space measurements; Faulkner makes fantastic difficulty about time and place both, and the result is beauty. Time after time Lawrence refuses to get his story told, to let his characters talk in any natural way; the story is held up forever, and through so delaying and through such refusal on the author's part, we enter the magical world of pure sense, of evocation—the shortest cut known through the woods.

Could it be that one who carps at difficulties in a writer ("Why didn't he write it like this? Why didn't he write another story?"), at infringements of the rules and lack of performance of duty, fails to take note of beauty? And fails to see straight off that beauty springs from deviation, from desire not to comply but to act inevitably, as long as truth is in sight, whatever that inevitability may mean?

Where does beauty come from, in the short story? Beauty comes from form, from development of idea, from after-effect. It often comes from carefulness, lack of confusion, elimination of waste—and yes, those are the rules. But that can be on occasion a cold kind of beauty, when there are warm kinds. And beware of tidiness. Sometimes spontaneity is the most sparkling kind of beauty—Katherine Mansfield had it. It is a fortuitous circumstance attending the birth of some stories, like a fairy godmother that has—this time—accepted the standing invitation and come smiling in.

Beauty may be missed or forgotten sometimes by the analyzers because it is not a means, not a way of getting the story along, or furthering a thing in the world. For beauty is a result—as form is a result. It *comes.* We are lucky when beauty comes, for often we try, but then when the virtues of our story are counted, beauty is standing behind the door. I think it may be wrong to try for beauty; we should try for other things, and then hope.

Intensity and beauty are qualities that will come out of man's imagination and out of his passion—which use sensitivity for their finding and focusing power. (This can't beg the question quite so hopelessly as assigning the best stories to genius.) It seems to be true that for practical purposes, in writing a story, beauty is in greatest accord with sensitivity.

The two things that cannot be imitated, beauty and sensitivity, are or may be kin to each other. But there is only one of them we can strive for. Sensitivity in ourselves. It is our technique. In the end, our technique is sensitivity, and beauty may be our reward.

A short-story writer can try anything. He has tried anything—but presumably not everything. Variety is, has been, and no doubt will remain endless in possibilities, because the power and stirring of the mind never rests. It is what this power will try that will most pertinently define the short story. Not rules, not aesthetics, not problems and their solution. It is not rules as long as there is imagination; not aesthetics as long as there is passion; not success as long as there is intensity behind the effort that calls forth and communicates, that will try and try again.

And at the other end of the stories is the reader. There is no use really to fear "the reader." The surly old bugaboo who wants his money's worth out of a magazine—yes, he is there (or I suspect it is a she, still wanting her money's worth and having yet to be convinced she's got it); but there is another reader too, perhaps with more at stake.

Inescapably, this reader exists—the same as ourselves; the reader who is also a user of imagination and thought. This reader picks up a story, maybe our new story, and behold, sees it fresh, and meets it with a storehouse of hope and interest.

And, reader and writer, we can wish each other well. Don't we after all want the same thing? A story of beauty and passion and truth?

EXERCISES

1. Miss Welty makes a distinction between (1) the creation and (2) the analysis of a short story. The person analyzing a story will isolate certain things or abstract them from the story: he will discuss tone, pace, the withholding of

information until the psychologically right moment, the moment of illumination, etc. The experienced writer of short stories is aware of these matters while he is creating a story even though he may not use these "critical" terms. An understanding of the method of analysis exists prior to the writing of a story and is necessary for the writer. Can you list any other terms that both the student and the writer of short stories will find useful?

2. In Section 3, Miss Welty discusses the uniqueness of the stories written by Hemingway, Faulkner, Lawrence or E. M. Forster. Sometimes critics talk about "Faulkner's world" or "James' world." In her discussion of Lawrence's characters (Section 7), Miss Welty says they would seem deranged people if we should meet them in real life. Does it follow that they seem deranged or unreal when we meet them in Lawrence's stories? Before answering this you might reconsider what is meant by a writer's "world."

3. In Section 4 and Section 5, Miss Welty analyzes "The Bride Comes to Yellow Sky" and "Miss Brill." Choose a story that has interested you and write your own analysis of it.

4. In her final section, Miss Welty says that the writer cannot consciously create beauty. After you have studied her comments restate her point in your own terms. Do you agree with Miss Welty?

2 STORY, THEME AND SITUATION

by Elizabeth Bowen

Elizabeth Bowen (1899–   ) was born in Dublin of an Anglo-Irish family and educated at Downe House in Kent. While still in her teens, she went to London, where she soon began to write. Her first novel, The Hotel *(1927), grew out of experiences she had had in Italy, but most of her fiction is about the upper middle classes in Ireland and England. In her work she especially explores frustration and unhappiness. Two of her short story collections,* The Cat Jumps *(1934) and* Look at All Those Roses *(1941), are well known. At her best, she is a subtle stylist.*

This essay was delivered as a three-part talk over the BBC in England. Miss Bowen explains that the good novel presents speculations and perceptions that will engage the attention of serious adult minds. As a story, it should be simple, turning upon some issue or crisis of general interest: it should begin well, and give promise of sustained interest. Miss Bowen also explores the nature of theme in a novel, discusses some methods of characterization and scene-settings, and concludes with a discussion of a novelist's rela-

tion to his own generation and to succeeding generations. Hers is a good general introduction to the problems of writing and reading serious fiction.

PART I: TRUTH AND FICTION

What is a novel? I say: an invented story. At the same time a story which, though invented has the power to ring true. True to what? True to life as the reader knows life to be or, it may be, feels life to be. And I mean the adult, the grown-up reader. Such a reader has outgrown fairy tales, and we do not want the fantastic and the impossible. So I say to you that a novel must stand up to the adult tests of reality.

The Novelist's Imagination

You may say: 'If one wants truth, why not go to the literally true book? Biography or documentary, these amazing accounts of amazing experiences which people have'. Yes, but I am suggesting to you that there is a distinction between truth and so-called reality. What these people write in their accounts of happenings is actually and factually true, but the novel is not confining itself to what happened. The novel does not simply recount experience, it adds to experience. I hope you will see what I mean. It is not news at all, not anything sensational or spectacular. And here comes in what is the actual livening spark of the novel: the novelist's imagination has a power of its own. It does not merely invent, it perceives. It intensifies, therefore it gives power, extra importance, greater truth, and greater inner reality to what well may be ordinary and everyday things.

So much is art—the art that, in common with poetry, drama, painting, and music, does, we all know, enter into the novel. But not less and absolutely joined with the art is craft, and craft—craftsmanship—is absolutely and surely an essential for the writing of a novel. I have said the novel is story. It is the story aspect that I am talking about first and now, and the craft of the novelist does lie first of all in story telling.

What is a good story? I give you three things which strike me. First, it is simple—by which I mean straightforward, easy to grasp, and therefore liable to be well remembered. Do you think by stressing simplicity I perhaps simplify too much? Do we say, 'Ah, but what about such books as *The Brothers Karamazov*; would you call such a story simple?' No, I would not; it is full of halts and magnificent confusions—at least to me. And therefore by my definition I would call *The Brothers Karamazov* a great book, but not, in the craftsmanship sense, a good novel. The novelists out-and-out do recognise what is a good story. It is part of their craft to perceive what story is. Look how brilliant in their choices—in their finding of stories—have been Dickens, Jane Austen, Balzac, Conrad, Hardy, Tolstoy, to name only a few of what we now call the classics. And, among contemporaries, is not the same true of Graham Greene, or E. M. Forster, Joyce Cary, Hemingway, and many others who pass with you and of whom you will probably think now?

The next mark of a good story is, surely, its general interest. The good story, to put it as shortly as I can, turns upon some crisis, or problem, which would be of importance, intense importance, to us; to you and me in our own lives.

Then the third essential of the good story—a good story takes off well. It takes off from a situation which holds promise, or at any rate it suggests that such a situation is to be. There I am generalising. I do say to you that it is not fair to judge all novels, even the best, by their opening pages. But, speaking as a reader, I must say that I myself am tremendously influenced for or against a book by the manner of the opening, and that as a novelist myself I have put great stress and interest into the openings of my own books. And though they are open to every criticism, I still would stand by the first two pages of most of the novels I ever wrote. However, to get to something more interesting and further from me, here are three examples of openings; and I want you to notice that in each we get the seed of the character of the whole book from this first initial scene.

While the present century was in its teens, and on one sunshiny morning in June, there drove up to the great iron gate of Miss Pinkerton's academy for young ladies, on Chiswick Mall, a large family coach, with two fat horses in blazing harness, driven by a fat coachman in a three-cornered hat and wig, at the rate of four miles an hour. A black servant, who reposed on the box beside the fat coachman, uncurled his bandy legs as soon as the equipage drew up opposite Miss Pinkerton's shining brass plate, and as he pulled the bell, at least a score of young heads were seen peering out of the narrow windows of the stately old brick house. Nay, the acute observer might have recognised the little red nose of good-natured Miss Jemima Pinkerton herself, rising over some geranium-pots in the window of that lady's own drawing-room.

'It is Mrs. Sedley's coach, sister', said Miss Jemima. 'Sambo, the black servant, has just rung the bell; and the coachman has a new red waistcoat'.

'Have you completed all the necessary preparations incident to Miss Sedley's departure, Miss Jemima?' asked Miss Pinkerton herself, that majestic lady; the Semiramis of Hammersmith, the friend of Doctor Johnson, the correspondent of Mrs. Chapone herself.

'The girls were up at four this morning, packing her trunks, sister' replied Miss Jemima; 'we have made her a bow-pot'.

'Say a bouquet, sister Jemima, 'tis more genteel'.

'Well, a booky as big almost as a hay-stack; I have put up two bottles of the gillyflower-water for Mrs. Sedley, and the receipt for making it, in Amelia's box'.

'And I trust, Miss Jemima, you have made a copy of Miss Sedley's account. This is it, is it? Very good—ninety-three pounds, four shillings'.

You will know that, I expect? The first page of *Vanity Fair*. What writing for the eye, isn't it? Doesn't that strike you? One is reminded that Thackeray was also a first-rate comic draughtsman, and do you notice how he whisks us from the outside into the inside of the house? Also what a foretaste: we know the note of the book. It is to be satire, you can see all those small, deft satirical flicks—the theme is going to be worldliness, success-mania and all its attendant absurdities. It is also magnificent stage setting; the stage is set. For whom? Who is to enter? Becky Sharp. I give you *Vanity Fair* as an extreme satiric example of one whole big group of fiction, the social novel.

Here is something totally different:

Hale knew, before he had been in Brighton three hours, that they meant to murder him. With his inky fingers and his bitten nails, his manner cynical and nervous, anybody could tell he didn't belong—belong to the early summer sun, the cool Whitsun wind off the sea, the holiday crowd. They came in by train from Victoria every five minutes, rocked down Queen's Road standing on the tops of the little local trams, stepped off in bewildered multitudes into fresh and glittering air: the new silver paint sparkled on the piers, the cream houses ran away into the west like a pale Victorian water-colour; a race in miniature motors, a band playing, flower gardens in bloom below the front, an aeroplane advertising something for the health in pale vanishing clouds across the sky.

It had seemed quite easy to Hale to be lost in Brighton. Fifty thousand people besides himself were down for the day, and for quite a while he gave himself up to the good day, drinking gins and tonics wherever his programme allowed. For he had to stick closely to a programme: from ten till eleven Queen's Road and Castle Square, from eleven till twelve the Aquarium and Palace Pier, twelve till one the front between the Old Ship and West Pier, back for lunch between one and two in any restaurant he chose around the Castle Square, and after that he had to make his way all down the parade to the West Pier and then to the station by the Hove streets. These were the limits of his absurd and widely advertised sentry go.

Undertow of Suspense

The first page of Graham Greene's *Brighton Rock*: straight off, we go into danger; the undertow of suspense and fear—the thing isolating one man from fifty thousand. Again wonderful scene-setting. You will have reacted to the immense contrast between the scene and the man; the irony of the band playing, the bright glistening paint, the Whitsun sunshine. This could be the opening of a first-rate thriller—and why not? Graham Greene's genius is contemporary; he is master of the technique which is in essence twentieth century. Tautness, quickness, and what Sartre has called the 'extreme situation'. There is something in that technique in common with the cinema; something, yes, in common with the thriller; swift moving and for the eye; dry, anti-emotional. Yes, but there is more to this. Graham Greene is using all this quick technique, this sense of imminent danger, for a purpose of his own. He deals in danger, yes; but the danger is more than danger to the flesh—it is danger to the soul. So the crisis is internal. And Graham Greene's novels head what is now a prominent group of fiction—the novel of action—though indeed he would not be what he is if he dealt only with action in the outward, physical sense.

Now I want an opening in another period of time:

There was no possibility of taking a walk that day. We had been wandering, indeed, in the leafless shrubbery an hour in the morning; but since dinner (Mrs. Reed, when there was no company, dined early) the cold winter wind had brought with it clouds so sombre, and a rain so penetrating, that further outdoor exercise was now out of the question.

I was glad of it: I never liked long walks, especially on chilly afternoons: dreadful to me was the coming home in the raw twilight, with nipped fingers and toes, and a heart saddened by the chidings of Bessie, the nurse, and humbled by the consciousness of my physical inferiority to Eliza, John, and Georgiana Reed.

The said Eliza, John, and Georgiana were now clustered round their mama in the drawing-room: she lay reclined on a sofa by the fireside, and with her darlings about her (for the time neither quarrelling nor crying) looked perfectly happy. Me, she had dispensed from joining the group; saying, 'She regretted to be under the necessity of keeping me at a distance; but that until she heard from Bessie, and could discover by her own observation that I was endeavouring in good earnest to acquire a more sociable and childlike disposition, a more attractive and sprightly manner—something lighter, franker, more natural as it were—she really must exclude me from privileges intended only for contented, happy, little children'.

'What does Bessie say I have done?' I asked.

Charlotte Brontë's opening into *Jane Eyre*. The key-note—immediate—and in how few words! We see the child Jane as life has already made her—solitary, sombre, isolated, unyielding. Exclusion seems to be her fate. But she does not sit down, you will notice, under injustice. Boldly she asks that point-blank question: 'What does Bessie say I have done?' This is to be the Jane of the after years; alone against the world and yet always flying her own flag.

Exile from Happiness

Charlotte Brontë, like Graham Greene, has used contrast to build up immediate drama. The exiled child on a bitterly cold day against the cosy, glowing family group in the firelight. This exile from happiness is to repeat and repeat itself throughout the novel. *Jane Eyre* is one of the most outstanding of a third group again, the character novel, and that is not simply a novel in which character plays a great part—because character does that in all novels—but one in which the story is architected round a single person, and one in which, usually, such persons show power to influence their own destiny so that the story springs from them. Things happen because of what they are and what they do. In themselves they precipitate situations. You will think of innumerable other examples of the character novel, *David Copperfield, Madame Bovary, Tom Jones.*

It seems to me today that we have fewer character novels. Is that because, do you think, we are less now concerned with individuals' destiny, or is it because the social novel with the questions it brings up, or the action novel with its clear-cut issues, appeals more to our kind of imagination?

There is a tremendous further thing in the story. I do not mean by 'story' simply the 'plot'—the outline of the happenings. There must be story in that sense: cause and effect, the keeping of suspense in play; the 'what next?' element. But something else is necessary to the story if the novel is to have the proportions it should have. We need a theme—an inner subject. The theme is what the novel is about, and, still more, it is the reason for the novel. You may know how difficult it is, if you are impressed by a book you are reading, and somebody says: 'What is it about?' You outline the superficial plot or story and your friend may say: 'Well, I've heard of all that before'. And really in order to convey the effect that the novel is having on you, you would have to plunge a degree more deeply and find words, if you could, if you had time, for the underlying idea which gives the reason why the story should be told, and the reason why the story is important and hits you.

I think that in almost all cases the theme, or the idea, of the novel has come first of all to the mind of the author, and he has shaped his plot in order to express it and conceives of his characters in terms of it. It is the kindling spark—the ignition spark—that is in his mind when he says: 'I've got an idea for a story!'

Let us consider some themes: *Vanity Fair* we have touched on—worldliness, its absurdities. Of *Brighton Rock*, one would say guilt and the danger which it involves. Other themes: conscience in Trollope's *The Warden*, and recently, in a novel of this year, Angus Wilson's *Anglo-Saxon Attitudes.* Love of power: *Emma, Barchester Towers;* and, in France, in many of the Balzac stories; in contemporary Britain in almost all of the Ivy Compton-Burnett novels. Self-deception: *Great Expectations,* and, again, *Emma.* (Often a novel may have a dual theme.) Self-redemption: *Lord*

Jim; The Power and the Glory. Frustration: *Jude the Obscure.* Real versus unreal values: *Howard's End,* and, indeed, I think all the E. M. Forster novels.

Two Attributes of the Theme

Two attributes the theme must have: the moral element, because it is through the theme that the novelist makes his evaluations or shows some new aspect of truth which has struck him: and again the theme must be deeply submerged in the story. If a theme or idea is too near the surface, the novel becomes simply a tract illustrating an idea. I do not mean theme in that way. It is something of which you will feel the effects and which works strongly for the novelist but which is down so deep that you may have to analyse the story to find what it actually is.

Besides theme, the story must have another thing: situation. The situation is something more than a series of episodes and happenings through which the story moves. There is nearly always an overall situation which is a 'controlling' thing. Often it is a situation between two persons: the unhappy passion of Anna and Vronsky in *Anna Karenina,* or in *Wuthering Heights* the stronger-than-death tie between Catherine and Heathcliff. There are endless variants of this situation between two persons which maintains through a book. For instance, enslavement—or disillusionment. But the situation can also be a circumstance. It can be the situation of somebody being extremely poor and being thrust into some kind of behaviour because of it. It can be a craving for education as in *Jude the Obscure,* or the idealisation of a great house and family as in Evelyn Waugh's *Brideshead Revisited.* And throughout Proust's long masterpiece there is his absorption in his own romantic conceptions of person after person who comes his way. I would call that situation.

I have said only exceedingly few of the things which could be said about the aspect of the novel as story. I have said that though the story is invented it must ring true through the power of imagination which is something higher than invention. It has a form of vision which makes for a peculiar truth. I have said that not only art but craftsmanship is necessary for the bringing alive of story, and that the story, besides its plot—however well built and exciting—must have an internal theme, and must hinge round some overall situation which must clearly be an interesting one. It is the presence of theme above all which demarcates the novel, and the greater the theme and the more imaginatively it is worked out the greater the novel.

There are excellent forms of story, like the detective story or thriller, which do not claim to have theme. We react to and we enjoy the sheer suspense element and the quick action. But I think the failure of theme—

the failure of a really important inside idea—shows in the kind of novel which is inferior. It is hard to say why: the story may be good, the characters may be amusingly touched in, but if at the end of a novel we put it down and it evaporates from our minds—if then we care to go back and see why that book has seemed less important and not worth more than the few hours which it entertained us—we will almost always find that the novelist has not had either a conception or a grasp of some inner, underlying important idea. And those ideas can be worked out perfectly well in comedy and satire. I do not want to leave in your minds the idea that a novel must be pompous or didactic.

Finally, you may say: 'Do you confine the novel to something which has an evident outward story?' And you will bring up some of the most interesting experiments of this century in which we live, the works, say, of Kafka or of James Joyce. I say that there is always story in a novel, but it may be on some different and unexpected plane: it may be psychological, emotional, or internal. And I cannot think of a better example of psychological story than the culminating masterpiece of James Joyce—*Ulysses*. It moves forward; it moves throughout a day—and the test of a story is that it does move forward.

PART II: PEOPLE: THE CREATION OF CHARACTER

Would you or I, as readers, be drawn into a novel—implicated with what may be its other issues at all—if our interest was not pegged to the personalities and outlooks and the actions of the people whom we encounter inside the story? They are the attractive element in the book.

This being so, which comes first actually into the mind of the novelist when he begins to work: the people, or character, or the plot? Do not think it strange when I say that the plot comes first. The actual idea or outline of a book is there—the possibilities of a situation—and then the novelist thinks, 'What would be the kind of person who would perform such an action? What would be the other kind of person who would react in a particular way?' I think to myself 'I need a proud man', or 'I need a woman so idiotically romantic in temperament that she will do unwise things', or 'I need perhaps an almost excessively innocent or ignorant young person'. In that sense the characters are called into existence by the demands of the plot; but I do not want you to feel that the characters are merely invented to formula. That is not so at all. Their existence having begun, they take into themselves a most extraordinary and imperative reality. And their relation with plot is a dual one because, though to an extent the demands of the plot control them, the plot also serves to give them force and purpose. And, because of the plot, those characters are so shown and so brought into action that as little as possible of them shall go to waste.

The people, the characters in a novel, must carry with them into the book their own kind of inevitability. We are conscious when we meet the people involved in a story that they have something within them which will probably take them towards some inevitable fate or end. If that inevitability breaks down—if the characters are compelled by the author to do what we instinctively know they would not do—then I think we feel that there is a flaw in the reality of the novel.

An Example from Henry James

How does the novelist bring his people in? A great question—and it comes early on—is the showing, or the presentation, of the characters. We want to see them, we want to feel them, and we want to have some idea of what they are about, as it were, in the story, and what kind of part it is highly probable that they will play. I want to give you an example first from the early Henry James, from the novel *Portrait of a Lady*. Visualise the scene: it is a summer day in the evening and on the lawn of an English country house by the Thames two gentlemen are strolling in conversation.

One of these was a remarkably well-made man of five-and-thirty, with a face as English as that of the old gentleman I have just sketched was something else; a noticeably handsome face, fresh-coloured, fair and frank, with firm, straight features, a lively grey eye and the rich adornment of a chestnut beard. This person had a certain fortunate, brilliant, exceptional look—the air of a happy temperament fertilised by a high civilisation—which would have made almost any observer envy him at a venture. He was booted and spurred, as if he had dismounted from a long ride; he wore a white hat, which looked too large for him; he held his two hands behind him, and in one of them—a large, white, well-shaped fist—was crumpled a pair of soiled dog-skin gloves.

His companion, measuring the length of the lawn beside him, was a person of quite a different pattern, who, although he might have excited grave curiosity, would not, like the other, have provoked you to wish yourself, almost blindly, in his place. Tall, lean, loosely and feebly put together, he had an ugly, sickly, witty, charming face, furnished, but by no means decorated, with a straggling moustache and whisker. He looked clever and ill—a combination by no means felicitous; and he wore a brown velvet jacket. He carried his hands in his pockets, and there was something in the way he did it that showed the habit was inveterate. His gait had a shambling, wandering quality; he was not very firm on his legs.

The first of those is a young English lord; the second is a highly intelligent American expatriate—something perhaps in common with Henry James and the type with whom he dealt so much. You will see how those small descriptive touches are none of them put in in a purely categorical way, and how the first young man is saved from being aggressively successful, aggressively privileged, by those odd little touches of eccentricity. His hat is too big, his crumpled gloves are rather soiled. And the second, there is something straggling—straggling in the moustache, straggling in the way he walks about—and yet we feel in that second man this sensitive, complex, deeply responsive strain. Neither of these two men is the central character. Isobel Archer is in a moment more to walk through the door of the house and across the lawn to meet them. These two characters are to play a tremendous part in her life, and I think the kind of role which each will play in their love for her and their desire to help her is indicated in those two very short paragraphs in which Henry James has first shown them to us.

Development by Analysis or by Dialogue

But there is not only the question of showing, of presenting, of introducing the characters. There is the still—I think—trickier one of keeping them in play, perpetually in the view of the reader, engaged in the action and also furthering the development of the plot. And this is done in two ways: either by analysis or by dialogue. Analysis has always been used. It was the original loose, comfortable, descriptive method which the late eighteenth-century people and the Victorians employed. The writer stepped in, he intervened, he explained the actions of his characters and he himself described their thoughts or emotions. But the other, the more recent and the more subtle kind of character analysis, which I think is most peculiar to the early part of the twentieth century, was called the 'stream of consciousness', and that had as its exponents such people as Dorothy Richardson, George Meredith, Proust, Henry James (increasingly as his work went on), James Joyce, and sometimes, though not to so great an extent, Virginia Woolf. This showed characters, not through explanations, but through the thoughts which occurred to them and the sensations which they had. Consider this from Dorothy Richardson, out of one of the novels in the Miriam sequence which is called *The Tunnel.*

At Gower Street it was eleven o'clock. She was faint with hunger. She had had no dinner and there was nothing in her room. She wandered along the Euston Road hoping to meet a potato-man. The shop fronts were black. There was nothing to meet her need but the empty stretch of lamplit pavement leading on and on. Rapid walking in the rain-freshened air relieved her faintness, but she dreaded waking in the night with gnawing hunger to keep her awake and drag her up exhausted in the morning. A faint square of brighter light on the pavement ahead came like an accusation. Passing swiftly across it she glanced bitterly at the frosted door through which it came. Restaurant. Donizetti Brothers. The whole world had conspired to leave her alone with that mystery, shut in and hidden every day the whole of her London time behind its closed frosted front doors and forcing her now to admit that there was food there and that she must go in or have the knowledge of being starved through fear. Her thoughts flashed painfully across a frosted door long ago in Baker Street, and she saw the angry handsome face of the waiter who had shouted 'Roll and butter' and whisked away from the table the twisted cone of serviette and the knives and forks. That was the middle of the day. It would be worse at night. Perhaps they would even refuse to serve her. Perhaps it was impossible to go into a restaurant late at night alone. She was coming back. There was nothing to be seen behind the steamy panes of either side of the door door but plants standing on oil-cloth mats. Behind them was again frosted glass. It was not so grand as Baker Street. There was no menu in a large glass frame with 'Schweppe's' at the top. She pushed open the glass door and was confronted by another glass door blankly frosted all over. Why were they so secret?

You see how that works. Outwardly we have a street and the entrance to the restaurant, but all of it is photographed in terms of subjectivity of a hungry, tired, and, above all, nervous and dread-filled young woman who is trying to make up her mind to go in and buy herself a meal. Why does the light show like an accusation? Because here is something that she must face—food; but has she got the nerve to go in and order her small cheap meal? . . . And the idea of secrecy and the restaurant being kept back as a sort of conspiratorial mystery. Here is somebody alone in London, and the entire five books of the sequence are devoted to this extraordinary reaction of one personality to what are outwardly perfectly ordinary circumstances to the Londoner who takes them for granted.

The 'Stream of Consciousness'

Two things may be remarked about the 'stream of consciousness' in the showing of character. It does take time and it deals almost always with prosaic experience seen or reacted to in a highly individual way. I do not know whether we should ever have, for instance, a stream-of-consciousness novel about somebody scaling Everest, because the scaling of Everest is exciting enough in itself. In the ordinary 'stream of consciousness', the excitement, the sense of crisis, resides in the personality, and all the other characters in the novel are likely to be slightly out of focus.

I want tremendously to go straight on to the question of the dialogue. Dialogue is much more the *contemporary* way of keeping in evidence—keeping in play—the characters in a book, and I think a satisfactory reason for this is that it is arresting and entertaining and clear cut and highly personal. Jane Austen, much in advance of her day, was a mistress of the use of the dialogue. She used it as dialogue should be used—to advance the story; not only to show the characters but to advance. Here, in this extract from *Mansfield Park*, you will find three characters—Fanny, the little poor relation; Lady Bertram, the overpowering and rather selfish aunt who is not only Fanny's relation but her employer; and Edmund, the son of Lady Bertram—all confronted by a situation which has never come up before. Fanny, mouse, accustomed to being ignored, has for the first time been invited out to a dinner party at the rectory.

'But why should Mrs. Grant ask Fanny?' said Lady Bertram. 'How came she to think of asking Fanny?—Fanny never dines there, you know, in this sort of way. I cannot spare her, and I am sure she does not want to go.—Fanny, you do not want to go, do you?'

'If you put such a question to her', cried Edmund, preventing his cousin's speaking, 'Fanny will immediately say, no; but I am sure, my dear mother, she would like to go; and I can see no reason why she should not'.

'I cannot imagine why Mrs. Grant should think of asking her?—She never did before.—She used to ask your sisters now and then, but she never asked Fanny'.

'If you cannot do without me, ma'am', said Fanny, in a self-denying tone—

'But my mother will have my father with her all the evening'.

'To be sure, so I shall'.

'Suppose you take my father's opinion, ma'am'.

'That's well thought of. So I will, Edmund. I will ask Sir Thomas, as soon as he comes in, whether I can do without her'.

'As you please, ma'am, on that head; but I meant my father's opinion as to the *propriety* of the invitation's being accepted or not; and I think he will consider it a right thing by Mrs. Grant, as well as by Fanny, that being the *first* invitation it should be accepted'.

'I do not know. We will ask him. But he will be very much surprized that Mrs. Grant should ask Fanny at all'.

Dealing with the Unprecedented

We learn something, as I said, of the relationships between these three, brought out by the small social crisis. We are in the grip of something which, in this undisturbed world of the big, bland country house, Mansfield Park, has not happened before. All good dialogue perhaps deals with something unprecedented. Here now is a totally different manner. It is a piece from E. M. Forster's *Howard's End*. The circumstances are that Margaret Schlegel, recently engaged to the widower Henry Wilcox, is on her way to the wedding of Henry's daughter, which is to take place in a house in Shropshire. She is in company with a number of other people, all of whom are the friends of the Wilcoxes, belonging to what might be described as their gang.

'That was the Grange,' remarked Albert, over his shoulder, and then he jammed the brake on, and the motor slowed down and stopped. 'I'm sorry', said he turing round. 'Do you mind getting out—by the door, on the right. Steady on'.

'What's happened?' asked Mrs. Warrington.

Then the car behind them drew up and the voice of Charles was heard saying: 'Get out the women at once'. There was a concourse of males, and Margaret and her companions were hustled out and received into the second car. What had happened? As it started off again the door of a cottage opened, and a girl screamed wildly at them.

'What is it?' the ladies cried.

Charles drove them a hundred yards without speaking. Then he said: 'It's all right. Your car just touched a dog'.

'But stop!' cried Margaret, horrified.

'It didn't hurt him'.

'Didn't really hurt him?' asked Myra.

'No'.

'Do *please* stop!' said Margaret, leaning forward. She was standing up in the car, the other occupants holding her knees to steady her. 'I want to go back, please'.

Charles took no notice.

'We've left Mr. Fussell behind', said another: 'and Angelo, and Crane'.

'Yes, but no woman'.

'I expect a little of'—Mrs. Warrington scratched her palm—'will be more to the point than one of us!'

'The insurance company see to that', remarked Charles, 'and Albert will do the talking'.

'I want to go back, though, I say!' repeated Margaret, getting angry.

Charles took no notice. The motor, loaded with refugees, continued to travel very slowly down the hill. 'The men are there', chorused the others. 'Men will see to it'.

'The men *can't* see to it. Oh, this is ridiculous! Charles, I ask you to stop'.

'Stopping's no good', drawled Charles.

'Isn't it?' said Margaret, and jumped straight out of the car.

She fell on her knees, cut her gloves, shook her hat over her ear. Cries of alarm followed her. 'You've hurt yourself!' exclaimed Charles, jumping after her.

'Of course I've hurt myself!' she retorted.

'May I ask what—'

'There's nothing to ask', said Margaret.

'Your hand's bleeding'.

'I know'.

'I'm in for a frightful row from the pater'.

'You should have thought of that sooner, Charles'.

Charles had never been in such a position before. It was a woman in revolt who was hobbling away from him, and the sight was too strange to leave any room for anger. He recovered himself when the others caught them up: their sort he understood. He commanded them to go back.

Albert Fussell was seen walking towards them.

'It's all right!' he called. 'It wasn't a dog, it was a cat'.

'There!' exclaimed Charles triumphantly. 'It's only a rotten cat'.

A Novel of Protracted Crises

You might call that a fight more than a conversation. The Schlegel-Wilcox antagonism has flared up and all because of 'a rotten cat'. Can Margaret Schlegel marry into this family, have this awful Charles as a stepson? *Howard's End,* for all its Edwardian surface, is a violent novel. It contains five—six—seven really explosive scenes. It is pitched high. What causes this protracted crisis? Conflicting values, opposing views of life. And such a novel, with such a theme of conflict could not, I am sure, have been written analytically. It is essential for the author's purpose to keep the characters human, spontaneous, and naturalistic. They must be close up to the eye, close to one's feelings the whole time, otherwise *Howard's End* could have been an abstract tract.

Both those authors, Jane Austen and E. M. Forster, have come into a renewed kind of prominence since the value of dialogue has been realised, and since we turn more and more to the dialogue-telling of the story. There have been changes in the use and the conception of dialogue. About thirty years ago the prevailing mode of expression was the analytical, which perhaps was a little misty and a little slow, and through this kind of smoke-screen of continuous analysis broke out, not long after the first world war, this sharp, clear-cut, almost rowdy dialogue of which the younger Hemingway was the great exponent.

But is there not now an emergence of dialogue of a different kind—stylised, formalised? I call your attention to the use of dialogue in two of our immediately contemporary authors—Henry Green and Ivy Compton-Burnett. In these we have a dialogue which is not representative of the person, which does not aim in its own way to sound either realistic or spontaneous. Here is an extract from Miss Compton-Burnett's novel *Elders and Betters:*

Thomas had heard his children in silence.

'Ought you not to be teaching Reuben, my boy?'

'I am teaching him, Father'.

'And how are you contriving that?'

'By my own odd methods, that will have a better result than ordinary ones. Or that is the kind of thing that would happen'.

'He is doing something for you, I suppose?'

'He is learning to use his brain for himself, which is the end of all education'.

'But is it the beginning?'

'The same thing is always both. The beginning and the end, we say. I never quite understand it'.

'I suppose you will go and point out his mistakes?'

'I shall let him see them for himself'.

'But if he could do that, he would hardly make them'.

'You must know that we learn by our mistakes, Father'.

'Has he any need of you?'

'Great need, the poor, untaught lad'.

'What does he think of your methods?'

'He does not think; that is not a thing he would do. He is gaining self-respect from them. And he will gain independence; and that is what I want, or I should have to spend my time with him'.

'What is his feeling for you?'

'A boyish veneration that will soon approach worship. I shall not feel so free when it reaches that. I shall find it has acquired its own value'.

'What would Anna say to your methods?'

'She would think that Uncle Benjamin ought not to pay me'.

'And do you think he ought?' said Thomas.

'Well, my service is of a kind that cannot be paid for in money. And that means it is paid for in that way, but not very well'.

'Does your uncle want that kind of service?'

'Yes, or he would have to pay better'.

'He has a larger income than we have', said Tullia. 'And yet they are to spend their lives in that awkward house'.

No: decidedly *not* a form of character portraiture. All the characters in a Burnett novel speak, as you will know, more or less alike—young and old, powerful and humble. Dialogue is used, as in a parallel way Henry Green does use it, apparently as an end in itself. And yet nothing in the novel is an end in itself. The novel is the end and aim of the author. Are we to take it—I leave you, in closing, with this suggestion—that this change in the manner and use of a dialogue denotes or symbolises some change in the form of the novel, and still more in the intentions of the novel in our day? Does it mark the ending of a study of individualised character, the individual for his own sake, as a theme? Are we going back to the symbolic, the masked speaker? Is this turning away from naturalism a lapse or suspension of interest in single people and a greater sense, on our part, of the importance of crisis or the meaning of group emotion and group feeling? Do we think more of *kinds* of people?

One thing we may be certain of—people are the novel's concern and with people the novel will remain involved; though who they are and what parts they are to play may change with time and the showing may change accordingly.

PART III: TIME, PERIOD, AND REALITY

Time is a major component of the novel. I rate it at the same value as story and character. I can think of few novelists who really know, and instinctively know, their craft who do not put time to dramatic use. Let us look at some of the ways in which this is done.

First, there are books in which time may rank almost among the characters and be even the chief character. What an example is *War and Peace!* In this, time acts on people; they react to it. We watch a large number of characters confronting each other in the presence of changing time and in the grip of the dramas and the solutions which time produces. Because of this, it is totally different from some imaginary, pleasant, topical, chatty little novel that we might have had some years ago called *The Joneses in War and Peace* which would have been a superficial view of people reacting to violent circumstances.

'A *Succession of Effective Nows*'

Another use for time is that it plays a great part in suspense: the 'what next?' which in a story is so essential. In the good thriller you hear almost the time-bomb-like ticking of a clock, but also in what we may call the serious novel we are, or should be, conscious of a clock that strikes from hour to hour and the leaves of a calendar which turn over. Again, time pins the reader to that immense 'Now' which is so important if we are to have a feeling of concern and reality with the novel. The good story is a succession of effective Nows—call them scenes, if you like—and those Nows are linked together by intermediate action. We may move backwards and forwards, but the present moment must grip and hold us, so that while we read it is as important—more important—than the moment in the room where we are in our chair.

I think myself that a master of the dramatic Now was Virginia Woolf, and I want to give you an instance of her use of that extraordinary simultaneousness in which a number of things may be made dramatic by happening close to each other. Here is an extract from *Mrs. Dalloway*. The scene is Bond Street, London, on a June morning. Everything is at its height, a car has stopped unaccountably outside the windows of a flower shop.

—oh! a pistol shot in the street outside!

'Dear, those motor cars', said Miss Pym, going to the window to look, and coming back and smiling apologetically with her hands full of sweet peas, as if those motor cars, those tyres of motor cars, were all *her* fault.

The violent explosion which made Mrs. Dalloway jump and Miss Pym go to the window and apologise came from a motor car which had drawn to the side of the pavement precisely opposite Mulberry's shop window. Passers-by who, of course, stopped and stared, had just time to see a face of the very greatest importance against the dove-grey upholstery, before a male hand drew the blind and there was nothing to be seen except a square of dove grey.

Yet rumours were at once in circulation from the middle of Bond Street to Oxford Street on one side, to Atkinson's scent shop on the other, passing invisibly, inaudibly, like a cloud, swift, veil-like upon hills, falling indeed with something of a cloud's sudden sobriety and stillness upon faces which a second before had been utterly disorderly. But now mystery had brushed them with her wing; they had heard the voice of authority; the spirit of religion was abroad with her eyes bandaged tight and her lips gaping wide. But nobody knew whose face had been seen. Was it the Prince of Wales's, the Queen's, the Prime Minister's? Whose face was it? Nobody knew.

Edgar J. Watkiss, with his roll of lead piping round his arm, said audibly, humorously of course: 'The Proime Minister's kyar'.

Septimus Warren Smith, who found himself unable to pass, heard him.

Septimus Warren Smith, aged about thirty, pale-faced, beak-nosed, wearing brown shoes and a shabby overcoat, with hazel eyes which had that look of apprehension in them which makes complete strangers apprehensive too. The world has raised its whip; where will it descend?

Everything had come to a standstill. The throb of the motor engines sounded like a pulse irregularly drumming through an entire body. The sun became extraordinarily hot because the motor car had stopped outside Mulberry's shop window; old ladies on the tops of omnibuses spread their black parasols; here a green, here a red parasol opened with a little pop. Mrs. Dalloway, coming to the window with her arms full of sweet peas, looked out with her little pink face pursed in enquiry. Everyone looked at the motor car. Septimus looked. Boys on bicycles sprang off. Traffic accumulated. And there the motor car stood, with drawn blinds, and upon them a curious pattern like a tree, Septimus thought, and this gradual drawing together of everything to one centre before his eyes, as if some horror had come almost to the surface and was about to burst into flames, terrified him. The world wavered and quivered and threatened to burst into flames. It is I who am blocking the way, he thought. Was he not being looked at and pointed at; was he not weighted there, rooted to the pavement, for a purpose? But for what purpose?

'Let us go on, Septimus', said his wife, a little woman, with large eyes in a sallow pointed face; an Italian girl.

You will have been struck by those intersections of different people, the ironies, the contrasts, the happy immunity of the lady buying her pink sweet peas apologised to by the shop woman because of the slight disturbance of the noise. The war-shocked man in his inner subjective torment—nobody's business except his wife's—at bay in his own strange unhappy world. The sublime, idealised, sentimental mystery surrounding the car, and, at the same time, the slight feeling of satire towards it: what *does* go on behind those grey blinds? And the mind moved also away from Bond Street, with that idea of cloud moving over roofs, moving even while the words go on towards the green hills of Hampstead, rising beyond London. It is an extraordinary drawing together in the moment, in the actuality of the Now, of the fortunes and the thoughts and the destinies of persons who gradually we are to follow as the day and the book goes on.

Dickens as a Master Scene-setter

And while I am discussing time, in its sense of creating a sharp Now, I want to make clear the importance of the actual scene which time can create. The hour of the day, the season of the year, whether it rains or the sun shines; all these give what I have called actuality and sharpness to the moment of the scene as described. We depend a great deal on the time-information which the novelist gives to us. Think what a difference there is between a street and a street in the middle of the night; a seaside town and a seaside town in the autumn gales. One of the master scene-setters was Charles Dickens. To remind you of that I want you to consider an extract from *Bleak House:*

The waters are out in Lincolnshire. An arch of the bridge in the park has been sapped and sopped away. The adjacent low-lying ground, for half a mile in breadth, is a stagnant river, with melancholy trees for islands in it, and a surface punctured all over, all day long, with falling rain. My Lady Dedlock's 'place' has been extremely dreary. The weather, for many a day and night, has been so wet that the trees seem wet through, and the soft loppings and prunings of the woodman's axe can make no crash or crackle as they fall. The deer, looking soaked, leave quagmires where they pass. The shot of a rifle loses its sharpness in the moist air, and its smoke moves in a tardy little cloud toward the green rise, coppice-topped, that makes a background for the falling rain. The view from my Lady Dedlock's own windows is alternately a lead-coloured view, and a view in India ink. The vases on the stone terrace in the foreground catch the rain all day; and the heavy drops fall, drip, drip, drip, upon the broad flagged pavement, called, from old time, the Ghost's Walk, all night. On Sundays, the little church in the park is mouldy; the oaken pulpit breaks out into a cold sweat; and there is a general smell and taste as of the ancient Dedlocks in their graves. My Lady Dedlock (who is childless), looking out in the early twilight from her boudoir at a keeper's lodge, and seeing the light of a fire upon the latticed panes, and smoke rising from the chimney, and a child, chased by a woman, running out into the rain to meet the shining figure of a wrapped-up man coming through the gate, has been put quite out of temper. My Lady Dedlock says she has been 'bored to death'.

There has been not only a physical scene, a landscape in heavy rain, but also a social scene. We have been given our first clue as to the secret of Lady Dedlock, and all that has been done in terms of the weather and the time of day. There is a close relation between the emotional effect of the atmosphere and the crisis of the character. Dickens has given us a scene by which any woman of fashion might well be what Lady Dedlock says she is—bored; but there is more to it. We are to know, as the story goes on, why she minds, why she is really tormented, by the sight of the child. And Dickens speaks of the rain-muffled axe blows and rifle shots, but his sentences are like blows or rifle shots which are not muffled. It is sharp, it is wonderfully actual, clean-cut: all that which stands out through the veil of rain.

Next, let us look at the question of time as timing: the expansion of some scenes—it may be a few moments into pages—and the contraction of long passages of time which must be felt to have passed and yet which are not actually described. The novelist, to a certain extent, opens and shuts time like a fan as he goes along, and this is important because every story demands, because of its proportion, some particular sort of timing of its own. There must be an allotment, a proportioning of time: time gives emphasis, as you will understand. The few moments in which we may stop and stare at some face passing at the other side of the street, or the moments in which our eyes will dwell on some particular line of print in a newspaper. All that demarcates that something important, though maybe only important to us, is occurring.

I would suggest that one reason why some novels, not bad—often making a good opening or a good start—lose their hold on us, is that as the plot goes on we feel the author losing his or her grip on actuality. There is a sort of slurring and we become impatient; we look back; we say 'Yes, but is this happening on a Tuesday or a Thursday?' We feel that the focus in which time should be has been lost, the thing is being mishandled. In a great novel, in a Tolstoy or a Balzac or a Trollope novel, I am certain that the author keeps in his mind that calendar on the wall and the clock on the table. Timing is the final important aspect of time *inside* the novel, on which I should like to leave time in that first class.

Time Outside the Novel

Now for time *outside* the novel. I am considering, as I suggested at the beginning, a time which is personal to us, which surrounds us like a climate or an atmosphere. It is time which is a page—or at any rate two or three lines—of history, although, in the foreground inevitably for most of us, stand the concerns and anxieties or the pleasures and fulfilments of our own individual day. And all this rootedness of the reader in his own time does inevitably affect his attitude to the novel he reads and his sense of whether or not it contains a reality. I have a great respect for people who say point-blank that they are attracted only by what is contemporary. They do not care for an old book. They feel alienated in some way by a time atmosphere or time climate which is not their own.

I thought of an instance of that in connection with the extract from *Mrs. Dalloway*. Why on earth, as we visualise a London street now, should there be any question of parasols or umbrellas opened on a top deck? The answer is that *Mrs. Dalloway* was written in 1925, and in 1925—as people of my generation will remember—the top deck of a bus was not roofed in. That, if it is not explained, can cause a shock to the sense of reality, to the reader of that passage. 'No!' they would be inclined to call out, 'That's wrong; that disturbs that picture in my mind, in my eye'. And there are other, more fundamental changes. The judgements or the proportion may seem wrong. We may perceive what seem to us absurdities or perhaps bad practices which were totally taken for granted in their own day. The heroines of Jane Austen, brilliant and charming as they are, may seem to us to be unduly concerned with getting themselves or their friends married. The great Thomas Hardy characters may seem overdrawn, made too gigantic, on the strength of what we now know about rural conditions in the south-west of England. The Henry James cosmopolitan, upper-class characters flit, it may seem, far too easily from capital to capital—they have no currency problems and apparently not many of them have any work to do. We must admit that a book originating in a time different from our own has certain differences of circumstance, and occasionally those differences may put up a sort of barrier between ourselves who read now and the novel and what is contained in it.

If that is so, or if that were so completely, how is it that any novels survive their time? I would say that a novel survives because of its basic truthfulness, its having within it something general and universal, and a quality of imaginative perception which applies just as much now as it did in the fifty or hundred or two hundred years since the novel came to life. A novel with force in it is durable, but the key is this thing to which I referred originally when we began these talks—the initial power to pierce through the surface to some cogent and important and general imaginative truth, about life, about experience, about human persons. A novel which survives, which withstands and outlives time, does do something more than merely survive. It does not stand still. It accumulates around itself the understanding of all these persons who bring to it something of their own. It acquires associations, it becomes a form of experience in itself, so that two people who meet can often make friends, find an approach to each other, because of this one great common experience they have had. And, like all experiences, it is added to by the power of different kinds of people in different times, to feel and to comment and to explain.

An Evolution in Form

What about the novels of our day? I suggested in two or three places, such as the changes in the manner of the dialogue and the liking for dialogue, that evolution and change and alteration in the form of the novel is going on. It always has been, and, please heaven, it always will. I think the novel will be perfectly all right if it moves forward in time along with us.

We ask: What is the quality in a novel written this year or last year, or a few years ago, which holds us? Is it perhaps a comprehension and a realisation of our own time? Is it that because of the stress of history and the extending consciousness we have of being people in a time, we are more time-conscious, we are more aware of the particular climate of our day? And therefore, though we cannot ever lose our interest in individuals, is there this slight shifting of interest from the individual to the circumstance, to the individual and the relation between him and others, which compose and make for society? And when I speak of a novel being truly contemporary I do not mean the purely topical, which bases itself on the events or happenings of one year. We want our time to live in art and in the comprehension of other people, as the times before us lived for us, and I do not doubt for a moment that we are raising up and finding groups of artists, among them the novelist no less than the poet, who will express the feeling and values of our day and at the same time seize what there is in it that is essential, the thing which has come from the past and will pass on into the future—in fact, universal experience.

Novelists now have to take in, to express, to comprehend, an enormous mass of new things. It is no good pretending that the circumstances of human life and the background of human judgement are not very different from what they were fifty years ago, and for this expression a particular kind of vocabulary may have to be found, a vocabulary not only of language but of ideas. There must be language, and a language that can be kept open at the edges, and if our young novelists are to exist, if they are to survive, they do need, I think, more attention and more response and more come-back on the part of the reader, than novelists have ever needed before. The relation between the writer and the reader is and needs to be closer than it has been. The writer needs reception, good reception in the radio sense, because of this forging ahead, this seeking for an expression which shall be unique to our age and yet hold in it the elements of all time. I ask you to look out for, to be aware of, the writers, the novelists, who seem to you to be making the literature of our age. Receive them, understand them, help them, and leave in our time, as there has been before, this close link, this identification, between fiction which we read and enjoy and the truths which through fiction we comprehend.

EXERCISES

1. What does Miss Bowen mean by the "theme of a story"?
2. In "Development by Analysis or by Dialogue," Miss Bowen makes a distinction between character-drawing in the earlier forms of the novel and in its twentieth-century form. What is this distinction?
3. In this article, Miss Bowen lists the elements or components of a novel (plot, theme, character, etc.). After a careful reading of the entire article,

go back to the beginning again and as you reread make a list of these components. After each item or component that you have listed write a sentence or two in which you summarize at least one important point that has been made about each of them.

3 WHY DO WE TEACH POETRY?

by Archibald MacLeish

Archibald MacLeish (1892–) took an L.L.B. at Harvard and practised law for a number of years. In the 1920's, he was one of the group of American expatriate writers in France. The poetry he wrote then (1923–38) shows the influence of Ezra Pound and T. S. Eliot. In the thirties, he became preoccupied with the social and political problems of the time, and this was reflected in his poetry. Conquistador *won the 1933 Pulitzer Prize. He wrote a number of verse plays for radio dealing with the fascist threat to democracy. From 1939–45, he was Librarian of Congress. In 1953, he again won the Pulitzer Prize, this time for* Collected Poems, 1917–51. *He is now a Professor of English at Harvard.*

In this article MacLeish examines the difference between science and art as modes of knowledge. Science, he argues, deals with abstractions; art, with things as we experience them. Science is the language of abstraction; poetry, the language of the particularized, the concrete. Abstractions and generalized knowledge are not concerned with the individual's relationship to an object or a situation, whereas poetry is. Thus, poetry should be read because it can give us knowledge of a very precious kind and, in the words of Matthew Arnold, because it has the "power of so dealing with things as to awaken in us a wonderfully full, new and intimate sense of them and of our relation with them."

1

There is something about the art of poetry which induces a defensive posture. Even in the old days when the primacy of poetry was no more challenged than the primacy of Heaven, which is now also challenged, the posture was habitual. If you published your reflections on the art in those days you called them a *Defense*. Today, when the queen of sciences is Science, you do not perhaps employ that term but you mean it. It is not that the gentlemen at the long table in the Faculty Club whose brains have been officially cleared to serve as depositories of scientific secrets of the eighth and thirteenth classes are patronizing in their manner. They are still gentlemen and therefore still modest no matter how great their distinction or how greatly certified. But one knows one's place. One knows that whereas the teachers of science meet to hear of new triumphs which the newspapers will proudly report, the teachers of poetry meet to ask old questions—which no one will report: such questions as, why teach poetry anyway in a time like this?

It is a relief in this general atmosphere to come upon someone who feels no defensiveness whatever: who is perfectly certain that poetry ought to be taught now as at any other time and who is perfectly certain also that he knows why. The paragon I have in mind is a young friend of mine, a devoted teacher, who was recently made headmaster of one of the leading American preparatory schools, and who has been taking stock, for some time past, of his curriculum and his faculty. Poetry, as he sees it, ought to be taught "as a most essential form of human expression as well as a carrier throughout the ages of some of the most important values in our heritage." What troubles him is that few teachers, at least in the schools he knows, seem to share his conviction. He is not too sure that teachers themselves have "an abiding and missionary faith in poetry" which would lead them to see it as a great clarifier—a "human language" capable of competing with the languages of mathematics and science.

But though teachers lack the necessary faith, the fault, as my young friend sees it, is not wholly theirs. The fault is the fault of modern criticism, which has turned poetry into something he calls "poetry itself"—meaning, I suppose, poetry for poetry's sake. "Poetry itself" turns out to be poetry with its meanings distilled away, and poetry with its meanings distilled away is difficult if not impossible to teach in a secondary school—at least *his* secondary school. The result is that secondary school teachers have gone back, as to the lesser of two evils, to those historical and anecdotal practices sanctified by American graduate schools in generations past. They teach "poets and not poetry." With the result that "students become acquainted with poets from Homer to MacLeish" (quite a distance no matter how you measure it!) "but the experience doesn't necessarily leave them with increased confidence in what poetry has to offer." I can well believe it.

The reason why modern criticism has this disastrous effect, the reason why it produces "an almost morbid apathy toward 'content' or 'statement of idea,'" is its excessive "preoccupation with aesthetic values." Modern criticism insists that poems are primarily works of art; and when you insist that poems are primarily works of art you cannot, in my friend's view, teach them as carriers "throughout the ages of some of the most important values in our heritage." What is important about Homer and Shakespeare and the authors of the Bible is that they were "realists with great vision . . . whose work contains immensely valuable constructions of the meaning of life"; and if you talk too much about them as artists, those constructions of the meaning of life get lost.

Now this, you will observe, is not merely another walloping of the old horse who was once called the New Criticism. It goes a great deal farther. It is a frontal attack upon a general position maintained by many who never accepted the New Criticism or even heard of it. It is an attack upon those who believe—as most poets, I think, have believed—that a poem *is* primarily a work of art and must be read as a work of art if it is to be read at all. It is a high-minded and disinterested attack delivered for the noblest of purposes, but an attack notwithstanding—and an effective one. What it contends is that an approach to poetry which insists that a poem is a work of art blocks off what the poem has to say, whereas what the poem has to say is the principal reason for teaching it. What the argument comes down to, in other words, is the proposition that it is a mistake, in teaching poetry, to insist that poetry is art, because, if you do so insist, you will not be able to bring your students to the meaning of the poem, the idea of the poem, what the poem has to tell them about man and world and life and death—and it is for these things the teaching of the poem is important.

Now, I can understand this argument and can respect the reasons for making it. Far too many of those who define poetry in exclusively artistic terms use their definition as a limiting and protective statement which relieves them of all obligation to drive the poem's meanings beyond the meanings of the poem: beyond the mere translation of the symbols and metaphors and the classical or other references—the whole apparatus of *explication du texte*. Far too many, indeed, of those who have to do with literature generally in our time, and particularly with modern literature, consider that meanings in any but a literary (which includes a Freudian) sense are not only outside, but beneath, their proper concern—that the intrusion of questions of morality and religion into the world of art is a kind of trespass and that works of literary art not only should but *can* be studied in a moral vacuum. Literature in the hands of such teachers is well on the way to becoming again that "terrible queen" which the men of the nineties raised above life and which Yeats, when he outgrew the men of the nineties, rejected.

But although I can understand this argument, and although I can respect its reasons, and although I believe it raises a true issue and an important issue, I cannot accept it; for it rests, or seems to me to rest, on two quite dubious assumptions. The first is the assumption, familiar in one form or another to all of us, that the "idea" of a work of art is somehow separable from the work of art itself. The most recent—and most egregious—expression of this persistent notion comes from a distinguished Dean of Humanities in a great institution of learning who is reported by the New York *Times* to have argued in a scholarly gathering that "the idea which the reader derives from Ernest Hemingway's *The Old Man and The Sea* comes after the reader has absorbed some 60,000 words. This takes at least an hour. . . . A similar understanding could come after a few minutes study of a painting by a skillful artist." Precisely, one imagines, as the Doré illustrations gave one the "idea" of the *Inferno* in a few easy looks!

2

It is the second assumption, however, which divides me most emphatically from my young friend. For the second assumption seems to be that *unless* idea and work of art are distinguished from each other in the teaching of a poem, the idea—and so the effectiveness of the teaching—will be lost. At this point my friend and I part company. I am ready, and more than ready, to agree that it is for the meanings of life that one reads (and teaches) poetry. But I am unable to see how there can be a distinction between a poem as a conveyer of such meanings and a poem as a work of art. In brief, the distinction between art and knowledge which is made throughout my friend's argument seems to me wholly without foundation. That it is a distinction almost universally recognized in our epoch I know well enough. Science makes it. Poetry makes it. And the world agrees with both. "Whatever can be *known*," says Bertrand Russell, "can be known by means of science." Poetry, say its professors, has no "messages" to deliver. And no one dissents from either. The exclusive proprietary right of science to know and to communicate knowledge is not only commonly recognized in our civilization: in a very real sense it is our civilization. For the characteristic of our civilization—that which distinguishes it from the civilizations which have preceded it—is the characteristic which knowledge-by-science has conferred upon it: its abstractness.

But though the agreement is general, the proposition is not one I can accept. I argue that the apologists for science are not justified in claiming, nor the apologists for poetry in admitting, the sole right of science to know. I insist that poetry is also capable of knowledge; that poetry, indeed, is capable of a kind of knowledge of which science is not capable; that it is capable of that knowledge *as poetry*; and that the teaching of poetry as poetry, the teaching of poem as work of art, is not only not incompatible with the teaching of poetry as knowledge but is, indeed, the only possible way of teaching poetry as knowledge.

To most of us, brought up as we have been in the world of abstractions which science has prepared for us, and in the kind of school which that world produces—schools in which almost all teaching is teaching of abstractions—the notion of poetry as knowledge, the notion of art as knowledge, is a fanciful notion. Knowledge by abstraction we understand. Science can abstract ideas about apple from apple. It can organize those ideas into knowledge about apple. It can then, by some means, introduce that knowledge into our heads—possibly because our heads are abstractions also. But poetry, we know, does not abstract. Poetry presents. Poetry presents the thing as the thing. And that it should be possible to *know* the thing *as the thing it is*—to *know* apple *as* apple—this we do not understand; this, the true child of the time will assure you, cannot be done. To the true child of abstraction you can't know apple as apple. You can't know tree as tree. You can't know man as man. All you can *know* is a world dissolved by analyzing intellect into abstraction—not a world composed by imaginative intellect into itself. And the result, for the generations of abstraction, is that neither poetry nor art can be a means to knowledge. To inspiration, yes: poetry can undoubtedly lead to that—whatever it is. To revelation, perhaps: there may certainly be moments of revelation in poetry. But to knowledge, no. The only connection between poetry and knowledge we can see is the burden of used abstractions—adages and old saws—which poetry, some poetry, seems to like to carry—adages most of which we knew before and some of which aren't even true.

But if all this is so, what then is the "experience of art"—the "experience of poetry"—which all of us who think about these things at all have known? What is the experience of *realization* which comes over us with those apples on a dish of Cézanne's or those three pine trees? What is the experience of realization which comes over us with Debussy's *Nuages*? What is the experience of realization which comes over us when Coleridge's robin sits and sings

> Betwixt the tufts of snow on the bare branch
> Of mossy apple-tree, while the nigh thatch
> Smokes in the sun thaw; . . .

or when his eave-drops fall

> Heard only in the trances of the blast,
> Or if the secret ministry of frost
> Shall hang them up in silent icicles,
> Quietly shining to the quiet Moon.

And if all this is so, why does one of the most effective of modern definitions of poetry (Arnold's in his letter to Maurice de Guérin) assign to that art the peculiar "power of so dealing with *things* as to awaken in us a wonderfully full, new and intimate sense of them and of our relation with them"?

The answer is, of course, that the children of abstraction are wrong—and are impoverished by their error, as our entire time is impoverished by it. They are wrong on both heads. They are wrong when they think they *can* know the world through its abstractions: nothing can be known through an abstraction but the abstraction itself. They are wrong also when they think they *cannot* know the world as the world: the whole achievement of art is a demonstration to the contrary. And the reason they are wrong on both heads is the reason given, quite unintentionally, by Matthew Arnold. They are wrong because they do not realize that all true knowledge is a matter of relation: that we *really* know a thing only when we are filled with "a wonderfully full, new and intimate sense of it" and, above all, of "our relation with" it. This sense—this *knowledge* in the truest meaning of the word knowledge—art can give but abstraction cannot.

There are as many proofs as there are successful works of art. Take, for obvious example, that unseen mysterious phenomenon, the wind. Take any attempt, by the familiar processes of abstraction, to "know" the wind. Put beside it those two familiar lines of George Meredith:—

> Mark where the pressing wind shoots javelin-like
> Its skeleton shadow on the broad-back'd wave!

What will be the essential difference between the two? Will it not be that the first, the analytical, statement is or attempts to be a wholly objective statement made without reference to an observer (true everywhere and always), whereas an observer—*one's self* as observer!—is involved in the second? And will not the consequential difference be that a relation involving one's self is created by the second but not by the first? And will not the end difference be that the second, but not the first, will enable us to know the thing itself—to know what the thing is *like?*

It would be quite possible, I suppose, to semanticize this difference between knowledge by poetry and knowledge by abstraction out of existence by demonstrating that the word, know, is being used in two different senses in the two instances, but the triumph would be merely verbal, for the difference is real. It is indeed the realest of all differences, for what it touches is the means by which we come at reality. How are we to find the knowledge of reality in the world without, or in the shifting, flowing, fluid world within? Is all this a task for the techniques of abstraction—for science as it may be or as it is? Is it through abstraction alone that we are to find what is real in our experience of our lives—and so, conceivably, what is real in ourselves? Or do we need another and a different way of knowing—a way of knowing which will make that world out there, this world in here, available to us, not by translating them into something else—into abstractions of quantity and measure—but by bringing us ourselves to confront them as they are—man and tree face to face in the shock of recognition, man and love face to face?

The question, I beg you to see, is not what we *ought* to do. There is no ought. A man can "live" on abstractions all his life if he has the stomach for them, and many of us have—not the scientists only, but great numbers of the rest of us in this contemporary world, men whose days are a web of statistics, and names, and business deals, held together by the parentheses of a pair of commuting trains with three Martinis at the close. The question is not what we ought to do. The question is what we have the choice of doing—what alternatives are open to us. And it is here and in these terms that the issue presents itself to the teacher of poetry.

3

Colleges and universities do not exist to impose duties but to reveal choices. In a civilization like ours in which one choice has all but overwhelmed the other, a civilization dominated by abstraction, in which men are less and less able to deal with their experience of the world or of themselves unless experience and self have first been translated into abstract terms—a civilization like a foreign language—in such a civilization the need for an understanding of the alternative is urgent. What must be put before the generation of the young is the possibility of a knowledge of experience *as* experience, of self *as* self; and that possibility only the work of art, only the poem, can reveal. That it is so rarely, or so timidly, presented in our schools is one of the greatest failures of our educational system. Young men and young women graduate from American schools and colleges by the hundreds of thousands every year to whom science is the only road to knowledge, and to whom poetry is little more than a subdivision of something called "literature"—a kind of writing printed in columns instead of straight across the page and primarily intended to be deciphered by girls, who don't read it either.

This sort of thing has consequences. Abstractions are wonderfully clever tools for taking things apart and for arranging things in patterns but they are very little use in putting things together and no use at all when it comes to determining what things are *for*. Furthermore abstractions have a limiting, a dehumanizing, a dehydrating effect on the relation to things of the man who must live with them. The result is that we are more and more left, in our scientific society, without the means of knowledge of ourselves as we truly are or of our experience as it actually is. We have the tools, all the tools—we are suffocating in tools—but we cannot find the actual wood to work or even the actual hand to work it. We begin with one abstraction (something we think of as ourselves) and a mess of other abstractions (standing for the world) and we arrange and rearrange the counters, but who we are and what we are doing we simply do not know—above all what we are doing. With the inevitable consequence that we do not know either what our purpose is or our end. So that when the latest discoveries of the cyclotron are reported we hail them with the cry that we will now be able to control nature better than ever before—but we never go on to say for what purpose, to what end, we will control her. To destroy a city? To remake a world?

It was something of this kind, I imagine, that Adlai Stevenson had in mind when he startled a Smith Commencement last spring by warning his newly graduated audience of prospective wives that the "typical Western man—or typical Western husband—operates well in the realm of means, as the Roman did before him. But outside his specialty, in the realm of ends he is apt to operate poorly or not at all. . . . The neglect of the cultivation of more mature values," Mr. Stevenson went on, "can only mean that his life, and the life of the society he determines, will lack valid purpose, however busy and even profitable it may be."

As he has so often done before, Mr. Stevenson there found words for an uneasiness which has been endemic but inarticulate in the American mind for many years—the sense that we are getting nowhere far too fast and that, if something doesn't happen soon, we may arrive. But when he came to spell out the causes for "the neglect of the cultivation of more mature values" Mr. Stevenson failed, or so it seems to me, to identify the actual villain. The contemporary environment in America, he told his young listeners, is "an environment in which 'facts,' the data of the senses, are glorified and value judgments are assigned inferior status as 'mere matters of opinion.' It is an environment in which art is often regarded as an adornment of civilization rather than a vital element of it, while philosophy is not only neglected but deemed faintly disreputable because 'it never gets you anywhere.' " It is true that philosophy is neglected, and even truer that art is regarded in this country generally as it seems to be regarded by the automobile manufacturers of Detroit: as so much enamel paint and chromium to be applied for allegedly decorative purposes to the outside of a car which would run better without it. But the explanation is not, I think, that we set facts—even facts in quotation marks—above values, or that we glorify the data of the senses, unless one means by that latter phrase not what the senses tell us of the world we live in but what the statistics that can be compiled out of the data of the senses would tell us if we were ever in touch with our senses.

In few civilizations have the senses been less alive than they are with us. Look at the cities we build and occupy—but look at them!—the houses we live in, the way we hold ourselves and move; listen to the speaking voices of the greater part of our women. And in no civilization, at least in recorded time, have human beings been farther from the *facts* if we mean by that word, facets of reality. Our indifference to ends is the result of our obsession with abstractions rather than facts: with the ideas of things rather than with things. For there can be no concern for ends without a hunger for reality. And there can be no hunger for reality without a sense of the real. And there can be no sense of the real in the world which abstraction creates, for abstraction is incapable of the real: it can neither lay hold of the real itself nor show us where to find it. It cannot, that is to say, create the *relation* between reality and ourselves which makes *knowledge* of reality possible, for neither reality nor ourselves exist in abstraction. Everything in the world of abstraction is object. And, as George Buttrick pointedly says, *we* are not objects: we are subjects.

4

But all this is a negative way of saying what a defender of poetry should not be afraid of saying positively. Let me say it. We have lost our concern with ends because we have lost our touch with reality and we have lost our touch with reality because we are estranged from the means to reality which is the poem—the work of art. To most members of our generation this would seem an extravagant statement but it is not extravagant in fact and would not have seemed so in another time. In ancient China the place of poetry in men's lives was assumed as matter of course; indeed, the polity was based on it. The three hundred and five odes or songs which make up the Song-word Scripture survived to the fourth century B.C., when Confucius is said to have collected them because they were part of the government records preserved in the Imperial Archive. For thousands of years the examinations for the Chinese civil service were examinations in poetry, and there is no record that the results were more disappointing to the throne than examinations of a different character might have been. Certainly there is no record that a Chinese civil servant ever attempted to deny an honor student in a military academy his commission in the imperial army *or* navy because he was friendly with his own mother! Idiocies which the study of science and of other abstractions in contemporary institutions of naval education in the United States seem to nourish were apparently cauterized from the mind by the reading of poems.

It was not for nothing that Confucius told his disciples that the three hundred and five songs of the Song-word Scripture could be boiled down to the commandment: "Have no twisty thoughts." You cannot have twisty thoughts if you are real and if you are thinking about real things. But if a mother is merely a biological event to you and if you yourself are merely a military event called an admiral, anything may happen: you may make your country ridiculous, humiliate a promising boy, and deprive the navy of a good officer, all in the twisted belief that you are being a wise man and a patriot.

One can see, not only in the three hundred and five songs, but in Chinese poetry of other periods, what Confucius meant. Consider two Chinese poems of the second century B.C. and the sixth of our era, both written by Emperors. The first is a poem of grief—of the sense of loss of someone loved: a poem therefore of that inward world of feeling, of emotion, which seems to us most nearly ourselves and which, because it is always in flux, always shifting and changing and flowing away, is, of all parts of our experience of our lives, most difficult to know. We cannot know it through science. We cannot know it by knowing things *about* it—even the shrewdest and most intelligent things, helpful though they may be to us in other ways. We cannot know it either by merely feeling it—by uttering its passing urgencies, crying out "I love" meaning "I think of myself as loving" or sobbing "I grieve" meaning "I think of myself as grieving." How then can we know it?

The Emperor Wu-ti wrote (this is Arthur Waley's beautiful translation):—

The sound of her silk skirt has stopped.
On the marble pavement dust grows.
Her empty room is cold and still.
Fallen leaves are piled against the doors.
Longing for that lovely lady
How can I bring my aching heart to rest?

Four images, one of sound, two of sight, one of feeling, each like a note plucked on a stringed instrument. Then a question like the chord the four would make together. And all at once we *know*. We know this grief which no word could have described, which any abstraction the mind is capable of would have destroyed. But we know more than this grief: we know our own—or will when it shall visit us—and so know something of ourselves.

The second is a poem of that emotion, that feeling, which is even more difficult to know than grief itself. The second is a poem of delight: youth and delight—the morning of the world—the emotion, of all emotions, most difficult to stop, to hold, to see. "Joy whose hand is ever at his lips bidding adieu." How would you *know* delight in yourself and therefore yourself delighting? Will the psychiatrists tell you? Is there a definition somewhere in the folios of abstraction by which we attempt to live which will capture it for you? The Emperor Ch'ien Wen-ti (again Waley's translation) knew that there is only one mirror which will hold that vanishing smile: the mirror of art, the mirror of the poem:—

A beautiful place is the town of Lo-yang:
The big streets are full of spring light
The lads go driving out with harps in their hands:
The mulberry girls go out to the fields with their
  baskets.
Golden whips glint at the horses' flanks,
Gauze sleeves brush the green boughs.
Racing dawn the carriages come home—
And the girls with their high baskets full of fruit.

In this world within, you see, this world which is ourselves, there is no possibility of knowing by abstracting the meaning out—or what we hope will be the meaning. There we must know things *as* themselves and it must be *we* who know them. Only art, only poetry, can bring about that confrontation, because only art, only poetry, can show us what we are and ourselves confronting it. To be ignorant of poetry is to be ignorant therefore of the one means of reaching the world of our experience of the world. And to be ignorant of *that* world is to be ignorant of who and what we are. And to be ignorant of who and what we are is to be incapable of reality no matter what tools we have, or what intelligence, or what skills. It is this incapacity, this impotence, which is the tragedy of the time we live in. We are spiritually impotent because we have cut ourselves off from the poem. And the crowning irony is that it is only in the poem that we can know how impotent we have become.

Why do we teach poetry in this scientific age? To present the great alternative not to science but to that knowledge by abstraction which science has imposed. And what is this great alternative? Not the "messages" of poems, their interpreted "meanings," for these are abstractions also—abstractions far inferior to those of science. Not the explications of poetic texts, for the explication of a poetic text which goes no farther ends only in abstraction.

No, the great alternative is the poem as itself, the poem as a poem, the poem as a work of art—which is to say, the poem in the context in which alone the work of art exists: the context of the world, of the man and of the thing, of the infinite relationship which is our lives. To present the great alternative is to present the poem not as a message in a bottle, and not as an object in an uninhabited landscape, but as an action in the world, an action in which we ourselves are actors and our lives are known.

EXERCISES

1. MacLeish says that those who like poetry as well as those who write it are usually on the defensive. What are some of the reasons you would give for

reading poetry? What are the reasons you would give for ignoring it altogether?

2. MacLeish writes about the difference between the knowledge of the world that we can obtain from abstractions and generalizations and that which we can obtain from the more concrete expressions found in poems. Do you agree or disagree with him? Give your reasons.

3. At the beginning of the article MacLeish discusses conflicting views of what poetry is and should be. What is MacLeish's own view? What is yours? Why?

4. Select a poem that you like and that you feel you understand. Explain why you like it.

4 THE ART OF THE SHORT STORY

Anonymous

The author of this article effectively demonstrates that in America the short story has been and remains a vital literary form. He lists a number of nineteenth-century short story writers but emphasizes that Poe was the first to explain the short story in critical terms—that the writer does not fashion "his thoughts to accommodate his incidents; but having conceived, with deliberate care, a certain unique or single effect to be wrought out, he then invents such incidents—he then combines such events as may best aid him in establishing preconceived effects." Having established the essential character of the short story, the author discusses many short story writers and comments on the nature and quality of their work.

In his excellent book *The Modern Short Story* Mr. H. E. Bates records that it was not until some years after buying Series I and II of *Selected English Short Stories*, published in the World's Classics Series, that he noticed that more than a third of the stories in Series I and exactly half the stories in Series II were written by Americans. "It was this discovery," says Mr. Bates, "that first gave me a clue to the poverty of the short story in nineteenth-century England, and an abiding respect for the short story in America." Remembering Scott, Stevenson, Conrad, Hardy, Kipling, Conan Doyle, W. W. Jacobs and the early Wells, we may feel that "poverty" is perhaps too strong a word. But Mr. Bates is right to praise the American contribution to the short story in the last century. If we cannot exactly agree with some American critics that the short story was an

American invention we can at least say that, even before the Civil War, it was practised in that country with an assiduousness and considered with a seriousness for which it had to wait half a century in England. Washington Irving, Hawthorne, Poe and Melville were pioneers of the American story, and after the Civil War William Dean Howells, Bret Harte, Ambrose Bierce, Sarah Orne Jewett, Frank Stockton, Stephen Crane, Jack London, Hamlin Garland, O. Henry, Henry James and Edith Wharton placed it firmly on the map.

William Dean Howells suggested that this extraordinary development and interest were fostered by the magazines. The most famous of these were *Godey's Lady's Book,* in which Poe published "The Cask of Amontillado"; *The Dollar Magazine* in which Hawthorne first published "Ethan Brand"; *The Gentleman's Magazine,* the *Broadway Journal, Scribner's Monthly* and *Scribner's Magazine,* and the long-lived *Harper's* and *Atlantic.* And no doubt the presence of so many flourishing magazines itself had something to do with the spread of popular education in America, the absence of class barriers and the increased pace of life in a society which was becoming very rapidly industrialized—all of which conditions, as we know from our own experience in the present century, lead, among other things, to the demand for entertaining and portable reading matter. Authors were not loth to supply the demand, for, as Mr. Somerset Maugham once pointed out, "writers quite naturally feel themselves impelled to write the sort of things for which there is a demand." Another reason for the early development of the short story in America lay, it has been suggested, in the absence of satisfactory copyright laws, which meant that English novels were pirated and American writers were driven by this competition into the short-story market, where the native product was preferred. Both these explanations are plausible, but they leave us with the feeling that this does not fully account for the seriousness with which, for example, Poe considered the form. It was Poe, after all, who, in his review of Hawthorne's *Twice-Told Tales,* gave us the first working definition of the short story. "If wise," said Poe,

> [the skilful literary artist] has not fashioned his thoughts to accommodate his incidents; but having conceived, with deliberate care, a certain unique or single *effect* to be wrought out, he then invents such incidents—he then combines such events as may best aid him in establishing this preconceived effect. If his very initial sentence tends not to the outbringing of this effect, then he has failed in his first step. In the whole composition there should be no word written, of which the tendency, direct or indirect, is not to the one pre-established design.

* * *

This is our first critical intimation of the birth of a new literary form which, Poe said, "belonged to the highest region of Art." It places emphasis upon structure, upon a careful ordering of thought and effect, which we now see to be fundamental. Whereas the *Gesta Romanorum, The Decameron* and the short tales which Dickens inserted into his novels are alike in that they are no different in kind from the longer narratives of their time, the modern short story is quite distinct, in intention and effect, from the modern long narrative or novel. It is, Miss Elizabeth Bowen has said, "in its use of action . . . nearer to the drama than to the novel." Its effects are gained through implication and suggestion, rather than through detailed description, or delineation of, character. It is essentially literary, the product of much careful craftsmanship, and this is perhaps what chiefly distinguishes it from the "told" tales of the past. And if in some cases it is nearer to the drama than the novel, in others it is nearer to the poem. And this perhaps may give us a clue to the peculiar interest the form held for Americans in the nineteenth century.

American society was unsettled. The state of the new nation, the growth and movement of population, the physical and mental challenge of a vast continent had the effect of stirring up writers' minds. These are conditions which might have inspired the poets, but the poets of America, with the exception of Whitman, were not to be stirred up. Perhaps because they sensed their alienation from a vital but crude and unformed society, they clung to a narrow circle and to narrow and superficial subjects. And so, to a certain extent, the short story became a vehicle for those speculations and explorations which may largely be termed "poetic." We may see how near Poe comes to defining the intention of a poem in his demand for the ordering of the short story and the attainment of a "single effect," and, as Dr. and Mrs. Leavis have at different times pointed out, Hawthorne's method can also be called "poetic." But American society in the nineteenth century, like our own in the twentieth century, was prose-conscious, and through a prose form the literary artist in America played a poet's part.

* * *

The Civil War marks the beginning of a critical phase in the American story. In the hands of Bret Harte, William Dean Howells and Ambrose Bierce it became realistic, and in Stephen Crane, Hamlin Garland, Jack London (no doubt influenced by Zola), naturalistic, reflecting the conditions of American society. "By God! I told them the Truth," said Frank Norris a few years later. "They liked it or they didn't like it. What had that to do with me? I told them the Truth, I knew it for the Truth then, and I know it for the Truth now." Even Henry James thought he was being realistic. We, remembering Stephen Crane or Sherwood Anderson, protest that that was the last thing James was. But it was in fact the first thing he was. In the sense that he used "real" situations and "real" people, in the sense that his work conveys the atmosphere of a scene or situation, he was being realistic, and this may be seen quite clearly by comparing his work with that of Poe and Hawthorne. Henry James was as much affected by his age as Hamlin Garland or Stephen Crane, but he chose to convey more than the sensuous vitality of everyday existence. Apart from an interest in symbolism which led him to praise Hawthorne's "allegorical glimpses . . . of the whole deep mystery of man's soul and conscience" his main preoccupation was the moral and psychological implication of various human situations.

* * *

It is odd, this praise of Hawthorne, for although in his best novels Hawthorne has a certain power which compels us to read on in spite of the tediousness of the prose, he was in his shorter pieces about as much of a short-story writer as Cotton Mather. We may suppose that it was Hawthorne's preoccupations which interested James, for, as stories, those amateurish, didactic attempts to "open an intercourse with the world" must surely have grated upon James's fine sensibility. So few of them have that level of interest and competence which must be present before we are inclined to swallow the real excuse for the story, the allegorical message. Even if we confine ourselves to the very best of the stories, lovingly chronicled and kept in circulation by American literary historians and preservers of Americana, there is only one, *Young Goodman Brown*, which makes some sort of impact. Most of them read like faintly disguised sermons, the efforts of a country parson who has just discovered Bunyan. From *Young Goodman Brown* and his novel *The Scarlet Letter* there are indications that he really wanted to write symbolically, but something seems to have prevented him, with the result that the majority of his stories are neither allegory nor symbolism but a very unsatisfactory confusion of both. Poe, on the other hand, may be seen to be the father of the art of the short story in America. As Mr. Bates points out in the book already quoted, Poe has "atmosphere, hypnotics, mathematical exactitude" and "of those it is interesting to note that at least two, the first and the last, are qualities of whose essential importance nearly every short-story writer of quality has given proof." Although his writing is mannered and his characters hardly realistic, it is in his power of conveying atmosphere, which in turn arises from power of personality, that Poe shows himself to be the forerunner of modern short-story writers, and that is why his stories are still read and enjoyed to-day.

If Poe is the father of the American short story then Henry James is its favourite son, but a son whose lustre so outshines the father's that comparison is not merely invidious but impossible. In the hands of Henry James the American story came to an early maturity. In his stories, perhaps more than in his novels, he "sees into the heart of things," and conveys a moment of truth. This, surely, is Poe's "single effect," a definition which critics have denounced because it has not seemed to them to convey the heightened awareness, the multiple consciousness of many facets of life with which the very best stories leave us. But the term "single effect" does not preclude artistic ambiguities. The "single effect" which James aims at in "The Real Thing" is the establishment of the idea that art is art and life is life. The two people who are really genteel do not look the real thing; the fakes do. And so the artist chooses the fakes because he is not concerned with moral standards but with art, and art consists in creating the right effect. One might say the same of the short-story writer's art. It lies in creating the right effect, and all the honesty, sincerity and experience in the world will be of no avail if the writer has not the requisite insight and skill to translate his vision into the right words in the right order.

* * *

The days are gone when Mr. Van Wyck Brooks's strictures on Henry James had positive meaning for young American writers. In those days Sherwood Anderson was felt to be more truly American, more "truthful." But either directly, or indirectly—through such polished writers as Miss Katherine Anne Porter—Henry James has had great influence on a sizable section of the youngest generation of American writers. They see, once they have got over their distaste for the effeteness of Henry James's characters and their distrust of the elegant society in which they moved, that the artistic preoccupations of Henry James, in spite of his alienation from the main stream of American life, were no less serious and no farther from the heart of things than those of William Faulkner or Ernest Hemingway. The English reader will think this perhaps a very odd thing to say, since it is to him self-evident. But one must not make the mistake of imagining good American taste to be exactly the same as good European taste. In some circles, in New England especially, it is very little different; but the majority of intelligent American readers have a different set of conditions which they "feel as facts": the land itself, whether it be the endless plains of Nebraska or the lush glades of Louisiana; the sense of native life and atmosphere which comes out of idiomatic American speech and a quite different set of habits and customs; the general predilection for the large, the loose, the carefree, the good-natured and the easy-going. Against such backgrounds Henry James can seem very alien, just as some of the stories which arise from the cauldron of American society can seem very alien to us. It is not a question of their being unable to see the wood for the trees; it is simply that the wood, the trees and the whole landscape is one seen from a different angle.

But which of their other short-story writers in the nineteenth century, apart from Henry James, do Americans now value? Only Stephen Crane seems to be really in favour. (One speaks, of course, of writers who genuinely appeal and not of writers who merely provide fuel for the American academic machine.) Crane, it is felt, was in the same line of country as Ernest Hemingway. The prevailing mood of American taste being for naturalism, his stories have an appeal and a flavour which the mannered constructions of Poe and Hawthorne do not. He is sharper on the tongue, carrying conviction through details which the modern reader can feel to be true. Beside him, Americans seem to feel, Bret Harte and Ambrose Bierce give the impression of artificiality, and Hamlin Garland and Jack London are lesser figures as artists. With these judgments we might not entirely differ except perhaps to put in a plea for Edith Wharton, who is a great artist in her own right and not merely a lesser Henry James, as many appear to think. We might also feel—not being quite so satisfied with the techniques of the naturalists as are the Americans—that Ambrose Bierce is receiving less than his due. He had the misfortune to be born before the age in which the raw details of life had only to be set starkly upon the page. He was, therefore, a clear, sure craftsman. O. Henry, too, is for most English people more than just another magazine writer with a click. He is a very skilful practitioner of the short story who, in his best work, manages to convey not only a sense of American life but also some significant, if small, truth about life itself. And, finally, if Frank Stockton is deservedly neglected, Sarah Orne Jewett is less deservedly so. Her world, as Mr. Bates says,

> like Jane Austen's, was small, but, like Jane Austen, if she had chosen it herself she could hardly have been born into a world more aptly suited to her gift of interpretation.

* * *

To leave the world of the American short story in the nineteenth century and enter that of the twentieth century is to come from a headlighted country road into the blaze of Main Street on a Saturday night. The concerted glare is confusing, and the apparent brightness of individual lights can vary with the viewpoint. When the picture is projected across the Atlantic some strange distortions occur, and if one takes an amateur Gallup poll to discover what modern American short-story writers are well known to the intelligent reading public in England, the results reveal a narrow and surprisingly unbalanced range of acquaintance. Almost everyone has, of course, at one time or another, read Ernest Hemingway, William Saroyan, Damon Runyon, James Thurber, and John Steinbeck, although not everyone has read William Faulkner, Erskine Caldwell, James T. Farrell or Eudora Welty. Fewer, among the younger generation, have read Sherwood Anderson, Dorothy Parker, Stephen Vincent Benét, F. Scott Fitzgerald, Thomas Wolfe, or Kay Boyle. Almost no one seems to have read, or in some cases even heard of, the stories of Ring Lardner, Ellen Glasgow, Ruth Suckow, Conrad Aiken, Glenway Wescott, William Carlos Williams, Katherine Anne Porter (even though her two volumes have been published in England), William March, Caroline Gordon or J. P. Marquand. Of the youngest generation of writers only the names of John O'Hara, Mary MacCarthy, Carson McCullers, Truman Capote, Irwin Shaw, Jerome Weidman, Ray Bradbury, Paul Bowles, and J. P. Salinger seem to be at all well known. But there are a great many more who are almost as good, among them Edward Newhouse, Allan Seager, Nelson Algren, Mark Schorer, Wallace Stegner, Walter Van Tilburg Clark, Frances Gray Patton, J. F. Powers, Shirley Jackson, Jessamyn West, Jean Stafford, Hortense Calisher, John Cheever, Robie Macauley, William Goyen, Robert Lowry, Wright Morris, Delmore Schwartz, Louis Auchincloss, Shelby Foote, Flannery O'Connor, and Peter Taylor.

* * *

This raises some interesting reflections. Let us take the first writer on our list, Mr. Ernest Hemingway. Mr. Hemingway, most people would agree, is outstanding, but it is significant that he should be the only serious American short-story writer that almost everyone has read. If the curious inquirer pushes his researches farther he finds that Mr. Hemingway is regarded as "typically American." Two things seem to be responsible for this assumption—his terseness and his toughness, for a considerable number of non-Americans not only have a preconceived idea of how an American should look and act but also, apparently, of how he should write, and Mr. Hemingway almost fills the bill. Erskine Caldwell and John Steinbeck add to the picture, William Saroyan and Damon Runyon round it off and, presto, we have the complete American short-story writer—tough like Hemingway, naturalistic like Caldwell, irresponsible like Saroyan, loquacious like Runyon, and sentimental like Steinbeck at his worst. These writers are at their best, of course, superb, and deservedly famous—Hemingway in "The Short Happy Life of Francis Macomber" or "The Snows of Kilimanjaro," Caldwell in "Kneel to the Rising Sun," Saroyan in "The Pomegranate Tree" and Steinbeck in "The Leader of the People." But they are not so often at their best that we could wish them the only representatives of the American stort story. There are others less well known, among the names already cited, whom one would certainly wish to have in any representative collection of modern American stories.

Perhaps the most neglected of these, in England, is Ring Lardner, a Middle Western journalist, who began writing the sketches he called

"You Know me Al" when he was a sports writer for the Chicago *Tribune*. Lardner is a ruthless, although not a bitter, satirist, whose best stories, like "Haircut," "Champion" and "Some Like them Cold," are written in a vernacular which makes Damon Runyon's seem like that of a stage American. William Carlos Williams is another whose collections, *The Knife of the Times, Life Along the Passaic River,* and *Beer and Cold Cuts,* have an authentic flavour of American life. Dr. Williams's stories, like his poems, give, at first sight, the impression of random jottings, but they are in fact far from being just that, as consideration of such stories as "The Knife of the Times," "The Use of Force" and "The Girl with the Pimply Face" reveal. They are instinct with humanity, and their casual tone and offhand manner are in fact the fruit of a long involvement in the lives of poor immigrants and Negroes in the New Jersey industrial towns he has lived in all his life. Mr. William March and Miss Caroline Gordon are both Southerners, but whereas Mr. March is a master of the short poignant episode, Miss Gordon's stories, like her novels, are long and finely wrought. Her world is the world of Virginia and fox hunting and classical values (as befits the wife of Mr. Allen Tate). Like so many American short-story writers—among them Conrad Aiken, Katherine Anne Porter, Kay Boyle, Wallace Stegner and Shirley Jackson—Miss Gordon is fond of symbolism. Perhaps her best story is "Old Red," the story of the indolent, scholarly Mister Maury, of which Mr. Robert Penn Warren has said,

[It is a story] about a basic conflict in our civilization—the conflict between a man's desire for a harmonious development of all his faculties and a set of social conditions which tend to compartmentalize life.

* * *

Conrad Aiken has been preoccupied with that land which lies between sleeping and waking. His "Silent Snow, Secret Snow" is a masterpiece of its kind. Of the other writers who are interested in symbolism perhaps the best (as well as the oldest) is Miss Porter, a highly intelligent and highly polished writer, whose "Flowering Judas" might perhaps be placed beside William Saroyan's "Sixty Thousand Assyrians" as an example of the inhibited and the uninhibited in the American story. Mr. Stegner, who is better known over here as the author of *The Big Rock Candy Mountain* and other novels, is, like Miss Porter and a good many other practitioners of the short story these days, closely associated with various writing centres. Whereas Mr. Stegner is a permanent member of that peripheral world which lies between the academy and the great world outside, however, Miss Porter is only an occasional professor. Mr. Stegner is a good example of the very satisfactory compromise which the short-story writer in America can make with the academy. In England the short-story writer must either become a lighthouse keeper or look for a job with the B.B.C. The university will have nothing to do with him because he is not a dedicated academic, and there are no liberal arts colleges. In America, however, the writer may fairly easily obtain a job at any one of the hundreds of universities and liberal arts colleges which have creative writing courses, and divide his time between writing his own stories and discussing those of his students. Mr. Randall Jarrell, in his recent "comedy," *Pictures from an Institution,* described the life of a writer who was a temporary teacher of writing at an advanced girls' college and who apparently, making no bones about it, spent as little time as possible on her students. It is, after all, she might have argued, the influence rather than any actual instruction which is beneficial. Permanent professors of creative writing are, through conscience or necessity or both, usually more conscientious, however.

* * *

It is fashionable in England to talk with a kind of pious horror of this professionalism, for we have a deep suspicion of anything which is not strictly amateur. But at the very least one can say that it does not seem to have affected the standard of short story writing in the United States. Mr. Stegner himself, in a volume of original short stories gathered this year in a paper-back edition from the Bread Loaf writing conference, puts it more positively.

> I have learned the most important part of my professional skill there [he says of Bread Loaf] by argument, analysis, lecture, conversation and osmosis, from the serious, intensive, responsible, non-arty, non-commercial, non-tendential, patient and informed discussion of their craft by the people I taught with.

One has only to compare the stories in the British and American literary magazines, or the former British *Penguin New Writing* with the present American *New World Writing,* to be struck by the difference in quality. The American stories are not only more skilful but in some indefinable way more "alive." The life of a situation, the tang and feeling of it, is presented accurately and vividly. A story in *New World Writing* 5, "Who Lives Alas Away," by Miss Clare McGrath Butler provides a good illustration of this. Miss Butler seems, as William Dean Howells said of Stephen Crane, to have "sprung into life fully armed." Her story, although it is a first publication, is both moving and vital, and this example, which may be multiplied from other numbers of the same publication and from the American smaller magazines, from the *Atlantic* and *Harper's* to *Epoch, Accent* and the *New Mexico Quarterly,* contrasts vividly with the amateurish pieces of reportage which used to appear in *Penguin New Writing* and the genteel and mannered vignettes which set the tone of the *London Magazine*. Does it arise from the difference between English and American life at the present time? Perhaps partly so, but equally it arises from the serious attention paid to the short story in America.

Every young man and woman in America seems to have a short story in his pocket. Undergraduates write them there as ours tend to write poems, not for this or that glossy magazine with its glittering prizes but as expressions of intense personal feeling, having their birth and sole reason for existence in this fact. This, perhaps, more than anything, contributes to the feeling of meaningfulness one gets from the American story. As one looks through Martha Foley's annual volume or the yearly O'Henry collection one feels that these stories vitally mattered to their authors, and this sense they convey to us. It is the legacy of Stephen Crane, of Sherwood Anderson, of Erskine Caldwell, of William Carlos Williams and Robert Penn Warren. It is a heartfelt activity, with that desperate honesty of intention which characterizes Sherwood Anderson's "I Want to Know Why." But although these stories are born of deep feeling they could not be what they are without the aid of skilful technique, and it is here that one can see that the lesson of Henry James has been well learnt. Of course, not every short story writer has dealings with creative writing courses, either as teacher or student. Some, like Miss Mary McCarthy, are very suspicious of them. But, while it is certainly true that not everyone comes up to the high standard already described, the spirit of the great majority of them could not be better, and it is this which matters. The creative writing course is a product rather than a cause, engendered by a state of mind which encourages both personal expression and concern with craftsmanship which is essential for true art.

Perhaps the best example of the polished craftsman among the younger writers is Miss Eudora Welty. Not that Miss Welty is exactly a "young writer"; but by "younger writers" one refers to those who have made their names during and since the last war. Miss Welty's first book was published in 1941 and it immediately established her reputation. In so far as she began with natural speech rhythms and developed her craft from this Miss Welty is in the main tradition of American short-story writers—in that of Hemingway and Caldwell and Steinbeck, not of Miss Katherine Anne Porter, who is polished in a more Jamesian way. Miss Welty has turned to writing longer and longer stories, the last one, "The Ponder Heart," filling a whole issue of the *New Yorker*. The stories immediately previous to this are collected in a volume called *The Golden Apples* which shows that the quality of Miss Welty's writing is growing steadily finer. The later stories are atmospheric. The air quivers with sounds. One is acutely aware of breathing, smells; feeling is finely caught. It is a much more exciting kind of writing than that of the stories collected in *A Curtain of Green*, yet one must admit that no one story quite stands up by itself like "A Piece of News," "The Petrified Man" or "Lily Daw and the Three Ladies." It is novels Miss Welty should be writing now, and yet she does not seem to be able to make the transition. Even *Delta Wedding*, long as it was, was not a novel; nor was it a short story.

* * *

Another Southerner, Peter Taylor, is at present the most admired of the very youngest short story writers. His first volume, *A Long Fourth*, appearing in 1948, contained seven stories published during the previous seven years. Mr. Taylor, like other good young writers, appears regularly in the *New Yorker*. Much has been said about the tendency of this excellent magazine to standardize the short story in America. The famous blue pencil is supposed to turn every piece, however individual, into a "typical *New Yorker* story." Since the reader cannot know what actually goes on in the *New Yorker* offices, he must judge by what he reads in the magazine, and from this the accusations do not appear to have much truth. If the *New Yorker* edits, it edits wisely, preserving the spirit and tone of the story. If one *New Yorker* story is at all like another it is because the *New Yorkers* prefers a certain kind of writer. It prefers those with the classical virtues, and its effect on the standard and polish of the short story in America has been considerable. One feels that the recent spate of nasty remarks about the *New Yorker* on both sides of the Atlantic must have come from disgruntled would-be contributors, for the magazine is highly selective and there is fierce competition for its space. Other writers who appear in the *New Yorker*, apart from Miss Welty and Mr. Taylor, are Mr. John Cheever, Mr. J. P. Salinger, Miss Frances Gray Patton and Mr. Edward Newhouse. Looking at Mr. Taylor's own stories one senses immediately why the *New Yorker* took to him. He is a leisurely, careful craftsman, not quite so obviously polished as Miss Katherine Anne Porter and with less interest in symbolism. He reminds one most nearly of the later Eudora Welty, exploring as he does the *minutiae* of life in small Southern towns; but he has less of Eudora Welty's sense of the physical life of the place. One of the most successful stories in his last volume is called "Cookie," in which the weekly visit of a doctor to the wife from whom he has apparently been separated is described with careful detachment and understatement. What Mr. Taylor is particularly good at is the pointed last line, which usually directs the reader, with the same apparent detachment, to the heart of the story. The South is strong in young short story writers. As with the established Southern writers, William Faulkner, Katherine Anne Porter, Robert Penn Warren, Caroline Gordon, Eudora

Welty and Carson McCullers, they make excellent use of the life of the region. The best of them, apart from Mr. Taylor, are probably Truman Capote, Flannery O'Connor and William Goyen.

One cannot call these writers "regional" because their work transcends the life of the region. A strictly "regional" writer usually has only a regional significance. But, as Miss Welty insists, you cannot write a good modern short story without conveying an intense sense of place and atmosphere. Walter Van Tilburg Clark, another of the outstanding names among the youngest generation of writers, uses the background of Nevada and Utah. Wallace Stegner's stories cover the Rocky Mountain region, from Iowa to California. Jessamyn West's stories are set among the Quakers of Indiana. Irwin Shaw and Jerome Weidman write of New York, Nelson Algren of Chicago. It is possible, as Miss Martha Foley has done, to make a collection of short stories which not only illustrates the excellence of the American story but also the divergence of regional background. A great deal is talked about the standardization of life in the United States by commentators who have at best travelled through various regions and noted that the same goods are on sale and the same cars fill the streets. But the standardization of goods does not necessarily imply standardization of life. One has only to live in the United States to realize how different life is even within state boundaries. Cairo, Illinois, for example, is in a different world from Chicago, Illinois, and the same can be said of northern and southern Ohio. Between Wyoming and Maine and Wisconsin and Louisiana there are more than miles.

* * *

It is this divergence within the vast area of the United States which is responsible for the sense that young writers have of the multifariousness of life. To reduce life to a story on paper is one way of subduing and ordering, and at the same time of preserving, one's experience. And perhaps it is this, as much as anything, which is responsible for the urge young Americans have to write stories out of themselves. But then they learn, the best of them, that, as Mr. Stanford Whitmore says in *American Accent*, the recent collection of stories from Bread Loaf, writing is "an honour and a severe responsibility." Like the poet, the short story writer must submit his work to a tireless process of analysis and polishing, until every word counts and every sentence is balanced. But first he must possess within himself the spring which sets men writing. He must have not only a desire to communicate the vision of his experience but a kind of fundamental innocence and integrity. And this the best young American short story writers have.

EXERCISES

1. What is the point the author of this article makes in his discussion of James's "The Real Thing"?
2. What is the theme of this article?
3. Write a brief historical account of the development of the American short story according to the author's viewpoint. Introduce whatever modifications you believe desirable.

X Writing and Revising the Term Paper

In most student themes, personal experience and attitudes supply the subject matter. In the research paper, the subject matter depends on primary sources. (Primary sources are facts and documents that have not been organized or interpreted. Secondary sources are those articles and books that interpret primary materials. A Supreme Court decision could be a primary source, an editorial written about it, a secondary source.) A good research paper requires examination of diverse sources and careful evaluation of them. Opinion undoubtedly enters into all writing, but in the well-done research paper one justifies his opinion. He shows documentary evidence as its basis. The whole enterprise of scholarship as well as business and industrial research involves respect for documentary evidence and the drawing of intelligent inferences from it. One of the most useful skills a student can acquire is the ability to investigate documents with an open mind and to write up his findings in a coherent and forceful manner.

A fairly common assumption is that highly documented articles and books are dull. There is no inevitable connection between documentation and dullness, and it is up to the writer to interpret and present his facts in such a way that a reader's attention is held.

We have suggested the general subject of censorship for the term paper, and if your instructor chooses to use this subject he will help you select a topic. Even if you choose to write in an altogether different area—Atomic

Missiles, the Smithsonian Institution, Television and the Movies, Women in Pre-Shakespearean Drama, or whatever—the general procedures will be much the same. You will have to choose a general subject, then limit it. Within the subject of censorship there must be hundreds and hundreds of topics that could be investigated—censorship under Queen Elizabeth, the Star Chamber in England, Socrates and the right to search out the truth, the Inquisition, the persecution of Roger Williams, etc., etc. (See the list of topics, pp. 497–498.) Before trying to settle on, or work out a topic, you should read a few encyclopedia articles on censorship and a book or two on the history of censorship. In this way you can get a sense of what the history of censorship is, the issues involved, and topics that might be interesting to write about.

We should point out that while the research paper depends upon documentation that there need be no set form for writing it. Frequently a term paper argues a thesis. For example, one might argue that it is fair (or unfair) to ask teachers to take special loyalty oaths. Perhaps most term papers are essentially arguments. But there seems to be no good reason why certain subjects should not also be cast in the form of biography. For example, one could write an interesting biography of Anthony Comstock or Senator McCarthy by seeing or presenting his personality in relation to the forms of censorship he sought to impose. Whichever form it takes, the research paper should create a unified impression. The research paper in other words should be creative, intelligent, and lively, and should exhibit the characteristics common to any piece of good writing.

No one can write a research paper who does not know how to use the library, to use the card catalogue intelligently, and to use the works in the reference room. The card catalogue is arranged by author, by title, and under general subjects. Thus, a specific book can be looked up by author or title. The subject matter index is particularly important for anyone trying to find his way around in a new subject matter. Under *Censorship*, for example, one could find a large number of entries.

In the reference room one will find encyclopedias, year books, biographical dictionaries, and guides to reference works. Perhaps it is wise to begin with the last item. One work that can be very helpful in learning how to locate reference works is *Guide to Reference Books*, American Library Association, 1951. This lists indexes to magazines devoted to special subjects, encyclopedias, books of quotations, dictionaries, etc. The following are works with which anyone wanting to do research should be familiar:

I

Encyclopedia Britannica
Encyclopedia Americana
Chambers's Encyclopedia

New International Encyclopedia
The Catholic Encyclopedia
The Jewish Encyclopedia
Encyclopedia of the Social Sciences

II

The World Almanac and Book of Facts
Britannica Book of the Year
The New International Year Book

III

Dictionary of National Biography
Dictionary of American Biography
Current Biography: Who's News and Why
Who's Who in America
Poole's Index to Periodical Literature (for 19th century)
Reader's Guide to Periodical Literature
Public Affairs Information Service
The Education Index
The International Index
New York Times Index
Index, London Times
Cumulative Book Index

A student should not hesitate to ask the assistance of the reference librarian, but he should also invest whatever time and attention may be required for him to become adept in the use of these reference tools.

After one has limited his topic and begun to read systematically, it is necessary to take notes. The most convenient and orderly way of doing this is to use 3 x 5 cards. On these cards one may copy a passage that seems significant or write the general sense of it in one's own words. In either case the source of the comment should be identified by author, title, volume number (if necessary), and the page on which it is found. Later, in incorporating the comment into the term paper, the source should be either footnoted or acknowledged as a source in the text proper. One should never present someone else's comments or ideas as one's own.

When the note taking is completed, one can begin to outline the paper. Usually various subsubjects will fall into place quickly enough. If some of them resist organization there is a reason; either the writer hasn't understood their significance in relation to his theme or they are irrelevant to what he is trying to say. In the latter case he should drop them; in the former he should try to understand them better.

Unfortunately, bibliographical forms have not been standardized. The system found in *The MLA Style Sheet* [1] however is favored by most English

[1] *The MLA Style Sheet* may be obtained for a small fee from the Secretary, Modern Language Association, 100 Washington Square, New York City.

departments and has been adopted by many literary journals. The following examples are taken from it:

Sample Footnotes

[1] Archer Taylor, *Problems in German Literary History of the Fifteenth and Sixteenth Centuries* (New York, 1939), p. 213.
(The simplest form of reference; the publisher, the MLA, might have been reported also.)

[2] Baldwin Maxwell "Middleton's *The Phoenix*," *Joseph Quincy Adams Memorial Studies*, ed. James G. McManaway et al. (Washington, D.C., 1948), pp. 750–752.

[3] See the unpubl. diss. (Columbia, 1949) by U. Fuller Schmaltz, "The *Weltschmerz* of Charles Addams," p. 7.
(Titles of unpublished works, regardless of length, are not underlined but enclosed in quotation marks.)

Sample Bibliograpy

[1] Baker, Ernest A. *The History of the English Novel.* 10 vols. London, 1924–39.

[2] Blenner-Hassett, Roland. "A Brief History of Celtic Studies in North America," *PMLA*, LXIX (1954), 3–21.

For the many questions that can arise in documenting a specific bibliographical item the student is referred to *The MLA Style Sheet.*

The documentation required in writing a term paper may sometimes be tedious work. Even so, it should be done carefully. But documentation is a minor task in comparison with the writing of the text proper. With the text, we meet the same problems we meet within any other piece of writing. Does the paper create a unified impression? Is the writing pretentious? Is attention sustained by an interesting variety of sentence structure?

Almost any piece of writing can be improved by revision. An unnecessary phrase or paragraph can be dropped; an illuminating sentence can be added, or a whole section expanded; a sequence of sentences or paragraphs can be altered for greater cogency; or the phrasing in a sentence can be changed to lighten its tone or to increase its intellectual vibrancy. Few of us think spontaneously in so orderly and appropriate a way that revision is unnecessary. We make false starts, scratch out a sentence or a paragraph, and start over again. Some writers sketch out a number of paragraphs or pages and then shuffle them to discover the best possible order, or they find that what should be the opening sentence has been tucked away in a paragraph where its effectiveness would be lost. The experienced writer gets into the habit of raising questions that may help to improve a piece of writing. Among them are these:

Is the title appropriate?
Is the opening sentence a good one?

Is the sequence everywhere logical?
Does the theme emerge clearly?
Is the composition as a whole an accurate statement of the theme?
Is the general conception original and worth saying?
Is there need for more or fewer illustrations?
Are there irrelevant sentences or sections?
Does any section, or the paper as a whole, need expansion or contraction?
Are any sentences ambiguous?
Are the sentences monotonously long or short?
Are there words or phrases that are imprecise or infelicitous?
Is the tone anywhere stilted, pretentious, or too light for the occasion?
Are the footnotes and bibliography in the proper form?
Are all sources of information and all borrowed statements properly identified?

Each of these questions raises a principle of good writing. As a matter of procedure, one's initial changes in revising are usually structural, for example, expanding a paragraph or improving the logical sequence of the sections, whereas the final changes are usually verbal, involving words and phrases. It goes without saying that one should check spelling, grammar, and punctuation. But to end on a higher note—the student should, as he revises, strive for some elegance. He should not disdain rhetorical effects. He should strive to make his paper not merely informative and intelligent but also arresting.

Censorship

It goes almost without saying that a society needs an orthodoxy, a certain degree of homogeneity or order if it is to avoid chaos. A country's constitution, tradition, laws, and even its games and manners help give it a homogeneity. But, as sociologists and political scientists put it, there are "closed societies" and "open societies." In the United States, we have an open society, with a nonauthoritarian government, a government that can be changed, and laws that can be changed. Each of us has the right to criticize laws, customs, and political or social theories and practices. A pamphlet published by the American Library Association puts the matter succinctly:

Totalitarian systems attempt to maintain themselves in power by the ruthless suppression of any concept which challenges the accepted orthodoxy. The power of the democratic system to adapt to change is vastly strengthened by the freedom of its citizens to choose widely from among the conflicting opinions offered freely to them. To stifle every nonconformist idea at birth would mark the end of the democratic process.

Inevitably there are groups who are quite certain that *their* beliefs are right and who insist upon trying to impose them on the community at large. They range from the Ku Klux Klan, insisting on the superiority and rights of Anglo-Saxon Protestants over Catholics, Negroes, and Jews, to the self-appointed censors of "liberal" textbooks used in the public schools. This is not to say that "conservative" elements alone try to impose their beliefs; there are so-called liberals who, while priding themselves on helping Negroes and Jews, still persecute Catholics. Again, there are certain Catholics who try to impose their dogmas and doctrines on their non-Catholic fellows. Bigotry and the authoritarian spirit can be found in almost any group.

The attempt to suppress opinions different from our own frequently identifies itself with righteousness, either in the form of patriotism or of religious piety. A group insisting that only a certain political or economic doctrine be taught in the schools will often proclaim all other doctrines to be "un-American." Self-appointed book censors frequently proscribe literature that is "shocking," and are apparently unwilling to admit that human experiences are often shocking, or that one best masters life by knowing what it involves.

The Constitution guarantees all of us the right to express our beliefs and the right to listen or to read free from persecution or punishment. The American Library Association pamphlet quoted from above concludes thus: "Ideas can be dangerous, but . . . the suppression of ideas is fatal to a democratic society. Freedom itself is a dangerous way of life, but it is ours." On the other hand, there are various laws, city, state, and federal, that prohibit the expression and distribution of seditious and pornographic literature. Since the distribution of seditious literature may be assumed to be infrequent we can here concentrate our attention on pornography. Most people agree that pornography should be censored—but there is frequent disagreement about what is and what is not pornography and about the methods of suppressing it.

Two of the articles in this section argue opposing theses. Mr. Millett apparently opposes all censorship. Father Murray sees great danger in too severe restraints, but he feels that some censorship is necessary to give greater freedom to man's rational and moral sides; he is very much in favor of censoring "pornographic violence."

Blanshard's article is not essentially an argument (he holds with a minimum amount of censorship); it is an evaluation of the contemporary situation in regard to censorship. The *New York Times* piece by George Steiner raises an interesting and difficult question—the qualifications of the censor. There are also three documents, two statements by the American Library Association, and a report of the American Civil Liberties Union on the conflicting evidence regarding the relationship between juvenile delinquency and the reading of crime comics.

Read singly and in relation to one another, these articles and documents show that the problems of censorship are complex and sometimes exceedingly subtle. It is hardly surprising that our courts and other agencies of censorship are frequently inconsistent.

Censorship occurs or can occur in many places and under many guises: in a newspaper monopoly that slants the news in favor of one group, through the refusal of the movies or TV to treat certain subjects, or even in the prohibition against printing certain four-letter words. Censorship is a perennial issue in our society, and all of us should try to have informed opinions about it.

Suggested Term Paper Topics

Ezra Pound and the Bollingen Award
Censorship of the Movies
What is Obscenity in Literature?
The Career of Anthony Comstock
The Purposes and Methods of NODL (National Organization for Decent Literature)
What is the Meaning of "Academic Freedom"?
Censorship and Realistic Novels in America
H. L. Mencken and the Censors
The Career of Morris Ernst
Roger Williams and Religious Freedom
The Censorship of Dreiser's Novels (*Sister Carrie* and *Jennie Gerhardt*)
The Supreme Court on Censorship
Censorship in Broadcasting
A One-party Press
Advantages and Disadvantages of "Top Secret"
The Career of Senator Joseph McCarthy
Milton and Seventeenth-Century Attitudes Toward Censorship
The Dismissal of Bertrand Russell by the New York Board of Higher Education (1940)
The Scopes Trial in Tennessee
The Censoring of Edmund Wilson's *Memoirs of Hecate County*
Book Banning in Boston
Massachusetts *vs. Forever Amber* and *Strange Fruit*
Legal Control of the Comic Books
D. H. Lawrence and the Censors
Early English and American Censorship
The Role of the Post Office in Censorship
Censorship of Foreign Books by Customs and the Treasury Department
Local Groups as Self-appointed Censors
The Fund for the Republic
The Ku Klux Klan in the Twentieth Century
Was Thomas Paine Persecuted?
The Local Police and Book Censorship
The Suppression of Textbooks Written by Harold Rugg
Mark Twain and Olivia, his Wife
Whitman and the Censorship of "Leaves of Grass"
Censorship Imposed by the Genteel Tradition
Loyalty Oaths for Teachers
Should Communists Be Allowed to Teach in American Schools?
Mill's Doctrine of Liberty
Supreme Court Rulings on the First Amendment
The American Civil Liberties Union and Censorship
State Control of the Movies for Public Release

Police Control of Burlesque
Book Censorship in Twentieth Century England

Some of these topics may be narrowed or broadened, or they may suggest similar topics.

1

THE VIGILANTES

by Fred B. Millett

Mr. Millett takes the position that censorship in the arts is "always unintelligent," "self-defeating," and "anti-democratic." Invariably, he says, censors are indifferent to aesthetic values, to the way a view is projected in literary form—they are hunting down attitudes and doctrines they find reprehensible. By "self-defeating" Mr. Millett means that when censors call attention to a book or play they advertise it, and many of the curious will go to great lengths to obtain a copy or to see it. Lastly, he says, that since democracy depends on the intelligent discrimination of the individual, it is "anti-democratic" of censors to deprive him of the obligation he has to make his own choices.

On the evening of December 21, 1953, in the course of a C. B. S. television program, "This is Show Business," the well-known American playwright, Mr. George S. Kaufmann, made the *ad lib.* remark, "Let's make this *one* program on which no one sings 'Silent Night.'" Before the show had ended, the switchboard of the Columbia Broadcasting System began receiving calls objecting to Mr. Kaufmann's remark on the grounds that it was "anti-religious." During the next few days, between 200 and 500 letters protesting the remark were received by either the Columbia Broadcasting System or the show's sponsor, the American Tobacco Company. As a result, Mr. Kaufmann was dropped from the show until calmer counsels prevailed and he was permitted to rejoin it. In the preceding May, an amateur production of *Mr. Roberts* closed after one performance at the Mitchell Air Force Base, Long Island, because several unidentified persons objected to Air Force personnel's being allowed to hear the salty language which had been tolerated by all and sundry members of its audience during the play's three-year's-run on Broadway. Last November, the Motion Picture Production Code Administration denied the appeal of Paramount Pictures to be permitted to retain in the dialogue of a picture depicting actual battle conditions in Korea three uses of the word "hell" and one use of the word "damn." A month or so ago, a most distinguished audience assembled for the private showing of a double-bill of moving pictures. The audience consisted of the Justices of the Supreme Court of the United States. The pictures were an old German movie entitled "M," and a French movie, entitled "La Ronde," which had played for two years in the most exclusive cinema in London's West End. In assembling to view these pictures, the Justices were not moved by a common interest in either abnormal psychology or licentious behavior. They were assembled to decide whether or not the sovereign state of Ohio had acted legally in banning "M," and whether the New York State Board of Censors had acted legally in banning "La Ronde" on the grounds that it "would tend to corrupt public morals." In that stronghold of public morality, Jersey City, the police recently advised booksellers to remove from prominent public display all copies of James Jones's novel, *From Here to Eternity*. In Detroit, booksellers were discouraged from offering for sale pocket-size editions of certain of the works of Hemingway, although they were permitted to sell the books in hard covers. In Cleveland, a dealer was told that he could sell a portfolio of reproductions of Renoir's paintings but that he should not display it. In March, 1952 it was not possible to buy at any price a paper-bound copy of Mailer's *The Naked and the Dead* in Boston, O'Hara's *A Rage to Live* in Cambridge, or *The Arabian Nights* in West Roxbury, Massachusetts. Here the technique of suppression was fairly elaborate. On the advice of an unofficial advisory committee on juvenile reading, the Attorney General wrote the two firms distributing pocket-size editions warning them to withdraw certain titles from unrestricted sale. Whereupon, the distributors recalled the forbidden titles and returned them to the publishers. It is important to note that no legal action was taken against anyone concerned. The Attorney General's letter, however, constituted a formidable threat. "I expect," he wrote, "immediate and appropriate action by you. . . . [These titles are to be] withdrawn at once from unrestricted sale. . . . Please acknowledge receipt of this communication and advise me what action you have taken in this matter." Here is the police state, with a vengeance. Not legal action but merely a peremptory order makes these books inaccessible to juvenile and adult readers alike. These instances involving censorship are only a few of many examples that might be cited of the wave of suppression that has swept over this free land of ours during the past two or three years.

Obviously, the ways of censorship are numerous and devious. As Judge Sidney Goldman of the Chancery Division of the New Jersey Superior Court wrote, "The way of the censor has been tortuous and tortured from the earliest times. His story is one of arbitrary judgment and the suppression of much that we consider good, true, and beautiful. Even the most cursory account of literary censorship will show its contradictions, the absence of valid standards, its lack of inner logic and outward consistency." To entrust censorship to "one fallible man, or a private body of men, is to set up an almost despotic arbiter of literary products." Censorship, generally, falls into two significantly distinct classes: hidden and public. Of the two classes, the first is, of course, the more insidious because it is uncontrollable. Such hidden censorship is part and parcel of the system in accordance with which motion pictures are produced in the United States. All pictures that are to receive the approval of the Motion Picture Producers Code Administration must secure the approval *before* the pictures can be released. There is plenty of evidence that many of the specific stipulations of the Code are hopelessly outmoded. A specific ruling of the Code bans "pointed profanity and every other profane or vulgar expression, however used." It was this specific ruling that brought about the enforced elimination of three "hell's" and one "damn" from the picture showing actual battle conditions in Korea. Public censorship is that exercised by a legally constituted body such as the New York State Board of Regents, which may refuse to permit the showing of a picture anywhere within the limits of the sovereign state of New York. A more dangerous form of public censorship, however, occurs when private individuals or pressure-groups exert their influence to prevent the public sale of books or the public showing of moving pictures.

II

Three recent instances of attempted censorship deserve somewhat more detailed comment. "La Ronde," a French moving picture, based on Arthur Schnitzler's classic dialogues, *Reigen,* directed by Max Ophuls, and acted by a distinguished French cast, has been shown legally not only in fifteen of the states but also in the District of Columbia. The Motion Picture Division of the New York State Board of Regents, however, refused, as I have said, to permit the showing of the picture within the state, and the ruling of the Board was sustained by the Court of Appeals by a three-to-two decision. The case was carried to the Supreme Court of the United States, and recently that court ruled that the New York State Board of Regents had no legal right to prevent the showing of the picture and that, in its judgment, the showing of it would not "tend to corrupt public morals." Thus, at long last, the innocent denizens of New York City were allowed to witness, if they so chose, a public showing of this famous film. Of "La Ronde," Mr. Bosley Crowther, the *New York Times* moving-picture critic, wrote, it "is a philosophical exploration of the delusions of illicit love. Some of it is obvious, some of it subtle and vague. . . . It is hard to imagine anyone without a good bit of sophistication understanding very well what's going on. It is ridiculous to think of this picture having been banned for being 'immoral.' Yet the only reason we're seeing it in this state is because the Supreme Court found the term 'immoral' inadequate as a standard for condemning a film." [1]

The case of the motion picture, "The Moon Is Blue," is even more preposterous. As a play, F. Hugh Herbert's little comedy had played for months in a New York theatre without arousing any great enthusiasm or attracting adverse comment. Then, a film, made from the play, failed to receive the approval of the Motion Picture Producers Code Administration but was passed by the New York Board of Censors. As the time came for the showing of the film, protests against it appeared in various places. In Chicago, the police allowed the film to be shown but only to adult audiences. In Kansas City, Missouri, the police censors asked for five elisions. The Motion Picture Censorship Board of the State of Kansas demanded sixty-six elisions. In New York, the picture was attacked as containing serious violations of morality and decency. A showing of the picture in Jersey City was raided by the police, led by the Director of Public Safety, and the theatre manager was haled into court. The description of the cause of all this to-do may be entrusted to the judicious Mr. Crowther. The movie, he wrote, is "a skimpy little story of a girl who is frank about sex but wondrously deft in deflecting the passes of predatory wolves." What apparently upset the guardians of the Motion Picture Production Code was not only the frequent use in the dialogue of such tabooed words as "virgin," "mistress," and "pregnant" but also a dissipated father's indifference to his daughter's sexual behavior. But, Mr. Crowther concludes, "the theme of this confection is as moral as a Sunday school book. . . . It is virtue that triumphs. The good little girl gets the man." [2]

Certainly the most momentous attempt to prevent the exhibition of a moving picture involved the film called "The Miracle." Directed by Roberto Rossellini, the picture tells the story of a half-witted Italian peasant girl who is seduced by a stranger whom she believes to be a vision of St. Joseph. Proud of what seems to her a miraculous pregnancy, she is tormented by the villagers, who stage a mock-procession in her honor. In the end, she crawls away to bear her child in the shadow of an empty church. The New York Film Critics voted *Three Ways of Love*, of which "The Miracle" was a part, the "best foreign movie of the year," but, under pressure, they made their award in the Rainbow Room of the R.C.A. building at Rockefeller Center, and not in a public theatre. The attack on this picture was violent and inflammatory; it was accused of being both blasphemous and sacrilegious. Angry picket-lines marched and counter-marched before the theatre; there were threats that the the-

[1] *The New York Times*, March 21, 1954, pt. I, p. 1.
[2] *The New York Times*, July 9, 1953, p. 18.

atre would be bombed. Although its showing had been licensed by the Motion Picture Division of the New York State Board of Regents, the License Commissioner of New York City immediately imposed a temporary ban on the showing of the film, and when he was enjoined from imposing this ban, the Board of Regents, after its special sub-committee had voted unanimously that the picture was sacrilegious, reversed the decision of its Motion Picture Division and banned the film. Legal recourse to the New York Court of Appeals resulted in a unanimous decision to sustain the Regents' ban. But Joseph Burstyn, the distributor of the picture, carried the case to the Supreme Court of the United States, and, finally, the Justices rendered a unanimous decision that the State of New York's banning of the film was unconstitutional. "New York requires," Mr. Justice Clark wrote, "that permission to communicate ideas be obtained in advance from state officials who judge the works and pictures sought to be communicated. . . . Such a previous restraint is a form of infringement upon freedom of expression to be especially condemned." On the issue of sacrilege, he wrote, "In seeking to apply the definition of 'sacrilegious,' the censor is set adrift upon a boundless sea amid myriad currents of religious views, with no charts but those provided by the most vocal and powerful orthodoxies. . . . Under such a standard the most careful and tolerant censor would find it virtually impossible to avoid favoring one religion over another." The Supreme Court decision in "The Miracle" case is without question an important step in the battle to win the same freedom of expression for the moving picture that, at least in happier days, was the possession of literature and the stage. And yet, in the face of this decision, the chief censor of the State of Ohio, who is also the State Director of Education, continued to ban the film "on moral grounds," and the Police Commissioner of Chicago refused an application for a license because the Chicago censor, namely, the Crime Detection Division of the police force, had banned the film, *before* the Supreme Court decision, on the grounds that it "features immorality" and "exposes a religion to ridicule." In the battle for freedom of expression, no victory is ever final.

III

These instances of censorship, proposed, attempted, or achieved, might easily be multiplied. What, however, is more important than the mere accumulation of absurdities and stupidities is the attempt to understand why in recent years the censorious spirit has made itself manifest with distressing frequency.

Various explanations of the strengthening of the spirit of censorship have been offered. Eric Larrabee, discussing the Gathings Committee reports before the American Library Association, raised the question as to "whether the stress of the current antiobscenity drive on paper-bound books does not demonstrate a fear of opening up literature to a greater audience, sharing as widely as possible what has in the past been available only to the privileged few." [3] In substantial agreement with Larrabee's explanation is David Riesman's interpretation of the current wave of censorship as the manifestation of a new class-struggle, "between the 'old' Eastern-oriented merchant and professional middle-classes and the 'new,' half-educated, small-business and small-town manufacturing classes. . . . City slickers," Mr. Riesman writes, "are no longer only bankers, lawyers, and drummers: they are drummers of ideas—that is, professors, teachers, writers, and artists. . . . The very ferocity with which these anti-intellectuals try to outlaw the worldly and the educated is a sign of their resentment of their inferior status in the traditional hierarchies of prestige and comprehension." [4]

I should like to suggest two other forces that may account for the strengthening of the censorious spirit with which we are concerned. I am inclined to think that the rise in the spirit of censorship is, in large part, a by-product of the extraordinarily wide diffusion of secondary education among our population during the last generation. Persons in every age-group are inclined to forget that in the past fifty years an educational revolution has taken place: the percentage of the age-groups now obtaining a secondary-school education has increased fantastically. America is conducting an experiment in mass-education such as the world has never seen, and most of the distressing phenomena characteristic of contemporary American culture are, I believe, the results of this audacious experiment. Optimists in educational circles have been too ready to assume that, if you taught the masses to read, a new day would dawn. Well, a new day has dawned, but what sort of new day is it? It is a new day in which the masses devote themselves to the consumption of comic books that are everything but comic, digest-magazines, and television programs; it is a new day in which pocket-books of various brands, bound in the most seductive covers the publisher's book-designer can devise, are available to the millions at modest prices at every corner drugstore and news-stand. The *rise* in censorship is in part due, I believe, to the concern of the half-educated for the well-being of the quarter-educated; the *concern* over the rise in censorship is the concern of the educated over the behavior of the half-educated. The sharply opposed views of the half-educated and the educated may be vividly illustrated if we juxtapose two quotations, one from the majority report and the other from the minority report of the Select Committee

[3] *American Library Association, Summary Reports,* 1953.

[4] "Some Observations on Intellectual Freedom," *The American Scholar,* XXIII (Winter 1953–54), 23, 15. Quoted by permission of the author.

on Current Pornographic Materials, House of Representatives, Eighty-second Congress. In the majority report, we read, "The so-called pocket-size books, which originally started out as cheap reprints of standard works, have largely degenerated into media for the dissemination of artful appeals to sensuality, immorality, filth, perversion, and degeneracy." On this sweeping indictment, the writers of the minority report—Representative Emmanuel Celler of New York and Representative Francis E. Walter of Pennsylvania—commented as follows: "There is no foundation whatsoever in its proceedings for the committee's conclusion. . . . More than 53 per cent of the sales of pocket books, according to the committee's report, comes from sales in such categories as mysteries, westerns, non-fiction, and miscellaneous publications, books in which, with few exceptions, the committee has found no serious faults. . . . The publishers of pocket-sized books are certainly deserving of better treatment than whole-sale condemnation. They have done much to bring within the reach of the entire population classics and great works of literature which were formerly available only to those who could afford to purchase higher priced editions. The books on the committee's dossier comprise only a fraction of the total sales of these publishers." Many of the phenomena accompanying the first generation or more of secondary education for the masses are, to be sure, extremely distressing, but they are, I believe, the unavoidable by-products of a magnificent experiment. In any case, there is no turning back. We can only hope that, perhaps in two or three hundred years, secondary education for the masses will produce results that are not ignoble.

But there is certainly a more immediate cause for the conspicuous rise of censorship in our time. This immediate cause, I believe, is a perfect illustration of the Freudian mechanism of "displacement," the transference of an emotion from the object that initiated the response to a quite different (and sometimes quite innocent) object. I find the cause for the intensified impulse to censorship in the general atmosphere of hysteria and fear of communism that is being systematically engendered in America and—it should be observed—nowhere else in the world. The conversion of communism into the national bogey-man has encouraged the transference of distrust, hostility, and fear to a great many other entities than communism. There is a type of mind easily given to obsessions that sees communism in everything it dislikes—in a collection of abstract paintings, in popular songs, in radio programs. A majority of the members of the Gathings Committee, confronted by a type of publication anomalously entitled "War Horror Comics," that has been "officially banned from distributions among United States Navy personnel," apparently concurred in the charge that "their objectionable features might be the work of a genuine pacifist organization but they were much more likely the subversive efforts of Communists." To these members of the Committee, there seemed no point in distinguishing between the publications of pacifists and the publications of Communists. The irrational fear that makes it impossible for people to study or discuss communism dispassionately quickly spills over and inundates any other product of contemporary culture that for some reason seems strange or baffling or threatening to the half-educated mind.

IV

I should like to conclude by commenting on three propositions concerning censorship which it seems to me follow logically from the evidence I have submitted and mountains of evidence that have accumulated through the centuries: (1) Censorship in the field of literature and the other arts is usually stupid, and always unintelligent. (2) The censorship of literature is almost invariably self-defeating. (3) The censorship of literature is anti-democratic; in other words, it is fundamentally opposed to the philosophy of democracy.

Censorship in the field of literature and the other arts is usually stupid and always unintelligent, because the critical assumptions that underlie censorship are aesthetically indefensible. The censor of literature does not condemn a literary work because it is a bad literary work; by his very nature, he is usually incapable of distinguishing between a good and a bad literary work, even if he thought it important to make such a judgment. The censor condemns a literary work and would prevent its circulation because it contains or implies ideas or attitudes that he regards as erotically, ethically, politically, religiously, or philosophically reprehensible, ideas and attitudes that he thinks would do damage, not to himself, mind you, but to other persons who might be exposed to them. Now, a literary work is not a good work because it contains ideas, of whatever sort, of which the censor would approve, nor is it a bad work because it contains ideas, of whatever sort, of which the censor would disapprove. If this were the case, a hymn embodying the soundest theology in the most banal style would be a good hymn, and a hymn expressing heretical ideas in a superb poetic style would be a bad hymn. Persons who are interested in rooting out heresies might condemn the second hymn as heretical; critics could hardly condemn it as being a bad hymn.

The relationship between the idea and the form of a literary work, and the relative significance of these elements in the evaluation of literary works are not, I admit, elementary problems. With regard to the relationship between the idea and the form of a literary work no less stern a moralist, no less great a poet, than T. S. Eliot has had this to say:

> Is the greatness, the comprehensiveness of the philosophy in any actual or theoretical relation to the greatness of the poetry? Actually, we may find a poet giving greater validity to an inferior philosophy, by realizing it more fully and

masterfully in literary art, and another employing a better philosophy and realizing it less satisfactorily. . . . The poet must be rated in the end both by the philosophy he realizes in poetry and by the fullness and adequacy of the realization.[5]

To put Mr. Eliot's position a little more simply, the excellence of a poem does not depend on the validity of the doctrine it expresses. The excellence of a poem depends finally on what is said, the manner in which it is said and, I should add, the relationship between the matter and the manner. If an artist is serious, he attempts in a work of art to express something that he regards as true and something that he considers it important to say. He also endeavors to give the most appropriate and appealing form possible to what he is trying to say. On both reader and critic, it is the form that makes the most immediate impression, but, if he is a good reader and a good critic, he will be able to grasp accurately not only the idea embodied in the form but the author's attitude toward that idea, his feeling about it. He is then, as either reader or critic, quite free to indicate that what the artist thought it important to say does not seem to him to be important or illuminating or weighty. But, so long as he is acting as a literary critic, he cannot condemn the work *merely* because its content seems dubious or dangerous. In the last analysis, the excellence of a literary work depends on a very subtle analysis and weighting of the content, the form, and the relationship between the content and the form.

That the censorship of literature is usually self-defeating is so obvious as hardly to need explication. The very fact that a censor openly designates a work as dubious or dangerous is enough to draw the attention of at least a considerable segment of the public to a work that might otherwise have gone unnoticed. When the official custodians of the public morals of Boston were most active, it used to be said that some publishers looked forward eagerly to having their books banned there so that a considerable sale would be assured elsewhere. I should never have dreamed of taking time to see *The Moon Is Blue* either as a play or as a motion picture if the latter had not been attacked. Then I certainly had no morbid curiosity about the piece nor—at my age—did I expect to be enlightened about the facts of life, or to profit by the knowledge if something novel was communicated. I did, however, feel an aesthetic, as well as a moral, responsibility to discover whether or not this moving picture was as bad as it was painted. And what did I find? A pleasant but innocuous little comedy, in which an emotionally immature but intellectually precocious young girl, in her perfectly innocent relations with the men she somewhat casually encounters, uses such

[5] "Poetry and Propaganda," in *Literary Opinion in America*, edited by Morton Dauwen Zabel (Revised Edition; New York. Harper & Brothers, c.1951), p. 106. Quoted by permission of the publisher.

words as "mistress" and "seduction" with a frequency uncommon to the teen-aged American screen. I cannot imagine an audience of adolescent girls finding either the situations or the language erotically stimulating. What I shall remember with pleasure is not the discussion of seduction but a little conversation about my *bête noir,* television. As the middle-aged tippler seems about to make passes at the heroine, she asks him if he would like to look at television. "Is it in color?" he asks. "No," she says, "that will take several years." Whereupon he replies, in terms with which I sympathize profoundly, "Let's wait." The unintentional effect of censorship may also be suggested by the fact that the touring company of *The Moon Is Blue* now uses as advertising slogans "SEE what the film couldn't show! *Hear* what the movie couldn't say!"

A further ironical consequence of the censorship of literature is the heightening not only of its psychological significance but of its objective value. This consequence is not, of course, inevitable. If a moving picture is banned by one state's board of review and passed by another, the curious citizens who live on the border of the first state may at small cost in time or money journey to the nearest moving picture house across the state line. If a book is banned in Boston, it will probably be found in considerable numbers in the bookstores of the independent little village of Brookline. But if a book is suppressed nationally, like certain of the novels of Henry Miller, the alternatives are awkward or expensive. If one wishes to complete one's studies of the contemporary American novel, one may have to go to France (or Mexico) to buy Miller's works, to persuade a travelling friend to smuggle a copy in, or to pay the exorbitant prices charged by under-the-counter dealers in America. It may be some consolation that in America it is probably easier to secure admission to Dr. Kinsey's collection of erotica than to the magnificent collection of modern paintings made by the late terrible-tempered Mr. Barnes.

V

Finally, the censorship of literature is in basic opposition to the principle of freedom of thought and expression that is one of the basic tenets of a philosophy of democracy. Since I am not a political philosopher, I may perhaps be permitted to use as my authority a distinguished member of the Council of the Association, Professor Ralph Barton Perry. In his essay, "What Does It Mean to Be Free?" he writes, "Freedom means *effective choice.* Man is free, in other words, in proportion as *he does or thinks what he chooses. . . .* It is choice that imposes on human life what is perhaps its greatest burden: for it is very hard to choose. It is because he has the capacity for choice that man is a moral being." Later, he says,

"It is surprising how many who consider themselves good Americans, after three centuries during which this creed has been proclaimed, embodied in our state and federal constitutions, and consecrated in our tradition, still do not understand what the principle means. They still tend to lapse into the primitive view that it means freedom to think and communicate *true or safe* opinions." [6]

The relevance of these principles to the problem of the censorship of literature requires no demonstration. An essential condition of freedom of thought and expression is the freedom of the artist to say what he believes to be true and important and the freedom of the reader to choose whatever expressions arouse his interest, satisfy his curiosity, or add to his understanding of the human plight. As Professor Perry says, "whoever determines what alternatives shall be made known to man controls what that man shall choose *from*. He is deprived of freedom in proportion as he is denied access to *any* ideas, or is confined to any range of ideas short of the totality of relevant possibilities."

The urge to censor literature has countless and tangled roots. But one of the major roots is a view of human nature that is in basic opposition to that implied in the philosophy of democracy. The view of human nature that is held by most censors is that expressed with terrifying eloquence by Dostoievski's Grand Inquisitor in the apologue Ivan recites in *The Brothers Karamozov*. The Grand Inquisitor, the anti-Christ of Dostoievski's apologue, holds the view that man is "weak, vicious, worthless, and rebellious." Man "is tormented by no greater anxiety than to find some one quickly to whom he can hand over that gift of freedom with which the ill-fated creature is born." Opposed to this view is the Christian view, the view of Christ, Whose view of man's capacity to choose, the Grand Inquisitor denounces. "Instead of taking man's freedom from them, Thou didst make it greater than ever. Didst Thou forget that man prefers peace, and even death, to freedom of choice in the knowledge of good and evil?. . . . Instead of giving a firm foundation for setting the conscience of man at rest forever, Thou didst choose what was utterly beyond the strength of men. . . . In place of the rigid ancient law, man must hereafter with free heart decide for himself what is good and what is evil."

The burden of choice is heavy, but, within the framework of democracy—I should even go so far as to say within the Christian framework—the burden is inescapable. In these contexts, not only must man be entrusted with the responsibility of choosing between what is good and what is evil, but he must have access to all kinds and varieties of literature in order that his choices may be as meaningful as possible. Within the increasingly complicated structure of the modern state, in the face of the confusing chaos of creeds, doctrines, and dogmas, man may, to be sure,

[6] *The Pacific Spectator,* VII (Spring, 1953). Quoted by permission of the Editor.

shift the responsibility of choice to whatever official or unofficial shoulders he may select, but in so far as he abnegates his own responsibility for choice, he becomes less than a mature and responsible moral or aesthetic being.

2 | LITERATURE AND CENSORSHIP *

by John Courtney Murray, S.J.

In "Literature and Censorship," John Courtney Murray, S.J., presents a sophisticated case for certain forms of censorship, at the same time recognizing the dangers inherent in censorship. It is a fact of history, he says, that governments hold police power and use it, as with censorship, for the protection of children and those "legally to be reckoned as children." But the proper use of constraint, he says, is to create freedom for rational and moral actions; excessive constraint may provoke worse disorders than those they are designed to check. It is Father Murray's position that censorship should be juridical, that is, subject to legal procedures; minority groups, he says, should restrict their censorship activities to the sphere of persuasion. He holds that the chief area where censorship is needed is in the "pornography of violence," and he concludes with a warning to members of his own Church, and presumably to society at large, that while willing censors are readily found, there is always great danger of discouraging the writing and reading of good literature.

In this difficult matter of censorship the casuistry is endless. Therefore, since this talk is supposed to have an end, it will be better to omit discussion of cases. Instead, I shall attempt to define certain central issues and to state some of the principles that bear upon their solution. We shall not be concerned with the problem of censorship in the areas of news or opinion, or of public morality in general, but only as it arises in the fields of literature and the arts. Here the perennial issue of obscenity has recently come to the fore.

The discipline of the Catholic Church in this matter is stated in canon 1399 of the Code of Canon Law. Among the eleven categories of books whose reading is *ipso iure* prohibited to Catholics the ninth is this: "Books which have for their principle purpose the description, narration or teaching of matter lascivious or obscene." However, this canonical discipline is outside our present subject, which deals with the issue of censorship as it arises in the civil order.

An argument is sometimes set afoot about whether "the state," abstractly conceived, has or has not some right of censorship over the media of communications. And there is the complementary argument whether the individual writer or artist has or has not a right to absolute freedom of expression. These arguments I leave aside. We can start from a fact of political history, that every government has always claimed what is called police power, as an attribute of government.

This power in itself is simply the principle of self-preservation and self-protection transferred to the body politic. It extends to the requirements of public morals, public health, public safety, public order, and the general comfort of society. The only question is, how far and in what circumstances does it extend to all these social values?

In virtue of the police power, society, acting through the agency of government, is entitled to impose restraints on property rights and on personal freedoms. The question is, what manner of restraints, under what conditions, is government thus empowered to impose, in restriction of rights and in restraint of freedom? These are the concrete questions that are relevant to censorship, which is, I take it, an exercise of the police power. It might, if you wish, be an exercise of what is called *patria potestas*, the emergency power which government is entitled to use, on occasion, to protect children and those who are *ad instar puerorum*, legally to be reckoned as children by reason of their helplessness. But the same concrete questions return: when and for what reasons and under what limitations is government empowered thus to act *in loco parentis?*

In addition to the problem of governmental or legal censorship there is the problem of censorship (at least in some wide sense of the word) as exercised by non-governmental bodies—by civic committees or voluntary associations of one sort or another. We shall also have to consider this aspect of the problem.

The Central Issue

The issue that is central in the whole problem is the issue of social freedom. More exactly, it is the issue of striking a right balance between freedom and restraint in society. This is the most difficult problem of social science, to such an extent that all other difficulties are reducible to this one. No complete discussion is possible here; I shall simply make certain assertions, general in themselves, but relevant to our special problem.

First, in society constraint must be for the sake of freedom. It seems a paradox to assert that the imposition of a constraint must be justified by an increase in freedom, since every constraint is a decrease of freedom. What I mean, however, is that the constraint must create a freedom in another respect. Traffic regulations, for instance, are a constraint on freedom of movement on the streets; but they are justified because they create a freedom to move—at least, nowadays, in some minimal sense! Tax laws are a constraint on your freedom to do what you want with your money; but they create other freedoms—to live in security behind a national defense establishment, for instance. The whole texture of civilization is a web of restraints, which deliver man from a host of slaveries—to darkness, cold and hunger; to ignorance and illness and wearisome labors. Delivered from these base slaveries man is free to be a man, to live the inner life of reason and love, the classic life of wisdom, the Christian life of faith.

The problem of constraint for the sake of freedom is difficult enough when it is only a question of organizing the material conditions of life. But it becomes even more inextricable when it is a question of organizing communications within society; for in this field religious and moral, intellectual and emotional values come into play. It is easy enough to see that the "press" (understood to mean all the media of communication) can be the vehicle both of corruptive and of beneficial influences. It is easy enough to say that corruptive influences ought to be put under reasonable restraints. And it is easy enough to define what you mean by corruptive influence; it is one which destroys or diminishes the rational freedom of man, either by damaging his power of personal reflection or by exciting his passions to the point where they interfere with his rational control of his thoughts and action.

On these grounds you can certainly make a case against sexual propaganda of certain kinds as corruptive of human freedom. The influence of inordinate and unregulated sexual passion on the life of reason in man is a commonplace of human and historical experience. The susceptibility of youth to dominance by carnal desires, to the detriment of rational freedom, is particularly well documented—and hardly in need of documentation.

However, when you have made your case against these influences as socially corruptive, you have only reached the threshold of the problem of social freedom. Many questions remain. For instance, when and under what circumstances do these influences become so corruptive that they require animadvertance by organized society itself? (It is presumed that the first solicitations of corruptive influences are resisted by the special resources of the family and the Church.) Again, what agencies are to be enlisted against these influences—the public agencies of government and law, or the private agencies known as voluntary associations? Either or both? And to what extent each? Above all, what is the norm whose requirements are to be enforced, in one way or another, against influences that are corruptive? It is, of course, the norm of public order. But what requirements of public order can be made valid against the claims of freedom?

Limitation of Freedom

Even supposing these questions to have been satisfactorily answered, a further complicating consideration remains. The fact is that the imposition of constraints, the limitation of freedom, has consequences. They are numerous; but two require special notice.

First, if you impose a constraint on freedom in one domain, in order to increase freedom in another, you may take the risk of damaging freedom in a third domain, with consequences more dangerous to the community. Social freedom is a complex, whose constituent elements are closely interlocked. You may, for instance, wish to "clean up" political campaigns by limiting the freedom of the contestants to attack each other's personal integrity; but the means you take to this end may damage the freedom of the electoral process itself. Every constraint has multiple effects; it may impose restraints on a freedom which you would wish to see untouched.

There is, secondly, a consequent consideration. Because social freedoms interlock so tightly, it is not possible to know antecedently what the multiple effects of a regulation will be. At best, the effect you want can only be foreseen with probability, not certainty. And unforeseen effects may follow, with the result that a regulation, in itself sensible, may in the end do more harm than good.

For this reason, the social reformer whose only strength is a sense of logic may well be a menace. For instance, if drunkenness and alcoholism are social vices whose effect is to diminish and impair the free will of men (as indeed they are), the logical thing is to ban alcohol. Here in America we learned by experience the disastrous effects of that type of mad logic. In contrast, the illogicality of the liquor law in Belgium commends itself. The retail sale of liquor in public bars is forbidden, but you can get liquor if you go to a store and buy two quarts at once! When you unravel its seeming lack of logic, you find that the Belgian liquor law protects the citizen against his own reckless impulses, but permits him the freedom to act deliberately. This, of course, is his essential human freedom.

I should call attention here to the somewhat unique difficulties presented by the problem of the public enforcement of standards of sexual morality. Jacques Leclercq, of the Catholic University of Louvain, who is no slight authority, concludes a brief advertence to this subject with this remark: "In short, it may be said that no government has ever succeeded in finding a balanced policy of combating unhealthy sexual propaganda without injuring legitimate freedom or provoking other equally grave or worse disorders."

Everybody agrees that debauchery of the sexual faculty is morally wrong, and that incitement to such debauchery should be legally forbidden. On the other hand, in the case of incitement as open as houses of debauchery, a view that goes back to St. Augustine's treatise, *De ordine*, warns against the dangers of attempting a total coercive repression of this particular incitement.

The strictness of traditional Catholic doctrine in regard to sexual lust appalls the libertarian; the laxness of many Catholic governments in the same regard equally appalls the Puritan. In 1517 the number of prostitutes in the city of Rome considerably surpassed the number of married women. And in 1592, under a Pope of formidable strictness, Sixtus V, there were more than 9,000 prostitutes amid a population of 70,000. This was in the capital of the papal states. The figures are not indeed edifying; but perhaps they are interesting, not least when one considers that during the same era the newly constituted Index of Forbidden Books was being used with extreme severity by successive Pontiffs (Paul IV, Pius IV, Pius V) against heretical propaganda. To this day the Italian who is merely amused by the obscene *pasquinade* is deeply offended by the earnest inanities of a Baptist minister from Texas.

To the proper Bostonian all this is profoundly shocking. Just as to the Continental European, especially if he is a Latin, the spectacle of the U.S.A. is infinitely puzzling. A man is free to call error truth, and truth error, if he likes, but he is not free to use the notorious four-letter word which, in direct French monosyllabic translation, is alleged to have escaped from the lips of Napoleon when he heard of the debacle of the sunken road at Waterloo. Again, the Supreme Court declares that the category of the sacrilegious is altogether indefinable, while the Post Office rules that Aristophanes' *Lysistrata* is an obscene book. This is indeed puzzling.

Considerations such as these would seem to indicate that the problem of social freedom is insoluble, if by solution is meant a simple formula that is applicable to all cases and similar for all countries. However, a community can do one important thing: it can decide on the general orientation it wishes to give to its particular solution. We have done this in the United States. We have constitutionally decided that the presumption is in favor of freedom, and that the advocate of constraint must make a convincing argument for its necessity or utility in the particular case.

I would only add that the presumption in favor of freedom does not rest on doctrinaire grounds. Its basis was not the philosophic rationalism that called itself Enlightenment, but only a political pragmatism more enlightened than the Enlightenment ever was, because it looked to the light of experience to illuminate the prudential norms necessary to guide it in handling a concrete social reality that is vastly complicated. In this light the option was made for the civil freedom of the citizen under a government whose powers are limited, and under a rule of the law whose reach is likewise limited, chiefly by the axiom that the constraints of law must serve the cause of essential human freedom.

In our case, the consequence of this fundamental option which gives a basic orientation to our constitutional law, is that freedom of expression is the rule, and censorship the exception. A more particular further consequence is the ban laid by the First Amendment (exceptional cases apart) on all prior restraint of communications. At the same time the government reserves the right to punish, subsequently, communications that offend against law. The freedom toward which the American people are fundamentally orientated is a freedom under God, a freedom that knows itself to be bound by the imperatives of the moral law. Antecedently it is presumed that a man will make morally and socially responsible use of his freedom of expression; hence there is to be no prior restraint on it. However, if his use of freedom is irresponsible, he is summoned after the fact to responsibility before the judgment of the law. There are indeed other reasons why prior restraint on communications is outlawed; but none are more fundamental than this.

Censorship as a Juridical Process

After this brief discussion of the central issue involved in censorship I come to my proposition. It may be briefly stated thus: censorship in the civil order must be a juridical process. In using the word "juridical" I mean that the premises and objectives of the program should be defined in accord with the norms of good jurisprudence; that the forms of procedure should be properly judicial; and that the structure and workings of the process should be sustained by the consent of the community. I should maintain that this concept of a juridical process should be verified, *mutatis mutandis*, in every form of censorship, whether governmental or non-governmental.

Censorship exercised by public authority is obliged to be literally juridical, in the sense described. As a legal process this censorship is controlled by the canons of necessity or utility for the common good. That some degree of punitive censorship is necessary is sufficiently evident. Pornography, for instance, the kind of obscenity that is a perverse and vicious profanation of the sacredness of sex seems to hold a permanent attraction for a portion of humanity. That it is a corruptive social influence is not to be denied; consequently, few would deny that its repression is necessary. Beyond this how much more censorship is useful, and how useful is it? That seems to be the central question.

A preliminary answer is furnished by the principle, basic to jurisprudence, that morals and law are differentiated in character, and not coextensive in their functions. It is not the function of the legislator to forbid everything that the moral law forbids, or to enjoin everything that the moral law enjoins. The moral law governs the entire order of human conduct, personal and social; it extends even to motivations and interior acts. Law, on the other hand, looks only to the public order of human society; it touches only external acts, and regards only values that are formally social. For this reason the scope of law is limited.

Moreover, though law is indeed a moral force, directive of human society to the common good, it relies ultimately for its observance on coercion. And men can be coerced only into a minimal amount of moral action. Again from this point of view the scope of law is limited.

The Aim of Law

Therefore the moral aspirations of law are minimal. Law seeks to establish and maintain only that minimum of actualized morality that is necessary for the healthy functioning of the social order. It does not look to what is morally desirable, or attempt to remove every moral taint from the atmosphere of society. It enforces only what is minimally acceptable, and in this sense socially necessary.

Beyond this, society must look to other institutions for the elevation and maintenance of its moral standards—that is, to the Church, the home, the school, and the whole network of voluntary associations that concern themselves with public morality in one or other aspect.

Law and morality are indeed related, even though differentiated. That is, the premises of law are ultimately found in the moral law. And human legislation does look to the moralization of society. But, mindful of its own nature and mode of action, it must not moralize excessively, otherwise it tends to defeat even its own more modest aims, by bringing itself into contempt.

Therefore the law, mindful of its nature, is required to be tolerant of many evils that morality condemns. A moral condemnation regards only the evil itself, in itself. A legal ban on an evil must consider what St. Thomas calls its own "possibility." That is, will the ban be obeyed, at least by the generality? Is it enforceable against the disobedient? Is it prudent to undertake the enforcement of this or that ban, in view of the possibility of harmful effects in other areas of social life? Is the instrumentality of coercive law a good means for the eradication of this or that social vice? And, since a means is not a good means if it fails to work in most cases, what are the lessons of experience in the matter? What is the prudent view of results—the long view or the short view? These are the questions that jurisprudence must answer, in order that legislation may be drawn with requisite craftsmanship.

It is, in fact, the differentiated character of law and morals that justifies the lawyer or judge when he insists that punitive censorship statutes should be clearly drawn, with the margin of uncertainty as narrow as possible.

Minimal Moral Force

The net of all this is that no society should expect very much in the way of moral uplift from its censorship statutes. Indeed the whole criminal code is only a minimal moral force. Particularly in the field of sexual morality the expectations are small; as I have suggested, they are smaller here than anywhere else. It is a sort of paradox, though an understandable one, that the greater the social evil, the less effective against it is the instrument of coercive law. Philip Wylie may have been right in saying that American society "is technically insane in the matter of sex." If so, it cannot be coerced into sanity by the force of law. In proportion as literary obscenity is a major social evil, the power of the police against it is severely limited.

This brings up the matter of consent. Law is indeed a coercive force; it compels obedience by the fear of penalty. However, a human society is inhumanly ruled when it is ruled only, or mostly, by fear. Good laws are obeyed by the generality because they are good laws. They merit and receive the consent of the community, as valid legal expressions of the community's own convictions as to what is just or unjust, good or evil. In the absence of this consent law either withers away or becomes tyrannical.

The problem of popular consent to the order of law and to its manifold coercions becomes critical in a pluralist society, such as ours. Basic religious divisions lead to conflict of moral views. Certain asserted "rights" clash with other "rights" no less strongly asserted. And the divergences are often irreducible. Nevertheless, despite all the pluralism, some manner of consensus must support the order of law to which the whole community and all its groups are commonly subject. This consensus must include, in addition to other agreements, an agreement on certain rules which regulate the relations of the divergent groups among one another, and their common relation to the order of law.

In what concerns our present subject of censorship, I suggest that there are four such rules. Before stating them I would note that in the United States at present all the religious groups are—from the sociological, even if not from the statistical, point of view—minority groups.

First, within the larger pluralist society each minority group has the right to censor for its own members, if it so chooses, the content of the various media of communication, and to protect them, by means of its own choosing, from materials considered harmful according to its own standards.

Second, in a pluralist society no minority group has the right to demand that government should impose a general censorship, affecting all the citizenry, upon any medium of communication, with a view to punishing the communication of materials that are judged to be harmful according to the special standards held within one group.

Third, any minority group has the right to work toward the elevation of standards of public morality in the pluralist society, through the use of the methods of persuasion and pacific argument.

Fourth, in a pluralist society no minority group has the right to impose its own religious or moral views on other groups, through the use of the methods of force, coercion, or violence.

I cannot pause here to demonstrate the reasonableness and justice of these four rules. I would only note that they are not put forth as rules that were made in heaven, necessarily inherent in the constitution of an "ideal" society. On the contrary, they are to be considered as rules made on earth, by the practical reason of man, for application in the conditions—by no means "ideal"—of a religiously and morally divided society. Agreement on them would seem to be necessary in the common interests of social peace. Their supposition is the jurisprudential proposition that what is commonly imposed by law on all our citizens must be supported by general public opinion, by a reasonable consensus of the whole community. At the same time they suppose that within a pluralist society the minority groups have certain definite, if limited, rights to influence the standards and content of public morality. The statement of these rules leads to the next subject.

Non-governmental Censorship

In the United States there are a multitude of voluntary agencies which exercise some measure of surveillance, judgment, and even control of various media of communication. For the most party they shy away from the idea of being called "censoring" agencies. We need not quibble over the word; the frequent fact is that many of them achieve the results of censorship, even when they refuse the name. With regard to these agencies I should maintain the general proposition stated above—that their censoring should also be a juridical process, if not literally, certainly in spirit.

The juridical premise of their action is not in doubt. In the United States it is generally acknowledged that the voluntary association is entitled to concern itself actively with matters that relate to the public welfare. It is invidious to stigmatize all such associations as "pressure-groups," pursuing "private interests." The fact is that, in their own way, they can perform a public function.

The more difficult question concerns the methods used by these associations or committees. There can be no slightest quarrel when they use simply the methods of persuasion; that is, when they appeal for voluntary cooperation on the grounds of a common moral and social responsibility. Thus, for instance, many associations interested in decent literature and movies (surely a public interest) seek the responsible cooperation of producers and theater-owners, of publishers and distributors, with a view at least to diminishing the volume of obscenity, or other objectionable features, in these media. Surely here all is entirely rightful and prudent.

Other methods—at the other end of the spectrum so to speak—seem to have at least the appearance of coercion. As an example one might take the organized boycott, against a merchant, a theater, etc. It is a sort of "consumers' strike"; it is sometimes accompanied by picketing; it normally involves some form of economic sanctions invoked against the offending party. What is to be thought of such methods?

It will be agreed that the use of formal coercion in society is reserved to public authority and its agencies of law. Coercion of a more informal kind—through economic pressures, etc.—is also employed by various associations that do not hesitate to identify themselves as "power-groups." Such for instance, is a trade union. It does indeed seem a bit incongruous that other types of voluntary association, concerned with values that are spiritual and moral, aesthetic and cultural, should pursue their ends by what appear to be the methods of power rather than of persuasion.

On the other hand, it is not possible to prove the position, taken by some, that an action like the boycott of a moving-picture is somehow "unrightful," or "unconstitutional," or "undemocratic." No one can show that such an action lies beyond the limits of a primeval American right to protest and object. The action may indeed be strenuous; but the American right to protest and object is permitted to run to some pretty strenuous extremes.

This said, against the doctrainaire, it remains true that methods of action which verge upon the coercive exhibit some incongruity when used by citizen-groups in the interests of morality in literature or on the screen. Even if they raise no issue of abstract right, they do raise the concrete issue of prudence, which, equally with justice, is one of the cardinal virtues.

The issue rises most sharply in the case of Catholic associations. The chief danger is lest the Church itself be identified in the public mind as a power-association. The identification is injurious; it turns unto a hatred of the faith. And it has the disastrous effect of obscuring from the public view the true visage of the Church as God's kingdom of truth and freedom, justice and love. Our purpose is to stand before the world as men and women of faith, and therefore of reason too, whose reliance is on the methods of reason and not of force. We would wish always to be men and women of courage, ready to face any issue; but also men and women of prudence, who understand the art of procedure, and understand too that we are morally bound, by the virtue of prudence, to a concrete rightness of method in the pursuit of moral aims.

The Competent Censor

It should be noted too that prudence is an intellectual virtue, a refinement of intelligence. It may therefore properly be asked, how intelligent is it to have recourse to methods that approach coercion in this delicate field of censorship? Few things are worse than to make oneself ridiculous. And when an effort to coerce is made at the dictates of stupidity, the result arouses ridicule as well as resentment.

This brings up the question, who is competent to censor, even in some extra-legal fashion? To say that all censorship should be a juridical process is to say by implication that it ought to be intelligently done. This means close attention to the qualifications of the censor.

Here the example of the Church is instructive. In his reform of the discipline of censorship Benedict XIV laid great stress on the rule that the censor is to possess professional competence in the particular field in which he is called upon to pass judgment. Censorship is no job for the amateur. Like stress is placed on the censor's obligation to perform his task impartially, in the fullness of the judicial spirit that forbids the intrusion of any private likes or dislikes. In the process of censorship there is no room for the personal, the arbitrary, the passionate. The censor is not called upon for a display of moral indignation; he is asked only for a judgment, calm and cool, objective and unemotional. So too in the civil sphere, the less we have of moral indignation, and the more we have of professional competence and an unclouded faculty of judgment, the better it will be for the juridical nature of the censorship process.

In what concerns the problem of obscenity I would not discount the value of what is called the "common estimation" of men. People in general have a fairly clear notion of what obscenity is. And people in general can make, for themselves, a pretty good judgment on whether a particular work is obscene. Certainly the Code of Canon Law seems to suppose that the ordinary Catholic can make this concrete judgment for himself. I repeat, for himself. The question is, who can make it for others, i.e., as a censor.

Here a distinction is in order. Certainly the ordinary father and mother ought to be qualified to act as censors within the family. And to decide what their children may or may not be prudently exposed to, in the way of reading, movies, etc. But I should not think that the ordinary father or mother, *qua* such, are qualified to act as censor within society at large, or to decide what literature and movies may be displayed before the general public.

Society has an interest in the artist's freedom of expression which is not necessarily shared by the family. If adult standards of literature would be dangerous for children, a child's standard of literature is rather appalling to an adult. If therefore any censorship is to be administered in the interest of society, the professional competence of the literary critic must play a role in the process.

Here perhaps the characteristic Catholic care for the welfare of children (often coupled with the typically American cult of the child-centered home) ought to be aware of a danger. The contemporary argument about censorship is sometimes described as a "battle between the literati and the philistines." The description is snobbish, if you will. But it would be lamentable if Catholics were to go over to the camp of the philistines. After all, we do stand, not only within the oldest religious tradition of the Western world, but also within its most venerable tradition of intellect, literature and art. The tradition has produced great achievements in writing, painting and the plastic arts. Not all of them are fit for children indeed—not even the Bible in all its parts. But that is no justification for any form of philistinism.

In one further and final respect the process of extralegal censorship ought to be juridical, pursued in the spirit of law—that is, in its adoption of minimal aims. Fussiness is out of order. There ought to be a few, only a few, areas of concentration, in which a little bit (if not much) can be done.

I suggest that the chief area is the "pornography of violence," as it has been called. Mischief enough is done by the obscenities that occur in the portrayal of illicit love (by literary hacks who never learned what the genuine artist knows instinctively—that, though art may "say all," there are certain things it is never allowed to say explicitly). But here sex is at least rescued from full profanation by its tenuous connection with love, as love is still resident in lust. However, when sex is associated with, and becomes symbolic of, the hatreds and hostilities, the angers and cruelties, that lie deep in men and women, the profanation of the most sacred thing in sex—its relation to love and to the hope of human life—is almost complete. It could move perhaps only one step deeper into the diabolical—in that association of sex and blasphemy that pervades the Black Mass.

The image of the truly evil thing in the obscenities of our day is seen on the typical cover of the "tough" kind of pocket-book—the seminude woman, with a smoking gun in her hand. The scene is one of impurity, but that is its lesser evil. The real evil is the violence in the impure scene.

There is the perversion. If some restraint could be imposed upon this pornography of violence—so damning in its revelation of a vice in our culture—it would indeed be a moral achievement.

The Chief Problem

It is a good thing to keep our problems in perspective. Our chief problem, of course, is not literary censorship, but literary creation. This is true in the Church. She has no trouble in finding censors; but she prays continually that God may give her men of learning who can write the works that are needed.

The American Catholic community particularly needs to attend seriously to this problem of literary creation. Leo XIII is indeed remembered for his revision of the Index of Forbidden Books. But he was not the first Pope to point to the dangers of reading bad books. It is his great glory that he was the first Pope to say, in substance and effect, in a multitude of discourses, that today there is great danger in not reading good books. This is why I think it is a fine thing for the Thomas More Association to sponsor a lecture on censorship—once every seventeen years! Now it may resume the high apostolic function which it has been splendidly performing.

3 | THE FUTURE OF CENSORSHIP

by Paul Blanshard

Mr. Blanshard believes that in two respects the American situation regarding censorship is relatively good: our freedom to discuss sexual matters openly and to favor labor interests is far greater than it was a generation or two ago, and our freedom of the press is second only to one or two other countries in the world. He is critical however of what he calls the taboos against serious and open discussion of the American economic system and of religious orthodoxies. In general, Mr. Blanshard favors fewer censorship regulations, and sees a need for individuals and groups to "organize for freedom."

The editor of the Lake Charles (Louisiana) *American Press* said in an editorial in 1954: "It would take volumes to outline the dangers of censorship, but they can be generally characterized by two questions: (1) Who will be the censors? and (2) Where will the censorship stop?" A third question might be added: When will censorship begin?

Men rarely agree on the answers to all three of these questions, and probably society is better off because of that disagreement. We are fortunate that Americans do not recognize any literary or clerical caste as having special fitness for censorship. There is safety for the nonconformist in diversity of standards. If men had a universally accepted criterion for measuring and appraising literary freedom in all countries, that fact would in itself be an evidence of intellectual stagnation. As Professor Hocking said in his *Freedom of the Press:* "Each society must recapture for itself, on its own terms, and by its own individual explorers, the beliefs it needs to live by. . . . even in this, the era of the liberal spirit at its height, liberty has a shape; it is not infinite."

Two-Way Comparison

If the shape of our liberty, as it emerges from the moral problem-areas we have discussed in this book, is not altogether pleasing, it is far from hopeless. Comparatively it may even be described as gratifying. If we look back over a long time-span and include all the facets of our reading history, we can see that we have improved in the scope as well as the stability of our literary freedoms. When we compare our present condition with that of many other peoples, we have a right to feel cautiously cheerful.

Probably it is fair to say that in respect to the right of the common people to read we are as well off as the citizens of any other nation. Our only possible competitors in this respect are in the British Commonwealth and the Scandinavian countries. Probably the treatment of Communist news in these countries is less hysterical than in our own press, and the presence of recognized left-wing newspapers is a healthful antidote to right-wing extremism. But in most other respects we are far more secure in our literary freedom than the average European. The continental press, particularly in France and Italy, is more partisan than our own and less adequate in news coverage. Many observers consider it far more susceptible to corruption.

Perhaps the nonconformist book or magazine has a slightly better chance of fair play in Great Britain and the Scandinavian countries than in the United States, but even this view may be challenged. The British newspapers of the largest circulation duplicate most of the sins of our mass-circulation newspapers and add a few of their own. They are no less sensational and certainly they do not maintain a higher level of non-partisanship and truth-telling during election campaigns. The scope of their treatment of world news is narrower than that of the American press, and their treatment of American life is more meager than the corresponding treatment of European affairs in the American press. In respect to the freedom to discuss sexual matters in print, the present British and American restrictions seem to be about equal in severity.

Of course the Communist countries have nothing but a state propaganda machine to offer as a "free" press; and Franco's newspapers and publishing houses are kept in censorial and clerical swaddling-clothes. Even outside the iron and the purple curtains in Europe, newspaper editors are frequently controlled by dictatorial governments—when they are not bribed by financial manipulators. If a considerable part of our press is dominated by investor-monopolies—as it is—the American newspaper at least has "standards." Usually our editors cannot be bribed directly; they may be owned but not bought. That is a distinction which does not impress Moscow critics, but it is substantial. We certainly have much more freedom to read than the people of the Soviet Union, China, Spain, Yugoslavia, Portugal, Iran, Egypt, Saudi Arabia, Argentina, Venezuela and Bolivia; and almost as much freedom as the people of the rest of the English-speaking world. Of course we have much more freedom to read than the illiterate peoples of Asia and Africa.

The divergence between American standards of freedom of the press and the restrictive standards of many totalitarian and non-democratic powers was dramatized in 1950 at the United Nations when the United States could not win majority support for a mild freedom-of-information agreement, after Congress and American editors had taken the lead in demanding such an agreement. A bloc of foreign nations which included not only the European Communist powers but also many Asiatic, Latin American, Moslem and Arab nations, instead of proposing more freedom for publishing, actually championed more restrictions and barriers to free information.

Some of the restrictive proposals of these nations would have sanctioned the complete suppression of opposition newspapers by governments even in peacetime. Carroll Binder [1] of the Minneapolis *Tribune*, who served as chief American representative in negotiations for a freedom-of-information agreement, declared that if the proposed restrictions had been accepted it would have been "illegal for an American magazine to publish a picture of Mohammed or for Hollywood to produce a movie about Fatima, Mohammed's daughter." The agreement would also have outlawed the American right to publish stories about "the romantic escapades of King Farouk of Egypt." Although the English-speaking countries, the Scandinavians and a few Latin American powers stood together as opponents of censorship, the result was a stalemate and all plans for establishing freedom of the press by international agreement had to be suspended.

Not the least of our comparative assets is the fact that in the United States the concept of freedom of speech is an organic part of a strong

[1] *Proceedings*, United Nations, 1956.

government. It is significant that our strongest defender of political tradition, the Supreme Court, is also our strongest defender of literary freedom. Although our reading rights are recorded rather sketchily in the Constitution, the document itself commands almost universal respect, and it is interpreted liberally in matters of intellectual freedom by a court under democratic control which is as near holy as anything can be in our irreverent society. Our bill of reading rights is top-sacred; there is no mystical image of a king or a dictator or a pope or a führer above the Constitution.

Comparisons between the past and the present states of our literary freedom are much more difficult to make than international comparisons. The right to read means much more to us than to our fathers and grandfathers, not only because of our increased capacity to read but also because we have the greatest supply of reading matter in all history, made available to us by a national system of distribution which for the first time can reach nearly all the people. In such an environment, all reading is incomparably more free for the common man than it was in the beginnings of our nation. In perspective the last century may well go down as the great reading century. In no other time-span has there been such a proportionate increase in the right to read or in man's ability to exercise that right.

Balance Sheet of Freedom

As we look back in perspective over the areas covered in this book we can see that in most areas the right to read is not seriously limited by law; the most serious curtailments come from pressure and prejudice. If we could measure changing literary tolerance on some kind of historical scale, we would probably conclude that the greatest change has taken place in the area of sex and decency. We have seen that a degree of frankness in print is now permitted in regard to sex which would have been unthinkable in the books and magazines of two hundred years ago. The areas of sexual taboo in print seem to be disappearing as rapidly as the forbidden portions of the body in pictorial art.

Is this a sign of decadence or of moral progress? Probably it is both. The obvious decadence of some of our underworld magazines and fiction may be a temporary phenomenon produced by the exploitation of a new-found liberty. Conventional family relationships are changing rapidly, and simultaneously literature is reflecting the weakening of traditional monogamous marriage and the decline of the authority of the paternal oligarch in the old-fashioned home. Personal happiness has been promoted to the position of the primary family value. Family power and stability are no longer regarded as supreme goods in themselves. The home is not the center of our economic life, and women no longer work under the direct control of their men. Having taken their places as equals in a world of men, they find that the sexual taboos which were supposedly created for their protection are disappearing. Now they read the same books, graduate from the same universities, drink the same liquor and embrace the same standards of sexual conduct. Their right to read about sex and life, with no four-letter words omitted, is an inevitable result of a bloodless social revolution. They have bought their new freedom with their pay envelopes.

There has also been a great change in the tolerance of our society for violence in print, and today the legal freedom to discuss crime and horror is almost unlimited. We have seen that the most significant and ominous feature of this new tendency is not the output of literary violence for adults but the deliberate exploitation of horror, crime and violence for the children's market. The child's right to read has an entirely new significance in our culture. As a literary consumer he stands on his own feet, and tenders his own dime. Gone are the days when parents and librarians could prescribe the Pansy books and the Little Colonel books for obedient and eager youngsters. Although publishers still produce millions of "good" books for children, and earnest parents earnestly endorse them, the big literary world of childhood today is the world of the comic book. In this world children are for the first time in history asserting a very vehement preference of their own. For the time being the chief reaction of the adult world to this phenomenon is one of simple dismay. As we have seen, a counter movement is beginning, but it is too early to predict its effect.

With respect to Communism and capitalism, our right to read is probably very much less than that of several European nations, and it cannot be said with certainty that freedom to discuss these two conflicting philosophies of life with candor has increased since World War I. While our laws nominally permit literary freedom in this area, in practice we attach such egregious penalties to any literary endorsement of collectivism that we have established a kind of post-publication censorship by vilification. Probably no democratic nation in the world is so enamoured of its own economic system or so unwilling to discuss fundamental changes in its "free enterprise" pattern.

However, in spite of this kind of immature hysteria, we have made immense strides in the last fifty years toward genuine freedom in discussing labor rights, poverty and social injustice. Pro-labor news, particularly pro-strike news, was virtually anathema in the American newspapers before World War I. The labor leader was pictured as an anti-social agitator and the strike leader as a dangerous "Bolshevik." In the steel strike of 1919 the Interchurch World Movement showed that the Pittsburgh papers were virtually organs of the steel companies, suppressing the news about constabulary violence, misrepresenting the working conditions in the mills and publishing false news about the "end" of the strike. In thirty-five years the whole climate of American information about labor has changed.

More than 16,000,000 labor union members now read their own newspapers. The labor leader is given almost as respectful treatment in the daily press as the capitalist—provided he professes belief in the economic system in which they have both found prosperity.

In this whole picture of changing freedoms, the two values which we protect with the most jealous solicitude are patriotism and religion. The man who is disloyal to America is still the archvillain of our literature. Of course the duty of allegiance to the nation-state may be questioned in discreet language, and the glories of a coming internationalism may be painted in pastel shadings, but let any man attack the whole pattern of national loyalties with forthright gusto in the language of the street-corner, and he will be doomed to social or legal discipline. If the attack is made in time of war, his negative suasion may be treated as a crime.

In perspective the right to read about religion seems to be, in spite of our complete formal liberty, the most frail and ephemeral of our literary rights. For the masses of men it consists simply of the privilege of reading one side of the story—or ignoring that side. An almost complete blackout is imposed on the critical analysis of orthodoxy in the mass media of information. No motion picture, no radio program, no theater, no newspaper and no magazine of mass circulation ever dares to make a forthright, frontal attack on current orthodoxies. The most that the mass agencies of information will venture is an occasional attack on some orthodox blunder of the past or some minor foible in an existing church. And in the meantime all of these media are constantly used for sectarian ecclesiastical promotion of one sort or another. Only in the world of hardcover books and in the small world of liberal magazines can a reader discover that a gigantic conflict between science and orthodoxy is still in progress throughout the world, and that its outcome is of deep concern to all believers in intellectual freedom. Usually the book-review editors exempt partisan religious books from independent analysis by assigning them for review to sectarian apologists of the same general outlook as the author.

Probably the present American taboo against what is called "religious controversy" is as bad for religion as it is for atheism. It means that the great concepts of religion are rarely discussed frankly in public by serious, independent thinkers. Religious literature suffers from too much tenderness; it lacks vitality and vigor. It is wrapped in the sterilized cotton wool of hypocritical respect. Most of the religious books which reach the best-seller lists are merely sentimental, and they systematically evade the critical issues that are the concern of serious minds. While the current taboo on controversy condemns the literature of religious iconoclasm to obscurity, this unofficial censorship does not benefit the literature of orthodoxy; in fact it carries the literature of orthodoxy down with it into a kind of quagmire of pious propaganda, scorned by intellectual readers and ignored by condescending critics. With a relatively few scholarly exceptions, our huge output of religious literature is the most pathetic exhibit in our non-fiction output. Nine-tenths of our religious books sink into deserved obscurity as soon as they are published. By operating under the taboo against candid criticism, orthodoxy has suffered a loss of prestige more damaging than any defeat which could be administered by the atheists.

More Law, No Law and Less Law

The censorship reformers may be divided into three groups: those who want no censorship law at all, those who want more censorship, and those who want less. In the first group Bertrand Russell is the most distinguished and persuasive. In a 1954 article on "Virtue and the Censor" he said, in discussing obscenity:

> For my part, if I had my way I should abolish all legislation on the subject. Perhaps for the first year or two after such abolition there would be a flood of "feelthy" pictures, but if there was no ban on them, people would soon get tired of them—except for a few with an exceptionally strong bent in this direction. At present a taste for pornography is almost universal among boys, but I think it is created by secrecy and tabu. If they were taught about sex in school, they would soon find it as dull as Caesar's Commentaries. However, I cannot hope that so extreme a measure as the total repeal of the laws against obscenity could possibly be carried.

Mr. Russell's last sentence applies with special force to the United States. Whatever may be the merits of his prediction concerning the effect of suspending all bans on obscenity, it is unthinkable that an American majority would accept such a program in the foreseeable future. If they did, the probable result would be a quick and violent reaction to an even stricter code, after a flood of postcards and films depicting copulation and perversion had swept over the juvenile market. The immediate reaction would be so hysterical that legislators would not wait for the ultimate readjustment predicted by Mr. Russell.[2]

The no-censorship program is equally unthinkable in the field of sedition, particularly in wartime, and probably Mr. Russell would be the first to recognize this fact. The conviction is deeply imbedded in our American tradition that no freedom comes ahead of national safety, and in wartime the tendency is to let the government and the military authorities define national safety in their own terms. In the light of this tradition, any effort to abolish all restrictions on treasonable and seditious literature would be a waste of time.

The facts we have marshalled in this book do not support a demand for

[2] *Encounter*, London, July, 1954.

extensive new censorship laws to augment the laws already on our statute books. We are already oversupplied with laws, ordinances and legal penalties. This is especially true in the field of loyalty oaths, alleged security information and seditious writings. Many responsible critics have contended that at least half the anti-espionage and anti-Communist laws passed since the beginning of World War I are superfluous and only tend to create popular hypertension. The Commission on the Freedom of the Press, after a long study of these laws, instead of advocating more legislation in this field, said: "We recommend the repeal of legislation prohibiting expressions in favor of revolutionary changes in our institutions where there is no clear and present danger that violence will result from the expressions."

But even if we hopefully assume continued "peaceful coexistence," it would probably not be worthwhile to attempt an outright repeal of any of our present anti-sedition statutes. The attempt would surely be interpreted as an unnecessary softening toward Communism, and in the ensuing uproar over alleged disregard of our national safety, the real purpose of reform, to free honest nonconformity from suppression, would be lost from sight. The efforts of liberal reformers could be more wisely expended in attempting to make enforcement of the present laws more moderate and fair. After all, very few of our laws are themselves totally and inherently obnoxious; they nearly all have exceptions and omissions which exempt the honest nonconformist from penalties. They become obnoxious only when they are enforced without mercy or a sense of proportion by narrow-minded and ambitious prosecutors.

We are also very well supplied with anti-obscenity statutes, and there seems to be no point in asking for more laws in this field. Most of the anti-obscenity laws passed as a result of purity crusades in recent years have added nothing important or essential to our prohibitory machinery, nor have they done anything new to get at the social roots of the evils involved. The federal government certainly has plenty of anti-obscenity laws; and nearly every state and city in the union is equipped with a sweeping statute or ordinance, often providing for rather vengeful over-penalties in the hands of a fanatical prosecutor or judge. In only one segment of the underworld of publishing is there a reasonably strong argument for more repression, and that is in the field of horror and crime comic books specially designed for children. But, as we have seen, no feasible scheme has yet been devised for the general legal regulation of this trade without at the same time threatening legitimate adult reading matter and establishing dangerous precedents for general pre-publication censorship.

In a few areas there is a convincing case for more laws curtailing unwise censorship. Most important of these areas is that of Post Office censorship. The present power of the Postmaster General even in peacetime to declare a book or magazine unmailable in advance of a judicial review is anomalous in a free society. The exercise of that power in an arbitrary manner seems to negate the lofty pronouncements of the Supreme Court against censorship. Most American liberals side with the American Civil Liberties Union in its long crusade for a law that will take away from the Postmaster General his present arbitrary powers. Professor Chafee and the Commission on the Freedom of the Press have suggested the goal for needed reform in this territory by recommending full judicial review in all obscenity mail cases, and by suggesting also that "Congress should treat mailed books like imported books and give either side a jury trial if it wants one."

There is also need for a federal freedom-of-information statute, and for new laws in many states and cities defining public records more adequately and guaranteeing citizens free access to them. The forthright language of the State of Florida and of the New York Public Service Commission law may well serve as models for such legislation. "All state, county and municipal records," says the Florida law, "shall at all times be open for a personal inspection by any citizens. . . ." "All proceedings of the Commission," says the New York statute on the Public Service Commission, "and all documents and records in its possession shall be public records."

Nevertheless, even with such laws, the press could be denied access to vital information in Washington about "internal affairs of government" if officials could fall back upon an overstrict interpretation of "security risks." To prevent that type of bureaucratic censorship in what Harold Cross has called "that vast, bewildering jungle which is the government of the United States," former Senator William Benton has proposed that there should be a "people's advocate" on the National Security Council, as well as departmental boards headed by outside newspaper editors to work within each federal department for public disclosure whenever feasible. Senator Benton's suggestion was not accepted by Congress, but its merit is self-evident.

Should We Smash the Monopolies?

Far more important than these proposed incidental reforms is a suggestion which has been hotly debated in the publishing world for several years that the government should halt the drift toward monopoly ownership of newspapers by use of its anti-trust legislation. As we saw [earlier], nearly 95 per cent of all American dailies today are non-competitive. Competition between independent local editors is dying, and the great ownership chains are taking over. As of January 1, 1955, America had 95 ownership chains or groups of newspapers with an average of five papers in each chain. We have lost at least 440 daily newspapers in the United States since 1909, while the population has gone up 63 per cent and the total newspaper circulation has increased 122 per cent.

Have we lost any substantial amount of literary freedom by this transformation? There is no doubt that we *could* lose a great deal. Ownership power is in its very nature censorship power, and it is exercised, or could be exercised, at the most dangerous point in the communication process, *before* publication, secretly, automatically and continuously. Monopoly power is a specially dangerous form of ownership power because it could destroy competition in the marketplace of ideas. Oswald Garrison Villard of *The Nation* sounded the alarm against the drift toward monopoly in his 1944 book, *The Disappearing Daily;* Morris Ernst in his 1946 work, *The First Freedom,* made an exceedingly effective case against monopoly; and Professor Chafee and the Commission on Freedom of the Press gave much thought and space to the issue in 1947. Mr. Ernst was so deeply concerned about it that he suggested a special exemption from income taxes for small newspapers, magazines and radio stations on the first $20,000 to $25,000 of their earnings, in order to help them to maintain their existence in the fight against the great monopolies.

The present monopoly situation in newspaper ownership is no better today than it was in the 1940's. Professor Raymond B. Nixon of the University of Minnesota has recently canvassed the developments since 1945. There are 18 states in which every city is either a one-newspaper city or a one-ownership city: Alabama, Arizona, Delaware, Georgia, Idaho, Minnesota, Montana, Nebraska, New Hampshire, New Mexico, North Dakota, Oklahoma, Rhode Island, South Carolina, South Dakota, Utah, Virginia and Wyoming.

One of the unpleasant realities is the character of the newspaper chains which have bought out the small papers in so many towns. Of course the Cowles chain in Minnesota and Iowa is of exceptional quality, but what can be said for Hearst's 16 dailies with a circulation of some 5,000,000 and the crackpot literature of reaction represented by such writers as Westbrook Pegler? Or the Chicago *Tribune-New York News* combination with its cranky and reactionary isolationism? Or the once-militant, 18-daily Scripps-Howard chain which has steadily lost its original crusading independence and become merely one more string of newspapers?

Professor Nixon [3] points out some mitigating facts. The 1361 non-competitive cities are nearly all below the 500,000 mark in population; the 87 competitive cities include all the large ones. And he believes that the industry is now stabilized— "The era of consolidations has about come to an end." Whether this prediction is sound or not, it seems clear that most of the newspaper mergers have been necessary steps toward economic sal-

[3] Raymond Nixon, *Journalism Quarterly,* Winter, 1954.

vation. Newspapers have no monopoly on the drift toward monopoly. Everybody is doing it in spite of the Sherman Anti-Trust Law; and today 135 corporations own 45 per cent of the nation's industrial assets.

No one charges that this trend toward bigness in newspaper control has impeded the flow of general news or reduced readership—the circulation of newspapers has gone up steadily through the merger period and the general news coverage has tended to expand. Big newspapers can frequently afford more journalistic features than small newspapers. But should a community trust any one man or any one corporation to own *all* its newspapers?

The best answer seems to be that at present the average community has no choice in the matter. Also there seems to be no proof that the actual presentation of news and opinion in monopoly papers is any more partisan or irresponsible than it was in the days of personal and small-scale journalism. One reason for this condition is that simultaneously with the trend toward monopoly within the newspaper industry there has been a very substantial trend toward destruction of monopoly of the news by newspapers. The machine age has produced a set of very vigorous competitors to the newspaper: the cheap book; the news and feature weeklies like *Time, Life, Newsweek,* and *United States News*; and the great TV and radio news services. There are also the syndicated columnists who develop audiences of their own fans, and sometimes disagree with local editors. And there has been in recent years a great development of schools of journalism, attempting to lift the craft of news-gathering to the dignity of a profession with responsible standards.

As far as cultural freedom is concerned, the gravamen of the complaint against newspaper ownership is not its drift toward monopoly; it is rather the nature of existing financial control. As a capitalistic enterprise the publishing industry puts power in the hands of the investor instead of the journalist, particularly when the flotation of a new daily newspaper in an American city takes many millions of dollars. Of course many publishers are also competent journalists, but they control their empires by virtue of their investments and not by virtue of their professional pre-eminence. Herbert Brucker, editor of the Hartford *Courant,* has put the complaint of the professional journalist on this point very candidly:

> It is largely held within newspaper ranks that the chief fault of our press is that the working newspapermen, who in their professional careers have rubbed up against all sorts and conditions of men and tend as a result to view the lot with the detachment born of disillusionment, are not allowed to control our newspapers. They are kept under the thumb of the business men who predominate among owners and publishers, who are self-interested members of an economic aristocracy rather than detached and objective reporters.[4]

[4] The *Nation,* June 18, 1938.

William Allen White, as both capitalist and working journalist, discussed this dependence of the journalist on the capitalist in a disarming article in *The Nation* in 1938. "The owners of newspaper investments," he said, "whether they be bankers, stockholders of a corporation, or individuals, feel a rather keen sense of financial responsibility, and they pass their anxiety along to newspaper operatives, whether these operatives be superintendents known as managing editors, foremen known as city editors, or mere wage earners known as editorial writers, copydesk men, reporters or what not. The sense of property goes thrilling down the line. It produces a slant and a bias that in time becomes—unconsciously and probably in all honesty—a prejudice against any man or any thing and any cause that seriously affects the right, title or interest of all other capital, however invested." [5]

This automatic built-in bias within the publishing industry is naturally intensified in all those enterprises which depend for their survival on advertising—and, as we have seen, the average American newspaper gets about two-thirds of its income from advertising. The censorship by advertisers is never direct or brutal; it is in the nature of a general requirement of approval by the business community. That general approval is a condition precedent of success for a newspaper, and it works in a negative way. No newspaper or magazine of general circulation can survive if its views are in constant conflict with the attitudes of its advertisers in respect to those vital economic matters on which business power is based. Even Henry Luce, head of the $130,000,000 *Time-Life-Fortune* empire, who is commonly rated both an able journalist and one of the most powerful individuals in America, would rapidly come tumbling down if his economic attitudes did not accord with those of the advertising community. William Allen White called him "a spot of capital."

The underlying pre-publication censorship by financial power in our newspapers is most evident in presidential campaigns. Then it expresses itself in editorial conservatism and in some shading or emphasis in the news. For many years American newspapers, in terms of presidential support, have been several degrees more conservative than the voters. They have chosen the Republican party in preference to the Democratic party even when the whole national drift has been directly contrary. In 1952 Adlai Stevenson was supported by only 11 per cent of the press, in terms of circulation, although he polled 44 per cent of the popular vote. In 1936, 86 per cent of the newspapers supported Landon; Truman won in 1948 with the support of only 16 per cent of national newspaper circulation.

However, when the Communists claim that the double-headed monster of investment power and advertising power completely destroys American

[5] On problems of a one-party press, see *Editor and Publisher*, Feb. 7, Sept. 6, Sept. 20, Oct. 25, and Nov. 8, 1952.

freedom of the press, they are overstating the case. There is still so much competition within the communications industry that all the grim possibilities of monopoly have not been realized. Some of the finest newspapers in America have no competition in their own morning or evening fields—the Washington *Post and Times-Herald;* the St. Louis *Post-Dispatch;* the Minneapolis *Star and Tribune;* and the Milwaukee *Journal.* The large newspaper may be more independent of specific advertising pressure than the small newspaper, which can too easily be destroyed by the withdrawal of a single large account. Also the large monopoly newspaper may be more able to resist the competitive pressure to cheapen and sensationalize the news.

The very eminence and power of the monopolist-publisher sometimes forces him into a position of neutrality among the community's warring interest-groups. The Stouffer survey . . . shows that, at least in a questionnaire, the publishers of leading newspapers were without exception the most tolerant toward the rights of nonconformists among all community leaders—more tolerant than labor union presidents, industrial leaders or politicians.

When all these factors are taken into consideration, the weight of argument seems to be against the use of the Sherman Anti-Trust Law to stop newspaper mergers, unless those mergers happen simultaneously to produce dangerous concentrations of power in publishing, radio and television.

Organizing For Freedom

If there is any single lesson to be derived from America's battle against censorship it is that intellectual freedom does not maintain itself automatically even in an open society. It must be ceaselessly defended by trained spokesmen for freedom who understand the psychology of the censorial pressure groups and know how to strike back at their most vulnerable points. In order to maintain the right to read, men need to organize themselves for freedom in the field of literature as systematically as they now organize themselves for freedom in the fields of politics and military power. Otherwise the professional enemies of nonconformist thought are bound to maintain those initial advantages which come from attack and from the appeal to fear.

The appeal to fear will always be with us, because men are human and they instinctively react with fear to any threat against their established ways of thinking. We cannot prevent this human reaction, even if we would, and if we have faith in democracy we should accept it as an inevitable part of a free society. The champions of censorship must be heard not only because many of them are sincere and they *might* be right, but also because if they are silenced, their suppression becomes a triumph for their own philosophy. Free men must act on the assumption that in a free society the most fanatical pressure group has the same right to state its case as the most august assemblage of impartial scholars.

The trouble with the august assemblages of impartial scholars in the past is that too often they have not organized properly for freedom. The open-minded citizen shrinks from the necessity of fighting for his literary rights in a noisy marketplace of controversy. He hates to meet attacks on nonconformist books and magazines with vigorous counterattacks. Sometimes he loses to the censorship claques by default because he contents himself with lofty quotations from Milton, Mill and the Constitution. Usually the quotations are admirable, but they cannot stand alone.

Happily, the American people are beginning to see the necessity of organizing themselves for freedom in order to maintain their right to read. Libertarian organizations have sprung up which are attempting to organize both the general public and the professions—the teachers, librarians, editors and writers—to resist every encroachment upon literary freedom. Foremost among these organizations is the American Civil Liberties Union which has served for thirty-five years as the legal watchdog for the common citizen in fighting any infringement upon constitutional rights. In the library world the American Library Association has organized a Committee on Intellectual Freedom which has done much to establish the Library Bill of Rights as the American code for freedom of reading in public libraries. The book publishers formed the American Book Publishers Council before World War I to advance their own interests, and they have repeatedly and successfully challenged the censorship of books in the courts. In 1954 a group of important leaders in the library, publishing and literary fields united to form a new National Book Committee, "to keep books free, make them widely available, and encourage people to read them." In the world of education the National Education Association fights for freedom of textbooks and teaching through its National Commission for the Defense of Democracy Through Education. Within the publishing industry, *Publishers' Weekly* carries the torch against every attempt at censorship. The Fund for the Republic (originally established by the Ford Foundation) is making a gigantic survey of the whole area of civil liberties, with a corps of trained research experts.

There are some Americans who doubt that an open society like ours can maintain its strength in the struggle against closed societies of the right and the left if it permits almost unlimited freedom to the literature of protest, iconoclasm and dissent. It seems to me that there are two answers to these critics, either of which is sufficient. Thus far America has remained strong in freedom, much stronger than the nations in which the minds of men have been systematically controlled by censorship. And, regardless of whether such freedom serves national strength or not, it is a good in itself, since it contributes to the growth of something greater than national glory, the development of the human spirit. Whatever men may think about the practical advantages and disadvantages of intellectual freedom in a world of militantly aggressive nation-states, there is no doubt that, as William Allan Neilson once said, "it is through freedom and not through compulsion that the human spirit gains in power and reach."

4 CLOSE-UP OF BRITAIN'S CENSOR

by George Steiner

Mr. Steiner says that although England prides herself on her freedom of the press and public utterances, she allows strong censorship of London's commercial theatre. Since he is highly critical of smutty newspapers and pocket books (both of which, he says, flourish in England), Steiner obviously is not asking that pornography be allowed on the English stage. He is protesting the banning of serious plays. It is difficult and perhaps impossible to inquire into the Lord Chamberlain's censorship principles, but Steiner denies the Lord Chamberlain's competence to censor. In support of his position Steiner points to serious plays that have been banned: Andre Gide's The Immoralist, *Lillian Hellman's* The Children's Hour, *and Tennesee Williams'* Cat on a Hot Tin Roof.

LONDON.

Englishmen boast that theirs is the freest nation on earth. All political parties are allowed to advocate their views in full and public liberty; no one need take refuge in a Fifth Amendment to conceal his beliefs; and on the soapboxes in Hyde Park speakers with turbans or kilts, bowler hats or flaming beards, can freely expound doctrines ranging from anarchism to theosophy. But there is one great medium of ideas, one great arena in which free minds have clashed and debated, to which the Englishman's access is barred by ancient inhibitions and rigorous censorship. It is the theatre.

The English theatre of today is less free than that of any other Western nation and is, in certain aspects, more severely controlled than the theatre behind the Iron Curtain. In the last few years alone, there have been half a dozen major Broadway productions which regular London producers have not been allowed to put on. They include: "The Children's Hour," "The Immoralist," "Tea and Sympathy" and "Cat on a Hot Tin Roof." Shortly after arriving in England, Arthur Miller was informed that his "A View From the Bridge" had not been cleared for performance.

Even those plays which are produced in London have been carefully censored. "Waiting for Godot" and "Waltz of the Toreadors" have been the toast of the town. But before allowing either play to be shown, censorship had used its scissors. Its acrimonious vigilance, moreover, extends far beyond serious drama. Musicals, operettas, revues and cabaret sketches are scrutinized lest they contain a line or a lyric dangerous to a formula established in the Seventeen Thirties—"the preservation of good manners, decorum and of the public peace." Hence, many a bright gag about the Prime Minister's mustache dies before curtain time.

Who are the guardians of morality and how do they carry on an art that goes back to the reign of Henry VIII? That is a difficult question, for the whole subject of theatrical censorship is shrouded in the courtly silence and evasive gloom with which English officials conceal and preserve some of their more outrageous traditions. The Lord Chamberlain and the four examiners of plays do not give interviews to journalists and it is fitting that in front of their offices in St. James's Palace there should be a constant picket of Guardsmen in tall bearskin caps.

Theatrical censorship is a direct prerogative of the crown and those who enforce it are members of Her Majesty's Household. As such, they stand above and beyond the kind of public control which a democracy can exercise over its elected representatives. The powers of censorship are vested in the Lord Chamberlain and he is assisted by a small group of examiners whom he can choose at will. The present Lord Chamberlain, Lawrence Roger Lumley, Earl of Scarborough, was appointed to his high and ancient office in 1952. What kind of man is he?

The letters after his name—K. G., P. C., G. C. S. I., G. C. I. E.—are like a drum roll of long years spent in the service of the crown and of a retreating empire beyond the seas. The noble earl was educated at Eton and at Sandhurst, England's West Point. Like so many of his proud generation, he fought bravely in the First World War for a way of life that was already passing into the shadow of history. After the war, he went to Magdalen College, Oxford, that beautiful and ancient house in which the Duke of Windsor spent some of his happier years. After serving in Parliament, the Earl of Scarborough went out to India and became Governor of Bombay. India and Asiatic affairs have remained foremost among his interests and he served as a distinguished president of the Royal Asiatic Society. After returning to England, he acted as Parliamentary Under Secretary for India and Burma and then retreated into the pomp and seclusion of the Queen's Household.

What emerges from this career is the portrait of an aristocrat and soldier, of one of that host of loyal proconsuls whose glittering regalia and white-plumed helmets represented the crown to its colonial millions in the aftermath of the Victorian Age. Standing in his robes of the Garter, the Earl of Scarborough (whose earldom goes back to 1690) aptly symbolizes a great tradition of *noblesse oblige* and service to the crown. But what is there in his training, experience or natural inclinations to qualify him as a judge of morality or as a censor of contemporary drama? Nothing whatever.

It is true that the Earl faced the problem of free speech and dangerous ideas while governing Bombay; he solved it rather neatly by putting Gandhi in prison. And he may feel himself qualified to deal with writers as he has himself published a definitive work—the "History of the Eleventh Hussars." To the outside world, most of which saw him performing his stately office during the coronation, the Earl of Scarborough remains a shadowy figure. To the theatrical profession, he remains a person in no way equipped to decide that Tennessee Williams and Arthur Miller are threats to public safety and morals.

When a producer wishes to put on a play in England, he submits the script to the Lord Chamberlain, who may either judge the play himself or pass it on to his four examiners, three of whom read English and one of whom reads Welsh. Little is known about Lieut. Col. Sir St. Vincent Troubridge, Baronet, and his three colleagues. It is rumored that they occasionally allow themselves a flash of wit. A producer who recently brought them a new play was asked whether it was about homosexuality. No, said he. "Is it about the Suez Canal?" Again, he said no. "Is it obscene?" He hastened to deny it. The four examiners looked at him and then one of them burst out, "If that is true, my dear sir, why in heaven's name produce the play?"

After the manuscript has been examined it will be returned with one of the following verdicts. It may be deemed entirely unacceptable, as was the case with the Broadway adaptation of Gide's "The Immoralist" and Julian Green's fine melodrama, "South." It may be returned with a list of necessary alterations and excisions. Some dramatists have enough integrity about their art to refuse to make such changes. Others, such as the author of "Waiting for Godot," put the phrase "the Lord Chamberlain" in place of the censored lines. Finally, a play may be termed "acceptable" and "licensed" for public presentation.

There is no way of appealing publicly against the ruling of the censors. They can declare that a play is unacceptable without specifying their reasons or indicating precisely what has to be changed. As the great critic William Archer put it at the end of the nineteenth century, the English theatre is at the mercy of "a secret tribunal, consisting of from one to three court officials, who at one stroke of the pen can annul the labor of months or years, giving no reason and allowing no appeal."

The history of theatrical censorship is fascinating and, like certain other English institutions, it has become respectable through senility. Ironically, it was Henry VIII, that connoisseur of immorality, who first created a dramatic censor and the whole process has remained closely linked to the crown. Charles I personally censored a number of plays. But the system of licensing as we know it today originated in the Seventeen Thirties as a sequel to the brilliant political lampooning in "The Beggar's Opera"—a masterpiece of fun currently to be seen off Broadway under the guise of Brecht's "The Threepenny Opera."

Since that time the history of English theatrical censorship has been the chronicle of individual censors, some of them enlightened but the majority obtuse and reactionary. Some of their decisions have been immortalized in anecdotes based on fact or invented by indignant playwrights. John Larpent, a censor active around the turn of the nineteenth century, excluded the word "gammon" from the English stage as Gammon happened to be the name of a close friend. When a play by Tolstoy was banned and a storm of public opposition broke out, the Lord Chamberlain of the day asked candidly, "Who is Tolstoy?" At various times, parliamentary commissions have inquired into the whole affair but they came up against a wall of obtuseness or evasion. A few officials were frank about their methods. Testifying in 1866, the Honorable Spencer Barbazon Ponsonby admitted that plays translated from the French could be examined very quickly, for were there any French plays that were not obviously immoral?

As in the drama itself, so in theatrical censorship fashions change. At certain periods, during and after the French Revolution, for instance, censors were particularly anxious to keep any hint of politics off the stage. At other times, all sexual problems were taboo, and such literary masterpieces as Shelley's "The Cenci" and Yeats' translations from Sophocles were barred from regular performance. At the beginning of this century, censors were especially fearful of any hint of atheism.

What is the situation today? The Earl of Scarborough has published no statement of his code of ethics. But a glance at the list of banned plays cited at the start of this article shows that they have one thing in common: reference, either implicit or open, to the problem of homosexuality.

This prohibition is, in actual fact, an absurdity. For although that delicate study of the subject, "Tea and Sympathy," cannot be shown, the Old Vic can put on a production of Shakespeare's "Troilus and Cressida," in which every costume and stage action underlines the homosexuality latent in certain characters. And the same Englishman who is not allowed to see "Cat on a Hot Tin Roof" can go to any book store and buy a copy of the play and can pick up, in the cheap Penguin edition, Angus Wilson's "Hemlock and After," a novel in which homosexuality runs riot.

Other themes which are barred from the London theatre are atheism and blasphemy—possibly the reason cuts had to be made in "Waiting for Godot"—and contemporary politics. It is one of the virtues of English political life that individual politicians are severely guarded from libel or gratuitous insult. But this doctrine can be carried too far, and it is significant that the modern English theatre has not produced a single good political play or anything that comes near Arthur Miller's "The Crucible" or Sartre's "Les Mains Sales." None of the major issues in present British affairs, neither the rise to political power of the laboring classes nor the end of imperialism and its effect on English life, has been reflected in the theatre. And consequently, the London repertoire is divided between inane drawing room comedies dealing with the alleged delights of debutantes and guards officers, and the supposed tragedies of retired gentlewomen fading away in boarding houses by the sea.

Fortunately, there is one way in which theatrical censorship can be, and sometimes is, circumvented. The Lord Chamberlain's powers extend only to the regular theatres. They do not include "unlicensed playhouses" which are, simply, theatres constituted as "clubs." In addition to buying tickets, "members" pay an annual subscription and this puts their "club" outside the range of censorship. At present, there are half a dozen such clubs in greater London, all the way from the Arts Theatre—the largest club of its kind in the world—to small, makeshift organizations in which Marxists or young actors can perform the masterpieces of O'Casey or such Elizabethan classics as "Tis Pity She's A Whore" without being summoned by the Earl of Scarborough.

But a playwright is at a disadvantage if he can only be produced at a theatre club. Only the Arts, with its 20,000 members, can tempt first-class actors to perform in an unlicensed play, and of twenty-four recent productions there, only three have been from the banned list. The other clubs lead a precarious financial existence. Unlike the off-Broadway houses—which are a product of economics—London's unlicensed theatres are the result of a legal necessity.

From the time of Dr. Johnson to that of Kenneth Tynan, the bright young musketeer of contemporary dramatic criticism, English playwrights and reviewers have protested against censorship, and some of them, such as Fielding, even stopped writing for what they considered a muzzled stage. But what of the public at large? Does it take this whole situation lying down or are occasional bricks tossed through the windows of St. James's?

The truth of the matter is that most English theatregoers are not even aware of the issue of censorship. They may notice the little phrase about "licensed by the Lord Chamberlain" in their programs, but the vast majority does not even know what it refers to. Millions are aware of the way in which movie censors work and of the way in which they classify pictures ranging from X (for adults only) to U (for the whole family). But a mere handful of enlightened people, many of them with an interest in literature or the stage, are conscious of the archaic rules and regulations enforced by the theatrical censors.

Certain observers go even further and argue that if the public at large were told the facts and if a representative poll were taken, the majority would favor the retention of censorship and praise the Lord Chamberlain! This does not mean that all Englishmen are Puritans, but it does suggest that their attitude toward the theatre is a special and rather complex one. Somehow, the theatre is in a different class from other media of communication. English newspapers, particularly certain Sunday papers with circulations in the millions, are full of every kind of smut and titillation. Literary pornography is a large industry and is passed on through specialized bookstores in London and other urban centers. Millions of Englishmen know that London by night is an increasingly unsavory spectacle. They accept all this and tend to regard it either as inevitable or as a necessary part of freedom. But when it comes to the theatre, a strong streak of Victorian pride and prejudice comes to the fore.

The Englishman's attitude to the stage is highly ambiguous. On the one hand, he considers theatrical people as somewhat shady characters living in a land of semi-respectability or downright Bohemia. Since the time of that great actor, Henry Irving, Englishmen have accepted the fact that actors can belong to good clubs and can even be knighted. But most English families would still be embarrassed at the news that one of their children "had gone on the boards." On the other hand, Shakespeare is England's greatest natural resource and consequently English people take immense pride in the history of their drama and tend to regard a visit to a theatre as something different from going to the local movie or buying a newspaper on the way home. Dramatic censorship appeals to both elements in this ambiguous attitude. It reassures those who instinctively distrust the theatre and it makes it safe for them and their families to patronize what is, after all, a great national institution. There is a good deal of hypocrisy in all this, but the genius of English history is a genius for compromise, and hypocrisy can be justly defined as a compromise between public morals and the truth.

There is a more sophisticated defense of the Earl of Scarborough's functions. With a twinkle in his eye, Harold Hobson, the dean of London reviewers, will admit that censorship is outrageous but will argue that it does not matter because English drama from Shakespeare to Congreve and

Sheridan to Shaw has flourished under it. That is a strong point, but it breaks down when one considers the past half century. Playwrights using the English language have either been Irishman such as Wilde, Shaw, Yeats and O'Casey or Americans such as O'Neill, T. S. Eliot, Arthur Miller and Tennessee Williams. The London theatre as such has produced little outside the minor excellence of Noel Coward or the brittle facility of Terence Rattigan. Is that fact unconnected with the Lord Chamberlain? Here is what Bernard Shaw said:

> We have got a censor of plays at present. We have had him for a considerable time. * * * I describe his function as an unmitigated nuisance. I repeat, an unmitigated nuisance. It prevents serious plays from being acted, and consequently, prevents them from being written.

That, surely, is the heart of the matter.

But what is involved is a rather abstract and subtle principle and, whereas Frenchmen will storm palaces at the mere thought of a principle, an Englishman doesn't get very bothered until someone is actually hanged or has his books burned. Critics and younger dramatists may be clamoring for the end of censorship, but behind the Lord Chamberlain stand the great forces of apathy and tradition. It is only in the House of Commons that something could really be done to put London's West End theatres on an equal footing with Paris and Broadway. But few members of Parliament care enough about the drama either to offend the moral susceptibilities of their constituents or to get entangled with the dangerous problem of royal prerogatives.

Despite the social revolution of the last decade, loyalty to the crown is stronger than ever and dramatic censorship is safely barricaded behind palace walls. Perhaps feelings will change if some major playwright is discovered in the next generation and if a play, which enough people consider outstanding and more wish to see, is barred from regular production. But as far as one can see at present, and unless the Earl of Scarborough bans "My Fair Lady" on the ground that it contains dangerous social doctrines, the censor's job is safe. And the delightful day may come when the Lord Chamberlain will caution a troupe of visiting Russian actors against putting on a play with too much controversy or freedom of ideas!

5 LIBRARY BILL OF RIGHTS

Adopted by Council of A.L.A., at Atlantic City on June 18, 1948

The First Amendment of the Constitution guarantees freedom of discussion. Despite this, one or another pressure group often attempts to force libraries to deny space on their shelves to books that express opinions which the group finds "un-American." As a way of resisting such pressure, the American Library Association has written a Bill of Rights. The American Library Association has also resisted pressure to "label" books, a more subtle attempt to limit one's right to read or to come to one's own conclusions. It should be observed, however, that neither of these two documents discusses the censorship of pornography, the right of publication of which is not guaranteed by the First Amendment.

The Council of the American Library Association reaffirms its belief in the following basic policies which should govern the services of all libraries:

1. As a responsibility of library service, books and other reading matter selected should be chosen for values of interest, information and enlightenment of all the people of the community. In no case should any book be excluded because of the race or nationality, or the political or religious views of the writer.

2. There should be the fullest practicable provision of material presenting all points of view concerning the problems and issues of our times, international, national, and local; and books or other reading matter of sound factual authority should not be proscribed or removed from library shelves because of partisan or doctrinal disapproval.

3. Censorship of books, urged or practiced by volunteer arbiters of morals or political opinion or by organizations that would establish a coercive concept of Americanism, must be challenged by libraries in maintenance of their responsibility to provide public information and enlightenment through the printed word.

4. Libraries should enlist the cooperation of allied groups in the fields of science, of education, and of book publishing in resisting all abridgment of the free access to ideas and full freedom of expression that are the tradition and heritage of Americans.

5. As an institution of education for democratic living, the library should welcome the use of its meeting rooms for socially useful and cultural activities and discussion of current public questions. Such meeting places should be available on equal terms to all groups in the community regardless of the beliefs and affiliations of their members.

By official action of the Council on February 3, 1951, the Library Bill of Rights shall be interpreted to apply to all materials and media of communication used or collected by libraries.

6 LABELING

A Report of the A.L.A. Committee On Intellectual Freedom

At the Midwinter Meeting, the report of the Committee on Intellectual Freedom dealt briefly with five or six cases. This morning, I ask your consideration of only one problem, but it is one which has manifold implications of a rather serious nature. This is the problem of labeling.

What is labeling and how has it become a matter of urgency? Approximately eight months ago, we received a report that the Montclair (N.J.) Chapter of the Sons of the American Revolution was exerting pressure on libraries in New Jersey to put a prominent label or inscription on "publications which advocate or favor Communism, or which are issued or distributed by any Communist organization or any other organization formally designated by any authorized government official or agency as Communistic or subversive . . . ;" furthermore, such publications ". . . should not be freely available in libraries to readers or in schools to pupils, but should be obtainable only by signing suitable applications."

The committee noted that the SAR resolution did not make clear who would do the labeling, who would decide what is communistic or "subversive" or by what criteria such decisions would be made. It would appear that labeling, if done in the local library, would require a member or members of the staff to examine carefully into the contents of, and attitudes in, every item acquired by the library in order to ascertain whether or not there was any communist or subversive slant, espousal or authorship therein. It is fair to assume that a variety of labels or statements would have to be fashioned to apply to the great diversity of shades of opinion or guilt in the light of whatever criteria might be established. It is conceivable that such a project could be handled centrally by the ALA or the government, but the implications of this sort of politburo arrangement are repulsive to people reared in the democratic tradition.

The committee felt that the practicability and financial problems of such a project were not necessarily relevant to its decision, which should be made on the basis of the principle involved.

As we looked more deeply into the problem of labeling, we found that it is not an uncommon proposal. In addition to the Sons of the American Revolution, we discovered that other groups have tried to use it as a technique of limiting freedom to read. Religious groups sometimes ask libraries to label, if not to ban, publications they find objectionable. There are also indications that so-called "patriotic" organizations other than the SAR are moving dangerously close to similar proposals.

In April, President Graham received a letter direct from the Montclair Chapter of the Sons of the American Revolution requesting this Association to adopt the SAR policy. This letter urged, as did the original resolution, that so-called communistic and subversive materials not only should be labeled but also should be segregated in libraries and given out only upon written and signed application.

By this time, members of the Committee on Intellectual Freedom had had an opportunity to study more fully the background of the problem and to submit their recommendations. When the issue was put to them formally, nine out of eleven members voted, and all nine were united against the idea of labeling as proposed by the Sons of the American Revolution. It was recognized by some of us that the committee's unanimity might stem from the fact that we were unusually sensitive to the subject of intellectual freedom. There was also some concern over the fact that, for the most part, we represented large public or institutional libraries; whereas the practical problems of labeling seem likely to develop in smaller libraries. It was therefore considered advisable to seek a slightly broader basis for judgment, and we proceeded at once to obtain the counsel of 24 other practicing librarians in libraries located geographically from Texas to Minnesota and from North Carolina to the state of Washington, the selection emphasizing but not being restricted to small and medium-size public libraries as well as college, university and state libraries.

Twenty out of the 24 to whom we wrote replied to our inquiry and without exception opposed labeling. Despite the smallness of our sample the unanimity among the replies seems impressive.

Although our request suggested possible pros and cons, plenty of leeway was left for individual points of view and the manner in which our colleagues took advantage of their right of free expression indicates that intellectual freedom is not yet dead. Without naming names, I would like to quote some of their remarks because they put the case more eloquently than I possibly could:

I

"Libraries must oppose the practice of labeling if they wish to maintain their positions as *impartial* agencies providing information on all aspects of any question."

II

"I am opposed to the idea of labeling books as pro or anti anything, because there can be no reasonable end to such an attempt once it is begun."

III

"Personally, I . . . think labelling is as dangerous as the evils it may attempt to correct—and I am aware that some real evils do exist. . . . Recognizing this time as a period of danger, and also realizing that the Soviet Communists do not play under the same set of rules as does a democracy, I still vote strongly against any labelling program such as the SAR requests."

IV

"I am opposed to such a procedure. . . . Those who read should be able to discriminate—to think for themselves."

V

"You may put me down as opposed to labelling any literature in American Public Libraries, regardless of the 'slant' or the subject. . . . Once labelling is started on behalf of one group or organization, libraries would have to label other material for its slant, political, religious, economic or whatever. (Imagine the book 'You Must Eat Meat' being labelled: 'This book is considered objectionable by the Vegetarians of America.')"

VI

"Labeling is not merely an 'attempt to prejudice the reader.' It is surely in the minds of some of its proponents an attempt to control or frighten him."

VII

"How soon after we start labeling books will we begin to burn them?"

VIII

"The suggested action if undertaken would seem to me (1) to invade the privacy of the individual and (2) to deny a democratic principle that people are able to weigh the evidence and to make sound conclusions. The outcome (of labeling) will be that public libraries will purchase only books which will not be challenged, with the inevitable result that the original and experimental will be driven out. . . . The idea of requiring readers to make written application for the use of materials labeled as Communist slanted seems in some ways more frightening than labeling."

IX

"If we wish to live in a free country, we must develop our minds to recognize propaganda and to *think*. A label is merely the thinking of one person or a group of persons."

X

"There is room in America for all people to read and form their own opinions. . . . In a democracy people must have the right to know facts about *everything*. (This) does not necessarily mean they advocate everything about which they know. Maybe quite the contrary. . . . I oppose all efforts to predispose readers for or against any materials. . . ."

XI

"To require labeling of material with any particular slant—such as communism—is to sacrifice the *principle* of free thought and opinion. American citizens of the future are going to be free to consider *all* points of view—or they are not going to have that freedom. Many of us—not only the professional anti-communist—have blind spots. But librarians must not agree to putting blinders of any kind on their readers. The principle of free inquiry, which is fundamental to American librarianship and American democracy, must be maintained against labelers as against all other censors."

XII

"Every group in the country, with an axe to grind, must be happy in the thought, that if one of them can make an opening wedge to wreck the 'Library Bill of Rights,' the rest of them can all come in, and the Free Public Library will be a thing of the past. . . . Everyone working here is against labeling. Where would the 'Sons of the American Revolution' be today if their great grandpas had been as 'scairt' of different viewpoints as they are?

"I spent an afternoon asking borrowers what they thought of labeling books (particularly subversive books) so they would not fall into the hands of the easily persuaded. Their answers were obvious, but the *shock* registered in their faces at such an idea, was something to see. Here are some of their comments:

"A well-educated old lady: 'Hitler began by burning the books. Isn't this another form of the same thing.'

"A college girl: 'It's an idea of old men. We young people are able to make decisions that are good. Give us credit and the chance to do it.'

"Another college student: 'They talk about the wonderful education we get in America. How are we going to make use of it, and really know that democracy is right if we are only allowed to read what they want us to believe.'

"Housewife: 'Stalin tells only one side of the question. I thought Americans didn't believe in his methods.'

"Man: 'I'm an adult. Sound mind. Good education. Who the hell has the right to tell me what to read or warn me what not to read?'

"Teacher: 'What are you trying to do? Take away freedom of thought and freedom of conscience? The Constitution gives me the right to read and think as I please, regardless of what anyone else thinks. I pay taxes to support the library and expect to find a good selection of books on the shelves. I'll be my own censor.'

"Housewife: 'It violates all principles of freedom of thought. It is treason to the principles on which the country was built.'

"High school senior: 'How can we tell that our way is right if we can't make comparisons. Are they afraid of comparisons? Then Democracy is sure on the skids.' "

RECOMMENDATIONS UNANIMOUSLY ADOPTED BY THE ALA COUNCIL

July 13, 1951

In view of our own convictions and those of other practicing librarians whose counsel we sought, the Committee on Intellectual Freedom recommends to the ALA Council the following policy with respect to labeling library materials:

Librarians should not use the technique of labeling as a means of predisposing readers against library materials for the following reasons:

1. Although totalitarian states find it easy and even proper, according to their ethics, to establish criteria for judging publications as "subversive," injustice and ignorance rather than justice and enlightenment result from such practices, and the American Library Association has a responsibility to take a stand against the establishment of such criteria in a democratic state.

2. Libraries do not advocate the ideas found in their collections. The presence of a magazine or book in a library does not indicate an endorsement of its contents by the library.

3. No one person should take the responsibility of labeling publications. No sizable group of persons would be likely to agree either on the types of material which should be labeled or the sources of information which should be regarded with suspicion. As a practical consideration, a librarian who labeled a book or magazine pro-communist might be sued for libel.

4. Labeling is an attempt to prejudice the reader, and as such, it is a censor's tool.

5. Labeling violates the spirit of the Library Bill of Rights.

6. Although we are all agreed that communism is a threat to the free world, if materials are labeled to pacify one group, there is no excuse for refusing to label any item in the library's collection. Because communism, fascism, or other authoritarianisms tend to suppress ideas and attempt to coerce individuals to conform to a specific ideology, American librarians must be opposed to such "isms." We are, then, anti-communist, but we are also opposed to any other group which aims at closing any path to knowledge.

7 CENSORSHIP OF COMIC BOOKS: A STATEMENT IN OPPOSITION ON CIVIL LIBERTIES GROUNDS

In recent years, many people professionally or otherwise concerned have said that horror comics or comics that portray violence and criminal acts are a strong contributing factor to juvenile delinquency. The American Civil Liberties Union investigated the allegation, publishing its conclusions in "Censorship of Comic Books." The study surveys the laws that relate to such publications, and observes the danger of any censorship, since one type of censorship can encourage further censorship. Presumably the ACLU would not oppose censorship when it can be shown that there is a "clear and present danger." Interestingly, the study shows there are considerable differences of opinion among experts about the correlation between horror and crime comics and juvenile delinquency.

Introduction

Within the past few years, the country has focused increased interest on the problem of juvenile delinquency and the relationship, if any, between this social evil and comic books devoted to crime and horror stories. Reflecting the widespread public concern, a number of solutions have been proposed that run the gamut from legislation forbidding publication of such comics or banning their sale to minors, to less drastic measures such as publishers' self-regulation.

As an organization devoted solely to the preservation of civil liberties, the ACLU's interest is confined to the civil liberties aspects of these proposals. We are not experts on juvenile delinquency, nor are we specially trained in the fields of sociology or psychology. And we do not claim to be particularly experienced in the skills of law enforcement. Our special field of knowledge, developed over 35 years, is civil liberties and the necessity of maintaining them in a society that practices and encourages freedom.

The problem of juvenile delinquency is of major importance and we believe that every legitimate effort must be made to deal with its causes and to seek its cure. As an organization concerned with the welfare of the American community, and as parents concerned with the welfare of our children, we are anxious that this alarming problem be solved.

Do Comics Breed Delinquency?

One of the main emphases in the public debate on the causes of juvenile delinquency has been the relationship between delinquency and the reading of crime comics. A large segment of the public has generally assumed that crime and horror comics do stimulate children to commit crimes. But this assumption does not reflect the spirited controversy among the experts in the fields of sociology, child psychology, psychiatry, and law enforcement. The debate indicates that there are almost as many opinions as there are experts about the degree of importance and significance of comic books dealing with crime, violence and horror and their connection with the rising tide of juvenile crime.[1]

Some experts state that crime comic books have the most direct relationship to the occurrence of criminal acts. A second group believes that crime comic books have some importance, but are not the controlling factor. Still a third group asserts that comic books play only a minor role in the development of a juvenile delinquent. A number of specialists feel that comic books do not have the slightest bearing on the problem. Finally there are those who feel that comic books actually help children by allowing them to give vent, vicariously, to their drives for adventure and thrills.

The ACLU believes that comic books, like the other mass media, may play an important part in the development of children's minds and behavior. But, in view of the divergent—even contradictory—opinions expressed by responsible and qualified persons, it believes there is lacking the assurance that crime comics are a significant cause of delinquency. This view is held by such an eminent crime authority as J. Edgar Hoover, Director of the FBI. In 1950, after commenting on the fact that certain crime stories and comics may be dangerous, particularly in the hands of an unstable child, he said:

"It is doubtful, however, that an appreciable decrease in juvenile de-

[1] An appendix of representative statements is attached.

linquency would result if crime comic books of all types were not readily available to children.

"Guidance by parents in the reading habits of boys and girls is the best defense against possible addiction to certain 'horror' stories. The love for this type of reading may reveal a lack of balance not only in reading habits but in the child's environment at home, in the school and in the neighborhood.

"The answer may lie not in wiping out objectionable crime comics but in substituting restrained presentations which will allow the child under guidance to logically set up standards as to what types of crime comics are good or bad."

It is not the function of the ACLU to decide the merits of the various and opposing contentions. It is appropriate to say, however, that at this time there has been no showing that the circulation of crime comic books constitutes a clear and present danger with respect to the occurrence, or continuance, of juvenile delinquency. Unless such a danger is shown—and further, the inadequacy of alternative means to combat this evil—there is no justification for cutting into a basic right guaranteed by the U.S. Constitution, a free press unhampered by governmental interference. In view of the anti-delinquency work being carried on by churches and synagogues, schools, social agencies, and civic and community organizations, it can hardly be said that there is insufficient time to combat whatever evils may be presented by crime comic books by means short of censorship or by legally banning their publication. Unless such time is lacking, then even the fact that some relationship is shown between the increase of juvenile delinquency and the distribution of crime comic books is no justification for their supression.

Can Censorship Be Limited?

The ACLU is not doctrinaire in its opinion about the various solutions that involve curbs on comic books which have been proposed to deal with the problem of juvenile delinquency. Although as individuals we may question the wisdom of a particular proposal for the solving of juvenile delinquency, we want to see this problem solved—without subverting civil liberties.

Some persons have suggested that, as a general rule, censorship is wrong, but that it might be proper to censor comic books since only children's reading would be affected. If the problem existed in a vacuum, it could be effectively argued that children's reading material should be handled differently than adult material, because the youthful mind has not matured to the level where it can assimilate and wisely evaluate a complex of ideas. But the problem does not exist in a vacuum, and this consideration is outweighed by others. First, it is most difficult to limit censorship only to the elimination of misdeeds and horrors to which children should not be exposed. Historical experience has shown that private groups who seek to inculcate their particular point of view are always eager to broaden the scope of banned material and seize on censorship as an ally. Once the wall has been breached, more ground may be lost. Second, if a system of censorship is established for children, it could pave the way for censorship of adult reading material. To institutionalize the censor and his scissors is a real danger. Governmental censorship, even in a limited form, has within it the means of destroying the climate needed to nurture the minds of free men.

However, it is unreal to discuss the problems of censorship of comic books in a context which implies that only children would be affected. There is ample evidence that a large part of the comic book readership is adult.[2] The ACLU is opposed to the prior censorship of reading material for adults, even if children may obtain access to such material, for we believe that the First Amendment flatly prohibits it. To condone pre-censorship for children is to risk abandonment of all reading material to the censor, since in one way or another youngsters are apt to obtain any book at some time. If the objective is to seal off tales of horror and crime from children, it will be necessary to ban classics of literature. Should we bar *Crime and Punishment* and *The Turn of the Screw?* Will we have repetitions of the attempt to suppress *Ulysses?* Or *An American Tragedy?* Will those who frown on the depiction of the intimate details of the commission of crimes turn their shafts on *Hamlet?* Is it still necessary to set forth the massive historical weight of evidence against prior censorship of books? Have we not yet finally passed this milestone of progress on the road to freedom?

The Specific Restraints

Some advocates of the theory that reading of comic books leads to delinquency and crime suggest that the sale of comic books to children under a certain age be banned.

Such legislation is aimed at banning distribution to under-age children rather than the comics themselves; in theory, no objection can be made, but the scope and administration of such legislation might draw ACLU protest. However, although we are not experts in law enforcement, we suspect that this solution will result in a great deal more confusion than benefit. There is ample evidence that a prohibition always heightens interest

[2] The Bureau of Public Administration of the University of California reported on February 28, 1955 that 25% of the nation's adults who were high school graduates were readers of comic books. 16% of the college graduates and 12% of the school teachers were comic book readers.

in the banned product, and it can be expected that "bootleg" sales will spring up, especially as children realize that comics are legally unobtainable. Some local ordinances allow sale of comics to young children if their parents consent, and there are many parents who will buy any comic book that their child requests. It is common knowledge that comic books are passed from one child to another and if one undesirable comic book gets into the hands of a single child, a great number of children will be exposed to it. In those communities where the law provides that crime comics may not be sold to children under a certain age, each bookseller is faced with the task of determining who is a qualified buyer, and deciding which comic book is outside the pale. This law may be more difficult to administer than the laws forbidding the sale of liquor to minors.

An extreme proposal, which has been incorporated into the law of many states, is an outright ban on publications devoted principally to criminal news and stories of bloodshed, lust, and crime—broad enough to include crime comics. In the ACLU's opinion, which has been upheld by the U.S. Supreme Court, such laws cannot meet constitutional standards.

In a key test case, the U.S. Supreme Court in 1948 declared a New York State law invalid because of vagueness (*Winters* v. *New York*, 33 U.S. 507). A New York State joint legislative committee subsequently studied the problem and attempted to enact new legislation whose language would be more definite. Former Governor Thomas E. Dewey vetoed two such bills on the ground that neither met the constitutional test of required definiteness and certainty. In 1955, a restrictive law aimed directly at comic books was finally passed and signed, but this, too, appears not to meet constitutional requirements. As the ACLU sees it, it may be impossible to legislate in this area without either making a frontal attack on civil liberties by setting up a licensing or censor system, or making indirect attacks on freedom of the press by enacting laws which are either too vague or indefinite for proper enforcement. In either case, they do not conform with the principles set forth in the First Amendment.

Still another technique, which has gained wide popularity, is the formation of volunteer citizen groups to serve as "watchdog committees" which attempt to influence book dealers not to handle the books that such "committees" consider improper. Recent newspaper reports indicate that the number of these groups has increased and that their influence is being felt more every day through different techniques of boycott and coercion.[3] Cer-

[3] The Providence *Evening Bulletin* on March 2, 1955 reported that several newsstands and drug stores have refused to carry books and magazines listed as "objectionable" by the National Organization of Decent Literature. The February list of "disapproved" publications include 316 book titles and 174 magazines. The *Evening Bulletin* reports: "Included in the February blacklist are works by some of the outstanding authors of these and recent times. Among the 'objectionable' titles are 'Nana' by Emile Zola, '1919' by John Dos Passos, 'To Have and Have Not' by Ernest Hemingway, 'Sanctuary' by

tainly individual members of the community have the right to decide what they or their children should read. Such discipline is entirely proper. But concerted action, designed to decide the reading fare of the entire community, imposes the will of one group on other persons and constitutes an attempt to enforce conformity, a practice alien to the American idea of free choice.

For some time suggestions have been made that the comic book publishers should impose censorship on themselves by the promulgation of a code of principles to which they would all adhere. Recently, Magistrate Charles F. Murphy of New York City was appointed as the Code Administrator of a newly-formed Comic Magazines Association, created by a number of the comic book publishers, and a code was formulated by the Association. There can be little doubt that a major purpose in the organization of the Association and the promulgation of the Code was to forestall legislative action against the publishers, which would have been for them much more unpalatable than the type of discipline which Magistrate Murphy might mete out.[4]

The Code adopted by the Association contains "do's" and "don't's" that follow the rules established by the "Hays Office" of the motion picture industry. In most instances, the precepts of the Code seem directly related to eliminating the more distasteful episodes of crime, bloodshed and violence appearing in a number of the comic books. In some cases the rules seem to go much further—and regardless of individual judgment as to their merits—they have nothing to do with protecting children against being exposed to horror, bloodshed, and violence.[5]

Because codes have inevitably had the effect of inhibiting the free expression of ideas, the ACLU has opposed their establishment among industry members of the mass communication fields, i.e., motion pictures, radio and television. Although a single publisher may prescribe for himself any set of standards he may desire for the publication of material, a different situation exists where a significant segment of the industry agrees

---

William Faulkner, 'The Forest and the Port' by Hervey Allen, 'The Catcher in the Rye' by J. D. Salinger, 'Forever Amber' and 'From Here to Eternity.' . . . Hemingway and Faulkner are winners of the Nobel Prize for Literature. . . . Although the list does not include the titles of objectionable comic books, it does contain a list of 'acceptable comics.' "

[4] Whether this effort will be successful in forestalling legislation is doubtful. The New York State Joint Legislative Committee has attacked the publishers' efforts, and despite numerous changes in the content and drawings of comics, critics are still assailing the books as a source of crime and delinquency.

[5] For example, the following rules are contained in the Code:

"In every instance, good shall triumph over evil and the criminal be punished for his misdeeds."

"Ridicule or attack on any religious or racial group is never permissible."

"Divorce shall not be treated humorously nor represented as desirable."

to abide by a code. Collective adherence to a single set of principles in a code has the effect of limiting different points of views, because individual publishers—as well as writers—are fearful of departing from the accepted norm lest they be held up to scorn or attack and suffer economic loss. (The "seal of approval" granted by the Code to approved publications also places economic pressure on local distributors, who are also under surveillance by local pressure groups.) But the variety of ideas is the lifeblood of a free society. Whatever evil exists in the restraint of competition in our economic life pales in significance when compared to the dangers of monopoly or uniformity of ideas. Experience has shown that the restrictive effects of codes goes far beyond their original purpose and intention. As described above, this is clearly evident in the Code published by the Comic Magazine Association where restraints unrelated to horror, crime and violence have been promulgated and are being enforced.

Therefore, while we encourage each individual publisher to develop his own standards of taste and decency in the publication of comic books, we are opposed to the establishing of rigid standards to which all publishers are constrained to abide.

What Can Be Done?

Is there anything that can be done to meet the comic book problem without creating the perils of censorship or other restrictions on freedom of expression? Let us consider obscenity laws, the manner of enforcing such laws, and the responsibility of parents. First, there is an area for proper enforcement of obscenity laws, and as we stated in 1952 to the Gathings Select Committee on Current Pornographic Material, the ACLU has not intervened in many "obscenity" cases.

It should be made clear, however, that the obscenity laws are designed to protect the community against smutty and salacious material. These laws were not intended to include within their orbit material which may offend the good taste of the majority of the public, but which nonetheless is not licentious. In reviewing the various reports describing crime comic books, we observed that the majority of these books—whatsoever other failings they may have—are not obscene. Even where obscene material is involved, a sharp distinction must be drawn between prior-censorship and post-publication punishment. Prior censorship, apart from preventing obscenity, also has great deterrent effects upon the publishing of proper material, for authors and publishers may eliminate passages or even whole books because of the fear that they will be considered obscene. Furthermore, prior-censorship places in the hands of a few public officials the power to make decisions affecting the community at large. On the other hand, post-publication punishment for violation of a law allows the defendant the rights of due process of law, including a jury trial. A jury far better reflects the community's current standards of taste than a few officials whose long labor in the vineyard of censorship may have given them a narrow outlook which refuses to broaden with the passage of time.

We are also interested in seeing that the manner in which such obscenity laws are administered by public officials does not have the effect of deterring publishers and booksellers from publishing and selling legitimate reading material. We are opposed to the wholly improper procedure of certain law enforcement officers who, instead of commencing prosecutions against the publishers and wholesale distributors of magazines—businessmen economically able to defend themselves against lawsuits—rather threaten the small, local retail booksellers who are in no position to resist official coercion. What happens in these cases, in effect, is that a ban on particular books results without any hearing on the merits of the book itself and the protection of a jury trial as set forth above.

Probably our best hope lies in the home itself—parental control over the reading habits of their children. A congressman's comment on television programs that portrayed crime and violence, "Did you ever think of turning the damn thing off?" suggests that parents sufficiently interested in the proper development of their children should keep a careful watch over their reading material. And, as the testimony of child welfare experts attest, an environment which embraces a wide range of interests will make comics less of an attraction to children. This is in line with accepted educational theory and practice which conceives of the child as a whole person, whose total needs must be considered. To those who argue that not every child's home environment can meet his total needs and something must be done to safeguard children who, unfortunately, live in an unwholesome environment, the answer lies in the work of schools, churches and community organizations. The creation of the healthy environment is their challenge.

Finally, additional study on the subject of juvenile delinquency and comic books should be encouraged. The research under way is a gratifying development. Experts are plumbing the depths of individual behavior and soon perhaps evidence will be forthcoming that will demonstrate the relationship, or lack of relationship, between comics and the wave of juvenile delinquency which has spread in recent years. As we have stated before, there is a healthy diversity of opinion already recorded, but there is by no means evidence that a clear and present danger exists in the publication of crime comic books, which would justify their suppression. Further investigations of the relationship between their publication and juvenile delinquency have the endorsement of ACLU. We believe such research will have broad ramifications, leading to study of the effect of all mass media on human behavior.

The Harm of Censorship

The ACLU understands the concern of American parents that their children are being subjected to a barrage of written material that may wield real influence on their impressionable minds. But there is another danger that must be equally considered—the danger of censorship. To suppress books in the absence of a clear and present danger, even offensive comic books, is in violation of the First Amendment. And the weakening of the First Amendment can lead to the undermining of our free institutions, which we want our children and their children to enjoy and respect. True, there may be a risk in allowing the circulation of books—all kinds of books—but risk is an indelible mark of democracy and a society of freedom. As the ACLU's executive director, Patrick Murphy Malin said, in his testimony before the Gathings Committee:

"All that I have said does not mean that action cannot be taken to curb the abuses that arise in this field. Such action is already taking place in American homes, schools, the churches and synagogues—all mustered to do battle with any evil tendencies, if such there be, that crime books may bring out. Are we to say that these forces are powerless? . . .

"There may be, in the absence of censorship, some risk that some persons along the line may possibly get hurt. But our life is founded upon risk. There is risk—and indeed certainty—that every day many people will be killed by automobiles, and yet we leave automobiles on our streets. I suggest to you that the institution of free speech is surely just as vital to our society as the automobile. Risk there is in all life, and we must take this risk on the side of freedom. That is the glory of our way of life. Censorship is abhorrent to Americanism."

APPENDIX

1. *Individuals taking the position that there is a direct or significant relationship between the reading of "crime" comic books and the increase of juvenile delinquency:*

(a) Frederic Wertham, *Seduction of the Innocent*, 1954, p. 164.

"Our researches have proved that there is a significant correlation between crime-comics reading and the more serious forms of juvenile delinquency. Many children read only few comics, read them for only a short time, read the better type (to the extent that there is a better type) and do not become imbued with the whole crime-comics atmosphere. Those children, on the other hand, who commit the more serious types of delinquency nowadays, read a lot of comic books, go in for the worst type of crime comics, read them for a long time and live in thought in the crime-comics world."

Frederic Wertham, "What Parents Don't Know About Comic Books," *Ladies Home Journal*, November, 1953, p. 219:

"Crime comics create a mental atmosphere of deceit, trickery and cruelty. Many of the children I have studied have come to grief over it. How best to summarize the attitudes most widely played up in crime comics? One might list them in some such way as this: assertiveness, defiance, hostility, desire to destroy or hurt, search for risk and excitement, aggressiveness, destructiveness, sadism, suspiciousness, adventurousness, nonsubmission to authority. Anybody could make up such a list by going over a thousand comic books. Actually, though, this is a literal summary of the traits of typical delinquents found by the famous criminologists Sheldon and Eleanor Glueck in a study of 500 delinquents when compared with 500 non-delinquents. In other words, the very traits that we officially wish to avoid we unofficially inculcate."

(b) Walter Lippmann, *New York Herald Tribune*, September 7, 1954:

"Third—There can be no real doubt, it seems to me, that the movies and television and the comic books are purveying violence and lust to a vicious and intolerable degree. There can be no real doubt that public exhibitions of sadism tend to excite sadistic desires and to teach the audience how to gratify sadistic desires. Nor can there be any real doubt that there is a close connection between the suddenness of the increase in sadistic crimes and the new vogue of sadism among the mass media of entertainment.

"Censorship is no doubt a clumsy and usually a stupid and self-defeating remedy for such evils. But a continual exposure of a generation to the commercial exploitation of the enjoyment of violence and cruelty is one way to corrode the foundations of a civilized society. For my own part, believing as I do in freedom of speech and thought, I see no objection in principle to censorship of the mass entertainment of the young. Until some more refined way is worked out of controlling this evil thing, the risks to our liberties are, I believe, decidedly less than the risks of unmanageable violence."

(c) Charles T. G. Rogers, Chief Probation Officer, San Diego, California, *Juvenile Delinquency, Special Committee to Investigate Organized Crime in Interstate Commerce, Senate Report, 81st Congress, 2nd Session*, 1950 (hereinafter referred to as *Juvenile Delinquency . . .*) p. 35:

"There is no doubt that a relationship exists between the reading of crime comic books and juvenile delinquency. Like the dime novels of an earlier era, the normal, well-adjusted child could read them without the experience being traumatic or sparking a pattern of behavior unacceptable to the society in which he functioned; the danger of such literature is to the juvenile whose psychological or emotional make-up predisposes him "to deviant reaction. The youngster of border-line or lower mentality who is susceptible to suggestion in any form may be stimulated to attempt to carry out activities depicted in a crime comic. The emotionally or psychologically maladjusted child who feels a greater need for attention or security than normal, and who has failed to achieve such attention or security through normal channels, may attempt to secure the attention or gain recognition by criminal acts. These may use crime comics as a source book." [6]

(d) *Report of the New York State Joint Legislative Committee to study the Publication of Comics, Legislative Document No. 37, 1954,* p. 11:

"4. So-called 'comics' are a most effective medium for the dissemination of ideas and when such a medium is used to disseminate bad ideas which may leave deep impressions on the keen, absorptive minds of children, the unrestricted publication and distribution of 'comics' becomes a matter of grave public concern.

. . . .

6. The reading of crime 'comics' stimulate[s] sadistic and masochistic attitudes and interfere[s] with the normal development of sexual habits in children and produce abnormal sexual tendencies in adolescents.

7. Crime 'comics' are a contributing factor leading to juvenile delinquency."

2. *Individuals taking the position that there is some relationship, though not necessarily a significant one, between the reading of "crime" comic books and the increase of juvenile delinquency:*

(a) *Interim Report of the Committee on the Judiciary, Senate Report No. 1064, 83rd Congress, 2nd Session, 1954,* p. 10:

"Through TV, radio, movies, and comics, children are fed a heavy diet of violence and crime. Although it is generally pointed out that law and order

[6] This report contains comments from a great many persons involved in probation work, guidance work, and from public officials and from comic book publishers, responding to questions asked by the Committee, three of which questions were: Do you believe that there is any relationship between the reading of crime comic books and juvenile delinquency? Please specifically give statistics and, if possible, state specific cases of juvenile crime which you believe could be traced to the reading of crime comic books? Do you believe that juvenile delinquency would decrease if crime comic books were not readily available to children?

eventually prevail in these presentations, the life of the underworld is frequently glamorized in the process. Lawlessness and evil are overcome only by brute force. Opinion thus far received is varied relative to effects of such programs upon the behavior of youth. That it has some influence is manifest in the play and garb of children. The old western tradition of checking your gun at the door is now literally carried on in the elementary classroom. The subcommittee has had called to its attention instances in which youngsters are required to leave their play 'shooting irons' outside the classroom, indicating the effect of mass media western programs have upon such children. Whether or not such programs also influence a child's attitude towards the standards of society and his sense of right and wrong is a matter to be explored by the subcommittee in its future work."

(b) Katherine F. Lenroot, Chief, Children's Bureau, Federal Security Agency, *Juvenile Delinquency* . . . , p. 8:

"There is general agreement in this country that delinquency is a product of multiple causes, that it is not a single act with a single determining factor or cause. We know that economic insecurity, parental neglect, domestic strife, lack of training, lack of love and affection, lack of spiritual guidance, lack of recreational facilities, inconsistent discipline, and physical handicaps are some of the factors which must be considered. I doubt, in the absence of some of these other factors, whether the reading of comic books *per se* will make a boy or girl delinquent. Any publication that glamorizes crime and criminals and presents in detail illegal acts and techniques may be harmful to some children. Boys and girls who have been exposed to unsatisfactory home and community conditions and, therefore, [are] vulnerable to delinquency may adopt certain illegal acts or techniques from these publications. Publications that provide schooling in crime for those youngsters who might have otherwise expressed their anti-social drives by less serious and less damaging misbehavior are obviously dangerous."

(c) Harold R. Muntz, Chief Probation Officer, Hamilton County, Ohio, *Juvenile Delinquency* . . . , p. 13:

"Some readers, we believe, easily follow the suggestions of the comic book pages, while others just as easily slough off these influences and are not impelled to try to imitate the activities of the comic book characters or improve upon their experiences and learn by their fictional mistakes. We believe there is a relationship between reading crime comic books and juvenile delinquency, but only as one factor in a great list of factors that cause delinquency."

3. *Individuals taking the position that there is little or no relationship between the reading of "crime" comic books and the increase of juvenile*

delinquency, or that there is insufficient information to make a useful judgment:

(a) Philippe Bauchard, *The Child Audience* (published by Unesco), 1952, pp. 13 and 14:

"In fact, where the influences affecting children are concerned, it seems essential to make a clear sweep of all preconceived ideas and prejudices, such as that the cinema encourages juvenile delinquency, pornography is dangerous for the young, accounts of crimes incite children to imitate the criminals, etc. In truth, strange as it may appear, we are forced to admit that we know almost nothing about what affects the child. It is thus for nonofficial bodies dealing with children, for the psychology and pedagogy departments of universities or, failing them, for the public authorities to initiate research which would enable us to say and, in many cases, to know how and why, when and in what circumstances, children react. (p. 13)

. . . .

"So long as this preliminary work is not done, neither educators, legislators, nor those publishing papers, directing films or producing broadcasts for children, will be in a position to achieve anything useful. To try to safeguard children without knowing what really endangers them, to set out to please them without knowing their tastes or understanding their development processes is to court failure. As of 1952, despite the efforts and goodwill of educators and legislators, the desire of those who produce papers, films and broadcasts to attract and retain the juvenile public, in short, despite the endeavors of all who have tried to take an interest in children, the results obtained are far from encouraging." (p. 14)

(b) Charles Y. Glock, Director, Bureau of Applied Social Research, Columbia University, "Juvenile Delinquency and the Mass Media," Sept. 15, 1954:

"In the midst of our deep concern with this problem, all sorts of ideas have been advanced to explain why juvenile delinquency has become a common characteristic of our cities and suburbs. One of these ideas is that there is a relationship between the increase of delinquency and the extent to which crime and violence have invaded the content of our mass media.

"This contention has gained wide acceptance and support, in part, because it seems so manifestly to be true and, in part, because it appears to offer the possibility of a relatively easy solution to the problem. However, upon close examination, the evidence which has been accumulated in its support is not conclusive. We are still groping to learn just what effects exposure to the mass media do have on our children."

(c) Erik H. Erikson, Senior Staff Member, Austen Riggs Center (see *New York Times*, Oct. 3, 1954):

"There is too much 'scapegoating' on the subject of juvenile delinquency and not enough careful search for the real causes, an authority on adolescent psychology said today.
"Erik H. Erikson, senior staff member of the Austen Riggs Center here, asserted there was an unfortunate and increasing tendency to blame without adequate evidence such media as comic books, television, movies and all the graphic representations of violence."

(d) Ellen Winston, North Carolina State Board of Public Welfare, *Juvenile Delinquency* . . . , p. 15:

"In our experience we have been unable to fix any reliable relationship between reading crime comic books and juvenile delinquency. On the whole, causes of juvenile delinquency have seemed to lie much deeper in the personal and environmental difficulties of the child rather than in stimuli of the type offered by comic books."

(e) Wallace H. Kuralt, Superintendent, Department of Public Welfare, Mecklenburg County, North Carolina, *Juvenile Delinquency* . . . , p. 18:

"The staff of this court believes that there is no direct connection. We have never had a case in which reading crime comic books seemed to be a motivating factor in the art of delinquency. Many seriously delinquent children frequently seem to be unmoved by what normal children seek in the way of thrills and excitement. If crime comic books and crime plays on the radio offer this thrill which satisfies the more seriously delinquent, and there is evidence that they may, the result is probably of a positive value rather than a negative value. We have noticed that chronically delinquent children almost always are poor readers."

(f) John J. Doyle, Probation Officer, Ramsay County, Minn., *Juvenile Delinquency* . . . , p. 28:

"You ask whether or not juvenile delinquency would decrease if crime comic books were not readily available to children. I doubt if crime comic books are any more significant as factors in the production of delinquency than their predecessor the dime novels were, and I would place the pool hall first, undesirable movies second, lurid magazines third, dramatic newspaper stories fourth, and comic books last.
"If you are measuring influences of a commercial nature, the delinquent is today what he always was: the product of the social milieu; i.e., the interplay of heredity and environment, and the child's everyday training in the

home, the places he plays, the education he receives in school, and the people he meets, together with his physical and mental inheritance, are all of them more important than something he may read or see."

(g) E. W. Brewer, Case Work Supervisor, Superior Court of King County, Seattle, Wash., *Juvenile Delinquency* . . . , p. 29:

"My professional opinion is that any relationship between the two is a nebulous one. Those of us who have had specialized training for this field and have worked in the field of treating the delinquent child firmly believe that delinquency is a symptom of a sick personality. Myriad factors make up the total personality; and, therefore, crime comic books only present one of thousands of influences in the forming of any personality."

(h) Joseph A. Homer, Probation Officer, Juvenile Court of Allegheny County, Pittsburgh, Pa., *Juvenile Delinquency* . . . , p. 37:

"On this question there is a difference of opinion among our staff members. However, the great majority of them believe that there is a very little relationship between reading crime comic books and juvenile delinquency. The consensus of opinion is that those who are apprehended for violating the law and attribute this violation to reading comic books would have found some other means of committing the same offense anyway."